Protestants

ALSO BY ALEC RYRIE

The Age of Reformation

Being Protestant in Reformation Britain

The Sorcerer's Tale

Protestants

THE FAITH THAT MADE
THE MODERN WORLD

ALEC RYRIE

VIKING

VIKING
An imprint of Penguin Random House LLC
375 Hudson Street
New York, New York 10014
penguin.com

Map drawn by Martin Brown. Used by permission of William Collins, an imprint of HarperCollins Publishers (UK).

ISBN: 9780670026166 (hardcover)
ISBN: 9780735222816 (e-book)

Printed in the United States of America
1   3   5   7   9   10   8   6   4   2

Set in Dante MT

In memory of Bill Ryrie (1928–2012)

Contents

PART III: THE GLOBAL AGE

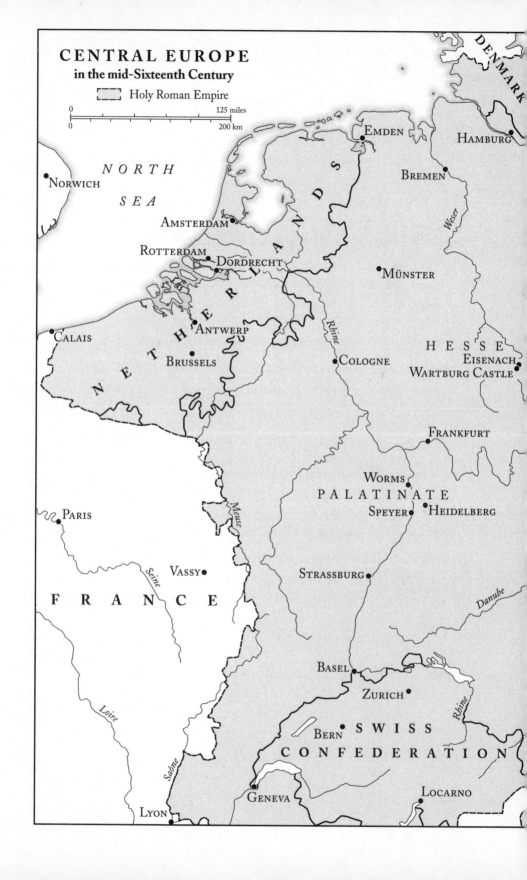

CENTRAL EUROPE
in the mid-Sixteenth Century

- - - Holy Roman Empire

0 ——————————— 125 miles
0 ——————————— 200 km

DENMARK

NORTH SEA

NORWICH

EMDEN

HAMBURG

BREMEN

Weser

N E T H E R L A N D S

AMSTERDAM

ROTTERDAM
DORDRECHT

MÜNSTER

CALAIS

ANTWERP

BRUSSELS

Rhine

COLOGNE

H E S S E

EISENACH
WARTBURG CASTLE

FRANKFURT

WORMS

PALATINATE

SPEYER   HEIDELBERG

PARIS

Meuse

Seine

VASSY

STRASSBURG

Danube

F R A N C E

BASEL

ZURICH

Rhine

Loire

BERN   S W I S S
C O N F E D E R A T I O N

Saône

GENEVA

LOCARNO

LYON

Protestants

Introduction

In 1524, Erasmus of Rotterdam wrote a blistering attack on a fanatical new cult that was spreading across northern Europe like a plague. These people claim to be preaching the Bible's pure message, he said, but look at how they actually use the Bible, twisting it to mean whatever they want:

> They are like young men who love a girl so immoderately that they imagine they see their beloved wherever they turn, or, a much better example, like two combatants who, in the heat of a quarrel, turn whatever is at hand into a missile, whether it be a jug or a dish.[1]

This book is about that cult and how it became one of the most creative and disruptive movements in human history. At present, about one-eighth of the human race belongs to it, and it has decisively shaped the world in which the other seven-eighths live. My aim is to convince you that we cannot understand the modern age without understanding the dynamic history of Protestant Christianity.

It turns out that Erasmus was right: Protestants are fighters and lovers. They will argue with anyone about almost anything. Some of these arguments are abstruse, others brutally practical. If we look at the great ideological battles of the past half millennium—for and against toleration, slavery, imperialism, fascism, or Communism—we will find Protestant Christians on both sides.

But Protestants are also lovers. From the beginning, a love affair with God has been at the heart of their faith. Like all long love affairs, it has gone through many phases, from early passion through companionable marriage and sometimes strained coexistence, to rekindled ardor. Beneath all the arguments, the distinguishing mark of a Protestant is the feeling and memory of that love, one on which no church or human authority can intrude. It is because Protestants care so deeply about God that they have been willing both to fight one another and take on the world on his behalf.

So this is both an interior and an exterior story, a spiritual and emotional drama with practical and political implications. The spirituality at Protestantism's center sends out waves that sometimes crest into tsunamis as they encounter the ordinary stuff of human life. This book will tell the stories of the changes they have left in their wake. Protestants have faced down tyrants, demanded political participation, advocated tolerance, and valued the individual. Equally, they have insisted on God-given inequality, valorized state power, persecuted dissenters, and placed the community above its members. They have fought religious wars against each other and have turned secular struggles into crusades. Some have tried to withdraw from the secular world and its politics altogether, and at times they have been the most revolutionary of all.

The Protestant Reformation was clearly an important event in world history, but that does not mean that it can take the credit or the blame for everything that has happened since. Nor does it make Martin Luther a prophet of individualism or a hero of self-determination. He and the Protestants who succeeded him were not trying to modernize the world, but to save it. And yet in the process they profoundly changed how we think about ourselves, our society, and our relationship with God. This book tells the story of that transformation: a story, in outline, of how three of the key ingredients of the world we live in are rooted in Protestant Christianity.

The first is *free inquiry*. Protestants stumbled into this slowly and reluctantly, but Luther's bedrock principles led inexorably in that direction. The insistence that all human authority in religious matters is provisional, and that the human conscience, constrained only by the Bible and the Holy Spirit, is ultimately sovereign, means that Protestants who try to police the boundaries of acceptable argument have in the end always failed. Protestants have always been divided among themselves both in their religious and in their political leadership, making it easy for new and dissenting ideas to find spaces both at home and across borders.

Protestantism is not a paradise of free speech, but an open-ended, ill-disciplined argument. How it has come to continuously generate new ideas, and revive old ones, is a recurring theme of this book. Protestants' bare-knuckle style of public debate wore down print censorship, and Protestant universities and scholars led the way in the emergence of the new natural sciences in the sixteenth and seventeenth centuries. Slowly and reluctantly, one notion which a few radical Protestants put about—that religious difference and free speech ought to be accepted as matters of principle, rather than merely tolerated as unavoidable necessities—became a new orthodoxy.

This is linked to Protestantism's second, more dangerous contribution: its tendency toward what we are compelled to call *democracy*. Virtually all Protestants before the nineteenth century, and many since, regarded that word with horror, yet the undertow was there. Protestants regularly found themselves having to deal with governments that did not share their beliefs. They asserted not a right to choose their rulers but a solemn duty and responsibility to challenge them. In performing that duty, the Scottish radical John Knox wrote in 1558, "all man is equal."[2] Few Protestants at the time agreed, and even Knox meant something very different from what we understand equality to mean today. Most early Protestants favored monarchy, order, and social stability. But their rulers had an intolerable tendency to act in defiance of God's will, and so, again and again, they were forced reluctantly to take matters into their own hands. This is what we should expect from consciences fired with love for God and ready to take on all comers.

Left to itself, this could lead to revolution or to the creation of self-righteous theocracies, and as we shall see, both have repeatedly happened. But these impulses have been tempered by the third, much less remarked-upon but perhaps more significant, ingredient of Protestantism's modernizing cocktail: its *apoliticism*. Protestants might have sometimes confronted or overthrown their rulers, but their most constant political demand is simply to be left alone. Returning to Christianity's roots in ancient Rome, they have tried to carve out a spiritual space where political authority does not apply and have insisted that that space, the kingdom of Christ, matters far more than the sordid and

ephemeral quarrels of this world. The results are paradoxical. Protestants have often been obedient subjects to thoroughly noxious rulers,
taking no interest in politics so long as their own separate sphere was
respected. It has also meant that rulers who would not or could not
respect that sphere have faced unexpectedly stubborn opposition. In
the process, Protestants have helped to give the modern world the
strange, counterintuitive notion of limited government: the principle
that the first duty even of the most righteous ruler is to respect his subjects' freedom and allow them to live their lives as they see fit.

These ideals, which seem natural to our own age, are in the span of
human history very unusual indeed. That we should all have a say in
choosing our own rulers *and* that those rulers' powers over us should
be limited—these principles are in obvious tension, as every society
that has tried to combine liberty and democracy has discovered. Without Protestantism and its peculiar preoccupations, that strange and
marvelous synthesis could never have come into being as it has.

This brings us to one of the most persistent puzzles of Protestant
modernity. Ever since the great German sociologist Max Weber advanced the notion of "the Protestant work ethic" in 1904, it has seemed
intuitively obvious that there is some kind of connection between Protestantism and capitalism. But for all the brilliance of Weber's arguments, the actual evidence he advanced to prove this intuition did not
really hold up, and his successors have not done much better.[3] It is true
both that capitalism has often flourished in Protestant societies,
and that Protestantism has often flourished in societies that are newly
embracing capitalism, from sixteenth-century Holland to eighteenth-
century England through to twentieth-century South Korea. Equally
plainly, capitalism and Protestantism can each prosper in the other's
absence. Two observations, perhaps, can be made. One is that the kind
of sociopolitical structure that Protestantism engenders—based on free
inquiry, participatory politics, and limited government—tends to favor
market economics.

The other is a matter of mood. As Weber pointed out, one of capitalism's odd features is its "restless activity."[4] Protestants are not always
driven to restless *economic* activity, although the need to fill the unforgiving minutes of their lives in a manner which is both blameless and
worthwhile can certainly push them in that direction. But a certain

generic restlessness, an itchy instability, is absolutely a core character-istic of the Protestant life. Settled peace and consensus does not come easily to Protestants. They are more usually found straining after new truths, searching out new sins or striving to recover old virtues. They have always known that their religious life is flawed and inadequate, and no sooner create an institution than they suspect it of calcifying into formalism and hypocrisy. They are forever starting new argu-ments and spawning new forms. This self-perpetuating dynamo of dis-satisfaction and yearning has helped to fuel and support the growth of capitalism. More broadly, it has also been, and still is, one of the engines driving modern history.

This book tells the story of how the first five centuries of Protestant history brought us to where we are now and asks what might be com-ing next. It is not chiefly a history of Protestant*ism*, of doctrines and churches and theological systems, although a certain amount of that can't be avoided. It is a history of *Protestants,* who see themselves as God's chosen people. There are towering thinkers like Martin Luther, the stubborn monk whose own overwhelming encounter with God began it all, and John Calvin, the brilliant and arrogant Frenchman who came tantalizingly close to forging a single, united Protestantism. There are outsiders like the self-taught Vermont preacher William Miller, whose apocalyptic hopes swept across 1840s America, and Choe Ja-Sil, the destitute Korean nurse who cofounded a tent church that became, by the time of her death in 1989, the world's largest congrega-tion. There are noblemen like Justinian von Welz and Count Nikolaus von Zinzendorf, whose conversions drove them from their German estates to cross the world spreading their subversive religion. There are women like Rebecca Freundlich Protten, one of the first ordained Prot-estant women, who risked reenslavement rather than compromise her faith, and Pandita Ramabai, the Indian widow whose campaign for women's rights was underpinned by her Pentecostal revivalism. There are heroes with clay feet, like Martin Niemöller and Johan Heyns, who only slowly and painfully realized that their faith could not square with Nazism or apartheid; and reactionaries, like Walter Grundmann and Gustav Gerdener, whose faith seemed to find its fullest expression in those doctrines.

The book falls into three parts. Part I takes the story from the great crisis of the Reformation through to the eighteenth century, when it finally became clear that Protestantism would not only survive but spread around the world. The story begins in chapter I with Martin Luther's attempt to work out the implications of his own personal spiritual crisis. What began as a decorous academic dispute quickly turned into a scandal, then a political crisis, and then, within less than a decade, the largest mass rebellion Europe had ever seen. Chapter 2 investigates how the fragmented, antagonistic reforming movements that emerged from this chaos tried to carve out space in which they could live. Some worked with the grain of existing power structures, while others openly defied them; all shared the deeply subversive assumption that Christ's kingdom was separate from and superior to human hierarchies of any kind. Chapter 3 looks at the most promising attempt at something Protestants have always longed for, namely reunion. Calvinism's failure to achieve this dream ended up proving that it was not only impossible but positively damaging.

Chapter 4 turns to one of the first consequences of the Protestant upheaval: more than a century of brutal religious violence, as a result of which, slowly and reluctantly, some Protestants began to harbor notions of tolerance. Chapter 5 stops for a more detailed look at one particularly significant example of that process: the English Civil War of 1642–46 and its aftermath, the most fertile nursery of new Protestant sects and ideas since Luther's day. Chapter 6 considers one vital consequence of violence: mass migration. Protestantism was profoundly shaped by the experience of exile, for good and for ill. In this first age of globalization, Protestants scattered not only across Europe but across the world, especially, fatefully, to North America. Here they tried and failed to build model societies, while initially making astonishingly little effort to convert non-Christian peoples.

In part 2, we see how Protestantism in Europe and North America recovered from its late seventeenth-century nadir only to face new crises in the modern world. Chapter 7 describes how, around the turn of the eighteenth century, Protestants rediscovered some of their old sources of spiritual strength and began a wave of global expansion that has scarcely paused since. This quickly led them to confront the defining spiritual and political crisis of the late eighteenth and early nineteenth centuries: Atlantic slavery. Chapter 8 looks at how slavery was defended and opposed by Protestants with equal vigor on both sides of the ocean. The slow but decisive shift to a Protestant consensus that slavery is intolerable would have lasting effects. Chapter 9 looks at another aspect of the early United States: the third great explosion of sectarian creativity in Protestant history, giving rise to a kaleidoscope of utopian, apocalyptic, antihierarchical, and Spirit-led movements, some of which continue to shape modern Protestantism to this day. Chapter 10 turns to a very different feature of nineteenth-century Protestantism, namely theological liberalism, a bold attempt to outflank the emerging secularist challenge. It was, if anything, too successful, and ended up being deeply implicated on all sides in World War I.

Chapter 11 takes up the role of Protestants in the rise of and resistance to Nazism in Germany, where old Protestant orthodoxies and new liberal ideals combined to smooth the path to genocide. Chapter 12 follows that story to the present in Protestantism's old heartland, arguing that the rise of secularism in Europe and in parts of the United States reflects many denominations' inability to find a distinctive voice after the immense moral shock of World War II. The real novelty of our own time is not the prominence of the religious Right but the silence of the religious Left.

In part 3, the book's final chapters look at what has now become a global story. Chapter 13 traces the longest and bitterest of Protestantism's African adventures: South Africa, where an indigenous African Protestantism took root quickly but ran up against a settler population that justified white supremacy in explicitly Protestant terms. Protestantism was crucial both to apartheid's beginnings and to its end. Chapter 14 turns to modern Protestantism's strangest success story, Korea, where colonial and cultural politics combined to give Protestants an opening unparalleled in Asia. The other great Asian story, that of China, examined in chapter 15, is very different; here a long-standing missionary effort bore relatively little fruit, but the pressures of Communist rule have now given China the world's fastest-growing Protestant population. Finally, chapter 16 looks at the greatest revolution in modern Protestantism: Pentecostalism, a global phenomenon from its inception, which for over a century has been quietly putting down roots in the United States, Africa, Latin America, and elsewhere, and now has a fair claim to be the modern world's most dynamic religious movement. Its persistent avoidance of politics has allowed it to deflect attention, but that may turn out to be its most subversive feature of all. The epilogue asks, in the light of this story, where Protestantism might be going next: for it may be that its history is still only beginning.

Protestantism has affected every sphere of human life. I have focused on its political effects, especially how it has eaten away at established orthodoxies and distinctions of race, nation, and gender, sometimes despite itself. I have not paid much attention to its role in driving economic change or in fostering modern science, though we will touch on both subjects. I have said virtually nothing about the arts. It would take a whole chapter to do justice to Johann Sebastian Bach; here he gets a single sentence. If you finish this book impatient to know about the parts of the story I have skated over or left out, I will feel I have succeeded.

It will already be obvious that I am using the word "Protestant" broadly. There are narrow definitions, restricting it, for example, to Lutheran and Calvinist Christians and their immediate descendants. One of the things Protestants like to fight over is who does and does not count as a proper Protestant. As a historian, I prefer a genealogical definition: Protestants are Christians whose religion derives ultimately from Martin Luther's rebellion against the Catholic Church. They are a tree with many tangled branches but a single trunk. So in this book "Protestant" includes those who are often shut out of the party, such as Anabaptists, Quakers, Unitarians, Jehovah's Witnesses, and Pentecostals. These groups have radically different beliefs, but they share a family resemblance. They are as quarrelsome and fervent as any other Protestants, and that first spark, the life-changing encounter between the individual believer and the grace of God, is visible in all of them.

One definition does need a little more attention: the one on which Erasmus focused. As a much-quoted seventeenth-century Englishman put it, "The BIBLE, I say, The BIBLE only is the Religion of Protestants!"[5] It is a truism that the Bible, the ancient library of Jewish and early Christian texts that Christians regard as Scripture, is close to Protestantism's heart. It is also clear that one of the things Protestants love to fight over is what the Bible is and means. To understand those battles, we need to ask just what Protestants' relationship with the Bible is—as a matter of historical practice, not of theological principle.

Some Protestants insist that Protestantism is "Bible Christianity," a religion that takes the whole, inspired Bible as the only and final authoritative source of truth. This view makes Protestantism's history of division easy enough to understand; these are simply arguments about the interpretation of a complex text. But the claim that Protestantism is mere Bible Christianity does not stand up. For one thing, there is that love affair. What Protestants share is an experience of God's grace rather than a doctrine of authority. Martin Luther had his life upended by God's grace before he decided that he could not be bound by any authority outside Scripture. Indeed, many Protestants have not treated the Bible as their sole authority. Some have found authority elsewhere, through (as they believed) the guidance of the Holy Spirit. Others have questioned whether and in what sense the whole text as we have it is authoritative at all.

Even those who do use the whole Bible as their sole authority do so in two different ways. They are Erasmus's lovers and fighters. The Bible has from the beginning been Protestants' weapon for defending their beliefs and dismissing their opponents', citing chapter and verse to prove the point. This works best if you believe in the word-by-word authority of the entire text, and the earliest Protestants were as adept as any modern evangelicals at that kind of close-quarters biblical combat.

And yet, before the Bible is a bludgeon that can be used to batter opponents into submission, it is a source of inspiration. Before you can wield it like a fighter, you must read it like a lover. We can see this through one of the strangest features of Protestant Christianity. Although Protestants have from the beginning vigorously *asserted* that the Bible is authoritative, they have been strangely slow to *argue* that that is so. When the case has been made, it has often been done without much energy: citing biblical texts to justify the Bible's authority, an obviously circular argument, or making shaky deductions to the effect that God must have inspired it. This is not because Protestants are avoiding an awkward subject or know they do not have a leg to stand on. It is because, in truth, their faith does not hang on these arguments. They do not need to convince themselves of the Bible's authority, because they already know it.

Early Protestantism's greatest systematic theologian, John Calvin, confronted the question head-on. In an extraordinary passage, he simply refused to argue the case for the Bible's authority at all. "We ought," he said, "to seek our conviction in a higher place than human reasons, judgments or conjectures, that is, in the secret testimony of the Spirit." In other words, we know that the Bible is the Word of God not by arguing about it but by reading it with "pure eyes and upright senses," for then and only then "the majesty of God will immediately come to view." The Holy Spirit inspired the Bible, and only the Holy Spirit can convince you that that is true. Therefore, Calvin concludes,

> Scripture is indeed self-authenticating. . . . We *feel* that the un-
> doubted power of his divine majesty lives and breathes
> there, . . . a *feeling* that can be born only of heavenly revelation.
> I speak of nothing other than what each believer experiences
> within himself.[6]

The Bible itself provides its own authority, and either you feel it (through the Spirit) or you don't. This is Scripture for lovers, who can talk rapturously of the vision before them but cannot in the end compel anyone else to see it.

Across the span of Protestantism's history, the experience Calvin describes is fundamental. The same argument, in essence, was made by seventeenth-century Puritans, eighteenth-century revivalists, nineteenth-century liberals, and twentieth-century Pentecostals. The Bible is woven into Western, and now global, civilization more deeply than any other book, and none of us can come to it cold. Yet in every generation, Protestants have felt that they are reading the Bible for the first time and have been enthralled by its stories, its poetry, and its arguments. This is why they persistently refuse to let anyone else tell them how to read their Bibles. "I acknowledge no fixed rules for the interpretation of the Word of God," Martin Luther told Pope Leo X, "since the Word of God, which teaches freedom in all other matters, must not be bound." The following century, John Bunyan gently refused to submit to anyone else's interpretation. "I am for *drinking Water out of my own Cistern;* what GOD makes mine by evidence of his Word and Spirit, that

I dare make bold with."[7] Protestants have been finding refreshment and boldness in their own cisterns ever since.

When Protestant groups have distanced themselves from the Bible, such as the Nazi-era "German Christians" for whom it was intolerably Jewish, they have ended up looking not very Protestant anymore. But if to read the Bible as a lover is common to all Protestants, whether and how to use it as a weapon is not. Many Protestants have concluded, as Calvin did, that the entire text must be fully inspired. This seems the most open-hearted way of honoring their encounter with God in the text and also makes the text much easier to use in combat. Others have for various reasons concluded that they cannot accept it as authoritative in that way, on some variant of a principle first articulated by Martin Luther himself. Luther argued that the Bible *contains* the Word of God rather than that it *is* that Word. He even called it "the swaddling cloths and the manger in which Christ lies."[8] But even those who have picked up that idea and run with it most daringly still keep coming back to the manger to worship.

Protestants have no consensus on the question of how and in what sense the Bible is authoritative. Some would defend every comma. Others are more free and easy with the text. Both positions are attractive and both present formidable problems. But for all their arguments, both parties continue to drink from this cistern out of a shared conviction that here, supremely, is where they hear God's voice—even if they are unable to agree on what he says.

A brief note about how and why I have written this book. I have written about a very wide range of religious movements. I find some of them admirable, some of them repellent, and some of them tinged with madness. In each case, I have tried to treat them with sympathy. This is not because I myself believe that witches should be put to death or that apartheid is God's will. It is because earnest, God-fearing Protestants who were no more inherently wicked than you or I did believe these things, even at the same time as other Protestants passionately opposed them. Condemning ugly beliefs is easy, but it is also worth the effort to understand why people once believed them. If we are lucky, later ages might be as indulgent toward us. We all live in glass houses. Those who are without sin are welcome to cast the first stone.

So I have tried to explain what all kinds of Protestantism felt like from the inside, but like each of us I also have my own corner to defend, and it is only fair to be plain about it. I am myself a believing Protestant Christian and a licensed lay preacher in the Church of England. This book was not, however, written to convert you to my views, and I should be amazed if it did. It was written to convince you of the richness, the power, and the creativity, as well as the dangers, of this vast religious tradition. If you are yourself a Protestant, I hope this book will show you your own tradition from a new perspective: to help you understand more about where it came from, how it ended up the way it is today, and where it might be going next. If you are not, I hope it will show you why so many people have been and still are. I hope you will also see how this tradition has not only made the modern world but also made itself at home in it.

PART I

The Reformation Age

CHAPTER I

Luther and the Fanatics

If God be for us, who can be against us?

—ROMANS 8:31

Everyone knew how it was supposed to end. The One Holy Catholic and Apostolic Church, headed on earth by the bishop of Rome, the successor of St. Peter and vicar of Christ, had endured in Europe for over a thousand years. Nothing survives that long by accident. For Christians in the early sixteenth century who reflected on that astonishing fact, the explanation was obvious. This was no human institution. It was the visible Body of its founder, guided by the Holy Spirit. It would outlast this fading world and the carping of its critics, enduring forever to God's glory.

Nowadays, we prefer more mundane explanations. Catholic Christendom was flexible and creative, a walled garden with plenty of scope for novelty and variety, and room to adapt to changing political, social, and economic climates. But it also had boundaries, marked and unmarked. Those who wandered too far would be urged, and if necessary forced, to come back.

So if a professor at a small German university questioned an archbishop's fund-raising practices, there was a limited range of possible outcomes. The archbishop might ignore it or quietly concede the point. Or the professor might be induced to back down, by one means or another. If none of this happened, the matter would be contested on a bigger stage. Perhaps one party or the other in the debate would persuade his opponent to agree with him. Or, more likely, the process would be mired in procedure until the protagonists gave up or died.

But if it reached an impasse, the troublesome professor would eventually be ordered to give way. In the unlikely event that he refused, the only recourse was the law, leading to the one outcome that nobody wanted: he could be executed as an impenitent heretic, in a fire that would purge Christendom of his errors and symbolize the hell to which he had willfully condemned himself.

This system had worked for centuries. But in 1517, when that professor, Martin Luther, challenged Archbishop Albrecht of Mainz, his challenge instead kindled a series of increasingly uncontrollable wildfires that swept away many of the Catholic Church's ancient structures and its walls. We call this firestorm the Reformation and the new form, or forms, of Christianity that emerged from it Protestantism.

This was not what Luther had intended. When he voiced his local protest, he was not trying to start a fire. He was working out the implications of his own recent spiritual breakthrough and trying to start an argument about it. It turned out that those implications reached much further than either he or his opponents initially imagined. Once the smoke began to clear, they were forced to realize that they were in a new world.

The Call of Reform

With hindsight, we can see that Luther's fire caught because fuel had been quietly building up for some time. The principal fuel was desire for reform of the church.

Churches always need reform. They are staffed by human beings, some of whom will inevitably be fools, knaves, or merely incompetents. The church of the later Middle Ages was no more "corrupt" than usual, and in many ways much less so. Yet three problems converged to make it appear worse than it was: money, power, and high principle.

The Western church was very rich. It had to be; it was responsible for a continental network of parish priests, church buildings, and monastic houses, supported by an international bureaucracy of unparalleled sophistication, and these things do not come cheap. It had to preserve its political independence in a dangerous world, which meant choosing leaders of royal and noble stock. These were men—and some women, the great abbesses—whose dignity and effectiveness in their offices depended on maintaining the high courtly style to which they had been born.

Yet this was also an age that actively valued poverty, lauding it as a positive virtue like no Christian society before or since. The ideal late medieval cleric was a friar, who was forbidden even to touch money and who was supposed not even to own the rough clothes on his back. The contrast between that ideal and the church's corporate wealth was disturbing. Surely all that money must be corrupting? Once, as a rueful proverb had it, golden priests had served from wooden chalices; now wooden priests served from golden chalices. Every time the church extracted rents, tithes, or other payments from its flock, it fed a resentment that went beyond ordinary taxpayers' grumbles. And when there were real or perceived financial abuses, the gap between high ideals and sordid reality yawned dangerously wide. Martin Luther was a friar as well as a professor. When a man in his position accused the church of moneygrubbing, people were ready to listen.

Then there was power. Back in the eleventh century, the popes had wriggled free from political control and established a vigilantly guarded independence. By the fifteenth century, they had quietly dropped some of their more startling claims. In theory, they were lords of Christendom, able to depose kings and demand universal obedience, but they knew not to push their luck. They had never really recovered from the ghastly schism of 1378–1417, when Europe was split between first two and then three rival popes. The schism was ended by a great reforming church council, which seemed to promise an era of renewal—a hope that slowly evaporated over the following decades, leaving a residue of bitterness. By 1500, virtually all Western Christians acknowledged the papacy, but they were not proud of it. Eye-popping tales were told about Pope Alexander VI (1492–1503), Rodrigo Borgia, who in 1501 supposedly held an orgy in the papal apartments for his son, to which he invited fifty chosen prostitutes and select senior clerics. True or not, it was widely believed.

Inadequate leadership and financial corruption make a dangerous mix. All the more so in the loose confederation of German, and other, north-central European territories known misleadingly as the Holy Roman Empire. The rivalry between popes and emperors was ancient, and as the papal court became dominated almost exclusively by Italians after the schism, it seemed increasingly foreign north of the Alps. National stereotypes came into play. Germans were, in their own minds, bluff, honest, easily duped, but firm in the defense of the right. Italians, by contrast, were scheming, malevolent, effeminate, avaricious, and cowardly. So when a German friar accused Italians of extortion and tyranny, German ears were ready to hear him.

There was also a matter of principle at stake. As well as some memorable popes, the Renaissance gave Western Christendom a slogan: *ad fontes,* "to the sources," an urge to return to the ancient, and therefore pure, founts of truth. By 1500, this fashion for antiquity was sweeping into every field of knowledge. Renaissance linguists tried to recover the glories of Cicero. Renaissance generals tried, with dubious success, to remodel their armies as Roman legions. The problem with the ancient world was that it happened a long time ago, and reconstructing it involved guesswork. But late medieval Europeans never doubted that it had been a world of pristine perfection. They measured their own age against that imagined ideal. Inevitably, it fell short. And so the most devastating critiques of the late medieval church came not from the discontented or marginalized but from within: from powerful establishment figures who believed in an ideal church and who would not hide their disappointment with the reality. They wanted to renew the church, not destroy it.

Leading these critics was the age's intellectual colossus, Erasmus of Rotterdam, a brilliant, sharp-tongued, penny-pinching, peripatetic monk who combined a deliberately simple piety, an acid wit, and a finely judged sense of when and with whom to pick a fight. The wit was displayed in his satire *The Praise of Folly* (1509), which told his readers that almost every aspect of the world they lived in was ridiculous. The piety and shrewdness were seen in his pathbreaking 1516 Latin translation of the New Testament from the original Greek. Its preface recommended that the Bible be made available in all languages so that it could be read even by those on the very extremes of Christian civilization: the wild Scots, the Irish, even—he strained himself—women. Characteristically, he wrote that dangerous preface in Latin. He knew what he could get away with. He also knew that the content of his New Testament mattered less than the fact of its existence. He was offering the chance to use the Bible to judge the church.[1]

The church's old guard was duly provoked. Erasmus himself always stayed on the right side of trouble, but others were less careful and more vulnerable. The great cause célèbre of early sixteenth-century Germany was Johannes Reuchlin, a pioneer of Christian Hebrew scholarship. Unfortunately, the only people who could teach Christians Hebrew were Jews, and late medieval Christians generally hated and despised Jews. Reuchlin, however, both was openly friendly with certain Jews and acknowledged his debt to Jewish biblical scholarship. Inevitably, he was denounced for crypto-Judaism, which the church regarded as heresy. His denouncer, with grim irony, was a Jewish convert to Christianity. German Renaissance scholars rallied to his defense, viciously mocking his opponents as self-serving obscurantists. For them, this was a war between fearless, cutting-edge German scholarship and corrupt, ignorant Italian power politics. The court case dragged on until 1516, and even then it was merely suspended; Reuchlin was never formally cleared. In the court of public opinion, however, the new scholarship was triumphantly vindicated, and the brethren sharpened their pens in readiness for the next skirmish. Enter Martin Luther.

An Accidental Revolutionary

Martin Luther was the Reformation's indispensable firestarter. Would there have been a Reformation if young Martin had followed his father's wishes and become a lawyer? Who knows, but the Reformation as it actually happened is unimaginable without him.

Luther does not fit the stereotype of a great Christian revolutionary. He never held high office, and he remained a professor of theology at the University of Wittenberg to the end of his life, squeezing his revolution in between his regular lectures. He was not a man of heroic virtues. He was grouchy, obstinate, and an unabashed sensualist, from his boisterous, flirtatious, and deeply affectionate marriage to his well-documented fondness for Saxon beer. In later life, he was frankly fat, and for most of his life he struggled with constipation. Fittingly enough, his religion was a matter less of the mind than of the heart and the gut. Spiritually as well as physically, he was larger than life. Even his flaws were outsized. His piercing insights, his raw honesty, and the shattering spiritual experiences that drove his life still leap off the page

five centuries later. They do so because they resonate with the modern
age, an age that he made.

Luther was born in 1483 or 1484, the eldest son of a family that was
newly prosperous from copper mining. He became a monk in 1505,
against his father's wishes, and remembered those early years in the
monastery as a torment. He felt imprisoned in his own sin, whose grip
on him grew stronger the more he struggled against it. Seemingly trivial sins tortured him. His exasperated confessor told him to go and
commit some real sins, but his superior, more constructively, packed
him off to the new university at Wittenberg for further study in 1507.
He drank in his studies. Over the following dozen years, as he rose
rapidly in both the monastic and the academic hierarchies, he gradually
came to understand the Christian Gospel in a way that seemed to him
completely new, authentically ancient, and utterly life changing.

Luther was not a systematic theologian, trading in logical definitions or philosophical consistency. The systematizers who followed in
his wake picked out two key principles in his thought: *sola fide* and *sola
scriptura*, "faith alone" and "Scripture alone." But this risks missing the
point. Luther's theology was not a doctrine; it was a love affair. Consuming love for God has been part of Christian experience since the
beginning, but Luther's passion had a reckless extravagance that set it
apart, and which has echoed down Protestantism's history. He pursued
his love for God with blithe disregard for the bounds set by church and
tradition. It was an intense, desolating, intoxicating passion, sparked by
his life-upending glimpse of God's incomprehensible, terrible, beautiful
love for him. Like any lover, he found it incredible that his beloved
should love him, unworthy as he was. And yet he discovered over the
long years of prayer and study that God loved him wildly, irresponsibly,
and beyond all reason. God, in Christ, had laid down his life for him.
This was not, as the medievals' subtle theology had taught, a transaction, or a process by which believers had to do whatever was in their
power to pursue holiness. It was a sheer gift. All that mattered was accepting it.[2]

This went beyond anything Erasmus had imagined. Erasmus
wanted to free Christians from superstition, not to interfere with Christianity's basic theological framework. Indeed, he thought that too much
attention to theology was a futile distraction from the pursuit of

holiness. He called Luther *doctor hyperbolicus,* the "doctor of overstate-ment."[3] But for Luther, it was impossible to overstate God's grace. He too wanted a radically simplified Christian life, but he wanted it be-cause the flood of God's grace had swept everything else away. All the structures that the medieval church had provided for the Christian life, from pious works through sacraments to the church itself, mediat-ing between sinners and their Savior—all of this was now so much clutter. Or worse, a blasphemous attempt to buy and sell what God gives us for free.

This talk of grace and free forgiveness was dangerous. If grace is free and all we need do is believe, surely that would lead to moral an-archy? The fact that free forgiveness can look like a license to sin has plagued Protestantism for centuries. But for Luther, even to ask this question was blockheaded. What kind of lover needs rules about how to love? What kind of lover has to be bribed or threatened into loving? God loves us unreservedly. If we recognize that love, we will love him unreservedly in return.

Luther's breakthrough had a dazzling, corrosive simplicity to it. The power of those twin principles, "faith alone" and "Scripture alone," lay in the word "alone." There is nothing and no one else other than God incarnate in Jesus Christ worth attending to. Being a Christian means throwing yourself abjectly, unreservedly, on Christ's mercy. Liv-ing a Christian life means living Christ's life—that is, abandoning all security and worldly ambitions to follow him "through penalties, deaths and hell." It is only then that we may find peace. That ravishing paradox is at the heart of Protestantism. It is a further paradox that such a profoundly personal insight should have such an impact on the out-side world.

The idea's initial impact was like that of Darwinism or Marxism in their own times: it was a concept that no one had thought of in quite those terms before but that seemed to many people, once they had grasped it, to be self-evidently true. Luther's themes were all familiar ones, either ancient or newly fashionable. St. Augustine had empha-sized God's grace, the late medievals had stressed God's absolute sov-ereignty, and Erasmus had called for simplicity. What Luther did was to combine those themes as never before.

However, his idea was also powerful because it was obscure. Luther suddenly became a public figure in late 1517 not because he was preaching free salvation but because his new theology made his archbishop's financial practices seem especially offensive. He denounced them and called for a debate on the principles behind them. It was only natural that Germans, primed to expect battles between a corrupt hierarchy and brave, pious scholars, should jump to conclusions. Luther was the new Reuchlin. Even Erasmus rallied to his side. The burgeoning scandal had run on for well over a year before it became plain that Luther was calling not only for moral reform and good scholarship but for a complete reimagining of what it meant to be a Christian.

Reuchlin had chiefly been a symbolic figure. The satires that destroyed his opponents' reputations were other people's work. But in 1518, Luther discovered that he could *write*: accessibly, pungently, mixing soaring ecstasies with brutal street fighting. He had a knack for unforgettable images and analogies and a sense of paradox that made his arguments seem almost irrefutable. He could do it in Latin, like a good scholar, but he could also do it wonderfully in German, seizing his readers by the throat and pulling them into the debate.

The new technology of print had found its first master. Printing with movable type was over sixty years old by this time. The industry seemed fairly mature, mostly producing hefty legal, medical, or liturgical texts for which there were steady, predictable markets. Luther stumbled into a new literary form, the mass-market pamphlet—short, cheap, quickly produced in large numbers. A pamphlet cost roughly the same as a hen in sixteenth-century Germany and could offer more lasting and spicier nourishment. These tiny books could reach a mass audience in a completely unprecedented way. Printers who caught the wave made fortunes. Luther's books changed the rules of religious debate, which was meant to be a game for educated elites, played in universities in the decent obscurity of Latin. Luther flung open the gates. Now anyone who could read German, or who knew someone who could read German, could join in. Already, Protestantism was breaking down walls.

Luther's literary achievement has no parallels in the whole of human history. If that seems an extravagant claim, consider the figures. During his thirty-year public career, Luther produced 544 separate books, pamphlets, or articles, slightly more than one every three weeks.

At his peak, in 1523, he managed fifty-five. That year, 390 separate editions of his books, new and old, were published. Luther alone was responsible for over a fifth of the *entire* output of pamphlets by German presses during the 1520s. One scholar has totted up the totals for his rivals and supporters and concluded that the top seventeen pro-Luther pamphleteers produced 807 editions between them during the years 1518–25, whereas Luther alone produced 1,465, nearly twice as many as all the rest put together.[4] No revolutionary leader in modern history has, without the aid of censorship or state backing, towered over a mass movement to the extent Martin Luther did.

Luther's opponents were left gasping. "Every day it rains Luther books," wrote one horrified churchman in 1521. "Nothing else sells." During those same seven years, barely three hundred editions of anti-Luther works were published in Germany. The printers of these books complained that they "cannot even be given away." More than half were in Latin, not even trying to reach a mass audience (only a fifth of Luther's editions were in Latin). Orthodoxy's defenders were entirely unprepared for the storm of print that had engulfed them. Who can blame them? No one had ever seen anything like this before. In some ways, no one ever would again.[5]

Even so, it should have blown over. The church had absorbed and co-opted mass movements before. If so many Christians found Luther's ideas appealing, surely, with a little house-training, they could be welcomed into the fold?

For decades afterward, plenty of Catholic Christians hoped and worked for reconciliation. From a modern perspective, it remains a tantalizing what-if. Was the whole thing just a ghastly misunderstanding? For myself, I suspect not. Luther's ideas were so radical that a Catholic Church that conceded them would have turned itself inside out. And Luther himself was never amenable to being house-trained. But he could, perhaps, have been outflanked and isolated, if his opponents had been wily and farsighted enough to poach some of his ideas.

Instead, they tried to face him down. He had launched his protest in October 1517 with a short set of "theses": bullet-point statements summarizing his views. It was a standard way of starting an academic debate, and Luther had done it many times before on different subjects. In this case, there were ninety-five theses, and the subject was the sale of indulgences: documents in which the church promised to bestow God's grace in recognition of a charitable gift. A great many thoughtful Christians reckoned that the indulgence trade stank, so much so that sales were dropping and the indulgence sellers were forced to redouble their efforts and coarsen their rhetoric. Luther had been preaching against indulgences since the start of the year. His October theses might or might not, as legend has it, have been nailed to the door of the castle church in Wittenberg.[6] More to the point, he sent a copy to Archbishop Albrecht, the sponsor and one of the chief beneficiaries of the current indulgence campaign.

It was a challenge that could not be ignored, and because Luther refused to back down, the argument steadily escalated. A series of set-piece debates between Luther and increasingly formidable theological opponents took place during 1518 and 1519. They settled nothing. Luther, in fact, found them intensely frustrating. He wanted to talk about God's grace, true repentance, and how nitpicking legalism was rendered meaningless by Christ's astonishing gift of salvation. But his opponents would not let him. From the beginning, they accused him of questioning superiors to whom he ought instead to submit. There were crude financial considerations at work; by attacking indulgences, Luther was threatening a major income stream. There were also institutional rivalries: the Dominican friars, watchdogs of orthodoxy, distrusted Luther's modish Augustinian order. After the first debate, in 1518, Luther was summoned to Rome to answer charges of heresy. He did not go. After the second, the pope required Luther, as a matter of obedience, to accept the official line on indulgences. Again Luther refused, insisting that the pope needed to produce arguments, not commands. The establishment had decided that this was a matter for lawyers, not theologians. But if there was one thing Luther's theology opposed, it was law.[7]

Most of us, in Luther's place, would have crumbled. Perhaps from prudence: a charge of heresy is not a game. Or from conscience: When the church, Christ's representative on earth, commands us to be silent, who are we to disagree? But Luther rejoiced in rejecting prudence, and his conscience was marching to a different beat. During 1518 and 1519, he discovered in himself an epochal, adamantine stubbornness. The more he was assaulted, the more firmly he stood.

At the third debate, a full-scale scholarly disputation at Leipzig in 1519, he faced the ablest theological opponent of his life, Johann Eck of Ingolstadt. Eck, who had no real hope that Luther would concede, aimed to unmask him as a heretic. He pursued the apparent points of agreement between Luther and the Czech theologian Jan Hus, who had been executed for heresy in 1415. Eventually, he forced Luther to concede and indeed to trumpet that he, too, held the beliefs for which Hus had been condemned.

Still Luther did not budge. If what he believed was incompatible with what the church had decreed, then, he insisted, the church must be wrong. To his opponents, this was almost comically grotesque. Luther was choosing his own frail opinion over the collective weight of the whole church, guided through the ages by the Holy Spirit. It was a textbook example of heresy: willful disobedience. But to Luther, it was a liberation. If the church's most authoritative decrees could be wrong, there was no longer anything that could separate him from the love of God. Only now did he realize how far he must go. Eck had succeeded in pushing Luther out of the church, but the result was not quite what he had intended. If 1517 was the beginning of the Luther scandal, 1519 was the real birth of Protestantism.

Luther, now outed as a plain heretic, should have been arrested and dealt with. He was saved by politics. Rome had more pressing concerns than this squabble between German friars. The Holy Roman Emperor Maximilian I had been dying for years and doing so unconscionably slowly. Since 1514, he had taken a coffin with him everywhere he traveled. Long before he finally died in January 1519, plans were being laid for the contest to follow. For the imperial title was not hereditary; it was elected, chosen by seven senior German princes and bishops. Since 1440, the electors had chosen members of Austria's Habsburg dynasty, but there was nothing to stop them from choosing someone else, and this time there was a good reason to do so: the Habsburg candidate, the eighteen-year-old Charles, was also king of Spain and of the Netherlands. The prospect of one man's controlling such a vast set of territories was alarming, not least to the pope. The king of France was a realistic rival. Even Henry VIII of England was considered. The looming election overshadowed everything.

It just so happened that one of the seven electors was Frederick of

Saxony, Luther's local prince and the founder of the University of Wittenberg. Frederick's relationship with Luther was an odd one. The two men never met in person, and Frederick, who was an avid collector of holy relics, never quite saw the point of Luther's theological preoccupations. Yet he was determined to defend the celebrity professor from his prized university. The celebrity was certainly part of it. Luther had put Wittenberg on the map in a very pleasing way, was beginning to attract star academics and distinguished students, and had vaulted the town's printing industry into the first rank. In this sense, Frederick's protection was a side effect of Luther's mass-market appeal. But Frederick also wanted to defy outside interference as a matter of principle. And in 1518–19, Frederick's wishes mattered. In the impending imperial election, he was seen as a crucial swing vote. He was even considered an imperial candidate himself. If, at this moment, he wanted to shelter a suspected heretic, no one was going to force the issue.

In the end, on June 28, 1519, Charles was unanimously elected emperor, and became Charles V. But the damage was already done. The crucial Leipzig disputation was unfolding when the election was held. Frederick had bought Luther enough time to turn his personal crisis of conscience into a mass movement threatening the church's entire structure of authority.

During 1520, Luther wrote a series of tracts laying out the core of his ideas. His legions of readers snapped them up like episodes of a serial drama. *The Freedom of a Christian* described his understanding of God's free grace in rapturous terms. Other books reviled the church's hierarchy and the corruption he thought it had spawned. Luther declared that the church's ceremonies and sacraments were an elaborate confidence trick, fleecing Christians before abandoning them to hell. All Christians, he insisted, had both the right and the responsibility to reform the church, and they should act on that right whatever the priests say. In fact, the distinction between priests and laypeople was meaningless. All Christians are priests. At the end of the year, he defiantly burned the papal bull that had condemned him as a heretic.

By then, his enemies were finally assembling. The new emperor formally assumed his imperial title in October 1520. Luther had had a magnificent run, but justice was closing in on him. An imperial Diet, the empire's highest legislative body, was planned at the southwestern

German city of Worms. Luther was summoned to attend and, undoubtedly, to be condemned. He was promised safe-conduct from Wittenberg to Worms and back, but promises made to convicted heretics were not necessarily binding. Jan Hus, whom Luther had praised in Leipzig, had been burned despite just such a safe-conduct promise. Luther fully expected the same fate, and friends urged him not to go. His correspondence as the Diet approached shows a man torn. Naturally, he was frightened and agitated. He prayed urgently for safety and doubted his prayers would be granted. Yet in another mood, he relished the Diet as an apocalyptic confrontation, at which he would at last testify to his doctrines, seal them with his blood, and win a martyr's crown. And so he went to Worms as Christ went to Jerusalem, a three-hundred-mile journey, pausing to preach on the way. When warned of the dangers ahead, he replied that if there were as many devils in Worms as there were tiles on the roofs, he would still go. He arrived on April 17, 1521, to find the rooftops crowded, not with devils, but with supporters and spectators. The streets were so thronged as to be impassable. He was borne through to the Diet and brought before the estates of the empire.[8]

Luther expected to have his long-delayed argument about God's grace. Once again he was denied. He was simply presented with his books and asked to repent of the heresies in them. To everyone's surprise, including perhaps his own, Luther asked for twenty-four hours to think it over. This unexpected request was granted, and it raised some hopes that he might actually concede. The one surviving letter which he wrote that night suggests such hopes were not entirely foolish. "With Christ's help," he wrote, "I shall not in all eternity recant the least particle."[9] Apparently, he feared that he might crumble. He could be forgiven for finding the empire's assembled glories a little overbearing.

He returned the following afternoon and was kept waiting outside the palace for two hours. The crowd pressed about him. Voices shouted that he should stand firm. One called out, "Blessed is the womb that bore you."[10] Finally, he was allowed in, and the previous day's question was put to him again. He answered carefully. Yes, they were his books. Would he disown them? Only if it could be shown to him, on the basis of the Bible and the Bible alone, that he was wrong. Otherwise, his conscience was captive to the Word of God. He might even—as one witness claimed, many years later—have concluded with a famous declaration of helplessness: "Here I stand. I can do no other."

Luther often looked back on that moment. In retrospect, his "humility and deference" troubled him: he reproached himself for having "held my spirit in check." He promised that "they would hear other things, if I would come before them again."[11] In other words, Luther at Worms was not quite the roaring lion of Protestant legend. He spent a week after that famous exchange locked in debate with a formidable roster of German prelates and princes. They had enough to talk about that the emperor extended his safe-conduct for forty-eight hours to allow the discussions to continue. But in vain. Neither side would budge. So Luther was condemned as a heretic and outlawed. The young emperor, principled, prudent, and a touch naive, honored the safe-conduct. Luther left Worms on April 26, having been granted neither his argument nor his martyrdom. Even so, the Diet of Worms would be the epicenter of his life and of what would become the Reformation: humble, unyielding defiance of the whole world in the name of Scripture and conscience.

"Captive to the Word of God"

Part of Luther's achievement at Worms was to enact, with unforgettable vividness, a new way of doing theology, which has defined Protestantism ever since. At the Diet, the archbishop of Trier's secretary, Johann Eck (a different Eck from Leipzig), accused Luther of being "completely mad." This was not just abuse. Eck was genuinely shocked. Luther had demanded to have his errors proved to him, from the Bible, to his own satisfaction. Eck pointed out the obvious problem:

> If it were granted that whoever contradicts the councils and the common understanding of the church must be overcome by Scripture passages, we will have nothing in Christianity that is certain or decided.[12]

If individual consciences are sovereign, then how can Christians ever again agree on anything? Eck's point was essentially unanswerable.

Much of the rest of this book is about the endless arguments that he correctly predicted. Some Protestants have tried to evade his charge. Others invert it: If the individual conscience is *not* sovereign, how can anyone call themselves Christian at all?

But it is worth noticing the detail of Luther's position at Worms. He took his stand on two authorities, which he saw as intimately linked: his own conscience and God's Word. The Word, he said, had his conscience captive, and it was neither safe nor right to disobey conscience.

The Bible's role here was crucial. To appeal simply to inner conviction would have indeed looked like madness. But for Luther, an acknowledged expert in biblical interpretation, to take his stand on the Bible was altogether different. His stirring, empty offer to submit himself to its correction was widely imitated in the years that followed. This is the "Scripture principle": the conviction that the Bible is the only and absolute source of authority and that all believers are equal before it. It is often taken to be Protestantism's central, unifying idea.[13] But, while it is certainly a pervasive one, it is not the whole story. Luther's own relationship with the Bible was subtler than that.

What made Luther's stance so outrageous was not that he valorized the Bible. That is hardly unusual for Christians. What was shocking was that he set it above *everything* else. He treated the views of the early church fathers, of more recent scholars, even of church councils, with great respect, but he would not be constrained by them. In the end, anything outside the Bible, including anyone else's interpretation of the Bible, was a mere opinion. This was the true and enduring radicalism of Protestantism: its readiness to question every human authority and tradition. The formulation of the English Thirty-nine Articles, half a century later, captures the same spirit in a careful double negative:

> Holy Scripture containeth all things necessary to salvation: so that whatsoever is not read therein, nor may be proved thereby, is not to be . . . thought necessary or requisite to salvation.

Not "everything in the Bible is essential," but "nothing that is *not* in the Bible is essential."

On the crudest level, this was a brilliant maneuver. In a Christian society which had always revered the Bible, which was rediscovering

its original text in the midst of a scholarly vogue for ancient truths, and
which was ready to measure the church's hierarchy against its own
ideals and find them wanting—in this context, for a monk and doctor
of theology to stand alone, at risk of his life, and wield the Bible against
all the forces of the establishment was dreadfully persuasive. Erasmus
had called for a simple Christian life informed by Scripture. What could
be simpler than the cry "Scripture alone"? It allowed Luther to shrug
off every authority the church could throw at him while still submitting to the highest authority of all. Best of all, the authority to which he
was submitting could not answer back. As Erasmus would soon argue,
this is Scripture for brawlers: turning the Bible into a stick with which
to beat your enemies. Protestants have been weaponizing Scripture
ever since, for use against outsiders and each other.

But this is too cynical. Luther was a superb scriptural street fighter,
but that was not why he valued the Bible. We need instead to notice
how apparently free and easy Luther could be with the Bible, to an extent that would shock many modern Protestants. It is not so surprising
that he threw out the so-called deuterocanonical or apocryphal books
of the Old Testament, the books such as Tobit, Ecclesiasticus, and Mac-
cabees, which survive only in Greek, not in Hebrew. Plenty of biblical
scholars agreed with him on that, though it conveniently got rid of
some theologically awkward passages. Yet he also dealt robustly with
the rest of the Old Testament. He wanted to expel the book of Esther
altogether. He thought that the books of Kings were more reliable than
the books of Chronicles, doubted that large chunks of the Old Testament were actually written by their supposed authors, and reckoned
that many of its texts were corrupted. He thought that most of the book
of Job was fiction and that the prophets had sometimes made mistakes.
He poured cold water on the huge numbers in the Old Testament narratives.[14]

On the New Testament, Luther was only a little more restrained.
He was famously scathing about the Epistle of James, whose teaching
on the role of faith and good works does not sit entirely easily with his
doctrines. He called it an "epistle of straw," claimed that it "mangles the
Scriptures" and "doesn't amount to much." Once he told a student, "I
almost feel like throwing Jimmy into the stove." In Luther's Bible,
James was yanked out of its normal place and sent to the end of the

New Testament, along with three other books that he doubted were written by apostles (the Epistle to the Hebrews, the Epistle of Jude, and Revelation). He treated other parts of the Bible with almost equally unnerving favoritism. John's Gospel was for Luther "the one, fine, true, and chief gospel, and is far, far to be preferred over the other three."[15] All of which suggests a Humpty-Dumptyish readiness to ignore what he disliked, choose what he wanted, and call it the Word of God.

That very brazenness tells us that this was not the whole story. Luther treated the Bible this way because of his understanding of what the Bible was. There is no doubting his profound debt to the Bible, where he had found the doctrines that shaped the rest of his life. Those doctrines were, for him, the Bible's true heart. As he advised Bible readers in 1530:

> Search out and deal with the core of our Christian doctrine, wherever it may be found throughout the Bible. And the core is this: that without any merit, as a gift of God's pure grace in Christ, we attain righteousness, life, and salvation.[16]

That was the message: the Gospel, the good news of Christ crucified and risen. The reason he called the Epistle of James straw was that for all its earnest moralizing "it contains not a syllable about Christ."

This is why, at Worms, Luther said his conscience was captive to the Word of God, rather than to the Bible. The two were not quite the same. John's Gospel teaches that Jesus Christ himself is the Word of God made human. The Bible, Luther argued, was the same Word of God "enlettered," clothed in a body of ink and pulped rag.[17] Therefore, much of its content was incidental and unimportant. If that included some factual errors or contradictions, they did not matter any more than the fit of Jesus' clothing. The message was what counted.

Luther used his Bible to fight his battles, and did so with relish, but before he was a brawler, he was a lover. The Bible had taught him about his beloved, and so he treasured it as a love letter. He understood it through the prism of that love. Everything that could not be read through this prism was unimportant. The Bible was not to be analyzed like a scholarly text but to be gazed at like a great work of art.[18] This was the only way that the Word of God could speak to your soul, and this was why every outside authority had to be rejected. Like that of a great work of art, the Bible's power was to Luther self-evident. Unless, impossibly, you could persuade him that he had not seen what he had seen, there was nothing more to be said. The difficulty, inescapable after Worms, is that not everyone who gazes on a great work of art sees the same message.

Although Luther was allowed to leave Worms in safety, he was merely given a head start. For the rest of his life, he was a wanted man, and to the end of his days he was conscious of the Diet's still-active condemnation hanging over him. The immediate effect was that halfway home he was kidnapped on the road by what seemed to be a band of brigands. His companions were aghast, but Luther had been warned to expect it. The "kidnappers" worked for his protector, Elector Frederick. They spirited him away to the Wartburg Castle, near Eisenach, where he remained in hiding for nearly a year. His captors took elaborate steps to conceal his whereabouts, even spreading rumors that he had fled to Bohemia.[19] He changed his monk's habit for the clothes of a country knight and grew his hair and beard: a disguise, but also an assertion of the Christian liberty he preached. Yet, as he joked, in his confinement he was now more truly a monk than ever. He did not waste his time in captivity; he translated the New Testament into German, among other projects. But he chafed. In the first few weeks he was "drunk with leisure."[20] Soon he was brooding over what was happening in his unexpected absence.

Luther was already displaying what would become an enduring feature of Protestantism: a queasy mixture of humility and arrogance. The humility was real. Luther knew that he was the worst of sinners. He begged his followers to call themselves Christians, not "Lutherans":

> What is Luther? The teaching is not mine. Neither was I crucified for anyone. . . . How then should I, poor stinking maggot-fodder that I am, come to have men call the children of Christ by my wretched name?

He denied that his movement's success was his own doing. In 1522, he gave this account of how it happened:

> I simply taught, preached, and wrote God's Word; otherwise I
> did nothing. And while I slept, or drank Wittenberg beer with
> my friends . . . the Word so greatly weakened the papacy that
> no prince or emperor ever inflicted such losses on it. I did noth-
> ing; the Word did everything.[21]

Vintage Luther, including the beer. But for all the humility, there are
some bold claims here. His teaching is Christ's teaching, and he wrote
God's Word. Increasingly, Luther saw himself not merely as a theologian but as a prophet, called by God to overturn the papacy. For one
obscure professor to mobilize an unprecedented mass movement, to
defy all the forces of church and empire, and to feel them crumbling at
his touch—this was heady stuff. And yet his confinement had sidelined
him. He still churned out books, but there was a dangerous vacuum—
especially back in Wittenberg, the eye of the storm.

Wittenberg was by now dominated by Luther's allies. The most
important of them was Philip Melanchthon, acknowledged on all sides
to be one of the most brilliant minds of his age. The unpronounceable
name is a sign of the times. He was born with the solid German surname of Schwartzerd, but Johannes Reuchlin, who happened to be his
great-uncle, suggested he adopt the Renaissance fashion of translating
his name into Greek. In 1518, Reuchlin also secured the job of professor
of Greek at Wittenberg for his nephew. Luther was immediately in awe
of Melanchthon, who, at only twenty-one, was thirteen years his junior.
He claimed that he had never written a book as good as Melanchthon's
Commonplaces, published in 1521. It was Melanchthon who fashioned
Luther's vivid, chaotic theological insights into a coherent system. But
while the two men were always close, Luther's faith in his younger colleague was shaken during his confinement in 1521–22. Melanchthon had
not kept a grip on Wittenberg. Where Luther was immovably stubborn, Melanchthon was calm and reasonable—to the point, his enemies
muttered, of timidity. Luther compared their respective styles by saying that Melanchthon pricked their enemies with pins, while he himself
stabbed them with pikes.[22]

If Melanchthon was timid, others in Wittenberg had the opposite
problem. After Luther's condemnation at Worms, some of his fellow

travelers began to take matters into their own hands. In September 1521, Luther's fellow Augustinian monks changed the way they were celebrating the Catholic Mass, the most prominent daily symbol of the theology they now questioned, eventually rewriting the service in German rather than Latin. Some began to abandon their cloisters. In January 1522, the university's chancellor, Andreas Karlstadt, even got married, in defiance of the long-standing Catholic requirement that clergy remain celibate.

A nervous Elector Frederick called for restraint, but these new radicals were only just beginning. In December 1521, three men from the mining town of Zwickau arrived in Wittenberg: a former student and two weavers. They claimed that God had called them to be prophets, predicted the imminent end of the world, and demanded further dramatic reforms. In particular, they criticized the practice of baptizing infants, which, as they rightly said, has no direct biblical basis. Meanwhile, Karlstadt and his allies were demanding the destruction of Catholic images, altars, and relics in the town's churches, so as to "cleanse" the buildings of idolatry and fit them for reformed worship. This was controversial in itself, but when the elector forbade it and some of the more excitable townsfolk started smashing images on their own initiative, it looked less like holiness and more like rioting.[23]

Luther was horrified. Partly this was because, for all his spiritual radicalism, he was deeply socially conservative. His instinct was to obey rightful authorities, to respect social hierarchies, and to preserve good order. For him, Christian freedom meant inner liberation, not political upheaval. He had defied established authorities, but he was a professor and had in any case been called by God. Self-appointed prophets like the Zwickauers and the iconoclasts had no excuse.

More significantly, Luther hated these impatient reformers' ideas. He wanted to set Christians free from rules and laws, but Karlstadt and the Zwickauers were burdening Christian consciences with new rules about baptism and images. They had missed the point. Luther wanted not to replace bad laws with good ones but to lift believers above the realm of law altogether, into the light of the Gospel of love. For him, these law-mongers were *Schwärmer,* "fanatics." It was a capacious category, which expanded over the coming decades to include almost everyone Luther disagreed with.

So in March 1522, Luther decided to risk returning to Wittenberg to take charge. Symbolically, he arrived in his monk's habit, shaved and tonsured. For a time, it worked. Karlstadt was reined in and then exiled to an obscure country parish. Luther's success in whipping his recalcitrant colleagues into line only confirmed his sense of his unique calling.

Yet while Luther could impose order on one town, the wider movement he had sparked was now beyond anyone's control. The early 1520s in Germany were revolutionary years. Priests, printers, peddlers, even (shockingly) women could all make themselves heard. In a ruthless, scurrilous, and almost ungovernable book market, talent rose rapidly to the top. Between 1518 and 1525, fifty-one editions of anti-Catholic works by a Nuremberg shoemaker, Hans Sachs, were published in Germany: not far off Philip Melanchthon's total of seventy-one. In parts of Germany's jurisdictional patchwork, reformist preaching and printing were banned, but preachers were hard to keep out, and books almost impossible. Those cities where the reformers found support were confronted with Wittenberg's dilemma: How was this Reformation actually to be *implemented*? By the time Luther himself finally abandoned his monk's guise, sealed his departure from the vowed life by marrying a former nun, and promulgated a German order for the Mass, he was scrambling to catch up with a splintering, restless, hydra-headed movement that offered a hundred different local Reformations in the name of the same Gospel.

The Fanatics' Reformation

With hindsight, we can see three broad strands of reform emerging from this chaos. One strand looked directly to Luther, with his appealing blend of spiritual radicalism and social conservatism. The other two strands were less unified. One, rooted in Switzerland and southern Germany, looked primarily to Huldrych Zwingli, the city preacher of Zurich, and several other loosely allied leaders; we will come back to them in chapter 3. The final strand was even more fractious. It lacked shared leaders, origins, or doctrines. What united it was a mood, a radically impatient determination to take Luther's insights about the futility of the old ways and to press them to their extremes. Karlstadt belonged to this radical strand. So too did Thomas Müntzer, a former pastor in Zwickau who became notorious after he was blamed for burn-ing down a shrine to the Virgin Mary in March 1524. That summer, he publicly demanded that the princes of Saxony take up arms on the re-formers' behalf. Luther denounced him as another fanatic.

Müntzer was starting to ride something bigger than he could con-trol. It is still unclear quite how the religious turmoil that Luther had unleashed was connected to the German Peasants' War of 1524–25, the largest mass rebellion in European history before the French Revolu-tion of 1789. The peasants had long-standing grievances about rents, rights, and property, but reforming preachers were a vital catalyst. Suddenly peasants were denouncing serfdom as incompatible with Christian liberty, demanding that the people be able to elect their priests, and claiming that the church's riches ought to belong to every-one. None of this was what Luther had meant, but they did not have to stretch his ideas very far to get there. The most widespread set of de-mands, first adopted by the peasants of Swabia, ended with a deliberate echo of Luther at Worms: they offered to desist if they could be proved wrong using the Bible.

Some of the rebels, influenced by preachers like Müntzer, wanted much more. Abolishing private property—didn't the Bible record that the early church had held all goods in common? Killing monks and priests—didn't the Bible teach that idolaters should die? Overthrowing princes—didn't the Bible promise a future kingdom of the saints? Even if these radicals were only clinging to the rebellion's tail, they gave the whole enterprise an apocalyptic feel. Something more than rents and landholding was at stake. It was a moment to establish a just social or-der in anticipation of Christ's imminent return.

To his credit, Luther was torn. In early 1525, he wrote *An Admonition to Peace,* accepting that many of the peasants' demands were fair but warning that rebellion was no way to secure them. To follow Christ meant meek submission, not pillage and insurrection. He advised the peasants, somberly and with a magnificent lack of realism, to return home and humbly petition their betters for redress. Once it became clear that matters had passed that point, Luther's deep social conserva-tism took over. His next pamphlet, *Against the Robbing and Murdering Hordes of Peasants,* blustered:

Nothing can be more poisonous, hurtful or devilish than a rebel. It is just as when one must kill a mad dog. . . . There is no time for sleeping; no place for patience or mercy. It is the time of the sword, not the day of grace. . . . I think there is not a devil left in hell; they have all gone into the peasants. . . . Stab, smite, slay, whoever can. If you die in doing it, well for you! A more blessed death can never be yours, for you die in obeying the divine Word.

Ironically, Luther justified this in the same apocalyptic terms as Müntzer. This was not a time for soft middle ways: "The destruction of the world is to be expected every hour." It was time to take a stand against the forces of Antichrist, whatever their guise.[24]

On May 15, 1525, nine days after Luther's pamphlet was written, the Thuringian peasants met a Saxon-Hessian mercenary army near Frankenhausen. Müntzer preached before the battle, pointing to a rainbow as an omen of victory and promising the peasants that bullets could not hurt them. Meanwhile, they were encircled with artillery. The peasants tried to flee to the town. Thousands died before they reached it. The wounded were left to die on the field. The town itself surrendered, but not quickly enough. The reprisals were on a genocidal scale. The victorious lords, one witness wrote, "seem bent on leaving a wilderness for their heirs." Müntzer himself was found hiding, in disguise, and was beheaded. A few weeks later, the southern German peasants suffered equally catastrophic defeats. The total number killed during the whole appalling business was probably well over eighty thousand. And while the peasants would certainly have been crushed with or without Luther's blessing, his moral responsibility for the slaughter is inescapable.

For the reforming movement as a whole, the Peasants' War was a calamity. Fairly or not, it was widely blamed on reformist preaching. By no coincidence, it was in September 1524, as the violence was bubbling up, that Erasmus finally decisively distanced himself from Luther. He argued, all too plausibly, that Luther's teaching on God's grace left no room for personal responsibility and so threatened moral anarchy and social collapse. If this was where conscience governed by Scripture alone led, perhaps the authoritative, binding interpretation of the church was not so bad after all.[25] In the early 1520s, it had been possible to hope that one of the various strands of the reforming movement might take over the old church wholesale. That hope died on the battlefields.

The radicals, those who survived, now began to preach withdrawal from Christian society, to form perfect communities of saints in expectation of the imminent Last Judgment. For many of them, the symbol of this withdrawal was adult baptism. All the baptisms described in the New Testament are of adults able to confess their own faith. So perhaps infants should not be baptized? In which case, all Christendom had been in error since at least the second century, and the community of the faithful could only be a small, self-selected group. This meant abandoning the ideal of a universal church, to which Luther and most other reformers still aspired, for sectarianism. Beginning in Zurich in January 1525, the radicals began to mark that withdrawal by baptizing adults. "Anabaptists," or rebaptizers, their enemies called them, and they were not short of enemies. To the old church, they were heretics like the rest. To Luther and other reformers who desperately needed to be thought respectable, the radicals risked discrediting the reforming movement as a whole. A sharp line urgently needed to be drawn in these shifting sands.

That effort to differentiate between radical Anabaptists and safe, mainstream, moderate reformers was strikingly successful. To this day, it remains controversial to describe the radicals as Protestants. Yet their shared heritage is unmistakable. The Anabaptists' doctrines were very similar to those of establishment, "magisterial" Protestantism. Even infant baptism was openly questioned by some supposedly mainstream reformers, before the subject became too hot to touch. One hundred twenty years later, the Baptists, a new group with its roots firmly in mainstream Protestantism, followed the Anabaptists in renouncing infant baptism, despite coming from a distinct theological tradition.

Like Luther's moderates, the radicals claimed to base their doctrines wholly on the Bible. And like Luther, they did so as lovers, perceiving the Bible's core message by God's grace and using it to interpret the rest. Some were more explicit about this than Luther. The south German radical Jörg Haugk complained that "many accept the Scriptures as if they were the essence of divine truth; but they are only a

witness to divine truth which must be experienced in the inner being."
Hans Hut, a survivor of the battle of Frankenhausen who became a
compelling Anabaptist missionary before his death in prison in 1527,
argued that the Bible, if taken literally, bristled with contradictions. It
could therefore only be properly understood by the direct guidance of
the Holy Spirit. In this way, theologically uneducated radicals could
defy learned professors like Luther. One self-taught Anabaptist preacher
called scholars "Scripture wizards," arguing that their hairsplitting
subtleties blinded them to the simple truth.[26]

Luther and the "fanatics" both exemplify Protestantism at work.
Both were driven by dazzling religious insights, which they discovered
by reading the Bible and which then taught them how to read the Bible.
Both denied that any human authority could teach them they were
wrong. The Christian liberty that Luther had preached reached far further than he had anticipated. That was his tragedy, and perhaps also
his glory.

For while 1525 was a catastrophe, Luther did win a kind of victory.
The first revolution was over. But for those princes, city councils, and
people who had imbibed the reformers' preaching, going back to the
pre-1517 world was hard to imagine. So Luther found himself representing a safe middle way, the acceptable face of reform. It was an outcome
that neither he nor anyone else had expected. His Reformation neither
transformed the church nor was crushed by it. Instead, a de facto partition took shape. One by one, a series of German and Scandinavian cities
and territories abolished the Catholic Mass, repudiated the church's
hierarchy, and required preachers to proclaim Luther's doctrines. A
new form of Christianity was starting to come into being. Luther's
revolution had, like all great revolutions, failed. But like all great revolutions, it had created a new world.

CHAPTER 2

Protectors and Tyrants

There is no power but of God: the powers that be are ordained of God.

—ROMANS 13:1

The Reformation became notorious for two fat men. The first, Martin Luther, we have already met. The second, King Henry VIII of
England, was in most things Luther's opposite. Yet the two men shared
a titanic stubbornness, near-messianic self-belief, a knack for dividing
Christendom into admirers and enemies, and a lifelong mutual hatred.

Henry VIII was not, except in his own eyes, a great spiritual leader.
And yet while the Reformation began as Luther's story, it quickly became
Henry's. Protestantism started in believers' souls, as a love affair with
God, but it could not be kept tidily in its place. It spilled out into every part
of life, and in particular, as we will see throughout this book, it collided
with politics, stymied and hijacked by it, but also subverting and occasionally transforming it. Like mating spiders, religious reformers and political
leaders needed and exploited each other, but they could never trust each
other. To the politicians, Luther's movement was both a threat to be negotiated and an opportunity to be seized. At the same time, it was either the
work of divine providence or a fearful scheme of Satan's. For politicians
are human beings. They felt the tug of Luther's teachings and of the
church's warnings on their souls like everybody else.

Taming the Reformation

The intertwined alliance-rivalry between church and state had been a
constant theme of medieval politics. The two sides were like an old

married couple, with plenty of accumulated grievances but held together by powerful bonds of affection, loyalty, convenience, and habit. Still, even placid marriages can be disrupted when an eye-catching interloper waltzes in.

For the reformers, breaking up this cozy twosome was a necessity. They knew that the pope's power depended on the cooperation of secular rulers: the kings, princes, and magistrates who actually governed Europe. In this sense, the Reformation was fundamentally a struggle for the backing of secular governments. Without their support, no religious dissidents could last for long. With it, the old church was at their mercy.

This was a matter of principle as well as of self-preservation. The church's hierarchy, Luther insisted, was illegitimate. It dominated and exploited when it should, Christlike, serve and submit. Priests, bishops, and popes should be mere functionaries, chosen by the Christian community to provide them with religious services. But then who *should* govern the church? The Anabaptists' spiritual anarchy was not to Luther's taste. Long-standing Christian tradition taught that emperors, kings, and princes had been granted their authority by God. The New Testament taught that Christians should obey such secular rulers as a matter of conscience. What's more, Europe's rulers were all baptized Christians, and Luther argued that all baptized Christians were the spiritual equal of any pope. Surely, because God has given princes power over secular matters, it would be natural for them to assume responsibility for religious affairs too.[1]

In 1520, Luther appealed to Germany's princes to take religious reform into their own hands. They did not do so—yet. Most preferred to wait and see what would happen, although some encouraged reformist preaching in their territories. Even after the disaster of the Peasants' War, there was no agreement as to what should actually be done. Worse, a terrifying Turkish invasion, which conquered most of Hungary in 1526 and would reach the walls of Vienna in 1529, meant that this was no time for intra-Christian quarrels. So when the princes of the Holy Roman Empire gathered at the Diet of Speyer in 1526, they unanimously agreed to postpone the decision. Until a proper council of the church (a much-hoped-for mirage) could resolve the religious questions, each prince should "so live, govern, and carry himself" in his religious policy "as he hopes and trusts to answer to God and his Imperial Majesty."[2] Almost by accident, this anodyne resolution created space for something that had never happened before. One by one, territories and cities began to peel away from the universal church. In the lead was Luther's own Saxony. Luther published a German order of service for Saxony in 1526, and the new church structure that coalesced there was widely imitated.

The breathing space created at Speyer was brief, but it was enough. In 1529, another Diet of Speyer overwhelmingly—but, this time, not unanimously—passed a resolution rescinding the implicit permissions granted three years earlier, horrified at how they had been used. Five princes made a formal "Protestation" against the new decree. They, their allies, and their spiritual descendants down to the present became known as Protestants.

Between them, those first Protestants encapsulate the tensions of political Reformation. There is no doubting the real religious conviction behind their stand. Elector Frederick of Saxony, who had protected Luther but never been persuaded by him, had died in 1525. His brother and successor, John, was a true believer. So was George, from 1527 the margrave of Brandenburg, who had been converted by Luther's courage at the Diet of Worms. Philip, landgrave of Hesse, had also met Luther at Worms, when he was only sixteen. By 1525, when he had commanded the troops who massacred the peasants at Frankenhausen, he was fully in the reformers' camp. All of these men knew the risk they were taking. Three days after the Protestation, Saxony, Hesse, and three leading Protestant cities—Strassburg, Nuremberg, and Ulm—signed a secret defensive pact.[3]

The risk the princes were taking was matched by the potential rewards. They had already begun to assume full control of the churches in their territories. Even during the Peasants' War itself, Philip of Hesse was drawing up an inventory of the property owned by monasteries in his lands. After all, Luther's theology made monasteries redundant and emphasized the rights of secular princes. Surely those hard-pressed and impoverished princes should be able to take over the monasteries' ill-gotten wealth, to use in God's service as they saw fit? Once the example was set, it proved too tempting to resist. There was safety in numbers. Each territory that jumped made it easier for the next one. It turned out that the Germans' modest and conscientious reforms were only a starting point for more rapacious regimes to come.

Outside the Holy Roman Empire, political Reformations first took root in two sets of territories that were in effect safe from outside interference: the ferociously independent cantons of Switzerland and the lands around the Baltic Sea. We will return to Switzerland's distinctive, republican Reformations in the next chapter. The Baltic story was, at first, simply an extension of Germany's. The grand master of the Teutonic Knights, a religious-military order that controlled territories in what is now Poland, was advised by Luther in 1523 that he could abandon his celibacy and turn his lands into a secular principality. He liked the prospect, and so in 1525 made himself duke of Prussia and his subjects into Lutherans. The wife he chose came from another northern early-adopter territory: the powerful kingdom of Denmark, which extended south into Germany and included modern Norway, and which by the 1530s was caught in a civil war between two claimants to the throne. One of them allied himself with the reformers, and when he emerged as King Christian III in 1536, he led his whole kingdom out of the Catholic Church. For the next century, Denmark would remain the single most substantial Lutheran state.

Sweden's case was more idiosyncratic. After more than a century under Danish rule, Sweden had broken free in the early 1520s. The rebel leader turned king, Gustav Vasa, had no intention of ceding an inch of his new sovereignty to anyone. So when German merchants in his ports began buzzing with tales of princes to the south sloughing off papal authority, his interest was piqued. The Reformation that he slowly imposed on a reluctant Sweden was clearly influenced by Luther and implemented by churchmen and ministers who were true Lutheran believers, but it was Gustav Vasa's Reformation, not Luther's. Its distinctive features were his seizure of huge amounts of church property and his iron insistence that the Swedish church's hierarchy and courts be under royal control.

Even Gustav Vasa, however, looks tame compared with the Reformation era's most megalomaniacal opportunist. Henry VIII was not a natural Lutheran. His greatest talent was political display, an invaluable skill for the ruler of a kingdom whose fading grandeur was not matched by much real power. His piety was as theatrical as the rest of his

persona—which is not to doubt its sincerity: no better way to persuade others than to persuade yourself first. So when Luther's movement erupted, Henry threw himself into the fray with characteristic
panache.

Like the Renaissance scholar he fancied himself to be, Henry wrote
a book. Despite his ghostwriters' efforts, *I Assert That There Are Seven
Sacraments* is no great piece of theology; but celebrity sells, and it became one of the few anti-Luther pamphlets to be a commercial success
in Germany. Whether anyone was persuaded by Henry's argument, we
may doubt. But in two quarters, at least, it struck home. For one, Luther
could not ignore such a high-profile challenger. He wrote a vitriolic
reply, much to the fury of the English king, who only liked polemical
rough-and-tumble on his own terms. More important, however, Henry's book found its mark in Rome. He had long resented the pope's gift
of glorious titles to the kings of Spain ("the Catholic King") and France
("the Most Christian King"), while England was left out. Now, finally
and after some negotiation, Henry got his prize and became "Defender
of the Faith."

So Henry's initial response to the Reformation was to remain ostentatiously Catholic and thereby to extort favors from Rome. Other Catholic kings were also discovering that the pope now needed them more
than they needed him. But for Henry VIII, this turned out not to be
enough. He ran up against one of the pope's few undisputed powers:
canon law, which included the law of marriage. In 1527, fretted by his
lack of sons and entranced by a young noblewoman named Anne
Boleyn, Henry convinced himself that his long-standing marriage to
the Spanish princess Catherine of Aragon was invalid. Only the pope
could grant the annulment Henry suddenly, desperately wanted. Yet
Henry's case in law was flimsy, and the pope was loath to offend Queen
Catherine's nephew, Emperor Charles V. Henry tried every diplomatic
trick in the book, but Rome would not cooperate.

In another generation, such a drama would have resolved itself some
other way. But the precedent set by the German princes, and the arguments made by some opportunistic English readers of Luther, raised an
enticing possibility. What if the pope did not, in fact, have the right to
judge an English king's marriage? What if God intended that the king
himself should be head of the church in his own realm? If German

princelings could get away with it, then why not the king of England, the Defender of the Faith? The idea grew on Henry until it had him absolutely in its grip. By the time he formally repudiated the pope's authority in 1534, his marital adventures had almost become a side issue. He was now convinced that he was, by God's appointment, Supreme Head of the Church of England.[4]

Lutherans might have swallowed that self-important title. They could not, however, accept what Henry did with it, which went beyond what any other prince of the age attempted and would not be surpassed until the French revolutionaries tried to impose the newly invented Cult of the Supreme Being. It was not merely that Henry took control of the church's courts and senior appointments. Nor that he seized its property, although the scale of the plunder was staggering; something like a third of the land area of England passed into royal control when the monasteries were dissolved. German princes usually simply closed the monasteries to new entrants and allowed them to wind down gradually, but Henry shut them down. Monks who cooperated were pensioned off. Those who resisted might or might not escape with their lives. He promised to use the proceeds on pious projects. Instead, he spent most of them on futile wars, such that, despite this vast influx of cash, by the end of his life he was facing bankruptcy.

Money and jurisdiction, however, were only the beginning. Henry earnestly believed he was Supreme Head of the church, and woe to those who defied him. Few did, but those few included some monumental figures. Erasmus's friend Thomas More and the famed bishop and theologian John Fisher were both beheaded in 1535. It was the public-relations equivalent of decapitating a pair of Nobel Prize winners, and won Henry a Europe-wide reputation as a tyrant, only underlined by the killing of his second wife the following year. More and Fisher died for their loyalty to Rome, but in 1536 the leading English Protestant theologian, William Tyndale, was burned alive, with Henry's approval and connivance, for daring to disapprove of the king's remarriage. That pattern, of parallel judicial murders of Catholics and Protestants, would persist to the end of Henry's reign.

The English church's new orthodoxy, in other words, was defined by its king's whim. Luther, appalled, claimed "that king wants to be God." Henry did not quite put it that way, but he did believe God had delegated a great deal of spiritual authority to him. He toyed with the idea that he could ordain priests. He certainly thought that he could tell his bishops what to believe, debating with them and browbeating them into submission. His own extensive notes on doctrinal reform include such choice snippets as his attempt to rewrite the Ten Commandments. The biblical text forbids coveting others' property, but Henry wanted it only to forbid coveting "wrongly or unjustly." Usually he was persuaded to pull back from the more outrageous positions, but his own fickle, inconsistent theological prejudices were at the root of his entire Reformation. He loathed the pope and eagerly promoted the English Bible. He also loathed Luther's doctrine of salvation and was extravagantly devoted to the Catholic Mass. It did not really make sense, but who was going to tell him that?[5]

When he died in 1547, England began to return to religious coherence. The regency regime of the new boy king, Edward VI, was controlled by a Protestant clique who had prudently kept their convictions muted while the old tyrant lived. Even so, Henry's legacy was pervasive. The principle of state control over religion was firmly established. England's religion changed with its monarchs. After Edward's death, a Catholic queen, his half sister Mary, returned the kingdom briefly to Rome, and after her death England obediently followed a Protestant queen, Elizabeth I, back into schism again.

Elizabeth was subtler than Henry VIII, and in any case, with orthodoxies hardening across Europe, the time for theological swashbuckling was over. Yet while she presided over an unmistakably Protestant church, her own prejudices could still override religious logic. She had a taste for trappings of traditional religion like vestments, choirs, and crucifixes, whether or not they were compatible with her new church's doctrines. Her Protestantism in medieval dress left her subjects split between ceremonialists who treasured those echoes of the old ways and "Puritans" who wanted to complete the journey to the new. Her idiosyncrasies are not exactly to blame for the Civil War that engulfed England forty years after her death, but they helped make it possible.

Henry VIII's legacy to England was a state church in the fullest sense. British monarchs and prime ministers continued to choose the Church of England's bishops until 2007. Parliament defined its liturgy, structures, and even doctrines deep into the twentieth century. The

Church of England has never quite been a puppet of the state, but it has certainly been kept on a short leash. Its liturgy purrs with approval of royal and state power and is filled with obsequious prayers for the Crown, without a whisper of acknowledgment that sometimes governments do bad things. It even stretched its Protestant principles so far as to anoint one king, the beheaded Charles I, as a saint. Yet when the Church of England has needed help from the state, such as when it was desperately trying to set up workable structures in colonial North America, the state has felt free to block it at every turn. For three centuries, the church did not dare even to question this arrangement. Since then, some of its leaders have wondered whether they should stay in this unequal marriage, but they have never yet walked away. The Church of England even now clings to its subordinate but privileged place in British public life, readier to celebrate than to challenge state power. Henry VIII would be proud.

The Two Kingdoms

Few other Protestant churches were so easily tamed, but they all faced the same dilemmas. How far should they submit to a ruler who was, or claimed to be, on their side? And how far should they resist a ruler who was not?

Luther's first instinct was to caution against any thought of rebellion, even against the "anti-Christian regime" of the papacy. In a tract written in 1521, he argued that it is always the innocent who end up suffering in rebellions and that politics is none of ordinary people's business. They could humbly petition their princes, but they could not take matters into their own hands. Who were they to think that they could tear down Antichrist's kingdom by themselves? Only God could do that. If they truly had faith, they would wait.[6]

This reflected Luther's own political context. Saxony was not a law-governed bureaucratic territory. Its prince, the elector, was the beginning and the end of government. Any alternative such as the "rule of law" meant handing power to corrupt local noblemen. Luther disliked *law* both theologically and politically. As one scholar puts it, he had "more confidence in one enlightened prince than in battalions of lawyers." In a sermon in 1528, he told his audience,

You aren't the one who ought to establish justice and punish injustice. When some wrong is done in my house, and my next door neighbor wants to break into my house and do justice there, what should I say to that?

Better to be still and wait on the Lord.[7]

Carte blanche for rulers, then? Not quite. In 1523, Luther published a longer book bluntly titled *Temporal Authority: To What Extent It Should Be Obeyed*. His starting point was that princes themselves are no better than plunderers:

They can do no more than strip and fleece, heap tax upon tax. . . . Since the beginning of the world a wise prince is a mighty rare bird, and an upright prince even rarer. They are generally the biggest fools or the worst scoundrels on earth.

That does not, however, detract from their authority. Rulers only rule with God's permission. The reason princes are so dreadful is that "the world is too wicked, and does not deserve to have many wise and upright princes." Indeed, the only reason God has established princes and governments at all is that human beings are sinners. "If the world were composed of real Christians, that is, true believers, there would be no need for or benefits from prince, king, lord, sword or law."

That might seem like a banal enough observation, but Luther's theology gives it immediate and practical importance. For him, all believers are "real Christians" of this kind, or rather, that is what they are in God's eyes, even if they are still outwardly mired in sin. In other words, Christians live simultaneously in two worlds. As redeemed and regenerate believers, they live for God and do not need laws to live by any more than trees need laws to tell them how to grow. But as sinners, subject to human frailty, they both need and deserve the smack of firm discipline.

This is Luther's theory of the "two kingdoms," the foundation of Protestant political theory. There is an earthly kingdom: the kingdom of secular politics, a place of law, justice, and punishment. Its purpose is to restrain human evil so that some semblance of peace and order is possible in this world. That is a limited aim but not an ignoble one. God has ordained this kingdom, and Christians can serve it, whether as princes, lawyers, or executioners. But existing alongside it, and far more important than it, is the kingdom of heaven, whose only king is Christ. Here there is no law, and no coercion, because all true Christians are one another's willing servants. And this is where Christians' hearts should be set, not on the lumpen business of human politics. It is an idea that has echoed through the centuries.

Plainly, however, it does not answer the question posed by Luther's title. Whenever two kingdoms exist side by side, there are boundary disputes. Where does the line fall? Luther had some partial answers. He argued that princes could regulate practical features of church life such as finance, property, and governance, but could not trespass onto matters of faith or doctrine. He did not spell out how to deal with issues which straddle that line. He did at least tackle some of the obvious hard cases. Could princes punish heresy? No, because errors should be corrected by loving admonition from ministers, not by persecution. Could they ban books? No. He suggested that if they tried, a Christian should reply,

> Gracious sir, I owe you obedience in body and property; command me within the limits of your authority on earth, and I will obey. But if you command me to believe or to get rid of certain books, I will not obey; for then you are a tyrant and overreach yourself.

Luther even argued that if a prince orders his people to fight in an unjust war, it is their duty to disobey him. Importantly, though, such resistance should *always* be passive. You should refuse an unjust order and then submit peacefully to punishment for that refusal. It is a bold theory, but not a practical one.[8]

Luther managed to maintain this position for the rest of his life. He happily accepted various princes' patronage and support. Yet he could still bite, or at least bark at, the hands that fed him. When princes enriched themselves with church property, he called them robbers. When a small Thuringian town tried to expel its pastor in 1543, Luther vigorously protested on two-kingdoms grounds: "You have not insti-tuted the office, but God's Son alone has done so. . . . Keep to your own office and leave God's rule to him."⁹ When he learned about the defen-sive pact that the Protestant princes and cities had agreed to in 1529, he angrily accused them of faithlessness for trusting in human aid rather than in God.

Yet pacts were made, and larger cities were not so easy to boss around. In practice, princes disliked laying down their powers at the gates of Christ's kingdom. Luther's Renaissance-minded colleague Philip Melanchthon took a more pragmatic view. If princes were called to punish sin in this world, surely that included punishing sin in the church? So, surely, they had a right—indeed, a duty—forcibly to reform a corrupt church in their territory, by, for example, expelling clergy who would not renounce the pope and imposing a new, Lutheran order of service? Indeed, is this not actually a prince's most important calling and responsibility?

Luther was forced to concede the point. Plainly, during the current crisis, with the church confined in its popish dungeon, no one but a prince could set it free. But he insisted that this was a temporary expe-dient. Once settled churches were established, princes must relinquish their hold. Likewise, he admitted that the princes should suppress Ana-baptists and other "fanatics." However, he denied that this was reli-gious persecution. It was simply the suppression of rebellion or the punishment of blasphemy, which was legitimate, he argued tenden-tiously, because openly defying God was a denial of natural justice.

His princely allies could live with the requirement that at some unspecified point in the future they would have to step back from their hands-on role in church life. Only slowly did they begin to argue that that time might never come. The duke of Brunswick-Lüneburg de-clared that he would always have an obligation to protect and oversee his church, like the kings of ancient Israel. Inexorably, this became Lu-theranism's entrenched orthodoxy. In 1555, German princes were granted legal authority to determine their subjects' religion.¹⁰

It was not too bad a deal for the reformers. Their princely allies might be overbearing, but they were sincere enough. Indeed, because they were now claiming that God had called them to reform their churches, they had to be seen to be doing so in good earnest. Still, the preachers needed the princes more than the princes needed the preachers, and both sides knew it.

A notorious crisis in 1539–40 showed just how badly wrong this could go. Philip, landgrave of Hesse, was one of the most powerful Lutheran princes. He was also a walking scandal. He had made a political marriage at the age of eighteen and had disliked his wife from the first—not that it stopped him from fathering ten children by her. His unabashed adultery was embarrassing, but he was tempted by a more radical solution: bigamy, like the Old Testament patriarchs. In this new religious world, when old rules were up for renegotiation in the name of Christian liberty, why not? The theologians disapproved, but not unreservedly. Luther had once publicly teased his wife with the prospect of polygamy, and Melanchthon had at one point suggested bigamy as a solution to King Henry VIII's marital crisis. In 1539, a brush with illness and the appearance of a suitable young lady crystallized Philip's determination. He gave Luther and Melanchthon a blunt ultimatum: if they did not support him, he would seek the pope's blessing instead.

They gave in. Of course they did. How could they not? Finding a sliver of theological justification, in December 1539 they reluctantly advised that a fresh marriage could proceed. They insisted that the whole affair be concealed, because "this act was not defensible before the world and the imperial laws." Keeping such an explosive secret would probably always have been impossible, but in the event Philip scarcely tried. To Luther's horror, in March 1540 he openly celebrated his new marriage, and the whole rotten scandal burst open. It permanently damaged Philip, although he stayed with his new wife for the rest of his life (they had nine children). It also permanently stained Luther's reputation. It did not help that instead of repenting, Luther merely grouched that the secret should never have come out. Asked about the matter by a visitor, he reportedly said, "Bigamy has well-known examples in the Scriptures and could have been kept secret. . . . Just be calm! It will blow over. Perhaps she will soon die."[11]

The point is not merely that Luther gave way under intolerable pressure but that his political theology had led him into a trap. He was too ready to believe in a benevolent prince, and he had mixed for that prince a cocktail of God-given authority and Christian liberty that would have proved heady for anyone, let alone an old goat like Philip. Innocence had been lost and would not easily be regained.

Chaos and Order

Other branches of the sundered Protestant family found other solutions. The Anabaptists and other radicals separated Luther's two kingdoms much more sharply. Agreeing with Luther's view that the secular state was little more than organized banditry, they concluded that Christians should therefore have nothing to do with it. They should obey its orders but not swear its blasphemous oaths, serve on juries that hang the hungry for stealing bread, or fight in armies that plunder the innocent. Perhaps they should not even pay taxes that funded such things. All they should do is live their lives in peaceful separation and prepare for the persecution that these rejections would inevitably bring down on their heads. The most enduring strand of Anabaptism was marked by pacifist withdrawal from a corrupt world, making Christ's kingdom visible in the godly communities they formed.

There was another, older Anabaptist reading of the two sharply separated kingdoms; short-lived, but it lingered in Christendom's memories. This view, first articulated by Luther's nemesis Thomas Müntzer, held that the kingdom of the world should in fact submit to Christ's kingdom. It was an apocalyptic doctrine. If the two kingdoms could be allied, then this world's violent methods could be used to usher in the next. Müntzer tried to turn the peasant rebellions of 1524–25 in this direction, to no avail, but the idea did not die with him. It was taken up, most notoriously, in the western German city of Münster.

When the city's pastor and several of its leading citizens were converted to apocalyptic Anabaptist doctrines in 1532, Anabaptists from across the region converged there and succeeded in throwing out the bishop and taking over the city's government. A Dutch baker named Jan Matthys prophesied that Münster was the new Jerusalem to which Christ would imminently return. Over a thousand adults accepted baptism. They began to muster an army. The expelled bishop raised forces too and laid siege to the city in 1534. Matthys was killed in a suicidal sortie early in the siege, but one of his comrades, a tailor named Jan Bockelson, was now proclaimed king and the successor of King David. Within his besieged Jerusalem, he abolished private property; all goods were to be held in common. He legalized polygamy, taking sixteen wives for himself. We are told that when one of them crossed him, he beheaded her himself, in public.

The "kingdom" of Münster ended as violent, apocalyptic cults usually do. After a yearlong siege, the city was overrun. Bockelson and his fellow prophets were tortured and executed. The gibbets in which their bodies were displayed still hang from the cathedral tower. Münster became a notorious atrocity, comparable to the September 11, 2001, attacks in our own age. It convinced plenty of sober observers that Anabaptism was an existential threat that could engulf all Christendom.

Protestants who wished to claim respectability now scrambled to distance themselves from the radicals. They distinguished radicals sharply from so-called magisterial Protestants: those who sought Reformation in alliance with the existing princes, magistrates, and other secular powers. The distinction was manifestly self-serving. In truth, the boundary between "magisterial" and "radical" was almost as arbitrary and porous as Luther's distinction between true Christians and "fanatics." Some of those who ended up on the "magisterial" side of the line had earlier dallied with "radical" ideas. The eminent Strassburg reformer Martin Bucer questioned infant baptism. John Foxe, chronicler of the English Reformation, opposed executing religious offenders and had qualms about oaths and church taxes.[12]

The radicals themselves only forswore state help when they had no prospect of receiving any. As in Münster, they set up governments when they had the chance. In 1526–27, something like a state-led Anabaptist Reformation unfolded in the small Moravian town of Nikolsburg. The Anabaptist preacher Balthasar Hubmaier baptized a string of converts there, including the dominant nobleman and the town's evangelical pastors. Hubmaier explained that he was trying to create "a Christian government at whose side God hung the Sword," with the secular power coming to his Reformation's aid.[13] The experiment lasted mere months. Austrian forces seized Hubmaier in 1527, and he was burned in Vienna the following year. Anabaptists subsequently glossed over this embarrassing lapse, but if more opportunities to lapse had arisen, there would surely have been more Anabaptists unable to resist the temptation.

Reformed, "Calvinist" Protestants, whom we will meet properly in the next chapter, accepted Luther's two-kingdoms theory but applied it in a very different setting. The Swiss and south German cities were much more politically complex than Saxony: republics and city-states with dispersed power, layers of law and bureaucracy, and wide political participation. From this perspective, Luther's ill-defined, arm's-length relationship with secular authority seemed like a missed opportunity. Surely the kingdom of this world should be summoned to the aid of Christ's kingdom, not merely by maintaining peace and order, but also by promoting education, caring for the poor, and institutionally re-forming the church. In Zurich, where political power and religious power were already so intertwined that the chief preacher was an employee of the city government, they now became almost indistinguishable. Erastianism, the supposed theory that churches ought to be subordinate to states, takes its name from a theologian of this party. That was not quite what Thomas Erastus meant, however, nor is it a fair representation of the Swiss Reformation. Swiss churches were not so much subordinate to the state as a part of the same organic whole.

This tradition's most important theologian, John Calvin, brought characteristic rigor to the question. Luther dreamed of good princes, disliked law on principle, and had little interest in institutions. As a result, Lutheran churches ended up with a mishmash of governing structures. Calvin, by contrast, had trained as a lawyer, knew that structures matter, and favored more participatory government. He insisted that pastors should never have control over money: A simple change, but who knows how many scandals it has averted down the centuries? More momentously, he distinguished *pastors,* the ordained ministers who preach and celebrate the sacraments, from *elders,* senior laymen who would take charge of discipline and who became the sharp edge of a cultural revolution.

The simple justification for the elders and their work was Christ's detailed prescription in Matthew's Gospel for how Christians should deal with sinners among the faithful: first private admonition, then progressively more formal reprimands, and finally, if repentance was not forthcoming, expulsion from the community.[14] Calvin saw the church as a covenanted community, a new Israel in which all were bound to be their brothers' and sisters' keepers. His elders were charged with systematically overseeing everyone's moral conduct, hauling adulterers, drunkards, and those who fell asleep during sermons before a tribunal, not to punish them, but to elicit repentance.

Nowadays, Calvinist discipline smells very totalitarian. "Repentance" could mean public humiliation, and penitents might be asked to prove their sincerity by denouncing others. However, most premodern societies were deeply communitarian and conformist. Notions of privacy and individual liberty scarcely existed. Calvinist discipline worked (and it did work) because of widespread consent. Maintaining moral order was in everyone's interest. Drunkenness led to injuries, damage, and lost working days. Fornication led to illegitimate children for whom the community would have to care. The system could be genuinely pastoral. To read disciplinary records is to be struck by the painstaking care these men (they were all men) took to reconcile neighbors, to resolve family disputes, and to protect the victims of domestic violence.[15]

Yet Calvinist discipline was ultimately neither a form of oppression nor a marriage-counseling service. It was God's instrument to form his church into a living example of Christ's kingdom. Hence its most radical feature: its egalitarianism. Every Christian fell under the elders' jurisdiction, including elders and pastors themselves, many of whom had at some time faced a grilling, although Calvin himself never did. Magistrates, noblemen, and other grandees could in principle be judged on the same basis as a street beggar.

That was the theory. Making it stick was almost impossible in rigidly hierarchical societies, but Calvinists at least tried. The laboratory was the city-state of Geneva, where Calvin was chief pastor from 1541 to his death in 1564. The city's councillors and leading families were all in favor of clearing out whorehouses, but being publicly humiliated for dancing at their own children's weddings was a different matter—especially at the hands of a French refugee, for Calvin was not even a native Genevan. They feared that immigrants were subverting the city's government. Calvin himself believed he was engaged in a simple contest between morality and immorality. Remarkably, morality won. In the faction-ridden city, Calvin and his swelling band of immigrants allied themselves with a grouping who in 1555 swept the elections to the city council. Their opponents were banished from the city and a swath of immigrants became citizens. In an unsettling echo of Münster, the refugees had taken over their asylum. Calvin's prize was not a royal title but something more tangible and enduring: the power of excommunication. His church was now empowered to expel obstinate sinners from Christian society, whoever they might be.[16]

Revolutionary Saints

This was not exactly a theocracy, but it was a church that was robustly independent of government. In particular, it cracked a problem that Lutheranism never even properly acknowledged: how to be Protestant in the face of an actively hostile state. Luther's advice was to pray. Calvin also wanted Protestants to organize. Informal groups of believers who chose elders to police themselves found that they had become cell churches, able to support and regulate one another even when under active persecution. Luther disliked the idea of secret meetings, which he said reminded him of rats. Calvin had found a way of forming the rats into a choir and then drilling them to march.

In the same year as his victory in Geneva, Calvin began sending missionary pastors into his native France to organize underground congregations there, riding a wave of dramatic Protestant growth in France over the following seven years. Variants on Calvin's model began appearing like mushrooms across Europe. One example can stand to show how far this model could go.

Scotland was a latecomer to the Reformation. In 1559–60, an inchoate evangelical movement fused with nationalist resentment to spark a rebellion against the pro-French Catholic regime. The man who crystallized this movement was John Knox, a disciple of Calvin's who lacked his master's subtlety and made up for it in zeal. He had seen the future as a refugee in Geneva and wanted to make it work in Scotland. Above all, he was entranced by the idea of spiritual equality. In a series of polemics in 1558, he warned his fellow Scots that they could not shirk their responsibilities to reform the church simply because they were commoners. In God's eyes, he insisted, "all man is equal": equal not in rights but in responsibilities. If you lived in a land of idolatry, it was your duty to demand reform and to take action to separate yourself from the sin around you. Otherwise, when God's judgment fell on the whole nation for tolerating blasphemies in its midst, it would engulf you too.[17] This frankly revolutionary agenda stretched Luther's two kingdoms to the breaking point.

After a decade of confusion, Scotland's Protestants succeeded in deposing their Catholic queen, Mary, and replacing her with her infant son, now King James VI. But having fought for Christ's kingdom against all odds, they were disinclined to submit to a king of their own making. James was raised Protestant, but spent his adult life in a running battle with Protestant churchmen who would not accept his power over them in any meaningful sense. They wanted a church that elected its own leadership—so-called Presbyterianism, from the Greek word for "elders." The king wanted the church to be governed by bishops, partly for tradition's sake, but mostly so that he could appoint them himself.

Worse, like the true Calvinists they were, the Presbyterians wanted comprehensive moral discipline and to be able to haul even the king before church elders. In 1596, the Presbyterian leader Andrew Melville expounded his turbocharged version of the two-kingdoms doctrine to James VI's face. There were two kingdoms in Scotland. James was king of one, but the other, rapidly turning itself into a recklessly expansionist empire, was the kingdom of Christ, "whose subject King James the Sixth is, and of whose kingdom not a king, nor a lord, nor a head, but a member!"[18] The effect was to reduce earthly monarchs to puppets, who on any matter of moral significance—that is, virtually every political decision—ought to take their steer from Christ's duly authorized representatives.

No actual government could accept this sort of arm's-length theocracy. All Protestants, therefore, potentially faced the same basic problem: how to deal with a secular government that would not conform to God's will. Luther's doctrine of strictly passive disobedience had theological clarity and long Christian tradition behind it. Unfortunately, it also had a tendency to crack under pressure. In a militarized, structurally violent society, when a community finds its principles repeatedly thwarted, when it is goaded beyond endurance or faces direct, sustained persecution, it will eventually fight back.

We will come back to those bloody struggles, but for now we simply need to notice how Protestants justified resistance to their divinely ordained rulers. These justifications were daughters of necessity, scrabbled together after the fact to legitimize self-defense. But once formulated, they took on a life of their own. The political cultures they created have shaped how Protestants relate to one another and to the world around them down to the present.

Early Protestants found two broad ways to justify resisting their sovereign lords. One, which started more slowly but mattered more in the long run, was legal. Most European monarchies were not absolute autocracies, but were governed by law, custom, and tradition. These laws, customs, and traditions often contained hints that rulers depended on some kind of consent from their subjects. By mixing a few carefully chosen legal and historical precedents with a hefty dose of wishful thinking, one could confect an argument for constitutional monarchy. Philip of Hesse, when he was not fathering children, was drawn to this approach. The Holy Roman Empire was not a hereditary monarchy: the emperor was elected, and traditionally made a series of promises when he acceded to the throne, including promises to respect the legitimate rights of the princes under him. Philip argued that the emperor's continued legitimacy depended on his keeping those promises. If he did not, the princes who had elected him could surely depose him and install someone better in his place.[19]

Likewise, French and Scottish Calvinist theorists used tendentious historical arguments to claim that their kings were implicitly chosen by the nation as a whole. Never mind that neither realm had consciously done this for centuries, if ever. It meant that Protestants who took up arms against their sovereigns could convince themselves that they were not defying the law but defending it. Excavating and reviving Europe's genuine, long-buried antimonarchical precedents suddenly became the Protestant reformers' business.

The other justification for resistance was being discussed by some of Luther's colleagues in the mid-1520s, by Martin Bucer, the influential Strassburg reformer, in 1535, and by Philip Melanchthon in 1546–47. It was fully formulated for the first time by Lutheran diehards besieged in the city of Magdeburg in 1550. In the 1570s, French Protestants would use it to justify resistance up to the point of assassinating a tyrannical king. This argument began from St. Paul's dictum that all ruling powers—plural—rule by God's permission: not just kings and emperors, but also the lesser princes, magistrates, and officials who hold authority under them. Those people, too, are obliged to uphold justice and defend true religion. So it may be that private citizens oppressed by a tyrant can do no more than resist passively and embrace martyrdom. But these other authorities—"lesser magistrates"—might have the right and the duty to stand firm for justice in the face of a tyrant. It was their obligation to reprimand an unjust king, to defy his orders, and even to defend their people with all necessary force. After all, their authority, like the king's own, comes from God.[20]

This theory's neat division between private citizens humbly submitting and lesser magistrates violently resisting was completely impractical. Yet it allowed Protestants fighting for their lives to convince themselves that they were not revolutionaries intent on anarchy but defenders of the existing social order. This quickly degenerated to the point where everyone who had any power of any kind to resist could claim that they therefore had the right to do so. Using Knox's principle that "all man is equal," even a mob could claim that its rough-edged power was granted by God. Knox went on to argue that any private citizen who had the power to assassinate an idolatrous prince could and should do so. Like the two-kingdoms doctrine itself, this theory could be used to justify almost anything.

The effects of all this can be overplayed. An inattentive Protestant prince in 1600 who compared himself to his great-grandfather a century before might conclude that things had not actually changed very much. Most of the time, Protestant politics worked better in practice than in theory. Churches believed in conscientious obedience and valued states that preserved peace and administered justice. Protestant princes believed the Gospel their ministers taught and valued the moral order, sobriety, and social cohesiveness their churches fostered. All sides usually rubbed along well enough.

Yet the ground had shifted under their feet. The tremors can, ultimately, be traced back to Luther's rejection of every authority beyond the believer's conscience bound by Scripture. Obedience was a Christian virtue, but who exactly should Protestants obey? A godly prince? A tyrant? A preacher—and if so, which one? In the end, only their own consciences, before God and informed by Scripture, could answer that question. Some Protestants found their consciences leading them on unexpected adventures. Even the vast majority who continued to obey their traditional rulers now had to justify their obedience in conscientious terms. Luther had argued that true Christians were subject to everyone, but only because, as redeemed and liberated souls, they voluntarily chose that subjection. When no human power can direct or absolve the conscience, it is the conscience that becomes the true sovereign.

King James VI feared that this line of thinking was leading "some fiery spirited men in the ministry" to envisage a "Democratic form of government."[21] That was not too wild an exaggeration. Compare the original "Protestation" of 1529, when the German princes first defied the emperor's authority:

> These are matters that concern the glory of God and that affect the salvation of each and every one of us; here we must . . . acknowledge our Lord and God as the highest King and the Lord of lords.

It was hardly a new idea that Christians should answer to a higher authority than the emperor. The novelty was bypassing the chain of command. They could not settle their consciences with the thought that they should submit to God's anointed authorities in church and state. "In this respect no man can conceal himself behind other people's acts or behind majority resolutions."[22] Every soul had to stand before God alone. In politics, as in faith, no other authority could hold.

CHAPTER 3

The Failure of Calvinism

Behold, how good and how pleasant it is for brethren to
dwell together in unity!

—PSALM 133:1

Protestantism was born in conflict, not only with the rest of the
world, but with itself. Its rejection of fixed authorities condemned
it to division from the very beginning, and it has repeatedly shown a
propensity to fissure into new, quarreling sects. But this is not the
whole story. If it were, then Protestantism would have blown itself
completely to bits, until there were as many churches as individual
believers. In fact, the centrifugal force spinning into sectarian chaos has
been matched by a gravitational pull toward unity.

As the dust of sectarian confusion settled during the late 1520s, two
major Protestant blocs appeared, alongside the smaller fragments: Luther's own, and a Swiss and south German grouping who lacked a single leader but whose most prominent figure was the city preacher of
Zurich, Huldrych Zwingli. For a time, it seemed as if his movement,
not Luther's, could be the center around which Protestantism's orbiting
fragments could coalesce. Calvinism, as it came misleadingly to be
called, was the last, best hope for serious Protestant unity. It failed, but
it came agonizingly close. Its story is a parable of what Protestantism
can and cannot do.

Parallel Reformations

Zwingli claimed that his Reformation owed nothing to Martin Luther's.
He claimed that the two movements arose almost simultaneously, with

strikingly similar ideas, because both were inspired by God. Believing
this does require a leap of faith. Zwingli's doctrine of salvation was very
similar to Luther's. It is natural to assume that, deliberately or uncon-
sciously, he had been influenced by his northern counterpart.

Yet the two men were very different. Luther was a monk and professor whose revolution was grounded in his own private spiritual
crisis. Zwingli was a more public figure. If Luther's Reformation was a
theology for lovers, Zwingli's was prosaic, politically aware, and more
self-consciously scholarly. Erasmus and the Renaissance scholars had
initially thought that Luther was one of them, discovering too late that
his earthiness and love for theological paradox were too raw for their
taste. Zwingli, by contrast, had exchanged letters with Erasmus in his
youth, and enthusiastically adopted both his biblical scholarship and his
zeal for social and political reform. Erasmus himself died a Roman
Catholic in 1536, but he lived out his last years in the Swiss city of Basel,
where a Reformation in Zwingli's tradition had taken hold. Many of
those who shared Erasmus's vision of a purified Christendom found
Zwingli's movement more congenial than Luther's.

Zwingli's Reformation was also unmistakably Swiss. Switzerland in
his day was, incongruous as it may now seem, a revolutionary entity: a
popular republic formed in the high Alps to resist the Holy Roman
Empire. Through the fifteenth century, it was expanding, reaching cities of the southern German plain like Bern, Basel, and Zurich. It would
grow no further, partly because the Reformation divided it, but the
danger that half of Germany might "turn Swiss" still seemed real. To
turn Swiss meant to assert one's liberty, but a liberty that was communal
and communitarian rather than individualistic.[1]

Sixteenth-century Switzerland was fiercely independent and politically idiosyncratic, but also poor. Its one lucrative export was its much-
feared mercenary soldiers, but being paid by foreigners to slaughter one
another has its drawbacks. The young Zwingli served as a military
chaplain, and in September 1515 he was present at the catastrophic battle of Marignano, when Swiss forces fighting for the pope were crushed
by a larger French army. About half of the Swiss soldiers present were
killed. For Zwingli, this was almost a conversion experience. He began
to denounce mercenary service, and his rural parish threw him out.
However, in the cities, which could afford to despise the mercenary

trade, he won a hearing. With the country still reeling from Marignano, in 1518 Zwingli was elected Zurich's city preacher.[2]

His sermons were a heady mixture: denunciations of blood money blended with doctrine akin to Luther's, faith alone, Bible alone, and rejection of church hierarchy. Soon, with cautious permission from the city's magistrates, Zurich's churches were purged of Catholic images and rites: the kind of cleansing that Luther called fanaticism. Basel and Bern followed close behind. Strassburg's great reforming minister, Martin Bucer, was also drawn to the Swiss reformers.

An alliance between Luther and this loose grouping seemed natural. They shared a Gospel of salvation, an exclusive loyalty to Scripture, and enemies in both Catholicism and Anabaptism. The Swiss reformers openly admired Luther. Politicians on both sides also wanted agreement, both to unite the sundered body of Christ and to seek safety in numbers. But despite repeated attempts, and a summit conference between Zwingli and Luther at Marburg in 1529, there would be no agreement. The sticking point may seem trivial to modern eyes: differing views of the sacrament variously known as the Eucharist, the Lord's Supper, Holy Communion, or (to Catholics) the Mass. It is worth pausing on this issue, because, abstract as it may appear, it was fundamental to early Protestants' religious experience.

At his Last Supper before his death, Jesus Christ gave bread and wine to his disciples, saying, "This is my body" and "This is my blood," and told them to eat and drink in remembrance of him.[3] Christians have done so ever since, but without agreement on exactly what is being done. In Catholicism, this rite became the Mass, a numinous celebration of Christ's saving presence in which his promise "This is my body" is literally fulfilled. For Catholics, the sacramental bread is wholly transformed, or "transubstantiated," into Christ's flesh, retaining only the outward appearance of bread and making the saving power of his unique sacrifice immediately present.

Luther and Zwingli alike saw this as wholly unacceptable. It sounded like manipulating God, re-crucifying Christ, and little more than magic. But there agreement ended. Zwingli's view was bluntly commonsensical: bread is bread. Yes, Christ said, "This is my body," but he also said, "I am the true vine." Obviously, he did not mean it literally. The rite was simply a symbolic memorial. For Luther, this was a worse blasphemy than the Catholic Mass itself. He insisted that Christ's words were literally true, because, in Christ, heaven touches earth. He rejected transubstantiation as a piece of Aristotelian sophistry but argued that Christ was wholly, physically present in the sacramental bread, just as the Son of God was wholly present in the man Jesus and just as the Word of God was wholly present in Scripture. Zwingli's cramped rationalism was, he thought, tantamount to atheism, reducing Christ to an abstract notion and denying Christians the greatest comfort their Savior offered: his own physical presence, dwelling within them as they ate and drank his body and blood.[4]

Zwingli looked at Luther's doctrine and saw unreformed dregs of popery, sodden in superstition. Luther looked at Zwingli's and saw intolerable blasphemies. Condescension versus outrage: not a promising mix. The colloquy at Marburg that tried to resolve the issue was carefully stage-managed, but on this key point there would be no budging. Luther began by writing Christ's words—"This is my body"—on the table in chalk and insisting that until Zwingli admitted those words were true, there was nothing to discuss. That fundamental disagreement was the rock on which attempts at pan-Protestant unity would founder for generations.

Luther characteristically claimed Marburg as a victory, and soon it began to look as if he were right. Zwingli's ideas might have reached into Germany, but much of Switzerland remained staunchly Catholic. In 1530–31, the tensions between the reformed and the Catholic cantons boiled over into the Reformation's first religious war. For the reformers, it was a disaster. Zurich's army was decisively beaten by the Catholic cantons at the battle of Kappel on October 11, 1531. The subsequent treaty banned Protestantism from advancing any further; Switzerland has been religiously divided ever since. Worse, Zwingli himself was killed in the battle, and his body mutilated by the victorious Catholic forces. Luther crowed mercilessly over his rival's shameful death, sword in hand, when he should have laid down his life in unresisting innocence like a true Christian martyr.

Zwingli's Reformation was left leaderless. His young successor in Zurich, Heinrich Bullinger, would eventually go on to steer his legacy with a cool head and steady hand for nearly half a century. For now, however, the most prominent figure was Bucer, in Strassburg. Bucer was the era's great ecumenist, forever churning out treatises and formulae to paper over doctrinal cracks, trying always to keep everyone talking. In May 1536, he secured an apparent triumph: the Wittenberg Concord, an agreed statement with Luther on the Eucharist. In fact, Bucer's view was distinct from both Zwingli's and Luther's. He disliked Luther's crude talk of Christ's physical presence but did insist that the bread and wine were no mere symbol; Christ was spiritually present in the faithful believer who received the sacrament, which mattered far more than any fleshly presence. So he and Luther did have some real common ground, and the Wittenberg Concord concealed their disagreement under ambiguous language. If both sides had been happy to bracket their dispute, it could have worked, but Luther loudly insisted that he had not budged an inch. Bucer sent the text to Basel with an accompanying note explaining *his* understanding of what it meant. In Zurich, however, where Zwingli's memory was kept pure, it looked like a sellout. And indeed, at the same time, Bucer was writing to Luther offering a different understanding of the text, explaining that he had told the Swiss what they needed to hear, because of their "weakness." Predictably, a copy of the letter found its way to Zurich. The Zurichers never trusted Bucer again. Basel and Zurich became alienated from each other, and Bern was contested between them. It was an utter fiasco. Protestantism's destiny to shatter into fragments was fulfilling itself.[5]

Calvin's Contribution

Enter, late in the day, John Calvin. Calvin has always been easier to admire than to love. As his best modern biographer, Bruce Gordon, puts it, Calvin "never felt he had encountered an intellectual equal, and he was probably correct."[6] He could not abide to be crossed by enemy or friend, and once he had begun an argument, he pursued it with unforgiving tenacity. While Luther's emotional theatricality gave even his faults a kind of grandeur, Calvin was a man of reserve and precision. But he was a spiritual writer of luminous clarity, fired by a ravishing vision of the light and sweetness of Christ. He also came closer than anyone else to unifying the disparate pieces of Protestantism. The

Reformed Protestant tradition that Zwingli started is commonly called Calvinism, inaccurately but not unjustly. Calvin did not found it, but he did keep it together.

Calvin was eight years old when Luther's revolt began: a mere child next to the theological giants who spent the period of his youth clashing with one another. He converted to the new German doctrines when he was a law student in Paris in the early 1530s. A clampdown on heresy in France in 1534 forced him to flee abroad, never to return. He went, initially, to Basel, where in 1536 he published the first edition of the book that would become his life's work: *Institutio Christianae religionis,* best translated as *An Instruction in Christian Religion.*

The *Institutio* had two immediate purposes. First, it was a letter to his home country, dedicated to the king of France. Calvin wanted to prove, in the wake of Münster, that Protestantism was not politically subversive and so could safely be tolerated. His other avowed purpose was nothing less than to unify Protestantism. All the hairsplitting arguments about Christ's presence in the Eucharist, he claimed, missed the point. The focus should instead be on how the sacrament spiritually nourished believers.

One book by a clever Frenchman was not, however, going to heal Protestantism's divisions. Its immediate effect was to derail Calvin's career. In 1536, his travels took him through the city of Geneva, where he intended to stay a single night. Geneva was then an independent French-speaking city-state under the military protection of the Swiss city of Bern. The previous year, the Bernese had encouraged a raucous little Reformation in the city, and a French preacher, Guillaume Farel, had been installed as minister. The city remained gravely divided, and Farel was conscious of needing backup. When the author of the *Institutio* strayed into his city, Farel confronted him with a prophet's certainty and convinced the reluctant Calvin that God was calling him to work in Geneva. Farel was more firebrand than theologian, but he managed to browbeat John Calvin into changing his mind: precious few could say as much.

Geneva was a briar patch for Calvin. The city's factional divisions continued, and in 1538 both Farel and Calvin were banished. For Calvin, it was a liberation. He went to Strassburg, spending three happy, fruitful years working with Bucer and revising the *Institutio.* His peace was interrupted in 1541, when Genevan politics turned again and the city invited him to return, without Farel. He felt obliged to accept, but he drove a hard bargain. He would now structure the Genevan church in his own way. As we saw in the last chapter, this meant imposing a systematic structure of moral policing. He set out to create a model of what a reformed Christian city could be. Calvin remained Geneva's chief pastor until 1564, when he worked himself into an early grave.

From his new Alpine Jerusalem, Calvin continued his dogged pursuit of Protestant unity. In 1540, he had criticized both Luther and Zwingli for their intransigence and called for reconciliation. With Zwingli safely dead, Luther let it be known that he liked the young Frenchman's book, a wisp of hope to which Calvin clung.[7] His first real opportunity came in the late 1540s, not long after Luther himself had died. In 1547, Emperor Charles V at last confronted the Protestants in battle and won a crushing victory at Mühlberg. Meanwhile, on the other side of the Alps in the Italian city of Trento (Trent), Pope Paul III had finally assembled a General Council to rebut the Protestant challenge. In this moment of dreadful urgency, Calvin persuaded Bullinger, in Zurich, to open theological negotiations. In May 1549, he went to Zurich himself, and the two men hammered out a full agreed statement on the Eucharist: the Zurich Consensus.

Despite the title, this was Calvin's achievement. It was he who had pursued the agreement and made concessions to make it happen. The result was an ambiguous formula that stuck fairly closely to Bullinger's views while still emphasizing that, in the Eucharist, Christ is received by faith. Crucially, though, there was enough goodwill to ensure that this was no rerun of the Wittenberg Concord. The Zurichers trusted Calvin, and even accepted two amendments he suggested to strengthen the text of the Consensus a few months later. One by one, the Swiss Protestant churches formally adopted the Consensus. Bucer, in exile after the wars in Germany, feared that Calvin had given too much ground. Calvin replied, "Let us bear therefore with a sigh what we cannot correct," but then persuaded Bullinger to accept the changes—to Bucer's evident surprise.[8] A stable, inclusive Reformed Protestantism had been born, with Calvin as its midwife.

Only one detail remained: bringing in the Lutherans. Calvin genuinely believed it could be done. His own position was reasonable and self-evidently correct, and many reformed Christians had already united around it. He also had considerable faith in his own persuasive powers. In particular, with Luther himself having died in 1546, Calvin's hopes were pinned on Luther's right-hand man, Philip Melanchthon. Melanchthon shared Bucer's eagerness for conciliation and Calvin's own scholarly brilliance. He was also mild mannered—to the point of spinelessness, his enemies muttered. The two men had met several times, and Calvin felt they were kindred spirits. Melanchthon was on friendly terms with other Swiss reformers; Bullinger's son even lived with Melanchthon for a year when he was a student. Surely something could be done.[9]

It was not to be. For one thing, Calvin the statesman could not always keep Calvin the theological street fighter muzzled. In the 1540s, Calvin and Melanchthon disagreed in print over the doctrine of predestination, and Calvin would not shut up and let it go. When Melanchthon was openly friendly toward one of Calvin's critics in 1557, Calvin could not bring himself to overlook it. More profoundly, Calvin never seems to have believed that he and Melanchthon really differed. He appealed repeatedly to Melanchthon to admit that he really did agree with him on disputed issues. Melanchthon tended to respond to these appeals by falling silent, and reportedly tore up one letter in fury.[10]

Calvin and his allies were wounded by Melanchthon's inexplicable reticence. They believed they represented a broad, centrist reformism drawing on the best scholarship. As their movement put down roots across Europe, in the British Isles, France, the Netherlands, Poland, Hungary, and parts of Germany, it seemed perverse that Luther's crude sacramental theology should be a barrier to unity.

In other words, Calvin and the Reformed theologians never took Lutheranism seriously. Calvin had the nerve to claim that Luther would have signed the Zurich Consensus had he lived.[11] Melanchthon at least continued corresponding with Calvin, but other Lutherans were less ready to accept his condescension. The Lutheran theologian Joachim Westphal denounced the Consensus in a book subtly titled *A Farrago of Confused and Divergent Opinions on the Lord's Supper*. Calvin, surprised and stung by Westphal's bitterness, responded in vituperative kind. It did not bode well.

Westphal's fury was a sign that Calvin had stirred a hornets' nest. By the 1550s, two parties of so-called Lutherans were at each other's throats. The split went back to that crushing military defeat in 1547 and to Melanchthon's penchant for appeasement. In 1548, facing threats to reimpose a virtually unreformed Catholicism, Melanchthon had persuaded Duke Maurice of Saxony to support a compromise, the so-called Leipzig Interim, which would have permitted Protestant preaching while conceding a great deal else in the ritual life and outward organization of the church. Such compromises were not ideal, Melanchthon admitted, but if the peace of the church and the will of princes demanded it, then so be it. It was, from one point of view, a brave stand.

From another, it was a cowardly betrayal, typical of a timid scholar whose spine had only ever been stiffened by having Luther at his side. A group of self-styled "Gnesio-Lutherans" or "true" Lutherans, who aspired to cherish every scrap of Luther's legacy, had holed up in the besieged city of Magdeburg, from where they poured contempt on Melanchthon's concessions. Men like Flacius Illyricus argued that even if outward ceremonies were unimportant, they should not be changed at sword point. It was a time for boldly confessing the faith, not for a faintheartedness that was tantamount to apostasy.[12]

The immediate crisis passed—the gyrations of German politics eventually produced a peace with established rights for Lutherans in 1555—but the rift between Gnesio-Lutherans and Melanchthon's "Philippist" supporters was not so easily healed. The Philippists were suspected of selling out not only to the Catholics but also to the Calvinists, whom the Gnesio-Lutherans loathed just as much as their master had loathed Zwingli. Even if Melanchthon did agree with Calvin, then, he could scarcely say so. No wonder he found Calvin's naive appeals frustrating.

Lutheranism in Search of Concord

The running battle between Philippists and Gnesio-Lutherans consumed the Lutheran world for thirty years. The Philippists were the establishment, even after Melanchthon's death in 1560. They controlled the universities of Wittenberg and Leipzig and held high office in most Lutheran territorial churches. They were politically much more palatable; it was, after all, the Gnesio-Lutherans who had been dreaming up dangerously subversive theories of resistance. Philippists, like Calvinists, had a patrician sense of themselves as the natural intellectual center of gravity. They were reluctant to stoop to polemical fistfights and disdained the quarrel that the Gnesio-Lutherans were forcing on them.

The Gnesio-Lutherans, by contrast, were revolutionaries. Luther had taught that worldly success was a sign of God's displeasure. His followers knew why they had been frozen out and why his intoxicating, world-upending vision had been diluted into insipid moralism. If the Philippists were condescending pragmatists, the Gnesio-Lutherans were bomb-throwing idealists, convinced that true faith never compromised and that criticism only proved them right. They deplored the Philippists' readiness to bend with the political wind. In particular, they feared that the Philippists' talk of ethics betrayed their Erasmian roots: this was not real Protestantism. Real Protestants would understand how absolutely pervasive human sin was and would not pretend it could be tidied up with a little good behavior.

In 1560, the tub-thumping Gnesio-Lutheran Flacius Illyricus claimed that humanity's fall from grace, in the Garden of Eden, had transformed human nature so fundamentally that men and women were made no longer in God's image but in the devil's: a kind of backward transubstantiation. Most Gnesio-Lutherans hastened to distance themselves from this bizarre idea, but it does tell us something about their movement. They were not interested in compromises between truth and error. Human depravity was absolute, and any softening of that line with oh-so-reasonable Renaissance idealism risked eviscerating the Protestant Gospel altogether.[13]

The standard to which Gnesio-Lutherans rallied was the Augsburg Confession: the statement of Lutheran faith submitted by the first "Protestants" to the imperial Diet of Augsburg in 1530 and written, ironically enough, by Melanchthon. The Augsburg Confession acquired totemic status. To Luther's friend Georg Spalatin to call it "the most significant act which has ever taken place on earth" was a little hyperbolic, but it was perfectly normal for Gnesio-Lutherans to place it on a par with the ancient Christian creeds.[14] To Philippists, by contrast, it was the product of a particular historical moment, subject to amendment or change. Indeed, Melanchthon himself later amended the text, making changes that Gnesio-Lutherans saw as weasel words contaminating

Luther's prophetic insights with brackish rationalism. In this battle for the Augsburg Confession, the Gnesio-Lutherans had one significant tactical advantage. The 1555 peace treaty made adherence to the original, unaltered Augsburg Confession the only legal alternative to Catholicism in the Holy Roman Empire. The Gnesio-Lutherans managed to position themselves simultaneously as fearless opponents of imperial tyranny and blameless upholders of imperial law.

Finally, in 1570–71, the Philippists were goaded into responding to their critics. A polemical counterattack labeled the Gnesio-Lutherans as fanatical perverters of Luther's legacy and accused them of a series of full-blown heresies, from misunderstanding Christ's nature to implying that the devil was God's equal.[15] No doubt it felt good, but these overblown caricatures only dented the Philippists' own credibility. German princes who had until now tried to broker compromise began to shift their ground. The turning point came in 1574, when the elector of Saxony, Augustus, purged the Philippists from the theology faculty at Wittenberg, on the grounds of crypto-Calvinism. In 1576, the Saxons set about trying to resolve the issue once and for all. The *Formula of Concord,* which six theologians under Saxony's sponsorship produced in May 1577, looked moderate only by comparison with Philippist hyperbole. Pressured by Augustus, one by one Germany's Lutheran territories adopted it as the only legitimate interpretation of the Augsburg Confession. In 1580, it was incorporated into a *Book of Concord,* a collection of Lutheran texts that became the canonical definition of Lutheran orthodoxy. Philippism's back was broken, and with it any wish to build bridges with Calvinism.

That, at least, was the story within Germany, the Lutheran world's center of gravity. On the periphery, there were different stories. Poland's history as a crucible of early Protestantism is now largely forgotten. Poland had a Catholic majority but also substantial numbers of Lutheran and Reformed Protestants mixed with radicals who denied the doctrine of the Trinity. There were also the Bohemian Brethren, who represented a tradition going back a century before Luther, to the Czech preacher Jan Hus, but who were broadly sympathetic to Protestantism. Out of this fragile and splintered situation emerged Jan Łaski, the Polish Calvin. A former student of Erasmus's, he returned home from a decade's exile in 1556 to try to unite Polish Protestantism. He

aimed to shore up relations between the Reformed church and the Bohemian Brethren and to cast this alliance in sufficiently open terms to
make it seem safe for the Lutherans to join too.

Łaski died in 1560, but his dream did not die with him. As the political
tides turned against Polish Protestantism over the following decade, the
pressure to unite increased. The Polish Lutherans were reluctant, but
their relations with the Bohemian Brethren were relatively warm,
and they eventually agreed to submit the Brethren's Confession of Faith
to the theologians at Wittenberg for their judgment. The Philippists at
Wittenberg were happy to approve it. Suddenly Lutherans and Calvinists
found themselves with a shared ally. A moment of goodwill opened up
and was seized. A three-way conference lasting a mere six days in April
1570 produced the Consensus of Sendomir.

The Consensus of Sendomir is a fair picture of what the much-
imagined Protestant unity might have looked like. It committed all
parties to mutual goodwill and peace. Its statement on the Eucharist is
masterfully ambiguous, along lines that Calvin and Bucer would have
recognized: Christ's body and blood are "truly" received, and what that
means is left to the individual believer. The Consensus was accepted by
Polish Protestants of all stripes, who urged their brethren elsewhere to
follow the Polish example. Instead, most ignored it and have done so
ever since.[16]

Denmark was no keener on Gnesio-Lutheran rigidity. Frederik II,
king of Denmark from 1559 to 1588, was the Lutheran world's most
powerful prince and was trying to forge an alliance with the more or
less Calvinist kingdom of England. On a Europe-wide scale, the *Formula of Concord* was far more divisive than unifying. Frederik accused
the Germans of behaving like miniature popes, and they accused him
of crypto-Calvinism. When his sister, Elector Augustus's wife, sent him
two beautifully bound presentation copies of the *Book of Concord* as a
gift in 1581, he publicly threw them on the fire. The *Formula* had pacified
Germany, but concord had its limits, and its price.[17]

Dreams of Union

By the 1580s, Protestant theological consensus seemed out of reach. But
there were other routes to unity. One looked back to Erasmus: Instead

of all this ridiculous doctrinal hairsplitting, why not simply live a good Christian life? In Strassburg in the early 1540s, Katharina Schütz Zell, the sixteenth century's most distinguished female Protestant theologian, made a valiant attempt to bring three of her colleagues—a Lutheran, a Zwinglian, and a radical—into dialogue on the basis of love of neighbors and a common acceptance of Scripture.[18] Significantly, like Erasmus himself, she lacked formal academic training in theology, and like Erasmus she suspected that the whole business of theology served only to breed dissent.

Such approaches were, therefore, less impartial than they looked, because they depended on belittling other people's deeply held convictions. It was, again, a Calvinist, or Philippist, approach rather than a Gnesio-Lutheran one. Calvinists were the more direct heirs of Erasmus and saw ethics as vital for defining a Christian community. That was one of the things Gnesio-Lutherans most disliked. For them, talk of ethics seemed to miss the point that sinful human beings simply cannot live ethically without the transforming power of true faith. Doctrine *had* to come first.

Where an appeal to shared ethics failed, however, more pragmatic considerations might succeed. Nothing unites like a common enemy, and early Protestants were under mortal threat from the Catholic powers. This was unity not for the sake of peace but to better fight. It was temporary: an agreement to shelve disputes only until the emergency was over. It therefore did not require absolute agreement, merely a broad recognition of spiritual kinship.

However, not all Protestants faced the same threats. As we shall see in the next chapter, in the religious wars of the later sixteenth century, Calvinists in France, the Netherlands, and the British Isles were on the front line. Some Lutheran princes and territories did provide logistical and diplomatic support, but it was the Calvinists who needed unity urgently. During the terrible existential crisis of the Thirty Years' War from 1618 to 1648, the entire survival of northern European Protestantism seemed at stake. Some Lutherans, especially the Scandinavians, discovered a renewed zeal for cooperation. Now, however, the premier Calvinist power, Great Britain, remained aloof. Unity at gunpoint was fleeting at best.

The battle with Catholicism did decisively shape Protestant

attempts at unity, however. Catholics mocked Protestants for their divisions and tried to damn them all with the worst excesses of a few extremists. Protestants therefore had a strong incentive to present a moderate, united front, rather than appear like a rabble of squabbling fanatics. The chief victims of this need were the radicals. It became imperative for mainstream Protestants of all kinds to draw a line between themselves and the radicals, by any means necessary. Hence the most notorious incident of Calvin's career. In 1553, a Spaniard named Miguel Servetus came to Geneva. "Radical" hardly does justice to Servetus, a brilliant physician and freethinker who denied the doctrine of the Trinity, the authority of the Bible, and virtually everything else that respectable Christians held dear. He was already on the run from the Inquisition. Virtually any territory in Europe would have executed him, and Calvin, who had read his books with horror, had warned him never to come to Geneva. When Servetus came nevertheless, he was arrested, tried for heresy, and, eventually, burned alive.

Calvin's defenders have advanced various excuses for his part in Servetus's death. It was the only such trial in which Calvin was involved, and most other leading Protestants were implicated in more bloodshed. Servetus was executed by the Genevan city government, not by Calvin, who petitioned for the more merciful punishment of beheading. All this is true. Yet Calvin testified against Servetus at his trial and solicited condemnations of him from a range of other Protestant leaders. When the city authorities considered banishing Servetus, on the grounds that they had no jurisdiction over him, Calvin insisted that Geneva be seen to take responsibility for stopping this menace to orthodoxy.[19]

Calvin's concern was not simply to stop Servetus's blasphemous mouth but also to vindicate his own model of a godly republic. In retrospect, Servetus appears like a harmless crank, but in the early 1550s, with radical ideas of various kinds bubbling up across Europe, it was not foolish to fear that the Reformation might dissolve into self-defeating revolutionary chaos. A line had to be drawn. Calvin positively wanted radical blood on his hands; it was a marker of respectability to the Lutherans and to potential converts, and a challenge to Catholics who could not, now, easily dismiss him as an extremist. But unsurprisingly, a quest for Protestant unity built on the ashes of Protestant dissidents did not succeed.

As Protestants' divisions hardened, they still dreamed of reconciliation. Many Calvinists nursed an unrequited love for Lutheranism. The English historian John Foxe was an unmistakable Reformed Protestant but also a dewy-eyed fan of Luther's who had a slew of Luther's works translated into English. He recognized that there were doctrinal differences, but refused to blow "one small blemish" in Luther's sacramental theology out of proportion and urged his readers to give "a moderate interpretation" to Luther's work. Other English theologians, like the royal chaplain Richard Field, tried to explain the doctrinal differences away altogether, arguing that it was all a misunderstanding. Some of Luther's English fans even argued that it was his German successors who were "ridiculous imitators" and perverters of his legacy, while they themselves were his true heirs. They were in love with an imagined Lutheranism, not the real thing.[20] This was the kind of condescension that Gnesio-Lutherans had come to expect from Calvinists.

Other Calvinists had more practical ideas. In out-of-the-way places, they just got on with it; in Batavia (modern Jakarta), the colonial capital of the Dutch East Indies, the Dutch Reformed Church simply admitted Lutherans to church membership. For those who wanted to turn local pragmatism into something more systematic, the way forward was obvious: a council, a full-scale theological conference that could thrash out the issues once and for all, on the ancient church's model. But who would convene such a council? Who would attend? Who would set the agenda? Worse, given that Protestants rejected all authority aside from the unmediated Bible, who could possibly compel anyone to accept what that council might say—if it did not degenerate into a grudge match and break down irreconcilably? For the advocates of a council, these were not reasons to despair, merely to lay their plans carefully.

Initially, some hoped for a big bang. Thomas Cranmer, the first Protestant archbishop of Canterbury, was a Reformed Protestant of Martin Bucer's kind. (He invited Bucer to England and gave him a plum job in Cambridge, where the climate promptly killed him.) At that moment, in the early 1550s, England was the most powerful Protestant state in Europe. The ancient councils had been convened and stage-managed by Roman emperors. Perhaps England's pious boy-king, Edward VI, could now serve the same function? In 1552, Cranmer invited

Bullinger, Calvin, and Melanchthon, the three most visionary Protestant leaders then alive, to England. Calvin, characteristically, was enthusiastic, though wary of the long journey. Bullinger had the same concerns and none of the eagerness. Melanchthon would have been the prize catch. Cranmer tried everything to lure him, even sending his travel expenses in advance, but Melanchthon's irrational fear of sea travel was matched by an entirely rational fear of Tudor England, a land of murderously capricious politics where Cranmer himself would meet a martyr's death less than four years later. Even if he had come, and even if some sort of deal had been reached, his involvement would hardly have persuaded the fledgling Gnesio-Lutheran caucus. But no one came. Then the English king died in 1553, Queen Mary briefly returned England to Catholicism, and the scheme died.[21]

In later generations, a multistage process seemed more prudent. The basic scheme, which resurfaced with many variations, was for an initial conference between the various Calvinist churches. This would allow them to present a common front at the second stage, when the Lutherans would be allowed into the room. Some imagined a third stage, of reconciliation with Catholicism. The scheme was like a child's plan to dig a tunnel to the other side of the world: utterly impossible, but easy to begin.

That is, uniting the Calvinists ought to have been easy. Calvinists across Europe recognized one another informally as brethren, studied at one another's universities, shared ministers, read the same books, and in some cases even shared formal confessions of faith. But those family ties were not enough for any kind of coordinated dialogue with the Lutherans. The *Formula of Concord* spurred an attempt to formalize matters; in 1577, German, Dutch, Hungarian, Polish, and French Calvinist theologians attended a conference at Frankfurt and prepared an agreed confession of faith, published in 1581. But it was merely a private initiative, with no formal status. The English regime even banned it.[22]

For the awkward truth was that even Calvinists were keenest on unity when their own situation was precarious. French Calvinists, who were fighting desperately for survival in a series of civil wars from 1562 to 1595 and who thereafter were a vulnerable minority, were cheerleaders for international Protestant solidarity. Elizabeth I's England, home to Europe's largest and oddest Calvinist church, was suspicious of any encroachment on national sovereignty. The weak pursued unity, and the strong distrusted it: not a promising situation.

Hopes were rekindled when, on Elizabeth's death in 1603, King James VI of Scotland inherited the English and Irish crowns, creating a formidable British monarchy that made him, at least in his own eyes, the leader of the Protestant world. Uniting that world, as a prelude to reuniting all Christendom, was a project fit for such a king. In 1613–14, a Franco-Scottish theological team sponsored by James drew up a kind of road map to Protestant unity, which was formally endorsed by a French Reformed synod at Tonneins. It proposed an initial meeting of a dozen Calvinist theologians, under James's patronage, to produce a common confession of faith. The churches involved would then commit not to decide any major controversies or make any innovations without consulting one another. A year later, there would be a second conference to which the Lutherans would be invited, where the delegates would condemn Anabaptism as beyond the pale while agreeing to tolerate one another. At that point, because we are already in lands of fantasy, the Catholics, too, would repent of their errors and be welcomed back into the fold.[23]

The idea was not altogether ridiculous. Determined politicians might have been able to bang the theologians' heads together hard enough to produce some grudging, temporary tolerance. Tonneins seemed as if it might have been such a moment. Another came in 1630, during the Thirty Years' War, when the Swedish warrior-king Gustavus Adolphus dramatically invaded Germany and so saved German Protestantism from what looked like certain destruction. John Dury, an indefatigable Scottish peddler of schemes for Protestant unity, smelled an opportunity and pestered his way into Gustavus's court, finally managing to meet him in December 1631. Dury outlined his vision, which amounted to the Tonneins plan reheated. Gustavus was enthusiastic and promised to give Dury letters authorizing him to summon Lutheran and Calvinist representatives from across Germany.

Or so Dury claimed. Unfortunately, Gustavus did not write anything down. Less than a year later, he was dead in battle, and Dury was once again without a patron. If anyone could ever have made this scheme work, it was Gustavus Adolphus in 1631–32. But even if

Gustavus had truly meant to, it would have been a tall order. The Germans were grateful to him, but they would not have taken orders, especially as the military situation moved on. The English would have been a harder nut still. Any conceivable agreement would have been both temporary and partial, with significant numbers of Protestants left carping outside.[24]

The same problems had left the Tonneins scheme stillborn. It bore a French endorsement and the British king's fingerprints, but no one else would actually pick it up. One of those stirred by it was the German Calvinist David Pareus, who published his own blueprint for unity in 1615, imagining a council that would be convened jointly by King James and by his brother-in-law, the Danish king Christian IV. Twinning the Protestant world's two premier princes would make the project look less like a Calvinist plot. However, James disliked Pareus's attitude toward royal authority and in any case would never have agreed to share equal billing with a king he regarded as his inferior. Nothing more was heard either of James's plan or of Pareus's. Only politics could have made such schemes work, and it was politics that made them impossible.

The Unraveling of Calvinism

In 1618–19, however, something very like the long-imagined international council did take place. The Synod of Dordt was called not to pursue some abstract project of unity but to resolve a bitterly divisive issue that is still almost synonymous with Calvinism: predestination.

Lutheranism and Calvinism alike stress that human beings cannot save ourselves. We are too mired in our own evil to dig ourselves out. Only God can rescue us, through Jesus Christ's redeeming sacrifice. But this doctrine, which Luther and others found so liberating, has a sting in the tail. If salvation is entirely God's work, then it is also entirely God's choice. Our human wills are too corrupt to choose God, too corrupt, even, to choose to accept God's offer of salvation. Only God himself enables us to accept that offer, and because God is sovereign, if he gives us that grace, we cannot refuse it. So, if God chooses to save us, we will be saved. We are not saved because we are good; we only become even partially good as a *consequence* of God's decision to save us. His decision to save us is free, sovereign, and inscrutable, and if he does not choose to save us, there is absolutely nothing we can do about it. In other words, our eternal fate is predestined.

Predestination was not Luther's idea. St. Augustine, Western Christianity's single most influential theologian, taught a strong doctrine of predestination, and the germ of the idea is in the New Testament. Luther did, however, quickly conclude that it was an essential consequence of his doctrines, and it was over this issue that Erasmus finally and decisively broke with him in 1524. However, most Lutherans chose to soft-pedal this part of their master's teaching. Like Erasmus and many others, they found it intuitively morally offensive. Melanchthon smuggled in a human ability to reject God's grace. On this point, at least, it was Melanchthon, not Luther, who shaped "Lutheran" orthodoxy.

Zwingli and the early Swiss reformers also had no affection for predestination, and Bullinger never embraced it fully. Calvin, however, would not evade the doctrine's iron logic and added the final deduction that Augustine and Luther had been too squeamish to make: if God predestines some people to heaven, he must therefore equally deliberately predestine the rest to hell.

Calvin initially suggested the preachers should be discreet in handling such a controversial doctrine. It was only when he was challenged on the point that, characteristically, he dug in and made it a test of loyalty. But he also found the idea unexpectedly nourishing. It fit his almost rapturous emphasis on God's absolute sovereignty. More practically, for those under persecution, predestination is liberating. If your salvation is wholly in God's hands, you do not need to fear that your courage will fail you when the torturer comes. One English Protestant awaiting a heretic's death enthused that the doctrine "so cheereth our hearts and quickeneth our spirits that no trouble or tyranny executed against us can dull or discomfort the same."[25] For Calvinists, who emphasized that Christians were a covenanted people, set apart for God, predestination seemed almost natural. They were God's chosen people: the new Israel.

By the end of the century, a hard-line doctrine of predestination had become orthodoxy across most of the Calvinist world, but it was never unchallenged. Moral revulsion refused to fade away. Predestination's ablest opponent was the Dutch theologian Jakob Arminius, whose ideas were confined to the academy while he lived. After his death in 1609, however, a group of his disciples presented the Dutch church with a public "Remonstrance," insisting that human beings can cooperate with God in salvation.

The Remonstrance provoked a dangerous split in Dutch Calvinism, to the point that civil war seemed a real possibility. Remonstrant militias were formed. The state of Holland, the Remonstrant stronghold, was on the point of seceding from the Netherlands. The federal Dutch government eventually intervened, purging Remonstrants from a string of Dutch cities and, following a show of force, persuading the Hollanders to abandon their quixotic stance without a fight. In August 1618, a series of Remonstrant leaders were arrested, and some executed. The crisis was over.

But it is unseemly to resolve theological arguments with armies, so during the winter of 1618–19 a national synod of the Dutch Reformed Church met at the town of Dordrecht, or Dordt, to pronounce solemnly on Arminius's doctrines. To lend it additional gravity, delegates from across Europe were invited. There were German, Genevan, Swiss, and English representatives, plus a solitary Scotsman. The French king banned his subjects from coming, but the French Reformed Church sent written submissions, and the synod symbolically kept chairs vacant for them in the assembly. Suddenly something very like the council of which so many had dreamed was actually taking place. Dordt could have been a template for international Reformed unity.

The synod did its job well. Naturally, it condemned Arminius's teachings, but without straying into some of the more extreme formulations of predestination. Most national churches quickly endorsed its rulings. Arminianism survived in the Netherlands, but the Remonstrant leaders were banished, and public preaching of their doctrines was banned. And yet no Protestant synod could bind the consciences of those who came after it. Soon the questions supposedly settled at Dordt were being reopened. A French theologian, Moyse Amyraut, published his own solution to the predestination problem in 1634, arguing that God's grace extended at least hypothetically to all humanity. He was accused of crypto-Arminianism, but he escaped formal censure, and his ideas stirred up fresh trouble in the Dutch church too. Protestant theological debate simply could not be closed down.

More immediately, Dordt was undercut by its own prominence.

The English delegates endorsed the synod's conclusions, but close interest in the event in England meant that Arminius's arguments were widely aired there for the first time. A group of avant-garde young ceremonialists felt that the Dutch disputes had awakened them from a "dead sleep." The most brilliant of these preachers, Lancelot Andrewes, mocked how the predestinarians claimed to know everything about God's secret and inscrutable will.[26]

So in fact Dordt, the high-water mark of Calvinist internationalism, did as much to spread as to contain disunity. The dream of councils and of consensus was dangerous as well as impossible. This was the objection that John Dury kept encountering during his thankless quest for unity in the 1620s, 1630s, and 1640s. He promised theological discussions, but in real life discussions caused divisions, not reconciliation.[27] When Protestants of different kinds seemed to be rubbing along tolerably well, starting to talk theology could only cause trouble.

By the later seventeenth century, Calvinism's promise of Protestant unity had dissolved, and Calvinism itself was splintering. In England, Arminian theology and ceremonial revival were fusing to form a weird hybrid called Anglicanism, which increasingly disowned its Calvinist heritage. The line between "orthodox" Calvinism and the "radical" Reformation, which Calvinists had tried to draw so clearly in the radicals' blood, was being blurred by constant passage across it.

In truth, this was nothing new. Bucer's ecumenism had extended to the more respectable Anabaptists. Even Calvin, as a young man, had given them unintended comfort. In 1537, he had been accused, falsely, of denying the doctrine of the Trinity. He rashly decided to try to refute the charge using only the language of the Bible itself, bypassing the ancient Christian theologians who had defined the doctrine and produced the relevant technical terminology. This seemed to give comfort to those radicals who had rejected all the early church's theological baggage in favor of the unadorned Bible. Worse, during this dispute, Calvin refused to sign the so-called Athanasian Creed, an exhaustive summary of Trinitarian doctrine that had been seen as a touchstone of orthodoxy since the sixth century. None of this meant that Calvin was a secret anti-Trinitarian, simply a little rash and overconfident.[28] But it does show that Calvinists' worries about the need to distinguish themselves from the radicals were not imaginary.

Soon fears that Reformed Protestantism might bleed into radicalism were coming true—in, of all places, Italy. Politically decentralized and intellectually sophisticated, Italy in the 1530s was fertile soil for freewheeling evangelical thinking. Most of the so-called *spirituali* made no open breach with Rome, hoping instead that the Catholic Church would take on the Protestants' most compelling ideas. When it finally became clear that that cause was lost, some returned to Catholic orthodoxy, others became more or less orthodox Calvinists, but others still plowed their own furrows. Some, following the logic that had entangled Calvin in 1537, questioned the doctrine of the Trinity. Italy was now too dangerous a place to think such thoughts, and the radical Italian fringe scattered, many of them finding refuge in east-central Europe: the thinly populated east of Switzerland, the borderlands of Hungary and Transylvania, or religiously fragmented Poland. In Transylvania, a Calvinist leader named Ferenc Dávid publicly abandoned the doctrine of the Trinity in 1565. Soon a Transylvanian anti-Trinitarian church was organized, teaching a rationalistic Christianity in which Jesus Christ was less divine redeemer than human exemplar. Polish Calvinism likewise incubated anti-Trinitarians. In 1565, the Polish radicals formally constituted the Minor Reformed church, which acquired its own university and printing press. They became known as Socinians, from their articulate Italian-descended leader Faustus Socinus. Anti-Trinitarian radicalism began to look less like a lunatic fringe and more like a serious alternative.

During the seventeenth century, as Poland's hardening religious politics scattered Socinians into exile, adventurous Calvinists kept stumbling across their ideas. It was a Dutch Reformed minister who, in 1642, first proved that the Athanasian Creed, about which Calvin had been so recklessly fastidious, was actually written two hundred years after St. Athanasius's death. Socinian or "Unitarian" Christianity became a stubbornly established part of the landscape, especially in Britain and the Netherlands. Its self-conscious rationalism, its emphasis on individual freedom of choice, its concentration on ethics rather than doctrine—all of these traits were like water in the desert to freethinkers who felt cramped by Calvinist orthodoxy. Calvinism had once seemed like the inheritor of Erasmus's mantle, but now Socinianism made a play for it. If Calvin had seen a fundamental threat in Servetus, the original anti-Trinitarian, he had been right.

Were Socinians and Unitarians Protestants? Lutherans and Calvinists denied it in horrified tones, citing the Trinity as a touchstone of all Christian orthodoxy. It is hard to see those denials as anything other than special pleading. Socinianism was an almost purebred descendant of Calvinism, and like most children it sheds some light on its parents' true nature. Its emergence on a wave of doubting and questioning makes Calvinism's failure to unify Protestantism seem all the more complete. It also makes the real achievements of that project, at moments so tantalizingly near to success, seem all the more remarkable.

CHAPTER 4

Heretics, Martyrs, and Witches

Be it known unto thee, O king, that we will not serve
thy gods.

—DANIEL 3:18

Protestantism was born in the fear and hope of bloodshed. From
Luther's first appearance on the public stage, it was clear he risked
execution as a heretic. The killing actually took a little while to begin;
the first of Luther's disciples to be burned alive as unrepentant heretics
were two Dutch friars who died in 1523. More soon followed. Over the
next half a century, more than three thousand men and women were
put to death in Europe for crimes of belief. The killings were neither
steady nor evenly spread, but were concentrated in short outbursts in a
few countries: France, England, and above all the Netherlands.[1] By the
1560s, judicial executions were giving way to full-scale religious warfare. Those casualties are much harder to count but certainly ran into
the hundreds of thousands. When the killing finally abated, in the middle of the seventeenth century, it left behind entrenched bitterness,
punctuated by ongoing spasms of brutality.

This violence marked Protestantism permanently. Because Protestants were often its victims, it kept many Protestants in a kind of defensive crouch for two centuries, a posture that had lasting effects. But
they traded in the same currency. When they had the chance, they
persecuted not only Catholics but also each other. And for all their differences with Catholicism, they readily closed ranks with the papists
against real or imagined threats from beyond Christianity's bounds.

The alternative—whispered by a few in the sixteenth century, spoken by a growing chorus through the seventeenth—was religious coexistence. Modern Protestants have often enjoyed telling themselves a self-congratulatory story in which their tradition gave rise to tolerance and freedom, and that is rather less than a half-truth. But it is not completely false. This was indeed the age when a measure of religious tolerance began to be possible, both in theory and in practice. Our subject in this chapter is how Protestants learned to die, to kill, and under some circumstances, not to kill.

Martyrdom and Heresy

Protestants thought about these questions using two ancient Christian categories: martyrdom and heresy. Martyrs are literally *witnesses*—believers who bear witness to their faith in the most vivid and unanswerable way, by choosing to die rather than to renounce it. Martyrs were supposed to go to their deaths with lamblike submission and defiant resolve—like St. Stephen, the first Christian martyr in the Acts of the Apostles, or indeed like Jesus Christ himself.

Because martyrdom was the highest honor for which any Christian might hope, to be persecuted was, paradoxically, proof of God's love. That paradox has helped give Christianity its tremendous resilience. The harder your enemies hit you, the firmer your convictions become. State violence normally works by intimidating its victims into compliance. Ancient Christians found instead that martyrdom served as a kind of spiritual judo, in which they derived strength from the very fact of their persecution. The blood of the martyrs, proverbially, was the seed of the church. The end of Roman persecution of Christians in the fourth century meant that the supply of martyrs dried up, and in medieval Europe it almost ceased, yet the rarity of true martyrdom only made the ideal more alluring.

At the same time as it nursed this hunger for martyrdom, Western Christendom developed its concept of heresy, a word that literally means "choice." A doctrinal error is not a heresy. Heresy is an act of the will: asserting your own judgment rather than submitting obediently to the mind of the church, guided by the Holy Spirit. An error only becomes heretical when someone consciously and deliberately defies the church's ruling. Orthodoxy versus heresy is more about obedience versus willfulness than truth versus error. Heresy is a moral offense, not an intellectual one.

In medieval Europe, heretics were seen both as threats to public safety, peddling seductive lies that might drag innocents down to hell with them, and as traitors against God, willfully spreading disgusting slanders against him. Good Christians could hardly stand idly by. So from the tenth century onward, heresy was treated as a crime. Because medieval justice was public, symbolic, and exemplary, this might ultimately mean death by burning: a symbol of the fires of hell to which heretics had condemned themselves, a vividly gruesome deterrent, and a practical way of disposing of a body unworthy of Christian burial. It also made a good show, and in northern Europe, where dry wood and good weather were rarities, often an extended one.

It is worth the effort to see these atrocities through our forebears' eyes. They lived in a much more publicly violent society than we do, but they did not impose such terrible punishments out of simple malice. The ideal outcome of a heresy trial was always repentance. Heretics who renounced their errors were usually spared, unless they were repeat offenders. This was why heresy inquiries were led by priests; they were pastoral processes, whose purpose was to reconcile sinners. Heresy both began and ended as a choice: to live in the true faith, or to die in error. The threat of fire was a merciful severity, helping waverers to choose wisely.

For centuries, this worked. A series of medieval dissident movements such as the Cathars and the Waldensians were suppressed or eliminated. In the late fifteenth century, a new variant arose in Spain, where Jews who had been forcibly converted to Christianity were treated as heretics if they kept the rites of their old faith. The Spanish Inquisition pursued them with unprecedented ferocity, killing over ten thousand. But this is better understood as a state pogrom, a spasm of Jew-hating that happened to make use of the heresy laws. Elsewhere, heretics were hunted sporadically, in ones and twos. It was a small price to pay for keeping a whole continent united in the faith. Not many contemporaries were troubled by the fact that their religion celebrated martyrs who chose to die rather than renounce their beliefs and also compelled dissidents to choose between death and renouncing their beliefs.

The problem, as St. Augustine had recognized in the fifth century, was that martyrs cannot in fact prove that their religion is correct by dying for it. People die for all kinds of beliefs, and they cannot all be right. Augustine concluded that the cause, not the death, makes a true martyr. If you die for the truth, you are a martyr, but if you die for an error, you are deluded or a servant of the devil. That may sound like self-serving relativism, but again, the role of the church is decisive. The truth is determined not by anyone's private judgment but by the church's collective voice, guided by the Holy Spirit. You might have honest scruples about doctrine, but how could your private doubts weigh against the certain authority of the church?

This was precisely the argument Martin Luther's opponents threw at him. And Luther, utterly convinced of the truth he had perceived in Scripture, concluded, logically enough, that any authority that denounced that truth must be false. He was driven to deny that the church could authoritatively denounce heresy. That was itself almost the greatest heresy of all. Across Europe, the church's traditional machinery ground slowly into action against the new Protestant enemy.

England's example is typical. In 1521, Henry VIII was still ostentatiously Catholic. With an eye on the burgeoning scandal in Germany, he sponsored a public burning of heretical books in London, accompanied by forceful preaching against heresy. This was a theatrical preemptive strike; there were as yet no English Lutherans, and the books had to be imported specially for the show. When the performance was repeated five years later, there were a few real English converts, some of whom made humiliating public recantations during the performance.[2] This was how the English had long dealt with their own indigenous heretics, the unsophisticated but stubbornly ineradicable movement known as the Lollards. Lollards were serial recanters, who mocked the church's rites scabrously in their private gatherings but were rarely willing to stand firm when their lives were at stake.

Yet it soon became clear that these new heretics were different: not peasants deploying crude commonsense rationalism, but clerics and scholars, hard to overawe and unseemly to burn. The bishop of London, Cuthbert Tunstall, spent long hours trying to woo individual suspects back to orthodoxy, smoothing over troubles and compromising where he could. He persuaded England's most outspoken early evangelical, Thomas Bilney, to make an ambiguous, carefully negotiated recantation in 1527.[3]

Not everyone shared Tunstall's instinct that the Reformation was a misunderstanding to be resolved between gentlemen. Thomas More, lawyer, friend of Erasmus's, and England's most famous scholar, was appalled by Tunstall's compromises; the law was "so far stretched forth that the leather could scant hold."[4] More, softhearted neither toward others nor toward himself, favored rigor, and as the heresy problem burgeoned, he took charge. Over the next five years, a swath of suspects were imprisoned, interrogated, and sometimes tortured, and a dozen were burned. Bilney, stricken by his conscience after his recantation and newly defiant, was one of the first to die.

Tunstall and More's dilemma—soft words versus exemplary rigor—was repeated across Western Christendom. Few countries had legal bureaucracies capable of full-scale campaigns of repression. Spain and Portugal had a battle-hardened Inquisition which ensured that no popular Protestantism of any kind ever took root there; a fledgling evangelical movement briefly appeared in Spain in 1558 and was swiftly exterminated. Italy is a more tantalizing case, because it did have a nascent evangelical movement in the 1530s. But when the Inquisition was reestablished across Italy in 1542, these reformers either fled to exile or returned to conformity. This was how it should have worked everywhere. If the response is tough and consistent enough, hardly any burnings should be necessary.

France shows how easily this could go wrong. Francis I, king from 1515 to 1547, was amused by fashionably daring scholarship and also locked in a generational struggle with Emperor Charles V, Luther's nemesis. He was therefore tempted to give houseroom to moderate reformers. Paris around 1530 was a tantalizing place for evangelicals; this was where John Calvin was converted. But as Tunstall had discovered, appeasement served only to embolden Protestants. One night in 1534, a series of outrageously provocative placards denouncing the Mass were posted anonymously across Paris. One found its way to the door of the king's bedchamber. A sudden wave of repression followed, and many reformers, including Calvin, fled abroad. But repression was not consistently maintained. France still hoped to recruit Germany's Lutheran princes as allies against the emperor. Calvin dedicated his *Institutio* to King Francis because he believed that he could still win him over.

In any case, the French state did not have the means to enforce a blanket policy of persecution. Nor did most of its neighbors. Even in centralized England, where Thomas More's repression would probably have succeeded if Henry VIII's marital drama had not intervened, English heresy hunters found themselves hamstrung by legal technicalities. It was harder still in the decentralized or fragmented polities that made up most of Europe, where the whim of individual bishops or judges could set local religious policy. Local persecution often merely pushed dissidents across porous borders. The problem was at its worst in the Netherlands, where a determined assault on heresy ran up against flimsy borders, entrenched local legal cultures, a cat's cradle of jurisdictions, and some very cosmopolitan cities. Well over a thousand deaths did no more than keep the lid on the problem.

As the church cried heresy, the fledgling Protestant movement countered it with martyrdom, an ideal that had been at the heart of Luther's thought from the beginning. He distinguished between what he called theologies of glory and theologies of the cross. A theologian of glory was self-serving and self-aggrandizing, whereas a theologian of the cross followed Christ's path of self-denial. Christ's true church must be a suffering, persecuted church, constantly assaulted by the devil. If a church was at peace, rich, and powerful, that alone proved it was already securely in Satan's bondage, even before it proceeded to attack the true, persecuted believers.

So Protestants embraced martyrdom, seeking out persecution as a sign that God loved them. One of Martin Luther's great spiritual crises came in the late 1520s when he realized that the sentence of condemnation that had hung over him since the Diet of Worms was unlikely ever to be carried out. Surely this meant God had rejected him?[5] In reality, of course, most Protestants never faced arrest or trial. Persecution was a fact, but it was also a myth, and that was what made it powerful. The tales of Luther's courage at Worms, and then of the first actual martyrs, were treasured, retold, and replayed in believers' imaginations as they put themselves in their heroes' shoes and asked themselves what they would do if they came to the time of trial.

In the 1550s, this storytelling culminated in collected volumes of martyr stories published in Dutch, German, and French, their authors joining individual atrocities into great national struggles between the suffering church of Christ and the cruel church of Antichrist. A still grander narrative was planned by an Englishman, John Foxe. Having originally conceived a vast Latin encyclopedia of cruelty, uniting English and Continental stories, he was eventually persuaded instead to produce an English-language martyrology, the *Acts and Monuments,* first published in 1563, in the wake of Queen Mary's sharp persecution of Protestants. Under the new Protestant queen, Elizabeth, Foxe set England's sufferings in the context of the whole of Christian history. Ancient Christian martyrs and modern Protestant martyrs were brethren. Persecution by Roman emperors had now been replaced with persecution by Roman Catholics.[6]

Foxe's *Book of Martyrs,* as it swiftly became known, would become fundamental to English-speaking Protestants' imagination and has been repeatedly reprinted, abridged, and updated. It is a thing of paradoxes. Foxe was a consummate internationalist, an idealistic radical who conscientiously opposed all religious violence and saw England's state Protestantism as badly compromised. But his book became an icon of national identity, a charter for that same state Protestantism, and a manifesto for religious hatred. To read it was to learn that Catholics always and forever seek Protestants' blood, and that their hatred may sleep but never dies.[7]

This was an exaggeration but not a fantasy. Catholics did not thirst for Protestant blood, but many did dream of wiping Protestantism out. But just because someone is out to get you does not mean you are not paranoid. The popularity of martyr stories shows how much Protestants saw the world in apocalyptic terms. Even those who lived in peaceful times under securely Protestant rule were ready to understand their lives as dramas of persecution, whether the villains were domestic political opponents, godless neighbors, or the devil himself. It was an alluring, all-consuming view of the world. The daily struggle of human life was a drama written by God's hand, in which the struggle itself was the surest guarantee of victory.

Turning the Tide

Protestants were formidably difficult to suppress. They were impervious to quiet reasonableness and only drew strength from persecution.

By the mid-sixteenth century, however, Catholic powers were developing two other ways of tackling the problem, two techniques that between them kept Protestantism on the defer ,ive for nearly two hundred years. Whereas in the 1560s it was reasonable to fear, or hope, that Protestantism would soon sweep all before it, instead it found itself contained and driven back across Europe.

The most effective engine of this Catholic opposition was the epochal reform program sometimes called the Counter-Reformation. Between 1545 and 1563, a great council of the Catholic Church met intermittently at Trent in northern Italy. It decisively rejected Protestant doctrines and laid out an ambitious vision for disciplinary reform and educational renewal of the church, which was implemented with verve by a reinvigorated papacy and by a series of religious orders. Over the next century, a more disciplined, better-educated Catholicism took shape, depriving the Protestants of some of their best talking points. Many Protestants believed that the Council of Trent had hatched a fiendish plot to slaughter Protestants. The truth was worse: it had hatched a plot to breathe new life into Catholicism, and Protestants struggled to respond.[8]

The other engine of Catholic revival was war. It began in France. By the 1550s, French Protestants, hardened by twenty years of intermittent persecution, were being fortified and organized by missionaries sent from Calvin's Geneva. The movement was on the march. High-profile converts were being won, and in 1559 the French Reformed Church even had the audacity to hold a secret national synod in Paris. In that same year, King Henry II, hammer of heretics, was killed in a gruesome jousting accident. Protestants naturally saw this as divine vengeance. In the political turmoil that followed, one party, led by the noble family of Guise, was staunchly Catholic, while the other, led by the king's widow, Catherine de' Medici, was still Catholic but willing to buy the Protestants' support in the currency of toleration. By the end of 1560, official persecution had largely ceased.

It was a moment of heady religious anarchy. France's Calvinist churches surged into the open. Street sermons attracted vast crowds, singing psalms to the plain metrical tunes that were becoming their battle hymns. By early 1562, something close to a tenth of the entire French population, and nearly half of the nobility, were affiliated with Calvinist churches. Not since Germany in the early 1520s had there been such an episode of breakneck Protestant expansion. A Protestant France suddenly seemed not only possible but inevitable.[9]

In Germany in the 520s, however, the Catholic establishment had been bewildered and paralyzed. Forty years later, its French counterparts fought back. Catholic preachers and polemicists matched the Protestants book for book and insult for insult. When official persecution ceased, vigilantism took over. As tinder-dry resentment and hatred piled up, eventually, inevitably, a spark caught. It happened on March 1, 1562, in the northeastern town of Vassy. The duke of Guise, leader of the Catholic hard-liners, stopped there to attend Mass. A large Calvinist congregation was assembled illegally in a converted barn nearby, and the duke's men tried to break up the meeting. A scuffle broke out. Someone threw a stone at the duke. He ordered the barn to be sealed and burned to the ground. Dozens of Calvinists were killed.

So began a series of civil wars that would last, on and off, for thirty-five years. The Protestant nobility mobilized for self-defense and to defeat the Guise faction. The Guise aimed, more simply, to exterminate French Protestantism. Two successive kings, Charles IX and Henry III, were caught in the middle: Catholic, but hoping for a compromise of some sort. Repeatedly, they declared pacifications granting restricted but real rights to the Protestant minority. Repeatedly, the kingdom collapsed into violence again.

The Protestants fought tenaciously and in the end secured a passably honorable stalemate that won them protected status for most of a century. The spring of 1562 was, however, French Protestantism's high-water mark. Once the fighting had begun, the conversions stopped, and the Protestants were on the defensive, in the streets as well as on the battlefield. Violence kills people but also divides them. Once blood has been spilled, it is very hard to remain neutral or persuadable. During the first religious war of 1562–63, virtually all French Christians became entrenched in one of the two religious parties, and thereafter viewed each other as enemies.

The violence ran both ways. Protestants took over several towns, sometimes slaughtering the Catholic leadership and often targeting Catholic priests and defiling Catholic churches. They mutilated the saints' statues, which they believed to be blasphemous idols. Female saints' statues were liable to have their noses cut off, as if they were syphilitic whores. But most popular violence was driven by the Catholic majority, urged by their preachers to purify communities polluted by heretics living in their midst. Paris became a cauldron of anti-Protestant hatred.[10]

In 1572, it boiled over. Yet another royal peace plan was being tried. But when the Protestant grandees gathered in Paris and their military leader was wounded by an anonymous sniper, tensions boiled up immediately. With both sides suspecting treachery and plotting preemptive strikes, the king decided he could no longer remain above the fray. Instead, he tried to eliminate the Protestant leadership at a stroke. Before dawn on Sunday, August 24, 1572, St. Bartholomew's Day, royal soldiers murdered the wounded man and several other Protestant dignitaries in their beds. It was intended as a surgical strike, but the people of Paris could read the signals. Crying, "The king wills it," Catholic mobs set out on an unprecedented orgy of destruction. In three days, some three thousand Protestants were killed, along with any Catholics who defended them. Over the following month, this massacre was echoed in a dozen French cities with histories of bitter interreligious tension; perhaps a further six thousand died.[11]

The St. Bartholomew's Day Massacre was the defining moment of the French religious wars. It was not exactly premeditated, nor did the perpetrators try to disown it. Pope Gregory XIII struck a medal in celebration of the massacre and commissioned commemorative frescoes. And not without reason: the massacre achieved something that individual trials and executions could not. It broke the bravado of Protestantism's martyr complex. The scale and speed of the killing dazed Protestants, who now questioned whether God was really on their side. Rumors spoke of fifty thousand, a hundred thousand dead. "The whole of France," wrote Geneva's city council, "is bathed in the blood of innocent people and covered with dead bodies." While in truth the numbers of the dead were only a tiny proportion of France's Protestants, the massacre virtually eliminated Protestantism from large areas of the country. In Rouen, for every Protestant who was killed, ten converted to Catholicism. Catholic Europe had finally discovered how to scare Protestants into conformity.[12]

Those who survived and stood their ground felt that every paranoid suspicion of Catholic treachery had been justified. Calvin's successor in

Geneva, Theodore Beza, saw the massacre as proof of a "universal conspiracy." French Protestants dug into their strongholds in southern and western France, and the religious wars resumed with fresh bitterness. They wore on until the mid-1590s, when a new king, Henry IV—a Protestant who converted to Catholicism in order to unite his kingdom—brought the Catholic hard-liners to heel. The wars were ended by the 1598 Edict of Nantes, which granted clear but limited rights to worship, self-government, and self-defense to "the so-called reformed religion." By then, the Protestant minority was half the size it had been in 1562. A lifetime later, in 1685, French Protestantism would once again be outlawed altogether.

France contained and rolled back Protestantism at the cost of three and a half decades of devastating civil war. The story would be repeated in the Netherlands, where in 1566 a sudden cessation of persecution let loose an upsurge of Protestant sympathy. Protestants called it the "Wonderyear," but prematurely. A swift crackdown gave way to a grinding eighty-year war between the Dutch and their Spanish Catholic rulers, splitting the Netherlands into a Spanish-ruled Catholic south and an independent Protestant north: the origin of the divide between the modern kingdoms of Belgium and the Netherlands. Again, the violence was both vicious and effective. Antwerp, the Protestants' former stronghold, was brutally sacked by a Spanish army in 1575. Protestants were all but driven out of the south.

The last and most terrible of the religious wars was the Thirty Years' War, which began in 1618 as an attempt by the Holy Roman Emperor Ferdinand II to suppress a Protestant rebellion in Bohemia. A crushing victory there emboldened him to try to wipe out Protestantism throughout the empire. First Denmark, then Sweden, and finally France (for political rather than religious reasons) intervened against the Catholic onslaught and managed between them to beat it back. The eventual peace confirmed the empire's religious pluralism and officially recognized Calvinism for the first time. But the Catholic victories that had been won at the start of the war were lasting. Protestantism was all but eliminated from large swaths of central Europe. The cost was unspeakable. Germany lost about a third of its entire population to disease, famine, and the flight of refugees as well as battle deaths.

None of these religious wars produced clear-cut victories. In each case, Catholic forces contained and rolled back Protestantism but failed to eradicate it. One result was that Protestants became convinced that Catholics were blood-soaked murderers who could only ever be fought, never persuaded or converted. Protestants' ambitions were blunted even as their determination to survive grew more mulish. But the wars also raised more troubling questions about how they themselves dealt with religious dissent.

The Luxury of Intolerance

From the time of Luther's first clash with the fanatics, Protestants had to deal with the problem of error in their midst. For the emerging establishments, this was a war on two fronts. There were the radical dissidents who tended to be lumped together as Anabaptists, but there was also the larger problem of what Protestants should do about their neighbors who remained stubbornly Catholic. Between them, these two problems virtually destroyed the inherited concept of how to deal with heresy.

For Protestants to treat Catholics as heretics might seem logical, but it was entirely impractical. There were simply too many of them, and moreover Protestant princes usually wanted to pacify rather than provoke their Catholic neighbors. Even Henry VIII, unmatched in his willingness to put Catholics to death, only once went so far as to burn a Catholic for heresy: an experiment he did not repeat.[13] England's Protestant rulers treated Catholics as political, not religious, offenders. By accepting the pope's authority, so the argument ran, English Catholics were traitors, serving a foreigner instead of their own natural sovereign. This allowed English monarchs to restrict their anti-Catholic fury to their own subjects and slotted papal loyalists into a convenient preexisting legal category, treason. It also subjected English Catholics to a death at least as horrible as burning, and more humiliating: being hanged, drawn, and quartered, an extended torture whose victims eventually died from being hacked to pieces from the belly out. Over two hundred English Catholics were killed this way in the sixteenth century, mostly under Elizabeth I. A few more were allowed a private beheading or deliberately starved to death in prison. Well over a thousand were killed in reprisals for failed rebellions.

No other Protestant state treated Catholicism as a capital crime. Yet Catholics in Protestant countries remained vulnerable to discrimination of all kinds, were routinely forbidden to hold public office or to worship in public, and were subject to penal taxation. England's official persecution wound down during the seventeenth century, but English anti-Catholic sentiment persisted. An entirely imaginary Catholic conspiracy to assassinate King Charles II triggered widespread panic and at least twenty-two executions between 1678 and 1681. A century later, an attempt to soften anti-Catholic legislation provoked the so-called Gordon Riots, a spasm of anti-Catholic violence across London that destroyed a great deal of Catholic property and left over three hundred people dead, most of them rioters killed by the army.

Anabaptists and radicals seemed more straightforward. Every government loathed them, and there were few enough for traditional anti-heresy techniques to be applied. Some Protestant territories did so—the English, naturally, and also several Swiss cities. But others were more squeamish. Many were reluctant to invoke heresy as a legal category, preferring to dress up their persecution of radicals as self-defense. The idea that Anabaptists posed an existential threat to Protestant establishments may seem risible with hindsight, but early Protestants were primed to see diabolical threats on every side. Anabaptists were naked flames in societies whose sins were tinder dry. They needed to be doused before disaster ensued.

Luther's approach was to treat Anabaptists as blasphemers rather than as heretics. Blasphemy was a civil rather than a religious crime, which helped Luther evade the charge of hypocrisy for seeking freedom of conscience while prosecuting dissidents. Respectable religion was free; insulting God was not. Most jurisdictions continued to treat blasphemy as a capital crime throughout the seventeenth century and beyond. The English Quaker James Nayler was convicted of blasphemy for restaging Christ's triumphal entry into Jerusalem on the outskirts of Bristol in 1656, casting himself in the starring role and claiming that Christ was in him. One admirer wrote, "Thy name is no more to be called James but Jesus." There was a clamor for his death, which the government only nominally resisted; he was in fact branded, whipped, bored through the tongue, and sentenced to two years' hard labor. His health broken, he died less than a year after his release.[14] The pretense that such prosecutions were not religious persecution was becoming hard to maintain. A Scottish student named Thomas Aikenhead was hanged for blasphemy in 1697, for ridiculing the Bible, calling Christ an impostor, and arguing that "God" was simply another word for nature. The punishment shocked his contemporaries. After him, Britain would execute no more blasphemers.

The alternative was some form of religious toleration. The notion of toleration was a familiar one, but it did not have the idealistic feel that it has in our own age. Errors might be tolerable rather as a minor infestation of vermin is tolerable, because eradicating them would be difficult and costly. The classic argument for toleration was that only God can know believers' hearts, and persecution produces hypocritical conformity rather than true belief. In other words, enforcing true belief is desirable but impossible. Against this pragmatism stood the principled case for persecution: truth cannot compromise with error, and giving simple Christians freedom to stray from the truth is as foolish as giving a child freedom to play with a razor.

On the face of it, Luther's defiance of the church made it hard to justify any form of religious compulsion. In his early enthusiasm, Luther took that view explicitly. His doctrine of the two kingdoms stated that compulsion applied only to worldly matters. He denounced executions of Anabaptists, declaring that "we should allow everyone to believe what he wills." But this was hardly a respectful pluralism. He added,

> Let them preach as confidently and boldly as they are able and
> against whomever they wish. For, as I have said, there must be
> sects, and the Word of God must be under arms and fight. . . .
> Let the spirits collide, and fight it out. If meanwhile some are
> led astray, all right, such is war.

False believers did not need earthly chastisement, he insisted, because they would be punished in hell. Yes, it was impossible to impose correct belief, but that did not make error any less culpable. And because Luther usually saw Anabaptists as rebels who deserved secular punishment anyway, there was much less to his proclaimed tolerance than met the eye.[15]

But the idea did not disappear. It would resurface in two streams, one philosophical, the other practical. The fountainhead of the philosophical tradition was Sebastian Castellio, a Protestant refugee in

Geneva who fell out bitterly with John Calvin. It was Castellio who made the execution of Miguel Servetus notorious. He argued that it was simply wrong in principle to kill someone for their beliefs, even someone as offensive as Servetus. Castellio's appeal to freedom of conscience was idiosyncratic in its day, but it was taken up in the seventeenth century and in the 1690s was canonized by two of Protestantism's greatest philosophers, John Locke and Pierre Bayle.

This tradition is inspiring but had its limits. Castellio famously argued that "to kill a man is not to defend a doctrine, it is to kill a man." Like Luther, he believed that compulsion was wrong, not that freedom of belief was right. He argued, "I must be saved by my own faith and not that of another." So religious compulsion is futile, but religious error is fatal. It is an oddly callous argument: my neighbor is hurtling toward hell, and I will do nothing about it. Locke's famous *Letter Concerning Toleration* is similarly measured. His core argument for religious tolerance is indebted to Luther's two kingdoms: princes simply do not have authority over their subjects' souls, because souls are under God's jurisdiction alone and no earthly power can compel them. But this does not mean an open-ended right to believe whatever you want. Princes can legitimately stamp out opinions that are dangerous to other people—such as Catholicism, the religion of bloodthirsty plots. Likewise, they can persecute atheism, not merely because atheists were assumed to be antisocial monsters, but because they had by definition denied God's authority over their souls, making it legitimate for princes to step in. The tolerance that Castellio and Locke taught was real, honorable, and costly, but it was a long way from what we would now recognize as genuine religious freedom.[16]

What gave their ideas increasing traction was the other, more pragmatic stream of Protestant toleration, arising chiefly from the experience of persecution. There was no logical reason why Protestants could not demand religious freedom for themselves while denying it to others. If error has a duty to tolerate truth, truth does not therefore have a duty to tolerate error. In practice, however, because Protestants made so much of tales of Catholic cruelty, it was only natural to try to differentiate themselves from their oppressors.

One dramatic way to do this was simply to refuse to kill people for their beliefs, a principle the Dutch rebels made their own. It was a

moral stance but also a prudent one, because it reassured the Netherlands' wildly plural religious communities that they would be safe under Calvinist rule. When the new Dutch Republic was established in
1581, "freedom of conscience" became one of its guiding principles.
Again, it is important to be clear what this "freedom" meant. The
Dutch Republic had an established Calvinist church, and non-Calvinists'
civil rights were restricted. Catholics were permitted simply to practice
their religion in private, without larger gatherings and certainly without the services of priests. Until 1648, the Dutch were locked in a war
of survival against their former Catholic rulers, and Catholics were
sometimes the targets of vicious reprisals.

Yet the Netherlands was by the early seventeenth century the
wealthiest and most cosmopolitan territory on Earth. Any real religious intolerance would be terrible for business. In the 1630s, the city of
Amsterdam allowed both Lutherans and Jews to build public places for
worship. The freedoms granted to Jews were particularly astonishing
at the time, not least to the city's Jews themselves. Visitors to the city
goggled at the synagogue, just as they do today at the red-light district
and coffee shops. Not everyone was impressed. The English poet Andrew Marvell wrote of:

Amsterdam, Turk-Christian-Pagan-Jew,
Staple of sects and mint of schism . . .
That bank of conscience, where not one so strange
Opinion but finds credit, and exchange.[17]

As he insinuated, it was commercial interest rather than principle that
had made the rapid growth of Amsterdam's Jewish community possible. Jews brought lucrative trading links, and they posed no real threat.
Like the Lutherans, all of whom were German or Scandinavian, the
Jews were understood to be a self-contained community of foreigners.
They could be used to demonstrate Dutch tolerance without any risk
that they would start winning converts.

Not that the indigenous population was short of choices. Although
the Dutch Republic was officially Calvinist, only a minority of the population, perhaps a fifth, were formal members of the Calvinist church.
Another third or more were loosely affiliated, attending services and

bringing their children to baptism without accepting the discipline that went with full membership. The rest were scattered between all churches and none. Mixed marriages and opportunistic conversions were widespread. One bewildered visitor to the Netherlands in 1618 stayed with a family where the mother and daughter were Calvinist, the father and son Catholic, the grandmother Anabaptist, and the uncle a Jesuit priest.[18] The Dutch did not have freedom of religion in the modern sense, and many, even most of them still believed that in principle a Christian society should enjoy religious unity. Even so, the achievement of Dutch religious liberty during the seventeenth century remains astonishing.

Can Protestantism claim that achievement? Certainly no Catholic territory could have managed such a thing. But Protestants neither had set out to achieve this nor were particularly proud of having done so. Protestant pluralism emerged in practice before it was articulated in theory. The principled pursuit of religious unity had taken France to the brink of ruin in the sixteenth century, and Germany over it in the seventeenth. Meanwhile, the Netherlands had become the richest society in the world. The single-minded pursuit of religious unity might have been ideal, but for many people it was better to be rich.

The most obvious Protestant beneficiaries of this policy were the radicals. The watershed moment for Anabaptists was the disaster at Münster in 1534–35, where an apocalyptic, utopian revolution had ended in a mass slaughter. After that, while a few still nursed violent fantasies, most radicals chose different paths. Two alternatives were open to them. One party of post-Münster Anabaptists withdrew into mysticism and into hiding, cutting themselves off from a world from which they expected nothing and to which they owed nothing. They would not fight, but they would deceive, feigning outward conformity while awaiting their deliverance. In 1544, their prophet David Joris moved incognito to the eclectic metropolis of Basel, where he lived out his life, continuing to publish works of mystical piety while remaining anonymous. Only in 1559, three years after his death, was his identity uncovered, at which point his body was exhumed and burned.[19]

Joris's exposure sent a thrill of fear around Europe. Who knew how many others remained hidden, binding each other to secrecy with devilish rites? Another mystical sect of Dutch origins, known by the sinister name the Family of Love, sparked a wave of panic in England in the early 1580s precisely because its members were almost impossible to detect. Familists called each other simply by their initials, and so although it eventually became plain that they had friends at Queen Elizabeth's court, it was impossible to establish the identity of the disciple they called "E.R.": not, we may assume, the queen herself. Familists conformed outwardly in all things, merely gathering to whisper forbidden doctrines. Movements like this terrified contemporaries, but their very secrecy doomed them to marginal status. It was very hard for underground sects to attract converts at all. They could even die out without anyone noticing that they had gone.[20]

A different path was chosen by Menno Simons, a Dutch Anabaptist whose Mennonite movement survives to the present. Simons preached pacifism and noncompliance with a positively suicidal integrity. Mennonites quickly became renowned for their readiness to lay down their lives for their faith and their refusal to lift a finger to fight for it. It was this small community, not the more numerous and more timorous mainstream reformers, that provided the bulk of the martyrs of the Dutch persecution. The tale of Dirk Willemsz became iconic. Willemsz escaped from a Catholic prison in the spring of 1569 and fled across a frozen river. He crossed safely, but the ice gave way under the officer who was following him. Willemsz turned back and saved the man's life by pulling him from the water. As a result, he was rearrested and, eventually, executed. In legal terms, this rigor made sense: he was still an unrepentant heretic. But such stories did not give the law a good name.

The Dutch Republic was content to tolerate Mennonites. Their closed communities were antisocial but not openly subversive. They had scruples about matters like swearing oaths and bearing arms, which took a little goodwill to accommodate politically, but the goodwill was there, greased by the Mennonites' willingness to pay hefty extra taxes to regularize their status.

The Mennonites' heroic virtues did not, however, extend to toleration. In the 1550s, they themselves divided bitterly, and by the end of the century there were at least six distinct, mutually reviling Mennonite groups in the Netherlands. The most divisive issue, with painful irony, was how far they ought to tolerate one another. One party, the Waterlanders, rejected the practice of formally excluding or "shunning" those who fell foul of the godly community's discipline. For this they were duly shunned by the others. They persisted in preaching reunion, and in the 1630s several Mennonite groups drew on Waterlander principles to form a body, the United Congregations, that decided to tolerate differences over minor issues in the faith. Unfortunately, it was unclear what counted as a minor issue. The Waterlanders themselves, who disliked binding rules of any kind, were not actually permitted to join the United Congregations, but by this time the Waterlanders had divisions of their own. In the 1620s, an educated, dissident movement of freethinkers known as the Collegiants had emerged, rejecting all hierarchies and structures and permitting any participant in their informal meetings to speak. The Waterlanders expelled them. The Collegiants themselves, in turn, expelled those who questioned Christ's divinity. The United Congregations then split over how to deal with the Collegiants. The faction who argued that Collegiants, anti-Trinitarians, and even the unbaptized should be admitted to the Eucharist were eventually expelled in 1664 and sought refuge among the Waterlanders. Naturally, the Waterlanders refused to admit such dangerous spiritual anarchists.[21]

This farce contains the paradoxes of Protestant tolerance and intolerance in microcosm. It shows Protestants' endless appetite for squabbling and their widespread conviction that separated brethren remained brethren. It also shows that the most divisive issue of all was tolerance itself. Even so, unwillingly, whether from political positioning, commercial opportunism, the exhaustion of alternatives, or even a degree of principle, Protestantism was by the late seventeenth century slouching toward a grudging, genuine tolerance.

The Devil's Minions

No more than a few thousand religious dissidents were judicially killed in the sixteenth and seventeenth centuries, but between 1450 and 1700, and especially between 1550 and 1650, some fifty to a hundred thousand Europeans were put to death for a slightly different religious crime: witchcraft. About 80 percent of these were women, whereas roughly 80 percent of executed heretics were men. The numbers are not vast; more people than that died of the plague in London in one year, 1665.

But the slaughter of tens of thousands of women for an imaginary crime is a phenomenon worth noticing.

For centuries, most Europeans had believed in witches: malevolent misfits who used uncanny powers to inflict harm on their neighbors. It was only from the fifteenth century on, however, that witches began to be judicially prosecuted in large numbers. Many jurisdictions now began treating witchcraft as a species of heresy, accusing supposed witches of making pacts with the devil. Petty crimes of personal malice were redefined in apocalyptic terms.

What, if anything, did this have to do with the Reformation? The witch hunts and the wars of religion took place in the same region, in the same period, and invoked the same murderous logic. Yet the two phenomena do not line up neatly, either chronologically or denominationally. Catholics killed more witches than Protestants did, but some Protestant witch-hunters worked very hard to stay competitive, and some Catholic territories, such as Spain, prosecuted very few witches. Protestants and Catholics read each other's anti-witchcraft treatises and competed to prove their zeal.

One key connection, however, has been made by the work of the historian Gary K. Waite. Witches were not alone in attracting both Catholic and Protestant persecutors; so did Anabaptists, who were often described as devilish, for their doctrines, their behavior, and their infuriating steadfastness under torture. One group of southern German Anabaptists, arrested in 1532, sang, laughed, barked, and brayed so that it sounded as if "the prison was full of devils." Or again, in February 1535, during the height of the Münster crisis, a group of Anabaptists (seven men, four women) burned their clothes in an upper room in Amsterdam and ran out naked into the street, proclaiming woe and claiming to be preaching "the naked truth." When forcibly dressed after their arrest, they tore their clothes from their bodies. Clothes had first been donned by Adam and Eve as a sign of sin, to conceal their shame. By shedding their clothes, the Amsterdam nudists proclaimed that they had overcome sin. At the same time, their nudity symbolically revealed and denounced the corruption that their godless neighbors had concealed under their fine clothing. To those appalled neighbors, this looked demonic. The Amsterdam nudists were discharged, but Anabaptists, sexual deviants, and demons were mixing together in people's minds. Two years later, a Dutch Anabaptist was burned as a witch. In the records, her crime was initially given as adult baptism, but that was scratched out and replaced with witchcraft.[22]

The leap from anti-Anabaptist paranoia to witch panic was easy. Anabaptists' secrecy seemed diabolical; David Joris's success in hiding among honest Christians was blamed on sorcery. Joris had in fact taught that there was no devil, but because the standard judicial view was that only witches deny the devil's existence, this hardly helped. Some radicals also questioned conventional sexual mores, even beyond nudity or permitting women to teach. One Thuringian sect, the Bloodfriends, supposedly taught total sexual freedom for the saved. Their secret outdoor meetings were said to end with the command "be fruitful and multiply," whereupon they paired off. Such deliciously appalling tales were widely told. One French gentleman, arrested in 1562 for attending a secret Protestant meeting, shamefacedly explained that he had gone along because he had hoped, vainly, that the rumors of orgies were true. The judges dismissed his case, our witness tells us, "trying not to laugh." Not everyone thought it was funny. A sectarian orgy is not too different from a witches' sabbat.[23]

Worst of all was the Anabaptists' refusal to baptize infants and their insistence that converts who had been baptized as infants be rebaptized. Catholic and Lutheran baptisms included a formal exorcism, casting the devil out of a child born in original sin. Anabaptism could be construed as a demonic scheme to fill the world with unbaptized slaves of the devil. Everyone knew that witches' sabbats involved sacrificing, and indeed eating, unbaptized babies. Suspicion came to focus on midwives, who were suspected both of concealing Anabaptists' babies so as to avoid baptism and also of witchcraft, especially when babies died suddenly. Adult baptisms only made matters worse, because the sabbat legend also held that the devil forced witches to renounce Christian baptism and to accept a foully diabolical baptism, with new devil-parents instead of godparents.

By the 1550s, the categories of "witch" and "Anabaptist" were becoming blurred. In the Lutheran territory of Baden, church authorities asked each parish in 1556 whether they were troubled by "Anabaptists, sorcerers, necromancers, or similar people." In Wiesensteig, in southwestern Germany, a secret Anabaptist group was discovered meeting by night in the summer of 1562. Weeks later, a freak summer hailstorm did terrible damage to crops in the area, and twenty women were arrested as witches, accused both of causing the storm and of having robbed children of their baptism. They were burned en masse, and at least forty more executions followed over the next few months. This was overseen by the local lord, Count Ulrich of Helfenstein, who had reconverted to Catholicism after brief flirtations with Lutheranism and a moderate strain of Anabaptism.[24]

This was the period's first true mass witch panic. From then on, persecution of Anabaptists began to dry up, to be replaced by a much larger-scale persecution of witches, in more or less the same areas. Fears of secret but real sects had metastasized into fears of invented ones. Tales of witches' crimes became as florid as each individual prosecutor's fantasies. Protestants and Catholics, having competed to stamp out one satanic sect, easily transferred their rivalry to the new target.

Protestants were deeply implicated in these killings. But in this as in almost everything else, they did not speak with one voice. Most assumed that witches were servants of the devil and fully deserved death, quoting Exodus 22:18 to prove the point: "Thou shalt not suffer a witch to live." A few, however, questioned whether it was correct to translate the Hebrew word *kashaph* as "witch." Reginald Scot, an English witch skeptic who might himself have had ties to the Family of Love, reckoned it meant "poisoner." Scot dismissed claims about old women's magical powers as superstition, insisting that the devil himself had been defeated by Christ and could do no more than spread lies.[25]

Scot was unique in his excoriating rationalism but not in his qualms about witch-hunting. The Dutch-born Lutheran physician Johann Weyer and the English preacher George Gifford did not question the devil's power, but both argued that most of the women accused of witchcraft were innocent, either accused out of malice or imagining themselves to be witches when they were not. By the mid-seventeenth century, there was widespread unease with the mismatch between the diabolical conspirators whom advocates of witch-hunting described and the pathetic wretches who were in fact dragged before most courts. Judicial persecution of witches quietly tailed away to nothing. The age's most notorious witch hunt, at Salem, Massachusetts, in 1692, was virtually the last of its kind. It may be significant that Massachusetts had reacted exceptionally violently to the appearance in the 1650s of the Quakers, the Anabaptists of their day: New England Quakers were frequently accused of witchcraft. Regardless, the Salem trials were remarkable chiefly for the near-universal disapproval they provoked.

Whether they were dealing with Catholics, radicals, or witches, Protestants could kill in the name of religion with a zeal that was second to none. They could also disagree with one another vigorously about doing so and could shift their ground with remarkable speed and flexibility. That combination of implacable fervor, conscientious stubbornness, and willingness suddenly to abandon and to repent of their old views is one of Protestants' most distinctive hallmarks.

CHAPTER 5

The British Maelstrom

Every valley shall be exalted, and every mountain and hill shall be made low. . . . And the glory of the Lord shall be revealed.

—ISAIAH 40:4–5

In the middle of the seventeenth century, the themes of Protestant-ism's early history came together in a bloody, chaotic, and exhilarat-ing symphony. They did so in an unlikely place: the island of Great Britain, which until then had played a supporting role in Protestant-ism's drama. The island's two kingdoms, England and Scotland, had both embraced the Reformation, allowing them to overcome their pe-rennial mutual hostility. Since 1603, both realms had been subject to the same king. During the religious wars, both countries sent volunteers, money, munitions, and—occasionally—formal armies to the Conti-nent, and England also completed a savage conquest of Catholic Ire-land. But they managed to keep their wars at arm's length. Spain's attempts to bring the war to Elizabeth I's England failed, most famously in the disastrous Armada expedition of 1588. From 1560, Britain enjoyed an unprecedented era of internal peace and of religious stability. After 1560, both kingdoms were more or less Calvinist, although the English church had retained some Catholic structures and a ceremonial streak in its worship. Religious debates in both countries could be lively, but they took place within a widely shared consensus, which included an almost universal commitment to the ideal of a comprehensive, national church.

And yet, between 1637 and 1642, first Scotland, then Ireland, and fi-nally England rebelled against their king, setting off two decades of

war, political turmoil, regicide, and wave after wave of religious revolution. When the smoke finally cleared and the blood washed away,
the monarchy and the old churches were restored in the 1660s almost
as if nothing had happened, but the new beliefs that took shape in this
crucible would make themselves felt around the world for centuries to
come.

An Unlikely War

The collapse during 1637–42 had many causes, most of them beyond our
concern. The immediate disputes over a dysfunctional system of taxation were symptoms of a deeper philosophical conflict. A century earlier, England's political classes had been utterly cowed by Henry VIII,
but by the early seventeenth century they had turned mulish. Perhaps
the turmoil of the Reformation and a series of nail-biting succession
crises had convinced them that politics was too important to be left to
kings. Perhaps Protestantism had simply corroded the ideal of obedience. For whatever reason, a broad class of gentlemen, merchants, and
lawyers were newly willing to stand on their rights and answer back to
their kings. James I, England's king from 1603 to 1625, had been raised
in Scotland's bare-knuckle politics and had learned to use his royal dignity to face down his opponents, but he understood that asserting his
divine right to rule was a political ploy. His son Charles I utterly believed it and had little interest in political realism. For all the deep forces
at work, the most obvious cause of the disaster was his profound inad-
equacy as a ruler.

Still, penny-pinching, idealistic legalism versus overweening, extravagant royal incompetence is the ordinary stuff of politics. What
made this nasty brew toxic was religion. In both England and Scotland,
royal power had long been associated with religious conservatism.
King James had had his fill of assertive Calvinists as king of Scots, and
when he became king of England after Elizabeth I's death, he eagerly
embraced the English church's ceremonialist strand, especially its government by well-behaved bishops. Yet he still allowed room for "Puritans," who thought the English Reformation was unfinished and who
dreamed of completing it.

King Charles shared his father's opinions but not his caution. He exclusively promoted ceremonialist priests and bishops, many of whom denied the core Calvinist doctrine of predestination and froze out anyone who disagreed. Leading the king's campaign was William Laud, bishop of London from 1628 and archbishop of Canterbury from 1633. Under Laud's eye, a counterrevolution was imposed on English parishes: Communion tables dressed and railed like Catholic altars, choral music instead of simple metrical hymns, sermons downgraded in favor of liturgy, and set forms of prayer favored over spontaneous outpourings.

For a great many English people, all of these things smelled of "popery": creeping re-Catholicization. Charles's queen, a French Catholic princess, maintained her own Catholic chapel in the heart of London, and Puritans suspected her husband was likewise smuggling popery into the English church. Of course Charles denied it, but he would, wouldn't he? Laud's campaign awakened English Protestantism's martyr complex. Puritans were being driven from office. In one notorious case in 1637, three outspoken preachers were imprisoned and had their ears cut off for defying the king. Meanwhile, Charles steadfastly refused to intervene in the Thirty Years' War to save his suffering Protestant brethren in Europe. Was he, in fact, now the puppet of Catholic plotters?

By the late 1620s, political trust had almost completely collapsed. A series of Parliaments clashed head-on with the king, until finally in 1629 Charles dismissed Parliament and set about governing without it. Which he could, but only as long as England remained at peace and could manage without the taxes that only Parliament could levy. Laud's agenda marched forward, and Puritans were left voiceless. It seemed like a victory.

Characteristically, Charles overplayed his hand. Despite ample warnings, he decided to extend Laud's counterrevolution to Scotland, whose church was much more straightforwardly Calvinist than England's and whose political culture was much less polite. The imposition of a version of the English Book of Common Prayer on Scotland in 1637 provoked first riots, then full-scale rebellion. In February 1638, a Scottish National Covenant was ostentatiously signed in Edinburgh and rapidly distributed across the country. The Covenanters affirmed their loyalty to the king while furiously denouncing popery. Declaring that King Charles's changes "tend to the reestablishing of the popish religion and tyranny," they swore to give the "utmost of our power, with our means and lives," to defend "the true religion and his majesty's authority." If that meant defending the king's authority from the king himself, so be it.[1]

Charles's instinct was to respond with force. Through 1639–40, he tried to cobble together an army. He could raise men from his third kingdom, Ireland, but paying them was another matter. In April 1640, he risked summoning an English Parliament, to ask for taxes. But England's political classes were not going to support a crypto-Catholic king in leading an army of Irish Catholics against Scottish Protestants. For all they knew, once the Scots were subdued, the Irish muskets would be turned on them, and a Catholic tyranny would be imposed openly. The "Short Parliament" was dismissed after three weeks of impasse.

Charles, typically, tried to attack anyway, but the Scottish Covenanters had assembled a formidable army, led by returned volunteers from the European war. There was only one serious skirmish, outside the English military town of Newcastle on August 28, 1640, at which the seasoned Scottish forces scattered the king's raw recruits. The Scots occupied much of the north of England, forcing the king to pay their expenses. Militarily defeated, financially exhausted, and almost completely politically isolated, Charles was compelled to summon another English Parliament. This one would endure in various forms for nearly twenty years.

This new Parliament shamelessly used its financial muscle to roll back Charles's counterrevolution. As well as extracting a series of constitutional concessions, it attacked the popish clique bewitching the king. Archbishop Laud was imprisoned. The earl of Strafford, the king's Irish deputy, whose army had been so much feared, was executed. Charles consented to Strafford's death only under excruciating pressure. His remorse at having done so would fortify him against sensible compromises for years to come.

For some in Parliament, that was enough: the point had been made, the clock turned back, and normal life could resume. Others, however, reckoned that the entire pre-Laudian settlement had been exposed as a sham. The bishops whom Puritans had once pragmatically accepted were now revealed as tyrannical miniature popes. Those who had spent a decade defying those bishops at considerable personal cost were not about to compromise. They had tasted freedom, and they wanted more.

It was not only the merchants, lawyers, and gentlemen in Parliament who wanted change. London was the world's largest Protestant city, a Babylon filled with Puritan agitators, unemployed soldiers, and volunteers returning from the war in Germany. With the hobbling of Charles's government and the release of Puritan prisoners, a carnivalesque anarchy had taken hold. A radical fringe was coming into the open as official censorship faltered. A storm of provocative, scabrous, and opportunistic pamphlets flew from London's presses and whipped up the urban fire over which Parliament was simmering.

In France in the early 1560s, and the Netherlands in 1566, the sudden withdrawal of government control produced an explosion of interest in and conversion to new religious choices. So it was in England in 1640–42. A petition calling for bishops and other ceremonial vestiges to be abolished gathered fifteen thousand signatures. An unknown young polemicist named John Milton published a foam-flecked diatribe against the "canary-sucking," "swan-eating" bishops. An emerging constituency was arguing that the old establishment was enslaved to Antichrist and so needed utter abolition, not mere reform. An uncontainable suspicion and fury was building.[2]

Still, the pull of consensus might have prevailed had it not been for Ireland. In October 1641, Irish Catholic landowners, emboldened by the political power vacuum and alarmed by the new mood in England, launched a coup. A surgical strike against leaders turned into a general rising almost by accident. Like the St. Bartholomew's Day Massacre seventy years earlier, the widespread belief that King Charles had backed the plotters gave the violence legitimacy. About four thousand Irish Protestants were killed, and twice as many died of exposure during the winter, having been expelled from their homes. Ireland seemed to have successfully shrugged off British rule.

This uprising raised the temperature of English politics beyond the boiling point. Irish atrocity stories, each more exaggerated than the last, fanned England's already-blazing anti-Catholic paranoia into a wildfire. Those who had been warning of a Catholic conspiracy to drown Protestants in their own blood felt vindicated. There were vigilante attacks on English Catholics. The "Grand Remonstrance," presented to the king by Parliament in December 1641, blamed England's woes on "a corrupt and ill-affected party" and "their mischievous devices for the alteration of religion and government" and insisted that bishops be abolished forthwith.[3]

The problem was, how was the Irish rebellion to be crushed? Could the king be trusted with an army? What would stop him from allying with the Irish papists and bringing them to England to slaughter Protestants in their beds? But if he could not stand to England's defense, then he had in effect abandoned his duties as king. In which case, his subjects' first duty was to bring him to his senses, by any means necessary.

For English moderates, this kind of talk was open rebellion. To accuse the king of treachery was to make a nonsense of all laws. Henry Burton, a radical minister whose missing ears were a token of his anti-Catholic bona fides, retorted that "if any human Laws be found to be contrary to Gods Word, they are invalid and void *ipso facto.*"[4] To some, this was common sense. To others, it was treason. In January 1642, Charles attempted a coup of his own and tried to arrest the parliamentary ringleaders. Westminster closed ranks to protect them, and the king fled London. It was no longer his city.

Even then, no one expected a full-scale war. As so often happens, both parties believed they would quickly defeat their opponents. Both seemed to themselves to be obviously right and moderate, and their opponents a fringe of extremists. Yet we cannot quite write this off as the naïveté of a people who had lived in peace for so long that they had forgotten what war means. For over two decades, the English had been transfixed by the ghastly spectacle that we call the Thirty Years' War, in which tens of thousands of English and Scottish volunteers and mercenaries had fought. As the political temperature at home rose, these men came pouring back, bringing with them up-to-the-minute military expertise and battle-hardened sensibilities. It was these veterans who made the Scottish mobilization and victory in 1639–40 possible. England, too, had all too many ex-soldiers: men with no skills other than killing, ready to be filled with martial zeal for whichever cause came calling. Continental butchery had inured a generation to war and had made it seem a natural state of affairs.

Now it was coming to England. As a 1641 pamphlet put it, "The same wheel of mischief that hath wrought the worst in Germany since the year 1618 hath for some years last past been set also at work in England, Scotland and Ireland." The Laudian counterrevolution, the Irish rebellion—it was all part of the same vast plot. Those who counseled peace were at best naive, at worst active agents of Antichrist.[5]

And so, in 1642, Europe's religious wars finally spilled across the English Channel. Both sides in the English Civil War drew on Continental veterans and imported Continental weapons. There was also a real threat of direct Continental intervention in England's wars, forestalled by Parliament's seizure of the Royal Navy. Parliamentarians, in particular, understood their war as part of a European struggle. The nickname Cavalier, applied to the royalist army, was a piece of Continental name-calling. ("Roundhead," a derogatory reference to typical Puritan hairstyles, was a homegrown English insult apparently first coined in 1641.) A woodcut dating from the 1650s gives this view of the wars in full. The two-headed eagle, symbol of the Catholic Habsburg emperors who had driven the Thirty Years' War, is seen straddling the North Sea, with one wing in the Netherlands and the other in Yorkshire. For those who feared a vast popish conspiracy, it was all one war: a war of desperate self-defense and also of liberation.

Winning the Peace

During 1642, each party found to its surprise that its rival did not crumble. Instead, both entrenched themselves in their regional strongholds. The supposedly swift war lasted three and a half years, during which more than eighty thousand people were killed and large parts of England, especially the heavily contested Midlands and West Country, were laid waste.

The king's aim was simply to put down a vast rebellion. Parliament's aims were more complex. At first, Parliamentarians believed they were fighting to defend themselves against the Catholic plotters who had deceived their king, a king to whom they still swore fealty. But as they began to realize what victory could mean, visions of a new England began to take shape, some more radical than others.

The most obvious route was the one endorsed in the summer of

1643 by a military alliance between the English Parliament and the Scottish Covenanters. The alliance, the Solemn League and Covenant, was sealed by a joint religious program which came close to making this a war for Presbyterianism: to import Scotland's national church into England. Several high-powered Scots now joined the Westminster Assembly, a gathering of theologians set up by the English Parliament in order to work out a postwar religious settlement. This was what English Puritans had long hoped for. England's unfinished Reformation would be purged of its popish dregs and brought into line with international Calvinism.

The Westminster Assembly set itself earnestly to work. In 1644, it produced a newly austere order of service for the English church in place of the uncomfortably traditionalist Book of Common Prayer. In 1646, the assembly produced a new confession of faith, which is still a touchstone for Presbyterians around the world. Parliament supported the assembly's work by banning the old Prayer Book, abolishing the office of bishop, and—to underline the point—executing Archbishop Laud. In place of the bishops, a Presbyterian structure of elected elders and regional assemblies was haltingly erected. However, to Presbyterian dismay, Parliament insisted on retaining oversight of those assemblies. The Scottish church's robust independence would not be imported. Presbyterian purists, whose temperament was not suited to seeing a glass as nine-tenths full, scented betrayal.

The moment when England might have turned Presbyterian came after a crushing defeat of the royalists by a Scots-Parliamentarian army at the battle of Marston Moor on July 2, 1644. There was talk of a negotiated peace in which a chastened king would have accepted a house-trained Presbyterian church. But if Charles had been the kind of man to accept such terms, the war would never have begun. By the winter, it was clear that Parliament would have to fight to the end, although no one yet knew what that end might be. And that meant defeating the king in his western heartlands, which required a new strategy. So, fatefully, in January 1645 Parliament voted to consolidate its various regional forces into a "new-modeled" army, a professional, national force that could fight the war to the finish.

In military terms, this was bruisingly effective. On June 14, 1645, the New Model Army crushed a veteran royalist force at the battle of

Naseby in Northamptonshire. In September, it took the ruined remains of Bristol, a royalist stronghold and once England's third-largest city. By early 1646, royalist resistance was virtually over. The army's career, however, was only beginning. In a series of further campaigns in England, Scotland, and Ireland over the following decade and a half, it was to prove itself an exceptionally formidable fighting force: man for man, a match for any army in the world. It also quickly became, and remained until 1660, the primary source of political power in the British Isles. The king was defeated not by Parliament but by the army. That fact determined everything that followed.

When armies intervene in politics in the modern world, we generally see them as authoritarian and conservative. But this army was created to be God's and the people's army, a meritocracy of true believers. It imagined itself to be a truer custodian of the godly cause than the House of Commons, whose aging electoral mandate dated from another world. In 1647, one zealous London artisan called it "our Army, . . . the Army that we had poured out to God so many prayers and tears for, and we had largely contributed unto. They were as our right hand."[6] The soldiers had earned their authority with their own blood, and God had plainly endorsed it by giving them an unbroken run of victories.

The army's godliness, however, was of a particular kind. The breakdown of religious authority since 1640 had given a vocal minority of English Protestants a taste for religious experiment. Even if they still believed in a unified national church, it took heroic patience to wait to reach it in lockstep. A vanguard of advanced reformers wanted to enjoy true Christian purity here and now. Already in 1641, some high-profile Puritans were advocating a network of "independent Churches," governed neither by bishops nor by presbyteries but by the law of Christ and by mutual consultation and advice.[7]

There were not all that many Independent congregations, but they were zealous and high-profile, and they bridled at all attempts to make them march to a slow, orderly national tune. John Milton, one of the Independents' publicists, bracketed bishops and presbyteries together as disciplinarian "forcers of conscience." Independents began to talk of toleration and religious freedom. In 1644, with Parliament trying to reimpose order on London's unruly printers, Milton famously defended a free press as a matter of principle. Castellio, a century earlier, had argued that "to kill a man is not to defend a doctrine, it is to kill a man." Milton now argued that "as good almost kill a Man as kill a good Book; who kills a Man kills a reasonable creature, God's Image; but he who destroys a good Book, kills reason itself, kills the Image of God." Making the classic Protestant appeal to conscience, he claimed the freedom "to argue freely according to conscience, above all liberties."[8]

The Presbyterians' retort was that liberty of this kind led directly to heresy and blasphemy. Thomas Edwards, Presbyterianism's painstaking and horrified chronicler of errors, warned that Independents were not merely orthodox Calvinists who had rejected external oversight, but concealed views that were "higher flown, more seraphical." That was untrue. Plenty of Independents were essentially orthodox in their theology, including the most famous of them all, Oliver Cromwell, a member of Parliament (MP) who became the army's most brilliant general. But for some, Independency was a gateway drug. Even as Presbyterianism's victory over royalist crypto-Catholicism was in its grasp, it was unraveling on its other flank, and Parliament could muster neither the votes nor the will for a serious crackdown.

In the long term, the most important of the new groups now emerging were the Baptists, who went from being a marginal sectarian movement in prewar England to a church tens of thousands strong by 1660. Their existence proves that the old barrier between "magisterial" and "radical" Protestants had collapsed. For over a century, magisterial Protestants had insisted on infant baptism as a necessary feature of a universal, all-embracing church. Now, in revolutionary England, it was becoming plain that such a church no longer existed. So why not stop pretending that infant baptism was biblical and embrace being a sect? Crucially, doing this did not make you a wild radical. Many Baptists were, theologically, pretty conventional Calvinists. But they had mixed magisterial doctrines with a radical structure: allowing congregations to organize themselves, and sharply separating their community of baptized believers from the mass of corrupt humanity. It was a potent mix. From this starting point, the Baptists would spread across the Atlantic and then across the planet, to become one of the world's leading Protestant denominational families.

The primary vector for this and other, even more radical infections

was the New Model Army. It is not simply that the army's zealous recruits were disproportionately Independent or Baptist. Independency's
essence was its denial of the network of parish churches; the army,
forever on the move, was by definition outside that network. Its chaplains were under its own discipline, and its soldiers, risking their lives
in God's service, had their own voices. We have testimony to this from
Richard Baxter, one of the most humane pastoral theologians of his
age. Baxter had believed that Parliament's war was being fought in defense of "our old principles . . . only to save the Parliament and Kingdom from papists and delinquents, and to remove the dividers, that the
King might again return to his Parliament." But shortly after the battle
of Naseby, he visited the army's encampment:

> Among Cromwell's soldiers, I found a new face of things which
> I never dreamed of: I heard the plotting heads very hot upon
> that which intimated their intention to subvert both Church
> and State. Independency and Anabaptistry were most prevalent;
> Antinomianism and Arminianism were equally distributed.[9]

Something shockingly new was brewing in the army's ranks. The "old
principles" were no longer to be had.

So when the king finally surrendered in 1646, he faced a divided
gaggle of victors: a staunchly Presbyterian and increasingly powerless
Westminster Assembly; an army seething with radicalism, keen to fulfill its providential destiny, and unwilling to demobilize until its soldiers' substantial arrears were paid; and Parliament, trying to balance
the books and retain the initiative. The king, trying to divide his enemies, spun out round after round of talks. As he did so, the mirage of a
settled Presbyterian church vanished over the horizon. Many parishes
and some regions did set up Presbyterian institutions, yet participation
in this supposedly national church was essentially voluntary. Every parish church had become de facto Independent, whether it used that freedom to submit to Presbyterian discipline, to stick to something very
like the supposedly banned Prayer Book, or to explore wilder shores.

Meanwhile, the army's frustration was growing. The symbolic
point at which the political initiative passed from Parliament to army

was June 4, 1647, when the army seized the king to forestall any attempt to impose a deal against their wishes. Those wishes were at this point still a work in progress. The leading officers were willing to contemplate a political settlement that permitted a fair degree of religious toleration but otherwise looked just about recognizably like precrisis England. For many of the men, however, the time for that had passed.

Enter the group known to history as the Levelers, justly famous as the world's first advocates of representative democracy. Their ambitions were first articulated in a series of pamphlets published in 1645 and 1646, but in 1647 the movement was taken up in earnest by the army's rank and file and reinforced by London-based petitions that gathered tens of thousands of signatures. The Levelers demanded that Parliaments be elected every two years, by something not too far from universal male suffrage, along with freedom of religion and equality under the law. As to the king, some openly called for a republic. They certainly refused to cede any real power to the man who had "intended our bondage, and brought a cruell War upon us."[10]

After that war, merely restoring the status quo felt inadequate. The Levelers in the army declared that their wartime service made plain "at how high a rate we value our just freedom." In any case, the past was irrecoverable. A new world needs new rules. Even some royalists were tempted by Leveler ideas; if you feared parliamentary tyranny, regular elections with a reformed franchise had an appeal.[11]

Underpinning all of this was an explicitly Protestant conviction that this was an apocalyptic crisis. The living God who acts providentially in history had renewed his Gospel through Martin Luther. Antichrist had mustered all his forces in response. Now this had come to a head in a catastrophic war that had convulsed all Europe and had at last come to the Gospel's last outpost, Britain, at earth's westernmost end. Finally, at terrible cost, victory had been won, and power providentially given to God's own army. It was a hinge in the world's history. God was about to do something new.

So the Levelers rejected Presbyterianism as "a compulsive mastership, or aristocratical government, over the people." They envisaged a government with no authority over religion at all, insisting that it was a sin to accept any externally imposed orthodoxy instead of "what our

Consciences dictate to be the mind of God." Respectable Calvinists generally held that orthodoxy was policed by the scholarship of university-trained ministers. But what if the universities had become self-serving guilds that excluded inconvenient truths? What use is book learning when the Spirit of God is at work? The Presbyterians' rule, claimed the radical army chaplain John Saltmarsh, was that "God must not speak till man give him leave." Saltmarsh instead appealed to "the infinitely abounding spirit of God, which blows when and where it listeth." The Levelers felt that breath on their necks.[12]

They could never have succeeded. Even if, impossibly, they had secured truly free elections, they would have been routed. Their awkward argument that Catholics and royalists should be disenfranchised shows that they knew it. But in any case, the discussions were cut short. It does not do to leave a live king out of your calculations. In December 1647, Charles escaped and gathered fresh supporters. Old royalists were joined by some Presbyterians, who had concluded that the army's radical ways were a more serious threat than the king. A second civil war ensued, which lasted for much of 1648, although Charles himself was swiftly recaptured. The new royalist coalition was potentially formidable but was disparate and disorganized, and the New Model Army did what it did best. Local revolts were put down one by one. A Scottish royalist army was taken unawares by a slightly smaller English force at Preston in Lancashire and beaten into a bloody surrender.

Now the army, officers and men alike, was unforgiving. King Charles was a war criminal, a "man of blood" who bore responsibility for his subjects' deaths. By restarting a war he had already lost, he had openly defied God. There was talk of forcing him to abdicate in favor of one of his sons, but even now such a compromise was not Charles's style. He tried to strike a deal with the parliamentary leadership over the army's heads. A parliamentary vote on December 5 that suggested it might happen triggered an open coup. The army moved into Westminster. Forty-five MPs were briefly imprisoned, and nearly 300 more were excluded, leaving a hard core of about 70 sympathetic to the army's views. Eventually, another 130 or so would be allowed to trickle back into the body known, cruelly but fairly, as the Rump Parliament. By then, it had already carried out the task for which it was created. It put its sovereign lord, King Charles I, on trial for treason, and on January 30, 1649, cut off his head.

Journeys into the Unknown

The king's death opened up three possible ways forward. One was to conclude that with this exceptionally awful king gone, normality of some kind could resume. This was the path chosen by the Scots, who proclaimed the dead king's eighteen-year-old son King Charles II as soon as the news from London reached them. The new "king," in Continental exile, was reluctant to accept the filleted crown that Presbyterian Scotland was offering him, but even royal beggars cannot be choosers, and in 1650 he landed in Scotland to claim it. Relations with his Scottish subjects were not warm. Nor was England's response. The army, under Cromwell's leadership, invaded, defeating the Scots royalists in a series of brutally effective battles. In 1651, Charles himself narrowly escaped to peripatetic exile once again. So the first option, a restored monarchy, failed, but not utterly. It slept until the second had run its course.

The second possible response, taken by the new regime in London, was to reform the state's abuses while still maintaining a degree of continuity. Following the king's execution, a republic was declared, but the purged House of Commons insisted in February 1649 that it was "fully resolved to maintain the fundamental laws of this nation."[13] It was in that spirit that the republican leadership experimented with a series of governing structures over the following decade. The Rump Parliament, ineffective and increasingly friendless, was forcibly dissolved by the army in 1653 when it tried to make its own rule perpetual. The army then made a brief and quixotic attempt to replace it with a nominated assembly, known derisively as Barebones's Parliament, many of whose members were drawn from the Independent churches. However, when its radical wing threatened to take control, this too was closed down. Oliver Cromwell, who as the army's most effective general had for some time been the de facto ruler of England, was now formally acknowledged as its Lord Protector.

The following five years brought a degree of stability. Cromwell proved himself to be a shrewd, effective, and even principled ruler,

imposing a semblance of order on his war-torn country and normaliz-
ing relations with England's neighbors. He held parliaments at which
dissident voices were muffled but not entirely silenced. He did make
some attempt to police the population's moral behavior, although this
was much exaggerated by subsequent legends, and he worked hard to
root out vestigial royalists. Yet, to howls of betrayal from the Presbyterians, he refused to impose a national church of any kind. Cromwell
became the first Protestant ruler anywhere to support religious toleration as a matter of principle, and as a result presided over a sectarian
flowering unmatched since Luther had first denounced the fanatics in
Germany in the 1520s. This toleration was not limitless. It did not extend to Catholics, whom the regime saw as a political threat, and in
principle anti-Trinitarians were excluded too. Yet the regime had no
stomach for actually persecuting anyone except Catholics. Cromwell
claimed his toleration could extend even to Muslims (of whom there
were none in England). He also ended England's centuries-old exclusion of Jews, in the hope of a boost to commerce (which happened) and
of mass Jewish conversions to Christianity (which did not).

And yet the republican regimes did not abolish the underpinning
structure of a national church. No one was now compelled to attend a
parish church, but most continued to do so. Presbyterian structures
were allowed to operate. The government vetted ministerial appointments. Most controversially of all, tithes continued to be legally required. Tithes were the makeshift local taxes that supported parish
churches and from which, very often, landowners took a considerable
cut. Radicals of all kinds railed against this, but tithes, as a symbol of
social order, became totemic for the establishment. The suppression of
Barebones's Parliament in 1653 was triggered by an attempt to abolish
tithes: for Cromwell, a step too far.

As lord protector, Cromwell became king in all but name. One of
his parliaments pressed him to accept the crown openly. He and the
army leadership refused, but when he died in 1658, he was succeeded as
lord protector by his son Richard Cromwell; it seemed pretty monarchical. However, during the next eighteen months the republican regime unraveled amid rising panic about sectarianism. The army, which
did not trust Richard, deposed him in May 1659. A bewildering succession of attempted governing structures came and went over the

following months, until eventually one of the most powerful of the generals accepted the growing clamor for what seemed like the only viable option: restoring the monarchy. Charles II returned to England in 1660, pledging forgiveness and moderation, promises that he did not violate as thoroughly as some had feared. And so in the end the second option failed utterly: it produced a republic that was simply old England in new dress and all too soon clothed itself in its old rags once again.

The third option, the impossible option, was the republic not of King Oliver but of King Jesus. This England would have been the Levelers' vision taken up and transfigured, the firstfruits of a world remade under Christ. This was the explicit aim of the so-called Fifth Monarchists, a group who deduced from the Bible that history would comprise four great human empires followed at the last by a fifth, Christ's kingdom on earth. In the turmoil of the 1640s, it was not foolish to think that the time had finally come. Immediately after the king's execution, a petition called on the army to encourage the godly to form themselves "into families, churches and corporations, till they thus multiply exceedingly." As this self-governing godly republic wriggled free from its cocoon, the husk of worldly government and law would simply wither away. In the meantime, those in power should prepare the way by abolishing tithes, imposing ferocious legislation against immorality of all kinds, redistributing land to the poor, radically simplifying the law, and purging the universities. Levelers wanted the rule of the people, but Fifth Monarchists wanted the rule of the godly.[14] The godly who were actually in power regarded these idealists with a certain patronizing tolerance. In return, especially after the failure of Barebones's Parliament, the Fifth Monarchists reviled their republican rulers as illegitimate. There was even fruitless talk of armed insurrection.

One of Cromwell's policies was a particular betrayal: he made peace with the Dutch in 1654 after a two-year naval war over commercial rivalries. This dashed the hopes that radicals had cherished as a result of Cromwell's genocidal reconquest of Ireland in 1649–50. Perhaps the Dutch, whose tolerance of Arminians showed them to be apostates, would be next. And then? "How durst our Army to be still, now the work is to do abroad?" one Fifth Monarchist wrote in 1653. "Are there no Protestants in France and Germany (even) now under persecution?"

Why could God's own army not ride all the way to Rome?[15] It is easy to laugh at the notion of Cromwell as a new Alexander the Great, setting out to conquer the world. But 150 years later, Napoleon proved that an army hardened by battle and fired by revolutionary zeal can do remarkable things. Cromwell's army, formidable as it was, would have had what neither Alexander's nor Napoleon's did: the certain knowledge that God was for them. Mercifully, it was not to be. The English republic turned into simply another human power, and the revolutionaries' restless hopes turned elsewhere.

In 1647, the army chaplain John Saltmarsh argued, borrowing medieval apocalyptic terms, that the age of the Gospel was coming to an end and that a new age, of the Spirit, was dawning. Christians should no more stay in the old church, stuck as it was in the old ways, than Christ's original disciples should have stayed in his tomb after he had risen from the dead. On that much, a great many people whom the 1640s had stirred into disquiet could agree. But where should they go?

The Levelers' ambitions turned out to be a dead end. After the second Civil War, the army high command suppressed the Leveler agitators, and a failed Leveler mutiny in May 1649 ended the movement as a political force. But their ideas did not die. A Leveler pamphlet a month earlier had asserted that because women had "an interest in Christ equal unto men," they too should have equal rights. This was, for the moment, a very marginal idea, but the prominence of women among the sectarians was inescapable. Another advocate of women's political equality, Anna Trapnel, became one of the best-known Fifth Monarchist prophets. In a religious free market, talent can sometimes rise to the top regardless of gender.

Later in 1649, another pamphleteer, Gerrard Winstanley, laid claim to the "true Leveler's standard." Winstanley's group, the so-called Diggers, had occupied a plot of land that had been shown to him in a dream and proposed to work it together, holding all property and produce in common. This now looks like Communism, but for Winstanley it was a prophetic act, prefiguring "a new heaven, and a new earth" in which

> none shall lay claim to any creature, and say, *This is mine, and that is yours, This is my work, that is yours.* . . . There shall be no buying nor selling, no fairs nor markets, but the whole earth shall be a

common treasury for every man, for the earth is the Lord's. . . .
Every one shall work in love: one with, and for another.

The commune's purpose was to show the world the true meaning of
the freedom for which the war had been fought, for "freedom is the
man that will turn the world upside down."[16]

The Diggers' experiment was soon forcibly broken up, and Winstanley eventually returned to a life of genteel respectability, but other
subversives were pushing in different directions. In the summer of 1649,
Abiezer Coppe, a preacher of questionable mental stability, produced a
book claiming that "Sword leveling, or digging-leveling" were

> but shadowes of most terrible, yet great and glorious good
> things to come. Behold, behold, behold, I the eternal God, the
> Lord of Hosts, who am that mighty Leveler, am coming . . . to
> Level the Hills with the Valleys, and to lay the Mountains low.

Coppe had his sights on the "plaguy holinesse" of Presbyterians and
Independents alike, people whose religion was no more than "horrid
hypocrisie, envy, malice, evill surmising": an engine for moral self-
satisfaction, as well-heeled believers used their self-awarded godliness
to despise the poor whom they ought to love. He urged Christians to
love not only the poor but thieves, whoremongers, and other notorious
sinners. He deliberately, even prophetically, abandoned both his own
dignity and his pretensions to morality. He ran through London's
streets, charging at the coaches of the wealthy, "gnashing with my
teeth . . . with a huge loud voice proclaiming the day of the Lord." He
prostrated himself before "rogues, beggars, cripples," kissing their feet.
He "sat downe, and ate and drank around on the ground with Gypsies,
and clip't, hug'd and kiss'd them, putting my hand in their bosomes,
loving the she-Gypsies dearly." Such comments, especially his claim to
"love my neighbor's wife as myself," made him notorious. But his
claimed sexual libertinism is a side issue. Coppe's point was that a true
Christian "must lose all his righteousnesse, every bit of his holinesse,
and every crum of his Religion." Only then could he reach the point
where he "knows no evil."[17]

Coppe was associated with a group of so-called Ranters, around whom a sudden moral panic ballooned in 1650. This panic was mostly about sex, and former Ranters did claim to have taught that "till you can lie with all women as one woman, and not judge it sin, you can do nothing but sin."[18] But this misses the point. The Ranters' assault on traditional moral norms was driven by their understanding of God. "They call him the *Being,* the *Fulness,* the *Great motion, Reason,* the *Immensity.*" Ranters taught a kind of pantheism, holding that all things are a part of God, including themselves. Hence the libertinism: If they were God and fully aware that they were God, how could they do wrong? But hence too the radical egalitarianism: Every human being is a part of God, so how could social barriers have any meaning? Like Saltmarsh before them, they believed that in this new age of the Spirit, most of received Christianity was simply out of date. They disliked talk of resurrection and judgment, instead thinking of the dead returning to "that infinite Bulk and Bigness, so called *God,* as a drop into the Ocean." Some even spoke of reincarnation.[19]

This tiny, quixotic movement, which had flared and disappeared by the mid-1650s, matters less in its own right than as a clue to the movement that contemporaries called Seekers. Seekers were in no sense a sect, but a mood: a restless conviction that the established forms of Christianity were simply inadequate and should be abandoned. Some Seekers waited for the new age of the Spirit to reveal itself. Others set out to create it.

Take Mary Springett, the kind of zealous Puritan for whom the early 1640s should have been filled with opportunity. Yet instead, when she saw the Independents' and Baptists' godly reformations, she "saw death there." "I changed my ways often," she recalled, "and ran from one notion to another, not finding satisfaction or assurance that I should obtain what my soul desired." She eventually abandoned the formal religious duties in which she had once been scrupulous, although "most of my time in the day was spent either in reading scriptures, or praying." Like the Ranters, during these years she developed a deep suspicion of outward religion. She actively sought out "the people of no religion," who were at least not hypocrites. She even began to explore worldly pleasures: not sexual libertinism, but "carding, dancing . . . and jovial eatings and drinkings," which for a former Puritan was quite bad enough. She became convinced that there had been no true religion in the world since the apostles' time and "resolved in my heart I would . . . be without a religion until the Lord manifestly taught me one."[20]

Being without a religion might sound like atheism, and that accusation was often made, but Springett was trying to be what the twentieth century would call a religionless Christian: gouging out hypocrisy and formalism even if, at the end, there was nothing left. That was what living on the cusp of the age of the Spirit meant. She was an avid Bible reader, but also needed a fresh revelation for the new age. The Ranters, too, valued the Bible, but as a channel of further revelation rather than a closed canon of Scripture. "*Paul* had the spirit of God, by which spirit he wrote the Scriptures," argued one Ranter. "I have the spirit, why may not I write the Scripture as well as *Paul?*" Coppe distinguished between "what is Naturally and Historically reported of Christ in the Scripture" and its true, mystical meaning, only now being disclosed. "The History is *Christ for* us, the Mystery is *Christ in* us."[21]

These radicals had come a long way. They had rejected and executed their anointed king, fundamentally challenged the structures of their society, and overturned inherited patterns of what it is to be a Christian church. Some of them were rejecting conventional morality and conventional views of the Bible. Even so, they remain recognizably Protestant. Coppe and Springett would not use their Bibles for close-quarters textual combat. Coppe described the inner voice tempting him to use it in that way as "the holy Scripturian Whore." However, he dismissed her raddled temptations as a distraction from his true reading of the Bible, as a lover. The Spirit spoke to him through the text, in a way that no theologian with dead book learning could gainsay. Like Martin Luther—who would have reviled them—these people had a profound experience of God's immediate grace and knew their consciences stood naked and shameless before God. Luther's advice to sin strongly but believe in Christ yet more strongly is not so very different from Coppe's intention to forswear righteousness and religion so as to know no evil. Even the extravagant mood is comparable. Like Luther, these radicals read their Bibles to make sense of their experience and would not allow any human authority to overrule them. The difference was that Luther defied the church with Scripture. These Seekers, like some of the early radicals in Luther's own time had done, defied the learned theologians with an appeal to an authority no one could refute: direct revelation from God.

Quakers and Anglicans

Mary Springett, like many other rootless Protestant radicals, eventually found her religious home in the most significant genuinely new sect to arise in this period: the Quakers.

The Quakers sprang up almost unnoticed in the north of England and were already formidable when they began to attract serious attention. They have their origin myths, mostly based on the story of their early leader George Fox, but Fox was one of many. What is clear is their astonishing success. From a standing start in the early 1650s, they numbered many tens of thousands by the end of the decade. It was exhilarating for them and terrifying for their neighbors.

Rather than forming around one prophet, Quakerism coalesced from a series of radical separatist groups who found echoes in one another. Many Seekers seem, when they encountered Quakerism, to have recognized it as something they had already known. For Quakerism's core doctrine is that the truth, the "inner light," is already within us. Those first Quakers read their Bibles avidly, but inspirationally and devotionally, as free-associating lovers rather than as textually precise fighters. The university-educated clergy, said Fox, had the written Bible, but Quakers had the living Word. Like Coppe and others who looked to the Levelers, the Quakers embraced a doctrine of absolute human equality. They accepted no titles or ministry and thundered against the self-awarded privileges and self-important learning of the clergy. They not only won large numbers of women converts but had prominent women leaders. And if they did not rant, they certainly quaked. Ecstatic shaking and trembling, roaring, crying, and foaming at the mouth were normal at their meetings. The label "Quaker" began as an insult and quickly became a badge of pride.

What marked the Quakers out from other sects, as Richard Baxter observed with distaste, was that they had turned from "horrid prophaneness and blasphemy to a life of extreme austerity." The Quakers' levelheaded energy was something new. Coppe had roared out against the rich, but the Quakers faced them in earnest, standing up in their churches to disrupt their corrupt services. Other sects had denounced tithes; it was the Quakers who conducted the first serious campaigns of nonpayment. They stubbornly refused to acknowledge social distinctions. A Shropshire Quaker, Elizabeth Andrews, waited at table for Lord Newport but refused to curtsy to him before his guests. He teasingly offered her £20 if she would. She replied that even if he offered her his entire estate, "I durst not do it, for all honour belongeth to God." Not everyone took such pertness in good humor. But the Quakers' utter disregard for human hierarchy won them moral authority as well as hatred.[22]

One shocking Quaker practice echoed earlier Anabaptists: nudity. Some 1640s sects were said to have been Adamites, believing they were free from original sin and shedding the clothes with which Adam had covered the shame of that sin. Quaker nudity, however, had a different meaning. In England's chilly northwest, Quakers preached stark naked in marketplaces, promising that God would strip the people bare of their hypocritical religion, exposing their shame to the world. One Quaker walked naked through Oxford in 1654 as a sign that Cromwell would soon be stripped of his seeming "Covering of Religion."[23] Those Quakers who remained clothed showed comparable zeal. Their itinerant preachers ate up the miles. No one was too grand for them to confront. In 1656, a Quaker named Mary Howgill made her way into Cromwell's rooms at Whitehall Palace, handing him a letter denouncing him as a "stinking dunghill in the sight of God." Cromwell, characteristically, patiently heard her out and let her go.[24]

By then, another Quaker, an unmarried serving maid named Mary Fisher, had made her way to Barbados and thence to Massachusetts; she was one of the first Quakers in the New World. She was promptly accused of witchcraft and shipped home, but undaunted, she and five others hatched a new scheme. After considering going to minister in Jerusalem, they instead set off to preach to the two great Antichrists of the Protestant imagination: the pope and the Turkish sultan. The party who reached Rome merely ended up spending three years in prison there, but in 1658, after many adventures, Fisher came face-to-face with Sultan Mehmet IV, encamped at Adrianople. "He was very noble unto me," she wrote. "He and all that were about him received the words of truth without contradiction. . . . There is a royal seed among them, which in time God will raise." He was presumably unused to Christians telling him that God's inner light was within him.[25]

For everyone who was converted, impressed, or amused by the Quakers, however, many more were horrified. Their exponential growth and willful disregard for social norms made them by far the most frightening of the sects, all the more so because Cromwell's regime showed no serious inclination to do anything about them. During the political chaos of 1659, with all government apparently dissolving, fears of Quakerism crescendoed. There were mob attacks and rumors of Quaker plots to burn cities. One preacher in July 1659 openly wondered whether God would "suffer *England* to be transformed into a *Munster* [and] the faithfull be every where Massacred."[26] Anti-Quaker panic helped to steer that year's political helter-skelter toward a restored monarchy. Presbyterians and even theologically conservative Independents and Baptists were beginning to fear Quakers and other sectarians more than they feared popery. In doing so, they were forming an alliance with by far the largest of all the Protestant sects to emerge from this period: the Anglicans.

Anglicanism is not used to thinking of itself as a Civil War–era sect. It traces its lineage back to the Church of England established by Elizabeth I after 1559, itself an echo of Henry VIII's more idiosyncratic national church. But Elizabeth's Church of England had been a comprehensive church to which virtually all English people belonged and which had held together would-be Presbyterians and proto-Laudian ceremonialists with the glue of loyalty to a national church. The Civil War wrecked that ideal irrecoverably, but many English people tried to preserve the wreckage as best they could. In the process, they created something new.

The Book of Common Prayer was now banned, but this rule was scantly enforced. Only a quarter of the serving parish clergy were ever expelled. Many of the rest continued using the old service book, either wholesale or by tweaking it to minimize offense. Some of the former bishops, deprived of their offices, were allowed to remain at liberty, and these men ordained clergy at a prodigious rate. Although these ordinations were outlawed, their numbers fell by less than half from the late 1630s to the late 1640s. More young ministers in the 1640s or 1650s were

illegally ordained by a bishop than were legally ordained by a presby-
tery. A few pragmatic souls had themselves ordained by both.[27]

The parliamentary and republican regimes, for whom bishops were
symbols of tyranny, nevertheless turned a blind eye to this. They seem
to have readily distinguished between those bishops who were actively
and dangerously royalist, such as those who had fled into exile with the
royal family, and those who were willing to be politically flexible. The
result was a new environment that changed Prayer Book religion profoundly. Freed from the constraints of legal uniformity and of active
oversight from bishops, these believers began to experiment with their
traditional religion in untraditional ways. The career of Jeremy Taylor
gives a flavor of what was possible. A rising clerical star in the 1630s, he
had defended the bishops in print in 1642 and served as a chaplain in the
royalist army. After the war, however, he was free to preach and to
publish, producing a string of devotional works arguing for a broad
Protestant toleration. In 1657, he published *A Collection of Offices or Forms
of Prayer,* a new set of liturgical texts intended to capture the spirit of
the Book of Common Prayer. At the Restoration of the monarchy, he
received the bishopric for which he was so obviously destined. He was
perhaps, to use a slightly anachronistic term, the first Anglican.[28]

As Presbyterians learned to fear the Quakers, they also learned to
relax about these proto-Anglicans. Likewise, some Independents, even
Cromwell himself, seem to have thought of them as a counterweight
to overbearing Presbyterianism. By 1660, the thought of permitting the
Book of Common Prayer to be used openly again no longer seemed like
an invitation to tyranny.

In the event, that was a misjudgment. Charles II restored the Church
of England's legal framework largely unchanged, as if his kingdom had
simply regained its senses after a twenty-year convulsion. In 1662, about
a quarter of England's parish ministers, more than two thousand men,
were once again ejected for failing to conform to the restored national
church. For the next quarter century, religious dissidents in both
England and Scotland were driven to the margins of society and sometimes beyond. But while the Presbyterians, Independents, Baptists, and
sectarians of the war years could be persecuted, they could not be
wished away. The "Great Ejection" confirmed that England's established church had become something new: Anglicanism, the largest of

the new sects, albeit with a residual ambition to be a comprehensive national church. The resulting tug-of-war has persisted to the present. Is England's established church the Church of England, an inclusive and rather shapeless church defined primarily by nationality? Or is it the Anglican Church, a more narrowly defined denomination with its own distinct identity?

Both Anglicanism and Quakerism have an uneasy relationship with Protestantism. Anglicanism's founding documents are straightforwardly Protestant, but many Anglicans have become wary of that identity, cherishing a myth of steering a middle way between Protestantism and Catholicism. Quakers reject large parts of classic Protestant doctrine altogether. In both cases, however, the family resemblance is too strong to be coincidental. Both Anglicanism's breadth and creativity, to say nothing of its awkwardly subservient relationship to the state, are familiar Protestant characteristics. So too are Quakers' passion and rigor, their mulish adherence to principle, their corrosive egalitarianism, and above all their willingness to allow a conscience lit up by God's grace to trump everything else.

England's astonishing eruption of religious creativity in the 1640s and 1650s left behind a kaleidoscope of identities, many of which have persisted to the present and spread across the globe. But that eruption was not entirely chaotic. The groups that emerged from it shared characteristically Protestant moods, impulses, and demands of conscience. The English Civil War killed any lingering notion of Protestant unity. It also allowed Protestantism to fully embrace the diversity that has been its greatest strength.

CHAPTER 6

From the Waters of Babylon to a City on a Hill

And a vision appeared to Paul in the night; There stood a man of Macedonia, and prayed him, saying, Come over into Macedonia, and help us.

—ACTS 16:9

It is one of the best-known stories in Protestant history: tiny ships inching their way across the ocean, filled with earnest believers choosing to cross the world rather than compromise their consciences. The *Mayflower* sailed from England in 1620 bearing 102 settlers; two more were born en route, but one of the newborns and three others died on the voyage. After a rough two-month voyage, they made landfall in what is now Massachusetts, somewhat to the north of their destination. Within a year, forty-nine of the hundred who had landed in early November 1620 were dead, from scurvy, accidents, and the bitter privations of a New England winter. That desperate group are now known to every schoolchild in the United States as the Pilgrims.

Those settlers exemplify one of early Protestants' most distinctive features: these were a footloose people, forever on the move. They traveled for urgently practical reasons, but for such people nothing is ever entirely mundane. The *Mayflower*'s voyage was understood as a pilgrimage, a spiritual journey undertaken in faith, just as Abraham had set out into the unknown and St. Paul had embarked on his missionary travels. The idea of pilgrimage was a fraught one for early Protestants, unpleasantly reminiscent of Catholic piety: gadding to superstitious shrines to pray blasphemously to dead saints. Yet Protestants would not let go of the idea. As John Bunyan's *Pilgrim's Progress* demonstrates, describing the Christian life as a pilgrimage, as a journey, or simply as "walking" was a persistent Protestant cliché. Protestantism was and is a religion of *progress,* of restless, relentless advance toward holiness, not of stagnation. The early English reformer William Tyndale urged believers to "go on pilgrimage unto thine own heart, and there pray."[1] He himself had matched that inner pilgrimage with an outward one; he had gone to Germany to publish an illegal English New Testament, knowing that once it was done, he would not be able to return.

An Age of Exiles

As Tyndale's example shows, before there was pilgrimage, there was exile. That was an even more potent biblical theme. The Hebrews had fled Pharaoh's wrath, passed miraculously through the Red Sea, and then endured forty years in the wilderness before entering the promised land. Nearly a millennium later, the Jews were carried off into exile in Babylon, but they did not forget Zion, and after seventy years they returned. Those two biblical exiles fired and haunted Protestant imaginations. "By the waters of Babylon we sat down and wept," the Psalm read. Protestants translated, paraphrased, quoted, and sang that Psalm more than any other, and understood their own exiles through it.[2]

Tyndale did not romanticize exile. He pined for home and had no patience for busybodies who could not be still and remain where God had placed them. Yet the idea of serving God through movement would not go away. Protestants compared St. Paul's energy and self-sacrifice with bishops who luxuriated in their palaces and would not lift a finger to bring the Gospel to their people. The idea helped make a virtue of necessity. As Europe became a religious patchwork, Protestants regularly found themselves having to trek for miles to attend worship; preaching might not be permitted in cities or might only be available on the estate of a particular nobleman. The thought that a grueling weekly journey was itself an act of worship could spur aching, ill-shod feet.

Spiritualizing travel like this also helped resolve a nasty moral dilemma. Arguably, Christians facing persecution should not run away. If you are a preacher, called by God to minister to your flock, you should not abandon them any more than a soldier should flee his post under fire. When persecution came, some Protestants did indeed stand their ground regardless of the consequences, and some who fled were stricken by conscience. Patrick Hamilton, a young Scottish nobleman, first tasted the new teachings at university in the 1520s and fled to Germany. There he drank more deeply from them, and in late 1527 he returned home, in effect handing himself over to be burned. He became Scotland's first Protestant martyr. He also wrote a succinct Latin summary of the Protestant doctrine of salvation, which was translated by a young English fugative, John Frith. Frith might have been the most gifted English theologian of his generation, but we will never know, for he, too, refused to remain in exile. Returning to England, he let himself be taken, spurned opportunities to escape, and went to the fire in July 1533.

Others argued that exile was not cowardice but a vocation. Christ, after all, told those who were persecuted in one city to flee to the next.[3] Exiles inevitably discovered that their travels changed them. Perhaps that was God's purpose. If all Christians are exiles on earth, and pilgrims to heaven, perhaps we should all taste the bitter clarity of literal exile? What better way to remember that your true home is in heaven than to leave your earthly home behind? Then you could be both an exile and a pilgrim, fleeing from danger to discover where God is calling you.

These were not small-scale concerns. It is impossible to count the Protestant exiles and refugees of the sixteenth and seventeenth centuries, but on any showing we are talking about more than a million souls. The biggest single exodus came at the end of the period, when the revocation of the Edict of Nantes in 1685 scattered about 400,000 French Protestants across Europe and beyond. Hundreds of thousands were also displaced during the Thirty Years' War (1618–48). Earlier, between 1550 and 1600, England hosted perhaps 50,000 Protestant refugees, mostly French and Dutch. The numbers who crossed the oceans were, again, smaller but noticeable. Something like 20,000 English settlers followed the first Pilgrims to New England over the next twenty years.

It began slowly, with a handful of individual converts who fled to save their lives but also to study, to write, and to publish. John Calvin left

France in a hurry in 1534 and promptly published the first edition of his *Institutio*. The small band of English reformers who joined William Tyndale in exile in the late 1520s fled chiefly so that they could further the cause in writing. The result was a persistent trickle of books smuggling the latest Protestant thinking back across the English Channel: few in number, expensive, and usually printed by typesetters unfamiliar with England's barbarous language. The exiles' more significant contribution came when they returned home during England's brief Protestant awakening under King Edward VI (1547–53), bringing their experiences with them. John Hooper spent almost a decade in Zurich before returning to become a bishop in Edward's church. He promptly set about re-creating Swiss purity by the banks of the river Severn.

The next English exile was on a different scale. During Queen Mary I's Catholic restoration (1553–58), more than eight hundred English Protestants fled. With numbers came better networks and greater financial security. As before, the refugees were exposed to their hosts' theological rigor. One result was the 1560 Geneva Bible, the first complete English Bible to be translated directly from the original languages. Its cover depicted the Israelites crossing the Red Sea: a symbol of the transforming exodus that had produced the book itself. But exile also brought division. Some of the exiles held fast to the way they had worshipped at home under King Edward. Others eagerly embraced the more radical purities of their hosts. When Elizabeth I's accession in 1558 brought a Protestant restoration, the exiles returned home and took their disputes with them. The so-called "Puritan" party, who now knew what a true Reformation looked like, were dismayed by the new queen's cautious conservatism. These cadres set about building the new Jerusalem they had seen abroad in their own land, whether their half-hearted queen liked it or not.

Among other things, that meant returning the hospitality they themselves had enjoyed. In 1548–49, Dutch and French Protestant refugees in London had been allowed to form self-governing churches of their own. They scattered in the 1550s but quickly reassembled after Elizabeth I's accession. Smaller refugee churches formed in a crescent of English coastal towns. These communities were shelters for their members and windows on the world for their hosts, but they were also springboards. The exiles were active players in their home countries' struggles, funneling money and even direct military support to their compatriots "under the cross," as well as providing the most valuable support of all, their prayers.

The Dutch exiles were the most militant. One of their first London ministers proposed to "attack our Flanders with fiery darts, and, I hope, take it by storm." Refugees were smuggled out of the Netherlands, some of them sprung from prison, and money, books, and weapons smuggled back in. In July 1562, a Protestant gang staged a daring open-air sermon at Boeschepe (nowadays in France), attended by armed guards. The preacher was brought in from England for the purpose and whisked back as soon as the event was over.[4]

Then came 1566, the Dutch "Wonderyear," when for a few short months open Protestant preaching was permitted, a riotous summer of religious liberty and iconoclastic destruction. A ferocious backlash followed, sending another wave of reformers abroad. The five years that followed were the crucible of the Dutch Reformation. In exile, an inchoate, diverse band of Dutch reformers discovered they needed unity. And because the preestablished refugee churches that received them were Calvinist, it was the Calvinists who offered the only unity available. In 1571, the Calvinists even convened a "national" synod of Dutch exiles, in the German port of Emden. From then on, their religious dominance of the Dutch Revolt was unquestioned.

As well as praying together, the fugitives fought. During 1567–68, a group of English-based exiles carried out vicious terrorist raids in Flanders, targeting Catholic priests, some of whom were castrated and tortured to death.[5] Another exile group formed a pirate fleet that raided Dutch coastal towns and attacked Spanish shipping. Initially, England and Emden hosted them, but in 1572 they became more trouble than they were worth, and they were sent on their way. The now-homeless pirates descended instead on the Dutch port of Den Briel, and to their own surprise their arrival sparked a wider revolt by Dutch towns. It was the beginning of an independent Dutch republic: first a few footholds, but within three years half of the old Netherlands.

Having made the rebellion possible, the exiles claimed their reward. Many of them had lost homes, property, and family and had been reduced to the status of legal nonpersons. Now they descended on rebel-held areas, claiming back their old houses or moving into those vacated by fleeing Catholics. They felt they were coming home, but both they and their old country had been changed.[6] Even when exile was over and done within a single generation, it transformed both those who endured it and the country from which they had been driven and to which they eventually returned.

Many other exiles never returned home. John Macalpine fled his native Scotland before a heresy charge in 1534. After a spell in England, he found his way to Wittenberg, met Luther, and studied with Philip Melanchthon. In 1542, the king of Denmark invited him to be his personal chaplain, and he lived out his life in Copenhagen, becoming sufficiently at home to translate the Bible into Danish. The king attended his funeral, and his son became a professor in Copenhagen and worked as an ambassador for the Danish Crown. Macalpine senior, who did not live to see the Scottish Reformation, could never go home. His son could have done so, but to him Scotland was a foreign land.[7]

For scholars like Macalpine, international travel was relatively easy; Latin speakers could slot into any university, even if they might struggle to buy a loaf of bread in a strange language. The Swiss Reformed city of Basel welcomed more than a thousand non-German-speaking students during the sixteenth century: French, English, Italian, Scandinavian, even Lithuanian. Many of them were given financial support by the university.[8] If students were welcomed, professors were actively courted. When war in Germany in 1546–47 forced several high-profile Protestant scholars onto the road, theologically backward England snapped them up. The new arrivals gently but firmly put their hosts through an intellectual workout.

Not all refugees were so welcome. In January 1555, nearly two hundred Protestants were banished from Locarno, in Italian-speaking Switzerland. Most of them came to Zurich, forming an Italian-speaking congregation in a German-speaking city. It was not a happy experience. The exiles prospered economically, because international contacts are good for business, but Zurich expected them to assimilate and learn German, and in the meantime restricted their civil rights. Italian-speaking preachers were suspected of heresy. Further Italian arrivals were discouraged, and the Locarnese slowly dispersed to other Swiss cities. The individuals survived, but the community perished.[9]

The Zurichers' testy attitude can look churlish, but 130 new arrivals in a city of 6,000 are, proportionally, the equivalent of a cohesive community of 150,000 or more arriving in modern London or New York. Plenty of religious refugees brought troubles down on their hosts—even leaving aside the nightmarish example of Münster in 1534–35. Geneva, as we have seen, was first flooded with and then effectively taken over by French refugees. Strassburg, in this period a German city, also welcomed French Protestant refugees, billeting exiles with local families and giving charity to the destitute. As France spiraled into civil war, Strassburg allowed Protestant armies to recruit men, buy arms, and borrow money. Not all Strassburgers approved. Some worried, presciently, that the city might not "remain a German city." There were religious tensions, too. By the 1550s, Strassburg was Lutheran, while the French were Calvinists. When Calvin himself visited the city in 1556, he was forbidden to preach. The French exiles' church was forbidden to celebrate the Eucharist from 1568 onward and was forbidden to meet altogether in 1577. But still the exiles came, until 1592, when the surrounding Catholic territories attacked the city. The war was brief but vicious, and while the city remained a Protestant one, its government was cowed. There would be no more welcome to dangerous foreigners.[10]

American Pilgrimages

Exile might mean moving no more than a few miles, but in an age whose geographic horizons were widening fast, it might mean half a world. A Zurich Anabaptist who escaped from prison in 1526 joked that he intended to flee "to the red Indians across the sea."[11] Soon that thought would be more than a joke.

In 1555, a swashbuckling and unreliable French nobleman named Nicolas Durand, the chevalier de Villegagnon, won his king's backing for a project he called Antarctic France. This referred not to the as-yet-undiscovered polar continent but to an attempt to compete with the huge Spanish and Portuguese empires in South America. Villegagnon led a force of six hundred men and established an island colony in Guanabara Bay, to the south of the main Portuguese settlements: the site of modern Rio de Janeiro.

We do not know very much about their first two years in Brazil. No doubt, like all early colonists, they suffered calamitous losses. Villegagnon was dismayed by the indiscipline of those first colonists, many of whom were convicted criminals: the only people desperate enough to volunteer for such a venture. In 1557, he requested another batch of settlers and sought them, among other places, from Geneva. Villegagnon, who may have met Calvin in his student days, seems to have thought the Genevans would give his colonists some much-needed moral fiber. Calvin saw a strategic opening. Fourteen Genevans, including two pastors, traveled to the infant colony. Guanabara Bay was almost certainly the site of the first Protestant worship ever to take place in the New World.

To Villegagnon's dismay, however, his Protestant settlers were more concerned with pure worship than with helping his colony to run smoothly. Soon France's bitter disputes between Catholic and Protestant were being replicated in Brazil. As in France, the flash point was the Eucharist: Were Christ's body and blood literally present? The Calvinists, to whom the Catholic doctrine was repulsively blasphemous at the best of times, found it doubly so in this new setting, surrounded as they thought they were by cannibals. The colony became polarized. Villegagnon, forced to choose sides, banished the Calvinist leaders. One group eventually found its way back to France in a tiny boat, near to starvation, and told their tale. Another group spent a surprisingly comfortable few months on the mainland, welcomed (not eaten) by the local peoples. When they returned to the colony early in 1559, hoping that tempers had cooled, Villegagnon had three of them drowned. He himself returned to France in the same year, thoroughly disillusioned; he would fight stoutly for the Catholics in France's religious wars. What remained of his colony was taken by the Portuguese in 1560.[12]

The scheme seemed to have caught other French Protestants' imagination, however. In February 1562, immediately before the first religious war began, a small Protestant-led expedition set out from France, explicitly aiming to create a New World refuge where they would be in charge. They settled near the modern town of Port Royal, in South Carolina, and loyally named their settlement Charlestown, in honor of King Charles IX, who was, unbeknownst to them, even then making war on their brethren. Thirty settlers overwintered while the ship returned to France. However, the colony was too small to be sustainable, and in 1563 those who had survived the winter decided to cut and run.

They built a makeshift ship and eventually made it home—or most of them: apparently, they ate one of their number en route.

One more attempt was made in 1564, when a larger French Protestant expedition landed in Florida, on the St. Johns River. They struck up good relations with the Timucuan Indians, and on June 30, 1564, the settlement gathered to sing a psalm of thanksgiving for God's grace shown through the Indians' hospitality: a pre-echo of the better-known Thanksgiving in Massachusetts a lifetime later. Then the Spanish learned of the settlement. The colony was destroyed in a surprise attack in September 1565, and several hundred settlers were massacred. They were, after all, heretics. The New World had proved to be a fire more dangerous than any frying pan.[13]

English Protestants were the next to risk their lives on this foolhardy venture. The English colonies were driven by commercial and imperial ambitions, but they were also set about with religious rhetoric. Some arguments were of the "because it's there" variety. In 1609, a London preacher drumming up business for Jamestown, England's first enduring North American colony, argued that all humanity was called by God to "spread abroad," in obedience to a "general law of replenishing the earth." Some found particular significance in journeying *westward*. Abraham had moved west to Canaan, and the Gospel had spread west from Jerusalem to Rome and then to England, the "end of the earth." Now, in a final leap toward the setting sun, the Gospel would "in the latter ages of the world . . . bend Westward, and before its setting, brighten these parts, with his glorious luster also."[14]

Whether anyone ever left home on account of these pretty word pictures, we may doubt. Most of the first English colonists were traders and adventurers. When some began to travel on religious grounds, they did so less as pilgrims than as exiles. England's more scrupulous Calvinists found that their consciences gagged at the thought of submitting to the half-Reformed English church. Most of them, however, were also deeply committed to the ideal of a single, national church, with no appetite for forming dissident sects. The only way to avoid being contaminated by the English church's corruptions, while not violating its unity, was to leave England altogether. So from the 1580s on, restless English Protestants began to trickle abroad, chiefly to the newly liberated Netherlands. Although tens of thousands of them eventually settled there, they were, like all expatriates, conscious of belonging in neither one place nor the other. In the second decade of the seventeenth century, when members of the English community at Leiden set their sights on America, they did so in order to assert that they were English. Their leader Edward Winslow lamented "how grievous it was to live from under the protection of the State of England; how like we were to lose our language and our name, of English." In America, the separatists might live under English sovereignty, but without having to conform to the English church.[15]

This odd possibility was open to them because England's imperial ventures were driven more by commercial opportunism than by geo-political strategy. England wanted North American colonies on the cheap, and if colonists were willing to bear the costs themselves, they could buy themselves some religious latitude in exchange. The Leiden separatists took the lead in negotiating a royal charter to found a new colony. They provided half of the passengers on the *Mayflower*.

In other words, the Pilgrims were not particularly interested in the New World as such. They simply wanted a place that was both English and free. It is a sign of the desperate seriousness of their quest that they were willing to cross the Atlantic to find it. It was no coincidence that they chose, and stuck to, the name "New England." A new England was what the settlers needed, even one halfway across the world.

To begin with, this solution only appealed to a few hardy souls. The westward voyage to New England took between eight and twelve weeks, sometimes longer. By the end, even the most carefully packed supplies were exhausted. Beer and fresh water stank, ship's biscuit was moldy, and any livestock that had not been eaten had long since ceased laying eggs or giving milk. Settlers described how, on arrival, the mere smell of the land was ravishing, even if not all were as lucky as those who in 1630 were greeted at their landing with fresh wild strawberries. Even so, as lands of milk and honey go, New England was a tough proposition. Weakened from the voyage, settlers faced disease, back-breaking work and consequent injuries, wild animals, indigenous peoples, and the astonishing, vise-like winters.[16]

The community remained tiny until 1630, when a fleet of a

thousand settlers led by John Winthrop arrived. As we saw in the previous chapter, King Charles I's Puritan subjects were finding their position increasingly unsustainable, and voyaging west seemed like the only solution. The chief purpose of their "errand into the wilderness" was, as one settler preached, simply the "enjoyment of the pure Worship of God." But there were also more apocalyptic concerns. The Thirty Years' War was visiting appalling destruction on Continental Protestants, and many in England wondered how long their own corrupt church could escape the same divine vengeance. Some cited the example of the woman who, in the book of Revelation, was sheltered by God in the wilderness while heaven was torn apart by war.[17]

Winthrop is best remembered for describing the Massachusetts colony as a "city on a hill," a phrase that has come to represent American exceptionalism. That is not quite what he meant. The biblical passage cautions that a city on a hill cannot be hidden. The colonists might be three thousand miles from England but were nevertheless in full public view. Hence, Winthrop warned, "if we shall deal falsely with our God in this work . . . we shall be made a story and a by-word through the world." They were a painfully visible laboratory of godly Reformation and could not afford to fail.[18]

In other words, their project was an inherently temporary one. Like all exiles, they hoped to return, and return they did. It is not part of America's founding myth, but we now know the sheer scale of the eastward journeying in the decades after 1640. England's religious politics suddenly changed that year, and the religious winds blowing across the Atlantic shifted too. Literal winds also helped; the eastward voyage was far easier, often lasting less than four weeks. Between 1640 and 1690, more English subjects returned from New England than embarked for it (there were many fewer returnees from secular Virginia). More than a third of the Protestant ministers who had traveled west in the 1630s returned in the 1640s. Almost half of the men who graduated from Harvard College in the 1640s and 1650s subsequently returned to England. After 1640, the price of land in the colony crashed. Those who remained lambasted the returnees as deserters, but from old England's perspective it was the stayers who seemed perverse. New England seemed to have outlived its usefulness. Oliver Cromwell, who dismissed New England as "a vast howling wilderness," wanted to relocate the remaining colonists to Ireland or to England's more lucrative and vulnerable Caribbean possessions. The errand into the wilderness was over.[19]

Preaching to the Nations

New England was saved by the Anglican Restoration of 1660–62, which did not produce a new flood of refugees but did at least turn the tide. By then, however, the need to find new justifications for going and staying in the New World had changed the nature of the project. One much-cited justification focused on the people whom the settlers had found in their wilderness.

Protestant settlers in the New World were sharply aware of the presence of non-Christian peoples. They complicated matters a good deal; an empty wilderness would have been much simpler, and periodically settlers tried to pretend that this was what they had found. In a macabre sense, it was half-true. The Spanish, French, and other early European settlers in the New World had brought with them diseases, which had already spread across much of the continent before the English arrived. The *Mayflower*'s Pilgrims arrived in Massachusetts to discover not the flourishing Algonquin communities of the previous century but the dazed and scattered survivors of a catastrophe—or, as Winthrop described it, of "a miraculous plague, whereby a great part of the Country is left void of Inhabitants." As such, he reasoned, the settlers were neither invaders nor thieves of land but occupiers of vacated space. "There is more than enough for them and us." Unlike the Catholic Spanish, whose "bloody invasion" of the New World Protestants piously condemned, Protestant settlers were careful to present the Native peoples as "the rightful owners of the country," from whom they were merely bartering a little excess land.[20]

Not that they saw the Native Americans as equals. They found them pitiable: "the very Ruins of Mankind," living like wild beasts, or at best like children, deserving compassion but also needing firm guidance.[21] This was not racist in the modern sense of the word. Europeans at this date assumed that all humanity shared a common descent and sometimes observed that their own distant ancestors had been equally sunk in darkness. But these attitudes did let the settlers see themselves not as invaders but as a light sent to enlighten the Gentiles.

It was a familiar scenario for them. On Europe's fringes, Protestant states were bumping up against peoples whom they saw as barbarians: the Sami of northern Scandinavia, the highland Scots, the Irish. Protestant states generally saw "civilizing" these peoples as both a Christian duty and a political necessity. This meant persuading or coercing them to live in settled communities, teaching them civilized languages like English or Swedish, and settling civilized people among them, to teach them by example. It did not work very well. Such peoples could, with effort, be subdued, but not persuaded to love their subduers. Still, that experience did mean that New World settlers thought they knew how to deal with barbarous and unsettled peoples. Civilize first; Christianize later.

Christianization was the settlers' best justification of all. One English preacher, shilling for the colonial effort, proposed the terms of trade: in return for a little unused land and some tobacco, fur, and fish, the settlers would give the Native Americans "1. *Civility* for their bodies, 2. *Christianity* for their souls." Winthrop dwelled on the theme. His initial meditations on emigration made no mention of the indigenous peoples' souls, but as the project gathered pace, he and others began to claim that "the propagation of the gospel to the Indians" was "the main end of our Plantation," "the thing we do profess above all." Winthrop's oath as the first governor of the Massachusetts Bay Colony bound him "to draw . . . the natives . . . to the knowledge of the true God." The colony's official seal rammed home the point. The central figure of the Native American quotes a momentous verse of the New Testament: St. Paul's vision of a man from Macedonia saying, "Come over into Macedonia, and help us" (Acts 16:9), which led to the Christian Gospel's being preached in Europe for the first time. Now the settlers were being called west to another new continent, taking the Gospel once more toward the setting sun.[22]

So the story went. However, surprising as it may seem to modern eyes, Protestant colonists in America and across the world were in fact astonishingly slow to make any kind of sustained missionary effort. This is in striking contrast with their Catholic rivals. In Spain and Portugal's burgeoning American, Asian, and African empires, there were mass baptisms and sustained attempts over generations to nurture Catholicism. Protestants tried nothing of the kind.

Take the case of Jaffna, in northern Sri Lanka. From 1621 to 1658,

Jaffna was a Portuguese colony, but in 1658 it was seized by the Dutch East India Company. The new Calvinist chaplain, Philip Baldaeus, inherited a Catholic population numbering just over sixty-five thousand, served by thirty-four churches, with fifteen thousand children in Christian schools. Under the Portuguese, this population had been served by some forty priests. But for the first three years of Dutch rule, Baldaeus was the only minister for that entire area. Thereafter, he sometimes had one assistant. Unsurprisingly, the community's previously rapid expansion stopped dead. During the first three years of Dutch rule, only thirty-six adults were baptized. So far from winning converts, Baldaeus found he was struggling to restrain his existing flock from their "strong Inclination to Paganism." And while Baldaeus was unusual in attending to missionary work at all, he was hardly burning with evangelistic zeal. His lengthy ethnographic study of the indigenous religions of the region gave no hint that converting such pagans to Christianity was possible or even desirable, until the very last sentence, which wished piously "that these poor Wretches, quite entangled in the Darkness of Paganism, may . . . be in time brought to the true Knowledge of the Gospel." Urgency is hardly the word.[23]

There are similar stories from across the world. We will return to the unhappy example of the Dutch way station at the Cape of Good Hope in a later chapter. The short-lived Dutch colony in northern Brazil saw some sporadic and unsuccessful attempts to convert the Catholic population to Calvinism and almost total neglect of other indigenous peoples and of slaves. The only genuinely ambitious Dutch missionary project took place on the island of Taiwan, much of which was under Dutch rule from 1623 to 1662. It so happened that two of the chaplains whom the Dutch East India Company posted to the island, George Candidius and Robert Junius, shared an interest in preaching to the indigenous peoples. They set about learning the languages and catechizing would-be converts. By the time they had both left the island in 1643, they had admitted more than six thousand people to baptism. They also did more than any Protestant contemporaries to separate Christianization from "civilization": conducting worship in indigenous languages, employing more than fifty native schoolteachers, and in two villages establishing proper Calvinist discipline, enforced by native elders. Plans were afoot for a seminary on the island. Even so, it was plainly a colonial enterprise. The newly erected wooden churches, lacking bells to announce services, used musket fire instead, a more naked symbol of imperial control than was perhaps intended. After Candidius and Junius's departure, the mission ran into the sand. Native teachers were dismissed, and local languages were abandoned. The planned seminary began to look like a reeducation camp for captured young natives. When a Chinese invasion abruptly ended Dutch control in 1661–62, even the most Christianized villages threw off their imposed faith, "delighted that they have been exempted from attending the schools." That was the high point of early Protestant missionizing.[24]

Lutherans were if anything less energetic missionaries than Calvinists. The 1626 charter governing Sweden's first colonial enterprises promised grandly that the heathen would be "taught morality and the Christian religion." When the colony of New Sweden, in modern Delaware, was established in 1638, Lutheran pastors were sent with the settlers. One of them, Johan Campanius, who worked there from 1643 to 1648, has a claim to be the first Lutheran missionary. He managed to learn some of the language of the Lenni-Lenape people and to explain some simple doctrines, but there is no evidence of his winning any converts. This was partly because he was operating entirely alone, supported neither by the colony's governors nor by his own successors. Campanius produced a translation of Luther's shorter catechism in 1648: the first European attempt to write down a North American language. It remained unpublished for fifty years, because no one would pay to print it. Campanius believed that actually winning Lenni-Lenape converts would be formidably difficult. Whether any sustained and creative effort would have proved him right, we shall never know.[25] As we will see in the next chapter, no sustained and earnest Lutheran missionary enterprise was launched until 1706.

English Protestant missionary rhetoric in Virginia and the Caribbean likewise came to almost nothing. Even the New England colonies had been established for a generation before any serious effort was made. The first and most effective mission took place on the Massachusetts islands of Martha's Vineyard and Nantucket, which were then home to some three thousand Wampanoags. In 1643, a man named Hiacoomes approached Thomas Mayhew, an English settler on Martha's Vineyard, to ask for religious instruction. He soon experienced a deep and enduring conversion, and Mayhew and Hiacoomes developed the mission to the Wampanoag together over the decades that followed. This was a spontaneous mission under local leadership, and it was highly successful. Virtually the entire population of the islands converted, and the tradition survives among the few remaining Wampanoag living there today.[26]

Nantucket was never going to change the world, but Boston might have done so. John Eliot, who was teaching elder at Roxbury, near Boston, from 1632 to 1688, is the century's best-known Protestant missionary. From 1646 onward, the "Apostle to the Indians" set himself to the evangelistic task, learning the daunting Algonquin language. In 1651, he organized the first "praying town," a settlement specifically for Native American converts, at Natick. Others followed, their inhabitants ultimately numbering a little over a thousand. It came to nothing in the end: the catastrophic settler-native conflict known as King Philip's War in the 1670s put a stop to New England's pretense of peaceful coexistence. The "praying towns" survived as a curiosity, not as models for the future. Still, the ambition and persistence of Eliot's efforts made him a hero to Protestant commentators at the time and since.[27] Is he a clue to another North America that might have been?

Probably not. Eliot's commitment to the mission field was entirely sincere, but it was highly unusual, and it came late. Until 1644, the New England colonists' missionary "effort" consisted merely of hoping that their Native neighbors might admire their exemplary lives. The winds only changed in the early 1640s, when the flow of settlers dried up and London began to question New England's usefulness. What actually goaded Eliot into action was the arrival in 1646 of an emissary from England linked to Massachusetts's bitter rival, the colony of Rhode Island. Suddenly it was urgent to demonstrate that Massachusetts really was an exemplary Christian community and could win converts. Eliot, who loathed the Rhode Islanders, swiftly organized two meetings to preach to local Native people through an interpreter. The first fell flat, but much to Eliot's surprise the second produced signs of real interest. It was only then that his own interest in winning converts was kindled and that he began his language studies. Having stumbled into the mission almost by accident, he became one of the very few New Englanders whose commitment to it was more than rhetorical.[28]

Generally, the closer a Protestant was to the mission field, the less enthusiastic he or she was about it. The pressure for mission in New England came almost entirely from old England. Those who had first-hand experiences of Native American peoples cooled rapidly to the notion. Puzzled do-gooders in England who complained about the lack of missionary progress were told that they "know not the vast distance of Natives from common civility, almost humanity itself, and 'tis as if they should reproach us for not making the winds to blow." No doubt Winthrop and his companions meant all their high talk of conversion, after a fashion. But it quickly withered in the face of real and startlingly alien people with histories, concerns, and minds of their own who would not readily play the roles that armchair missionaries had scripted for them.[29]

There were also deeper reasons for the dearth of early Protestant missions. Many Lutherans were actually opposed to mission on principle. The classic proof text for missionary work was Christ's so-called Great Commission to his apostles: "Go ye therefore, and teach all nations." Seventeenth-century Lutheran orthodoxy held that this instruction was intended specifically and exclusively for the apostles, not their successors. The theology faculty at Wittenberg formalized this position in 1651, adding that heathen peoples' faithlessness was their own fault. Because the apostles *did* preach the Gospel to all nations, the heathens' ancestors must have rejected it. They could not expect a second chance.[30]

Most Calvinists, by contrast, believed that the Great Commission was still in force. It is often assumed that the Calvinist doctrine of predestination impeded missionary work: Why bother preaching to the heathen when their fate is foreordained, so you can do nothing either to save or to imperil their souls? In fact, however, most Calvinists believed that they were obliged to spread the Gospel as a simple duty, regardless of whether or not conversions would result. So predestination did not prevent missionary projects, but it might have taken the wind out of them. If you believe that your preaching is unlikely to bear fruit, you are more likely simply to go through the motions. Eliot's evident surprise when some of his audience responded to his message is a sign of this. It is starkly different from the urgency of contemporary Catholic missionaries, desperate to snatch each soul from hell and confident in the power of their sacraments and their teaching to do so.

Calvinists had other theological problems, however. Many of them, especially in New England, shared a distinctive view of how the world would end. First, popery would be destroyed and the Jews would convert en masse to Christianity. Only then would the heathen be converted. Mission to non-Christian peoples was not wrong, but it was premature. As Roger Williams, one of the founders of Rhode Island, put it, "God's great business between Christ . . . and Antichrist" must be resolved before any other missions could be undertaken. In the meantime, at best, a few stray individuals could be saved from the general destruction. Williams himself doubted even that was possible.[31]

Some missionaries, including Campanius in New Sweden and Eliot in New England, found a way around this problem. Based on some dubious similarities of ritual and language, they convinced themselves that the Native Americans were descended from the ten lost tribes of Israel. It was a quixotic theory, but if the Indians were in fact Jews, then perhaps *their* conversion would truly mark the beginning of the endtime. That would make mission not only acceptable but urgent. The fact that missionaries had to embrace such a far-fetched theory shows that the theological obstacles were real.[32]

Williams's focus on the "great business" with Rome alerts us to a more systemic problem. The Lutherans' distaste for mission was largely based on scrupulous observation of the 1555 Peace of Augsburg, which required that "no Estate shall try to persuade the subjects of other Estates to abandon their religion." To Germany's embattled Lutheran churches, cross-border religious initiatives of any kind looked like dangerous meddling with a fragile status quo.[33] Calvinists were excluded from the 1555 settlement, but their attention, too, was consumed by the existential, apocalyptic conflict with Rome. Hence one of the oddities of early Protestantism's few missionary efforts: they tended to be directed not at non-Christian peoples but at Catholics. Baldaeus proudly recalled how his schoolboys in Jaffna "could refute the Popish Errors concerning Purgatory, the Mass, Indulgences, Auricular Confession, &c"— as if this were his most urgent pastoral task in southern Asia. The Dutch in Taiwan and in Brazil also focused, with no success, on the small Catholic populations left by previous Portuguese colonists. In North America, there was no Catholic problem, but one reason often cited by settlers for evangelizing the Native peoples was to prevent Catholic missionaries from infiltrating them first. When these missions did begin, their bemused subjects were made to sit through denunciations of popery. Early modern Catholic missionaries aimed to convert anyone and everyone. Protestant missionaries really only wanted to convert Catholics.[34]

It did not help that Protestants, especially Calvinists, had a very exacting and culturally specific understanding of conversion. They wanted converts to embrace the Protestant love affair with God and to express that love both sincerely and according to European norms. This was a tall order. Eliot only petitioned for his first few "praying Indians" to be admitted to church membership in 1652, fully six years after his mission began. Amazingly, they were rejected. The first admissions finally took place in 1659. In Jaffna, where Protestant ministry was first introduced in 1658, the first Calvinist Communion was offered in 1661, and twelve indigenous converts participated. Baldaeus was proud that by the time he left Jaffna in 1665, that number had risen to thirty—from an avowedly Christian population of sixty-five thousand. One New Englander made a virtue of this: compared with Catholics, he observed, "we have not learned as yet the art of coining Christians, or putting Christ's name and Image upon copper metal." But taking pride in your ineffectiveness is rarely a good sign.[35]

Then there were structural problems. The New Englanders were Congregationalists, which meant that each church was independent and called its own minister to serve it. There was no mechanism to commission or indeed to pay missionaries. Nor did more hierarchical Protestant churches find this much easier. Lutherans also insisted that ministers had to be called to serve a particular congregation. A vocal Lutheran advocate of foreign missions named Justinian von Welz exemplifies the problem. After repeated rebuffs, von Welz eventually decided to act unilaterally. But while he was wealthy enough to support himself in the mission field, he had no means of being properly appointed to it; the structures did not exist. In the end, he persuaded a friend to ordain him, in 1666, as "Apostle to the Heathen" and set off for Suriname. He was apparently dead within eighteen months. With no structures, his mission died too.[36]

Generally, Protestantism is a cheap religion, but foreign missions cannot be carried out on a shoestring. They need training, support, supply networks, and a flow of talented people. Above all, they need institutions able to commit to such things for decades on end. Committed individuals such as Baldaeus, Candidius, Junius, Campanius, Mayhew, Eliot, and von Welz were all very well, but without sustained continuity nothing would be achieved. The Catholic Church's religious orders could provide all of these things, but in the seventeenth century no Protestant institutions could. This was one sour legacy of early Protestantism's Faustian bargain with the state. The princes' seizure of church property during the Reformation robbed Protestantism of the institutional potential to propagate itself, and instead condemned it to merely maintaining a parochial network.

The story does not end there. As we will see, from the eighteenth century onward, Protestants discovered and funded a new missionary verve. There are a few glimpses of this in the earlier period, championed by those armchair missionaries enthusiastic for spreading the Gospel to lands they would never visit. This was how the New England mission was in the end sustained. In 1644, an English enthusiast established a £20 annuity to support "the Preacher to the poor Indians in New England," even though there was not yet any such person. It was the beginning of a flood of donations, many sparked by a wave of optimistic pamphlets about Eliot's early achievements. Some £16,000 was raised from private donors to support the New England mission before 1660. It provided salaries for Eliot and Mayhew, printed books in Algonquin, and even funded the short-lived Indian College at Harvard.[37] Not much came of this in the end; money may be necessary for missionary success, but it is not enough. But it did pioneer the model that Protestants would later take around the world. In increasingly prosperous countries, the private donations of the faithful could match anything that ancient endowments could achieve.

The first two centuries of Protestant migration left a mixed legacy. Most early Protestant travelers were exiles, not pilgrims, and simply wanted to be able to go home. Even so, their travels changed them, changed their hosts, and changed Protestantism. The movement of refugees sustained embattled Protestants and kept their religion international. If exiles did return, they returned transformed, and also left their mark where they had been. Some hitched a ride on imperial expansion and began, hesitantly, to open up the world to conversion. Some who never left home still found exile a potent metaphor for their own spiritual journeys. And, increasingly, the stay-at-homes dreamed of what their Gospel could achieve in far-off countries. In the centuries to come, those dreams would change the newly connected world.

PART II

The
Modern Age

CHAPTER 7

Enthusiasm and Its Enemies

I will pour out my spirit upon all flesh; and your sons and
your daughters shall prophesy.

—JOEL 2:28

A dispassionate observer in the 1660s might well have concluded that Protestantism was doomed. Its churches were crumbling at the edges, unable to stop the leakage of members to radical sectarianism, and sagging in the center, as secularism and skepticism seeped into their hearts. Their chief defense was a brittle authoritarianism. Meanwhile, an incoming Catholic tide lapped at them, slowly swamping outposts and turning settled heartlands into frontiers.

Some threats were new, some perennial. Sectarianism had been gnawing at establishment Protestantism ever since Luther had set himself against the fanatics, but its hunger was now sharper than ever. The established churches of the Netherlands and England were now merely the biggest fish in sectarian seas. The Lutheran world policed its own orthodoxies more rigidly but suffered from a comparable problem. A mystical-esoteric secret society known as Rosicrucianism emerged in Germany in the early seventeenth century, cross-fertilizing with the Freemasons, another faux-ancient group that had appeared in Scotland a couple of decades earlier. In 1624, Jakob Böhme, a shoemaker from what is now western Poland, began to publish accounts of his visions and the secrets of creation he had gleaned from them, visions that became the basis for a theosophical system increasingly at odds with orthodox Lutheranism.

Alongside mysticism, by the early seventeenth century establishment Protestantism was in full-scale moral panic about atheism, a bogeyman that the panic helped to conjure into reality. It was not long before thinkers like Thomas Hobbes and Baruch Spinoza began to earn the label. Neither was an atheist in the modern sense, but both had gone a long way from any established orthodoxy. The burgeoning revolution in natural science was questioning conventional Christian metaphysics and subjecting received authorities of all kinds to experimental testing, putting Protestant orthodoxy's weak points under pressure. The doctrine of the Trinity began to seem like an overelaborate mathematical theorem that ought to be replaced with something more elegant. The English mystic and scientist Isaac Newton abandoned his belief in the Trinity in the 1670s. Newton also, in his famous laws of motion, provided ballast for a rising skeptical philosophy widely seen as tantamount to atheism: deism, the belief that God exists but does not interfere with his creation beyond providing it with inexorable natural laws. Protestants had traditionally taught a doctrine of special providence, in which God is the direct cause of every worldly event. Deism is less a passionate love affair with God than a dignified arranged marriage.

An additional point of vulnerability was Protestantism's weapon of choice, the Bible itself. Minor niggles about its text kept appearing. The Hebrew language indicates vowels with inflection marks instead of actual letters. It now appeared that the inflection marks in the Old Testament were of relatively recent origin. Were they part of inspired Scripture or not? In the New Testament, variant versions of some passages were being discovered in ancient manuscripts. Which were the right ones? In its traditional form, 1 John 5:7 declares that "there are three that bear record in heaven, the Father, the Word and the Holy Ghost, and these three are one": the Bible's most explicit affirmation of the Trinity. By the mid-seventeenth century, it was increasingly clear that the verse was a late addition to the text. The dispute over this verse was crucial in persuading Isaac Newton to abandon the Trinity.

These may seem like points of detail, but attentive Protestants recognized them as tremors warning of a major fault line beneath their feet. Who knew what core element of the faith might be undermined by the next scholarly discovery? Believers were submitting no longer to the Word of God but to the judgments of scholars, men with grudges and agendas, many of them heterodox or even Jewish. But other than wishing the problem would go away, what was the alternative?

All the while, the perennial threat of Catholicism was advancing. The Thirty Years' War ended in 1648 with a bitter compromise. Protestantism was driven to the margins in large swaths of central Europe, and believers remaining in those territories faced bleak choices. In 1684 and 1685, for example, about a thousand adult Protestants were expelled from an upland valley near Salzburg and ordered to leave children under fifteen behind them to be raised as Catholics. A great many of those who were expelled died or were sold into slavery in the course of desperate attempts to return for their children.[1]

Elsewhere, the 1648 settlement permitted Protestantism to survive, but for how long? Europe's new dominant power, Louis XIV's France, was aggressively Catholic. In 1685, the compromise that had ended France's religious wars nearly a century earlier was abruptly abandoned. French Protestants found their religion banned. Hundreds of thousands went into exile. In the same year, England itself acquired a Catholic king, James II. Unsurprisingly, his subjects, already at a fever pitch of anti-Catholic paranoia, did not believe his promises to be more tolerant than his French ally. He was deposed three years later in favor of a safely Protestant Dutchman, William of Orange. England subsequently banned any Catholics from the throne by law. That law is now an embarrassing relic, but at the time it was deadly serious. The deposed king and his descendants continued to claim the British crowns, and their supporters staged rebellions in 1689, 1715, and 1745. The last of those led to a brutal, decades-long military occupation of the Scottish Highlands.

If the Catholic sky never actually fell on English heads, in Germany it was ratcheting steadily lower. The electors of Saxony had traditionally been Germany's premier Protestant princes, but in 1697 Elector Augustus converted to Catholicism in order to claim the Polish crown. A few years before, French troops had occupied the Palatinate, in southwestern Germany. Catholic churches were built, Protestant ones seized, and a new Catholic establishment created, all in violation of the 1648 settlement. In 1719, a new elector of the Palatinate took the attack further, censoring traditional Protestant texts and seizing the Protestants' iconic church in Heidelberg. Protestants barricaded themselves into the building, but Catholic officials climbed the church tower and lowered themselves into the nave on ropes. The doors were pried open,

Catholics let in, and Protestants forced out. This was blatantly illegal, and the elector partly relented the following year, but he continued to starve the Palatinate's Protestant churches of funds. Thousands of his Protestant subjects emigrated.[2]

The cause célèbre of the age came in 1731, when the prince-archbishop of Salzburg suddenly expelled the Protestants who had survived, churchless and leaderless, in his territory for a century. They were given eight days to leave, in an Alpine November. The scale of what followed surprised everyone, not least the archbishop himself. Thirty thousand people were soon on the move, supported by a swiftly organized international Protestant relief effort that, remarkably, ensured that the large majority of them survived their winter exodus. In retrospect, it was a fiasco. Salzburg's mining industry was crippled by the loss of its workforce, and the hapless archbishop only drew attention to how many heretics he had been sheltering. We also now know that it was the Counter-Reformation's high-water mark. At the time, however, the tide still seemed to be rising.

Protestant alarm was amplified by a new industry: news. Two centuries on from Luther's revolutionary use of print, the publishing industry was more sophisticated than ever. Protestant countries, especially the Netherlands and England, had big cities, literate populations, booming economies, and relatively lax censorship. The burgeoning newspapers wove together events from France to Salzburg into a story of relentless popish encroachment and served them up for their appalled and eager readers in Berlin, Frankfurt, Amsterdam, London, and Boston. Fear, especially secondhand fear, sells.

The Pietist Adventure

The Protestant establishments' reaction to these multiple threats was to draw sharp lines and hold them as best they could. The 1648 peace settlement made Lutheranism and Calvinism the only legal alternatives to Catholicism in the Holy Roman Empire. Protestant churches and princes shared an interest in defining those two categories clearly and keeping their subjects firmly within one or the other of them. What resulted is commonly called the age of Orthodoxy. Protestant churches devoted considerable energy to tracking down, flagging up, and freezing out error, on the principle that those who were given an inch would take a mile.

This no-surrender defensiveness was embodied in Francis Turretin, professor at the Geneva Academy from 1653 to 1687, who made his name by unbudging hostility to the new biblical scholarship. Where Luther's generation had talked about the Bible as *sufficient,* containing everything necessary for salvation, Turretin insisted instead that it was *perfect.* Moreover, he reasoned, the God who had provided it in the first place must also have providentially preserved it from error. So 1 John 5:7 and the Hebrew vowel markers were inspired Scripture, whatever the ancient manuscripts said.[3] The Bible was Protestantism's weapon, and he would not let scholarly irresponsibility blunt its edge.

The obvious danger was that the spirit of the Protestant Gospel would be obscured by arid dogmatic precision. In this atmosphere, to suggest that the Christian life was about following Christ, not about doctrinal correctness, was to court suspicion that you were advancing a heretical agenda. This problem was particularly acute among Lutherans, for whom the doctrine that Christians are saved by faith alone, and not by good works, threatened to degenerate into a self-satisfied conviction that outward conformity to Lutheran dogma was a sufficient manifestation of faith.

This, at least, was how things looked to Orthodoxy's critics, chief among them the Frankfurt Lutheran minister Philip Jakob Spener. Spener's devastating 1675 manifesto *Pia desideria* (Pious desires) claimed that his was an age of "showy human erudition, of artificial posturing, and of presumptuous subtleties." Christianity, he insisted, was not about refuting errors but about love. Echoing Erasmus a century and a half earlier, Spener claimed that if St. Paul were to try to follow a modern German theological debate, he would "understand only a little of what our slippery geniuses sometimes say." But at the Day of Judgment, he warned, "we shall not be asked how learned we were," but rather "how faithfully and with how childlike a heart we sought to further the kingdom of God."[4]

Spener's case has obvious moral force, but Orthodoxy was not as bankrupt as he made it appear. Sometimes it is sensible to respond to attacks by pulling up the drawbridge. We will meet the same instinct, in different forms, in the nineteenth and twentieth centuries. For

Orthodoxy did see one thing more clearly than some of its idealistic opponents: the tides of skepticism, sectarianism, and Catholicism that were lapping at Protestantism's foundations could not be appeased. Building walls to keep them out was neither a bold nor an imaginative strategy, but, we are forced to admit, it worked. The Protestant establishments were battered but did not collapse. If Orthodoxy had not policed itself so firmly, who knows into what mystical-sectarian welter seventeenth-century Protestantism might have collapsed or how far milk-and-water deism would have advanced? If German churches and states had not clung so tightly to the 1648 settlement, who knows what pretexts might have been given to the Catholic powers to roll back Protestantism still further? Defensive victories are not inspiring, and with hindsight missed opportunities loom larger than disasters averted. But the view from the front line is different.

Nor was Orthodoxy the desert its critics made it out to be. After the pillage of the sixteenth century and the devastation of the Thirty Years' War, this was a golden age of church building and of baroque art, giving us astonishing buildings such as the Frauenkirche in Dresden. And any culture that produced Johann Sebastian Bach cannot be all bad.

Even so, Philip Jakob Spener struck a chord, giving voice to a Protestant tradition that, while sometimes submerged, had never disappeared. His most important antecedents were English Puritans who, stymied in their ambitions to reform their church's structures, had often transposed their political aspirations into a spiritual key. The result was an outpouring of "practical divinity": devotional writing and preaching teaching Christians how to grow in holiness. What these ministers wanted from the state was, momentously, to be left alone. They wanted to train up individual believers in rigorous, enriching lives of private prayer, study, and fellowship. Readers of bestselling books like Lewis Bayly's *The Practice of Piety,* which ran through more than eighty English editions in the century after its publication in 1612, learned how they should pray: twice or thrice daily, for at least fifteen minutes at a time, ideally in their own words rather than following a set form. And they learned what inner experiences to pursue in prayer: an intense, heartfelt devotion, a proper horror at the sight of their own sins, a burning desire for redemption, and a ravishing joy in God's presence.

Most of this material was pretty orthodox Calvinism, but not narrowly so. One of the first "practical divinity" bestsellers was a lightly adapted Catholic tract. Others drew on medieval sources and on Lutherans—especially Luther himself, who was read avidly by English Calvinists he would have called fanatics. The compliment was soon repaid. The German translation of Bayly's *Practice of Piety* ran to at least sixty-eight editions, and it also appeared in languages as varied as Hungarian, Romanian, Italian, and Welsh. It became a truism in seventeenth-century Protestant Europe that theology came from Germany but devotion came from England. More than five hundred English devotional works had appeared in German translation by 1750.[5]

The most popular German devotional work, however, was homegrown. Johann Arndt's *True Christianity* (1605) ran through some ninety-five German editions and twenty-eight more in nine other languages, including Icelandic, by the mid-eighteenth century. Arndt's work was more enraptured and mystical than the English Puritans' practical advice, but unlike in England, where top-rank theologians were producing devotional works, writers like Arndt remained outside the theological establishment. Spener's *Pia desideria* marks the moment when this pious undercurrent made a bid for the German mainstream. Significantly, that book originated as a long preface to an edition of Arndt's sermons. To the consternation of Lutheranism's doctrinal police, Spener was also immersed in English and Dutch devotional writers.

Spener took pains to stress how banal *Pia desideria* was. Indeed, much of it is a bland assembly of platitudes from irreproachable Lutheran worthies. To modern readers, it seems as controversial as a preacher being against sin. No revolutionary manifesto has ever been more reassuring. What gave his book bite was that rather than merely lamenting the state of Christendom, he offered practical solutions. The first, which would become his hallmark, he called "the ancient and apostolic kind of church meetings." He had already pioneered such meetings in Frankfurt, calling them *collegia pietatis*, "schools of piety." There were Dutch, French, and English precedents. In the Lutheran world, however, they were both new and alarming. Spener made them sound harmless: discussion groups, led by ministers, in which interested laypeople could read the Bible together and discuss its application to their lives. The minister would ensure that the conversation stayed off controversial issues, and that everyone went home enriched.[6]

Spener's *collegia pietatis* would become the cadres of a wholesale Protestant reawakening. Inoffensive as they might sound, they marked a decisive shift in religious power. He urged his readers to the "diligent exercise of the spiritual priesthood," the equal dignity that all baptized Christians share. And he had a pointed, ringing silence on one crucial topic. His scheme simply had no role for Christian princes, Protestant churches' protectors, guides, and masters.

Orthodoxy's policemen smelled heresy. Praising lay leadership while ignoring the godly prince sounded Calvinist, if not Anabaptist. More fundamentally, Spener's whole approach to the Christian life was un-Lutheran. Salvation, for him, was less a fundamental change in the categories of being than an experience. Worse, his emphasis on building a life of progressive holiness instead of on conversion seemed to be obscuring the Gospel's foundational truth.

Yet Spener's message resonated with some of Germany's Protestant princes. Governments generally like religions that promote moral effort: orderly citizens pay more taxes. Spener also offered a solution to one of the age's perennial political headaches: endless intra-Protestant quarrels. The message that some things matter more than doctrine was particularly welcome in Protestant Germany's rising power, Brandenburg-Prussia. The ruling Hohenzollern dynasty were Calvinists, but most of their subjects were Lutherans. A religious movement that could unite different Protestants in a common cause was very attractive.

Hohenzollern support turned Spener's ideas into the movement we know as Pietism. In 1691, Spener was given a court appointment in Berlin, and his disciple August Hermann Francke a plum posting at the Hohenzollerns' new pet university, at Halle. Francke, one of history's great religious entrepreneurs, turned Halle into the engine room of a Pietist revolution. He established a huge orphanage, which eventually became one of the largest single buildings in Europe. "Orphanage" has a grimly Dickensian sound to it, but this was more boarding school than workhouse, and its boys and girls received an enviable education. Halle also produced medicines on an industrial scale and marketed them across Europe. And of course books of all kinds surged out as from a geyser: Bibles and Pietist tracts for every budget, in virtually every language spoken in central Europe. Nor was Francke's influence limited only to Europe. In 1706, inspired by what he had heard of John Eliot's work in Massachusetts, he launched the first-ever organized Lutheran overseas mission, sending two German missionaries to the Danish colony of Tranquebar, in southern India.

Pietism became a branded product. Students flocked to Halle; medicines and books sold; and donations poured in, allowing the medicines and the books to be circulated for free. The books in particular became Pietism's ubiquitous missionaries. Regions in which Protestant churches were banned found themselves flooded with pamphlets urging believers to form themselves into *collegia pietatis* and to train one another in godliness, ministers or no ministers. Catholic and Lutheran Orthodox authorities alike tried to ban such meetings, but it is not easy to prevent neighbors from gathering to talk.

By their nature, these fires were more easily lit than controlled. The further Pietist enthusiasm spread, the clearer it became that Spener's and Francke's efforts to keep it house-trained were not always working. Pietism quickly cross-fertilized with other, more alarming strains of religious renewal.

Chief among these was a movement that had first emerged in the mountains of southeastern France after Protestantism was outlawed there in 1685. In February 1688, Isabeau Vincent, a sixteen-year-old shepherdess from Dauphiné, began singing the Ten Commandments in her sleep. Over the next few nights, the sleeping girl also prayed aloud and warned of coming judgment. She quoted the prophet Joel: in the last days, daughters shall prophesy. She became a phenomenon. She was arrested in June, but other Protestant children and teenagers took up the torch. Soon the region was bubbling with child prophets, many of them warning of imminent divine judgment for France.

For a time, the movement was suppressed. Hundreds of children were arrested; some of the older ones were executed, and many of the younger girls were banished to convents. In 1700–1701, however, the prophecies began again. Children too young to remember any settled Protestant ministry were walking on burning coals or weeping tears of blood for the people's sins. Newborn babies reportedly spoke aloud to revile Catholic baptism. There were open-air assemblies. Worshippers fell to the ground and howled like wolves. Catholic churches were attacked. Again, more than three hundred prophets were arrested, and some of them sentenced to galley slavery.

When a wider European war broke out in 1702, so did war in the French mountains. In July, fifty psalm-singing Protestants attacked a village prison, freeing their tortured comrades, killing three Catholic priests and castrating a fourth. The so-called Camisard rebellion that followed saw more than two hundred Catholic churches burned that year. It took twenty thousand French troops two years of indiscriminate brutality to put down the insurgency. More than four hundred villages were completely destroyed.

By the rebellion's end, the surviving prophets were angry young men, not teenage girls. Inevitably, some made their way to London, Europe's largest city, already home to some fifty thousand French Protestant refugees. In 1706, three men began prophesying in London; they would fall into trances, trembling or convulsing, and then speak prophecies to be recorded by scribes. Their warnings of coming doom were directed chiefly at the leaders of London's French Protestants, whom the prophets saw as self-satisfied sellouts. Some of their English neighbors, however, began to take an interest. The prophets' suffering won them widespread sympathy, and plenty of levelheaded Protestants shared their apocalyptic worldview. One English bishop openly backed them. Soon respectable English men and women were prophesying themselves. By early 1707, the movement still known as the French Prophets was dominated by its English converts.

What drove them was their fear that the Protestant establishment was asleep at the helm, and their hope that God would raise up new leaders for a time of need. At their meetings, one hostile observer wrote, "all may set up for Teachers that have but a sufficient stock of Confidence. . . . Women teach as well as Men. . . . Rapture and Exstacy supply the place of Order and Regularity."[7] The prophets would fall senseless, whistle, hiss, or roar. One convert began to speak Latin, having supposedly never learned it before. Precise, dated prophecies began: within a week, the French war would come close enough that the Tower of London's guns would be fired. The guns, however, remained ominously silent. Worse, when one of the English prophets died on

December 22, 1707, his colleagues confidently predicted that on May 25 next, he would be raised to life. The day came and went; the huge crowds who had gathered dispersed, and the Prophets' career as eighteen-month wonders was over. They were remembered as a notorious symbol of what happens when learned authority is trampled by— the word was an unvarnished insult—"enthusiasts."

Yet they also represent a wider pattern of how Protestantism would be reinvented in the eighteenth century. French Protestants' predicament after 1685 was hardly unique. In large areas of central Europe, Protestant populations under Catholic rule were forbidden to practice their religion. The churches of Protestant Orthodoxy, bound to princely establishments and wary of stirring up trouble, had nothing to offer these people. But Pietism, which could bypass both princes and churches, did.

As the French Prophets' reputation was cresting in London, Pietism bore sudden and unexpected fruit eight hundred miles farther east. In late 1707, Swedish troops, engaged in a grueling war with Russia, occupied the duchy of Silesia, in modern Poland, a territory whose once-numerous Protestants had been driven to the margins. While there, Pietist Swedish soldiers held open-air worship meetings. Their example provoked something remarkable.

Early in 1708, groups of Silesian children began following the Swedish pattern. Boys and girls, aged from fourteen down to five or six, sometimes hundreds together, gathered in the open, three times daily, to pray and sing. Parents claimed to be powerless to stop them. Magistrates were at a loss to know how to deal with crowds of orderly, pious children. In one town, soldiers fired blanks at them, but they stood firm. In another, the public hangman was sent to disperse them with a whip, but "seeing the Children in so serious and kneeling a Posture," he was "highly moved at so wonderful a Sight" and refused to comply. How far this was genuinely led by children is unclear. The facts that adult crowds gathered to watch them, and that the children prayed pointedly for God to "move the Emperors Heart, . . . [that] they might have Liberty to serve and Worship God," suggest some role for adult agitators. If so, it was a highly effective ploy.[8] The children's action was widespread, utterly unexpected, mostly peaceful, and universally seen as having enormous moral power.

Francke rushed to exploit and publicize this unexpected movement.

By the summer of 1708, Londoners recovering from the collapse of the French Prophets could read about it. Readers eagerly seized on hints that the Silesian stirrings not only had invigorated latent Protestants but had won Catholic and Jewish converts. Orthodox Protestantism, stuck in its defensive trenches, was discovering that Pietism could take the battle to the enemy.

Over the next half century, this pattern would become almost familiar. Protestant populations without any effective Protestant ministry were reached by Pietist books, preachers, and principles and organized into lay-led, mutually supporting groups. It was just such a grassroots Protestant resurgence in Salzburg that provoked the infamous expulsion in 1731, and Pietism's most faithful political backer, the Hohenzollern kingdom of Prussia, took the lead in rescuing the Salzburg refugees. But as well as reaching south into formerly Protestant upper Germany, Pietist influence spread in every direction.

East: A crushing Russian battle victory over Sweden in 1708 left thirty thousand Swedish Lutheran prisoners, men and women, in Russian hands. They were transported to Tobolsk in Siberia, remaining there until peace was settled in the early 1720s. Two Pietist-influenced officers began preaching to them. When Francke got wind of it, he flooded the encampment with books and medication. Pietism swept through the prisoners. When Russian soldiers began to be drawn in, too, a Pietist school was established in Tobolsk for their children. When peace finally came, and the Swedes returned to spread Pietism in their home country, Russians clamored for places in Moscow's small Pietist school.

North: The war-ravaged Estonian island of Oesel acquired a Pietist-influenced minister in 1738. Under his eye a lay-led movement began in 1740. There were open-air meetings at which "vanities," from bagpipes to ornate clothing, were ostentatiously destroyed. The moral transformation was so profound that the island's courts supposedly did not hear a single criminal case from 1740 to 1745. Converts fell insensate and had visions of heaven and hell. A messiah figure, Tallima Paap, claimed to be a prophet greater than Christ, might have practiced ritual nudity, and forbade his followers to plant or harvest, because Christ's imminent return made it unnecessary. Estonia's Russian rulers, hostile to

Lutherans at the best of times, cracked down hard. Tallima Paap managed to return in peace to his farm, but the ministers were imprisoned and only released after two decades. Pietists' books and even their houses were confiscated. Only in the early nineteenth century did the movement emerge from hiding.

West: The principality of Wales had been incorporated into the English state in 1536 but had remained more a conquered province than an equal partner, its church mostly staffed by Englishmen who despised the Welsh language. One rare exception was a Carmarthenshire shepherd turned minister named Griffith Jones. Jones devoured Pietist books and briefly considered joining the mission in India, but instead pursued mission at home. In 1731, he established a Welsh-speaking charity school in his parish of Llanddowror, which became the taproot for a series of temporary schools that began to sprout across Wales: typically lasting for a single winter, providing crash courses in Welsh literacy and Protestant piety. By Jones's death in 1761, 158,000 people had passed through more than three thousand such schools. One of his converts, a fellow cleric named Daniel Rowland, was at the forefront of a wave of Welsh Pietist-evangelical preaching that surged from the mid-1730s on.

As Spener had been at pains to insist, Pietism was nothing new. It was a rekindling of the love affair with God that had been Protestantism's beating heart since Luther and that had run through its veins ever since. Its recipe was disarmingly simple: believers supporting one another in pursuing holiness, with or without ministers to help them. And it was proving that it could take the Protestant Gospel to places quite beyond Orthodoxy's reach. The price was loss of control. Once French peasant girls, Silesian children, Swedish prisoners of war, Estonian farmers, or Welsh shepherds took responsibility for their own religious lives, there was no knowing what they might do.

Spener himself knew it. Not all of the members of his original *collegia pietatis* in Frankfurt took kindly to suddenly becoming a model for the renewal of Lutheranism. Their close-knit group of earnest believers was being thrown open to a more mixed public. Shortly after *Pia desideria* was published, a subgroup broke off to meet under lay leadership, and eventually withdrew from Sunday worship altogether. The

Orthodox establishment was right to fear that such meetings could be nests of schism and heresy.

Moravian Riders

The most spectacular demonstration of this was the unlikely figure of Count Nikolaus Ludwig von Zinzendorf und Pottendorf, a German nobleman born in 1700 who was trained in Pietism as a teenage student at Halle. In 1722, he bought an estate at Berthelsdorf, in Saxony, bordering Moravia in the modern Czech Republic, where Pietist missionaries had been finding a hearing. As Protestant refugees trickled north, Zinzendorf established a village for them: Herrnhut—literally, "the Lord's Safekeeping."

Herrnhut's settlers were an eclectic bunch: self-taught Protestants influenced both by Pietist Lutheranism and by the Moravian branch of the Bohemian Brethren, whom we met in chapter 3. It did not take long for their divisions to surface. In 1727, Zinzendorf, who had only paid them intermittent attention, took the matter in hand. He imposed a self-governing structure on the community that drew on Pietist and Calvinist patterns but also on the older patterns of the Brethren. His arrival, and approval of the Brethren's texts, sparked a summer of intense debate, Bible study, and prayer.

This culminated in the so-called Moravian Pentecost. At the center, once again, was a child, a newly orphaned eleven-year-old named Susanne Kühnel. She experienced a powerful conversion, and her first Communion turned that into a general movement. One witness wrote,

> On 23 August, such an impulse of prayer came upon the boys and girls that it was not possible to hear them without heartfelt emotion, and through Susanne Kühnel an extraordinary movement arose in their assembly. . . . So powerful a spirit prevailed among the children as is beyond words to express.[9]

Riding this wave, the community accepted Zinzendorf's new structures and adopted a name for themselves: the Moravian Brethren.

Zinzendorf saw his Moravians as a voluntary society within the Lutheran church, like the Pietists. But Lutheran and even Pietist establishments were suspicious. Halle's Pietism had become systematized, especially after Francke's death in 1727. Pietism, which had always been morally austere on matters like drinking and dancing, was now becoming prescriptive about religious experience, too, laying out a series of fixed stages for believers' struggle with sin. Zinzendorf ridiculed this "self-induced sickness." The Moravians' experience of salvation was more immediate: if you could identify imaginatively with Christ and his sufferings, then you had made the leap. "A Pietist," he commented wryly, "cannot be converted in so cavalier a way as we can. . . . We ride and the Pietists go on foot."[10]

The Moravians were what Pietists had been falsely accused of being: freewheeling tolerationists who bypassed theological rigor with waves of emotion. It briefly looked as if they might sweep all before them, until the 1740s and 1750s, when their reputation was badly damaged by financial scandals and by a spiral into such weird spiritual practices as crawling imaginatively into the spear wound in Christ's side. But for a few brief years, their impact was immense. Zinzendorf traveled almost constantly, as did many of the Herrnhuters, refugees who were already by definition footloose. Their emotional, anti-theological, and antihierarchical Protestantism found fertile soil wherever it fell.

The Moravians had a particular enthusiasm for mission. Like the Pietist missionaries in India, they looked first to the overseas territories of Denmark, the only Lutheran power with any sort of non-European empire. In 1733, a Moravian mission set off for one of the most hostile territories imaginable: Greenland. Progress was slow, but unlike their predecessors in Protestant mission the Moravians were institutionally committed and patient. The first Inuit converts were made in 1739. Two years later, the Moravians persuaded their nomadic flock to move to a permanent settlement, helping them to secure a regular food supply. In 1747, they shipped a prefabricated meetinghouse to this community of New Herrnhut: Greenland's largest building. By 1762, there were five hundred baptized Inuit. A modest harvest, perhaps, but a testament to the Moravians' dedication and impact. New Herrnhut would become the nucleus of Nuuk, now Greenland's capital city.

A more dramatic story unfolded on the Caribbean island of St. Thomas, now in the U.S. Virgin Islands, but then also under Danish rule. Two Moravian missionaries arrived in 1733 and set out to preach

to a population of some 3,700 African slaves. They were appalled by
what they found; the cruelties of the slaveholders, one wrote, "would
make a stone wail."[11] They carefully avoided openly criticizing slavery,
but they did preach Christian spiritual equality. The slaveholders,
frightened by recent rebellions, were openly hostile. Stories began to
be told of slaves' denouncing their masters' behavior as unchristian and
calling down divine judgment on them. Missionaries were threatened
and converts whipped. One master set fire to the Bibles his slaves had
been given and then beat the flames out on their faces.

The crisis came in 1738. Rebecca (at that time she had no surname)
had been a house slave whose master had raised her in his own Reformed Protestantism and freed her on his death. She quickly fell in with
the Moravians and, not yet twenty, became central to their mission. She
visited slave quarters, preached to women in a mixture of languages,
and organized self-supporting study groups. Spener's *collegia pietatis* had
come to the Caribbean. She was "very accomplished in the teachings of
God," the Moravians said. "Everything depends on her." One of them,
Matthäus Freundlich, went further: he married her, despite some initial
misgivings on her part. They promptly adopted at least nine orphans.
He might have hoped the marriage would give Rebecca some protection
from the rising hostility of the plantation owners. If so, the plan back-
fired, for the marriage was also a deeply provocative statement about
racial equality. Rebecca and Matthäus were arrested, tried, and convicted on fabricated charges of burglary and fomenting rebellion. She
was sentenced to be sold back into slavery. She refused repeated offers
to save herself from this fate by renouncing her Moravian faith and her
marriage. Disaster was only averted by the chance arrival on the island
of Zinzendorf himself. He spoke to the island's governor, nobleman to
nobleman, and the matter was smoothed over.[12]

Not that Rebecca Freundlich's adventures were at an end. She and
her husband traveled to Herrnhut in 1741, but he died en route. Nevertheless, she was warmly welcomed there and in 1746 was ordained a
deaconess, one of the first Protestant women ever ordained. In the
same year, she was married again, this time to a Moravian convert
from West Africa, Christian Protten. In the 1750s and 1760s, the Prottens
would travel together to the Danish fort of Christiansborg, in modern

Ghana, to establish a school; and there they lived out their days.[13] She was evidently a remarkable woman, but her story would only have been possible among the Moravians.

By the 1760s, when the rest of the Protestant world finally began to wake up to what Moravian missionaries were doing, there were over three thousand Moravian converts on St. Thomas and two neighboring islands. Over two hundred Moravians had become missionaries, working in Jamaica, Labrador, Suriname, Guinea, and, as we will see, South Africa. A 1747 Moravian painting of the kingdom of heaven gives a glimpse of their unparalleled internationalism. Christ himself is still white, but the remainder of the group, from a skin-clad Inuit to an African slave, is as remarkably multicultural a gathering as you could hope to find. Protestantism was finally becoming a world religion.

Methodism: Pietism's English Stepchild

England, long accustomed to practical divinity, embraced Pietism as if it were nothing particularly new. An immigrant German preacher in London established the first of several *collegia pietatis* on Spener's model as early as 1678, and by the second decade of the eighteenth century more than a quarter of London parishes featured meetings of this kind. Pietist moral severity found an echo in one idiosyncratic species of English Protestant: the ceremonial High Church Anglicans, for whom Protestant Orthodoxy was a close cousin to the regicidal sectarianism that had almost destroyed their country in the 1640s. One such high Anglican grouping, which gave itself the callow students' nickname the Holy Club, was established at Oxford University in 1729. Their severe, ascetic regime of fasting and prayer was described in a tract that gave them a more enduring name and was quickly translated into German: *The Oxford Methodists* (1733). The "Methodists" themselves, however, did not feel like anyone's model. Like good Pietists, they were fighting their inner spiritual battles, and had not achieved any kind of breakthrough when they left Oxford to go their different ways.

In 1737–38, one of these discontented seekers, John Wesley, made a trip to Britain's newest North American colony, Georgia. He had heard of the religious excitements in North America, of which more shortly, and wanted to try his hand. In preaching terms, his visit was a failure, but it bore fruit for him personally. For among his shipmates were a group of Moravians, who introduced him to Arndt and other greats of German spirituality and deeply impressed him with their hymns.

Wesley became the Moravians' English contact. When Moravian emissaries arrived in England in 1738 to seek privileges for their colleagues in Georgia, Wesley found them lodgings and introduced them to London's religious societies. With Wesley's encouragement, the delegation's leader founded a new religious society at Fetter Lane in London. Three days later, the Moravians left for America. The Fetter Lane Society they left behind them was not exactly Moravian, but where its Anglican counterparts enforced a strict moral code, Fetter Lane was open to anyone of goodwill. That heady liberty was a sign of things to come.

On May 24, barely three weeks after Fetter Lane's establishment, Wesley attended a meeting at a neighboring religious society. As he described the event, somebody was reading from Martin Luther, "describing the Change which God works in the Heart thro' Faith." As Luther spoke to Wesley,

> I felt my Heart strangely warm'd. I felt I did trust in CHRIST, CHRIST alone, for salvation: and an Assurance was given me, That he had taken away *my* sins, even *mine,* and saved *me*.[14]

It was the archetypal conversion of the age. Wesley sensed in his heart ("I felt . . . I felt") that the salvation which he had so often preached was finally personal: God's gift directly to him.

Wesley went on to visit Herrnhut, and might have become a Moravian. Instead he became something new. Fetter Lane became a crossroads for restless and adventurous Protestants of all colors. High Churchmen like Wesley rubbed shoulders with old-fashioned Calvinists, German expatriates, aging French Prophets, and the heralds of the kindling Protestant fire in Wales. When "proper" Moravians next passed through London in October 1739, they were shocked. Instead of the simplicity and stillness of Moravian worship, the crowds at Fetter Lane were "sighing, groaning, whimpering and howling," straining every sinew in their devotion.[15]

Wesley, like the Pietists, now suspected that the Moravians' easy path to joy meant that they neglected good morals. He himself went to the other extreme. English High Churchmen had always disliked Calvinist predestination, and Wesley became the most outspoken advocate of the alternative doctrine, Arminianism, which dominates evangelical Protestantism to the present and teaches that we are free to accept or reject God's offer of grace. Wesley even taught that faithful Christians could achieve moral perfection in this life. Whether you liked it or not, this was an explosive theological synthesis. Luther's dizzying experience of free grace; the Moravians' ease in reaching that grace; Pietist moral rigor; high Anglican perfectionism and commitment to structures. None of the elements of this "Methodism" were new, but Wesley combined them into a formidable alloy of heartfelt spontaneity and rigorous order.

The order emerged almost by accident. Methodism was not a denomination. It was what Zinzendorf had wanted Moravianism to be, a voluntary society within a larger church. Wesley himself was determinedly loyal to Anglicanism, and English Methodism remained a movement within the Church of England until after his death in 1791. Its emergent structures were informal and parallel to the established church. Methodism grew like ivy on an old tree, swiftly and flexibly, using Anglican structures where possible and working around them where not. Informal groups sprang up in response to Wesley's restless itinerant preaching. Soon these groups were organized into "classes" of between nine and eighteen believers, which were grouped into societies, which were grouped into circuits and conferences. Suddenly Wesley found himself in charge of a national para-church network. He led it for almost half a century: sometimes generously, sometimes crankily, but usually shrewdly. His gift was to hold the structure together with little more than the force of his personality, while also usually being open to the possibility that God might do something new and unexpected with individual believers in the community he headed.

Methodism's greatest success, however, would come not in England but in Britain's North American colonies, a scattered set of communities that by the mid-eighteenth century numbered about one million settlers and slaves. It was a unique Protestant society, and not only because it was exuberantly plural. Its most religiously vibrant region,

New England, had been founded by refugees from Old World corruptions, but the refugees' children, and the commercially minded later generations who joined them, did not necessarily share the founders' ideals. So almost from the start New Englanders were in the shadow of their lost godly past. The more they subsided into worldliness, the more the imagined purity of the founders glittered in memory. Elsewhere, from the Cévennes to Silesia and from Herrnhut to St. Thomas, children and teenagers were in the vanguard of Protestant renewal. In New England, refugee parents lamented their children's godlessness.

How could a once-godly society be restored to its pristine virtues? Institutional reform could hardly help; godly institutions had not saved them before. All that could help would be the renewed gift of the Holy Spirit that the prophet Joel had promised. Their language, as they prayed for that gift, always looked backward: begging God that "the Work of Conversion . . . may be revived," for "present revivings," for "the resurrection of Religion," for the gift of the Spirit to be "renewed."[16] And it happened, at least to some extent. It became part of the rhythm of New England's life that once or twice in a generation a town saw a "harvest" in which young people in their teens and twenties would be swept up into conversions. Often these were set-piece events, usually in high summer, festivals of preaching and prayer that might last all night and for which scattered rural populations might gather from a wide area. Preachers delivered sermons that they had neither prepared beforehand nor could remember afterward, yet that melted every heart in the meeting. Their hearers wept, trembled, panted, fainted, convulsed, or fell as if dead. Little of this was new. The pattern had originated among radical Presbyterians in Scotland and Ireland in the 1620s and 1630s.[17] In America, these events acquired a new label, which has since become standard Protestant jargon: "revivals."

What changed in the 1730s was that these regular, local revivals became media events. This was largely the work of two men, one American, one English. The American was the brilliant, humane minister Jonathan Edwards, whose book *Some Thoughts Concerning the Present Revival of Religion in New-England* (1742) helped to popularize the notion of revival. Edwards owed his fame to a revival in the small Massachusetts town of Northampton in 1734–35. Like many other revivals, this one began with the conversion of one loose-living young woman, who then became "the greatest occasion of awakening to others." Teen-agers move in herds. However, Edwards had seen periodic revivals be-fore and believed this was something new. Teenage girls and young women were revivals' core constituency, but this time men and women of all ages were being converted. He even cautiously detected a hint of the miraculous. Illness virtually ceased in the town while the revival was at its height. He dwelled on the impossibly precocious piety of one four-year-old convert. Edwards's account of the event, *A Faithful Narrative of the Surprizing Work of God,* was written in a careful, sober style that made its contents all the more astonishing. Readers on both sides of the Atlantic devoured it and longed to emulate it.[18]

One such reader was the revivals' second great publicist, the English-man George Whitefield. Like Wesley, he was a graduate of the Oxford Holy Club, but he was straightforwardly Calvinist and saw Wesley's Arminianism as heresy. He, too, was drawn to North America, but where Wesley had seen little success, in 1738–41 Whitefield preached himself into the first rank of celebrity. One witness from rural Con-necticut described traveling to hear Whitefield, seeing a huge cloud of dust, and hearing a low rumble as of thunder. It was the crowds coming to the event:

> Every horse seemed to go with all his might to carry his rider
> to hear news from heaven for the saving of Souls. . . . The land
> and banks over the river looked black with people and horses.
> All along the 12 miles I saw no man at work in his field, but all
> seemed to be gone.[19]

Those who fought their way to within earshot of the young English-man heard a captivating, demotic speaker. He warned his hearers that outward religious conformity was worthless. Instead, they must recog-nize their sinfulness, embrace Christ, and be renewed from within by the transforming power of the Holy Spirit.

The sharp edge to that plain evangelical message was Whitefield's attitude to the colonies' churches. American Protestantism was plural but not ecumenical. Anglicans, Presbyterians, Congregationalists, Bap-tists, and Lutherans generally remained in their own religious and lin-guistic silos. Whitefield was an Anglican priest, but he ignored Anglican parish boundaries and jurisdictions. He worked promiscuously with other denominations and was gentle with none of them. Church leaders' godless corruption was one of his main themes. He told Anglicans that "the generality of their teachers do not preach or live up to the truth as it is in Jesus" and accused Congregationalist ministers of having "a bare, speculative knowledge of the doctrines of grace, but never experiencing the power of them in their hearts."[20]

Whitefield's preaching became the whirling center of the so-called First Great Awakening. In the early 1740s, New England's periodic local revivals coalesced into something wider. Or at least publishers presented it that way, and so turned what they had invented into a reality. When Whitefield finally returned home, he brought American revivalism with him. The 1742 Cambuslang awakening in Scotland, to which Whitefield's preaching was critical, matched anything in the New World. Whether real or illusory, these revivals would set the pattern, and the bar, for evangelical religion for generations to come.

The Revivals' New World

Revivalist religion of this kind was classically Protestant, rekindling the old love affair with God, but it had new features. One of these is the prominence of women. Jonathan Edwards was right to be surprised when his Northampton revival produced as many male as female converts. In the informal, household-based discussion groups that sprang up everywhere, from Spener's *collegia pietatis* to Methodist bands, women were often the hosts and enablers, and women's social networks were the veins through which these groups' lifeblood spread. A fairly consistent 60 percent of early Methodist converts were women.[21]

These women did not all wait quietly to be taught. The French Prophets, again, had shown the way; because the Holy Spirit bypassed normal authority to speak through the uneducated, and indeed through children, surely he could and would also speak through women. Wesley, whose instincts were patriarchal and who accepted that the "ordinary rules of discipline" forbade women to preach, was willing to believe that God overturned such rules in special cases and that some women manifestly had exceptional gifts for preaching. When the Essex Methodist Mary Bosanquet made the jump from leading classes to preaching in the early 1770s, she did so against Wesley's advice. Yet he admitted that "her words are as fire, conveying both light and heat to the hearts of all that hear her." She continued preaching five times weekly into her seventies.[22] In America, a splinter denomination, the Separate Congregationalists, was formed in 1744–45, partly on the principle that men and women alike should be able to speak in church. In theory, this did not extend to formal preaching, but one Separate church on Long Island enjoyed weekly sermons from one Sarah Wright Townsend for fifteen years. When the pastor, her son-in-law, tried to put an end to it, she and the rest of the church faced him down. Some Separate churches may have had African American women as teachers.[23]

Such defiance of social norms usually petered out in a generation or two. The Separate Congregationalists abandoned female exhortation in 1787, and the Wesleyan Methodists tried to ban women's preaching in 1803. At the height of the Great Awakening, however, anything was possible. If a minister has been invoking the Spirit's power and thundering against stifling formalism, what is he to do if the women who form the bulk of his congregation start proving him right? In October 1741, one Bathsheba Kingsley of Westfield, Massachusetts, was disciplined by her church for stealing a horse and riding off on a Sunday without her husband's permission. She explained that she had had "immediate revelations from Heaven" commanding her to spread the Word. Two years later, she was disciplined again for wandering "from house to house, and very frequently to other towns, under a notion of doing Christ's work and delivering his messages." Some of those messages were denunciations of specific sinners, including the ministers who opposed her. When her husband tried to stop her with "hard words and blows," she prayed that he "might go quick to hell." Jonathan Edwards himself was called in to resolve the case. Edwards firmly reproved the husband for his violence, and while he forbade Bathsheba any public ministry, he allowed that she might visit her neighbors for "mutual edification" and continue to testify to her faith.[24]

Women preachers are eye-catching, but they can distract us from the deeper change here. The expectation that the Spirit pays no heed to gender, age, or status corroded hierarchies of all kinds. Mary Bosanquet and Bathsheba Kingsley were seeking spiritual, not social, empowerment. During the Cambuslang awakening in Scotland, one young married woman took part in an all-night prayer meeting in the minister's house. When she felt "the promises of the new Covenant rushing with great sweetness into [her] heart," she

> could not forbear . . . taking the Minister in my arms & crying out O My Dear Minister and going about and with an Unfeigned love, shaking hands with severals of the Company.[25]

The minister crossed out those scandalous lines when he prepared her testimony for publication. But the reality, as she experienced it, surpassed any innuendo. This was simply one redeemed soul embracing another, shockingly enacting the cliché that "souls have no sexes."[26]

In other words, there were alarming undercurrents in these revivals. From the beginning, respectable evangelicals worried that the entire movement risked being discredited by a few fanatics. On the whole, respectability won this argument, so that we nowadays tend to divide the revivals into a safe moderate mainstream and a colorful lunatic fringe. It is not at all clear that we should.

Revivals were often accompanied by deep sighing, trembling and shaking, howling and barking, uncontrolled laughing or weeping. Some fell insensate to the floor, an experience that one Scotsman described as God "sheathing the Sword of Justice in my heart." Others saw visions or heard voices. In America, several visionaries saw the Book of Life and then testified as to who was in it and who was not. The testimony from Cambuslang is full of converts' claiming words of Scripture "darted into my mind" or being woken at night by a voice crying, "Awake thou Sleeper, and call upon God." One woman, hearing a Bible verse "sounded loud" in her mind, was thunderstruck. "I was not," she explained, "at that time used to such secret ways of God's communicating his mind." Some converts even felt the need to state that they had *not* experienced visions. In such a moment, there could be anguish in being left out. One young woman at Cambuslang "fell under great distress, fearing I was passed by, and cried, that everybody will get good, but I."[27]

And then there were out-and-out miracles. A Connecticut girl named Mercy Wheeler was left unable to walk after a serious illness in 1726. In 1733, she published a pious pamphlet describing how God had sustained her through her afflictions. Ten years later, at the height of the Great Awakening, she became convinced she was going to be healed. While a skeptical minister prayed with her, she was overcome with trembling, rose from her bed for the first time in seventeen years, and walked across the room. She remained alive, able to walk, and in tolerably good health until at least 1771. Her case became famous, because the evidence of the earlier pamphlet made it very hard to accuse her of fraud. But she was not alone. Any unexpected or unexplained recovery from illness could be seen in the same light.

When the healthy begin to fall to the floor as if dead and the sick leap from their beds, it is hard to keep a level head. Prophecies and miracles inevitably disturb religious establishments. Visions and revelations authorize ordinary men and women to speak out against their teachers. If you have had a dramatic experience of God and your minister has not, what becomes of his authority? Like the French Prophets, or the Quakers, or Luther himself, these evangelicals readily denounced the entire clerical caste as conspirators who preferred to save their own livelihoods rather than their people's souls.

When ministers themselves were caught up in the moment, the results could be dramatic. James Davenport, a revivalist Presbyterian minister on Long Island, excluded anyone who did not share a dramatic conversion from his church. The crowds who did come screamed, laughed, and fell insensate. He once attempted, unsuccessfully, to preach for twenty-four hours without a break. In March 1743, matters came to a head. He staged a book burning in his church, destroying not only Catholic or unorthodox works, but Protestant classics and works whose support for the awakening seemed to him lukewarm. The fire represented "the Smoke of the Torments of . . . the Authors" in hell. The following day, he held a classic bonfire of the vanities, encouraging his people to bring velvet, lace, or other fripperies to be destroyed. He himself added a pair of "plush Breeches" to the pile. That was the last straw. New Yorkers' sense of the absurd was lively even then: one of those present snatched them off the pile and gave them back to him, lest he be "obliged to strutt about bare-arsed."[28] Ridicule cascaded in on him, and he became anti-revivalists' favorite icon of ludicrous excess. The bubble was burst.

Anti-revivalism, after all, was much more than establishment self-interest. We should not forget how frightening *disorder* was in all premodern societies, where policing scarcely existed and social peace essentially rested on consensus. And these events could arouse ridicule as well as fear. Groaning, convulsions, roaring, and fainting looked more like lunacy than the Holy Spirit's work. Some explained that the brains of enthusiasts were choked with vapors rising from hot black bile. Others diagnosed conspiracy and manipulation. A preacher might use exaggerated voice and gesture to provoke the "weak Women" present to cry out. Then "the Shrieks catch from one to another till a great Part of the Congregation is affected. . . . Some . . . cry out themselves, on purpose to move others and bring forward a general Scream."[29]

What made revivalism truly offensive was its dependence on religious experience. For the old tribunes of Protestant Orthodoxy, Pietist claims were simply inadmissible. God had decreed an orderly church consisting of teachers and pupils: "the former govern by divine right, the latter obey."[30] Citing religious experience to challenge established practices was like trying to refute a mathematical theorem by claiming that it feels wrong. It was commonplace to claim that once the madness had passed, nothing would change, and supposed converts would quietly revert to their former sins. Meanwhile, the structures of Orthodox Protestantism would endure, and the route to salvation remain as rigorous and institutionally prescribed as ever.

By the mid-1740s, it was clear that this was wishful thinking. Evangelicalism was not going away. What was needed was a means of giving its energy and insights a sound theological base and durable institutional expression. The trail was blazed by Jonathan Edwards. In a famous 1741 sermon, Edwards considered the accusation that all the visions, fainting, and cries were merely natural phenomena. Of course they were, he answered: natural and also rational. This is what human beings do when they suddenly realize they are in terrible danger. It is those who stand on the brink of hell *without* terror who are irrational. As to the visions and voices, yes, very often these are simply natural actions of the imagination, but the fact "that Persons have many Impressions on their Imaginations, don't prove that they have nothing else."[31]

In other words, none of these manifestations proved anything about whether or not the Holy Spirit was truly at work in the revivals. The proof, he insisted, had to be paid in orthodox Protestant currency:

sober and enduring conversions, regenerate lives, honest affirmations of Reformed doctrine, quiet obedience to lawful authority. What Edwards bought with that transaction was legitimacy. If the revivals' dramatic experiences did indeed renew the Protestant churches in that way, then who could gainsay them?

This is how, unexpectedly, the Protestants who had been so embattled in the seventeenth century found themselves in the vanguard of the modern world a few decades later. The evangelicals' appeal to *experience* was very modish. In the age of rationalist, experimental progressivism we call the Enlightenment, old orthodoxies were being interrogated with new knowledge, and established authorities overturned by observed evidence. The evangelicals' achievement was to place themselves on the side of the new. From the social programs of Francke's Halle to Wesley's writings on electricity, these were children of the Enlightenment. Edwards even unwittingly gave his life to science: he was killed by a pioneering form of vaccination, not yet properly safe. It was of a piece with their experiential religion, which was, as Calvin had said of the Bible's authority, self-authenticating. The new experimental scientists appealed to what they had seen with their own eyes. Evangelicals appealed to what they had felt in their own hearts.

And so evangelical Protestantism became mainstream. Awakenings became a part of the rhythm of Protestant life. State power over Protestant churches was permanently weakened. When the new American republic was founded in the 1770s, deistic skeptics and pious Protestants united in opposing state-sponsored religion. Ministerial hierarchies survived, but ever more aware of their dependence on the consent and the money of their people. Protestants remained patriarchal, but learned to look to women and to children for examples of active godliness.

The result was a noisy, turbulent, and creative culture, without much respect for traditional hierarchies and identities. To focus on that social consequence is, however, to miss the point. The pietistic-evangelical movement was not a social revolution but a rediscovery of Protestantism's first love. It is no accident that this was a great age of hymn writing. The experiences that the evangelicals were trying to share lent themselves better to poetry than to treatises. Take a hymn originally written in Welsh by Ann Griffiths (1776–1805):

Earth cannot, with all its trinkets,
Slake my longings at this hour;
They were captured, they were widened,
When my Jesus showed his power.
None but he can now content me,
He, the Incomprehensible;
O to gaze upon his Person,
God in man made visible.32

This is about *desire:* the craving for God that is at the heart of Protestantism's great love affair. Like all great loves, it is a desire that the believer seeks to sharpen, not to satiate. Griffiths's meager, earthly desires are not only *captured* by Jesus; they are *widened,* giving her a breadth of longing beyond anything she previously knew to be possible.

The sentiment would have been shared by the first generation of reformers, to say nothing of their ancient and medieval predecessors, and by the English Puritans and the German Lutheran mystics. It is shared around the world by Protestants of all kinds today. It was on this wave of agonized, enraptured desire that Protestantism was borne into the modern world.

CHAPTER 8

Slaves to Christ

He that is called in the Lord, being a servant, is the Lord's freeman: likewise also he that is called, being free, is Christ's servant.

—I CORINTHIANS 7:22

In late 1596, a Dutch privateer brought a captured Portuguese ship into the port of Middelburg in order to sell its cargo: 130 African men and women. They had been destined for the slave markets of Brazil, and now they were spoils of war. To the landlubbers of Middelburg, however, they looked like human beings. The provincial authorities ruled that they should "be restored to their natural liberty." And so, apparently, they were, although what happened to them for the rest of that cold Dutch winter is a mystery.[1] The following year, Middelburg adopted a policy that soon spread to the rest of the Netherlands: any slave who steps onto Dutch soil is, at that moment, freed.

Yet from the 1630s onward, Dutch traders delivered some 460,000 enslaved Africans to the New World. A further 100,000 died aboard Dutch slave ships. There is no knowing how many were killed in Africa resisting capture. And the Dutch were only supporting players in a horror whose scale is almost beyond grasping. Across four centuries, European slave traders shipped around twelve million people across the Atlantic. The largest share was carried by another Protestant power, Great Britain. Ten to fifteen percent of these people died en route. The same or more died within a year of arrival. The survivors, and any children they might have, were faced with perpetual enslavement.

It is worth being clear what *slavery* actually meant. Irrevocable abduction from home and family. A voyage of incalculable horror, chained

in the dark aboard tiny, heaving ships, packed in with hundreds of naked strangers, living, dying, and dead. If you survived that, you faced
the prospect of being worked to death. Slaves sometimes worked the
sugar boilers for twenty-four hours or more at a stretch. Any relationships you might form would be fleeting; slaveholders could and did
separate couples at will and normally separated parents and children.
Enslaved women were routinely raped. Resistance of any kind was met
with breathtaking, exemplary brutality. After a slave rebellion in Suriname in 1790, adults deemed complicit were "hanged from the gibbet
by an Iron Hook through his ribs, until dead," or "bound to a stake and
roasted alive over a slow fire, while being tortured with glowing
Tongs." Children, by contrast, were "tied to a Cross, to be broken alive,
and their heads severed."[2] Nonlethal, but still appallingly violent, punishments were applied for lesser crimes, such as learning to read or
trying to discover the date of your own birth.

Those who escaped the worst of slavery's horrors did not escape the
horror of enslavement. Arbitrary subjection even to a kindly master
warped the soul. In 1849, an American slave named Henry Brown escaped to the free city of Philadelphia by having himself mailed there.
He spent twenty-seven hours squeezed into a box scarcely large enough
to hold him, silent and unmoving while the box was roughly handled
and stacked the wrong way up. It was a unique escape, but also a metaphor for every enslaved person's existence.

The Emergence of Protestant Slavery

By any measure, Atlantic slavery was one of humanity's greatest crimes.
It was also intimately connected with Protestantism. As the Middelburg incident shows, some Protestants concluded that slavery is wrong
from the beginning, a view that never disappeared and that eventually
brought about slavery's downfall. Equally, many Protestants accepted
and collaborated with slavery. Some even developed a biblical defense
of it as a Christian ideal.

Enslavement is almost ubiquitous in human history. What made
Atlantic slavery unique was its vast, industrial scale, its racial
determinism, and its absolute nature, in which slaves' legal status was
hardly distinct from that of animals. One of the few good things to

have emerged from it is the modern conviction that slavery in any form is unacceptable. That judgment would have seemed almost incomprehensible to most of our premodern forebears. Slavery was often compared to poverty: an inescapable fact of life, which individuals might escape but which could hardly be abolished. What better alternative was there for the destitute, prisoners of war, or conquered peoples? Even now, when slavery is formally illegal throughout the world, tens of millions of people endure some form of it. One of the things that human beings do is enslave other human beings.

The Bible is full of both matter-of-fact references to enslavement and regulations governing slavery. Christianity was formed in the Roman Empire, one of the most slave-based societies ever seen. The early Christians' response to this situation was characteristically spiritualizing and nonconfrontational. They insisted on the spiritual equality of all believers. St. Paul taught that in Christ the distinction between slave and free vanishes, and he spoke of being freed from spiritual enslavement. But this led him and others to conclude that physical slavery was of little consequence and that Christian slaves ought humbly to submit to the masters whom God has providentially given them. Indeed, Paul once sent a Christian runaway slave back to his Christian master, urging the master to receive and forgive the slave as a brother in Christ, but not suggesting that the man be freed.

In ancient times, for individual Christians to free their slaves was seen as a work of exceptional piety, but there was no shame in not doing so. Nor were Christian slave masters always models of loving kindness: so we learn from a fifth-century bronze neck collar unearthed in Sardinia, stamped with the words "I am the slave of archdeacon Felix: hold me so that I do not flee."[3]

The economic changes of the Western Middle Ages, however, saw Christian slaveholding morph into serfdom. After the plagues of the fourteenth century, even serfdom was eased. In England, the Netherlands, and elsewhere, it faded away entirely. There was of course still grinding poverty and exploitation, but the Protestant Reformation inherited something very unusual in human history: societies without slavery.

Already, however, an entirely new slavery was emerging. From the 1430s onward, first the Portuguese and then the Spanish were enslaving the populations of their burgeoning overseas empires, on the convenient principle that they were not Christians. The mainstays of this slave economy came to be West Africans, hardy against tropical disease and readily purchased or captured for shipping to the New World. When Protestants first met the Atlantic slave trade in the 1590s, it was already a large-scale enterprise nearly a century old. Only with hindsight can we see that it was still in its infancy.

Protestant theological opinion was generally against slavery. The most widely used Calvinist catechism condemned enslavement as "man-stealing." In 1618, the Synod of Dordt found the time alongside its decrees on predestination to consider slavery. Dordt stopped short of ruling that Christian slaves ought to be freed, for fear that this would deter Christian masters from baptizing their slaves—a dilemma that would bedevil Protestants for centuries. It did, however, insist that once baptized, slaves could not be sold and that they "ought to enjoy liberty."[4]

The Protestant powers did not deliberately set out to join the Atlantic slave economy. They drifted into it like a ship moving with the current. The Dutch trading companies' initial preference was to staff their planned colonies with freely employed indigenous laborers, not slaves. But the economic realities already established in the Americas were not easily defied. In 1627, a charter for a new Dutch colony in Guyana envisaged using African slaves. In 1630, when the Dutch conquered the Portuguese colony of Recife, on Brazil's eastern tip, they took over Recife's slave economy and began importing fresh slaves on their own account. Within twenty years, the Dutch were a major supplier of African slaves to the whole region.

The English, too, were initially resistant. One English pioneer of trade with Africa, when offered slaves for sale in the early 1620s, could still reply with pride that "we were a people, who did not deal in any such commodities, neither did we buy or sell one another, or any that had our own shape."[5] English colonists generally hoped to use indentured laborers: destitute or adventurous English men and women who freely bound themselves to unpaid labor for a fixed term of years, with a promise of land at the end. Yet indentured laborers were in short supply, had tiresome legal rights, insisted on tolerable working conditions, and died in the tropics at a prodigious rate. Meanwhile, Spanish and Portuguese slavers had temptingly cheap alternatives readily available for purchase.

On Barbados, England's sugar island, indentured servants outnumbered slaves ten to one in the 1630s. But by the early 1650s, there were twenty thousand slaves on the island, a majority of the population. Even Providence Island, a self-consciously Puritan English colony off the coast of modern Honduras, found itself importing slaves. The colony's London governors fulminated against slavery, and some idealistic colonists argued that no good Christian could own slaves, but the colony found it could not manage without them. By the time Spain captured the ill-fated colony in 1641, a majority of its people were African slaves. A further attempt to found a slaveless colony in the 1730s, in Georgia, only lasted a few months. The colonists reported that "a white man in these lands, if he cannot buy a slave, must work himself like a slave." It is, after all, very hard to compete with unpaid laborers who can be worked to death.[6] By the end of the seventeenth century, English ships were already taking a dominant place in the transatlantic slave trade.

A few voices opposed this, a stance usually taken at no personal cost. One statement, a Quaker manifesto of 1688 from Germantown, Pennsylvania, is famous as the world's first unreserved denunciation of slavery. But the petitioners' reasons included the fear that a slave economy was bad for free laborers whose wages would be depressed and good for the slave owners to whom the colonies' wealth accrued. Colonists were often also loath to introduce shiploads of black pagans into their new Jerusalems.

Some Protestants did find slavery simply repugnant. Take Samuel Sewall, the only one of the judges at the 1692 Salem witch trials to publicly repent of his actions. Perhaps that experience left him wary of neat justifications for brutality. In 1700, he was provoked to write a pithy pamphlet on the burgeoning slave business. "All Men," he insisted, "have equal Right unto Liberty. . . . Originally, and Naturally, there is no such thing as Slavery." Man-stealing, he warned, is a capital crime. In England, John Wesley was similarly categorical: "Liberty is the right of every human creature as soon as he breathes the vital air." His warning to slaveholders was stark: "The blood of thy brother crieth against thee from the earth."[7]

For the time being, these were isolated voices. Few other Methodists followed Wesley. The most consistent early Protestant opponents of slavery were Quakers, with their radical doctrine of human brotherhood. Even among Quakers, however, only cranks harped on the issue. Take Benjamin Lay, an Essex Quaker troublemaker who moved to Pennsylvania in the 1730s. Lay cut a distinctive figure: four feet seven inches tall, dressed in clothes of his own making, never wearing leather, a strict vegetarian, opposed to capital punishment, alcohol, tobacco, tea, and, above all, slavery. Once he burst into a Quaker meeting dressed as a soldier, declared that slaveholding was tantamount to murder, and stabbed his Bible with a sword. The Bible dramatically spurted red; he had hidden a bladder of juice between its pages. Lay's moral clarity is admirable, but we can appreciate that his neighbors might have sniggered rather than cheered.[8]

To most mainstream Protestants, this was naive. Better to work with and improve slavery than to rail pointlessly against it. Perhaps it was even a good thing. Was not rescuing Africans from the horrors of their native continent and bringing them to orderly New World plantations a kind of liberation? Some slaveholders sincerely believed this, priding themselves on their paternalistic care and on the affection that they believed their slaves had for them. They compared their slaves' happy, childlike simplicity with the desperate plight of the free and destitute poor in England's cities. Because no slave could set foot in England, it was an argument no slave could answer. Not that slaves were foolish enough to try to answer their masters' arguments.

Living with Slavery

Not all of slavery's defenders were so self-interested. In 1742, a book in defense of slavery by Jacobus Elisa Johannes Capitein, a newly ordained minister in the Dutch church, became a bestseller, running through five Latin and Dutch editions within a year. The book's argument is succinct and eloquent, but its unique selling point was its author's story. For Capitein was African by birth and had been enslaved as a child. The Dutchman who bought him and gave him the name Capitein recognized his quick mind and at the age of nine sent him to the Netherlands to be educated, freeing him in the process. He eventually spent five years at Leiden University. From the beginning, his ambition was to take the Protestant Gospel back to his native land as a missionary.

Capitein, the first black African ever to be ordained a Protestant minister, was everything that Europe's Protestant establishments hoped for from their empires. This was how Christian civilization would spread into heathen darkness. In 1742, he was sent to Elmina, in modern Ghana. Of the 240 employees of the Dutch West India Company stationed there, only the governor had a higher salary. The Netherlands cheered him on his way. A friend published a celebratory poem: "His skin is black / but his soul is white, since Jesus himself prays for him. . . . / [W]ith him, the Africans, once whitened, will always honor the Lamb."[9] It was kindly meant.

In reality, Capitein found himself resented by his new colleagues in Elmina. He managed to found a school, which within a few months had more than forty children, but his plan to create a Pietist-style orphanage was stymied. His attempt to translate Christian texts into the local vernacular was opposed by the church back in Amsterdam, which feared doctrines might be distorted. He tried to marry a local woman and was forbidden. In 1745, in frustration, he tried to resign but was forbidden. When he died in 1747, aged only thirty, his school died with him. The experiment had failed, and the Dutch ordained no more Africans.

The argument with which Capitein defended slavery was fairly routine. Like Luther before him, he distinguished "between freedom of the spirit and freedom of the body. . . . The New Covenant demands only *spiritual* freedom in order that we can worship God, not necessarily *external* freedom." What stands out from his book is his avowed purpose in advancing this argument. The book arose, he insisted, from his determination to preach the Gospel to the heathen. A key obstacle to this was "that some Christians fear that through the evangelic freedom slavery will disappear entirely from those colonies which Christians own, to the great detriment of the overseers of those colonies."[10] If he reassured slaveholders that they truly owned men's and women's bodies, perhaps preachers would have a chance to save their souls.

It caught the mood of the moment. The need to Christianize slaves was becoming a consensus, but like most Protestant missionary schemes it was more popular in Europe than on the front line. Ministers in the colonies, caught between frighteningly alien enslaved people and the planter class's entrenched prejudices, generally put converting slaves at the bottom of their priorities. In 1725, when the London-based missionary agency the Society for the Propagation of the Gospel (SPG)

ordered its missionaries to instruct and baptize the slaves they themselves owned, its impractical metropolitan idealism produced howls of
protest. The SPG itself owned a slave plantation on Barbados, but initial
hopes to turn it into a model of paternalistic Christian slaveholding
quickly withered. For a time, slaves there were even branded with the
word SOCIETY, so that runaways could be returned.[11]

Those who did earnestly attempt conversion found not only that
slaves were often unenthusiastic about adopting their captors' religion
but that slaveholders were openly hostile. They feared that Christian
slaves might refuse to work on Sundays, demanding to attend church.
Worse, if slaves could contract Christian marriages, it would be difficult
to split up families for sale. Christian slaves might even discover notions of spiritual equality, inviting slaveholders' perennial nightmare:
rebellion. It did not help that the most assiduous missionaries came
from groups like the Moravians and Quakers, whom many Europeans
saw as seditious anyway. It was easy to conclude that such missionaries
were spreading a "Fanatic's spirit of Obstinacy, against all Laws and
Government," and would end by persuading slaves, "out of pure Conscience, to murder their Masters."[12] In 1681, Barbados's rulers voted to
ban any attempt to Christianize the island's slaves.

One persistent worry was that slaves would be freed by being baptized. In 1656, Elizabeth Key, born a slave in Virginia, successfully sued
for her freedom on these grounds. Everywhere, laws were rapidly
changed to close off this avenue, but the laws are easier to change than
cultures, fears, or rumors. It was not uncommon for converted slaves—
especially house slaves, personally intimate with their owners—to be
freed, perhaps on their owners' deaths. Others followed Dordt in arguing
that even if Christian slaves need not be freed, they should not be sold.

For all these reasons, slaveholders tended to oppose missionary
work, often with preemptive violence. In 1723, a group of Virginia
slaves who petitioned the archbishop of Canterbury for preachers to be
sent to them did so anonymously: "If they knew that we have sent
home to your honor, we should go near to swing upon the gallows
tree."[13] As we saw in the previous chapter, the Moravian missionaries
on St. Thomas in the 1730s discovered that such threats were not idle.
One of the missionaries was even beaten to death. As for the slave converts, one was chained to the ground "until he promised that he would

learn nothing more from the brethren about Christianity." Another convert, Abraham, was attacked on the road one night, tied up, viciously beaten, and then dumped at the Moravians' church. With steely, nonviolent defiance, Abraham sent the ropes back to his attackers by name, apologizing for the damage their property had suffered while on his person.[14]

Like Capitein, most would-be Protestant missionaries dealt with this hostility by arguing that converting slaves was actually in their owners' best interests. Christian slaves would be loyal, honest, and hardworking. The more passionately Protestants believed in slaves' spiritual equality, the more earnestly they affirmed the legitimacy of slavery. The Moravian mission to St. Thomas was saved, in part, by Count Zinzendorf's sermon to slave converts in 1739, in which he told "kings, masters, servants, and slaves" that "everyone must gladly endure the state into which God has placed him."[15] One early critic of Virginia slavery felt the need to insist that Christianity "establisheth the Authority of Masters, over their Servants and Slaves, in as high a measure, as even themselves could have prescribed," and to deny the pernicious rumor that baptized slaves should be freed.[16] Such ministers could only buy their own freedom to preach by trading away slaves' hopes for liberty.

This was not mere cowardice. In 1676, an English Quaker wrote an impassioned appeal to a slaveholder she had met in Barbados on behalf of the people "whom thou callst thy Slaves." She begged not that the slaves should be freed but that they should be free to worship. Then, she promised, "the Lord God Almighty will set them Free in a way that thou knowest not, for there is none set Free but in Christ Jesus. . . . All other Freedom will prove but a Bondage."[17] Could any serious Protestant, believing that the soul's fate matters more than the body's, disagree? Some slaves were drawn to the missionaries' preaching in the belief or hope that it would ease their captivity. The missionaries, wary of being used in this way, insisted firmly that they offered something different and better. If slaves converted, their bodies would still be enslaved. But, asked the missionaries, "why should you be Men's Slaves and Satan's too?"[18] The option of not being slaves at all was not on offer.

These arguments did not persuade slaveholders. They not only feared the prospect of Christianizing their chattels; many of them loathed it. Slaves in the Atlantic world were of course predominantly black Africans. Atlantic slavery and racial prejudice blended to produce a uniquely poisonous brew. Protestantism's role in this is as ambivalent as ever.

The Bible, most Protestants agreed, clearly teaches that all humanity descends from a single stock. Africans, and indeed Native Americans, were as human as anyone else. As so often with principled egalitarianism, this matter was theorized in the abstract and then qualified by those with firsthand experience. Slaveholders had obvious motives for denying that their slaves were human; it was the only truly effective way of sidestepping all of slavery's moral problems. When a slaveholder challenged a Baptist missionary in Jamaica to give Communion to his horse—or a pious Barbadian slaveholder told her minister that he "might as well Baptize a Puppy, as a certain young *Negro*"—they were not joking. Slaveholders had, in their own minds, successfully dehumanized their slaves.[19] On St. Thomas, slaves were told "that Negroes must not be saved and that a baptized Negro is no more than kindling wood for the flames of hell." One South Carolina slaveholder asked, with almost disarming honesty, "Is it possible that any of my slaves could go to Heaven, & I must see them there?" How they might feel about seeing *him* there would not have occurred to him.[20]

Such views were widespread but theologically indefensible, and anyone who thought about it knew it. Phillis Wheatley, a Massachusetts slave girl and Protestant convert who became a published poet shortly before she was freed, put it this way in 1773:

> Some view our sable race with scornful eye,
> "Their color is a diabolic die."
> Remember, Christians, Negroes, black as Cain,
> May be refin'd, and join th'angelic train.[21]

The point was unanswerable, yet the scorn she described was all too real. Readers who had to concede she was right about salvation could still ask whether Africans were an inferior variety of human.

The Bible did not have much comfort to offer these racist speculations—aside from one deeply peculiar story. Genesis 9 describes how Noah invented wine, became drunk, and was accidentally seen naked and paralytic by his son Ham. When he woke, soreheaded, Noah cursed not Ham himself but Ham's son Canaan, condemning him to slavery. This weird tale had long since been used as an awkward proof text for enslaving Africans, the supposed descendants of Ham. We may doubt whether it ever truly persuaded anyone. It rarely features in serious attempts to defend African slavery, except as a throwaway debating point. It could, however, help quiet slaveholders' consciences, should they stir. It also provided a story that slaves themselves could be told: God had not made all humanity equal but had decreed that they and their descendants should forever be enslaved.

The real value of the curse of Ham was not to convince anyone that Africans *should* be enslaved but to explain the fact that they *were*. It made sense of a puzzling "fact" on which most European observers agreed: African slaves' subhuman nature. It was a truism that Africans were by nature "cowardly and cruel . . . prone to revenge . . . libidinous, deceitful, false and rude."[22] Even Europeans who cherished abstract notions of common humanity found their beliefs challenged when they met people who had been systematically dehumanized. William Knox, a slaveholder and an outspoken advocate of converting slaves, pondered at length on the problem of "the dull stupidity of the Negroe":

> Whether the Creator originally formed these black people a little lower than other men, or that they have lost their intellectual powers through disuse, I will not assume the province of determining; but certain it is that a new Negroe (as those lately imported from Africa are called) is a complete definition of indolent stupidity.[23]

A more fashionable and optimistic alternative was to see Africans as a childish race, capable one day of attaining full European maturity. The SPG's annual report in 1757 concluded that Africans "must be reduced from their Barbarity, I had almost said Brutality, and be made Men, that is rational considerate Creatures, before they will become good Christians."[24] Until that far-off day, enslavement was perfectly justified.

Only slowly did some Europeans begin to wonder if slavery was the cause, not the consequence, of slaves' degradation. It began to be apparent that some Africans could be as civilized as any European. As British merchants began to trade *with* Africans as well as *in* them, they found that Africans could be estimable business partners. Some were even invited to London for a charm offensive. In the American Revolutionary War of 1775–83, slaves fought with honor on both sides. Most were promised, and many received, their freedom in return for their service. George Washington commanded a racially integrated army, which no American general would do again until the mid-twentieth century. Perhaps Africans were more human than they appeared?

Yet if slavery itself made slaves unfit for freedom, surely it was irresponsible simply to set them free? William Wilberforce, whose commitment to the antislavery cause is undoubted, balked at the notion of immediate emancipation. "Our poor degraded Negro Slaves are as yet incapable" of enjoying freedom, he lamented in the year Britain's slave trade was abolished. "To grant it to them immediately, would be to insure not only their masters' ruin, but their own."[25] Slavery should be ended the moment slaves were ready for freedom, but not before.

Unsurprisingly, black commentators had a different view. For Capitein's generation, working with the slave system was unavoidable. Not so for their successors. Philip Quaque, like Capitein before him, was sent from Cape Coast, in modern Ghana, to London for an education in 1754, aged thirteen. In 1765, he became the first African to be ordained in the Church of England, and he returned to Cape Coast as a missionary. His career was longer than Capitein's but no happier. Unlike Capitein, he openly recognized the impossibility of being a missionary in a slave-trading station. "The vicious practice of purchasing flesh and blood like oxens in market places," he wrote, drove out all religion. The slave trade debased Europeans' morals, quite apart from what it did to "my poor abject Countrymen . . . whom you without the Bowels of Christian Love and Pity, hold in cruel Bondage." He would become a vital informant for the British abolitionists' effort to expose the cruelties of the slave trade.[26] Earlier missionaries had concluded that Africans could not be converted until they were first civilized. Quaque helped his age to conclude that Africans could not be converted until they were free.

The most incisive commentator of all arose in the following century. Frederick Douglass was born a slave in Maryland in 1818 and escaped to America's free North in 1838 to become the age's shrewdest and most searing critic of slavery and racism. Douglass demonstrated not merely that enslavement is dehumanizing but that American slavery was systematically designed to brutalize. Even slaves' supposed privileges played their part. On the traditional slave holidays between Christmas and New Year's, when slaves were actively encouraged to drink eye-watering quantities of cheap rum, Douglass observed, "their object seems to be, to disgust their slaves with freedom, by plunging them into the lowest depths of dissipation." Likewise, slaves who stole food were sometimes force-fed until they vomited. When Douglass illegally taught fellow slaves to read, "it was necessary to keep our religious masters . . . unacquainted with the fact, that, instead of spending the Sabbath in wrestling, boxing, and drinking whisky, we were trying to learn how to read the will of God."[27] Brutalization was not an accident but deliberate policy. It was how slavery was justified in the eyes of a white population that badly wanted to believe that Africans were not quite or not yet fully human.

The Road to Abolition

In the last quarter of the eighteenth century, the consensus that slavery had to be lived with was disrupted by an emerging conviction that slavery in general and the transatlantic slave trade in particular were intolerable evils that must be abolished.

This conviction spread unevenly through the Protestant world. In 1791, French Quakers urged their new revolutionary rulers to abolish slavery—to no avail, for all their boasted devotion to the "Rights of Man." The Netherlands, by contrast, preserved slavery until 1863, longer than any other European power. It is Denmark, whose slave economy was modest, that has the honor of being the first state actually to outlaw the transatlantic slave trade, in 1792. That was the personal initiative of Count Ernst Schimmelmann, the Danish minister of finance, a slaveholder who had been moved by the piety of his slaves and who hoped that ending the supply of fresh slaves would force masters to treat their slaves better. The 1792 law, however, allowed the trade to continue for a further ten years as a transitional measure. Danish slaveholders spent the next decade stockpiling, driving up both the number of captives and their prices to record levels.

In the main, however, abolitionism was an English-speaking drama. First British Quakers and Methodists and then some American Methodists, Baptists, and Presbyterians began to insist that enslavement was wrong, that ministers and even laypeople ought not to own slaves, and that slavery itself ought to be abolished. Laws were changing. A 1772 lawsuit introduced the long-standing Dutch legal doctrine into England: any slave setting foot on the mother country's soil was immediately freed. Massachusetts went the same way in 1783. In 1777, the (briefly) independent republic of Vermont adopted the world's first constitution that outlawed slavery. Back in Britain, a campaign to prohibit the slave trade materialized as if from nowhere in 1787. A petitioning effort against the trade swept the country, gathering 1.5 million signatures between 1787 and 1791, from a population of some 12 million. Nothing like this had ever happened before.

Britain's abolitionists almost succeeded in that first headlong rush. A bill to abolish the British slave trade passed the House of Commons by 230 to 85 in 1792, only to fall in the House of Lords. That turned out to be a high-water mark. The fear and violence spiraling around the French Revolution made it a bad time for an idealistic campaign about human equality. A violent slave rebellion in the French colony of Saint-Domingue (modern Haiti) made abolitionism look dangerously naive. British abolitionists knuckled down to a further fifteen years of campaigning, building and sustaining a mass movement alongside tortuous parliamentary maneuvering. Finally, in 1807, for a brief moment, the mass movement, Britain's military interests, and the shifting party-political forces all aligned, and the act was passed. Britain banned a huge, lucrative trade that was one of the principal props of its own empire.

How did this happen? It is sometimes portrayed as a moment of heroic national virtue, but the wealth generated by the slave trade was concentrated in relatively few hands. Most British people and parliamentarians had no personal stake in slavery, beyond access to cheap sugar and tobacco. And there were secular principles in play. Political philosophers worried that slavery endangered British liberties, and a new breed of economists argued that wage labor was more efficient than slavery.

Yet abolitionism was a religious movement first and last. The

Protestant argument against the slave trade was simple. Even if the Bible had not specifically condemned "man-stealing," Christ's so-called Golden Rule—"do unto others as you would have them do unto you"— could hardly justify kidnapping people, shipping them across the world in hellish conditions, and selling them into perpetual slavery. Even if you accepted slavery itself, it was almost impossible to construct a Christian defense of the slave *trade,* and hardly anyone tried. Even so, earlier Protestant generations had not been moved to abolitionism, and Protestants beyond the English-speaking world were mostly untouched by it. Why this sudden localized change of heart?

Abolitionism's origins as a public movement lay in the global Anglo-French conflict of 1754–63, known in America as the French and Indian War. Under attack, American Protestants asked themselves for what national sins they were being judged: Slavery, perhaps? That danger passed, but the worry did not. As colonists began to fear British oppression more than French, slavery resurfaced as an explanation for the judgment that was evidently being visited on them. During the Revolutionary War of 1775–83, American abolitionism started to win real victories. Wiping the new nation's slate clean of the guilt of slavery was not only an opportunity; it was an urgent obligation.[28]

In the event, slaveholding interests in the new United States were too strong. After fierce debates, the Constitution ratified in 1787–88 froze the unfinished battle against slavery. In Britain, American independence had the opposite effect. With the American colonies gone, Britain's slaveholding lobby was badly weakened. The shock of unimagined defeat again posed the question: For what sin are we being punished? The year Britain finally conceded American independence, 1783, was also the year of a grotesque lawsuit. The crew of a British slave ship, the *Zong,* had deliberately drowned 131 men and women from their cargo hold in order to make an insurance claim. The case was about insurance fraud, not mass murder, and in the end the court ordered the insurers to pay, but abolitionist publicists used the scandal to confront the British public with what "slavery," that distant, abstract word, really meant. Anthony Benezet, a longtime Quaker abolitionist, seized the moment. In the same year, he mobilized the first mass petition against the trade and had eleven thousand copies of his pamphlet *The Case of Our Fellow-Creatures, the Oppressed Africans* printed and circulated. The line from there to the petitions of 1787 and William Wilberforce's parliamentary campaign is a straight one.

Benezet, Wilberforce, and the other leading abolitionists emphasized the trade's cruelty, but like all Protestants they were more concerned with spiritual than material evils. Many evangelicals, including Wilberforce, had concluded that slavery itself was a block to conversion. How could those who were denied every other freedom possibly choose freely to follow Christ? What made this urgent, however, was their conviction that their own souls were in graver peril than the slaves'. The slave trade was a national sin, and defeat in the American war was only a warning of worse punishments to come. England's slaving ports could, Wilberforce warned, expect the judgment once visited by God on the ancient slaving cities of Tyre and Sidon. Blood was crying out from the ground for justice. Josiah Wedgwood's famous abolitionist miniature, "Am I Not a Man and a Brother?," posed a question that could only have one answer, and to answer it was to speak judgment on yourself and be stirred to action. And ordinary English Protestants acted, in enormous numbers. They signed petitions, bought periodicals, and boycotted sugar and other slave-grown produce: "If we purchase the commodity, we participate in the crime."[29] For a growing swath of the British public, men and women who had rarely seen a black face, this far-off crime was becoming intolerable. And so, eventually, it ended.

The journey from Britain's abolition of the slave trade to the abolition of slavery itself was agonizingly slow, but fast enough to leave businessmen all over the Atlantic bewildered by this sudden moral spasm. The United States banned the import of slaves in the same year, 1807. Britain, dominant in Europe after the defeat of Napoleon in 1815, progressively strong-armed other European powers into banning the trade. A large-scale illicit slave trade continued for much of the century: more than 2.5 million people were shipped from Africa after 1807, mostly on Portuguese, Spanish, or American ships. The British navy, with a convert's zeal, harassed traders, blockaded and closed ports, and freed some 160,000 slaves from ships it intercepted. Some of this was flagrantly illegal, but Britannia ruled the waves, and few traders had the stomach to take their cases to a London court.[30]

Slavery remained legal in Britain's colonies until the 1830s. Most

trade abolitionists assumed it would simply die out and consoled themselves that in the meantime slaveholders would need to take better care
of their now-irreplaceable assets. Any thoughts of immediate emancipation posed formidable problems. Who would compensate slaveholders
for the loss of their "property"? Worse, what would be done with all
those free Africans? Many abolitionists, in a scheme as impractical as it
was racist, favored transporting freed slaves "back" to Africa. This did
give rise to two troubled resettlement colonies, Britain's Sierra Leone
and the United States' Liberia, but it chiefly served to delay any serious
effort to end slavery. The hope instead was gradually to erode slavery's
worst abuses. The title of a new antislavery society formed in Britain in
1823 catches the mood: the Society for the Mitigation and Gradual Abolition of Slavery.

This time the pace was forced by Methodist, Baptist, and Anglican
missionaries, who were at last beginning to build genuine communities
in the Caribbean. In 1823, a crisis blew up on the British island of Demerara, fanned by optimistic rumors about reforms coming from London. The rebellion began as a studiedly nonviolent protest to demand
certain limited freedoms. The participants met in an Anglican mission-
chapel and swore an oath on the Bible. The Anglican missionary John
Smith celebrated Communion for them, telling them that "we must
end in Christ, whether dead or alive": a recognition that slave protests,
however nonviolent, did not go unpunished. He was right. About 250
slaves were massacred or judicially murdered during and after the rising. Smith, too, was condemned, and died in prison before a royal par-
don could reach him. The death of the "Demerara Martyr," far more
than those of the slaves, caused a storm in England. Britain's pious political classes did not like slaveholders who murdered missionaries.
Slavery's defenders were becoming isolated.[31]

The drama replayed itself on a larger scale in Jamaica in 1832, in the
biggest slave rising Britain ever faced. A Baptist deacon and slave named
Samuel Sharpe led many of his congregation in a general strike at Christmas 1831. The so-called "Baptist War" that followed was in fact, as Sharpe
urged, astonishingly peaceful, although some sixty thousand slaves took
part. Again, restraint would not save them from vicious reprisals. Sharpe
spent his brief time in prison preaching to his fellow inmates. He told a
missionary friend that "he learned from his Bible, that the whites had no

more right to hold black people in slavery, than black people had to make white people slaves," and declared, "I would rather die upon yonder gallows than live in slavery." On May 23, 1832, he did.[32]

Sharpe is now a Jamaican national hero, but again, what outraged the British public was the reprisals against white missionaries. One was tarred and feathered by a white mob. His still-soiled neckerchief was solemnly taken home and exhibited, to much fascinated horror. In the same year, 1832, a bitter constitutional struggle in Britain led to the election of a new Parliament on a broadened franchise less beholden to special interests. Among its first items of business was ending slavery altogether.

British emancipation arrived stumbling and unheroic. The 1833 act subjected freed slaves to a transitional period of unpaid "apprenticeship," a plan that was cut short in 1838 when it was manifestly not working. Slaveholders were also compensated handsomely for their financial loss. It is a sorry fact of nineteenth-century emancipations that, in every jurisdiction except the United States, slaveholders were financially compensated. That compensation has never been returned, and no systematic reparations were or have ever been given to those who had actually been enslaved or their descendants. All they received was freedom, which often meant the freedom to be near-destitute plantation laborers. Still, freedom it was and is.

The Gospel of Slavery

Slavery in the southern United States differed from the Caribbean model in several ways. It did not depend on new imports; this was the only place in the Americas where slaves' birthrate exceeded their death rate, thanks to a milder climate and to an agricultural economy centered on tobacco rather than sugar. Slavery's legal status was different; while Caribbean slavery was becoming subject to tighter legal restrictions, most slave states in the United States progressively closed down any routes by which slaves or their descendants might attain freedom or betterment, by, for example, banning any attempt to teach a slave to read. In the Deep South, it even became legally impossible to free a slave. The legal status of free African Americans was very tenuous— even in the North, where they were generally denied citizenship and most civil rights, but much more so in the South, where their very existence was seen as offensive and where they faced a constant danger of enslavement.

And unlike elsewhere in the New World, slavery in the United States was not dying out. The Caribbean sugar economy was crumbling, but the American South was discovering a new and lucrative use for slaves: the cultivation of cotton. Visionary southern slaveholders believed they were designing an alternative modern world, founded on enduring and perpetual enslavement. They also believed that this was a more truly Christian model than the one offered by the free North. Abolitionists were, to their astonishment, being challenged for the moral high ground.

The idea of a conscientious Christian argument for slavery now seems so ridiculous that it is worth dwelling on. Grossly self-serving as it was, in its day it had real power. Most Protestants had always believed that God had ordained a well-ordered hierarchical society in which everyone knew his or her place. Mixing America's emergent democracy with abolitionist idealism threatened anarchy. Martin Luther, surely, would have called the abolitionists fanatics. Southerners argued that the "free" wage slaves of the North's industrial slums, whom employers could exploit and discard at will, were far worse off than slaves laboring honestly in the open air, freed from responsibilities, whose benevolent masters were compelled by mere prudence to take a long-term interest in their welfare. Slavery, the argument ran, was a time-hallowed human institution, working with the grain of God-given human inequality and racial difference. It would endure when the North's naive industrial egalitarianism had long since consumed itself.

The slavers also had a compelling biblical case. The Bible never condemns slavery and implicitly condones it. Where abolitionists appealed to the Golden Rule, "do unto others as you would have them do unto you," their opponents impatiently explained that this meant treating others as you would wish to be treated *in their situation:* a father may still treat a child as a child, and a master may treat a slave as a slave. Where abolitionists condemned the reduction of human beings to property, slavery's defenders agreed. Slaves were not property but a sacred trust, people over whom their owners had certain (rather extensive) rights, and for whom they had equally extensive responsibilities.

Slave and slaveholder were bound together in a Christian household. If Abraham had bought slaves, if Paul had sent a runaway slave home, if Christ himself had never spoken a word against slavery, who were these upstart prophets to proclaim a new abolitionist gospel of their own invention?

Not that any of this bore much resemblance to the reality of American slavery. Even if we leave aside its racial basis, for which there was no serious biblical argument, the problems were legion. Slaves' almost total lack of legal status sat poorly with the claim that they were a sacred trust, to say nothing of the specific cruelties routinely visited on them. Their marriages had no status in law, and families were very often broken up for sale. The laws against slave literacy were acutely embarrassing for Protestants, whose identity was founded on making the Bible available to all. But abolitionists who turned gratefully from general principles to these specifics found themselves in a quagmire. Southerners readily acknowledged that their system needed reform but claimed that this reform was being blocked by abolitionist agitation. If the abolitionists would only stop stirring discontent, the result would be a reformed, godly slavery, America's gift to the world.

Many antislavery white Protestants recognized the power of these arguments. They conceded that slavery could be tolerable in principle while maintaining that in practice it was deeply undesirable. So while they still pressed for reform and eventual emancipation, they admitted that the matter was debatable. In the American context, that meant admitting that each state might make its own rules. It also meant this was not a matter over which to break Christian fellowship. Southern Christians might be wrong to hold slaves, but they were still Christians. No major church in the United States, north or south, called for immediate abolition before the outbreak of the Civil War in 1861. The northern churches aimed to persuade their southern brethren to reform and ultimately to abolish slavery. Peremptory denunciations would not work.

A minority found this gradualism morally bankrupt. "Immediatist" abolitionism arose in the 1830s among Quakers and Unitarians energized by abolition in the British Empire. They were also galvanized by black American Protestants, who found it much easier to answer proslavery arguments than their white brethren. They focused not on textual niceties but on the evils clustering around slavery like maggots, and the few white Americans who were willing to listen to such testimonies found their worlds changed. William Lloyd Garrison, who became immediatism's vehement, polarizing standard-bearer, was converted by his encounters with African Americans who manifestly deserved respect as well as sympathy. And "converted" is the word. Garrison described a speech by the escaped slave Frederick Douglass as something like a revivalist meeting. "I shall never forget . . . the extraordinary emotion it excited in my own mind. . . . I never hated slavery so intensely as at that moment." Once Douglass had concluded, Garrison rose to ask the meeting if they would allow him to be sent back to slavery,

> law or no law, constitution or no constitution. The response was unanimous and in thunder-tones—"NO!" "Will you succor and protect him as a brother-man?" . . . "YES!" shouted the whole mass.[33]

Immediatism was not a coolly reasoned philosophy but a very Protestant moral awakening. The Gospel's power pierced the hearts of hardened sinners and left the world transformed.

For such converts, there could be no slow persuasion. To counsel patience, Garrison argued, was to "tell the mother to gradually extricate her babe from the fire into which it has fallen." He was not a politician, looking for practical solutions to complex problems, but a prophet, rousing his people from a death-like moral sleep to see the evil that surrounded them. Slavery was a sin, and all slaveholders, however individually benevolent, bore a terrible and immediate guilt. So, too, did northern moderates, slavery's "watchdogs," whose mealymouthed gradualism gave slavery moral cover. The Massachusetts Anti-slavery Society resolved in 1843 that "the sin of slaveholding . . . is the sum of all other sins" and that any church which refuses to treat it as such "is not a Church of Christ."[34]

For slavery's defenders, immediatism was an opportunity. They aimed, one said in 1851, "to push the Bible continually, to drive abolitionism to the wall, to compel it to assume an anti-Christian position."[35] They pointed out that Garrison and his allies embraced a series of other controversial stances, such as teetotalism, pacifism, and women's suffrage. Because none of these had precise biblical proofs, the immediatists rejected the notion of precise biblical proof. One Presbyterian abolitionist tried simply to sweep away pro-slavery biblical arguments:

> The whole Bible is opposed to slavery. The sacred volume is one grand scheme of benevolence—beams of love and mercy emanate from every page, while the voice of justice denounces the oppressor, and speaks his awful doom![36]

Stirring words, but what southerners heard was an implicit admission that the immediatists had no biblical case.

It was an old Protestant battle: the spirit of the Word against the letter of Scripture. Faced with southern exegetes' learned subtlety, self-taught black theologians condemned "scripturians" who would rather parse the text than meet God in their hearts.[37] Some abolitionist radicals were driven to the only truly logical position: if the Bible endorsed slavery, then the Bible must be wrong. As one Baptist ethicist put it, we know slavery is wrong, not because Scripture says so, but as "a matter of immediate moral consciousness." It is self-evident. Anyone who cannot see this, another immediatist argued, is "an incurable Idiot who cannot distinguish good from evil." But if this most pressing question was decided by moral intuition, then surely Scripture itself must be tested against "the oracle God places in the breast"? It was not far from there to the abolitionist minister who in 1860 preached that "slavery is not to be tried by the Bible, but the Bible by freedom."[38]

Some abolitionists, indeed, openly rejected Christianity. Garrison's newspaper carried articles with titles such as "The Bible, if Opposed to Self-Evident Truth, Is Self-Evident Falsehood," although Garrison himself never went quite so far. Frederick Douglass, whose anger with the religion that had justified slavery never mellowed, became profoundly alienated from organized Christianity. America's thriving black churches were, he feared, merely "strutting about in the old clothes of the masters." In particular, he deplored how Christianity made a virtue of suffering and patience, a doctrine calculated to keep slaves in their place.[39]

Most immediatists, however, reconciled their biblical faith with their political convictions. They suggested that the biblical regulations permitting slavery applied only in specific historical circumstances. They suggested that Christ and the apostles had stayed silent on the subject of slavery not because they condoned it but because they knew that an antislavery message would drown out the Gospel they had come to preach. Most daringly of all, they suggested that revelation was progressive. God had not yet shown the early church the full truth. Only now was Christendom ready to see that slavery is and must always be evil.

What tipped the balance between immediatism and gradualism was gradualism's self-evident failure. Southern slavery was neither dying nor being reformed. None of the schemes mooted to protect slaves' families from arbitrary division could actually have been put into practice in a functioning slave economy. As it became plainer that slavery was unreformable, its defenders simply became more strident. The northern Protestant establishments refused to break fellowship with slaveholders, but the slaveholders broke fellowship with them. When the southern Presbyterian, Methodist, and Baptist churches broke away in 1837, 1844, and 1845, respectively, in each case the decisive fact was the northerners' refusal to endorse slavery. In particular, northerners' qualms about ministers' owning slaves felt like an intolerable slur. A bitter political compromise in 1850, which legally committed northerners to send escaped slaves back, and an explosively controversial court case in 1857, which threatened to extend slavery deep into America's West, exposed gradualism as a fantasy.

The southern establishment felt its economy and "way of life" to be under siege by fools, fanatics, and barbarians, while the safeguards and rights it demanded seemed increasingly intrusive and unacceptable to the North. In 1860, the avowed abolitionist Abraham Lincoln was elected president, exclusively on northern votes. Most of the southern states promptly seceded from the United States. The North treated this as rebellion. The resulting war lasted from 1861 to 1865 and was fought with unforeseen savagery, leaving more than 600,000 dead.

So it turned out that the immediatists' warnings of wrath, judgment, and blood had been correct. When the war was almost over, Lincoln framed it as a divine judgment on a national sin. He prayed for the fighting to end but, echoing Garrison and the British abolitionists before him, added,

> If God wills that it continue until all the wealth piled by the bondsman's two hundred and fifty years of unrequited toil shall be sunk, and until every drop of blood drawn with the lash shall be paid by another drawn with the sword, as was said three thousand years ago, so still it must be said, "the judgments of the Lord are true and righteous altogether."

Instead, within weeks, it was over. The victorious North dictated peace terms. All slaves were freed, no compensation was paid to slaveholders, and all native-born persons were granted citizenship. The era of discrimination and segregation that would eventually follow was perhaps not much of an improvement, but no serious Protestant would ever defend slavery again.

Despite its many hypocrisies, the awful truth is that pro-slavery Protestantism was sincere and consistent. It is less a unique aberration than an example of Protestantism's protean adaptability. Southern society needed a religious justification for slavery, so Protestants provided it. There was no central religious authority who could tell them that they were wrong, and when their national churches expressed qualms, they simply walked away. Pro-slavery Protestantism did not lose the argument; it lost a war. That catastrophe was accepted by most of slavery's former religious defenders as divine judgment. The consensus came to be that they had failed to build a truly Christian slavery and had tolerated too many abuses. If some continued quietly to believe that slavery might sometimes be justified, they nevertheless accepted the reality that American slavery was gone.

Slavery's Lessons

Two lessons about Protestantism's history emerge from this ghastly saga.

First, its priorities. Pro-slavery Protestantism eventually became little more than a religious veneer for a political cause. Almost the same criticism could be made of Protestant abolitionism. Hard-liners on both sides abandoned the eighteenth-century missionaries' consensus that the Gospel matters more than slavery. But even in the midst of the crisis, the consensus persisted. The free African American revivalist preacher Zilpha Elaw certainly condemned slavery and occasionally attended abolitionist meetings, but her heart was elsewhere. In 1828, she met another preacher, himself a slave, who, she wrote disdainfully, "seemed to manifest an undue anxiety for his freedom." Although the Bible told slaves to be content with their condition, this man "anxiously sighed for liberty." Happily, his prayers were soon heard. "In the same week he was taken ill, and finally fell asleep in Jesus, departing to be 'where the wicked cease from troubling, and the weary are at rest.'"[40] This kind of attitude infuriated Frederick Douglass, who despaired at how promises of heaven were used to keep slaves quiescent. Yet if you believed, as Elaw did, that this life is a passing shadow and that humanity's only true happiness lies in God, how could temporal slavery or freedom compare with the momentous and eternal question of salvation or damnation?

This underlying logic persistently reasserted itself. Many abolitionists in the United States wanted missionaries working with Native Americans to denounce the slavery practiced by the Cherokee and the Choctaw. The missionaries themselves retorted that this would simply bring their mission to a swift end and proposed to treat slavery as they did polygamy, as a social wrong to be righted with forbearance. They did not defend slavery, but were ready to tolerate it for the sake of spreading the Gospel.

The same pattern resurfaced in Atlantic slavery's last redoubt, Brazil, where promises of abolition were repeatedly postponed, and slavery did not finally end until 1888. Brazil was in that era overwhelmingly Catholic, but not exclusively so; by 1888, it had sixty Protestant churches with a combined membership of some three thousand. As the nation wrestled with slavery, Protestant missionaries, who could have had a powerful tale to tell on the subject, kept a monk-like silence. Their Portuguese-language newspaper, produced from 1864 onward, scarcely touched on slavery, except in spiritual terms. An 1878 article titled "Are You Slaves or Free?" argued that true slavery was the oppression of

Catholic ritual and ceremony. Only in the mid-1880s did the newspaper finally acknowledge the rising abolitionist tide, urging "gentle responses and calm arguments on the topic."[41]

The missionaries' calling was to evangelize, not to emancipate. Many Protestants became extremely exercised about slavery, but just as their religion taught them that slavery was wrong (or right), it also taught them that the Gospel mattered more than any worldly issue. Those hoping to recruit Protestants as political allies have often found this insistence awkward, but it will not go away.

The second lesson is that abolitionism set some powerful precedents. The first battle, against the slave trade, was hard but not complex; Protestants slowly allowed themselves to notice a vast and all but indefensible atrocity and then repented for it. Nineteenth-century American abolitionists, however, faced a principled Christian defense of slavery. They needed not only to repent of a deeply ingrained sin but to denounce a long-standing error.

For many Christians, condemning previously held orthodoxies is very difficult. Churches that claim to define doctrine authoritatively cannot easily admit to making mistakes. For Protestants, however, it comes naturally. Even instinctively conservative Protestants know that being sinful means being fallible. They will tear up cherished interpretations of the Bible if they have to. And as the abolitionists' confrontation with the Bible shows—and as Protestantism's prophets have shown from Luther's time on—when the heart of the Gospel is at stake, Protestants will not even let the biblical text itself stand in their way.

In the great matter of slavery, Protestants performed this maneuver in full dress for the first time. Generations had worked with or even defended slavery. Yet ever since 1865, the doctrine that slavery is evil has become a fixed reference point on Protestantism's moral map, despite its shaky biblical basis. It is indicative of the flexibility Protestantism can show when it must. But it is also an important precedent. By God's grace, a long-tolerated practice had been exposed as a terrible evil. Who knew what other long-standing truths might suddenly have to be denounced as errors in the years to come?

CHAPTER 9

Protestantism's Wild West

Surely I come quickly. Amen. Even so, come, Lord Jesus.
—REVELATION 22:20

The world had not seen anything quite like the United States of America before. In 1776, it had the nerve to declare independence and union for a vast wilderness whose scarce two and a half million people were a kaleidoscope of languages, nationalities, and beliefs. Amazingly, as its population rose almost tenfold by the mid-nineteenth century, and its territory grew to span the continent, this phantasm of a country not only held together but became the richest society in human history. It also turned democracy, an idea that had been almost universally reviled for centuries, into a virtue. In 1828, Andrew Johnson, a future president, explained what he thought that meant:

> The voice of the people is the voice of God. . . . The democratic party . . . has undertaken the *political redemption of man,* and sooner or later the great work will be accomplished. In the political world it corresponds to that of Christianity in the moral.

The time was coming when that political redemption would be complete, when "the millennial morning has dawned and that the time has come when the lion and the lamb shall lie down together."[1]

As Johnson implied, America's democratic adventure and its religious adventure went hand in hand. The United States in the early to mid-nineteenth century saw one of Protestantism's great bursts of sectarian creativity, akin to Germany in the 1520s or England in the 1640s. It gave rise to major movements that have prospered down to the present and set the pattern for how Protestantism could thrive in a democratic age.

Big-Tent Protestantism

The new republic's governing elite was laced with deism and outright skepticism, and much of New England's old Puritan establishment was turning to rationalistic doctrines like Unitarianism. Meanwhile, the newly enfranchised mass population was going the other way. Like 1520s Germany and 1640s England, post-Revolutionary America saw a revolt of the uneducated against professional elites: lawyers, medics, and above all ministers. Self-taught men and women asserted themselves against the self-satisfied and self-serving priesthoods of knowledge. The Revolutionary spirit meant that traditional learning and expertise were not only disregarded but actively distrusted. Simplicity was valued over subtlety. Alarming as it might be, this attitude was and is authentically Protestant. It is the attitude of believers who know they must stand before God and who are confident that they can.

As America's population surged westward, the establishment churches of the East Coast, the Congregationalists and the Episcopalians, could not keep up. New waves of immigrants were reinforcing other Protestant denominations, such as Lutherans and Presbyterians, but the real growth was in the light-footed evangelical denominations who made the frontier their own: the Baptists and, above all, the Methodists, who by 1850 counted over a third of the republic's entire population as their adherents. Not that they were denominational monoliths. The Baptists and Methodists especially were competing families of churches. As well as the North-South split over slavery, they were divided by theology, by language, and above all by race. America's fast-growing population of black Protestants, slave and free alike, had by now largely split off from the white-led denominations that disdained them. Black churches mushroomed across the country, from stand-alone independent congregations to major denominations such as the African Methodist Episcopal Church, founded in 1816. The racial division in America's churches has remained stark ever since.

Much of America's population, however, had no formal church membership at all. They managed their own religion. It was said of

Scotch-Irish (Ulster Scots) settlers that when their crops failed, they could live off their catechisms. The printed page brought Christian community to scattered populations, as radio, television, and the Internet would in the future. By 1830, the United States had some six hundred religious magazines and newspapers. The old denominations were struggling to keep up with freelance itinerant preachers. In 1775, there were fewer than two thousand Christian ministers in the thirteen colonies, a number that had risen to almost forty thousand by 1845: a growth rate three times faster than that of the population.[2] A Second Great Awakening was said to have begun around 1800, but in truth the first one had never really ended. What changed was the shift to the new, more dynamic denominations, led by growth on the frontier, where respectability cut no ice. In this free market, revivalist preachers who could gather the greatest harvest would succeed. They shared and copied the most effective techniques—such as the trick of praying publicly for a single sinner in the crowd, by name and with juicy details.

To the elites back east, all this looked like ignorance and fanaticism. They knew what happened when you gathered a mass of lusty humanity for a weeklong revivalist meeting, and they assumed that "more souls were begot than saved."[3] "Religious insanity" was beginning to be a medical diagnosis. The revivalists' dramatic spiritual manifestations, from healings and prophecies to laughing, fainting, and "the jerks," ill became a rational age.

For frontier folk, these new forms of Christian life seemed modern and vital compared with the old denominations, obsessed with their dry theological quibbles. Frontier preachers often disowned any denomination, claiming with that characteristically Protestant blend of humility and arrogance simply to be Christians. Elias Smith, a Connecticut-born preacher and publicist, insisted that properly republican churches ought to be democratic, governed by the conscience and common sense of ordinary believers rather than by theologians' self-serving obscurantism. Many Americans, he lamented, were only half-free from their European fetters, "being in matters of religion still bound to a catechism, creed, covenant or a superstitious priest." The title of his newspaper, founded in 1808, invoked an idea as potent in religion as in politics: the *Herald of Gospel Liberty*.[4]

So many itinerant preachers joined Smith's anti-denominational movement, the Christian Connection, that it became a denomination too. Its aversion to any other fixed orthodoxies made it a Babel of competing views, divided over the Trinity, women's preaching, the validity of prophetic revelations, and old-fashioned personality clashes. In 1830, it merged with a parallel movement, the Disciples of Christ, another self-conscious attempt to forge a primitive, nondenominational Christianity, and eventually settled down to become an established minor player on America's ever more crowded religious stage.

Like Smith, most of those caught up in the Second Great Awakening remained more or less traditional in their doctrines even as they abandoned the traditional churches. As in every age of renewal, however, the potential for radicalism lurked just below the surface. The story of William Miller, for example, began as a very typical one. Massachusetts-born and meagerly educated, he moved to Vermont in 1803 at the age of twenty-one, discovered a public library, and gave himself an eager crash course in radical politics. Shaken out of his Baptist upbringing by scathing polemics against the Bible's "history of blood, tyranny and oppression," he became a deist. It was the spirit of the new republic.

Then, suddenly, the new republic needed more than philosophy. Miller went to fight for his country in the War of 1812 and took part in the bloody battle of Plattsburgh in September 1814. It was a life-changing experience. The Americans were outnumbered three to one by the British and yet emerged victorious. It was, for Miller, "the work of a mightier power than man." The slaughter moved him as much as the victory. "How grand, how noble, and yet how awful!" Trite deist optimism seemed inadequate in a world capable of such glory and horror. After a drawn-out crisis, he finally experienced a dramatic conversion. Stern Calvinism could explain what bland deism could not. In a dark world, "I saw Jesus as a friend, and my only help."

So far, so typical. But how could he reconcile this new conviction with his long-standing doubts about the Bible? It was no use asking a minister to set his worries at rest; Miller had all his age's prejudices against learned authority. So he set out to solve the problem himself: to "harmonize all those apparent contradictions [in the Bible] to my own satisfaction, or I will be a Deist still." He would rely on hard work, common sense, and simple faith. As a result, he did indeed quiet his doubts, but he also made a startling discovery.[5]

Like many Bible readers before him, he was drawn to the tantalizingly obscure prophecies of the books of Daniel and Revelation. It seemed to him that they laid out a map of human history, past and future. There was a long Christian tradition of reading those texts that way, and while it is unclear how well Miller knew that tradition, he certainly picked up the idea, dating back at least to the twelfth century, that when the text spoke of a "day," it in fact meant a year. What Miller brought to the problem was ingenuity, an eye for detail, and an almost scientific conviction that God's plan for the world is susceptible to numerical analysis. The pieces slowly fell into place. After many false leads and blind alleys, Miller eventually found several different calculations that led him, independently, to the same conclusion. Daniel 8:14 promises, "Unto two thousand and three hundred days; then shall the sanctuary be cleansed." If "days" mean years; if the "cleansing of the sanctuary" means Christ's return; and if (as Daniel 9:25 can be seen to imply) that 2,300-year period began with the order to rebuild Jerusalem in 457 B.C., then a simple calculation showed that Christ would return in glory in the year 1843.

We now think of such predictions as the business of cranks and fanatics, but Miller was no fool. The date rested not on one single calculation but on a complex, interlocking system of calculations, all of which could be made to point to 1843. It was bold but not self-evidently crazy. When skeptics quoted Christ's words—"of that day and the hour knoweth no man"—Miller readily agreed: he was predicting a year, not a day or hour. The idea that this world, so full of hectic, exciting, and terrifying novelties, was hurtling toward its end seemed almost self-evidently true. For millennia, prophetic excitement had been doused by the world-weary biblical principle that "there is no new thing under the sun." In this new democratic world, that plainly no longer applied. A careful, scientific analysis that both explained what the helter-skelter of recent history meant and foretold its imminent end was all too plausible.[6]

Miller took a long time to convince himself that he was right, and even then was slow to act. He had no wish to become a traveling preacher, not with his fragile health. Yet the years were running short.

Finally, in 1831, he began to preach his message around New England. His hope was simply to visit churches of all denominations and persuade them that the moment for repentance was now. To his surprise, he was mocked as a fanatic. Even when ministers allowed him to speak, they cast doubt on his predictions. Even so, he persisted, convinced that once people understood his calculations, they would accept them as self-evidently true.

The crucial moment was his conversion in 1839 of Joshua Himes, a Christian Connection preacher and a gifted publicist. Having been convinced by the message, Himes was alarmed that Miller's amateurish efforts at presenting it were inadequate. The hour was becoming late. "The whole thing is kept in a corner yet," he protested. "No time should be lost in giving the Church and the whole world warning, in thunder-tones." The men formed a formidable partnership. Himes quickly launched a newspaper, *Signs of the Times*. It was the first of many: about four million copies of "Millerite" publications appeared in the next four years, many of them illustrated with vivid symbols drawn from the book of Revelation. Himes secured speaking engagements, raised funds so that Millerite publications could be given away, and organized conferences. In 1842, he had a meeting tent made, supposedly America's largest ever, seating over four thousand. Crowds came simply to see it. It became a kind of symbol of the movement: a colossal circus-church, both grand and, by nature, temporary. Supposedly, it inspired P. T. Barnum's traveling circus.[7]

Now the message won tens of thousands of fervent converts. Inevitably, it changed in the process. Miller had wanted simply to fire up Protestant believers in their home churches, but what happened to convinced Millerites whose ministers ridiculed the message or were slow in preaching it? What about laypeople whose churches would not let them preach, but who were too fired with the message to stay silent? What about the increasing number of new converts, who had no home church? Meanwhile, those burning with advent hope began gathering together for worship rather than sharing pews with their skeptical, lukewarm brethren. The Millerites did not want to found a denomination, but they were turning into one despite themselves. They grew increasingly impatient with skeptics, and the skeptics' mockery and contempt grew sharper. Miller himself remained a member of his own

Baptist church for as long as he could, but eventually he was expelled. Meetings were disrupted, tents pulled down, greased pigs set loose in crowds. Vandalism might have been to blame for the giant tent's collapse in a storm in 1843. It was partially repaired, but the damage to the Millerites' relationship with the wider world was not so easily mended. Once again, an anti-sectarian movement had become a sect.

Miller's early vagueness about the precise date was now unsustainable. Under pressure, he reluctantly declared that the end would likely come between March 21, 1843, and the same day the following year. When March 22, 1844, dawned, Miller was philosophical: "We have no right to be dogmatical . . . we should consider how fallible we are." But if he could live that way, a mass movement built to work toward a crescendo could not. That summer, a previously obscure preacher named Samuel S. Snow declared he had found the glitch in Miller's reckoning. The actual date of Christ's return would be the Hebrew Day of Atonement, October 22, 1844.[8]

The memoirs of that summer resonate with calm, solemn joyfulness. Believers put their affairs in order and gave what they could toward publicity for the cause—some holding guiltily on to reserves, others offering up all they had. One Millerite, looking back a quarter century later, wrote, "Not for all the world would I have missed going through my advent experience; nor for all the world would I want to go through it again." There were visions, prophecies, conversions that defied unbelief. One meeting was visited by strangers come to gawk at the fanatics. Instead, when they heard their hosts singing, the spirit of the meeting caught them. They tried to slip away quietly, back to everyday life:

> One man and his wife succeeded in getting out of doors; but the third one fell upon the threshold; the fourth, fifth and so on, till most of the company were thus slain by the power of God [that is, they fainted]. . . . Some thirteen, or more, were converted before the meeting closed.

Even the couple who had left came back the following night and were converted. Or so one of their hosts said, and so others readily believed. It was a season of miracles.[9]

Himes and Miller were wary of the October 22 prophecy but were won over by the fruit the message was bearing in believers' lives. The prophecies of 1843, Himes admitted, "never made so great, and good an impression as this has done upon all that have come under its influence. . . . I dare not oppose it." The October 16 issue of his weekly newspaper, the *Advent Herald,* confidently declared, "We shall make no provision for issuing a paper for the week following." Miller could not quite bring himself to endorse Samuel Snow but conceded, "I see a glory in [the October date] which I never saw before," and admitted, "If the Lord does not come in the next three weeks I will be twice as disappointed as I was in the Spring."[10]

The stories told about the day itself—the white ascension robes, the crowds gathered on hilltops—seem mostly to be malicious inventions. One believer who was supposedly killed leaping from a treetop into God's arms wrote indignantly to his local paper to deny it. But the crushing emptiness of the "Great Disappointment" could not be denied. "Our fondest hopes and expectations were blasted . . . we wept, and wept, till the day dawn."[11] The ribald mockery of families and neighbors, no doubt a little relieved to have won their wager on skepticism, could hardly help. Some Millerites now threw over the whole movement as phony. The premillennialist doctrine that Christ might suddenly return at any time has never fully recovered from this scandal. Christ had not come; perhaps he wasn't coming. The biblical calculations had proved fruitless, so evidently the Bible shouldn't be read that way. Perhaps it shouldn't be read at all.

But what of those whose lives had been changed by the advent message? What if, as Himes wrote in November 1844, you were compelled to admit that God "has wrought a great, a glorious work in the hearts of his children; and it will not be in vain?" The simplest, hardest road was taken by Miller and Himes themselves. They admitted that there had been a mistake in their calculations. Some went scurrying back to their Bibles for another try, but Miller warned against further date setting. God had taught them a bitter lesson, and they should learn it. Himes, in particular, emerges from this period with some honor. Facing a slew of accusations from property speculation to robbery, and rumors of arrest or suicide, he patiently and successfully defended his own and the movement's honesty. He organized relief funds for those who had abandoned jobs or homes or who had left their crops unharvested. Further editions of the *Advent Herald* and his other periodicals did eventually appear, although the *Western Midnight Cry!!!* discreetly dropped two of its exclamation points.

This Adventist movement, still looking expectantly for Christ's return, tried not to become just another denomination, but it was inescapable. It slowly became a family of small, conservative Protestant churches, distinguished by preaching Christ's imminent second coming with a little more urgency than most others. Adventism became an identity, based on a shared memory of one extraordinary year, and even a pastime for biblical hobbyists. One Adventist recalled how, traveling through Indiana in 1845, he was longing to meet someone with whom he could have "pleasant conversation on the advent question." The man he eventually met was "a perpetual motionist, about as much that as an adventist," and was more interested in talking about his latest invention; he claimed that the interruption had prevented him from finishing it that afternoon. "Rather a sad misfortune to the world, as it has not got the machine perfected to this day," his visitor commented drily.[12] Miller ministered to this odd community until his death in 1849. Himes did so until 1876, when he finally returned to the Episcopal church of his youth. He was ordained an Episcopal priest in 1878 and served a parish in South Dakota for sixteen years. He died in 1895, aged ninety, still faithful and expectant.

The Communitarian Alternative

For other Millerites, subsiding into churchly respectability was not an adequate response to the glory they had glimpsed and the bitterness they had endured. Some bewildered groups tried to summon Christ by sheer force of will, forming prayer communes until they were worn down by exhaustion and disillusion. One group decided that the world had now entered its Sabbath rest and that they should therefore do no work. The men who conceived this notion rebuked the women in their community for Sabbath breaking and then backtracked very rapidly when food stopped appearing on their plates.[13] Several ex-Millerites formed more enduring communes, including one near Jerusalem that endured until 1855.

In doing so, they joined themselves to a quite different, long-standing radical impulse in American Protestantism. Alongside the anti-denominational mass movements like the Millerites and the more respectable Christian Connection, other Protestants had been choosing depth over breadth. They set about building their new worlds within closed communities, either refuges from an irredeemably sinful world or seeds from which God's kingdom might grow. Long before Miller proclaimed Christ's advent, such groups had been working to make a new earth and heaven in earnest. Some of them had moved from Europe, such as the Society of True Inspiration, led by a Prussian prophet. Others were homegrown. Jemima Wilkinson, an ex-Quaker prophet who became known as the Public Universal Friend, established a community at Keuka Lake, New York, distinguished by its strict gender equality.

Most of these communities held all property in common. That raised an awkward question about marriage. If you no longer had the right to have things for yourself alone, how could you have the right to have a person for yourself alone? One alarming answer was advanced by John Humphrey Noyes, who moved from an ordinary revivalist conversion in 1831 to some very idiosyncratic ideas. Christ, he believed, empowered his people to live perfect lives, and he set about creating a community that would embody this. At first, he simply taught radical equality of the sexes. When his community relocated to Oneida, New York, in 1847, however, he added a doctrine of "complex marriage." Every man in the community was married to every woman. This entire web of relationships ought in principle to be sexually consummated, albeit with strict mutual consent. The result was not quite the endless orgy that the community's prurient critics eagerly imagined. Noyes also believed in the moral virtue of self-control, by which he meant rigorously practicing coitus interruptus. Younger men were trained in the method by postmenopausal women. Actual breeding was rigorously regulated, not least to control incest, and the community collectively decided which pairings ought to be permitted a child. Only about a quarter of the community's pregnancies were unplanned. The children were then raised collectively, without forming attachments to individual parents. It should be said that the community's children generally appear to have become stable and well-rounded adults. It should also be said that over a sixth of all the children born to this nearly hundred-strong community were sired by Noyes himself. He eventually fled to Canada to escape charges of statutory rape.[14]

The more respectable answer to the marriage problem was strict celibacy. Protestant communities gave old monastic traditions a radical twist: strict gender equality became possible, untroubled by matrimonial rights, childbearing, or child rearing. This was the pattern long since adopted by America's oldest and best-known utopian community, the Shakers. Their founder, the eighteenth-century English Quaker Ann Lee, had been forced unwillingly into marriage, and each of her four pregnancies ended in an exceptionally terrible birth and in the child's death. She became convinced that sex was the world's besetting sin and that all Christians were called to celibacy, not least because Christ's return was expected imminently. In 1770, she received a revelation that that long-hoped-for day had in fact already come. She herself was Christ: a second, female Christ, a counterpart to Jesus' maleness. Through her, Christianity would transcend gender and reunite humanity.

In 1774, she and her little group of English disciples immigrated to America, and after her death in 1784 the disciples formed communities. There were eighteen such groups by 1830, scattered across New York and New England, comprising around four thousand Shakers. They lived out a serene, rigorous vision of heaven: celibate, strictly egalitarian, with each community led jointly by a woman and a man. The Shakers became a byword for calm order and mutual love, and also for forward-looking working practices, eagerly embracing the latest science in their farming and manufacturing. Converts and adopted orphans kept the numbers growing, in keeping with the teaching that Christ's second appearing would be gradual, like a sunrise. Lee herself was the first glimmer of dawn. The Shaker communities were the beginnings of light. The pure kingdom, liberated from sin and sex, would gradually form around them until the whole world basked in the new day.

Shakerism's crisis came in 1837, the first community's fiftieth anniversary, the point at which the last of those who had known Lee were dying, and the year of an acute economic crisis in the United States. A group of girls in one community began to shake, whirl, sing unknown songs, and report visions, including of Lee herself. We have seen preteen and teenage children at the heart of revivals like this before, but among the Shakers that age-group faced more than the usual stresses.

They were beginning to discover how much it would cost to belong to the community that had raised them. The manifestations, especially rapid spinning on the spot, spread across the entire Shaker family. One Shaker song from this revival, "Simple Gifts," has become an American folk favorite, still bearing the mark of the Shakers' characteristic whirling—"to turn, turn will be our delight." Some communities began gathering to share intangible gifts such as celestial wine and "silver sacks filled with the bread of life" or to contemplate a fountain of life only visible to those with spiritual insight. Other Shakers took to walking through their communities at midnight, bearing lamps like the wise virgins they were, and rousing their sisters and brothers with the song "Awake from your slumbers, for the Lord of Hosts is going through the land / He will sweep, he will clean his holy sanctuary."[15]

This ill became the Shakers' normal orderly peace. Soon visionaries were starting to deliver messages not only from Ann Lee but from Jesus, Christopher Columbus, and George Washington. One hopeful young medium claimed that Lee had told her to abandon celibacy. The community drew down the shutters, promulgating new rules imposing tight discipline on spiritual manifestations and regulating men's and women's interactions more strictly than before. Most of the young visionaries left. The Shakers were saved from spinning into disintegration, at the cost of renouncing much of their spiritual power.

That was the Shakers' condition when the Millerites, reeling from the Disappointment, found them. Unlike almost anyone else in America's raucous religious scene, the Shakers could understand and sympathize with the Millerite predicament. One former Millerite, told by a Shaker that Adventists ought to press on in their spiritual journey, felt at last that he had met "a person that speaks as though he comprehends our whereabouts, and understands our path ahead." He and a decent trickle of Millerite survivors joined, and found peace in, these communities. Shakerism provided an answer to the great Adventist problem after 1844: What should believers *do*, other than simply wait? "Do you not," the Adventist-turned-Shaker Enoch Jacobs urged his former brethren, "want to find a place where Advent *work* takes the place of Advent *talk*?" These communities were working for Christ's second appearance, and the settled holiness of their lives was a standing rebuke to the fretted consciences of disappointed believers.[16]

Only a handful of the tens of thousands of Millerites took this route, however. Those who did often found, eventually, that they were not pure enough for this austere heaven. Lifelong celibacy might have had an appeal in the urgent rush of a religious crisis, but as the sun's ascent remained imperceptibly slow, the cost rose. Enoch Jacobs himself eventually left, reportedly saying that he would "rather go to hell with Electa his wife than live among the Shakers without her."[17] The Shakers slowly withered: tolerated, even admired, but doomed by their own principles to a slow extinction.

The Narrow Way

Two groups emerged from Millerism that managed to resolve this conundrum, finding ways to be rule-bound communities of believers dedicated to the arduous work of holiness, while also engaged with the wider world and capable of winning converts.

The first was grounded on one believer's sudden insight on the bleak morning of October 23, 1844. Hiram Edson and his friends had kept watch all night, and he now stared into the abyss:

> I mused in my own heart, saying, My advent experience had been the richest and brightest of all my christian experience. If this has proved a failure, what was the rest of my christian experience worth? Has the Bible proved a failure? Is there no God—no heaven—no golden home city—no paradise? Is all this but a cunningly devised fable?

As he prayed with renewed urgency, he was given an explanation. Miller's calculation had foretold when the sanctuary would be cleansed. Edson now realized that that did not actually refer to Christ's return to earth in glory. The date had been right after all! Christ had now entered the heavenly sanctuary, the Holy of Holies, in final preparation for the Last Judgment. The world might look the same, but while the Millerites had wept and prayed the night before, it had moved a decisive step closer to its end.[18]

It was a very satisfying solution, allowing Adventists to affirm the message they had first believed while explaining its apparent failure, and Edson rushed it into print. It was taken up by a seventeen-year-old Millerite from Portland, Maine, named Ellen Harmon. In December 1844, she had a vision in which Adventists were walking on a narrow way toward the new Jerusalem, their eyes fixed on Christ. But some now "rashly denied the light behind them, and said that it was not God that had led them out so far." Those poor fools stumbled and fell off the path into darkness.[19] Only those who embraced Edson's sanctuary doctrine remained on the straight and narrow.

Harmon then added two further doctrines. One was the "shut door": an argument made by several Millerites that during this, presumably brief, interlude between Christ's entry into the sanctuary and his final return, the door was shut on fresh conversions. The world had had its chance before October 22. This meant that Harmon's efforts were focused exclusively on the scattered Adventist community. The other addition came in a vision in which Jesus showed her the original tablets of the Ten Commandments. One commandment was encircled by a halo: "Remember the sabbath day, to keep it holy."

Since the sixteenth century, Catholics had taunted Protestants by asking why, if they rejected all authority aside from the Bible, they still worshipped on a Sunday. Worship on Sunday, the first day of the week, is a very ancient Christian practice, but the only Sabbath the Bible explicitly teaches is the Jewish one, on Saturday, the seventh day. Very few Protestants had ever shifted their Sabbath, however, whether because of the radical rejection of tradition it implied, because of its unwelcome tang of Judaism, or simply because of its disruptive challenge to social norms. Harmon's little band now did so, distinguishing themselves sharply from a sinful world. Perhaps this was the last step in their purification before the sanctuary was cleansed.

The Joshua Himes to Ellen Harmon's Miller was a young preacher named James White, her chaperone, publisher, and then husband. They were a formidable team, not least in turning a movement with a very short-term outlook into one capable of functioning indefinitely. By 1851, the "shut door" was becoming a problem: new converts were being won, and others were being born. A rigidly consistent movement might have withered, but the Whites recognized the new situation and quietly dropped the shut-door doctrine. They also disowned any further date setting. The reason Christ had entered the sanctuary in 1844, Ellen was told in a vision, was to conduct his "investigative judgment": working steadily through the record of humanity's sins in advance of the end. By its nature, this might take a while. Rather than playing guessing games with the calendar, they should use this providential delay to make themselves a truly holy people.

In 1860, this community reluctantly organized itself as a church. The name they chose—the Seventh-day Adventists—encapsulated their distinctive double focus. Their eyes remained fixed on Christ's imminent return, but in the meanwhile they urgently pursued personal and corporate holiness, of which the Saturday Sabbath was only the most prominent symbol. In the 1860s, that quest for holiness took a new direction. Ellen White had long suffered from poor health, and like many other American Protestants she distrusted the learned priests of medicine as well as those of theology. Many Adventists expected miracles of healing in these latter days, and some toyed with rejecting human medicine altogether, but White was too levelheaded for that. She accepted that God worked through human medicine. She did not, however, mean the medicine practiced by learned and expensive MDs. It was not merely socially exclusive and cruelly ineffective; it also offended her notions of purity, simplicity, and natural perfection.

These notions were hardly original. Sylvester Graham, still famous for his trademark crackers, had become a celebrity on the back of an eccentric vision of dietary purity during the 1830s. Graham was a Presbyterian pastor, and his quest for health was a spiritual one. A Grahamite society in Boston, founded in 1837 to make "worthy disciples of the Great Reformer of men, and the Redeemer of their bodies and spirits," made an explicit link between Miller's prophecies and their own quests:

> The millennium, the near approach of which is by many so confidently preached, can never reasonably be expected to arrive, until those laws which God has implanted in the *physical* nature of man are, equally with his moral laws, universally known and obeyed.[20]

Ellen White picked up the theme following a vision in 1863. As well as denouncing alcohol, she urged Seventh-day Adventists to abstain from the "filthy weed" tobacco, and disapproved of tea and coffee, dangerous stimulants that fostered gossip. Pork was forbidden, in line with Old Testament prohibitions. White in fact abandoned all meat, fish, eggs, cheese, and cream for a time, although unlike some of her disciples she continued to permit milk, sugar, and salt. The spread of vegetarianism in Seventh-day Adventism was slow and uneven. White's own final conversion to absolute vegetarianism came late in life, in 1894, after an Australian Catholic woman reproached her with "the selfishness of taking the lives of animals to gratify a perverted taste."[21] It was a novel way of thinking about the subject. Vegetarianism has periodically surfaced in Protestantism, but has usually focused on the health and purity of believers' bodies, not the ethics of butchering fellow creatures.

Diet was only the beginning. White was also a convert to hydrotherapy, a technique that consisted chiefly of wrapping yourself in soaking bandages and drinking copious quantities of pure water. She credited this harmless technique with saving two of her sons from a dangerous illness in 1863, and a vision led her to declare the merits of "God's great medicine, water, pure soft water, for diseases, for health, for cleanliness, and for luxury." She also had firm views on sexual health and on the dangers of excessively frequent sex. When her sons were teenagers, she wrote vehemently against masturbation, which she blamed for "imbecility, dwarfed forms, crippled limbs, misshapen heads, and deformity of every description." That streak of Victorian prudery meant she would never advocate nudism, as some Christian perfectionists had done in previous centuries. She did, however, have stern views on dress, and her recommendation of a "short" (calf-length) skirt for women, with loose-fitting trousers worn beneath it, was almost more scandalous in her age than public nudity would be in ours. A vision in 1875 finally gave her permission to abandon that particular lost cause.[22]

Nurturing good health became central to Seventh-day Adventism's identity: a means not only of purifying believers but of winning converts. The church began to publish journals such as the *Health Reformer* aimed at a general reader, and to establish sanatoriums and spas where patients of any religion might "become acquainted with the character and ways of our people, see a beauty in the religion of the Bible, and be led into the Lord's service."[23] One result of this was the long and fruitful, though eventually unhappy, partnership between White and John

Harvey Kellogg, nutritionist, health reformer, and the inventor of corn-flakes. White, who did not particularly like cornflakes, turned down the opportunity for the church to own the Kellogg's brand. It was an expensive decision, but it might have saved the church's identity from being swallowed up in a commercial empire. After she had kept her church's soul pure throughout her long life—she finally died in 1915—it would have been a shame to have sold it for breakfast cereal.

Thanks not least to White's own legacy of levelheaded pragmatism, Seventh-day Adventism has repeatedly escaped vanishing into extremism while keeping its distinctiveness. It moved from its early view that the United States was one of the anti-Christian beasts described in the book of Revelation to a more constructive, pragmatic apoliticism. It never allowed its apocalypticism to tip it into madness, although some of its splinter groups—most notoriously, the Branch Davidians who were immolated in Texas in 1993—show how easily that could have happened. Nor did Adventist health reform take the blind alley represented by White's near-contemporary Mary Baker Eddy, whose superficially similar Christian Science movement became trapped in a ghetto by her occultish preoccupations and her blunt rejection of medicine. The Adventists, by contrast, were able quietly to abandon quackery and fully embrace mainstream medicine in the twentieth century.

Cautious, pragmatic, untroubled by scandal or open fanaticism, focused both on this world and the next—no wonder their numbers have grown so steadily. Seventh-day Adventism has grown from some two hundred members in 1850, to 3,500 in 1860, to 75,000 worldwide by 1900, to some eighteen million at the time of writing. It has quietly mushroomed into one of the world's major Protestant denominations.

Is it a Protestant denomination, however, or a heretical sect? It has in some ways come closer to the Protestant mainstream. Whereas many early Seventh-day Adventists openly questioned the doctrine of the Trinity, White herself was studiedly cautious on the subject. Her eventual split with Kellogg was caused in part by his radical pantheistic speculations. Some Adventists remain anti-Trinitarian, but the church formally affirmed the Trinity in 1931 as part of its alliance with the burgeoning Fundamentalist movement. In the 1960s and 1970s, Adventists began to engage with other evangelical organizations and with the

World Council of Churches. But if a time will ever come when Seventh-day Adventists are simply conservative Protestants who worship on a Saturday, it is not yet here. Although Ellen White's visions have never been elevated to the status of Scripture, accepting them as genuine is a decisive test of fellowship. For all the embrace of modern science and scholarship in Adventist universities, historical study of White herself remains painfully sensitive. To question her status is to question Hiram Edson's sanctuary doctrine, the foundational significance of 1844, and the entire culture of what Seventh-day Adventism has become. Other Protestants are sometimes impatient for Adventists to decisively choose between retreating to sectarian irrelevance or joining mainstream orthodoxy. So far, however, Adventism's knack for adapting to the world while retaining a firm grip on its own soul has not done it any harm.

Witnessing for Jehovah

Millerism's last, untimely apostle was Charles Taze Russell, born in 1852 and converted as a teenager by a preacher from the mainstream, post-1844 Adventist tradition. Like Miller, he turned to self-taught study of biblical chronology. Unlike the Seventh-day Adventists, he assumed that Miller's calculations had been wrong and set himself to find the mistake. By 1876, he had an ingenious solution. One of Miller's arguments for his date of 1843 had been a tenuous calculation that there would be an interval of 2,520 years during which Israel's enemies reigned over it. Miller counted this as beginning in 677 B.C., when the first exiles were deported from Jerusalem, which took him to 1843 A.D. Russell argued that a much more natural start date would be the actual fall of Jerusalem in 606 B.C. That pointed to the crux year as being 1914 A.D.: helpfully, still in the future.

Russell was hardly the first to come up with a new date. What set him apart was a separate set of calculations, based on the ancient Jewish years of jubilee. This led him to conclude that the millennium, Christ's rule on earth, would begin not in 1914, but forty years earlier, in 1874. That year had recently passed without obvious cosmic incident, but far from torpedoing Russell's theory, that fact became central to it. He preached not Christ's second coming but his second *presence* on earth, a slow process that had already begun. During the years leading up to

1914, Christ would slowly harvest the souls of his faithful, eventually reaching 144,000, the number foretold in Revelation.[24]

Russell was no keener than any other prophet to found a new church or sect. Like the century's earlier "Christians," his disciples were known with studied humility only as "Bible students." They would keep that anonymous title until they adopted the modern term "Jehovah's witnesses" in 1931, and that, too, was meant to be a plain description: people who bore witness to the God whose name is Jehovah. Outsiders' habit (which I will follow) of calling them "the Jehovah's Witnesses" or "the Witnesses" thrusts onto them a denominational identity that they reject. What Russell founded was not a church but, like every nineteenth-century American religious movement, a publishing enterprise. He began with a self-published book in 1877, and in 1884 established the Zion's Watch Tower and Tract Society as a legal corporation.

It was a very American way to form a sect. As a corporation, the Society, renamed the Watch Tower Bible and Tract Society in 1896, has unchallenged legal rights over its publications and a simple, autocratic structure of internal governance. As a result, under Russell and his successors as president, the Witnesses have become Protestantism's most rigidly controlled large-scale movement. They have also become by far the most persecuted Christian movement in modern times.

Russell's understanding of the window of opportunity before 1914 gave his Bible students their ethos. He adopted a variant of the shut-door doctrine: this was a time not for winning fresh converts to Christianity but for calling nominal Christians out of their false churches while there was still time. Distinguishing his movement from false churches became, and remains, a central concern. So, like other anti-sectarians before him, he rejected the Trinity, "the unreasonable theory that Jehovah is his own Son and our Lord Jesus is his own Father," thus giving his own movement and the mainstream churches an enduring pretext for reviling each other. Hence, too, his self-conscious use of the word "Jehovah," the traditional Latin form of the Hebrew name of God. That not only set his movement apart; it also became a way to assert that Jesus, who has a different name, is not God, merely "a god."[25]

The need to fill up the numbers of the faithful gave Russell's Bible students their only priority. It is hardly novel for Christians to decide that saving souls matters more than anything else. Russell's achievement, however, was not only to create the most determinedly conversionist movement in Christianity's history. His Bible students lived to bear witness to the truth, regardless of whether they were believed. If there will be only 144,000 chosen, that means most of humanity will spurn the message. The legions of Witness "publishers" who work door-to-door and in public places across the world do so in deadly earnest, after careful training in managing difficult encounters and turning conversations so as to have a chance to save another soul. But they neither expect a high rate of success nor regard rejection as a failure, and they find camaraderie in shared tales of doorstep rebuffs. Their responsibility is to bear witness faithfully, whether or not that witness is heard. Later Witnesses told of how Russell himself, as a young man, "would go out at night to chalk up Bible texts in conspicuous places so that workingmen, passing by, might be warned and be saved from the torments of hell."[26] In the 1920s, American Witnesses sometimes descended on quiet neighborhoods with loudspeakers so that locked doors could be no barrier to the Word. This is proclamation whose primary purpose is proclamation itself.

That was the Witnesses' answer to Millerism's unresolved question: How should you live in the shadow of Armageddon? Only snatching souls from the fire mattered. The whole world, all its governments and nations and churches and families, was shortly to be judged and destroyed. True students of the Bible should, therefore, renounce all worldly ties. Nations mean nothing; Russell's movement could only have been born in America, but while he would not defy the American state, neither would he actively support it through such means as voting or military service. His disciples were pacifist until the time came to fight for God in the Battle of Armageddon. In the meantime, they would bear witness by rigidly refusing to conform to this world's norms.

The movement's most obvious problem was its preprinted expiry date of 1914. As the year grew closer, Russell began to backpedal, but his earlier predictions had been very specific. He now began to embrace more eccentric theories, such as that the date of Armageddon could be deduced from the dimensions of the pyramids of Giza. The movement ought to have disintegrated. Instead, two new developments saved it.

First, although the world did not actually end in 1914, the year did indeed bring a global catastrophe of biblical proportions in which the world's corrupt nations set about each other's destruction. It was possible, although a little awkward, to argue that this was what Russell had been predicting all along. In which case, prophecy was vindicated and the end was near. Second, when Russell himself died in October 1916, the Society's presidency was seized in a boardroom coup by Joseph Franklin Rutherford, the movement's second founder and creator of the modern Witnesses. Rutherford forcefully made the best of the new circumstances. On the authority of a newly published volume of what he claimed were Russell's writings, he argued that 1914, like 1874 before it, was the beginning of a process. In early 1918, Rutherford delivered a speech, later a tract, titled "The World Has Ended—Millions Now Living Will Never Die!" Time was short, and Jehovah's witnesses had to separate themselves from the world's death throes. As the United States entered a short-lived, intense war fever in 1917, Rutherford vehemently denounced both the war itself and its cheerleaders, the clergy of the mainstream churches.

He and seven of the Society's other directors were arrested, found guilty of sedition, and given lengthy prison sentences. They were released in 1919, as war fever abated and the courts became warier of locking up Americans purely for their political opinions, but the damage was done. By the war's end, the Society's main periodical, the *Watch Tower,* which had boasted forty-five thousand subscribers in 1914, had only three thousand left. Rutherford led a short-lived recovery based on a further, confident prediction that the end would finally come in 1925. When that prophecy also failed, this time without a world war as consolation, the movement reached its lowest ebb.

So Rutherford reinvented it. Along with the new name, in 1931, went central control of the appointment of elders in local congregations. Teaching offered in those congregations, whose buildings were renamed Kingdom Halls, would now be uniform across the globe. Russell's original works, many of them embarrassingly obsolete, were allowed to go out of print for good. Publications began to appear anonymously, as the collective, unchallengeable wisdom of the Society, which in 1927 declared itself to be God's "faithful and discreet slave," with authority to determine matters of faith. Its new books typically had sweeping one-word titles such as *Life, Riches,* or *Vindication.*

The Witnesses' apocalypticism is undimmed, as any glance at their publications will show, but since 1925 there has been no further authoritative date setting. There have been excitements around other dates, in particular 1975, which some of the Society's directors apparently endorsed. Yet in 1976, the Society's vice president could confidently reproach an assembly of Canadian Witnesses: "Do you know why nothing happened in 1975? It was because you expected something to happen." For most of the twentieth century, the Society simply held tight to 1914, declaring week by week in its main magazine that the new world would dawn "before the generation that saw the events of 1914 passes away." In 1995, this increasingly implausible claim, too, was redefined, explaining that "generation" was a spiritual rather than a literal term.[27]

The Witnesses' global growth is built not on their apocalyptic hope but on the abrupt, disconcerting separatism of their lives in the present. Rutherford continued Russell's pattern of distancing the Witnesses symbolically from Christian norms, for example by insisting that Christ was impaled rather than dying on something so popish as a cross. For this, other Christians have duly reviled them, but the real hatred has come from governments. The most extreme example, their fate in Nazi Germany, we will return to. Nowhere else have they faced actual extermination, but during World War II they were subject to state bans in much of the British Empire and were more likely to be imprisoned than any other religious conscientious objectors in the United States. The Witnesses' refusal to salute flags or stand for national anthems led to their children's being expelled from some American schools. In all of these countries, with grim irony, the Witnesses were accused of Nazi sympathies. Since 1945, their sharpest trials have been in one-party states. Malawi banned the Society in 1967 after Witnesses refused to join the ruling party, and over twenty thousand were expelled to brutal camp conditions in Zambia in 1972. Some eventually ended up in Mozambique, where after 1975 some seven thousand Witnesses were interned in Communist reeducation camps.[28]

The Witnesses' best-known ethical stance, the rejection of blood transfusions, is characteristic. Russell, citing Acts 15:20, argued that it was wrong to eat meat in which blood remained. In 1945, Rutherford ruled that this prohibition extended to blood transfusions. No other religious group of any kind has found this argument persuasive, and it is an odd fit in an organization that has no general aversion to modernity or to science. Its value, apparently, lies in compelling Witnesses to assert a highly visible difference that challenges social notions of religious tolerance.

It is not easy for outsiders to love the Witnesses. They have endured appalling persecution with astonishing stoicism, but facing and even courting persecution are part of their identity. Their steady growth—they currently number some eight million active members worldwide—can easily be ascribed to their missionary barrage and to their formidable system of control rather than to any real attraction offered by their faith. There is a large constituency of ex-Witnesses with little good to say about the Society. The Society has no culture of intellectual openness or of scholarship and does not reply to critics.

Yet there is more to the Witnesses than hostile caricature admits. Their determined internationalism and disregard for racial differences have made them—along with the Seventh-day Adventists—among America's most racially integrated religious groups. They are capable of winning real respect from their neighbors, especially in tough social environments. When other churches have reputations for clericalism, hypocrisy, or financial corruption, the Witnesses can justly boast that they have no paid ministers, take no collections, and maintain strict moral discipline. The rigorous training that all Witnesses undertake, from carefully directed study of texts to sharing in leadership, can be as rewarding as it is demanding. Outsiders need not admire the Society, but they should try not to hate it, not least because hatred is one of the fuels on which it thrives. Neither Witnesses nor mainstream Protestants like to admit it, but they belong to the same extended family.

Latter-Day Protestants

One last new movement is a more distant cousin. Indeed it is not normally seen as a Protestant movement at all, nor do I claim it as such. Yet it arose from and in a Protestant milieu. For all that it has gone in a radically new direction, that Protestant inheritance lingers around it. It provides a unique example of how far Protestantism can stretch and of how, in the end, it can break.

Joseph Smith was a poor boy and visionary from upstate New York, America's most fertile nursery of new sects. In 1823, aged seventeen, he was visited by an angel named Moroni, who explained that under a hillside near where he lived, a set of fourteen-hundred-year-old gold plates were buried: plates whose inscriptions recorded the lost gospel of Christ's ministry in the New World and the history of the ancient Israelites who had crossed the ocean.

The story of how the Mormon church grew from that strange seed is too complex to be told in any detail here. In 1827, the angel permitted Smith to recover the supposed plates, and he spent the next three years transcribing and translating them. Several of his disciples testified to the plates' existence, but they were taken up into heaven before skeptical eyes could examine them. Eventually, Smith published the resulting document, the Book of Mormon, beneath whose biblical-pastiche style are some very striking spiritual claims. The book itself was not the heart of the new faith, however. Smith's visions and revelations did not cease. In 1829, he was ordained in a vision by John the Baptist, and in 1830 he organized a church, then comprising six people, with himself as its prophet. As the new church moved—first to Kirtland, Ohio, then to several settlements in Missouri, and then to Illinois—Smith's flow of revelations took his community ever further from its Protestant roots. By the time of his murder in 1844, Mormonism was effectively a new religion. That identity crystallized when, from 1846 onward, Smith's successor as prophet, Brigham Young, led the embattled but defiant Mormons to a new home beyond the frontier, in the deep wilderness around the Great Salt Lake.

Mormonism arguably does not belong in this book at all. It is a religion which teaches that God is a physical, embodied entity and that Jesus is another, and indeed denies the entire category of "spirit" as usually understood. It teaches that human beings were not created by God, are coeternal with him, and have the potential to become divine. It has a central, magisterial authority that is the custodian of ongoing revelations, although these have slowed dramatically over the past century.

It places great importance on the secret rituals performed in its temples, and therefore also on the two grades of consecrated priests to which virtually all Mormon men—but no women—belong. The result is a complex theological system that is at least as far removed from Christianity as Christianity is from Judaism.

Yet just as Christianity is pervasively influenced by its Jewish origins, Mormonism is still Protestant-accented. Smith was raised Protestant, as were almost all of his converts. Part of Mormonism's appeal was its heady mixture of traditional Protestant themes. Like Millerism, it could be made to look modern, scientific, and evidence based. Where Miller had his calculations, Smith had his plates and his book. Smith's rejection of all other sects, and of awkward abstractions such as the Trinity and predestination, was also widely shared. The appeal to prophetic inspiration was made, in different ways, by Shakers, Seventh-day Adventists, and Jehovah's Witnesses. Mormonism also, in classic Protestant mode, appealed to the inner witness of the Holy Spirit in the believer. Just as Calvin had seen the Bible as self-authenticating, the Book of Mormon challenges the reader to ask God if the book's teachings were true: "If ye shall ask with a sincere heart, with real intent, having faith in Christ, he will manifest the truth of it unto you, by the power of the Holy Ghost." Another verse promises that if the seed of belief takes root in you, it will grow by its own power. "Because ye have tried the experiment, and planted the seed, and it swelleth and sprouteth, and beginneth to grow, ye must needs know that the seed is good."[29] What could be more Protestant than this simultaneous appeal to God's Spirit within and to that most modern of ideas, *experiment*?

Yet Mormonism could also make promises that Protestantism could not. Its priesthood of progressive, secret knowledge was anathema to Protestants in general and to the egalitarian, anticlerical mood of the Second Great Awakening in particular. *Knowledge,* as distinct from mere *faith,* remains central for Mormons. Brigham Young disparaged the standard Protestant-revivalist pattern, in which conversion is the pivotal moment and a believer's life consists of trying to hold on to that first ardor. As he put it, Methodists are "always the biggest when they are first born," whereas Mormons' religious life is one of continuous growth in virtue and knowledge. One result is a certain intellectual openness in Mormonism. Mormons are not supposed to allow the church to do their thinking for them, although they are not supposed to critique its doctrines either. Like the Seventh-day Adventists, but unlike the Witnesses, Mormonism has founded universities.[30]

If these claims could appeal, they could also repel. The early Mormons were the focus of venomous hatred. They were loathed for their aggressive proselytization, their offensive religious claims, and their secretive, authoritarian governing structures, and they made no serious attempts to allay those concerns. Instead, blazing the path the Witnesses would later follow, they thrived on persecution and to an extent sought it out. Smith, who had been threatened with lynching as early as 1832, took pride in being "persecuted the worst of any man on the earth. . . . I should be like a fish out of water if I were out of persecutors."[31] Mormons did not merely deny the nation's claim on their loyalty, but substituted new, theocratic claims of their own. Smith claimed to be king of the kingdom of God and a new Muhammad, and instructed Mormons how to vote. It was a genuine challenge to republican norms. When the Mormons settled at Commerce, Illinois, and renamed it Nauvoo in 1840, they transformed it in four years from a small town to the state's second-largest city, numbering more than ten thousand, with its own militia under Smith's command. Anti-Mormon mobs were threatened with "a war of extermination," and Smith himself declared that "if they come to molest us . . . we will trample down our enemies and make it one gore of blood from the Rocky Mountains to the Atlantic Ocean." This was mostly rhetoric: where there was killing, it was done by anti-Mormon vigilantes. But the assertion of power was real. In 1844, Smith ordered the destruction of a Nauvoo printing press that had dared to publish an anti-Mormon newspaper. This was not the American way. He was eventually arrested and then murdered by a mob in the insecure prison where he was left deliberately unguarded. He did not go quietly. A six-shooter had been smuggled into his cell by a friend, and he managed to shoot and wound three of his attackers before he himself was shot leaping from a window.

The final move west in the years that followed did not end this pattern of defiance. The federal government disliked having Brigham Young as governor of the Utah Territory. When President Franklin Pierce tried and failed to replace him in 1854, Young exulted that "President Pierce and all hell could not remove me from office. . . . I shall be governor of Utah territory just as long as [God] wants me to be." When Pierce tried to impose federally appointed judges for the territory, Young told the Mormon representative in Washington to

> tell Mr. Franklin Pierce that the people of the territory have a way . . . of sending their infernal, dirty, sneaking, rotten-hearted, pot-house politicians out of the territory and if he should come himself it would be all the same.[32]

Pierce had no interest in setting foot in such a wilderness, but in 1857 his successor, James Buchanan, did launch a full-scale military campaign against the Mormons. Before the "Utah War" had properly started, however, on September 11, 1857, more than 120 California-bound settlers passing through the Utah Territory were slaughtered by Mormon militiamen. There had been rumors that some of the travelers were guilty of anti-Mormon atrocities back east. The massacre brought the war to a swift end. The Mormons, well aware that Washington would now refuse to accept any compromise, conceded federal oversight of the territory, and Young was replaced as governor, in return for pardons for everyone except those involved in the massacre. Even so, actual convictions proved elusive. Utah's sheer remoteness meant that Mormon self-rule remained the de facto reality.

Anti-Mormon sentiment now centered on one issue: polygamy. Like his contemporary John Humphrey Noyes, Smith had been cautious on the subject. The Mormon church did not openly avow polygamy until 1852. It is a subject with which Protestantism has repeatedly flirted, but in Mormonism it had its own logic and reflected the Mormon valorization of the family and of married fertility. If raising children is a sacred act, the more the better. Polygamy was not, in practice, a license to sexual depravity. Smith had as many as forty-eight wives, but although his first wife was not at all happy about this, many or most of the others were "eternal" or platonic relationships. It is uncertain whether any of his other wives bore him any children. Thereafter, relatively few Mormon men took multiple wives, and most of those did so under pressure, as a pious obligation to be borne. By 1890, when the church formally dropped the practice, not only the federal government but the vast majority of Utah Mormons opposed it.[33]

By then, polygamy had served its purpose. It bound the community and especially its leaders together with multiple webs of obligation, as marriage ties proliferated. It was no coincidence that Brigham Young, cementing his role as Smith's successor, swiftly married three of Smith's widows. Polygamy was also a rough-and-ready way of providing for a Mormon population in which women outnumbered men. Most important, while polygamous families were not especially happy, they were often astonishingly fertile. Population growth on the American frontier was dramatic at the best of times; polygamy turbocharged it. One man might sire thirty or more children. Even when polygamy was abandoned, the norm of large or very large families persisted. The comparison with the Mormons' near contemporaries the Shakers is instructive. The fact that the former now claim fifteen million members worldwide, whereas the latter have dwindled virtually to extinction, represents their different levels of success in attracting converts but also their different attitudes to reproduction. The success of religious movements over generations is sometimes as much about raising children as about winning converts.

Can the remarkable, worldwide growth of the Seventh-day Adventists, Jehovah's Witnesses, and Mormons continue? It may depend on their adaptability. The Mormons have a proven ability to jettison previously authorized beliefs and practices that cause trouble, abandoning polygamy in 1890 and overturning the ban on black men in the priesthood in 1978. That 1978 pronouncement was, however, the only full prophetic revelation the church has received in the past century, so Mormonism may not be as flexible as it once was. The Witnesses' characteristic approach to change, by contrast, is to deny that new doctrines or practices are in fact new. They have been able to make quiet changes in this way, such as accepting, in 1996, that Witnesses facing military conscription could perform civilian service in lieu. Even so, the Witnesses' ethics and practices remain comparatively rigid. The Seventh-day Adventists' situation is the closest to that of Protestants generally. They are committed to biblical authority but have no authoritative norms beyond their own tradition with which to interpret the Bible. Their culture of nonconfrontational pragmatism and their continued openness to the idea of prophetic innovation mean that even as a large international institution they can remain light on their toes: with, for example, some regions pressing ahead unilaterally toward women's ordained ministry. These groups' future rivals will probably not be each other, or the established Protestant denominations, so much as the new movements that continue to spring up across the globe. One of the lessons of Protestantism's Wild West is that groups that arise from the most obscure or unimpressive beginnings can stumble on ways of being Protestant so powerful that by the time the old establishments notice them, they have put down roots across the world.

CHAPTER 10

The Ordeals of Liberalism

No man putteth new wine into old bottles: else the new
wine doth burst the bottles, and the wine is spilled, and the
bottles will be marred.

—MARK 2:22

A fashionable, forward-looking group of young friends in the big city are carving out their generation's place in the world. One of their circle, incongruously, is a young clergyman. They are mystified by their friend's interest in something so out of date as *religion*. Because they are a literary coterie, he writes a short book explaining himself to them. He has no doubts about where they stand. It is not simply that their lives have nothing in them "that would in the least way resemble religion" and that "you have succeeded in making your earthly lives so rich and many-sided that you no longer need the eternal." If they think about religion at all, they imagine it is about "fear of an eternal being and reliance on another world," beliefs they find contemptible. They conclude, therefore, that "religion everywhere can be nothing other than an empty and false delusion."[1]

All this could plausibly have come from our own age, but Friedrich Schleiermacher wrote it in Berlin in 1799. Already, at the end of the eighteenth century, it was in some corners commonplace to dismiss Christianity as self-evidently false. As the existential threat of Catholicism receded over the course of the eighteenth century, the challenge to Protestantism from skepticism and secularism took its place. The Enlightenment philosophers of that century—earnest, experimental, and rationalistic—were deeply indebted to Christian ethics but balked at anything supernatural or "superstitious." This included the Bible's prima facie claim that the world is some six thousand years old; by the 1780s, both scientists and historians were becoming convinced that could not be true. Perhaps, the English poet William Cowper wondered caustically, when God revealed Earth's age in Scripture, he was mistaken? But more than individual doctrines were at stake. Because the Enlightenment embraced religious toleration on principle, it had to assume that doctrine was relatively unimportant. Your moral character mattered more than whether or not you accepted the Trinity as traditionally formulated. Christianity's roots in a specific historical moment, in the miracles of Christ's incarnation and resurrection, began to feel crass. Surely a mature philosophy would be more generic and universal. The Enlightenment's greatest philosopher, Immanuel Kant, argued that the only absolute that human beings can actually know is morality. Kant then tried to deduce God's existence from that starting point, but at best this resulted in an etiolated, austere God, not the living God of history. Meanwhile, the philosophers attacked churches as self-interested peddlers of superstitious cruelties or, as the English revolutionary Tom Paine put it, "human inventions set up to terrify or enslave mankind and monopolize power and profit."[2] The revolutionaries who overthrew France's political order in 1789 embarked on an explicit program of de-Christianization, even creating an alternative state religion, the Cult of the Supreme Being.

Naturally, many Christians fought back simply by reasserting their old-time religion, but some, most of them Protestants, tried another approach, which they called liberalism. Liberal theology's project was to reconcile the best of Christianity (whatever that might be) with the secularists' critiques. For this, they were opposed by hard-liners on both sides. Their presence turned what might have been trench warfare into a more dynamic struggle. In the process, they not only shaped the nineteenth century but helped lead the twentieth into trench warfare of a more literal kind.

Most readers will instinctively feel sympathy for one of the three parties in this struggle: conservatives, secularists, or liberals. Be cautious. The struggles of our own times do not map neatly onto those of the nineteenth and early twentieth centuries. Those early struggles did, however, make both conservative and liberal Protestantism what they are today.

The Liberal Project

Two things drove Protestant liberalism. One was a conviction that this was the only way to defeat secularism, and so both save Christian civilization and keep the power of the Gospel alive in people's lives. In an 1892 book tellingly titled *The Evolution of Christianity*, the American Congregationalist theologian Lyman Abbott explained that he was trying "to maintain faith by expressing it in terms which are more intelligible and credible" to the age of religious ferment in which he lived. The Baptist Walter Rauschenbusch warned a quarter century later that by trying "to keep Christian doctrine unchanged, we shall ensure its abandonment."[3] In the previous century Samuel Taylor Coleridge, a keen and liberal amateur theologian as well as a poet, had argued that an intelligent reinterpretation of contentious doctrines offered "the means of silencing, and the prospect of convincing, an alienated brother."[4] The same message came from the mission field, which nineteenth-century Protestants were embracing with unprecedented enthusiasm. John Colenso, a missionary bishop in South Africa whose questioning of the Bible scandalized the Church of England, was spurred forward by his Zulu flock. They found the literal details of some biblical stories hard to credit. In Noah's flood, had water really, literally, covered the entire world, up to the tops of the newly measured mountains? Colenso, who had a Gospel to proclaim, would not let such details become stumbling blocks.

Liberal theology was more than simple pragmatism, however. The liberals were deferring not only to skeptics' and pagans' doubts, but to their own. Colenso came to believe that biblical literalism was actually untrue, not merely unhelpful. The conviction that miracles were neither credible nor particularly attractive had seeped into educated Protestants' bones. So too had the powerful moral critique that the Enlightenment had made of certain core Protestant doctrines, a critique often made in Christian terms: contrasting Jesus' love and forgiveness with the churches' intolerance and callous rigidity. The traditional Christian doctrine of original sin, which deemed babies guilty even before their birth, stuck in the craw of an age that was learning to romanticize childhood innocence. To say nothing of the doctrine of hell, which (in its traditional form) consigned the majority of humanity to everlasting torment for not believing a Gospel that they had never heard.

William Ellery Channing, who was born in Rhode Island in 1780 and would become one of the first leaders of American liberalism, liked to tell of how, as a boy, he had heard a revivalist preacher whose talk of hellfire filled him with terrified urgency. He was all the more shocked that his father, who was with him, simply commented to a neighbor, "Sound doctrine, sir," whistled on the way home, and then took off his boots to read his newspaper in front of the fire. Channing junior concluded that no one actually believed these fearsome doctrines. He made it his life's work to make Protestantism honest again.[5]

Traditionalists naturally countered that it was the liberals who were the real unbelievers, crumbling before each fresh secularist challenge. Sometimes that was true, but the more thoughtful and creative liberals were not merely grudgingly abandoning old truths one by one. They believed they were using their age's insights to see the Protestant Gospel in a more faithful light than ever before. They were not tagging along behind an intellectual agenda set by skeptical thinkers, but trying to outflank or overtake it and to embrace an authentically Christian radicalism.

The trail was blazed by Friedrich Schleiermacher, with his worldly Berlin friends. The skeptical challenge had been in full spate in Germany for a generation or more. Theological rationalism had produced a decaffeinated version of Protestantism, stripping the Bible of anything miraculous and leaving a moral code of which Jesus was the exemplar. Devotionally, this was a pretty meager diet, but it was popular with the Protestant churches' political patrons, who were always keen on moralizing. The encyclopedias beloved of the Enlightenment age defined "churches" as "institutions for religious and moral questions."[6]

Schleiermacher was a young minister who had passed through a Moravian upbringing, a revelatory encounter with Enlightenment skepticism, and enthusiasm for and then disillusionment with the French Revolution, all filtered through a first-rate theological education. His 1799 book *On Religion: Speeches to Its Cultured Despisers* laid out the territory that liberal Protestants would claim for centuries. Schleiermacher's flowery, arch writing style has aged badly and can nowadays be hard going. But it repays the effort.

The basic rhetorical maneuver of *On Religion* is the disarming feint. Having laid out his readers' contempt for religion, Schleiermacher proceeds to agree with them. The idea that religion's purpose is to inculcate morality insults both religion and morality. As for the "cold argumentation" and "calculating proofs" of theology, they are no more than the burned-out ashes of religion's fire. Religion, he insists, is not about how we act or think but how we feel: the "heavenly sparks that arise when a holy soul is stirred by the universe." Philosophical speculation is futile unless grounded on "an original beam of the inner light." The philosophers imagine that they are God, sitting in detached judgment over creation, not limited and contingent creatures who can only see from their own perspective. It is only in feeling the power of those limited, contingent intuitions, and sharing them humbly with one another, that any true religion can be found. Schleiermacher did not defend miracle claims or revelations, but argued that the truly religious see miracles and revelations everywhere. He did not call on the reader to accept specific doctrines but rather to "become conscious of the call of your innermost nature . . . and follow it." He did not even urge the reader to believe, but rather to "see with his own eyes."[7]

A pretty peculiar defense of Christianity, then. Schleiermacher's orthodox critics felt that this pantheist mush conceded virtually everything to the skeptics. Yet in his second great book, *The Christian Faith* (1821), Schleiermacher demonstrated that you could get to a more or less orthodox Christianity from this unpromising starting point. This unusual route was a way to revive Protestantism's experiential power for his post-Enlightenment contemporaries, rescuing its original love affair with God from dead formulae and a "mania for systematization." He insisted that true religion is a matter of the heart, of longing to be "grasped and filled," of "feelings . . . like a holy music." Schleiermacher was, in fact, trying not to argue a case, but to awaken his readers' intuitions and to reveal the Reformation's original emotional power to the new, Romantic age. If your soul does not long "to drink in the beauty of the world and be permeated in its spirit," if you have never sensed something beyond yourself, then, he says despairingly, you have no religion. "Any further word about it would be an incomprehensible speech."[8]

Most professed Christians of his own time, he feared, were stone-hearted, secondhand believers. Almost two decades before *Frankenstein* was written, Schleiermacher compared this kind of religion to trying to assemble and bring life to a corpse. For the truly religious, by contrast, the church is about not structures and dogmas but a community for sharing intuitions and for mutual caring, like the Pietist *collegia pietatis*. Schleiermacher admitted, wryly, that in a sense he had come full circle back to his Moravian upbringing. He had found a way of embracing the new philosophies while still feeling the classic Protestant encounter with God burning in his heart.

By insisting that Christianity be approached experientially, from the unshakable starting point of our own humanity rather than from historical claims or abstract doctrines, Schleiermacher offered the prospect of a Protestantism that nineteenth-century skepticism could not assault and that could rekindle some of its smoldering fire. But could it work? Schleiermacherian liberalism instead led some believers to self-centered transcendentalism and off the Christian map entirely. Channing, the American liberal pioneer, claimed that "God is another name for human intelligence raised above all error and imperfection, and extended to all possible truth"; in other words, he had deified his own moral convictions. Theodore Parker, an avid reader of Schleiermacher, claimed that "each man must be his own Christ, or he is no Christian." He at least remained a Unitarian minister. Ralph Waldo Emerson, who insisted that as a believer you must "make your own Bible," left the ministry in 1832; despising all outward forms and rituals, he could no longer bring himself to celebrate the Lord's Supper.[9] Following your religious intuitions wherever they led could mean leaving historic Christianity behind entirely.

Those examples may sound like a few eccentrics, but liberal Protestantism was never a mass movement. It appealed chiefly to a thin slice of the male, educated elite and was led by academic theologians rather than by preachers or by popular devotion. This now seems inevitable, but a more broad-based liberal Protestantism ought to have been

possible. Liberalism—the belief that societies should be free, politics
should be open, and everyone should be equal before the law—was one
of the century's great ideals. Surely liberal Protestants could claim their
part in pressing those claims? A few did, Schleiermacher himself among
them. He had once said that for a church to accept state patronage and
control was to stare at Medusa's head, forever frozen into a dead semblance of itself. When that prospect actively threatened in Prussia after
1817, he was one of a handful of liberals who stood against it. Schleiermacher died in 1834, but in the early 1840s the Friends of Light, a movement blending political and theological liberalism, bubbled up in
Saxony, campaigning against state control of religion and for political
reform. This movement and others aligned with it were involved in
the abortive liberal revolutions that swept across Germany in 1848. In
the United States, too, early theological liberals took up positions at the
leading edge of political reform, opposing slavery and supporting democracy. Theodore Parker coined the phrase "government of the people, by the people, for the people," which Abraham Lincoln made
famous. He also supplied the weapons for the Harpers Ferry raid of
1859, which was intended to trigger a slave uprising.[10]

Most liberal Protestants, however, were too deeply invested in the
status quo to ally themselves with radical political reformers. Like almost everyone else of their class, they were terrified by the French
Revolution's excesses and swayed by the fact that the Protestant powers
spent a generation at war with revolutionary and Napoleonic France.
The churches became pillars of German national resistance; Schleiermacher was so effective in preaching to soldiers that he was dubbed the
second Luther. Following Napoleon's final defeat in 1815, princes con-
solidated the new order. In 1817, King Frederick William III of Prussia—
a pious Reformed (Calvinist) Protestant married to a Lutheran—imposed
by fiat the scheme his Calvinist brethren had dreamed of two centuries
before: a merger between the Reformed and Lutheran churches. The
new body was a creature of the state, and its bishops royal officials. In
Britain, meanwhile, the Tory establishment's grip on the Church of
England was undisguised, and the established Church of Scotland was
dominated by the so-called Moderate party, which entrenched the
power of the landed classes. Even the United States' far more open

religious landscape was dominated by a conformist political consensus that prioritized national unity over matters of principle such as slavery. Everywhere, Protestant clerical establishments were co-opted by political establishments and resolutely opposed not only revolution but liberal political reform. The long-term damage that this did especially to Europe's churches is hard to overstate. Liberal reformers came to see the churches as the stooges of tyranny, if not as its puppet masters.

Insofar as there was opposition to the new political order, it came not from theological liberals but from obstinate conservatives. The liberals who spoke against the German church mergers of 1817 and after were easily sidelined, whereas the refusal of unreconstructed "old Lutherans" in Prussian and Silesian parishes to accept the new structures led to arrests, to troops' being sent in, to a wave of emigration, and finally, in 1840, to a new Prussian king's accepting defeat and granting the old Lutherans a degree of toleration. The same king had no difficulty in suppressing the Friends of Light a few years later.

Likewise, Britain's Tory religious establishment was challenged not by liberals but by staunch traditionalists. In England, old High Church Anglicanism was joined in the 1830s by a new "Anglo-Catholicism," vigorously asserting the church's right to govern itself against the pretensions of an increasingly secular state. These Anglo-Catholics explicitly disavowed the Church of England's Protestant past, and several of their leaders ultimately converted to Roman Catholicism. At the same time, a resurgent evangelicalism across most of Britain's Protestant denominations became the religious backbone of the great reforming Whig-Liberal governments of the 1830s and thereafter. In Scotland, evangelicals chafing against the landed Moderates' grip on the Church of Scotland finally decided, in 1843, to walk out and form a Free Church, leaving behind them both the legal status and the buildings and finances of the established church. More than a third of all Scotland's ministers, and as many as half of its laypeople, took this step into the unknown. Within four years, the Free Church had built 730 churches, housed their ministers, and built 500 schools. The confident modernity of the new church is symbolized by the famous painting of 457 signatories of the Act of Separation, the world's first group portrait aided by the new science of photography. (One of my ancestors is there in the crowd.) It was the century's most dramatic and effective Protestant revolution, and an achievement that liberals never came close to matching.

God's Successive Revelations

To begin with, most Protestants shrugged off the ominous rumbles of skepticism and secularism, but slowly the darkening skies became unmistakable. A persistent drip-drip of new ideas first eroded Protestantism's certainties, then threatened to wash them away entirely. Many Protestants experienced this simply as a storm to be weathered as best they could. Some discovered that it had its own appeal and tried to ride the wave.

The most immediate challenge came from scholarship on the Bible. This problem had been there in embryo since the beginning. As we have seen, Luther and several other first-generation reformers had been surprisingly relaxed about factual accuracy or minor contradictions in the biblical narratives. The Bible was God's love letter to them, and they read it with that sense of passionate inspiration. Yet they also, of necessity, used it as a weapon, and the sharp need to defend their respective positions quickly led them to cling much more tightly to the precise letter of Scripture. In particular, they dismissed medieval theology's allegorical and symbolic methods of Bible reading, arguing that allegory run wild could make a text mean virtually anything. The plain, literal sense of the words, they insisted, must be primary, as it was—a fateful thought—for any other book.

The problem was that much of the Bible consists of detailed historical narratives whose doctrinal or moral relevance to Christians is not obvious. Traditionally, these passages had been read allegorically, but if they were to be taken literally, readers would inevitably ask, "Are they literally true?" The problems with those historical claims were not glaring, but they were niggling and persistent. The book of Genesis appears to date the creation to approximately 4000 B.C. Even in the sixteenth century, it was apparent that the historical traditions of Egypt, China, and other ancient civilizations reached back further than that. Or consider the two different genealogies of Christ in Matthew and Luke's Gospels. Traditionally, they had been given different symbolic meanings, but in a world of biblical literalism this looked like a simple contradiction. Miracle stories were a different kind of problem; here, eighteenth- and nineteenth-century rationalists were struggling against not the text's inconsistencies but their own incredulity. Could you really believe (it became the totemic example) that a whale had swallowed the prophet Jonah, kept him alive in its belly for three days, and then spat him out unharmed on a beach?

If the Bible had to be read like any other book, then perhaps it had to be analyzed and critiqued like any other ancient text. When the English cleric Henry Hart Milman published *The History of the Jews* in 1829, it proved so controversial that he feared his own parishioners might attack him, but not because he had actually denied the biblical account. Rather, he had recast the Old Testament narrative into the mode of secular history, treating the ancient Jews as a Near Eastern tribe, assessing and critiquing the documentary evidence. The whole approach was profoundly subversive. Milman survived the controversy and went on to become dean of St. Paul's Cathedral in London, but other boundary stretchers were not so lucky. In Germany, the home of the new biblical scholarship, pioneers' careers and reputations were destroyed. Yet they kept coming. David Friedrich Strauss was a Hegelian mystic who found the whole notion of a religion rooted in specific historical events distasteful. His *Life of Jesus* (1835) was a frontal assault, dismissing John's Gospel as mythical and rewriting the other Gospels' accounts so as to remove anything miraculous and to render Jesus a mere preacher. It cost him his job, and when the University of Zurich subsequently offered him a post, the resulting outrage triggered a popular revolution and the overthrow of the canton's liberal government.

Within a generation, however, using new biblical scholarship explicitly to attack Judaism and Christianity became a route to commercial and scholarly success. In 1901, the German Assyriologist Friedrich Delitzsch claimed that virtually the entire Old Testament was based on earlier Babylonian texts. By the time it became clear how gross an exaggeration his claims were, his fame was already established. Skeptical scholarship did not debunk the Bible, but it did make it possible for laypeople honestly to conclude that the Bible had been debunked. By the early twentieth century, it was possible for a nonspecialist like the scientist Ernst Haeckel, whose works were bestsellers in both German and English, to claim offhand that the Gospels were forged in the fourth century, without attracting too much outrage or ridicule.[11]

As these ideas slowly seeped out of the academy, most believers shared the Zurich peasantry's instinct to reject them. Because most Protestants' everyday religion does not hang on the date of creation, the precise genealogy of Christ, or the edibility of seaborne prophets, it was possible for many of them simply to ignore these problems for a remarkably long time. To begin with, only a relatively small group of liberals directly faced the problem of how to absorb the new scholarship into their faith without losing that faith's heart.

The guiding principle of this new approach, as laid out in 1790 by Johann Gottfried Herder, was that the Bible "must be read in a human way; for it is a book written by men for men." For Coleridge, an acute reader of both Herder and Schleiermacher, this opened an alluring possibility. Rather than claiming that "whatever is contained in the Bible is religion, and was revealed by God"—a claim that, for Coleridge, strained credibility—he could claim more modestly that "the Bible contains the religion revealed by God." Channing, too, saw the Bible not as an actual revelation but as "the records of God's successive revelations to mankind": a *human* (and therefore fallible) record of the infallible divine Word.[12] The claim that God's revelations are *successive* was crucial, for it suggested that modern believers' experiences and intuitions need not simply fall in line behind the ancient faith but could stand beside it and even augment it.

This approach allowed Protestants to believe that the Bible they loved was *inspired* without having to believe it was *infallible*: to focus, as Quakers would say, on the living Word rather than the dead letter. The Bible, Schleiermacher had warned, could become "merely a mausoleum of religion," "a weak reproduction" of past religious experiences. Liberal theologians could therefore claim that their faith was more alive than the traditionalists'. The American Presbyterian David Swing, charged with heresy by his church in 1874, urged his congregation,

> Always distrust any one who rigidly follows the letter of God's
> word, for thus you will be plunged into a world of discord, and

the Bible will lie at your feet a harp, broken, utterly without
music for the sad or happy hours of life.

On this view, Protestants could read the Bible *either* as lovers *or* as fighters.
It could be a source of inspiration or a polemical weapon, but not both.[13]

However, this approach also posed formidable problems. A set of
English liberal position papers published in 1860 under the anodyne
title *Essays and Reviews* argued that the Bible should be read "like any
other book." Examples were soon on hand to show what that meant.
Bishop Colenso's 1862 treatise on the opening books of the Old Testament took a disarmingly plain approach, arguing that the text simply
could not be read literally. For example, Leviticus 8:3–4 claims that
Moses assembled the whole congregation of Israel at the door of the
tabernacle, a door whose dimensions are given elsewhere. Colenso calculated that nine people could have fit in front of it, whereas figures
given elsewhere count the entire Israelite congregation at around two
million.[14] Professional biblical scholars found Colenso's bluntness
simpleminded, but his claims were easy to understand and hard to rebut. Reading the Bible like any other book apparently meant accepting
that it might contain mistakes. In which case, it was simply a fallible
record of one ancient people's religious experiences: admirable perhaps,
but no more authoritative than Babylonian myths.

The fear of a slippery slope mobilized eleven thousand English clerics
to sign a declaration opposing *Essays and Reviews*. An attempt was made
to try Colenso for heresy. But once the first wave of fear had died down,
a weird period of calm ensued. It slowly became clear that real Christian
faith was still possible in a world of biblical criticism. In Germany, the late
nineteenth century was a time of renewed Protestant self-confidence,
thanks to the newly unified German Empire's aggressive promotion of
Protestantism as a marker of national identity. Britain, too, successfully
house-trained the new ideas. In the 1880s, a group of Cambridge biblical
scholars used the new methods to reach some reassuringly conservative
conclusions, and the problem faded from public view. Its chief legacy was
a rash of literary "lives" of Jesus, imaginative, often fictionalized attempts
to re-create the Gospel narrative as a human story within an entirely
orthodox frame. Astonishingly, more than five thousand English lives of

Jesus were written between 1874 and 1906. It almost looked as if liberal
Protestantism had successfully ridden the wave.[15]

The Book of Nature

The stereotypical Christian view of the universe—that it was created
in six days a few thousand years ago, with Earth at its center—had
never been universally accepted. It was openly questioned by the new
astronomy of Nicolaus Copernicus, published under Lutheran auspices
in 1543, which put the sun instead of Earth at the center. That was a
disorienting idea, but one easily absorbed into Christian orthodoxy.
Seventeenth-century astronomers then began to suggest that the universe was infinitely large and that the stars might themselves be distant
suns. This did not contradict claims for humanity's or for Jesus Christ's
uniqueness, but it did unsettle them. More unsettling were the gathering hints that creation's traditional timescale was far too short. Some
astronomers began to revive the ancient Platonic argument that the
universe is without beginning or end. Isaac Newton stuck fast to the
traditional timetable of creation, but his great rival, the Lutheran-raised
deist Gottfried von Leibniz, suggested that the six "days" of creation
might have been periods lasting far longer than twenty-four hours. Was
this an attack on Christian orthodoxy or a reimagining of it?

The real trouble came not from the sky but from the ground, as the
spread of mining in the early industrial age made geology an urgently
practical science. The rocks told a story that was hard to reconcile with
traditional Christian history, and some geologists became openly skeptical. The scathingly antireligious British geologist George Hoggart
Toulmin argued in 1780 that both Earth and humanity were eternally
ancient and that anyone who disagreed was "cramped by the fetters of
superstition." But others drew different religious conclusions from the
same geological findings. The Scottish polymath James Hutton agreed
that, as he famously claimed in 1785, geology could find "no vestige of
a beginning—no prospect of an end" to the world's history. The next
century's greatest geologist, Charles Lyell, was too cautious to specu-
late about Earth's creation, but he, too, insisted that the world was far,
far older than six thousand years. Yet neither man found that his conclusions troubled his faith. In what was by then a scientists' cliché, Lyell

claimed to be reading the truth from the Book of Nature, a counterpart to the Book of Scripture. Earth's crust, he argued, was a "book . . . written in characters of the most striking and imposing kind," and its testimony was unambiguous.[16]

Accommodating the apparent contradiction between these two divine books was not terribly difficult. For Lyell, the creation story in Genesis 1 was "elliptical in the extreme" and "makes no pretensions whatever to supply those minute scientific details which some would endeavor to extort from it." To read it as a geology textbook was a category error. Once that was accepted, reconciling geology and Genesis was easy. Perhaps the six "days" of creation were figurative. The sun, after all, does not appear until the fourth day. Perhaps untold aeons had passed between verse 1, when God created the heavens and the earth, and verse 2, when God's spirit moved over the formless waters and the creation of living things began. More to the point, for Hutton and Lyell, the geological revelation had its own appeal. Their conviction that Earth had been shaped by slow, ancient, continuous processes, not by sudden catastrophic events like Noah's Flood, was as much aesthetic as it was scientific. A perfect divine designer, they reasoned, would not be so vulgar as to wrench his creation around like a drunken rider. Lyell liked to quote the great Swedish naturalist Carl Linnaeus: "Nature does not make jumps." That was not a scientific fact but an article of faith.[17]

Protestant readers of the new geology had three choices. They could abandon their faith, and some did. They could try to deny the new findings, a position that became ever more difficult. Ignoring the mounting scientific evidence could be done, but it was not easy. "If only the Geologists would let me alone, I could do very well," wrote the artist and idealist John Ruskin in 1851, "but those dreadful hammers! I hear the clink of them at the end of every cadence of the Bible verses." A genuinely watertight solution to this problem was advanced in 1857 by the zoologist Philip Henry Gosse, who conceded that the world *appeared* to be ancient but argued that God had created it looking that way, like a forged painting. The idea was perfectly logical and utterly irrefutable. To almost all his contemporaries, it was also completely ridiculous.[18]

But there was a middle way: to rebuild the old faith on these new foundations. Charles Kingsley, now chiefly remembered for his children's book *The Water Babies,* was also a keen amateur scientist. He found his own faith enlivened by geology, but he also called the new science "the devil's spade, with which he loosens the roots of the trees prepared for burning." That is, science exposed lazy and merely formal Christians for the unbelievers they truly were. Accepting its religious implications required a leap neither of faith nor of the intellect but of the imagination. It meant seeing that the universe was dizzyingly vast and ancient, and finding in that not an alienating, dreadful emptiness but what Schleiermacher had called "an astonishing intuition of the infinite."[19]

It could be done, and liberal Protestantism was uniquely well equipped to do it. But the bedrock on which this new synthesis was being built turned out to be less solid than liberals blithely assumed. For geology was only the warm-up act for the greater crisis that had been slowly brewing in biology for decades and that broke in 1859 with the publication of Charles Darwin's *On the Origin of Species.*

The notion of evolution—that different species were somehow related and that simpler, lower creatures might develop into more complex, higher ones—had been widely accepted by scientists for decades. Darwin's contribution was twofold. First, he provided a plausible account of how it happened. "Natural selection," by which individuals who prosper in the "struggle for life" pass their advantages on to their descendants, could lead to the gradual alteration of an entire species, allowing it to morph seamlessly into something subtly, and eventually radically, different. This formidably powerful idea has since been refined and developed, but it has never yet been successfully challenged. Almost equally important, Darwin successfully planted his idea in the center of educated culture. His book became a bestseller, and a large swath of the educated public found his arguments intuitively true. The notion that all living things—including humans—are tied together by a web of interrelations was an idea whose time had come.

Again, Protestants faced the same three alternatives. A few decided that evolution made a creator God redundant and so abandoned their faith, more often with enthusiasm than with regret. Karl Vogt, Darwin's great German advocate, bluntly claimed that science had now disproved God's existence and that the universe consists entirely of physical matter, which was never created but simply exists eternally.

He famously dismissed thought as a substance excreted by the brain, "as gall from the liver, or urine from the kidneys."[20]

Orthodox believers pushed back, and a few became redoubtable anti-Darwinists, seeding the persistent myth of the battle between science and religion. Denying evolution was easier than denying the new geology, because Darwin's evidence was more piecemeal and (for the time being) incomplete. For Christian antievolutionists of the first generation, however, the stakes were different. Their problem with Darwinism was not chiefly that it contradicted Genesis. Evolution was a little tougher to reconcile with the Bible than geology, but it could be done. The anti-Darwinists' worries were more philosophical. They viscerally disliked the notion of one species shading gradually into another, with its implied seamless continuity from primordial soup to humanity. Endlessly fluid change, in which everything is always slowly turning into something else and nothing has any unchangeable essence; the lack of any clear direction to evolutionary history; the suffering and endless extinctions that, for Darwin, were the driver of evolutionary change—none of this contradicted any core Christian doctrine. Some traditional Calvinists cheerfully embraced evolution; they had always seen the world as mired all but irrecoverably in corruption, and found Darwinism's unsentimental rigor appealing. But to many Victorians, this shaking of the hierarchies by which they lived felt as unscientific as it did impious. In the United States, some white Protestants had been claiming that white and black people were different species and that only whites were descended from Adam and Eve. One even argued that the "serpent" who tempted Eve in Eden referred to a black man. Darwinism's claim that all humans were of one stock and that even the "master races" were descended from dumb animals offended white Protestants' sense of their own dignity. None of this had very much to do with Christianity.[21]

Once again, however, there was a third way: to see what spiritual insights Darwinism had to offer. Like gradualist geology, Darwinism suggested a God who worked patiently within his universe, an ever-present creating hand. On these grounds, the Oxford theologian Aubrey Moore called Darwinism "infinitely more Christian than the theory of special creation."[22] But what captured the late Victorian age's imagination was not natural selection's austere simplicity but the more seductive notion of evolution, a word that became almost synonymous with "progress." Perhaps, under God, evolutionary change was not directionless but a life force driving inexorably toward higher forms. Perhaps that principle of gradual, inexorable progress was everywhere. That, after all, would explain how nineteenth-century Europe had become such a pinnacle of civilization. It became common knowledge that Darwin had proved that progress was a law of nature.

Darwin had of course done no such thing. The true begetter of this pattern of thought was Herbert Spencer, a political philosopher who had entirely abandoned Christianity for a progressivist philosophy and who took Darwin's neutral term "natural selection" and repackaged it as "the survival of the fittest." Evolution now became a moral imperative. Those who prospered, by definition, deserved to do so. Wealth and power were signs of virtue. The poor and the weak were "unfit" and thus doomed by the law of nature. Attempting to protect or even to educate them was not only naive but arguably immoral. It was kinder to let nature take its course, or indeed to help it along, accelerating the inexorable progress toward a better humanity. If some unfortunates suffered, that was the law of nature and was in any case as nothing to the progress that the master races might make.

Darwin himself was rather less racist than the average Victorian Englishman. His successors and interpreters had no such restraint. The German popular scientist Ernst Haeckel explicitly argued that European imperialism proved white racial superiority. Darwin's cousin Francis Galton coined the term "eugenics" for his scheme to give natural selection a helping hand by choosing which humans should be allowed to breed. John Fiske, whom Darwin called his best American expositor, reckoned that what he called "the English race" would inevitably crowd out the indigenous populations of North America and Africa. Fiske coined the term "manifest destiny" to describe this, a phrase whose queasy elision of what *will* be with what *should* be sums up what we now find repellent about this whole pattern of thought.[23]

Fiske's other distinctive contribution was his claim that Darwinism proved the existence of God. He argued that because religion was a universal feature of humanity, it must have evolved and that it could not have evolved unless it were true.[24] As that dubious argument demonstrates, evolution in general, and Spencer's social Darwinism in particular, were ideas liberal Protestants could embrace, despite the very poor fit between traditional Christian morals and Spencer's callous collectivism. So Darwinian natural selection, overlaid with Spencer's triumphalist moralizing, became sanctified. An endless struggle for existence was God's will, and the victors were the blessed. *Evolution* became not a biological process but a divine principle. Evolution, wrote the Scottish Free Churchman Henry Drummond, "is Advolution; better, it is Revelation . . . the progressive realization of the Ideal, the Ascent of Love."[25] This not only made a spiritual virtue of the age's most powerful secular idea but provided the perfect riposte to any conservative Christian naysayers: they were simply out of date. Liberal Protestantism had out-evolved them.

Liberalism in the Trenches

In 1914, two of the world's three great Protestant powers, Germany and Britain, went to war. In 1917, the third, the United States, rode into the fray. In all three cases, liberal Protestants were at the forefront of the clamor for war. They did not cause World War I, nor was their faith doomed to warmongering, but the experience does show where liberalism's bold ideals could lead.

German Protestantism, far more so than its British and American counterparts, was unified and dominated by the state. It was common for late nineteenth-century German pastors' homes to feature paired portraits of Luther and of Otto von Bismarck, Germany's two liberators. Luther, often described simply as "the German man," was celebrated more for freeing the nation from the papacy than for preaching salvation by faith. He had once been celebrated as a harbinger of freedom, but Lutherans' political radicalism had long since faded. Socialists increasingly despised Luther for having betrayed the revolution he began, by substituting slavery to the state for slavery to the church. The now-united Protestant church loathed and feared socialism in return, and instead embraced a pungent German nationalism.

Germanness had come to be associated with certain specific Christian or quasi-Christian virtues. German character was said to be courageous, honest, and honorable, cherishing truth and beauty above advantage and profit. And, in keeping with the social Darwinism with which Germany was particularly enchanted, the country's impressively fast rise to world power was a sign of the superiority both of German culture and of the German race.

Yet German Protestant self-confidence was an anxious, brittle thing. While Germany saw itself as a new power, struggling to get the corrupt old hegemons to recognize its legitimate claims, German Protestantism felt itself to be in retreat before socialism, secularism, and ever-present Catholicism, with the country's huge industrial cities almost lost to it. Perhaps Germany might win the new industrial age and lose its soul.

So when war came, liberal and conservative Protestants found themselves in resolute alliance, and they remained in lockstep until the bloody end. At the start, they hoped it would be a moment of spiritual awakening, turning Germany away from its creeping commercialism. This was a war for honor—or, as the great Protestant philosopher Ernst Troeltsch put it, "for the freedom of hearth and home, for the right of the German spirit." When Germany's parliamentarians gathered for a service in Berlin's cathedral on August 4, 1914, the day Britain entered the war, the preacher declared a war of "German civilization against barbarism," claiming that "German faith and piety are intimately bound up with German civilization."[26] The medievalist Walter Lehmann, preaching that autumn, declared in excitement that "the God of the Germans had come to life!" This God, he admitted with some understatement, was "perhaps not entirely orthodox Christian," but omitting divisive doctrinal questions was a means to unite "the most valuable things in Christianity" and "the unique character of German nationality." Some began to talk of how Christianity needed to be Germanized.[27]

This outburst of clerical excitement was based in part on the claim that Germany was fighting a just war of self-defense: a claim bolstered by official propaganda which alleged, falsely, that France had attacked Germany rather than vice versa. Germans' righteous outrage, however, focused especially on the British, supposedly their fellow Protestants, now unmasked as grasping, imperialistic hypocrites. How could Britain, which had invaded so many countries on the flimsiest of pretexts, possibly discover self-righteousness in claiming to defend poor innocent Belgium—when Germany had only sent its troops through

Belgium in desperate self-defense against the French attack? Surrounded and outnumbered by these treacherous enemies, Germany ought to have been crushed. Yet it swiftly won battle victories in 1914. Evidently, Germans' purity of spirit and God's love of justice were more than a match for their craven enemies. Could a victory be won? asked the minister Bruno Doehring in 1916. If so, "there is only one power that can do it . . . the German, Martin Luther, the man of the gospel, who found courage through the power of the gospel and the sword of the spirit to assault the whole world and its money politics."[28]

During August 1914, congregations doubled in size in much of Germany. This seems to have been due to families saying farewell to, and then praying for, conscripted young men, but to excitable clerics it felt like a revival. The moment of national unity swept normally sober souls away. More than 10 percent of all Germany's Protestant clergy volunteered for military chaplaincies. And notoriously, in October 1914, ninety-three leading German academics across all disciplines signed a Declaration to the Cultured World, giving full-throated support to a war to defend the land of Goethe, Beethoven, and Kant against the barbaric hordes massing at their gates. Among them was the greatest liberal Protestant theologian of the day, Adolf von Harnack.

The mood soured as the war ground bloodily on, but German Protestantism had made its bed and resolutely lay in it. As shortages of war matériel became urgent, churches were stripped of copper, brass, and nickel, including organ pipes and bells. With political discontent rising as food shortages bit tighter by 1917, liberal and conservative Protestants alike reinforced their support for the regime, opposing plans for political reform and any hint of peace initiatives. In a holy war for righteousness fought against the odds, the threat of defeat should only renew your courage. The volunteer military chaplains came to be loathed. When both army and regime finally buckled in October and November 1918, one of the first signs that military discipline was breaking down was the near-total withdrawal of soldiers from the now-hated religious duties. German Protestantism paid dearly for its folly. The people it cheered to war paid more.

Liberal Protestantism was not to blame for Germany's war, but it played its part. At the very least, it now became plain that if the world decided to go mad, liberal Protestantism could do nothing to keep it sane. Schleiermacher's insistence that religion was a matter of intuition and feeling meant that an outpouring of nationalistic rage could be a religious experience. Liberal Protestantism's flexibility also made it easy to discard awkward Christian principles such as loving one's enemies. In his 1906 *Quest of the Historical Jesus,* the great liberal Albert Schweitzer depicted Jesus not as a moralizing teacher but as an apocalyptic prophet whose ethic of nonresistance and love for humanity applied only to his specific historical situation. Since then, religious truth had evolved, reaching its apogee in Germany. Troeltsch, the eminent philosopher who claimed to be acting in "the spirit of Kant, Hegel and Schleiermacher," spoke of "reshaping" Christianity into "an idealism of freedom" that would demand and justify victory at any cost. In this social Darwinist world, defeating the lesser races by any means necessary would be God's will, because victory is always and by definition justified. "God," Walter Lehmann preached, "is nothing but our moral activity, our honest and righteous behavior, the deepest, final reason for our fighting." Liberal Protestantism was not actually responsible for Germany's destruction, but not for want of trying.[29]

Britain's Protestantism was much less centralized and politicized than Germany's, but scarcely less enthusiastic for the war when it came. Like their German counterparts, British preachers in 1914 believed they stood at a hinge of history. "The world is passing out of one thing into another," declared Randall Davidson, the archbishop of Canterbury. "Much that we set high is being lowered, much that we placed low is being lifted up." There was a whiff of evangelistic opportunism in that comment.[30] Yet attempts to spark renewals of religion among British troops had at best modest success. The constant movement of troops, the attrition of casualties, and the arrival of newcomers made building cohesive believing communities difficult. British soldiers regarded their chaplains and preachers more warmly than did the Germans, and many of them found solace, strength, and even sanity in their religion, but there was no mass revival.

In Britain as in Germany, Protestant clerics alarmed by growing secularism and materialism hoped that a good dose of war might draw their people back to the true faith. "Perhaps," the hymn writer Percy Dearmer mused in 1915, as the scale of the war's horrors was becoming unmistakable, "God has allowed us to pull down the temple of modern civilization over our heads in order that the survivors may be cured of the modern habit of regarding man as a calculating machine." Germany reckoned Britain had sold its soul to moneygrubbing commerce, and British Protestants feared it might be true. Like their German counterparts, they hoped that war might help their countrymen rediscover honor and sacrifice.[31]

This was because they saw the moral case for war as unanswerable. Britain was simply trying to stop German aggression. Much was made of the invasion of innocent Belgium and of the wanton damage done by German troops in Louvain, Rheims, and elsewhere. These incidents, however, were not in themselves enough to steel a nation for total war. What the preachers did was connect them into a narrative of Germany as a rogue nation. They blamed this, above all, on liberal Protestant theology.

Britain's diagnosis was that Germany had become intoxicated by social Darwinism, and in particular by the notion that neither law nor morality could apply to states. This was labeled kaiserism, Prussianism, or the "Gospel of Force." The state takeover of the Protestant church and the liberal theology's abandonment of Scripture had turned German Protestantism into a militarist neopaganism in which nation and race were preferred above humanity and universal principles. Britain's responsibility was to bring Germany back to its senses, which meant, first, bringing it to its knees. As the bishop of London put it,

> We are on the side of Christianity against anti-Christ. We are on the side of the New Testament which respects the weak, and honors treaties, and dies for its friends, and looks upon war as a regrettable necessity, and we are against the spirit that war is a good thing in itself, that the weak must go to the wall, and that might is right.

The result, he added with a straight face, was "a Holy War, and to fight in a Holy War is an honor." It was, as one pamphlet put it, a war between the "mailed fist" and the "nailed hand," albeit one in which the nailed hand was firing a machine gun.[32]

The irony of German and British Protestant propaganda in World War I is that both sides were uncomfortably accurate. The German account of the British, the self-righteous, moneygrubbing imperialists who are sticklers for rules that somehow never apply to themselves, was fair. So was the British account of a Germany that abandoned law, believed force to be self-justifying, and prized national and even racial superiority over justice and mercy. Britain's stance was more traditionally Christian and more profoundly hypocritical. What gives the lie to both sets of justifications is the constant aversion to talk of negotiated peace from churchmen in both countries, liberal and conservative alike. Each side reviled the other's aggressions, but neither would accept a return to the prewar status quo. They wanted punishment for the warmongers—that is, revenge. In Britain as in Germany, liberal Protestants were not exactly to blame for the war, but nor did they manage to demonstrate the inexorable moral and spiritual progress in which they believed.

That belief had taken deepest root in the United States. There, unlike in Europe, the war split Protestant liberals and conservatives from each other. By the early twentieth century, a self-styled "progressive" Protestant theology had attained a remarkable dominance among American church leaders. Just as the United States saw itself as the nation of the future, so many of its Protestant ministers and theologians saw themselves as preaching what Charles W. Eliot, the president of Harvard University, called "the Religion of the Future." Christianity had once promised to redeem a few chosen souls from a lost world, the progressive preacher Lyman Abbott wrote, but the new Social Gospel promised something greater: "the transformation of the world itself into a human Brotherhood . . . the great world-wide democratic movement." This was an evolutionary idealism, but it had little in common with Spencer's callous individualism. Instead, the whole world was struggling toward a higher moral plane. A widely used seminary textbook published in 1898 dismissed traditional notions of Christ's second coming. "If our Lord will but complete the spiritual coming that he has begun, there will be no need of a visible advent to make perfect his glory on the earth."[33]

What this meant in practice was moral reform. Following in the footsteps of their abolitionist heroes, progressive Protestants targeted the evils enslaving their own times: divorce, gambling, the exploitation of workers, commercialism, and—their signature issue—alcohol. The

American campaign to prohibit alcohol was grounded on concerns about the real social ills of alcoholism in an industrial society, but also on a conviction of moral progress. Like slavery, if alcohol was once prohibited, it seemed inconceivable it would ever be restored. But as with slavery, no one expected it to be easy. Evolution is always a struggle. America's progressive churches were full of talk of battles and crusades. So when a real war thrust itself onto America's attention in 1914, they were ready.

America was neutral but from the beginning leaned toward the Allies, commonly depicted as fighting for democracy and republicanism against monarchical tyranny. Progressive Protestants were in the vanguard. This war to end war, they suspected, was the next, decisive stage in humanity's moral ascent. German aggression needed not merely to be contained but to be punished. When President Woodrow Wilson made a (doomed) attempt to broker a negotiated peace in December 1916, sixty prominent church leaders denounced him. "There are," they warned, "conditions under which the mere stopping of warfare may bring a curse instead of a blessing. . . . Peace is the triumph of righteousness and not the mere sheathing of the sword."[34] It seemed to make sense that an organization pressing for the war to be fought to the finish should call itself the Church Peace Union.

Progressive Protestants did not actually drag the United States into the war—Germany's use of unrestrained submarine warfare from February 1917 did that—but they certainly tried. On April 1, 1917, the ministers of New York's Plymouth Church, the progressives' most influential pulpit, wrote to Congress urging a declaration of war. The first Russian Revolution, which briefly looked as if it would turn the Allied powers into a fully democratic coalition, only spurred the progressives' sense that this was a war of destiny. It was America's moral duty, as the nation that was the world's last, best hope, to save the world from militarism. The dean of Yale Divinity School claimed, without irony, that America "is called of God to be . . . a Messianic nation."[35]

American progressives echoed Britain's critique of Germany but, like German liberals, were willing to part company with conventional Christian ethics. It is unclear whether Newell Dwight Hillis, a minister at Plymouth Church, really did say that he would forgive the Germans "just as soon as they were all shot," or claimed that "if we forgive

Germany after the war, the moral universe will have gone wrong." But he certainly called Germany "a mad dog let loose in the world's schoolroom" and reviled talk of a negotiated peace for putting "too much stress on human life. . . . What is human life? All the great things of the world have been done through martyrdom."[36]

War was declared following a congressional vote on April 6. During the debate, one antiwar congressman read aloud a letter from a constituent, dismayed by pulpit warmongering:

> We heard a minister state with vehemence . . . that the great question today is "Christ or Prussianism." His idea was that we should shoot Christianity into the Germans with machine guns and cannons. Just how much Christianity he could cram into a 10 or 12 inch cannon he did not say.[37]

Soon the whole country would be swept up by such sentiments. The United States has now almost forgotten its brief participation in World War I, but for a couple of years the nation was gripped with a militaristic nationalism to match anything in Europe.

If liberal and progressive Protestants were deeply implicated in this warmongering, America's conservative and evangelical Protestants took a different tack. A much-despised but very substantial grouping of American Protestants were premillennialists; that is, they believed that the world was irreformably sunk in sin, that Christians ought to be saving souls rather than reforming society, and that the world would be saved only by Christ's literal return. The premillennialists reviled progressive theology in general and the Social Gospel in particular, and when war came in 1914, they wanted nothing to do with it. William Jennings Bryan, a giant of progressive politics whose theology was staunchly conservative, resigned as secretary of state in 1915 in protest against President Wilson's drift away from strict neutrality. When war finally came, some premillennialists remained pacifist and were accused of betraying their country, or even of being German agents.

Not many evangelicals had the nerve to hold that line. Some, like Bryan, accepted the war with loyalty but without enthusiasm. Others discovered that they were the true patriots, because this was a war against the very same liberal-progressive theology that was taking over their own country. Evolutionary thinking, a consensus quickly decided, was at the root of all of Germany's evils. Back in 1904, Bryan had denounced Darwinism as "the law of hate—the merciless law by which the strong crowd out and kill off the weak." Ten years later, Germany had put that law into practice. The revivalist preacher Billy Sunday, who moved seamlessly in 1917 from denouncing progressivism's evils to (literally) pulpit flag-waving, claimed that "if you turn hell upside down, you will find 'Made in Germany' stamped on the bottom." If conservative Protestants would not fight for heaven, they would fight against hell.[38]

The establishment Protestant churches of Germany, Britain, and the United States all survived World War I. They had faithfully channeled their people's nationalisms and had ministered to those people through years of terrible butchery. Some of the war's survivors did emerge with their religious faith broken, but others emerged with it strengthened or renewed. There was no immediate change in the churches' social position in postwar Britain and America, and even in Germany, now a secular republic, the churches remained deeply woven into the social structure. Postwar Protestantism did not face a crisis. Rather, its status and its self-assurance slowly ebbed away, just as Europe and America slowly came to doubt that World War I had been a just struggle after all.

In the next two chapters, we will see how that erosion of confidence played out in its different contexts and how Protestants tried to fight back against it. What is plain is that, like so many nineteenth-century ideals, liberal Protestantism never truly recovered from World War I. Liberalism's dilemma was, and remains, how to discard some parts of traditional Protestantism while retaining a defensible core. It was far subtler, more modern, and more rational to treat the Bible as a collection of historic religious experiences rather than as a direct revelation from God, but if Christianity was to be simply a religion of intuition and of reason, was it not doomed to follow the secular world rather than to lead or shape it? The "Religion of the Future" proclaimed at Harvard was not, a *New York Times* reporter commented drily, a religion anyone would die for. It was hardly a comfort to discover that plenty of people would kill for it.

Conservative Protestants reviled their liberal brethren for having abandoned the historic faith for a malleable mush of modernism. It is true that liberal Protestantism is—and makes a point of being—exceptionally adaptable. And yet conservative Protestantism is in practice almost equally pliable. All Protestants adapt; the difference is that liberals admit it. The theologians on all sides might have come up with different rationales for war, but they all sent their young men to the same trenches.

It is easy to condemn those early liberals for their reckless naïveté. It is worth remembering that even before 1914 they were enduring a formidable bombardment. The secularist threat in the early twentieth century was, in intellectual terms, stronger than ever before or since. The best modern scholarship was telling Christians that the universe was eternal, with no beginning and no end; that a progressive life force of some kind drove the world's development; that the Bible was a collection of myths and forgeries with almost no roots in real history; and that humanity was evolving to ever greater wisdom and virtue, "virtue" being defined in social Darwinist terms that left little space for quaint notions like justice and mercy. We now know, or think we know, that none of those claims are true. Our forebears had to digest them as best they could.

CHAPTER 11

Two Kingdoms in the Third Reich

And who is my neighbor?

—LUKE 10:29

Not many people saw it coming. While most Europeans and Americans were expecting the great struggles of the twentieth century to pit them against old dynastic empires, Communism's godless legions, or the fanatical Asiatic hordes, another, more pernicious ideology was taking root. Even those who found it distasteful were slow to realize that it was worse than any other supposed threat. Nazism was eventually crushed, but the price was the bloodiest war and the most terrible genocide in human history.

This happened in the cradle of Protestantism. A handful of German Protestants stood heroically against it, but many more were its collaborators or cheerleaders. If we are to understand modern Protestantism, we need to understand why so many Protestants went along with Nazism as far as they did, and why some of them decided they could go no further.

Nazism itself was neither religious nor atheistic, in the normal senses of those words. Adolf Hitler never openly renounced the Catholicism in which he was raised, but he was vehemently anticlerical, and he came to view Christianity as "a fairy story invented by the Jews" and a Jewish-Communist conspiracy against the German people. Yet he also dismissed atheism, the Communists' creed, as subhuman and mocked attempts by some Nazis to revive ancient Nordic paganisms. Since the Nazi Party's first formation in 1920, it had been formally committed to "positive Christianity," but this slippery concept was a code for opposing individualism and "the Jewish-materialistic spirit." Nazism actively rejected Christianity's ethic of compassion and humility, in favor of the supposedly German virtues of heroism, strength, and patriotic pride. Although Hitler thought Nazism should foster some "notion of divinity," it found its spiritual meaning not in any god but in the purity of the Aryan race, a purity whose highest expression was the Nazi state itself.[1]

So Nazism was not in any meaningful sense a Christian ideology. But at its heart was hatred of Jews, a hatred built on many centuries of Christian anti-Judaism. The chief pretext for Christian Jew-hating has long been the peculiar accusation that the Jews, collectively, killed Christ; the Romans, who actually crucified him, were somehow forgiven. Beneath that lay a simmering resentment at Jews' continued existence. How could these people not see that their Messiah had already come and that their whole religion was out of date? Perhaps their obstinacy was diabolical. Perhaps God had blinded them to the truth in punishment for their faithlessness. As a result, while they were mostly allowed to continue their stubborn lives, they were hemmed in, exploited, induced or compelled to convert to Christianity, and subject to periodic spasms of violence.

Protestantism added its own distinct twist to this poisonous legacy. Protestant theology was built on a fresh reading of St. Paul, who contrasted his Christian convictions with a sometimes crude caricature of the Judaism of his youth. Judaism, for Protestants, came to represent legalism, self-righteousness, and hypocrisy. Contempt for this imagined Judaism was deeply woven into Protestant thought, especially for Lutherans, for whom the Hebrew Bible—what Christians call the Old Testament—was more a historical witness to God's patient dealing with his obstinate chosen people than a model for contemporary Christian living. Luther's 1523 pamphlet *That Jesus Christ Was Born a Jew* aimed to win Jewish converts by offering Jews kind treatment, which was at least a novel approach. When it seemed not to be working, Luther lurched as far the other way as any Christian theologian had ever done. The best that can be said of his 1543 tract, *On the Jews and Their Lies,* is that it does not openly call for genocide. Instead, he demanded that Jewish synagogues, books, schools, and homes be destroyed, rabbis forbidden to preach, and Jews' property confiscated. He recommended that Jews have no legal rights and be either used as forced labor or banished. While he did not actually advocate murder, he did argue that Christians have no moral obligations toward Jews and that there is no sin in killing them. The Nazis, for whom Luther was a German national hero, made sure this work was copiously reprinted.

During the eighteenth and nineteenth centuries, Protestantism seemed to be leaving these prejudices behind. As tolerance changed from a pragmatic concession to a liberal principle, European and North American Jews slowly won legal rights and a measure of popular acceptance. But Protestant anti-Judaism changed with the times, assuming two contradictory faces. For politically conservative Protestants, Jews became symbols of godless, socialist, commercial materialism. If you hankered for the old, simple, spiritually unified Germany—a naive and not quite innocent longing—the Jews might represent everything that stood in your way. In 1928, the leading Luther scholar Paul Althaus warned against a "disintegrated and demoralizing urban spirituality, whose representative now is primarily the Jewish race."[2]

Theologically liberal Protestants, by contrast, found that new scholarship was letting them discard the old restraints on their anti-Jewish impulses. Almost-respectable historians began to suggest that ancient Galilee's people had been mostly Gentile, and the supposed miracle of Jesus' virgin birth was invented to conceal the fact he had been sired by a Roman soldier. Jesus' parentage had once proved he was divine; now, even better, it proved he was a Gentile. With the new categories that cutting-edge scientific racism was producing, he could even be optimistically classified as Aryan. Those who could not quite swallow that might accept other sweeping reinterpretations of the Gospel. The best-selling French historian Ernest Renan accepted that Jesus was Jewish by birth but saw his mission as being defined by his opposition to Judaism and all its many evils. Adolf von Harnack, the lion of German liberal theology, thought Christianity had moved so far beyond Judaism that the Old Testament might not belong in Christian Bibles at all. Few 1920s German Protestants would go that far, but many felt it was tasteful to downplay the Old Testament, to cease giving children Old Testament names, and quietly to drop embarrassing Hebraisms such as "Hallelujah" from modern church use.

The Institute for the Study and Eradication of Jewish Influence on

German Church Life, inaugurated in 1939, was not some ersatz Nazi project. It was launched in the Wartburg Castle, where Luther had lived in hiding and translated the New Testament in 1521–22. Its director, the distinguished New Testament scholar Walter Grundmann, asserted in his inaugural lecture that the institute's work was nothing less than a second Reformation. Luther had thrown off the pope's stranglehold on Christianity. Now, Grundmann declared, scholars had likewise revealed the "deformation of New Testament ideas into Old Testament preconceptions, so that now angry recognition of the Jewishness in the Old Testament and in parts of the New Testament has arisen."[3] Christianity had to be purged of Jewishness. Any listener might logically conclude that it was therefore also time for Christendom to be purged of Jews.

Making Peace with Nazism

For most of Germany's Christians, the 1920s were an ordeal. Their country had suffered an unexpected military collapse in 1918, a humiliating victors' peace, devastating hyperinflation, and then a cultural takeover by liberalism, licentiousness, and a mocking, anticlerical secularism. Almost all German Protestants belonged to the national Protestant church, fruit of the previous century's state-sponsored mergers in which the Lutheran majority had been forced to accept the Calvinist minority. But now a newly secular state had cast them adrift. Communism and socialism, on the rise both internationally and at home, looked like a threat to Western civilization as a whole. Frightened, angry Protestants, longing for old certainties, voted overwhelmingly for right-wing parties. Increasingly, this included the National Socialist German Workers' Party, known in their characteristic abbreviated style as Nazis. Their distinctive promise was a synthesis of ancient German values and the modern world. It was a message aimed at those who found the present intolerable but knew the past was irrecoverable. And if the Nazis' violent style was distasteful, at least it showed they would stick to their guns. In the national election of July 1932, when the Nazis looked like the only force capable of stopping Communism, they won 37 percent of the overall vote. In Catholic-dominated regions of Germany, they took "only" 23 percent, but in Protestant-dominated regions it was over 56 percent.[4]

When Hitler took office as German chancellor on January 30, 1933, no one mistook it for a routine constitutional transition. This was avowedly the birth of a new German Reich, and Germans had to choose sides. Many Protestants supported the new order. Many did not, and by 1934 some of these opponents had formed themselves into the so-called Confessing Church. The struggle between these two parties dominated German church life throughout the Reich, but we should not be too distracted by it. The Confessing Church was a broad coalition, and most of its members were not anti-Nazis in any active sense. They were not active collaborators with the regime, but they were often its silent accomplices.

The pattern was set in the spring of 1933, when the Nazis' brown-shirted storm troopers unleashed a wave of anti-Semitic violence. The Nazi regime was announcing its arrival. Hundreds of Jews were murdered. Alongside this went a boycott of Jewish businesses, and the "Aryan Paragraph," a law expelling Jews from all public offices. Foreign observers were shocked. So, too, were many ordinary Germans, who neither loved Jews nor liked to see thugs smashing windows and beating up people in the street. Ahead of its regular meeting in Berlin on April 26, the national Protestant Church Committee was deluged with pleas to speak out.

At that meeting, most speakers did show some distaste for what was happening. The vast majority, however, favored discretion. Plenty of them thought the new regime was at least partly right, comparing the new regulations to the status of German Jews before emancipation in the nineteenth century. Perhaps this was simply the return to an old status quo, in which Christianity had been closer to the heart of national life. Some truly believed that there was a threat of Jewish-Communist "infiltration" and takeover. Otto Dibelius, a Protestant bishop who had preached at Hitler's inauguration, wrote,

> I have always considered myself an anti-Semite. One cannot ignore that Jewry has played a leading role in all the destructive manifestations of modern civilization.

In June, a memorandum from the Protestant church's central office to its brethren overseas went further. With a prickly resentment of foreign

criticism, it claimed that "the Jewish question . . . can only be understood from within Germany," before explaining that "Jewish infiltration" and the "Jewish mentality . . . [were] undermining the Christian
faith and ethic, family life and the national culture." While any excesses
were deplorable, tackling Germany's Jewish problem was a matter of
national self-defense.[5]

Even so, there was real disquiet, much of which focused on the
status of baptized Christians who were of Jewish ancestry. For most
Protestants, such people were simply Christians, but Nazi racial theories did not allow the stain of Judaism to be washed away by baptism.
All anti-Semitic regulations applied to baptized as much as to unbaptized Jews. It was not too much to expect Germany's Protestants to
make some mild protest about these issues, but in April 1933 they decided not to, a decision to which most of them stuck for the next twelve
years. The reasons include fear and wishful thinking, but they were
also grounded in earnest theological principles.

Martin Luther's doctrine of the two kingdoms insisted that church
and state not encroach on each other's territory. This had by now
evolved, or degenerated, to the point that the church doubted its right
to express political opinions at all. This apolitical instinct is a recurrent
theme in Protestantism. In its milder forms, it has often served Protestantism very well, but in Nazi Germany it infected the churches with a
fatal lassitude. The June 1933 memorandum to the foreign churches
deplored violence in the abstract but added that it was "scarcely possible
for any general comment to be made by the church . . . in view of the
complexity of the factors involved." When the regime appealed to reasons of state to justify its actions, Lutheran churches had no reply. God
had permitted the Nazis to take power. The church could hardly defy
his manifest will.

Even ministers of the supposedly anti-Nazi Confessing Church felt
a deep tug of loyalty to the state, a loyalty for which they were prepared
to compromise what might seem like fundamental principles. Karl
Barth, whom we will meet shortly as the Nazis' most formidable theological opponent, wrote in 1939 that the two-kingdoms doctrine "lies
like a cloud over the ecclesiastical thinking and action of more or less
every course taken by the German Church."[6] He had in mind an

incident in which a pro-Nazi pressure group had challenged Germany's Protestant ministers to take an oath to Hitler as Führer. Virtually all of them did so. Yes, the oath was terrifyingly plain, promising total submission with no heed to God, conscience, or law. But Christian kings had demanded oaths from their subjects for centuries. When the nation's rightful Führer asks this of his people now, how dare they refuse? Farcically, the regime then refused to accept the oath. Martin Bormann, Hitler's vehemently anti-Christian personal secretary, dismissed it as a purely voluntary and internal matter. The lesson: even when the state did not demand loyalty, Germany's Protestants could not stop themselves from giving it.

Insofar as anyone avoided this trap, it was Dietrich Bonhoeffer, a young minister who was unusually quick to see Nazism for what it was. Yet in 1933, even Bonhoeffer, Lutheran to his core, accepted that there was a "Jewish question" that the state needed to solve and that it had considerable freedom to do so as it saw best. The best he could do was to argue, in classic two-kingdoms mode, that the state's basic function was to preserve order. Churches could therefore speak out when it failed to fulfill that function, by permitting lawless street violence. As he came to appreciate that street violence *was* the policy of the Nazi regime, Bonhoeffer avowed that the regime was no longer a state at all but a criminal conspiracy. This was a blunt solution, but few other German Protestants found one at all. Bonhoeffer became an active plotter against the Nazi regime, and in April 1945 he was hanged for it. In prison, he reflected on why so few Germans had been willing to defy "the radical evilness of evil" that was Nazism. He blamed a fatal humility, which led to Germans' being readier to trust their rulers' decrees than their own instincts. It was virtuous in its way. But it meant that when the regime gave evil orders, Germans obeyed with "an irresponsible unscrupulousness," scarcely bothering to consult their consciences. Yet when they considered defiance, those same consciences awoke into "an agonizing scrupulosity which invariably frustrated action."[7] Submission and obedience were the paths of least resistance.

Those paths were smoothed by less high-minded impulses. The regime terrorized the churches, not in most cases by direct attacks, but by ominous, implicit threats. In that first debate on anti-Semitic violence in

April 1933, the president of the German Protestant church's executive committee admitted that he had not dared raise the matter with Hitler in person. It was already clear that this was not a regime which took kindly to opposition. In the years that followed, the Confessing Church was permitted to exist, but its people were regularly subject to frightening harassment. If Gestapo surveillance was not constant, it was assumed to be. There were periodic arrests, and while most victims were soon released, some were not. It was, Karl Barth wrote, a form of "death by strangulation," slowly squeezing the spirit from churchmen until, after years of jumping at every shadow, they had little stamina for real defiance.[8]

More damaging than fear was hope. The primary reason that the church committee chose not to make an issue of anti-Semitism in April 1933 was that it had more exciting priorities. To worry about a few Jews, whose sufferings were probably exaggerated, was to miss the point: the Nazi seizure of power was a moment of national spiritual renewal, as 1914 had been. The epochal battle against Communist secularism had been won. Congregations were surging across the country, and the new government, unlike its secular predecessors, was committed to "positive Christianity" and traditional Christian morality. When Paul Althaus, the Luther scholar who had earlier linked Jews to moral decay, exulted that "our Protestant churches have greeted the turning point of 1933 as a gift and miracle of God," he was referring not to the Nazi seizure of power as such but to a national awakening that transcended politics.[9]

This miracle still hung in the balance. The opportunity of 1914 had been squandered. This one must not be. "Use the hour!" one church newsletter urged in mid-1933, "so that our church will once again be a people's church and able to participate in the construction of our *Volk*."[10] *Volk* was a word to conjure with. It has no precise English equivalent, but combines "nation," "people," and "race." Its use here implies that "non-Aryans" were not welcome in this people's church. But if that seemed tasteless, carping over such details risked letting the moment slip through your fingers. Many Protestants saw Nazism as a stepping-stone to national revival. When that happened, surely Nazism's uglier features would fade away. In the meantime, the battle for the *Volk*'s soul mattered more than a few Jews. And did a renewed Christian Germany want Christ-killers in its midst anyway?

Like so many other false dawns, this one faded. Congregations ebbed again, and it became clear that the Nazis were using the churches more effectively than the other way around. Yet German Protestants clung determinedly to the hope that the regime was ultimately on their side, a hope that the regime naturally encouraged. When elements in the Confessing Church produced a wide-ranging protest against the regime's evils in 1936, they sent it directly and discreetly to Hitler, apparently genuinely believing he did not know what was happening.[11] Believers told each other stories of how Hitler carried a well-thumbed New Testament in his vest pocket. Even in 1941, a rumor spread "that Hitler had experienced a conversion [and] now confesses the Christian faith." A Confessing Church synod lamented the same year that "this trust in the Führer contends desperately with a realization of the truth."[12] In dark times, it was natural to grasp at comforting lies.

De-Judaizing Christianity

Yet there is more to Protestantism's story in the Nazi era than a centrist establishment muddling through ingloriously. Some Protestants' support for the Nazis was full-throated. In 1932, a regional Nazi Party leader organized a forum for party members and sympathetic churchmen, a group that he planned to call the Protestant National Socialists. Hitler, always protective of the Nazi brand, suggested a simple alternative: the German Christians.

For a short moment in the spring and summer of 1933, it looked as if the German Christians might end up as a formal part of the Nazi state. In April, Hitler appointed a hitherto-obscure German Christian minister, Ludwig Müller, as his special adviser on church affairs. He also pressed the Protestant church, then a loose national federation, to create a new, centralized structure led by a Reich bishop. The new constitution, eventually adopted in June, was rather less centralizing than the regime had wished, and there was an impasse over the appointment of the Reich bishop. The regime broke the deadlock by calling national church elections on less than a week's notice. The German Christians, forewarned, presented slates of candidates everywhere, while the old establishment was left, dazed, on the starting blocks. The day before the elections, Hitler made what would be his plainest ever intervention in church politics, in a radio broadcast praising the German Christians for their "solidarity

with the national and cultural movement." He urged Protestants to support them over "the unrealistic forces of religious ossification."[13] German
Christian candidates duly won two-thirds of the votes and took control
of twenty-four of Germany's twenty-seven regional churches. The new
Reich bishop was none other than Hitler's adviser Ludwig Müller. From
then until 1945—for there would be no more church elections—most of
the formal structures of Germany's established Protestant church would
be firmly in German Christian hands.

The German Christians expected this to be only a beginning. Their
ambition was nothing less than to create a new Christianity organized
around Nazi racial ideology. Humanity's racial divisions, they reasoned, were not only a fundamental fact of nature but also God's will.
Aryans were created superior to other races, just as men were created
superior to women. Any realistic Christianity had to embrace that self-
evident truth, instead of Bolshevik claptrap about human equality.

That idea had enormous theological consequences. If the *Volk* was
the fundamental unit of Christian life, then traditional Protestant preoccupations with individual salvation and eternal life were not only
beside the point but tasteless. Liberal Protestantism's this-worldly focus
was much more welcome. At least as momentously, a truly German
Christianity would have to be a Christianity for all true Germans. The
German Christians wanted a single Reich church that would forcibly
encompass all Protestants and, many of them hoped, Catholics, too,
even though neither the regime nor German Catholics were remotely
interested in creating such an entity. More fundamentally, what of traditional Christian ethics? "We are not unacquainted with Christian
love," the German Christians' first manifesto reluctantly conceded in
1932, but again liberal theology's trick of selecting the principles it likes
proved invaluable. The "living, active Christianity" of the modern age,
they declared, had left behind such outmoded ethics as "mere pity" and
"charity." True Christian love means protecting the *Volk* "from the
feckless and the inferior." In 1939, the Reich bishop, Müller, was arguing that Christian love "hates everything soft and weak," which has to
be "cleared out of the way and destroyed" for the *Volk*'s true life to
flourish.[14]

The first targets for this "love" were Christians of Jewish descent,
of whom there were some fifty thousand. Some German Christians

toyed with the idea that Aryan and Jewish Christians might coexist in separate churches, "both specially suited to the members of their *Volk*." Others taught ever more plainly that mere baptism could not erase racial inferiority, refused to baptize would-be Jewish converts, and drove non-Aryan Christians from their churches. In December 1941, German Christian church leaders issued a declaration excluding all "racially Jewish Christians" from their churches, on the grounds that the "racial essence" of Jews cannot be changed by baptism.[15] By then, this was a symbolic statement. Germany's remaining Jews were either in hiding or en route to the death camps.

For all this, the German Christians' bid to become the Protestant wing of the Nazi Party failed. After the triumph of the church elections in 1933, the regime backed away. Hitler's deputy Rudolf Hess laid out a policy of strict religious neutrality, a stance whose wisdom soon became clear. In November 1933, the leading German Christian Reinhold Krause told a huge rally at the Sports Palace in Berlin what a truly German Christianity meant. It meant "liberation from the Old Testament . . . one of the most questionable books in the world's history." It meant "that the whole scape-goat and inferiority-type theology of the Rabbi Paul should be renounced."[16] Tellingly, the twenty-thousand-strong crowd cheered. Only when his words were widely reported did they become a scandal. The broad center of German Protestantism was content to accept both Nazi rule and casual anti-Semitism, but openly attacking the Bible was another matter. Hundreds of German Christians resigned from the movement. One of these was Reich Bishop Müller, whose vain attempt to protect his reputation only succeeded in undermining what authority he still had.

The regime deliberately kept its distance from the whole fiasco, and from then on kept church factions of any kind at arm's length. After repeated warnings, the German Christians were finally forced to stop using the swastika. Members of the SS, the Nazis' paramilitary wing, were barred from holding any church office. In 1938, Hess explained that the party's policy was to remain aloof from religious politics so that the churches could quarrel themselves into oblivion and the people would "recognize that National Socialism is a God-ordained order and institution."[17] When war came in 1939, the German Christians longed to provide military chaplains, to help the nation celebrate this great, uniting sacrament of blood. To their dismay, chaplains' numbers and rights were systematically restricted. A so-called Uriah law even had them deliberately sent to the front of combat, to accelerate Hitler's view that "the best thing is to let Christianity die a natural death." He would not, yet, mount a frontal attack. "The ideal solution would be to leave the religions to devour themselves, without persecutions." But in another mood, he would add, "If I ever have the slightest suspicion that they are getting dangerous, I will shoot the lot of them."[18]

Still the German Christians tried, vainly, to demonstrate the compatibility of their beliefs with Nazism. In 1939, eleven regional churches produced a declaration describing Christianity as "the irreconcilable religious opposite of Judaism." Still the regime would not bite. During the war, some German Christian churches took to declaring themselves "officially anti-Jewish." In 1944, one German Christian publication even looked forward to a postwar world "completely purged of Judaism."[19] Still the Nazi regime was not interested.

The final throw of the dice was the Dejudaization Institute at Eisenach, a top-level theological think tank. For its participants, the project of de-Judaizing Christianity was a moral as well as a political priority. If Christianity was to flourish in a postwar world purged of Jews, it had to prove that it could decisively rid itself of its own Jewish roots. Otherwise it risked giving the future to secularists and neo-pagans.

The institute's proudest achievement, published in the summer of 1940, was *The Message of God,* generally known as the *Volkstestament.* This was nothing less than a de-Judaized Bible. It is quite brief. The entire Old Testament is of course gone. The three "synoptic" Gospels, Matthew, Mark, and Luke, are merged into a single text in which Jews and Judaism appear chiefly as Jesus' enemies. Some extracts from John's Gospel, Paul's letters, and the Acts of the Apostles are also included. The following year, a hymnbook appeared, its nearly three hundred lyrics carefully vetted for any hint of Jewish influence. Both books ran to over 200,000 copies, which, given that access to paper was tightly restricted in wartime, shows that the institute was not without friends. Soldiers at the front—the very embodiments of Nazi virtue—were using them. Perhaps the German Christian dream was not dead after all?

In fact, nothing could demonstrate its futility better than these books. De-Judaized Christianity turned out to be pretty thin gruel. Nearly half of the hymnbook consisted of secular German lyrics. The rest had been purged of anything reflective or penitential, and of references to Christian doctrine. Militaristic triumphalism and domestic sentimentality were all that was left. The *Volkstestament* was more complex, for its editors had not been able to eliminate Judaism entirely. Although Jesus' racial identity is not stated, he still teaches in the Jewish temple and even, daringly, quotes a Jewish psalm. Nor could St. Paul's Jewishness be avoided; this was why some German Christians had wanted to drop him altogether. A few even argued that the very idea of Scripture was a Jewish perversion. "Whereas the Jews were the first to write out their faith, Jesus never did so."[20] It is often said that you can twist the Bible to mean anything, but the Dejudaization Institute's efforts prove that even if you abandon almost all of it, there are still meanings it will simply refuse to bear.

In return for this effort, in 1941 Walter Grundmann, the institute's director, was bluntly told by an official in the Propaganda Ministry that "there is no interest in synthesizing Christian teachings with National Socialism, nor proving that a reshaped Christianity is not fundamentally Jewish."[21] It is almost pitiable. Emptying Christianity of all its substance did not make anyone want the husk. But it will not do to feel too sorry for Grundmann. His institute, while it lasted, seems to have been a thoroughly agreeable place to work. Most of its alumni managed to shake off any unpleasant associations after the war and to go on to very successful academic careers. Grundmann himself, after a cursory show of repentance, became both the rector of a prestigious seminary in East Germany and an active informer for the East German secret police.

Shades of Opposition

A handful of German Protestants were uneasy about the new regime from the beginning. Bonhoeffer could not evade the issue of anti-Semitism: his sister had married into a Jewish family. When her father-in-law died in April 1933, Bonhoeffer was advised not to conduct the funeral—advice that he heeded, to his immediate and lasting regret. Most of his fellow ministers were more concerned with the Nazi regime's interference in the church's self-governance. When the snap elections were called in June, a fledgling movement calling itself Gospel and Church tried to organize against the German Christians, arguing for a church "independent from the state and from the pressure of all political powers" that "declares the Word of God in complete freedom."[22] Given the electoral juggernaut they were facing, their achievement was impressive enough. Their inchoate campaign managed to deny the German Christians control of three of Germany's twenty-seven regional churches, namely Bavaria, Hanover, and Württemberg. Those three—soon known as the "intact churches," as against the "destroyed churches" in the rest of Germany—would be both a crucial power base for non-Nazi Protestantism and a steady drag on real anti-Nazi activism.

The German Christian triumph tied the substantive problem of anti-Semitism to the constitutional question of the church's independence. The flash-point issue became the status of Protestant ministers who were classed as racially Jewish, whom the German Christians wished to remove from office. There were only around thirty such men nationwide, but for the nascent opposition a vital theological principle was at stake. For most Protestants, Jewishness was a religious rather than a racial category, and a Jew who converted to Christianity was no longer a Jew. To apply the Aryan Paragraph to the church was to devalue both the sacrament of baptism and the grace of God.

The new movement was headed by an avowed anti-Semite and former U-boat commander who had first voted for the Nazis back in 1924. But Martin Niemöller's anti-Semitism was lazy and conventional rather than passionate. He was now discovering that he needed to make a stand. He organized the Pastors' Emergency League, whose members committed themselves, in classically Protestant terms, to accept no religious authority beyond Scripture and the historic Protestant confessions of faith, and bound one another to mutual assistance. In particular, they agreed to defy the Aryan Paragraph as an intolerable trespass by the state into the kingdom of Christ. Within weeks, more than a thousand ministers had joined.

In 1934, emboldened by the chaotic lurches in church politics under Reich Bishop Müller's inept leadership, Niemöller's league and its allies hardened into the Confessing Church, consisting of the three intact regional churches as well as ministers and people across Germany. That year over a third of Germany's eighteen thousand Protestant ministers affiliated with it, and although that number did fall away somewhat, it remained higher than the number who were avowed German Christians. Nothing else quite like this happened under Nazi rule—the formation of a genuinely independent nationwide organization defined by its rejection of parts of Nazi ideology. Its survival throughout the Nazi Reich demonstrates that for all the regime's pretensions to totalitarianism it could not in fact police hundreds of thousands of believers, and dared not risk confronting them openly. But it also shows the weakness of the Confessing Church itself, which never truly stood against the Nazi regime. Its achievement was to defend its own independence. The price was to let the regime have its own way on almost everything else.

The Confessing Church was defined not by politics but by theology. It was the church of old-fashioned Protestant orthodoxy: Scripture, the historic confessions, justification by faith alone. The chief accusation it leveled at the German Christians was heresy. For many Confessors, the German Christians' worst offense was not the Aryan Paragraph but their doomed overtures to Catholicism. Plenty of Protestants still remembered that the pope was Antichrist. For a while, the German Christians worked with an anti-Catholic nationalist outfit named the Protestant League, but in 1937 the league could stand the German Christians' inclusiveness no longer and managed to publish 130,000 copies of a pamphlet opposing them, titled *National Church?* The Confessing Church's surviving bishops, in the intact churches, also warned that the German Christians had been "heavily infiltrated" by Catholics.[23] A similar principle lay at the heart of the Confessing Church's rejection of state control. One of its formative synods in 1934 implicitly accepted that the "Führer principle . . . and the consequent demand for unconditional obedience" were acceptable in secular politics but insisted that in the spiritual realm they amounted to "a Papal hegemony unthinkable within the evangelical church."[24]

Along with old-fashioned anti-Catholicism went old-fashioned anti-Judaism. Confessing Church propaganda commonly dismissed the German Christians' obsession with race by comparing it to the Jews' claim to be a chosen people. They even called the Dejudaization

Institute's purged Bible "Pharisaical." These were more than cheap shots. For most in the Confessing Church, Judaism was and remained a symbol of theological error—in particular, of quasi-scholarly nitpicking that twists truth out of recognition until it becomes its very opposite.

Insofar as the Confessing Church had a clear line on anti-Semitism, it was drawn by a synod in September 1935, in the same month as the Nuremberg Laws stripped German Jews of citizenship. Marga Meusel, one of the most senior women in the church's administration, drafted a forceful document for discussion. It denounced "the idolatry of Blood and Race" and argued that "persecution of Jews . . . *must* of necessity be followed by a persecution of Christians." Unusually, she was explicit in defending Christian and non-Christian Jews alike. Bonhoeffer, Niemöller, and a few others supported her. The synod as a whole, however, saw the document as dangerously political. One minister threatened to resign if it was adopted. The synod instead issued a simple statement merely affirming Jews' right to seek Christian baptism. As Niemöller acidly commented, what might happen to Jews after they were baptized was a subject the church preferred not to touch.[25]

The Confessing Church was chiefly composed not of heroes like Bonhoeffer but of men like Otto Dibelius. Dibelius preached at Hitler's inauguration, only to be ejected from his bishopric before the 1933 elections for insisting on the church's independence. In 1938, he was provoked to public protest by a speech in which the regime's minister for church affairs had argued that being a true Christian meant living a Christlike life, not recognizing Christ as God incarnate. An outraged Dibelius pointed out that the regime had no right to comment on doctrine. He was also appalled by the minister's claim that Jesus was not Jewish, on the grounds that a secular government had no business openly contradicting Scripture. However, Dibelius was content, in 1940, to propose a compromise solution to the ongoing impasse between Confessing and "constitutional" churches; both would formally be established as parallel state churches, recognizing the Führer's authority and restricting their ministry to German citizens. It did not trouble him, as a self-described anti-Semite, that this was a category from which Christian Jews were now excluded.

The Confessing Church's symbolic leader remained Niemöller, who slowly came to understand that compromise with Nazism was impossible. In 1937, he became one of the very few Confessing ministers actually to be imprisoned. A court order freeing him the following year was personally overruled by Hitler. He remained a prisoner until 1945, when he became the chief prophet of German Protestantism's national repentance. Niemöller's anti-Nazism, however, remained focused on the church and its rights. Although he opposed the Aryan Paragraph as an unacceptable intrusion on church life, he advised Christians of Jewish descent to withdraw from leadership roles voluntarily, for the sake of the church's internal peace. When war came in 1939, Niemöller, as a former naval officer, wrote to Hitler from his concentration camp to volunteer for service. There is some justice in the fact that Niemöller is now best remembered for his apocryphal admission that he was silent when Jews, Communists, and trade unionists were arrested, so when he himself was taken, no one was left to speak for him.

One reason why Niemöller has become the Confessing Church's symbol was that its intellectual giant was also one of its least representative figures. Karl Barth was the twentieth century's greatest Protestant theologian, but in the Confessing Church he was an outlier. He was Swiss rather than German, a social democrat in a church full of nationalist conservatives, and a Calvinist, heir to a tradition that had always been more skeptical of state power than the Lutherans. In 1914, when German Protestantism's liberal establishment cheered Europe on to slaughter, Barth, a twenty-eight-year-old minister in a rural Swiss parish, took another road. He believed liberalism's fundamental error, ever since Schleiermacher, had been its insistence on basing "religion" on human experience. That kind of religion, Barth warned, could only ever be a mirror, in which humanity saw and worshipped an imagined version of itself.

He was modern enough in many ways, and no friend to Fundamentalism, but his faith was based on reading the Bible and meeting in it a God who was utterly transcendent, before whom all human attempts to construct reasonable religions are like so much straw in a furnace. His contemporaries had become so used to making God in their own image that they had almost forgotten they needed salvation. Their obsession with "progress" had ended in four years of blood. In neutral Switzerland, young Barth had the perfect vantage point on his age's folly. As World War I ended, he published his volcanic commentary on Paul's letter to the Romans. A church that had almost forgotten how to say such things was reminded of the radical otherness of God, of humanity's depravity and desperate need for Christ, and of how nothing but divine revelation and divine grace could bridge the gulf between God and a fallen world.

Barth was, however, very much an academic theologian. Only the Nazi seizure of power dragged him into public life, for by then he held a university post in Germany. Naturally, he opposed state interference in church life and loathed the Aryan Paragraph, but for him these were secondary issues. Characteristically, he thought churchmen defending their institutions were almost as far from the true Gospel as were the German Christians. He was one of the first Protestants in Germany to affirm not only that Jesus was of course Jewish but that the Jews were and remain a people chosen by God's unconditional and irrevocable grace. The German Christians' central error, he insisted, was their claim that the German *Volk,* its race, history, and culture, constituted a "second revelation" superseding the Bible, a claim that put them beyond the bounds of Christianity altogether.

When German Protestantism's theological heavyweights gathered in the western town of Barmen in May 1934 to sketch out a way forward, Barth was at the heart of their councils. The Barmen Declaration, which became the Confessing Church's founding charter, was not solely Barth's work, but his intellect and personality so overawed his colleagues that it is hard to see their stamp on it. Thanks to Barth, the declaration was formulated not as a response to the immediate political crisis but as a timeless confession of faith, in the style of Protestantism's historic formularies and intended to take its place among them. Its contents were therefore almost entirely theological, but they were bold—too bold for many Lutherans. Since the sixteenth century, Calvinists had been trying to create Protestant unity by bleaching out Lutheran principles, and some Lutherans, especially the surviving establishments in the intact churches, suspected Barth of playing the same game. The declaration's insistence that church and state ought both, reciprocally, to respect each other's rights, even speaking of "the responsibility both of rulers and ruled," sounded to many traditional Lutheran ears as if the duty of obedience were now conditional.

Barmen did not explain what these broad principles might mean in practice. That would have to wait until a synod held in Dahlem, a suburb of Berlin, in October 1934. This bluntly stated that the German church had "collapsed" and no longer had any legitimate leadership, and unilaterally declared a wholly new structure that would henceforth be the legitimate Protestant church of Germany.[26] For the leadership of the three intact churches, this was a step too far. The result was a formal split in the Confessing Church, which was never fully reconciled. A group of moderates, led by the intact churches, repudiated the Dahlem synod's authority and accused it of reckless, Calvinistic divisiveness. Bishop August Marahrens, from the intact church of Hanover, claimed that Barth posed a greater danger to the church than Hitler.

That danger would soon be removed to a safe distance. In 1935, Barth was expelled from his university for refusing to swear allegiance to Hitler and deported to Switzerland. From then on, he was a voice crying in the Alpine wilderness. He denounced most of Germany's Christians, including most Confessors, as an

> army of neutrals . . . whose symbol consists of two thick blinkers and whose ecclesiastical desire is to be dangerous to no one, thus letting themselves be in no danger.[27]

He himself was very willing to be dangerous. During the Munich crisis in 1938, Barth wrote to a Czech friend that "every Czech soldier who fights and suffers . . . will also do it on behalf of the church of Jesus Christ"—so vindicating his German critics who had always suspected him of being too political.[28] When war finally came, Barth was in neutral Switzerland, but he worked with Jewish refugees and joined a Swiss civil defense organization.

The contrast between Barth's courageous clear-sightedness and his co-religionists' compromises can seem stark. But Barth was Swiss. Having neither been weaned on myths of German national greatness and humiliation nor endured the 1914–18 war, he had some immunity to Nazi cant. He was instead susceptible to his own national myths. He supported Swiss neutrality in 1914 as a prophetic sign of the possibility of peace. He backed it again in 1939, even as he argued that other countries had a duty to fight Nazism, claiming awkwardly that Switzerland's peculiar calling among the nations was to be a place of tranquillity amid the storm. He was sincere in these beliefs; they were also safe and easy ones to express. Moreover, Barth was first and last an academic theologian. His critique of Nazism was shaped accordingly. It was Nazism's theological errors rather than its crimes against humanity that truly fired his rage, although he recognized that the two were connected. On a visit to England in 1938, he was asked why the Confessing Church had said so little against the concentration camps, whose existence, if not their full horrors, was already well known. Other than begging the audience's understanding of the Confessors' precarious situation, he had no answer.[29]

The Limits of the Possible

What is true of Germany's national Protestant church is also true of its much smaller independent Protestant groupings—with one startling exception. Almost all of Germany's Protestant churches, from Methodists through the New Apostolic Church to American-rooted sects such as the Christian Scientists, were concerned primarily with protecting themselves. In most cases, they and the Nazi regime decided essentially to leave each other alone, although some sects positively supported the Nazis, whose conservative moralism was more appealing than 1920s secular permissiveness. Hitler's own well-known asceticism was another draw; Mormons and Seventh-day Adventists could not but notice that the Führer was a teetotal vegetarian. Adventists' interest in hygiene and health reform also chimed with the regime, and Mormons could see scope for reconciling Nazi racial theories with their own. For its part, the regime chiefly wanted to reassure itself that the sects were not crypto-Jewish, a concern that led the Seventh-day Adventists to drop the awkwardly Jewish term "Sabbath." Most sects made it their business to be noisily, demonstratively patriotic and were rewarded with the designation "nonpolitical," which allowed them to continue operating. When they did face restrictions, they quietly complied.

Youth groups were closed without protest. The Christian Scientists were banned altogether in 1941, and healing by prayer was criminalized; the church's tens of thousands of German members quietly dispersed, some meeting occasionally to pray together. None of this was heroic, but these groups survived.

One telling exception is the Seventh-day Adventist Reform Movement, a devoutly pacifist splinter group formed in 1916. The Nazi state did not take kindly to Germans who refused to fight for their country. The group was formally banned in 1936, its members interned and their children forcibly removed. The campaign against them was assisted by the mainstream Seventh-day Adventists, who were keen both to demonstrate their own bona fides and to rid themselves of a troublesome rival.

Yet this was a sideshow compared with the one major Protestant group that openly defied the Nazi state: the Jehovah's Witnesses. There were about twenty thousand of them in Germany in 1933, and nobody liked them. They, too, were pacifists and had refused to fight in 1914, and that, in the end, seems to have been what made them intolerable for the Nazis. But it did not help that they were fiercely opposed to any claims of nation or to any notion of race. That, plus their unshakable attachment to the Hebraic word "Jehovah," was enough to convince the Nazis that the movement was a Jewish-Communist conspiracy. The Watchtower Society's president, Joseph Franklin Rutherford, insisted, truthfully, that the Witnesses in general and he in particular hated and despised Judaism as much as every other religion. To no avail: the Nazis were determined to make the Witnesses their enemies, and while the Witnesses might have thought they were used to persecution, they had never faced anything like this before.

The Witnesses were banned nationwide as early as June 1933. At least eleven died in prison following a wave of arrests in November 1933, for refusing to vote in the regime's stage-managed national elections and refusing to use the greeting "Heil Hitler." A Witnesses' convention in Switzerland in October 1934 directly defied the Nazi regime, declaring, "We will, by His grace, obey Jehovah-God and fully trust Him to deliver us from all oppression and oppressors." They were not empty words. On December 12, 1937, the Witnesses managed to distribute in one day 300,000 copies of a leaflet, which they had had printed in Switzerland and smuggled to Witness groups across the country, condemning Hitler as the apocalyptic beast.[30] The Nazi state simply could not tolerate this.

By 1936, so many Witnesses were in custody that the state of Bavaria was having trouble arranging foster care for their children and ordered that Witness parents only be imprisoned one at a time. When war broke out, most of the remaining Witnesses were arrested for their refusal to support war work. Over ten thousand were sent to concentration camps. Uniquely among the Nazis' prisoners, they were offered the opportunity to free themselves by renouncing their faith. Almost none did so. Instead, according to the bewildered accounts of their fellow prisoners, they dealt exceptionally well with their ordeal. Suffering at the hands of Antichrist was exactly what their faith led them to expect, and their mode of resistance was scrupulous, obedient honesty. One SS officer commented that Jehovah's Witnesses were the only prisoners who could be trusted to shave their captors with cutthroat razors. It did not save them. More than five thousand died for refusing to renounce their faith. No other Protestants of any kind offered defiance like this or paid this kind of price. And because they were the most widely despised sect of all, no one spoke out for them.

A few German Protestants did manage to stand up for people other than themselves. The Confessing Church's letter of protest to Hitler in 1936, denouncing "a totally alien morality to that of Christianity," was naive, but it was not craven.[31] The mood shifted after the pogrom of November 9–10, 1938, glamorized by the Nazis with the title *Kristallnacht,* when tens of thousands of Jews were arrested, thousands of synagogues and businesses destroyed, and more than a hundred people killed. When one of Bonhoeffer's seminary students commented that this was another example of divine punishment for the Jews' faithlessness, Bonhoeffer retorted, "When today the synagogues are set afire, tomorrow the churches will burn." He and others were already helping Jews to emigrate. The Berlin pastor Heinrich Grüber organized a scheme that arranged safe passage abroad for more than seventeen hundred Jews. Most were Christians of Jewish descent, but his increasing willingness to help Jews regardless of religion might have persuaded the regime to shut him down in December 1940. Grüber spent the next three years in Dachau.[32]

Other initiatives were on a smaller scale. The Confessing Church's underground seminary in Berlin provided illegal employment to several Jews until it was broken up in May 1940. In 1941, three Mormon teenagers in Hamburg took it upon themselves to print anti-Nazi pamphlets, with titles such as *Hitler the Murderer,* on a church press and scatter them through the city. Two were imprisoned, and the third, despite his youth, was beheaded with an ax by the Gestapo.[33] Bonhoeffer, who had refused safe passage to the United States, became involved from late 1940 onward in a network of anti-Nazi conspirators at the highest level of military intelligence. It was his peripheral involvement in the failed July 1944 attempt to assassinate Hitler that in the end had him killed, but he was more central to a complex, risky plot in the summer of 1942 that succeeded in smuggling fourteen Jews to safety in Switzerland. By then, that was a remarkable achievement beyond most individuals' power. When the last free German Jews were arrested in 1941–42, their neighbors could do little for them. Confessing Church community groups met to pray with their Jewish-Christian members before their deportation, leading them in Bible studies to prepare for the ordeal ahead, training them to minister in the camps, even helping them to pack. If they feared that all this was futile, they could still hope that rumor had exaggerated the truth.

The dreadful extent of that truth remained largely hidden for the time being, if only because most people prefer to avert their eyes when faced with horrors. Even so, the Confessing Church remained silent until very late in the day. In January 1943, Theophil Wurm, bishop of the intact church of Württemberg and one of the Confessing Church's long-standing moderates, protested to the Interior Ministry about "the manner in which the war is being conducted against other races and peoples" and in particular "the systematic murder of Jews and Poles." This was not only a gross violation of God's law but, he added shrewdly, unbecoming of a cultured people. Pointing out Germany's recent, unexpected military reversals, he wondered if perhaps the nation had forfeited God's favor.[34] It is telling, however, that he preferred discreet lobbying to any kind of public protest. Later the same year, a

Confessing Church synod at Breslau offered something unique in Nazi Germany: a public condemnation of genocide. Insisting that all human life, "including the life of the people of Israel," is sacred, it warned, "Woe unto us and our nation . . . when the killing of men is justified on the grounds that they are unfit to live or that they belong to another race."[35]

Mere words, of course. How could even the bravest of protests have slowed the Nazi death machine? And yet the churches had already proved that it could be done. On September 1, 1939, Hitler authorized the so-called Action T4 program: mass extermination of invalids. Nazi eugenic theory had long called for the *Volk* to be purified of contaminants, and supporting such useless burdens in wartime was more than the Reich could endure. Typically, patients would be moved from one hospital to another on short notice, and the family would then receive a boilerplate letter informing them that their relative had unexpectedly died of a heart attack or similar cause and had been immediately cremated for reasons of hygiene. The letter offered condolences and the comforting thought that the patient had been released from a life of torment that was scarcely worth living. By the end of 1940, more than 35,000 patients had been murdered.

Within the health system at least, the secret could not be kept for long. In June 1940, Paul Braune and Fritz von Bodelschwingh, two Confessing Church ministers who were also directors of sanatoriums, petitioned the justice minister to stop the killing. The minister, an establishment lawyer now largely sidelined by Nazi ideologues, offered helpless sympathy. Braune then sent a carefully documented memorandum to the Interior Ministry, an altogether more sinister outfit. Von Bodelschwingh, fearing repercussions for his own patients, refused to sign it. Again, Braune achieved nothing apart from having himself arrested by the Gestapo, which held him for a month.

Yet the two men had stirred up genuine disquiet. A judge named Lothar Kreyssig, a member of the Confessing Church, now questioned Action T4's legal basis and was forced into premature retirement to his country estate, where he sheltered two Jewish women until the war's end. Bishop Wurm himself wrote an open letter denouncing the policy. The Confessing Church's synod in October 1940 discussed the matter but decided against speaking out. Many of those who actually worked in sanatoriums were torn between their desire to challenge the policy and their responsibility to their own patients, whom they feared they might make into targets. The middle way was to keep trying to work with the system, through private petitioning and networking.

Meanwhile, the crematoriums kept busy. By the summer of 1941, some seventy thousand patients had been killed. What tipped the balance was a public intervention, not by a Protestant bishop, but by a Catholic one. On August 3, 1941, Clemens Graf von Galen, the bishop of Münster, preached a devastating sermon against Action T4. With forensic care, he laid out both the horror of what was happening and its moral implications. He also took steps to ensure that this remarkable intervention reached beyond his audience in the St. Lambert Church that day. The sermon was printed in secret and circulated widely. British bombers dropped copies. A Confessing Church synod claimed that the sermon was "whispered from mouth to mouth throughout Germany."[36]

"I am quite sure," Hitler fumed, "that a man like the Bishop von Galen knows full well that after the war I shall exact retribution to the last farthing."[37] But he also backed down. Action T4 was becoming more trouble than it was worth, and on August 24, Hitler signed an order ending the program. Murders continued, including deaths from deliberate neglect and medical experiments, but the rate of killing slowed dramatically.

Braune, von Bodelschwingh, Kreyssig, Wurm, von Galen, and others had demonstrated that when a broad enough swath of Germany's Christians took a stand, it was possible to save lives. The effort was not exactly safe, but it was not impossibly dangerous either. The churches might not have been able to prevent the Nazi regime's other crimes, but they could have blunted their edges. Those crimes depended on the consent and cooperation of ordinary German civilians, and the Christian churches were the most prominent public arbiters of morality in German society. If they had insisted more regularly, in public and in private, that murder and hatred are wrong regardless of race, then it is all but certain that more of those civilians would have been given pause, and more of the regime's intended victims would have lived.

From a safe distance, the central and terrible fact of Protestantism in Nazi Germany is that most Protestants were either complicit or indifferent as unimaginable crimes unfolded around them. Yet condemnation is too easy. I am neither Jewish nor a Jehovah's Witness. We might imagine, or hope, that had we been there, we would have done something or taken some stand, but we are fooling ourselves. We would have understood what was happening around us in the same way they did. We would have shared their hopes, resentments, assumptions, and prejudices. We, like them, would have lowered our heads and muddled through increasingly terrible times as best we could. There is only one reason why we do not share in their guilt: we were not there.

CHAPTER 12

Religious Left and Religious Right

A prophet is not without honor, but in his own country, and among his own kin, and in his own house.

—MARK 6:4

The simple story of Protestantism's history in the Western democracies over the past century is one of steady decline, while secularization marches inevitably on. This much-told tale is really a claim about the future: a prediction that organized religion is doomed. Perhaps so, but the story so far is messier than the myth of decline suggests. Christianity has not collapsed intellectually during this period. If anything, the case against it is weaker than it was a century ago. The shifts we will be tracing in this chapter are cultural and political, and they have not been steady. Western Christianity seemed to be reviving in the 1950s but went into free fall in the 1960s. In the 1970s, the patterns on either side of the Atlantic diverged. Europe's churches continued to hemorrhage, while conservative Christianity in the United States began a dogged fight back.

The story begins where we left it at the end of chapter 10, with American Protestantism riding the crest of World War I's nationalistic wave. Protestant liberalism had led the United States' charge to war, but conservatives and premillenarians, having come late to the party, made up for lost time. They quickly diagnosed the war as a struggle against liberal theology, which they blamed for German militarism. The second Russian Revolution, in November 1917, added a new bogeyman, Communism. For conservative Protestants, the world seemed to hang in the balance. Christian civilization was both in danger of collapse and on the point of inheriting the earth. Battle had to be joined.

The first victory was sudden. The war gave the long Protestant-led campaign against alcohol a decisive boost. With half of Europe on the edge of starvation and the nation on a war footing, how could Americans justify turning precious grain into beer rather than bread? In December 1917, Congress passed a constitutional amendment banning the manufacture, sale, or import of "intoxicating liquors." National Prohibition came into force in 1920. We remember it now as an illiberal and impractical measure whose only beneficiaries were hypocrites and criminals. At the time, it was a moment of national moral renewal.

President Wilson claimed America was fighting to make the world safe for democracy. But conservative pastors warned that only Christ could "make democracy safe for the world." The dangers crowded in on every side: alcohol, dancing, the cinema, evolution, Communism, the sinister secular idealism of the League of Nations, and modernist theology. It was to fight all of these evils that the World's Christian Fundamentals Association (WCFA) was founded in 1919. The name was a nod to a series of defiant antimodernist manifestos published between 1910 and 1915 titled *The Fundamentals,* which asserted not only that the Bible was entirely infallible but that salvation simply meant individual sinners being redeemed by Christ's sacrifice and that there was no such thing as a Social Gospel. The WCFA, seeing that "the Great Apostasy was spreading like a plague throughout Christendom" and "false science had created many false apostles of Christ," gathered "to do battle royal for the Fundamentals" and proudly adopted the name Fundamentalists.[1]

Fundamentalism's enemies were quick to brand it a newly invented sect, as much a modern innovation as the "modernists" it reviled. But while some specific Fundamentalist doctrines were new, the continuity with historic conservative Protestantism is also real. Fundamentalism was never a denomination but a movement within all of America's main Protestant churches. Doctrinally, it was close enough to eighteenth- and nineteenth-century evangelicalism and even to seventeenth-century Protestant Orthodoxy. What was new about Fundamentalism was its mood, not its beliefs. Rather than focusing on winning converts, or even on wider campaigns for moral renewal on issues like alcohol, the Fundamentalists were openly contesting the nation's soul. They felt that the foundations of Christian America were being shaken and that it was time to stand and fight.

Fundamentalism was that conviction's respectable face, but not its only one. It is no coincidence that the early 1920s was the heyday both of Fundamentalism and of the revitalized Ku Klux Klan (KKK). Most Fundamentalists were quick enough to denounce the KKK, but they were drinking from the same well. The original KKK had been a terrorist movement in the American South in the late 1860s whose members dressed as the ghosts of the Confederate war dead to intimidate and murder blacks and northerners. It was revived in 1915 by a former Methodist minister in Georgia inspired by the notorious film *The Birth of a Nation,* and turned itself into a movement campaigning for white Protestant America. It was never a mass movement; at its peak in 1924, its weekly magazine *Dawn: The Herald of a New and Better Day* had a circulation of fifty thousand. Yet Klansmen believed that they were the future: the spearhead of a second Reformation through which Protestantism and the white race would triumph.[2]

For Catholics, Jews, and above all blacks, the Klan remained a symbol of faceless terror, in an age when lynchings claimed dozens of lives every year. Yet to many white Protestants it was a secret club, a downhome Freemasonry with self-parodying titles and deliberately kooky spellings. Its hooded members were knights, defending Christ and southern womanhood. Its initiation ceremony included a quasi-baptism and a rewritten evangelical hymn. Klansmen were urged to model themselves on Christ and to give a tenth of their income to "humanitarian service." The white robes, it was claimed, symbolized neither ghosts nor white supremacy but the robes with which Christ will clothe the redeemed, while the hoods were the mark of humble Christians who give the glory to God rather than take credit for their own good deeds. The "Exalted Cyclops" of the Texas Klan enthused,

> Who can look upon a multitude of white robed Klansmen without thinking of the equality and unselfishness of that throng of white robed saints in the Glory Land?[3]

Not, perhaps, the uppermost thought in every spectator's mind.

Fundamentalist leaders readily condemned the Klan, but like it or not, Fundamentalists and Klansmen were fighting the same enemies. Above all, that meant evolution, which for conservative Protestants was by now less a biological theory than an all-purpose symbol of modernity's evils. Racists loathed the claim that all humanity had a common origin, and antiracists disliked the implication that some human "races" were less developed than others. Anti-Communists feared that evolution's blurring of divinely ordained differences between species would lead to God-given human hierarchies being eroded too. Billy Sunday, the age's iconic populist preacher, warned that if the Communist evolutionists had their way, "the turtle dove would marry the turkey buzzard; . . . chickens would crow and the roosters would squeal," and indeed, with an apparently unintended biblical echo, "the least would be the greatest." Worst of all, as an editor of *The Fundamentals* warned, evolution gave "the strong and fit the scientific right to destroy the weak and the unfit."[4] It had produced the moral vacuum of German militarism. This was not fair to Darwinism as a scientific theory, but it is true that social Darwinist ideologies were even then shaping Nazism.

Antievolutionism was a left-wing as well as a right-wing issue. Indeed, its standard-bearer was William Jennings Bryan, the greatest left-wing populist of his age, a legendary orator, three times the Democratic Party's nominee for president, three times defeated, a scourge of bankers and the moneyed interest, a trenchant opponent of World War I, and a tireless campaigner for Prohibition. Now, arguing that evolution corroded Christian faith and had "laid the foundation for the bloodiest war in history," he campaigned for laws against teaching it in public schools.[5] In 1925, the American Civil Liberties Union persuaded a Tennessee high school teacher named John Scopes to defy one such law and provoke a test case. The WCFA took up the challenge and supplied a special prosecutor: the ailing Bryan himself, who had not tried a case in thirty-six years.

The trial was a farce. Scopes was in fact convicted and fined, but the trial was never about him. Bryan's plan was to expose the moral and spiritual corruption of evolution, while the defense attorney, Clarence Darrow, intended to do battle with "bigots and ignoramuses" and put Fundamentalism itself on trial. Bizarrely, Darrow was permitted to call

Bryan as a hostile defense witness, and he hammered him on the scientific impossibility of biblical inerrancy. Bryan, no scientist and no intellectual, was helpless. In the most excruciating exchange, Bryan tried to brush off Darrow's questions by arguing that his was a practical faith and he did not bother with highfalutin ideas. Darrow repeatedly pressed him, but he stood firm:

> BRYAN: I do not think about things I don't think about.
> DARROW: Do you think about things you do think about?
> BRYAN: Well, sometimes.[6]

Perhaps it was a joke. Perhaps he did not exactly say that at all. But that was how the national press reported it, snickering at the small-town southern simpletons. It made Fundamentalism, once so formidable, look ridiculous. As for Bryan, he died five days after the trial ended. His mockers hardly skipped a beat. Every further legislative attempt to ban the teaching of evolution failed.

The mood shifted quickly. The press began to pick up other scandals, such as the case of a Texas Fundamentalist pastor who shot and killed a Roman Catholic in his church parlor in 1926, and used them, fairly or unfairly, to depict Fundamentalists and their allies as crazy. Finding themselves in a hole, some Fundamentalists dug harder. Baroque conspiracy theories circulated, claiming that liberal theology was a plot by German spies to seduce America into moral collapse. More significantly, by the mid-1920s, conservative Protestantism's flagship moral achievement, Prohibition, was plainly fomenting contempt for the law, not national moral renewal.

The decisive battles were within the churches. A substantial majority of American Protestants agreed with the Fundamentalists on most theological issues, but Fundamentalism was about mood more than about doctrine. The Fundamentalists in each denomination tried to drive out the minority who had embraced liberal or modernist theologies. Hounding fellow Christians for their conscientiously held beliefs did nothing to dispel the Fundamentalists' growing reputation as intolerant obscurantists, and left them isolated. Some withdrew to their own splinter groups, and the rest piped down. Fundamentalism faded from public view. Educated, metropolitan America believed it had gone for good.

Saving Civilization in the Age of World War II

It might have been of some comfort to the Fundamentalists that their opponents fared little better than they did. Breezy Jazz Age mockery, always a pretty thin cosmopolitan crust on a rural, pious nation, was not much of a defense against the bitter economic hardships of the 1930s. And Protestant liberalism never truly recovered from the moral shock of World War I, which made bromides about human perfectibility seem like a joke in poor taste. The philosophies of the future, it seemed, were fascism and Communism.

Protestantism did offer an alternative to liberalism and Fundamentalism: Karl Barth's "neo-orthodoxy," which we met in the previous chapter. Its American prophets were the brothers Reinhold and Richard Niebuhr and a German refugee, Paul Tillich. The Niebuhrs' project was to show that Protestants could embrace modern science and biblical criticism while still holding on to the essentials of the Gospel. Their view was dubbed "Christian realism": recognizing the pervasiveness of evil both in individuals and in social structures and arguing that Christians had to work within that reality, giving way neither to utopianism nor to despair. This was classic Protestant two-kingdoms thinking, but with the accent on political skepticism rather than on obedience.

It was a steely philosophy for an age that badly needed one. Christian realism could conceivably stand against fascism, Communism, and even corporate capitalism, and so save humanity from itself. In this spirit, the "realists" took up the ecumenical idealism of the pre–World War I era and set about reforging it with sharper edges. An ecumenical conference held at Oxford in 1937 talked of what Tillich called "evangelical Catholicism"—a transnational Christian unity of the kind not seen since medieval times. In 1940, T. S. Eliot, one of the conference's participants, wrote that a "new Christian culture" was all that could stand against the encircling horrors.[7]

Eliot's view was a little eccentric in his adopted British homeland but not in the America of his birth. The United States entered World War II in 1941 as it had entered World War I in 1917: cheered on by interventionist Protestants. The secular republic's struggle was a holy war. It rolled together America's three main religious groups into a newly imagined "Judeo-Christian civilization." All soldiers were assumed to be either Protestants, Catholics, or Jews. The American armed forces, dominated by Protestants and in particular by Episcopalians, were a unique military-ecclesiastical complex. They provided a better resourced ecumenical chaplaincy than any mass army in human history. While Nazi Germany's military chaplains were marginalized and despised, the United States' were exalted. Sixteen million Americans served in the armed forces during the 1940s, of whom almost three-quarters served overseas; that is one in nine Americans, or about 80 percent of the men born in the 1920s. The armed forces were their university and the war their moral education.

One incident came to symbolize America's crusade. In February 1943, the American troopship *Dorchester* was torpedoed off the Canadian coast. Four chaplains—two Protestants, a Catholic, and a Jew—worked together to hurry men into lifeboats, then distributed life jackets. When the life jackets ran out, they gave their own to four young soldiers. They then joined hands, singing and praying together as the ship sank. Reportedly they were reciting the Shema, the Jewish affirmation of God's oneness, as the waters took them. The "Four Chaplains" became symbols of an America united for Judeo-Christian civilization against its godless foes. American soldiers were told that Nazism was anti-Christian so often that many of them, when they at last entered Germany, were surprised that church buildings still stood there.

Plenty of servicemen were cynical about this kind of propaganda. Paul Fussell's acerbic memoir of wartime service recalled how most GIs "sneered or giggled" at the word "crusade." In this particular war, however, the joke went sour. Allied troops in Germany discovered more than just churches. Outsiders had heard about concentration camps, but even had they believed all they were told, nothing could prepare them for what they found at Buchenwald and Dachau. When horrified American soldiers summarily shot dozens of captured SS officers at Dachau, General Eisenhower grimly reflected, "We are told that the American soldier does not know what he is fighting for. Now at least he will know what he is fighting against." Fussell agreed that this was where cynicism died:

> They had seen and smelled the death camps, and now they
> were able to realize that all along they had been . . . fighting for
> something positive, the sacredness of life itself. . . . After the
> camps, a moral attitude was rampant. . . . The boys' explosive
> little tour in France had been a crusade after all.[8]

Every Christian army tells its soldiers they are fighting evil. Just this
once, it turned out to be true.

It was the defining moral event of the modern age. Since 1945, the
Western democracies have had, in Nazism, something they did not
have before: an all but universally accepted definition of evil, a fixed
point on our moral compasses. As a result, our notions of morality have
changed, among other things becoming more secular. The old definitions, which failed to see Nazism for what it was, have been exposed as
inadequate. The story of Christianity in the Western democracies since
1945 is largely the story of how this moral shock has been faced and assimilated, a process that is still under way.

The year 1945 was a moment of defiant, hardheaded hope for what
still thought of itself as the Christian West. Secularism looked like a
busted flush. Only (Judeo-)Christian civilization had had the moral
power to defeat fascism, and only (Judeo-)Christian civilization had the
moral power to confront Communism. In Germany, the Western occupiers quickly identified the Confessing Church as the body that could
be most trusted to rebuild a free Germany. In the late 1940s, politics in
Germany, Italy, Belgium, much of Scandinavia, and elsewhere was
dominated by Christian Democratic parties, uniting Catholics and
Protestants in opposition to Communism. Even in Britain, the new
postwar social-democratic settlement drew heavily on a Christian identity, in particular the manifesto *Christianity and Social Order* by William
Temple, the wartime archbishop of Canterbury and a pioneer of
Anglican-Jewish reconciliation. Europe's surge of Christian politics was
not exactly matched by religious revival, but there were modest hopeful signs. The churches' role in rebuilding a devastated Europe was
hard to ignore. Britain saw a modest uptick in Anglican numbers, led,
as churchmen eagerly noticed, by the young and especially by students.
John Robinson, a chaplain at Cambridge University through the 1950s,

found its Christian environment so lively that he speculated that secularization's tide had finally turned.

In America, the change was unmistakable. In 1954, when the Cold War was at its iciest, the United States added the phrase "under God" to the Pledge of Allegiance and adopted "In God We Trust" as a national motto. The previous year, the proportion of the U.S. population who were formal members of a church reached its highest level ever, 59.5 percent. Polling indicated that the American public respected religious leaders far more than any other group in society, a dramatic turnaround from the prewar years. Weekly church and synagogue attendance in the United States rose from 38 percent in 1946 to 49 percent in 1955. Bible sales doubled over the same period. Again, students led the way.[9]

Alongside numerical growth, the two alienated sides of American Protestantism were cautiously recognizing each other as fellow travelers. On one side was the clerical and intellectual elite of the "mainline" Protestant churches; the term was a railway-era joke that hardened into a truism. They made much of their stance as detached critics of the age's complacent social and economic assumptions, Communist and capitalist alike, yet at the same time they were the coziest of establishments. Their ecumenical association, the National Council of Churches (NCC), sat in a prime Manhattan location in a building, the "God Box," whose cornerstone was laid by President Eisenhower. The NCC had been critical in launching the World Council of Churches in 1948, a movement that was avowedly anti-imperialist while explicitly aiming at global unity. This was the old Christendom, still effortlessly assuming its own perennial importance.

On the other side, it turned out that Fundamentalism was not dead. The label was not worn so proudly after the fiascoes of the mid-1920s, but every Protestant denomination still nurtured large numbers of believers who combined conservative, evangelical beliefs with a hostility to modernism and all its works. Such people had been driven out of the mainline churches' institutions and had for a time withdrawn into a subculture, showing a profoundly American distrust of establishments and compromises. If their country succumbed to liquor, the cinema, and other sins of modernity, they at least would remain pure. But they could not quite shake off the sense that they were responsible for America's soul. They established a formidable presence for themselves on local radio; by 1942, Charles E. Fuller's *Old Fashioned Revival Hour* was being carried by 456 stations across the country, the largest reach of any prime-time radio program in America.[10] By then, their ministry was becoming more than mere denunciation, partly inspired by the shared struggle against Hitler and Mussolini, whom they had long ago decided were agents of Antichrist. In 1943, a new National Association of Evangelicals was formed, bringing together some old Fundamentalists with the Dutch and Scandinavian Protestant churches of the American Midwest, which had been shut out of the mainline's Anglo establishment and had retained a steadfast but scholarly theological conservatism.

The symbol of this newly optimistic conservatism was a charismatic young evangelist named Billy Graham. Graham learned his preaching style from the radio, became a full-time preacher in 1944, and rapidly became a big fish in what was still a small pond. His preaching tours across America in 1945–46 won him the title of United Airlines' top civilian passenger, and the following year he made the first of several visits to Europe. In 1947, still aged only twenty-nine, he was strong-armed into accepting the presidency of a major evangelical seminary. Instead of harping on divisive moral issues such as beer and the movies, Graham focused on the anxieties of the atomic age, suggesting that the conversion and renewal for which he tirelessly called might bring national as well as individual salvation.

In 1949, Graham was planning a revival campaign in Los Angeles, a bold venture onto such a prominent stage, when he had a crisis of confidence. Like many bright young evangelicals, he found the Fundamentalist insistence on the Bible's absolute inerrancy difficult to stomach, but knew that if he gave modern biblical criticism an inch, it would take all the miles he had. He resolved his dilemma neither by throwing over his youthful certainties nor by retreating into a Fundamentalist bunker but by laying the matter before God. He could not resolve his doubts, but decided as a matter of faith that he would accept the Bible nevertheless. It was an existential decision of the kind Karl Barth and, indeed, John Calvin would have recognized. It was also a sign that Graham was about to become something extremely unusual both in Protestant and in American history: a genuinely unifying figure.

The first half of the Los Angeles campaign bumped along, with sponsors preparing to spin anticlimax as success. Then a loose-living local radio presenter was dramatically converted, and the city took notice. As the story goes, Graham was surprised to find reporters gathering at his tent one evening, and he asked them why they had come. One said he had received instructions directly from the ailing and fiercely anti-Communist press baron William Randolph Hearst: "Puff Graham."[11]

Hearst thought he had discovered a mouthpiece for his anti-Communist views. The mainline establishment, too, assumed Graham was just another southern preacher, Billy Sunday in a sharper suit. Reinhold Niebuhr called him an obscurantist and accused him of presenting "Christianity as a series of simple answers to complex questions."[12] Graham was an easy man to underestimate. He refused to lash back at his critics the way evangelicals were supposed to. He would go on to spend seventy years in the public eye without attracting the faintest hint of financial or sexual scandal, and showing a remarkable talent for reconciliation. He has had scarcely a harsh word to say of anyone. Repeatedly, people who feel they ought to dislike him have tried to do so and failed. He visited Union Theological Seminary, the modernist lions' den, in 1954 and impressed his hosts as honest, thoughtful, and ecumenical. Some noticed that evangelicals, unlike the neo-orthodox, were actually winning converts. Graham brought Niebuhr into the planning of his New York revival campaign of 1957, professing to be "inadequate before his brilliant mind and learning." Before long, Niebuhr was praising Graham's modesty and honesty.[13]

We can almost imagine that it could have lasted, and a new Judeo-Christendom could have been built. But the Western democracies in the 1950s were not waking from a ghastly secularist-totalitarian nightmare. They were trying to subside back into a pleasant dream from which they had been roughly awoken. In the aftermath of World War II, a certain numbness was only natural. But before too long, its lessons would need to be absorbed in earnest.

Not all Protestants responded to secular modernity by simply restating old truths. What if God was calling his people not to sing the old Gospel in a different key but to play a different tune altogether? What if the churches, hierarchies, liturgies, sacraments, and all the struggling inheritance of Christendom should be allowed to die rather than being preserved on life support? In the 1880s, the campaigning British journalist W. T. Stead experienced a conversion in which God told him to "be no longer a Christian, be a Christ." He now argued for what he called a "civic church," which would serve all humanity regardless of race, gender, or religion and would be open to anyone willing to work selflessly for the common good. In an 1894 pamphlet, *If Christ Came to Chicago!,* a bestseller on both sides of the Atlantic, he argued that this was how Christ himself would serve the people of that iconic modern "shock city." The measure of true Christianity was not churchiness but "the extent to which we succeed in restoring in man the lost image of God." Many of Stead's contemporaries struggled to see how "being a Christ" like this actually spread the Gospel. It would surely be better, as one critic put it, "if Chicago came to Christ."[14] But the idea did not go away.

In the summer of 1944, strikingly similar ideas were pressing on the conscience of Dietrich Bonhoeffer. Imprisoned in Berlin, with bombs falling and all trace of Christian civilization apparently gone, the bravest theologian of his generation began groping toward an understanding of what Christian faith might mean in this new world. "We are," he wrote to a friend, "proceeding toward a time of no religion at all: men as they are now simply cannot be religious any more." Perhaps, he wondered tentatively, this was God's will? Perhaps "religion" was an infantile stage that "a world come of age" had outgrown? What if "religion" could be separated from Christianity and is in fact no more than its "garment"? In which case, what would then be needed would be "a religionless Christianity."[15]

In letter after letter, Bonhoeffer circled around what this religionless Christianity might actually be. He did not mean some milk-and-water rationalization of the faith, stripped of revelation or divine power. He meant instead to strip away hierarchies, forms, jargon, wealth, and power, leaving a truly Christlike Christianity, serving the world in weakness from the cross. What he never did was to specify how this religionless Christianity might actually work. "I shall be writing to you about it again soon," he promised in letter after letter. "I am thinking over the problem at present. . . . More about that next time, I hope."[16] If he made any further progress before the Nazis hanged him, his surviving letters do not record it. His death itself was perhaps a kind of answer, but hardly a practical model for any church to follow.

Bonhoeffer's theological reputation in the West was considerable even before he acquired the aura of martyrdom. It was cemented by the publication of his prison writings in English in 1953. His inconclusive reflections on "religionless Christianity" spoke profoundly to many of his British and American readers. They shared his impatience with "religion"—that is, with churchiness which looks after its own institutional welfare rather than loving the world regardless of cost. Like so many other Protestants before them, they wanted to cut through the formalism and hypocrisy that they felt had become encrusted on their faith, to reach the authentic heart of the Gospel. "Authenticity" became their watchword. They felt that church-religion was, like the whole patched-together postwar society that hosted it, a sham.

This burgeoning discontent first took shape not in the margins or the religionless spaces but at the heart of Western Christian privilege, the universities. Student groups were groping toward ways of living an "authentic" religionless Christianity. Joseph Wesley Mathews was a former Fundamentalist preacher whose faith had been turned upside down by the butchery of the Pacific war. Studying under Richard Niebuhr and reading Bonhoeffer set him off on a search for a "breakthrough" to authenticity. He once ripped out the pages of a church Bible during a sermon to demonstrate what breaking free from religion might mean. In 1956, he took over the leadership of a Christian student community in Austin, Texas. Not all of its members appreciated his drive to break through their self-deceptions to discover their authentic selves. A few ended up in psychiatric institutions. Others accused him of "destroying every belief, every shred of self-confidence," and deriding anyone whose spirituality he found inauthentic. But others found it immensely liberating. One former member said that Mathews's unyielding quest for authenticity had given her "Cosmic Permission to LIVE." In 1962, a member of the community declared defiantly,

> I think the Community is more like the early Church than other groups are today, because the early Church didn't give a goddamn about life after death. Neither do we.

The claim about the early church was entirely wrong, but the focus on this world rather than pious abstractions was true to Bonhoeffer. The deliberate profanity, using blasphemy to cut through pious conventions, was America's own contribution.[17]

Like many earlier movements of Protestant renewal, this one sought inner authenticity. Unlike most of its predecessors, however, it refused to focus on inward piety. That was religion, disengaged from the world. Instead, it valued Christlike service, given with defiant disregard to cost. An awakened conscience was searching for a cause to serve. In postwar America, it did not have to search very hard.

The Gospel of Civil Rights

The American Civil War and Reconstruction had ended slavery and, in principle, granted legal equality to all races. Yet new structures of systematic oppression soon ensured that African Americans were segregated and stripped of most civil and political rights. The system was powerfully entrenched by law, by violence, by near-universal racism, and by a political establishment comfortable with the status quo. Bonhoeffer, who spent nine months in Harlem in 1930 and 1931 and acquired a lifelong love of jazz, was appalled by American racism, which seemed to him worse than German anti-Semitism. Some Nazis hailed American segregation as a model to which an Aryan state could aspire.[18]

Determined civil rights campaigners, Christian and secular alike, had been making slow, uneven progress on several fronts for decades. In the 1940s and early 1950s, buoyed by a war fought to destroy an anti-Christian tyranny that defined itself by racism, they began to win substantial victories. The place and time when the cause finally came to the nation's attention, however, was Montgomery, Alabama, in 1955, where a particularly egregious arrest had sparked a boycott of the city's segregated buses. The boycott's initial organizers were secular civil rights campaigners, but they knew an effort of this sort needed a preacher's moral and rhetorical leadership. Whether from disagreement among themselves or simple fear, none of the city's established black Protestant ministers came forward. So the choice settled on Montgomery's newest black Baptist minister, a twenty-six-year-old who had been in town barely a year: Martin Luther King Jr.

King only reluctantly took on the role for which he had, unwittingly, spent his life preparing. He had been raised in what he now called Fundamentalism but had received a doctorate from Boston University, at the heart of the white Protestant establishment. His ability to connect the very different worlds of the black and white churches would be crucial to his achievement.[19] In seminary, he met classic Protestant liberalism, whose focus on social evils struck him as self-evidently right, and neo-orthodoxy, whose recognition of the pervasive fact of evil rang truer than the liberals' sunny bromides. He found the beginnings of a reconciliation between the two in an unlikely place. Mohandas K. Gandhi was not a Christian, but his principle of nonviolent resistance, made famous by the struggle for Indian independence, owed something to Christianity, and like many Western readers King was moved by its moral power. As he later recalled, "I came to see for the first time that the Christian doctrine of love operating through the Gandhian method of nonviolence was one of the most potent weapons available to oppressed people."[20]

It was only a theory, but it meant that when King was thrust into leading the Montgomery bus boycott, he knew what he was doing. The key moment of the campaign, and perhaps of King's career, was the night of January 30, 1956, less than two months into the boycott, when King's house was bombed. He was not at home, but his wife, Coretta, and their two-month-old daughter were; they escaped unhurt. By the time King had hurried home from his meeting, hundreds of supporters had gathered. They came, Coretta later recalled, "to do battle. . . . It could have been a riot, a very bloody riot." The city's mayor and its police commissioner, trying to disperse the crowd, only stirred up further anger. Everyone present knew that the police were part of the problem. Then King spoke from the bomb-damaged porch. It was not the high oratory he was capable of, but the impromptu, knife-edge words that the *Montgomery Advertiser* reported the following day were crystal clear:

> Don't get your weapons. He who lives by the sword will perish by the sword. . . . We want to love our enemies. I want you to love our enemies. Be good to them. Love them and let them know you love them. . . . If I am stopped our work will not stop. For what we are doing is right.

The reporter added that by the time King had finished, the mayor and the commissioner "looked very much like members of the beet family." The crowd remained, singing hymns, for much of the rest of the night.[21]

There, already, are the three core elements of King's theology of nonviolence. Practicality: violence leads to defeat. Principle: nonviolence is not a tactic but the Gospel ethic of love in action. And power: Gospel nonviolence cannot be defeated by violence. Houses can be bombed and people can be killed, but neither love nor justice can be stopped.

Like his German namesake nearly four and a half centuries before, King was working out the implications of his ideas in the midst of a storm. He had already made contact with some of America's long-standing theorists of nonviolence, both black and white. Initially, they were a little condescending to him: "so young, so inexperienced, so good." Advisers descended on Montgomery. King asked them to "teach me all you know about nonviolence" and always acknowledged his debt to them. Yet he was also clear that "the experience in Montgomery did more to clarify my thinking on the question of nonviolence than all of the books I had read." Like most of the best Christian theology, his was forged in fire. Pretty soon his advisers were admitting that King had come "to a profoundly deep understanding of nonviolence through the struggle itself" and that he had achieved far more in a few months than "any of our so-called non-violence experts" had in decades.[22]

That achievement was not, primarily, the desegregation of Montgomery's buses, a victory that was won after a yearlong boycott but made hollow by a violent backlash in the city. What King had done was claim America's moral high ground. It was, he insisted in February 1956, a struggle "between the forces of light and the forces of darkness," not between white and black Americans.

> We are concerned not merely to win justice in the buses but rather to behave in a new and different way—to be non-violent so that we may remove injustice itself, both from society and from ourselves. This is a struggle which we cannot lose, no matter what the apparent outcome, if we ourselves succeed in becoming better and more loving people.

By contrast, at a segregationist rally in Montgomery earlier the same month, a handbill titled "A Declaration of Segregation" was distributed, stating, "We hold these truths to be self evident that all whites are created equal with certain rights; among these are life, liberty and the pursuit of dead niggers."[23] The contrast, at least for those Americans who were not themselves in a deep pit of hate and fear, could hardly be plainer.

The civil rights campaign was broad and inclusive, but its foundations were unapologetically Christian. King's own Baptist spirituality was unmistakable. His account of a spiritual crisis one sleepless night in January 1956, shortly before his house was bombed, became famous. Daunted by implacable opposition and murderous threats, he admitted to God that he was at the end of his powers:

> At that moment . . . I experienced the presence of the Divine as I had never experienced Him before. It seemed as though I could hear the quiet assurance of an inner voice saying: "Stand up for righteousness, stand up for truth; and God will be at your side forever."[24]

The same words could have been said in any century of Protestantism's history.

After the Montgomery protest, King formed the organization through which he would work for most of the rest of his life. The word "Christian" was a late and deliberate addition to the title of the Southern Christian Leadership Conference (SCLC), partly to rebut the charge that civil rights campaigners were Communists but also to set the campaign's ethos. The SCLC was run by ministers, and its avowed aim was "to redeem the soul of America." SCLC volunteers were required to pledge to "MEDITATE daily on the teachings and life of Jesus," "WALK and TALK in the manner of love, for God is love," and "PRAY daily to be used by God."[25]

Civil rights campaigning had an air of old-fashioned revivalism to it. There was a whiff of the miraculous: moments of prophetic certainty, claps of thunder during sermons, ministers raised from their sickbeds to preach with unaccustomed power. The greatest miracle of all was marching straight-backed toward brutal police and watching their power ebb away. As Thomas Gilmore, who would himself become one of Alabama's first African American sheriffs, put it,

> You really get the feeling that somebody bigger than you is walking beside you, and you feel that, well, man, nobody can hurt you if he wanted to.[26]

For whites, the movement offered a different Protestant revivalist trope: repentance. Civil rights preachers, like their abolitionist forebears, named evil for what it was, challenged their hearers to slough it off, and offered them redemption if they did.

America's white churches were not necessarily persuaded by this, but they were silenced. They had never been in the forefront of segregation's defense, in part because they found it all but impossible to construct a positive Christian argument for segregation. During the 1950s, the Southern Baptists and Presbyterians were in fact quietly desegregating their seminaries and other institutions. All the opposition they could offer was to plead that segregation was permissible and to urge caution, moderation, and consensus. King was justifiably angry to see them "stand on the sideline and merely mouth pious irrelevancies and sanctimonious trivialities," but they did not give much active support to the segregationist cause, despite their congregations' overwhelming preferences. Many white churches outside the South were less hesitant. Billy Graham himself, who since 1954 had refused to allow segregated seating at his "crusades," welcomed King, his fellow Baptist minister, to the stage at a New York rally in 1957 and praised the "social revolution" he was leading. In his newspaper column, replying to a correspondent who assumed Jesus was white, Graham gently pointed out that he was probably "a swarthy color—or light brown." In 1965, Graham held a desegregated rally in Alabama, calling his work there "the most strategic and most important of any crusade." Four years earlier, a South Carolina newspaper had dropped Graham's syndicated column in protest against his integrationist views, only to be met with a surge of protest from readers who valued his Gospel more than they disliked his racial politics. After that, the southern press tended to celebrate Graham while avoiding any mention of his racial views. It was a sign that the battle was lost. As King had promised, it had been lost not in white southerners' segregated schools and shops but in their hearts. Most of them still wanted segregation, but now they neither knew how to defend it nor had the will to fight for it. And so, slowly, at times bloodily, but inexorably, it ended.[27]

One particular group of American Christians, however, were entranced by King's message. The authenticity-seekers of the 1950s were drawn to civil rights like moths. The cause was—for a while—a living example of what Bonhoeffer had struggled to imagine, religionless Christianity in action. The movement's Christian basis was as unmistakable as the Reverend Dr. King's leadership, but it was never about churchiness, piety, or institutional safety. It was led by Christians but not only for Christians, and it welcomed allies regardless of their faith. Christian-led and Christian-inspired civil rights organizations such as the Student Nonviolent Coordinating Committee (SNCC) deliberately refused to claim a Christian identity. They would live the Gospel, not boast of it. The experience of campaigning, even for those who only read about it, was transformative. It seemed much more like true Christianity than another self-satisfied Sunday service.

Above all, the civil rights movement was prophetic. King insisted that the Christian church be "not merely a thermometer that recorded the ideas and principles of popular opinion" but "a thermostat that transformed the mores of society."[28] We have seen Protestantism's endless adaptability throughout this history, and in democratic America churches tended to provide what their people demanded. But there are moments to lead the social consensus rather than follow it. Many American Protestants were ready to be asked not what God could do for them but what they could do for God, and King looked like a prophet of what religionless Christianity could be. Unfortunately, not all of the self-appointed prophets who followed his example were so successful.

Prophetic Christianity in the 1960s

It was a moment of heady possibilities. A postwar generation was coming of age. In West Germany, the *Spiegel* affair of 1962 reopened some of the hastily bandaged wounds of the Nazi era, questioning how far the 1950s establishment, to which the churches were so central, was in fact implicated in Nazi crimes. In Britain, the 1960 prosecution and triumphant acquittal of the publishers of D. H. Lawrence's *Lady Chatterley's Lover* dramatically widened the scope of public discourse. Earlier the same year, the contraceptive pill was approved for general use in the United States. Television satire and irreverent popular music were booming. The new American president, John F. Kennedy, was young and glamorous and, with his talk of moon shots, had a touch of the prophet to him. And he was Catholic, vindicating America's promise to itself that it was no longer narrowly a Protestant country.

One of the star witnesses at the *Lady Chatterley* trial was a newly minted Anglican bishop, John Robinson. At Cambridge University in the 1950s, Robinson had hoped that a Christian resurgence was dawning. His arrival in 1959 as bishop of Woolwich, in southeast London, was a rude awakening. His shock on meeting the English working class up close was not unlike Bonhoeffer's shock on meeting his jailers: people apparently utterly indifferent to religion. His courtroom defense of obscenity was calculated to shock too. The public expected priests to drone self-serving platitudes. Robinson wanted to offer them a Christianity that was unexpected, candid, and authentic. He capitalized on the trial's notoriety with a 1963 book whose title, *Honest to God,* promised that instead of party-line religious cant, for once a bishop was going to tell the plain truth.

In fact, Robinson's praise of religionless Christianity, and his call to adapt Christian ethics, language, and imagery to a rapidly changing society, would have been pretty standard fare in academic theology. But this sort of thing was not usually laid before the general public in vivid and provocative language. His book sold more than a million copies worldwide. Many readers found it liberating, a means of holding on to a faith they cherished while sloughing off rules and orthodoxies they could no longer stomach. Others vilified him as the "atheist bishop" or mocked him on the grounds that making Christianity exciting and relevant was self-evidently impossible.

His cause was taken up most enthusiastically not in the secularized cities, but in his old university stomping grounds. The story of student Christianity in the 1960s is a microcosm of the decade's religious convulsions. The dominant Christian presence in British universities was the Student Christian Movement (SCM), whose ethos was broad, socially engaged, and ecumenical. Between 1963 and 1973, when total British student numbers were rising fast, the SCM's membership fell by an astonishing 90 percent. This was almost a deliberate act of self-destruction. In 1962, the SCM appointed a new general secretary, Ambrose Reeves, a Bonhoeffer enthusiast who had served as a bishop in South Africa until 1961, when he was deported for his blunt antiapartheid views. Reeves introduced an "openness policy," committing the SCM to ignoring distinctions between Christians and non-Christians. Like Bonhoeffer, he argued that Christians needed to recognize that secularism was not their enemy but God's will for a "world come of age." The SCM, therefore, should be "primarily concerned with students who are not Christians. . . . We can best serve the churches by ceasing to be a 'religious' society."[29]

This bold abandonment of institutional self-interest certainly felt prophetic, but did not by itself answer Bonhoeffer's unresolved problem: What does religionless Christianity actually mean? Reeves admitted that "many of us have been uncertain as to what exactly the new emphasis on 'openness' involves." His answer, inspired by American civil rights activism and the antiapartheid cause, was working alongside groups of all kinds that were "seeking to promote justice and world peace." In 1965, Reeves was succeeded by a like-minded radical named David Head, who in 1968 formally committed the SCM to "revolutionary change" and to supporting Marxist movements worldwide. A 1969 SCM communiqué stated,

> The overall purpose of the movement would be to bring about a better and just society. . . . Call it "the revolution," call it "the Kingdom," call it what you will.[30]

The policy was courageous, sincere, and utterly disastrous.

For one thing, most Christian students did not share these political views and simply left. The SCM's leaders, knowing that prophets are not honored by their own people, felt this as a vindication. Yet even those who stayed had little idea what they were actually supposed to do. In 1967, one SCM branch complained that its members were in a state of "utter apathy," which "will only be removed when the leaders make clear what they are trying to do." The only consistent answer—to work alongside secular campaigners—did not answer the increasingly urgent question of why the SCM itself existed at all. It was deliberately suppressing any assertion of a distinctively Christian identity, instead subsuming that identity into radical politics. So Christians who disliked radical politics withdrew from the SCM, and Christians who embraced radical politics increasingly saw themselves simply as radicals and no longer as Christians. In a decade, Britain's main student Christian organization willed itself almost out of existence.[31]

The SCM's story is extreme, but it was widely paralleled. Its smaller American affiliate, the University Christian Movement, wound itself up in 1969 after a decade of bitter internecine conflict. The international body of which both were part, the World Student Christian Federation (WSCF), immolated itself with the same prophetic certainty. The WSCF's 1972 Assembly committed the organization to "the common class struggle against capitalism and its psychological/cultural consequences." All of the assembly's resolutions focused on left-wing political causes, and none on matters of specific Christian interest. One resolution deplored the failure to invite official representatives from the People's Republic of China, where at that date Christian practice of any kind was illegal.[32] The WSCF alienated most Christians with its radical politics, while refusing as a matter of principle to try to attract political radicals to Christianity.

Grown-ups were caught up in the same ferment. The World Council of Churches' assembly at Uppsala in 1968 took Bonhoeffer and King as its theological guides and chose a slogan—"The world sets the agenda"—that explicitly refused to assert a Christian identity. Its focus was anti-imperialism and antiracism, and it set up a program to support guerrillas in southern Africa. In the United States, the main ecumenical body, the NCC, did not actually embrace Marxism, but it did campaign on the Vietnam War and other bitterly divisive issues. The point is not who was right on those issues but that these organizations were leading their member churches toward radicalism without heed as to whether ordinary believers wished to follow. It could not have gone on indefinitely. In the early 1970s, after some years of issuing resolutions that were ignored and resented by its member churches, the NCC was subjected to savage cuts by those churches, reducing its radical international affairs department from five staffers to one.[33] In Britain, which stayed out of Vietnam, temperatures were lower, but in 1965 one radical London cleric, who had transformed his own church into a community center, called on his fellow clergy to "leave their parishes and take secular jobs, especially in the welfare and social services run by the State"—advice that he later took himself.[34] In 1968, Bishop Robinson, yesterday's radical, wrote sympathetically of the modern Christian's dilemma: to stay in the church despite its many flaws, or to say "'This is so irrelevant,' that there is nothing to be done but come out." He admitted that "creative disaffiliation" from the church could be liberating and that sometimes "non-involvement in organized religion is indeed a Christian vocation." In political terms, he, too, believed by 1969 that "only a revolutionary and not a radical solution is going to be adequate."[35]

If Robinson peered over the edge, his American friend James Pike leaped over it. Pike was an Episcopalian radical with a long-running Sunday morning TV show who was elected bishop of California in 1958. In the early 1960s, he began publicly to question core Christian doctrines such as the Trinity and Christ's virgin birth, not so much doubting their truth as questioning their relevance. They represented the kind of jargon a religionless Christianity must leave behind. In 1966, he resigned his bishopric in contempt for the "standard-brand churches" and in 1969 left the church altogether to form what he called a Foundation for Religious Transition. Its aim was to scrape away centuries of self-serving doctrinal pablum to reveal the true historical Jesus, who was, of course, a political revolutionary. In the same year, he traveled to Israel, confident of making "the big breakthrough" to a post-religious consciousness. Instead, he and his young, third wife lost their way in the Judaean desert. She eventually walked out. His body was found a few days later. It was a kind of prophetic end, if not exactly what he had intended.[36]

By then, the civil rights campaign itself, religionless Christianity's model, was in trouble. King's methods—nonviolence, multiracialism, the ethic of love—had become an establishment, and new prophetic voices moved ahead of them. In the wake of King's murder in 1968, the Student Nonviolent Coordinating Committee dropped the "nonviolent" from its name and began building links with Communist

Cuba. A black New York pastor and U.S. congressman named Adam Clayton Powell brought the term "black power" into public use. In 1967, a black Detroit minister, Albert B. Cleage Jr., published the sermons he preached at the time of the city's recent riots under the title *The Black Messiah.* "Jesus was black," he argued, "and he did *not* preach universal love. . . . Almost everything you have heard about Christianity is essentially a lie." Cleage later adopted a Swahili name meaning "liberator, holy man, savior of the nation."[37]

Some of these figures could be dismissed as cranks, but James Forman, the international affairs director of the SNCC, could not. In April 1969, arguing that African Americans were a "colonized people inside the United States," he presented a "Black Manifesto." This declared a "war," which might include "armed struggle" against America's "racist, imperialist government" but also against "white Christian churches and synagogues." Specifically, he demanded reparations from the churches and synagogues, a sum he initially named at $500 million and then raised to $3 billion. In any other era, those churches would have laughed off such a demand from an unelected campaigner, but this was an age of prophets. The churches' leaders knew the truth of their long complicity in American racism and felt the moral force of Forman's demand. Many churches were spurred to designate significant sums of money for social and minority projects. The Congregationalists invited Forman to speak at their General Synod and offered his fund $10 million.[38]

These church leaders, however, were spending not their own money but that of ordinary American believers: the people of a nation who had elected Richard Nixon as president in 1968 and who had been left behind by their prophetic leaders. In the end, they rebelled. When it emerged in 1972 that the Episcopal Church had been giving money to groups who supported violent revolution, parishes' donations immediately fell sharply. The presiding bishop resigned, and his successor formally ended the national program of support for minority groups. Donations stopped falling but never returned to their previous levels.

Western Protestantism would in any case have faced powerful cultural headwinds in the 1960s, but its fateful seduction by the half-developed notion of religionless Christianity made matters far worse. A swath of Christian leaders became convinced that it was their duty to stop talking about Christianity and to subsume themselves into radical politics. Some completed the journey and became secular revolutionaries. Others discovered that in practice being a religionless Christian was an unchallenging lifestyle and joined the large majority of the population who, when pushed, professed a Christian identity but showed little sign of it in their everyday lives. Others remained in the churches, voiceless and disillusioned, scolded from the pulpits for their traditionalism. They had already learned that, in Judeo-Christian America, Protestantism ought not to assert its own identity too much. Now they were being told that any public assertion of Christianity was "irrelevant." Preachers hoped that that message would at least be appealing to secular society and to nominal or disillusioned Christians, but what such people heard was a series of charismatic Protestant leaders telling them that belonging to a church was unimportant. It was a message they were all too ready to hear.

It was not Bonhoeffer's fault. He knew he had not yet worked out what form religionless Christianity might take, and his inconclusive musings in private letters were never intended to be a manifesto. His diagnosis of a crabbed, formal institutionalization in the churches strangling the Gospel was authentically Protestant. It is no surprise it touched a nerve. What he could not have known, but his successors should have, was that the future was not actually as inhuman as it looked from a Berlin prison in 1944. In retrospect, one feature of that prison environment stands out: the guards and prisoners whose irreligion so shook Bonhoeffer were all men. Christianity across most of the world, since the eighteenth century at least, has been predominantly a women's religion. Patriarchal Christians, among whom we have to include Bonhoeffer, have often worried that this makes Christianity seem weak. The postwar prophets of religionless Christianity, like most radicals before the arrival of new-wave feminism in the 1970s, were men. Their quest for revolutionary relevance was very masculine. There is an instructive contrast with twentieth-century Chinese Christianity, which (as we shall see) embraced its huge numerical preponderance of women and thrived as a result. Religionless Christianity was a stirring vision. Attempts to put it into practice, however, both denied the lived reality of its believers and treated faithful pew-fillers with presumption and disdain rather than recognizing them as their community's life-blood.

The Crisis of the Religious Left

By 1970, the establishment Protestant churches of the Western world were in free fall, bleeding members, clergy, and money, with the Catholic Church not far behind. That downward trajectory has continued ever since, with a few pockets of good news amid the gloom. That is not to say those churches are doomed. They still have a good way left to fall, and their fortunes may revive as they have often done before. The claim that secularization is an unstoppable historical force is no more than a prophecy. As yet, though, there is no sign of the tide turning.

For western Europe, that is almost the whole story. But even there, some conservative, evangelical, and fundamentalist churches have not lost members as fast as their establishment brethren, and there have been occasional, localized gains. Many of these churches are independent, entrepreneurial outfits from outside the denominational establishments, often serving immigrant communities. It is hard to see how, in modern Europe, these churches can become more than a vibrant countercultural minority, but if there is energy in European Protestantism, it is here.

The story in the United States is different, but not because America has successfully resisted secularization while Europe has succumbed to it. America's experience shows both that modern Western Protestantism is alive and kicking and also that it still faces formidable and possibly lethal cultural challenges.

A straw in the wind appeared in California around 1967. While the Protestant establishment was busily using the principle of religionless Christianity to saw off the branch on which it sat, an inchoate movement known as the Jesus Freaks set out to throw off church structures and churchy jargon as enthusiastically as Bonhoeffer, Bishop Robinson, or even Bishop Pike while maintaining conservative doctrines. They were dressing evangelical Christianity in the hippie counterculture. The best-known Jesus Freak, Arthur Blessitt, walked across America in hippie clothing carrying a hefty cross. The movement claimed a radical identity—one group called itself the Christian World Liberation

Front—and presented Jesus as the ultimate countercultural icon. They produced a hip paraphrase of the New Testament, *Letters to Street Christians,* and a journal, *Right On.* As one early researcher put it, they "rediscovered Jesus as a funky character to groove on."[39]

This counterculture within the counterculture was a sign of what was to come. By the early 1970s, it was becoming plain that while radical American Protestants had dug themselves into a hole, their conservative and fundamentalist brethren were relatively unscathed. In 1970, the California student evangelist Hal Lindsey published *The Late Great Planet Earth:* a space-age title for a book that used biblical prophecies to make detailed, apocalyptic predictions about world events. Lindsey's details, such as his claim that the European Economic Community was the new Roman Empire, were novel, but he shared his basic framework with Protestant preachers stretching back two centuries and more. The book was widely ridiculed, but at sixteen million copies sold, it was also the bestselling book in 1970s America.

If not all of Lindsey's readers swallowed his predictions wholesale, his dystopian frisson was still a welcome change from the dreamlike optimism of 1960s radicalism. Lindsey's fundamental point was that revolution is a fool's quest. This world and its societies cannot actually be saved. All that can be saved are individual human souls, snatched from a doomed world by God's grace and through Christ's sacrifice. If you believed that old orthodoxy, then the establishment churches had made a disastrously wrong turn. They had deliberately subsumed their Christian identity into futile projects to build God's kingdom on earth and abandoned their calling to save souls.

So a fight back began. While the hierarchies of America's establishment churches winced at such crass evangelicalism, those churches were much more democratic than their European counterparts both in their structures and in their cultures. Nor, bluntly, could church leaders afford to disregard the views of the ordinary believers whose giving kept their churches solvent. Those believers, especially those who remained after the winnowing of the 1960s, were rather more traditionalist than their leaders, and they kept evangelical concerns on those leaders' agendas. So when a conservative evangelical magazine in the early 1970s mooted a scheme for a massive, "simultaneous evangelistic thrust" across America, it produced a groundswell of enthusiasm that the denominations could not ignore. The result was the Key '73 campaign, launched in 1973 with the consent of most of the major Protestant denominations and a good many Catholics, which promised "a gigantic offensive in which every person in North America will be challenged with the claims of Jesus Christ." The point is not that Key '73 succeeded. Few secular Americans wanted to be "challenged," and in any case many local ministers dragged their feet, wary of cross-denominational poaching and uneasy with tub-thumping evangelism, and especially conscious of American Jews' fears that they might be targeted for conversion. The campaign's significance is that it happened at all, and that it did so using such bluntly aggressive language. In America's decentralized and antihierarchical religious culture, clerical qualms were not enough to tame lay evangelicalism.[40]

What was not yet clear was the political direction this newly energized evangelicalism would take. Plenty of evangelicals, like Billy Graham himself, had recognized the moral significance of civil rights and other radical causes. In 1974, Graham organized a global conference on evangelization, believing that "there is a vacuum developing in the world church" left by the World Council of Churches' abdication of its responsibility for preaching the Gospel. Almost half of the nearly 2,500 delegates who gathered in Lausanne were under the age of forty, and over 40 percent of them came from beyond the traditional West. Latin American evangelicals, some influenced by Marxism, made decisive contributions to the conference. The final communiqué committed evangelicals to social action as well as to seeking converts.[41] Choosing between these two aims, insisted the Ecuadorian Baptist René Padilla, was like choosing one of the two wings of a plane. This radical turn was not what Graham and his allies had expected, but they accepted it. Perhaps, following the Jesus Freaks' example, the future for theologically conservative Protestants was on the political Left.

The American evangelical Left's great moment came during the 1976 presidential election. With the Republican Party's moral authority shredded after the Watergate scandal, a Democratic Party candidate emerged who was, unprecedentedly, a bona fide born-again evangelical Protestant. Jimmy Carter promised moral renewal to a country that had lost its way. His election poster—J.C. CAN SAVE AMERICA!—was a joke, but it says something about the hopes invested in him.

Evangelical voters, who had rarely been noticed by the American national media, turned out in unprecedented numbers in the early primaries and caucuses and helped Carter to clinch the Democratic nomination. The televangelist Pat Robertson interviewed Carter on his show and later claimed that "Carter was the one who activated me and a lot of others."[42] A flood of political novices volunteered for the campaign. The general election turned out to be unexpectedly close. Carter's victory, by a mere two percentage points, depended on the fact that, unprecedentedly for a Democrat, he had won more than half of the evangelical vote.

Yet when Carter ran for reelection in 1980, five million evangelical voters switched to his challenger, Ronald Reagan, a divorcé whose Presbyterianism was more conventional than pious. Since then, America's white evangelical and conservative Protestants have been consistently identified as a right-wing bloc of voters and activists. The surprise is not that there is a vocal religious Right, but that since 1980 there has not been a vocal religious Left. Many American Christians have political concerns associated with the Left, such as poverty, openness to immigrants, and environmentalism. A sizable minority of white Christians and large majorities of nonwhite Christians typically vote Democratic. But repeated attempts to mold an organized and vocal religious Left have run into the sand.

In modern America's partisan bear pit, this is usually seen as a matter of which party benefits, but Protestantism's longer history gives a different perspective. Becoming openly partisan is dangerous for any religious movement. In January 2016, a junior Republican congressman claimed, "We own the entire [biblical] tradition." Inevitably, outraged Democrats leaped to deny it, but for Protestants—left or right—the danger is that it seems so nearly true.[43] For a religion to be wedded to one political party, however broad, is to condemn it to rise and fall in tandem with that party's shifting fortunes and to write off that large part of the nation whose political views are different. The failure of the religious Left, therefore, is a problem not for the political Left but for American Christianity.

During and after the Carter presidency, the religious Left foundered on one acute problem, which was a symptom of a more intractable difficulty. That problem was abortion, legalized nationwide in 1973 by the

Supreme Court's decision in *Roe v. Wade*. To begin with, Protestants paid relatively little attention to what had traditionally been a Catholic issue. But with well over a million abortions taking place annually from 1975 onward, Christians of all political persuasions discovered in themselves an apparently intuitive moral revulsion. Although there is no direct biblical guidance on the subject, it came to seem self-evident to most serious believers that abortion was murder.

For Christians on the political right, this was a rallying point. By 1980, the Republican Party was formally proposing a constitutional amendment to overturn *Roe*. On the left, matters were harder. The campaign for legal abortion was a feminist cause, and the Democratic Party was committed to feminism for reasons of politics and of principle. And so left-leaning Christians were torn between pro-feminist and antiabortion impulses, none more so than Carter himself. He personally disagreed with *Roe,* opposed providing abortion on government-funded health-care programs, and appointed an antiabortion Catholic as health secretary. Yet he also refused to campaign on the subject. The bulk of his staff were, in the jargon, "pro-choice," a position that was becoming Democratic Party orthodoxy. Carter's unsuccessful challenger for the party's 1980 nomination, Ted Kennedy, was a late but loud convert to the pro-choice cause. Carter was caught in the cross fire. Many feminists found his antiabortion views increasingly unacceptable, whereas evangelicals (and Catholics) felt he had betrayed them. The 1980 election had a more bitter evangelical slogan than four years earlier: "Abort Carter."[44]

This issue fired up the Christian Right and flummoxed the Christian Left. There were attempts to resolve it in the 1980s. The campaign group JustLife tried to claim the antiabortion cause for the Left by allying it with other "pro-life" causes such as antimilitarism and opposition to the death penalty. But despite a good deal of publicity, it had little success in actually supporting candidates. It is not simply that it faced powerful opposition from pro-choice Democrats. Antiabortion Democrats were themselves reluctant to press their views, lest they undermine the feminist cause in which they also believed. They made their arguments tentatively, with nuance and moderation. And so they were either ignored or never heard at all.

This debate was only a sign of a deeper, systemic problem: the inability of the white Christian Left to assert its religious identity. It has been muzzled not by secularist opponents but by its own profound commitment to inclusion and opposition to discrimination. Its aim is to serve society as a whole rather than its own narrow confessional self-interest, a commitment that blends a noble Bonhoefferian instinct for self-sacrificial service with a lingering sense of white Protestant America as normative America, which cannot abandon its universal responsibilities by claiming a particular identity for itself. So the powerful and politically active black Protestant churches are pigeonholed as black rather than as Protestant. And white Protestant America has been subsumed first into Judeo-Christian America, then into multi- and non-faith America, making it very hard for white Protestants on the left unapologetically to put their faith at the center of their politics.

Take the campaign in the mid-1980s against President Reagan's support for the contra rebels in Nicaragua. More than eighty thousand Americans signed a Pledge of Resistance, vowing mass, nonviolent resistance in the event of direct American intervention in Nicaragua. The Pledge was an evangelical initiative, but its religious identity was quickly abandoned in the interest of breadth. If Jews or gay rights activists were to support it, naturally it could not be assertively Christian, nor could its campaign meetings include Christian prayer. Another evangelical initiative, the Witness for Peace movement, placed more than four thousand unarmed Americans as human shields in Nicaraguan villages at risk of contra attack. Again, the movement was deliberately broadened, initially to being a "prayerful, biblically based community" open to anyone who was "comfortable" with that ethos. But as it drew in liberal Protestants, Catholics, and secular idealists, that ethos was progressively diluted. "The last thing you want to be doing when people you love are getting killed," said one frustrated evangelical volunteer, "is worrying about whether your prayer is going to offend someone." Yet the fear that prayer might offend had become one of the fundamental realities with which the Christian Left had to live.[45]

In 2015, a senior Democratic strategist was quoted as saying that "the right wing has no problem using religious language to push its agenda, but liberal faith leaders hesitate to use religious language when speaking with secular coalition partners.'[46] It is true, but not because Protestants on the left lack conviction. It is precisely that their convictions make it intensely difficult for them to assert their religion.

The plainest symbol of this is Martin Luther King Jr. himself. Not that King ever hesitated to use religious language. Yet he is remembered and celebrated as the hero of a secular political cause, not for being—as he surely was—modern America's greatest Christian leader. His murder is not celebrated as a Christian martyrdom, even though it was how his path of Christlike nonviolence was always likely to end. And all this for the best of reasons. He is and should be a unifying figure, who belongs not to his church but to the ages.

In the meantime, the old white establishment Protestantism of the West is adrift. Those who are on both the theological and the political right can still assert themselves, often as a counterculture, and they do so especially vocally in the United States, where theological conservatism is strong and church hierarchy weak. The rest cannot find their voice. The problem is not some inexorable deep-historical force of secularization but the ongoing impact of the cultural revolution of the 1960s and its mantra of inclusion, itself the result of the moral shock of World War II.

The most remarkable symbol of this comes from the 1960s' greatest adventure: the space program. The idea of reaching to the heavens in order to peacefully defeat godless Communism should have been a gift to Christians. It was in this spirit that on Christmas Eve 1968 the crew of Apollo 8, who were orbiting the moon and looking back at Earth, read the first ten verses of the book of Genesis in a live television broadcast. This prompted a lawsuit from a secularist campaigner who alleged that NASA was violating the constitutional separation of church and state. The case was dismissed, but it had its effects. One of the first two men to land on the moon the following July, Buzz Aldrin, was a Presbyterian elder as well as an astronaut, and he had brought consecrated bread and wine from his home church. And so, before either he or Neil Armstrong went outside, the first food and drink ever consumed on the moon was a Presbyterian Eucharist. (Armstrong did not receive.) The real significance of this event, however, is the discretion that surrounded it. Aldrin wanted to broadcast it, like his predecessors on Apollo 8, but NASA's flight operations manager discouraged him, wanting to avoid any further controversy. Aldrin therefore invited "each person listening in, wherever and whomever he may be, to contemplate for a moment . . . and to give thanks in his own individual way," and then closed down the radio to celebrate his Communion. The point is not that a Christian witness was silenced by secularist bullying. Aldrin wrote about how much the event had meant to him but also, years later, wondered whether he had been right to do it at all:

> Perhaps if I had it to do over again, I would not choose to celebrate communion. Although it was a deeply meaningful experience for me, it was a Christian sacrament, and we had come to the moon in the name of all mankind—be they Christians, Jews, Muslims, animists, agnostics, or atheists.[47]

An earnest and committed Protestant could now feel that he had a duty to speak in the name of all humanity and therefore, as a matter of conscience, regret privately celebrating the central rite of his faith.

It may be that as white Americans and Europeans slowly come to terms with the traumatic fact that their cultural hegemony is over, they will discover a way to be genuinely pluralist while still having an identity of their own. If Protestants, or indeed the Judeo-Christian religions more widely, can find a way of asserting their religion's meaning and power while maintaining their hard-won commitment to a genuinely inclusive society, then a new chapter in the history of religion in the West will begin. As we will see in the final chapter, there are hints of how this could happen. But first, we must turn our attention away from the becalmed Protestantism of the old Atlantic world to see how different the twentieth century's story has been elsewhere.

PART III

The
Global Age

CHAPTER 13

Redeeming South Africa

> He hath made of one blood all nations of men for to dwell on
> all the face of the earth, and hath determined the times be-
> fore appointed, and the bounds of their habitation.
>
> —ACTS 17:26

In the twentieth century, Protestantism became a global religion. The change has been most dramatic in Africa. Much of sub-Saharan Africa was untouched by Christianity before the later nineteenth century but is now dominated by it. The broad-brush story is of Europeans nibbling progressively at Africa's coast from the fifteenth century onward; then capturing and shipping slaves, especially in the West; then, during the later nineteenth century, moving decisively into the interior, establishing colonial rule over almost all of sub-Saharan Africa by 1900. Christian missionaries arrived with the conquerors, although not always in lockstep with them. For a little less than a century, the continent was ruled by Europeans, under whose umbrella enormous effort was poured into missionary work, and respectable numbers of converts were won.

In the 1950s and 1960s, however, the European powers found that they had little further practical need for African empires and that they lacked the military resources and the political will to keep them. They scrambled out of Africa even faster than they had scrambled to seize it. Their political and economic legacy to the postcolonial states was at best mixed, but their religious legacy was more surprising. We might have expected African nationalists to throw off their colonists' religion, and some did. Yet it was after independence that African Christianity's really dramatic growth began, a growth led not by missionaries but by independent churches that answered to no one but God and their congregations.

If we are to go beyond these sweeping generalities, it is no use talking about "Africa," a vast, diverse continent. We must look at the local stories. All are worth telling, but this chapter will focus on one, entirely unrepresentative experience. South Africa was the site of the continent's first Protestant presence and is now one of Africa's most Protestant countries. Alongside the movement from missionary-led churches to African leadership and independence, however, is another story. South Africa had a larger population of European descent than any other colonial territory on the continent. Uniquely, it became independent as a white-ruled state, in which the nonwhite population was suppressed with increasingly systematic brutality. This system, known from 1948 onward as apartheid (separateness), justified itself explicitly in Protestant terms. Yet Protestants were also central to the opposition to apartheid and to its sudden, unexpectedly peaceful collapse in 1990–94. This is a story of how Protestants made one corner of Africa their own, how they came to sanction one of the most notorious injustices of modern times, and how they helped to bring it to an end.

Settlers and Missionaries

For early European explorers, sub-Saharan Africa was principally an obstacle, a large and barren blockage en route to the Indian Ocean. Portuguese sailors made landfall in South Africa, and in 1501 a short-lived Catholic chapel was built at what is now Mossel Bay. But there was no permanent European settlement until 1652, when the Dutch East India Company established what is now Cape Town. Despite the normal vague pieties about civilizing native peoples, the colony was plainly intended as a refuge from the sea rather than as a foothold on the land. Yet the land was fertile and the climate temperate. Dutch farmers began to spread beyond the fort to make their own fortunes. This brought them up against the region's indigenous inhabitants.

Of all of Africa's peoples, none were more different from Europeans than the Khoikhoi. They were nomadic pastoralists, a lifestyle incompatible with the newcomers' weird habit of claiming specific patches of land for their own exclusive use. To the Dutch, the Khoikhoi language, in which the most numerous consonants are clicks made with the tongue, sounded more like hiccups, gurgles, or animal noises than speech. This fed their suspicion that the Khoikhoi were an unusually bestial branch of humanity. So did their inability to discover anything that they could recognize as a Khoikhoi religion. One Dutch Protestant minister who had served all around the Indian Ocean declared that the Khoikhoi were "the most savage, stupid, and filthy heathens I had ever met." A great many Dutch settlers described them as "filthy" or "stinking." They were referring to the Khoikhoi custom of rubbing their bodies with animal fat, but taking it as a symbol of barbarism and depravity. As early as 1655, ministers at the Cape declared missionary work with these creatures to be impossible, "because," as one put it, "they are so used to running about wild, that they can't live in subjection to us." The possibility of converting them without subjecting them would not have occurred to him.[1]

Not all of the Dutch despaired so easily. Soon after 1652, a Khoikhoi girl named Krotoa became a servant in the household of Jan van Riebeeck, the colony's founding commander. Krotoa swiftly mastered Dutch and was soon baptized as a Reformed Protestant, taking the name Eva. She ate Dutch food, wore Dutch clothes, and later described herself as having a "Dutch heart." When she traveled inland to visit her family, she was mocked for her new, alien faith. Undaunted, she taught a sick relative to pray to Christ for healing. The wider family "listened with tears in their eyes," the patient recovered, and Eva claimed she had been urged to send them further religious instruction.[2] Perhaps this Eva might become the mother of a new Christian Africa.

The gap, however, was too wide for one woman to bridge. When van Riebeeck moved to Indonesia in 1662, Eva was cast adrift. By the colonists' unforgiving account, she descended into drink and apparent prostitution, a decline only temporarily arrested by a short-lived marriage. In 1669, after a confrontation with the colony's commander, she fled, leaving her five children behind, but was overtaken, arrested, and imprisoned in the colony's new prison on Robben Island. The official record of her death in 1674 observed, "With the dogs she returned to her vomit, until finally, in death, she put out the fire of her lust, affording a clear illustration that nature, no matter how tightly muzzled by imprinted moral principles . . . reverts to its inborn qualities."[3] Neither baptism nor education could change the Khoikhoi's fundamentally inferior nature. A handful of other early converts taught the Dutch the same lesson: some scornfully renounced the faith when it no longer suited them, one committed suicide, and one spent his life imprisoned on Robben Island for some unspecified, heinous crime.

The Dutch concluded, as one minister put it in 1678, that "this nation is totally opposed to our religion, no matter what means are directed toward them."[4] Because converting the Khoikhoi was impossible, there was no need to try. What the Dutch really wanted from the Khoikhoi was for them to disappear. The Dutch did not plan the smallpox epidemic that devastated the Khoikhoi in 1713, but nor did they regret it.

The colony's labor force consisted not of Khoikhoi but of slaves imported from India, the East Indies, and elsewhere in Africa. Here, too, only minimal attempts were made to spread Christianity, although for a different reason. The colony's religious life was governed by the Reformed Church of the Netherlands, which had decided in 1618 that baptized slaves could not be sold. Naturally, slaveholders therefore refused to allow their slaves to be baptized. Christianity remained the exclusive preserve of white settlers.

Idealistic newcomers might have felt differently, had there been any. By around 1700, however, European immigration had all but dried up. The few thousand remaining settlers prospered and multiplied: a tiny, isolated outpost of Protestant Europe on the shores of the Southern Ocean. Dutch officials regarded the frontier lifestyles of these Boers—"farmers"—with increasing contempt. If the cultural gulf with the Khoikhoi had been narrower, the Boers might have intermarried and assimilated. Instead, they jealously asserted their distinct identity, not as free, white, European, Dutch, or (a later term) "Afrikaners," but simply as *Christians*: as the "natives" could never be.

What was these settlers' Christianity? The colony's official Reformed church, six of whose seven congregations were in Cape Town itself as late as 1795, could not provide more than occasional, itinerant service to a scattered Boer population. It could, however, prevent other Christian churches from establishing themselves, and it could set cultural norms. The settlers appear to have been a people of the Dutch Bible, who learned from the Old Testament how God had led his people on an exodus through deep waters to a new land, fertile and filled with heathens. They read these stories through the prism of the Calvinist doctrines that Christians are God's chosen, covenanted people and that children born into that covenant belong to it from the moment of their birth. In their context, the meaning was obvious: European equals Christian, slave or African equals heathen, and it must always be so.

Protestants from other backgrounds did not agree. The first challenge came from evangelicalism's ubiquitous advance guard, the Moravians. In 1737, a Moravian missionary named Georg Schmidt arrived and established a commune on a farm at Genadendal, eighty miles east of Cape Town. He gathered a group of Khoikhoi who eventually numbered twenty-eight, and in 1741 he baptized five of them in a nearby river. However, the Reformed church consistently opposed him. In 1743, isolated and worn down, he returned to Europe. As a parting gift, he left his Dutch New Testament with a girl whom he had baptized Magdalena.

In 1792, Moravian missionaries were able to return to Genadendal. When they arrived on Christmas Eve, they were greeted by the now elderly Magdalena, who unwrapped her treasure from its sheepskin case. Her failing eyesight meant that she could no longer read, but she had a young woman read the story of the Magi's journey to Bethlehem for the newcomers. The community had endured in isolation for half a century, meeting to read and pray under the pear tree Schmidt had planted. The visitors' sudden appearance did not surprise them, for God had told them in dreams to expect their return.

Perhaps we suspect that the story has grown in the telling. But if nothing else, it is an early sign of an indisputable truth: Protestant missions to southern Africa's indigenous people could be far more successful than those first Dutch settlers had assumed. When the Cape Colony was seized by the British—first in 1795 and definitively in 1806—it was opened up to Protestant missionaries, although the new regime maintained the privileges and position of the Dutch Reformed Church (DRC). The missionaries were from the beginning scandalously interracial. In 1806, one of the first, Johannes van der Kemp, began ordaining his converts as deacons and deaconesses. In the same year, he scandalized his Boer neighbors still further by marrying. The outrage was not because Sara Janse was fourteen years old to his fifty-nine but because she was a former slave of Malagasy descent.

The missions quickly reached beyond the Cape Colony's boundaries, with considerable success. It is not simply that missionaries could help negotiate with the government at the Cape and facilitate access to European weapons. The Europeans' religion was a plausible explanation for their power, whereas conventional African spiritual defenses were not working well. In 1823, the Tswana people of Kuruman, north of the Cape, were attacked by a larger force from the neighboring Tlokwa. Fortunately for the Tswana, Robert Moffat, a Scottish missionary, was able to secure assistance from a nearby group who had guns. The victory fomented a widespread belief that the presence of a missionary was a guarantee of battle victory—a belief only reinforced the following year, when a Tlokwa raiding party defeated another Tswana group, having attacked on a day when their resident missionary happened to be traveling.

Protestantism offered more than worldly assistance, however. From the beginning, missionaries reported intense, dramatic conversions. The Christian sacraments of baptism and the Eucharist made self-evident sense to peoples for whom water and blood had long-standing religious significance. African Christians were swiftly interpreting dreams, singing, and displaying vivid emotion in prayer, their cries sometimes drowning out preachers' voices. In 1816, a German missionary with the London Missionary Society reported, "My hearers were drowned in tears, others were unable to sit or stand." Once his service was over, they withdrew together into a field to pray. Their unconverted neighbors tended to despise these displays, seeing it as shameful for adults to weep. Missionaries were taken aback too. When a revival struck Kuruman in 1829, Moffat wrote,

> We were taken by surprise. . . . Although it was impossible to keep either order or silence, a deep impression of the Divine presence was felt. They sang till late hour and before morning dawned, they would assemble again at some house for worship, before going to labor.

Moffat was a little alarmed by this outpouring of emotion and was keen to channel it toward a mature faith; to this end, he remained with the Tswana for a total of forty-nine years. Another Scot, the age's best-known explorer-missionary, David Livingstone, disagreed, arguing that the "native Church" should be left to its own devices rather than being infantilized by continued missionary support.

> We have great confidence in the essential vigor of Christianity. It blooms in imperishable youth wherever it is untrammeled by the wisdom of men. Sow the seed, and it never dies. The Divine Spirit will see to it.

That was an article of faith rather than the result of sober observation. But there was no shortage of evidence.[5]

Consider an apparently futile interlude in Johannes van der Kemp's pioneering mission, his 1800–1801 attempt to preach the Gospel to the Xhosa, east of the Cape Colony. By the time of his death in 1811, his mission there had borne no evident fruit. It was only in around 1815 that Ntsikana, a highborn but outcast Xhosa singer to whom van der Kemp had preached, was converted. Following a vision in which he saw a single bright sunray strike the side of his prize ox, he found himself inspired to begin humming and then chanting early versions of what would become the first Xhosa-language Christian hymns. He also set himself against a millenarian Xhosa prophet who was attempting to mobilize his people for war against the encroaching Europeans, promising supernatural immunity to bullets. Ntsikana accused him of self-aggrandizement and of lying to the people and preached repentance and reconciliation instead, attracting a substantial following, many of them Khoikhoi refugees and other outcasts. It was a sign of things to come. Protestantism had already been transposed into an authentically African key.

Blood River

When the first significant wave of British settlers arrived in 1820, they joined around 43,000 descendants of the seventeenth-century settlers. The British called these people "Dutch," but by now they were less transplanted colonists than an almost indigenous people. The labels "Afrikaner" and "Afrikaans," for those people and for the distinctive language that their form of Dutch had become, were not yet coined.

But their distinct identity certainly existed. It also, already, felt itself to be under mortal threat.

British conquest, British immigration, and a hostile British colonial administration were bad enough, but the missionaries' work with non-white peoples threatened Afrikaners' core identity, that sharp division between Christian and heathen. Missionaries' repeated interventions to protect indigenous peoples' rights looked to Afrikaners like treason. They even suborned the Afrikaners' own Dutch Reformed Church, which the colonial administration now began to staff with British subjects and which in 1829 obediently decreed that the sacraments should be administered equally to all Christians regardless of race.

The last straw was the abolition of slavery throughout the British Empire in 1833. One Afrikaner later recalled her outrage at "the shameful and unjust proceedings with reference to the freedom of the slaves . . . their being placed on an equal footing with Christians, contrary to the laws of God and the natural distinction of race and religion." "Christian" was a tribal identity, "race-and-religion" a single word. For this Afrikaner, there was only one solution: "We withdrew in order to preserve our doctrines in purity."[6] It was a pilgrimage into the unknown, like that of the American Pilgrims, and also a mass migration, like those of many other southern African peoples of the early nineteenth century. The so-called Great Trek of the late 1830s saw around twelve thousand Afrikaners leave the Cape Colony and move north and east. The DRC's synod denounced the trek and banned its ministers from joining, but the "Voortrekkers," undaunted, knew that they were leading their covenanted people from British captivity into the promised land.

This myth was powerfully reinforced on December 16, 1838, when a trekker group of some 470 was attacked by a Zulu army of at least 12,000 at the Ncome River in what is now KwaZulu-Natal. The trekkers had firearms and an excellent defensive position, but they were still vastly outnumbered, and the Zulus had a formidable military reputation. The story goes that the besieged trekkers vowed to commemorate God's mercy in the event that they survived. We can certainly believe that they saw God's hand in their victory. The Afrikaners suffered no deaths and only three minor injuries, while the Zulu eventually retreated, leaving three thousand dead. The carnage gave the battle its name: Blood

River. Who now could doubt that the Afrikaners were God's people? The commemoration of the vow every December 16 would become Afrikanerdom's holiest ritual. It proved that, as the Dutch Reformed minister and poet J. D. du Toit put it in 1909, the "handful of trekkers . . . the freedom seekers, creators of a People," were "another Israel," beset by "stark naked black hordes, following tyrants," but delivered by God's hand to the paradise providentially set aside for them.[7]

And so the Voortrekkers carved out independent Afrikaner republics north and east of the Cape Colony and, with them, independent Reformed churches. The whole point of the trek, one leader explained, was not to be forced "to sit at table in Church with Bushmen and Hottentots," or to accept "that baptism and confession destroys the eternal and thus necessary difference between white and black."[8] In 1853, an independent Dutch Reformed Church was founded, in defiance of that egalitarian doctrine, as the state church of the emerging Transvaal Republic. The DRC establishment back at the Cape, desperate to reunite with these separated brethren, was now badly split. On the one side were advocates of mission, many of them Scots rather than Dutch. On the other were so-called neo-Calvinists, committed to maintaining the covenanted people's distinctiveness. The critical issue was the status of nonwhite converts. The 1829 ruling that they should be accepted as church members had, in practice, bolstered the Afrikaner assumption that it was better not to convert nonwhites at all. The solution was proposed in 1857 by the missionary moderates' leader, Andrew Murray. A synod resolved that racially integrated congregations were "desirable . . . wherever possible." However, recognizing that "this measure, as a result of the weakness of some, impedes the furtherance of the cause of Christ among the Heathen," the synod permitted congregations to be segregated.[9] As some outraged missionaries insisted, in this fatal permission, the DRC had returned to its original sin.

Yet at the time it seemed wiser than launching a doomed assault on Afrikaners' prejudices. Moreover, it succeeded. The missionaries were let off the leash, making progress especially among Afrikaans-speaking peoples of mixed race, known in South Africa's racial jargon as "coloreds." In 1881, these "colored" congregations formed the separate Dutch Reformed Mission Church. Meanwhile, the establishment DRC regained its reputation in the Voortrekker republics, which were prospering immensely. The total Afrikaner population rose from 43,000 in 1820, to 140,000 in 1850, to some 700,000 in 1900.

By then, the British rule the Voortrekkers had fled was catching up with them. Fatally, the Afrikaner republics turned out to be sitting on vast deposits of diamonds and gold. Britain launched an abortive attack in 1880–81 and a far more serious assault in the Second Boer War or South African War of 1899–1902. It is not to defend the republics' own racial tyranny to point out that this was one of the ugliest episodes in the history of British imperialism. It was a war fought against the entire Afrikaner population, using what Britain's leader of the opposition called "methods of barbarism." Huge tracts of land were emptied of people, who were interned in concentration camps: a new invention, Britain's gift to the twentieth century. Twenty-seven thousand imprisoned Afrikaners and unknown numbers of nonwhite people died.

The British imperial war machine ground out its victory in the end. But the Afrikaners did not learn to love their conquerors, especially when the victorious British establishment tried to stamp out education in the Afrikaans language and other symbols of Afrikaner identity. As any Calvinists might, Afrikaners interpreted their defeat as martyrdom, calling them to further defiant faithfulness. Hence the formation in 1914 of the National Party (NP), a political vehicle for asserting Afrikaner identity. In 1918, it was joined by the Afrikaner Broederbond (Brotherhood), a secretive body committed to "the eternal existence of a separate Afrikaner nation with its own language and culture" and to Afrikaner mutual assistance.[10] Alongside these two, the third institutional prop of Afrikanerdom was the DRC. It would eventually become routine to joke that the only difference between the NP and the DRC was the day of the week. Daniel F. Malan, an NP hard-liner who became party leader in 1934, was also an ordained Dutch Reformed minister. For him, preserving the Afrikaner nation was not mere self-defense but a religious duty:

> We hold this nationhood as our due for it was given to us by the Architect of the universe. . . . The history of the Afrikaner reveals a will and determination which makes one feel that Afrikanerdom is not the work of men but the creation of God.[11]

Like all good Calvinists, nothing encouraged Afrikaners more than defeat, isolation, discrimination, and contempt.

For the time being, this defiance was confined. After victory in 1902, the British tried to bind up the wounds of war with a promise of white unity, which was the keystone of the newly formed Union of South Africa in 1910. British and Afrikaners would together exercise what, in the 1930s, the governing United Party called the "Christian Trusteeship of the European Race" over the "Natives."[12] What this meant in practice was that the supposedly nonracial legal structure of the Cape Colony, in which certain nonwhites had some limited rights to political participation, would be restricted to that section of the new country. The former Afrikaner republics would remain under exclusively white control. Even in what was now the Cape Province, nonwhites' rights were progressively curtailed. In the 1930s, the vote was formally restricted to whites and "coloreds," with "blacks"—people of pure African descent— instead being given the Native Representative Council, whose effectiveness one commentator compared to a toy telephone. Because few nonwhites qualified to vote anyway, that change was largely symbolic. The 1913 Natives Land Act was a much more severe assault, reserving the vast bulk of the country's best farmland and of its cities exclusively for white ownership. Legislation through the 1920s and 1930s progressively restricted nonwhites' employment rights and regulated where they were permitted to live and work. South Africa's British establishment claimed that this was a society evolving toward equality under the law, but for those on the law's receiving end most progress was in the other direction.

If English-speaking South Africa's myth of color blindness had any truth, it was in its churches. English-speaking churches only established themselves slowly at the Cape, lagging behind their missionaries. During the nineteenth century, those missionaries' focus had shifted to Africans working on white-owned farms and, especially, to migrant laborers in the rapidly growing cities and mines. Workers at the vast diamond mine at Kimberley from the late 1860s, restricted to closed compounds and suffering ghastly death rates, were not much more than contracted slaves. What the mining companies did provide was chapels, which Methodists, Lutherans, and even African American churches from the United States readily staffed. There and elsewhere, missionaries provided what few social services migrant laborers had, including decent burials for the dead.

These missionary-led churches were of necessity multiracial. So although few congregations were actually very mixed (language alone ensured a good deal of self-segregation), most of these churches aspired in principle and eventually began in practice to train nonwhite leaders. The first black South African to be ordained a Protestant minister was Tiyo Soga, a Xhosa whose father had been a follower of the Xhosa preacher Ntsikana. Soga was taken to Scotland as a teenager on one missionary's private initiative, baptized, trained, and ordained there in 1856. He returned to South Africa and worked as a missionary for the remainder of his life, translating Bunyan's *Pilgrim's Progress* into Xhosa. By the 1870s, the Anglicans, too, were ordaining black clergy. By 1910, some four hundred black South Africans were serving as ordained ministers in various denominations, and more than eight thousand as teachers or evangelists.

Even so, white missionaries retained administrative control. The natural result was the emergence of so-called African Independent churches—Protestant churches entirely controlled by black Africans, outside denominational structures. As we have seen, this phenomenon was almost as old as southern African Protestantism itself. Magdalena, the Moravian leader at Genadendal, has a claim to be recognized as South Africa's first independent church leader; or perhaps Ntsikana and his Xhosa following. What distinguishes the first classic Independent church, Nehemiah Tile's Thembu church, founded in 1884, is that it deliberately broke off from an existing denomination. Tile was a Methodist evangelist among his own Thembu people on the Cape's eastern frontier, but he broke with his white superiors over politics. He hoped to help the Thembu's paramount chief to negotiate an independent British protectorate. In order to cement the chief's authority, boost his credibility with the British, and save his people's souls, Tile proposed to establish a state church in Thembuland, headed by the chief, much as the Church of England was headed by Queen Victoria. It did not last. The British establishment swiftly decided that this church was seditious, and after Tile himself died in 1891, the chief admitted defeat and returned to orthodox Methodism.[13]

Tile had imitators, however. Another disgruntled Methodist, an ordained minister named Mangena Mokone, visited the Thembu church shortly before breaking with his denomination in 1892. He concluded that

> no African pastor is respected by the White brethren. . . . The White pastors do not even know the members of their own congregations. They always build their own houses one or two miles away from their parish. The separation shows that we cannot be brothers.[14]

Mokone called his new church the Ethiopian Mission, an invocation of the Bible's only unambiguous references to sub-Saharan Africa. He was the first of many black church leaders who, belittled or ignored by white denominations, decided they had to go it alone. These schisms generally reflected breakdowns of trust rather than any disagreement over theology or even politics. A particular source of friction was the assumption, shared by even the most liberal whites, that black people could not be trusted with money. Some "Ethiopian" churches promptly tried to negotiate new relationships with established denominations. African American churches were particularly interested; one of Mokone's community, James M. Dwane, was consecrated a bishop in the African Methodist Episcopal Church in 1898 and was received with honor when he visited America the following year. Yet the South Africans quickly realized that the Americans, too, believed themselves to be more civilized than their new brethren. Dwane eventually negotiated a deal with the Anglicans instead, was ordained an Anglican deacon, and became the head of the new, autonomous Order of Ethiopia within South Africa's Anglican church. The order endured until 1999, when it was refounded as the fully independent Ethiopian Episcopal Church, with Dwane's grandson as its first bishop. For most "Ethiopians," however, the only path was full separation.

Livingstone had hoped for fully native churches, but now that they were here, few missionaries liked them. Departing black ministers usually took their congregations with them. Missionaries were left on the hook for maintaining empty churches and often accused their former brethren of excessive pride or financial greed. Beyond these base jealousies, missionaries worried that independent churches might veer into heresy, compromising with traditional African religions or forming personality cults. Even more alarming was the possibility that these churches, having rejected white religious authority, would become sites of political dissent. Governments kept a close watch on independent churches for signs of sedition.

Only as it became clear that most independent churches were studiedly apolitical did some of the established English-speaking denominations warm to them. Maybe Livingstone had been right: Africa would be evangelized by African churches. At a global missionary conference in Geneva in 1904, Édouard Jacottet, a Swiss missionary with decades of southern African experience, argued that shepherding Africans into white-run churches was misguided. Even if such churches ordained the occasional black minister, he would be seen by his own people as a "colored European." Meanwhile, as Jacottet knew from bitter experience, white congregations simply would not accept black converts as their spiritual equals. Perhaps it was better for all sides simply to have their own churches. So the independent churches, arising from black Protestants' assertion of their own spiritual worth, inadvertently helped to foster separation.

"Separate Development"

After World War I, South Africa's white ruling class found itself at an ideological crossroads. Anglophone whites and Afrikaners were perched precariously atop an extremely unequal society. It was only natural that they would hate and fear the rising ideology of Communism, which remained white South Africans' favorite bogeyman for the rest of the century. But what form would their anti-Communism take?

Anglophone whites mostly followed their mother country's example. British imperial liberalism aspired to a nonracial capitalist democracy under the rule of law, knew that good order and gradual change were the ways to get there, and was in no particular hurry. This ethic took sincere pride in its commitment to law, democracy, and human equality but was compatible with an effortless sense of cultural and racial superiority. Liberalism did not threaten South Africa with revolution. Nor was its soft gradualism a solid bulwark against change.

The beckoning alternative, especially for Afrikaners, was an ideology of racism and anti-Communism, which despised democracy, preferred republics to monarchies, and celebrated violence and manly, peasant virtues. What could be a better fit to Afrikanerdom than the new movement gathering strength in Germany? All the more so when Nazi Germany confronted the Afrikaners' own, bitterly resented conquerors, Britain. Fascistic Afrikaner movements emerged from 1933 onward. The centenary of the battle of Blood River in 1938 produced a surge of Afrikaner nationalism, out of which came a new outfit called the *Ossewabrandwag* (OB), the "Ox-Wagon Sentinel": a folk reenactment society with paramilitary ambitions, whose stated aims were to protect "the religious, cultural and material concerns of the Afrikaner."

When Britain went to war with Germany in 1939, South Africa's long-serving Afrikaner prime minister, J. B. M. Hertzog, tried to keep his country neutral, failed, and resigned. Afrikaners were now dragged into a war for their despised imperial masters against an enemy many of them respected. Hertzog, freed from office, inveighed against "the democratic-parliamentary form of government" and urged South Africans to be part of the "creation of a new world order"; he cited Nazi Germany as a model. As Anglophone whites signed up for the army, Afrikaners flocked instead to join the OB, which by mid-1940 numbered 200,000. Its manifesto of that year demanded an Afrikaans-speaking republic in which "the Jewish question, the poor-white question and the question of the coloreds would be settled without delay" and in which "pure white descent and service to the Afrikaans ethnic calling" would be a precondition for citizenship. The OB's *stormjaers* began a campaign of sabotage, cutting telephone lines and dynamiting railways. Its leader explained that he wanted "blood rather than votes" and that the fulfillment of the OB's hopes depended on a German victory.[15]

Remarkably, however, the OB failed not only in its bid for South Africa but also in its bid for Afrikanerdom. The Afrikaner National Party was never at ease with the OB and by 1941 was openly opposing it, a rift that went deeper than the tactical split between direct action and parliamentary politics. The NP's leadership was committed to creating a white-supremacist Afrikaner republic, but they were not Nazis. This lugubrious distinction between two kinds of racism matters profoundly, because at its heart was the NP's commitment to its Christian identity.

The OB defined its nationalism by race and blood. This caused an immediate problem, because talk of the "white race" lumped Afrikaners in with their British oppressors. The NP's intellectual powerhouse, Hendrik Verwoerd, opposed the OB on these grounds. Worse, emphasizing blood rather than covenant changed Afrikanerdom's meaning. In OB hands, Afrikaner history was not a sacred narrative of divine protection and redemptive suffering, but a story of triumphalist violence. Instead of the miracle of Blood River and the sufferings of the concentration camps, the OB emphasized the victory over the British at Majuba Hill in 1881 and the daring feats of Boer War commandos. This was part of what finally pulled the Afrikaner Broederbond, the secret society for whose allegiance both the NP and the OB were competing, into the NP's camp. The Broederbond's 1941 political manifesto called for a state that was not "cast in a foreign mold," whether British or German, but was instead "free and republican and Christian National." Unlike the Nazis' vacuous "positive Christianity," the Broederbond explained that such a state "must acknowledge as basic the eternal legal principles of the Word of God" and that "no inroads may be made upon the freedom of conscience and independence of the social spheres which are grounded in creation." To be sure, the same manifesto also wanted citizenship restricted to what it called "ethnically constructive" whites, a provision that Malan, the NP's leader, disliked. This was not liberal democracy, but nor was it fascist totalitarianism.[16]

As it became clear how World War II was going to end, the OB crumbled. Everywhere else in the world, racist structures and assumptions found themselves without ideological props, surviving on raw prejudice and social inertia. What made Afrikaner nationalism unique was that racist policies continued to be openly and defiantly defended in principle as well as in practice. Apartheid was often compared rather loosely to fascism, but this was not true, except in the sense that different boots feel the same to the person being kicked. Apartheid was a form not of fascism but of Calvinism. That fact is central both to its creation and to its dissolution.

Apartheid was of course far more about money, power, and fear than it was about religion. Almost all of South Africa's productive land, mines, industries, and cities were controlled by its white minority. That minority naturally found this status quo agreeable and also feared that if they ever loosened their grip, the resulting explosion of resentment would sweep them away. Yet human societies do not act on bald calculations of self-interest. Generally, we need to believe that what we are doing is right, or natural, or inevitable, or serves some higher purpose. Ideologies can be bent and stretched, but they are not infinitely malleable, and if they eventually snap, the cause they are holding together can fall apart. So it was in the case of apartheid and the Dutch Reformed Church's Calvinism.

The theology of apartheid was based on the apparently innocuous principle that human diversity is God's will, a doctrine that the most cursory observation of the world or reading of the Old Testament readily confirms. The Old Testament also implies that the primary unit of that diversity is the nation, and its story of the Jews' conquest and exile makes plain that nationhood is defined neither by territory nor by political independence. A nation is a spiritual entity, defined by its common culture and way of life. It is easy to conclude that not only nations themselves but their cultures are created by God, and it is their duty to preserve those cultures to the glory of the God who created them.

The Afrikaner "nation," a conquered minority in a very diverse country, thus came to have a horror of mixing, blending their God-given national distinctiveness into a soulless, cosmopolitan, modernist soup. This principle even stymied the achievement of a great Afrikaner hope, the full reunion of the sundered branches of the Dutch Reformed Church after the Boer War. An attempt to do this in 1911 foundered because the Cape DRC, in keeping with its notorious 1857 ruling, did not actually *require* racial segregation. It retained a handful of "colored" members and two "colored" congregations. A fully united DRC would be governed by a synod including an elder from each of those congregations. For the other, exclusively white branches of the DRC, this was intolerable. One Transvaal delegate insisted that "if there were even one Coloured among 1000 delegates, he would vote against unification." Full union was not achieved until 1962.[17]

That Transvaaler's comment certainly arose from profound racial loathing and fear, but it had a rationale. The argument was that "colored" and black Christians should belong to their own national churches, not the Afrikaners' church. They were another nation, with their own divinely created culture and way of life. Mixing them into the DRC would contaminate not only Afrikanerdom but the "colored" minority themselves, preventing them from attaining their own true national destiny.

The argument had its own momentum. During the 1920s and 1930s, the DRC turned in earnest toward the task of Christianizing the non-white population. This was partly raw self-interest. As one DRC missionary put it in 1931, "Who is today the best friend of the white man in this land? The native who got his education from the D. R. Church. He is the greatest opponent of the political agitators."[18] But there were theological principles at stake too. The DRC believed that the English-speaking churches' missionaries were wrong to force African converts into white-led churches where their God-given national character would be lost. It would be better for each nation to attain the fullness of its own distinctive divine calling. From around 1929, DRC writers on this subject began to borrow a word coined by a small DRC splinter group to describe their struggle to protect a separate Afrikaner identity: "apartheid."

This early, church-led vision of apartheid was idealistic. In 1931, the Orange Free State's DRC called for black churches to be established "on their own terrain, separated and apart," as part of a community that "shall take care of its own economic life apart from yet, where possible, in cooperation with the white community." Blacks living in the white community would be treated with "equity and justice" but not as equals; nor could whites living in the black community expect full "equalization." The federal DRC's mission policy of 1935 did not go quite so far, but it did insist that "each nation has a right to be itself and to try to develop and uplift itself," and it supported "social differentiation and spiritual and cultural segregation, to the benefit of both sections."[19]

This policy, it seemed, was in everyone's interests—apart from the Anglophone capitalist elites of cosmopolitan liberalism, with their project to mash South Africa's God-given diversity of nations into bland, mongrel homogeneity. DRC and NP idealists argued that apartheid was morally superior to the interwar status quo, a de facto system of white supremacy in which nonwhite peoples were deliberately deprived and exploited, unjustly and unsustainably. One theorist cited the Afrikaners' own suffering at the hands of the British to argue that the Boer nation can therefore understand the sufferings of the Bantu [black South Africans]. It is the same imperialism and capitalism, having them believe that the foreign is better than what is their own, which seeks to destroy their tribal life.[20]

Apartheid could allow each nation to discover its own true destiny in its own sphere. The way to make the races good neighbors was to build good fences.

How this might be done in practice was sketched out by a group of theologians at Stellenbosch University, led by Gustav Gerdener, professor of missions and himself the son of a German missionary. Gerdener preferred the term "separate development" to "apartheid" and emphasized that separation should not mean inferiority. In 1945, he persuaded the DRC to amend its mission policy so as to call for "co-equal education and instruction, in their own sphere, of the Coloured and the Native with what the European enjoys." He was included on the five-man commission that formulated the NP's "color policy" in 1947, a policy which, thanks to him, insisted that

non-whites are to be actively and powerfully led to make the Christian Religion the foundation of their whole life, so that a healthy Christian-National life-view is also built up among them.[21]

This was entirely consistent with his other priority: a ban on interracial marriage. Just as the Jews had, in the book of Ezra, been saved by a rigid prohibition on marrying Gentiles, so South Africa's many nations ought to be preserved in their individual purities from the dangers of mongrelization. It was possible to say, with a straight face, that none of this was about racism.

The test came in 1948. The National Party, having successfully crushed the OB, ran a moderate campaign for that year's election, focusing on anti-Communism, protecting the Afrikaans language, and the emerging policy of apartheid. It lost the popular vote, taking 38 percent against 49 percent for the governing United Party, figures virtually unchanged from the previous election. But constituency boundaries had been redrawn, and the NP's success in thinly populated rural

seats delivered it and a small allied party a slender parliamentary majority. Malan became prime minister. Soon after, Verwoerd became minister of "native affairs," a post he would turn into a virtual fiefdom
before becoming prime minister himself in 1958. The NP would remain
in power without a break until 1994.

Gerdener and his allies had some worries. Would apartheid actually
be constructed so as to permit what he called "really equivalent and
autonomous development"? One of his associates warned in 1947 that
apartheid could only be justified if inspired by "Christian love and not
by racial egotism or a feeling of racial superiority." In 1950, Gerdener
chaired a DRC conference on "the native question" which insisted that
nonwhites be permitted to own substantial, sustainable amounts of
land. He also argued that the use of black labor in the white-run economy, from mining to domestic service, ought to be wound down and
that in the meantime black laborers ought to be treated with the respect due to an equal, separate people. These views were reflected in
the 1956 report of the Tomlinson Commission, a review of racial policy
set up by the NP government. It recommended a major, renewed missionary effort among nonwhites, in the hope of winning converts not
merely to Christianity but to the merits of separate development. A
surge of DRC missionary work within South Africa duly followed, and
membership of the DRC's black sister churches rose sharply.[22]

More radically, the report recommended that South Africa itself be
partitioned. The white-ruled state ought to relinquish enough land to
form a series of viable independent states, with most blacks becoming
citizens of these new states. Decolonization was gathering pace across
the continent, and the Tomlinson report suggested a kind of internal
decolonization, to leave a rump white South Africa alongside its black
neighbors. In order for this to be done justly, the new states were to be
set up with paternalistic care, endowed with appropriate resources.

Squint hard, and it is almost possible to imagine that this could have
been just. There were other contemporary examples, from Austria-
Hungary to India, where partition had seemed like the least bad way of
dealing with irreparably riven societies. It was possible for apartheid's
theorists honestly to believe that this was the only way for all of South
Africa's nations truly to be themselves.

There were only two problems with this fantasy. First, partition could only have been just if it was mutually agreed upon by all the peoples concerned, which was tricky, because the underlying purpose of the entire project was to deny nonwhites any real political voice. As Manas Buthelezi, a Lutheran bishop in Soweto, patiently explained in 1977,

> If we came together, and then agreed that the solution is that we should separate, then separate development would have a moral basis. But now only one section says we must separate and dictates how we should separate.[23]

Second, neither the NP government nor the white population as a whole was ever willing to contemplate the sacrifices that the Tomlinson Commission called for. Enormous amounts of white-owned land would have had to be renounced and enormous sums of money invested in setting up the new states. In any case, the white-run economy depended wholly on cheap black labor. As early as 1950, Prime Minister Malan had been warning Gerdener that "apartheid as envisaged" by his circle "is not at present feasible" and that the best that could be hoped for was a distant "eventual separation."[24] Verwoerd, less burdened by personal Christian commitment than Malan, was blunter. He roundly rejected the commission and did his best to purge Gerdener's idealists from Stellenbosch. Any talk of separate development, he warned, had to take into account the "innate hereditary factors" which ensured that blacks' development would inevitably lag behind whites'.[25]

Apartheid as actually implemented drew on the idealistic vision of "separate development" but fell well short of it. Interracial marriages were banned in 1949, and all other interracial sexual contact the following year. The 1950 Group Areas Act banned nonwhites from owning land in most of South Africa. Houses owned freehold by black families for generations were bulldozed and the land seized. Entire communities were forcibly relocated to new, purpose-built "townships" such as Johannesburg's South-West Townships (SoWeTo), confined slums deliberately kept a safe distance from the cities. All schools for nonwhites were brought under government control in 1953, to the dismay of the churches that had run most of them. The purpose of these "Bantu schools" was to train unambitious, politically quiescent manual laborers for the white economy.

Once he became prime minister in 1958, Verwoerd appeared to change direction. He began to use the language of separate development and in 1959 proj osed the creation of so-called Bantustans, or "homelands," carved out of South Africa for the black population. This turned out to be no more than a parody of the notion of partition. The homelands as eventually erected constituted some 13 percent of South Africa's land area and did not include any of the best farmland or any of the cities. Almost all blacks, who formed a large and growing majority of South Africa's population, were now supposed to be residents of these reservations. The millions who worked in the white-run economy were reclassified as migrant workers, stripped of many of their remaining rights, barred from bringing families with them, and made liable to arbitrary "deportation." The vestigial structures for representing "native" views to South Africa's government could now be dissolved, because blacks were supposedly represented by the governments of the "homelands"—puppet police states funded by the NP government.

The point is not that Verwoerd betrayed some ideal vision of what apartheid could have been. That vision was both contradictory in its conception and utterly impossible to put into practice. Apartheid's theologians were less the NP's dupes than its enablers, providing a vital idealistic veneer to a policy that was actually grounded on the white population's desire to maintain a fragile dominance and their profound alienation from and fear of their black compatriots. The DRC had, for the time being at least, legitimized apartheid.

South Africa's English-speaking Protestant churches were in an awkward position. Their long-standing commitment to multiracialism and equally long-standing prejudice against Afrikaners made it easy for them to oppose apartheid, and from 1948 onward most of them issued regular, formal denunciations of NP policy. Yet they tended to advocate the pre-1948 status quo rather than any dramatic democratization, and they preferred issuing resolutions to, for example, choosing to pay their black and white employees equally for equal work. Some spoke more clearly, such as Trevor Huddleston, an English Anglican missionary in a Johannesburg township. His 1956 book *Naught for Your Comfort* insisted that apartheid was "inspired by a desire which is itself fundamentally evil and basically un-Christian: the desire to dominate in order to preserve a position of racial superiority." It also laid bare what that meant for the ordinary lives of apartheid's victims and did more than any other one publication to place apartheid on the world's conscience.[26] Yet Archbishop Geoffrey Clayton of Cape Town refused to fully back Huddleston, and he was recalled to England. Such incidents infuriated the apartheid state but did not threaten it.

The opposition the churches could have mounted is made plain by the one contrary example from the 1950s, the Native Laws Amendment bill proposed in 1957. The bill would have made it very hard for non-white Christians to attend churches in designated white areas, making multiracial congregations almost impossible. Like the Confessing Church in 1930s Germany, South Africa's English-speaking churches might do little about wider social injustices but mobilized forcefully when under direct attack. Even the DRC, drawing on the long tradition of Calvinist defense of church against state, publicly denounced the proposal. The Anglicans went beyond routine denunciation and threatened mass civil disobedience. "I don't want to end my days in prison," Archbishop Clayton declared, "but I'll go if I have to." He was spared the necessity by dying of a heart seizure the following day.[27] Verwoerd, for once, backed down. The law was enacted, but he promised not to enforce the relevant clause, a promise the apartheid regime never dared break. When the churches chose to, they could make themselves heard.

The mood changed more decisively in 1960. When the radical Pan-Africanist Congress called nationwide demonstrations against the much-hated pass laws, which required nonwhites to carry identification papers at all times, the regime responded forcefully. At one march near Cape Town, a police baton charge killed three protesters and injured twenty-seven more. Another march was dispersed by low-flying jet fighters. And notoriously, at Sharpeville, south of Johannesburg, police opened fire on a mostly female crowd. They kept shooting until sixty-nine people were dead and 186 wounded, most of them shot in the back. The regime, instead of investigating the atrocity, imposed a nationwide state of emergency and arrested thousands of opposition activists. It also banned both the Pan-Africanist Congress and its more moderate, avowedly interracial rival, the African National Congress (ANC).

This was enough to awaken the sleepiest of consciences. Joost de Blank, the new Anglican archbishop of Cape Town, called peremptorily for the DRC to be thrown out of the World Council of Churches. Instead, the WCC organized a formal consultation at Cottesloe, in Johannesburg, in December 1960. It was a remarkable event. The representatives of one small DRC offshoot kept themselves clearly separate from all the others throughout and were rumored to be feeding news to Verwoerd. The main DRC's delegates, however, mingled freely with those of the other churches, including eighteen nonwhite participants (and one woman). Over a week, they discovered sufficient mutual understanding that on the last day Archbishop de Blank made an uncharacteristically gracious apology for misjudging his DRC colleagues. The consultation's final communiqué, agreed to by all present except that DRC offshoot, denounced the ban on mixed marriage and the system of migrant labor and even insisted that every adult regardless of race had "the right to own land wherever he is domiciled, and to participate in the government of his country." The only concession made to the DRC's traditional stance was the admission that some present still believed that "a policy of differentiation can be defended from the Christian point of view."[28]

The Afrikaner Broederbond, the entire theology faculty at Stellenbosch, and Verwoerd himself denounced the communiqué. The DRC's Transvaal synod, which had sent most of its officeholders to Cottesloe, not only rejected their conclusions but withdrew from the WCC and threw all those involved out of office, including the synod's acting moderator, Beyers Naudé. The consultation had evidently failed, but it had also plainly changed the mood. The DRC, once a proud outpost of the Protestant world, now felt besieged. It was also clear that enemies might be within as well as outside the laager. No one shows this more spectacularly than Naudé, for whom Cottesloe triggered nothing less than a full-scale conversion. Naudé became convinced that reconciliation between peoples was the only defensible Christian ideal. Liberated from office, he agitated against apartheid and the DRC's role in it. In 1963, he founded the Christian Institute to foment antiapartheid views within the DRC, but after the church expelled him and banned its members from joining the institute, Naudé turned his attention to the English-speaking churches. As one Presbyterian observed in the same year, those churches' pro forma denunciations of apartheid were not merely toothless:

They may have soothed the conscience of the Church's members, who can point to them and say, "There you are—that is what my Church thinks" and then go back to their reading of the Sunday paper.[29]

Naudé's Christian Institute was no home for such placid liberals. He developed a root-and-branch theological critique of apartheid, bringing the antiapartheid radicals of Europe and North America into partnership with the slowly awakening consciences of white South African church people and, momentously, with leading black South African Christians, a constituency who had generally been ignored up to this point. Naudé not only succeeded in funneling significant amounts of foreign money in their direction, allowing them to build up theological training, but created networks through which they could communicate with one another and the outside world. The threat was profound. In 1968, Prime Minister John Vorster warned the Christian Institute that anyone aiming to "do the kind of thing here in South Africa that Martin Luther King did in America" should "cut it out, cut it out immediately for the cloak you carry will not protect you."[30] It was no idle warning. The apartheid regime had the firm ideological basis for racism that American segregationists lacked, and it had already proved that it was willing to defend that position with a degree of indiscriminate violence that no American government could contemplate.

The noose slowly tightened around Naudé. In 1975, he was banned from receiving foreign funds and briefly imprisoned. After his outspoken support of the 1976 Soweto uprising, in 1977 he and a swath of other antiapartheid activists of all races were placed under strict, incommunicado house arrest. In retrospect, the regime should have silenced him far sooner. He had galvanized the English-speaking churches from nominal to earnest antiapartheid activism and turned their struggle into a genuinely multiracial one. He had also shown where the DRC's own Calvinist conscience might lead it.

Under Naudé's influence, the English-speaking churches' moribund ecumenical body, the Christian Council, was refounded in 1968 as the South African Council of Churches (SACC). Many of the independent churches were now included in what was for the first time a multiracial forum, whose members were willing to do more than issue statements.

The Anglican dean of Johannesburg helped carry messages for exiled activists and was arrested, brutally interrogated, and imprisoned for a year before being allowed to flee the country in 1972. There was talk of defying conscription into South Africa's army. In 1976, the SACC's white president resigned so that a black church leader could take the helm. The choice fell, propitiously, on the new Anglican dean of Johannesburg, a forty-five-year-old rising star named Desmond Tutu, who argued that the antiapartheid cause was a struggle for white as well as for black liberation. Drawing on the successes of the American civil rights movement, he led the SACC into advocating peaceful civil disobedience in 1979 and was crucial in the mass civil-disobedience campaign that challenged the apartheid state's new 1984 constitution, a doomed attempt to divide "colored" and Asian South Africans from blacks. None of this destroyed apartheid, but it made it plain that the state was not going to reacquire even tacit popular consent. From 1986 to 1990, South Africa remained under a continuous state of emergency. Tens of thousands were arrested and thousands killed. President P. W. Botha talked of South Africa's facing a "total onslaught." It was clear that the apartheid state was no longer even faintly stable. Most of the world assumed it would eventually fall, that it would go down fighting, and that it would take the country into chaos with it.

The Trek to Repentance

Instead, between 1989 and 1994, a new president, F. W. de Klerk, gambled that there was another way. Through a combination of skill, luck, and, above all, the remarkable vision and astuteness of his counterparts in the ANC, he succeeded. It is not to devalue the ANC's decisive role to point out that this was the apartheid state's initiative. The National Party was not forced to the negotiating table. Its military and intelligence advisers favored a political solution, but they were also clear that they still had the situation in hand and could hold out for a long struggle. If anything, the regime had won the bloody confrontations in the townships through the later 1980s. Had it chosen to fight on, even in a state of low-level civil war, it could have done so for many more years. The cost would have been high, but dictatorial regimes have often been willing to pay much higher costs to preserve themselves. There were reasons to hold on to the bitter end. Fear of retribution or even extermination in the event that the white minority lost its grip on power was very real. The rider of a tiger may not have a viable long-term strategy but still clings on.

Instead, the apartheid state guessed that a deal could be made. It helped enormously that in 1988, as the Soviet empire was collapsing, South Africa finally won its own drawn-out war against Soviet- and Cuban-backed guerrillas in Angola. The specter of Communism behind the ANC was suddenly less frightening. The moment was, de Klerk said, a "God-sent opportunity"—not a throwaway phrase from an earnest Calvinist.[31] And if the ANC's liberal-capitalist wing was in the ascendant, so too was the NP's. Botha's government had embraced neoliberal economics, carrying out a string of privatizations and abolishing certain apartheid regulations that were causing economic headaches, including the much-hated pass laws. All this had cost the NP a significant amount of working-class Afrikaner support, while persuading the white economic elite that apartheid in general and burdensome rules such as workplace segregation in particular were bad for business. As the NP had long feared, the homogenizing logic of cosmopolitan capitalism was eroding Afrikanerdom's distinctiveness. By the late 1980s, as many as a quarter of all white marriages were "mixed" between Afrikaners and English speakers. With the ANC apparently converging on the same ideological spot, what was there really left to fight for?[32]

These secular themes, however, are only half the story. One survey of Afrikaner business leaders found that between 1968 and 1988, almost half ceased believing that humanity's division into nations was an expression of God's will. This was not because they were secularized. As late as 2001, 90 percent of Afrikaners (compared with a mere 40 percent of South African Anglophone whites) told pollsters that they considered religion more important than politics or money. Afrikanerdom was losing not its faith but its moral self-confidence. A senior intelligence officer who would later hold secret talks with Nelson Mandela recalled that in the mid-1980s "nowhere was the situation out of hand, but it was clear that politically and morally we were losing our grip."[33] As early as 1979, an Irish visitor to the Afrikaner university of Potchefstroom described his hosts as "good men who had inherited certainties, which no longer seemed certain, and who were now groping their way, in considerable intellectual, and some moral, discomfort."[34]

The crucible of that discomfort was the Dutch Reformed Church. Its instinctive response to Beyers Naudé's challenge was a defiant reassertion of its views on "mixing," but loudly singing old songs was not enough. Some in one of the DRC's small offshoots, the puritanical Dopper Church, were drawing attention to the ever-plainer brutality with which apartheid was being defended, and they began to criticize the main DRC's apparent subservience to the state. Reformed churches in Germany, Switzerland, and the Netherlands were also becoming increasingly critical of their South African brethren, and while the DRC could dismiss the World Council of Churches as a gaggle of crypto-Marxist heretics, other Calvinists were harder to ignore.

In 1974, the DRC produced a full-scale report on racial issues, titled *Race, People, and Nation,* which set out to persuade skeptics inside and outside South Africa that it was legitimate for a country or a church to "decide to regulate its inter-people relationships on the basis of separate development."[35] The tone was cautious and moderate. South Africa's churches had begun an experiment with segregation in 1857, and the churches had been blessed with prosperity ever since, yet churches must never simply subordinate themselves to any one nation's culture. Apartheid was a justifiable policy in principle, but some of its features were deplorable, such as the ways that the systems of migrant labor and residential segregation destroyed families. The report even lamented the fact that "social contact between the different groups of people is restricted to the minimum" and blamed this for fostering prejudice.[36]

The synod that debated the report found itself badly split. A vocal minority tried to push the critique further, while the majority's instinct was still to circle the wagons. The crux issue was mixed marriage. The report had argued that because different cultural backgrounds can "impede the happiness and full development of a Christian marriage," mixed marriages were "undesirable." For DRC traditionalists, this altogether missed the point. The synod eventually added a clause stating that mixed marriages were "impermissible," on the grounds that they "destroy the God-given diversity and identity" of the nation.[37] This was about racial duty, not marriage counseling.

Skeptics in Europe and in the Dopper Church were unpersuaded, but the decisive challenge came from an unexpected direction: the Dutch Reformed Mission Church, the DRC's "colored" daughter church, which had long been quietly apolitical. Leading the charge was Allan Boesak, a young "colored" minister recently returned from studying in the Netherlands, where he had learned about the "black theology" emerging in the United States. In 1978, in the wake of the Soweto uprising, he persuaded the Mission Church's synod to declare that apartheid was a sin and to join the South African Council of Churches. Boesak addressed the SACC the following year and helped spur it to adopt a policy of civil disobedience, but his most significant impact was within the Reformed church family itself.

In 1982, the World Alliance of Reformed Churches (WARC) met in Ottawa. The WARC had criticized apartheid before, but Boesak now intended to force the pace. He led nine other South African delegates in publicly refusing to take Communion at the opening service, on the grounds that DRC representatives were present: a vivid statement of the gravity of the situation. The WARC was impressed. It formally declared "that apartheid is a sin, and that the moral and theological justification of it is a travesty of the gospel, and in its persistent disobedience to the Word of God, a theological heresy." Declaring that a fundamental question of the faith was at stake, it suspended the white DRC and elected Boesak, who was only thirty-six, as its new president.[38]

The Mission Church now had an opportunity to define the crisis, and a group led by Boesak promptly drafted a new confession of faith. Like the 1934 Barmen Declaration, on which it was explicitly modeled, the new Belhar Confession was framed not as a response to a specific political situation but as a potentially timeless statement of Christian doctrine. It condemned any doctrine that "absolutizes either natural diversity or the sinful separation of people," especially "the forced separation of people on the grounds of race and color," and asserted unity and reconciliation as fundamental Christian values.[39] The Mission Church's synod overwhelmingly approved the draft and, after the extensive consultation that its procedures required, in 1986 formally adopted it as a full confession of faith. The 1986 synod also elected Boesak as its youngest-ever moderator.

For the white body that still thought of itself as the "mother" DRC, this was a genuine crisis. The debacle at the 1982 WARC fostered soul-searching as well as anger. A defiant motion to withdraw from the WARC failed to muster the necessary two-thirds majority in the DRC's 1982 synod. Everywhere, previously sound men started to express doubts. Johan Heyns, one of the church's most prominent theologians and most prolific authors, now denied that apartheid was God's will and came out in favor of mixed marriage. Another highly respected academic, Willie Jonker, demanded that "we distance ourselves from every form of racism, not because of Ottawa, but because racism is a sin."[40] When the synod resolved to set up yet another commission to produce yet another report, the outcome, for once, did not seem pre-determined.

The next DRC synod did not meet until 1986, but four years had apparently not been long enough. The commission's report, *Church and Society,* was chaotic and full of points on which the authors had not been able to agree. Even so, it denied that forced separation of peoples or a ban on interracial marriage could be justified. It even stated that

> the application of apartheid as a political and social system by which human dignity is adversely affected, and whereby one particular group is detrimentally suppressed by another, can-not be accepted.[41]

The reference to "the application of apartheid" shows the limits of this denunciation. The report denounced racism as an evil but only called apartheid an error, suggesting that it could have been intended honor-ably and done differently. Even so, the change is astonishing. The DRC had crossed a theological Rubicon, hesitantly, ungraciously, but volun-tarily. Apartheid's hard-liners recognized that their cause was lost. In 1987, they formed the breakaway Afrikaans Protestant Church, a refuge for a few tens of thousands of bitter-enders. Afrikanerdom's conscience had moved on.

Johan Heyns, who was elected as the DRC's moderator in 1986, now took charge of the process. He had *Church and Society* sent back for further revisions, resulting in a 1989 draft that was less a statement of doctrine and more a confession of past errors. Heyns also helped per-suade the government to permit some antiapartheid protests from late 1989 onward, and in 1990 he bluntly declared, on behalf of the DRC, that apartheid as such was a sin. His conversion, like those of many of his colleagues, was late but in earnest. Unlike most of them, he sealed it with his blood. He was shot and killed by an unknown assassin in 1994 while playing cards at home with his wife and grandchildren: one of apartheid's last martyrs.

In December 1989, President de Klerk—a member of the Dopper Church rather than of the DRC—called for a conference of all South Africa's churches to address the emerging new world. This eventually took place at Rustenburg in November 1990. It was the most diverse ecumenical gathering in South African history and included, among others, the long-silenced Beyers Naudé. The show was stolen, however, by Heyns's ally Willie Jonker. Four pages into his lecture, Jonker pulled out a handwritten scrap of paper and told the startled delegates,

> I confess before you and the Lord, not only my own sin and guilt, and my personal responsibility for the political, social, economical and structural wrongs that have been done to many of you and the results of which you and our whole community are still suffering from but vicariously I dare also to do that in the name of the D. R. Church of which I am a member, and for the Afrikaans people as a whole.[42]

The DRC's awkward, crabbed journey to repentance had not prepared the delegates for this unscripted moment. Desmond Tutu now interrupted proceedings from the floor and asked to be allowed to speak:

> I believe that I certainly stand under pressure of God's Holy Spirit to say that . . . when confession is made, then those of us who have been wronged must say "We forgive you." . . . It [the confession] is not cheaply made and the response is not cheaply made.[43]

The delegates present applauded. The exchange made headlines around the world, and the DRC's formal delegates, as surprised as everyone else by Jonker's sudden intervention, rushed to declare that they endorsed his remarks. And they all lived happily ever after.

Church politics does not work that way, of course. A good many

DRC members, including the former president P. W. Botha, objected to being told they were penitent. Some talked of further schism. On the other side, the nonwhite Dutch Reformed churches, who understood the fine gradations of the DRC's language better than most, felt Jonker's statement was suspiciously vague and wanted to know exactly what the DRC was now confessing. Tutu himself was criticized for offering too quick and blithe an absolution, criticism that he stoutly rebutted, insisting that he had been speaking for himself and that he personally trusted that the DRC would make good on Jonker's promises.

It has done so haltingly. In 1994, the DRC synod finally abandoned its attempt to produce a theological statement on racial matters. The same synod invited an outsider to address it, a lifelong Methodist of discreet but fervent faith: the newly elected president, Nelson Mandela. In 1998, the DRC was readmitted to full membership of the WARC. It also aspired to formal union with the nonwhite DRCs, which had themselves merged into a single body in 1994. This union was long delayed by disputes over the status of the Belhar Confession, which the DRC was reluctant to impose retrospectively on its old membership. It finally accepted that it must do so in 2011. Likewise, the DRC has been slow to admit that apartheid had been evil from the beginning, rather than an innocent idea wickedly implemented. The church's formal submission to South Africa's postapartheid Truth and Reconciliation Commission (TRC) claimed that "apartheid was allowed to degenerate" into injustice, not that it was unjust by nature.[44]

Plainly, the DRC's repentance has been neither perfect nor consistently gracious, but repentance of any kind is not so common in human affairs that it can pass unremarked. It is part of what makes this an authentically Protestant story. The DRC had sanctified racial prejudice from the very beginnings of Dutch settlement and was intrinsic to apartheid. Some of those who did these things believed they had good intentions, but that failure of moral insight only deepens their culpability. Protestantism's immense theological malleability made it uniquely able to play this role. Yet Protestantism's restlessness and its incorrigible tendency to revisit and question its own orthodoxies also meant that support for apartheid was not graven in stone. Protestants can dig deep holes for themselves, but they can also dig themselves out. They can even help to save a nation in the process.

And perhaps a soul or two. One participant in the TRC recalled a private conversation with a witness who was a member of one of the state's death squads. During the 1980s, this man had carried out sickening atrocities. "I did all those things because of my Christian faith," he explained; he believed he was fighting a just war against Communism. "You have to understand, I really believed that I was being a good Christian." But he had changed his mind. Some of the murders he had seen committed went beyond what he could accept as honorable. So he decided to confess his former crimes, to tell survivors as much as he could, and to denounce his former colleagues. His interviewer asked him why he had done this. "He looked me straight in the eyes and said, 'You see, I'm a devout Christian. I was changed by my profound Christian faith.'"[45] There are layers of self-deception, self-justification, and wishful thinking in that statement. There may also be truth.

The Independent Witness

During the course of this monumental struggle, South Africa quietly became a Christian nation. The 1980 census revealed that 77 percent of South Africans of all races described themselves as Christians. Seven-eighths of those Christians were black or "colored," and fully 30 percent of the black population belonged to "independent" churches. Some of these were the old "Ethiopian" churches founded around the turn of the century, but the vast majority were more doctrinally adventurous outfits, often linked to Pentecostalism, such as the Zion Christian Church or the Nazaretha Church, offering healing and practical spiritual assistance and sometimes teaching idiosyncratic variants on historic Christianity.

These independent and Pentecostal churches were, as a rule, determinedly apolitical during the apartheid years. Some openly curried favor with the government. One independent leader, Isaac Mokoena, was repeatedly used by the regime to denounce international sanctions. The Zion Christian Church, the largest independent church, invited President P. W. Botha to preach at Easter 1985 and invested him with a church honor. Some of its ministers accepted roles in the puppet governments of the homelands. At the TRC, one prominent "independent" church leader came forward to "ask forgiveness for not having fought in the struggle, for not having been beaten up, detained and killed. . . . We are cowards and we admit it. We are cowards because we did not stand up and fight.'[46] More generously, we might say that it was enough of an achievement for such churches to exist.

Political struggle was simply not what these churches were for. Many of them valued humility, obedience, and submission as virtues. The early Pentecostal preacher Elias Letwaba once visited a white farmer who sent him to sleep in the chicken coop because he would not have a black man in the house. Letwaba joyfully accepted: "My Master slept in a stable, and I am only a black worm." He insisted that because whites had first brought the Gospel to South Africa, "my nation must learn to . . . be obedient to them, because there would be no heaven for us poor Blacks if it were not for the White man." In other hands, apoliticism became less craven and more steadfast. Another early Pentecostal evangelist, Nicholas Bhengu, insisted on racial equality but also forbade his flock to engage in politics. National redemption, he taught, would come through believers' individual virtues, their obedience to the law, and their faith in God.[47]

This was the more consistent witness of those independent churches who addressed the TRC. The Zion Christian Church's submission emphasized that it had defied apartheid by teaching its members to respect themselves, one another, and the law. They were "not to hurt others, but to refuse to be hurt by others." The members of the Nazaretha Church struck a slightly different note. When confronted by oppression, they testified, "all they had to do was to ask the congregation to kneel down and have Isiguqa, which is a special prayer to God." This sort of talk led establishment Protestants to despair that the independent churches would only ever offer supernatural placebos rather than providing what one black theologian called "the kind of political direction which the black community needs." When, in 1985, the main English-speaking churches produced the Kairos Document, a stirring theological declaration of the evils of apartheid, the "independent" churches that constituted such an enormous part of South African Christianity were neither included nor even mentioned.[48]

The independent churches would reply that providing "political direction" was not their purpose. What the "black community" truly needed, in their view, was not mobilization but spiritual assistance in the midst of this world's troubles. As a more sympathetic black South African theologian, Simon Maimela, pointed out, the establishment churches had much to say to the people about the distant hope of political liberation but little about "their daily misfortunes, illness, encounter with evil and witchcraft, bad luck, poverty, barrenness—in short, all their concrete social problems." The independent churches, by contrast, positively encouraged believers to bring these troubles to church with them. The establishment churches were learning to defy evil, but the independents offered instead to defeat it.[49]

To outsiders, Protestantism may seem admirable for its role in promoting racial equality and in fighting apartheid, or it may seem culpable for its role in promoting racism and defending injustice. Yet it was only incidentally and temporarily a vehicle for those causes. Protestant movements that become too deeply attached to such social and political issues tend to find that they are running out of steam. Like it or loathe it, the heart of Protestantism's message is a spiritual one, a message of salvation and of divine power. South Africa's independent churches have prospered, not because they collaborated with the apartheid regime, but because through them many of its victims discovered a power and a dignity which defied anything that regime could throw at them. Who can say that they were wrong?

CHAPTER 14

Korea in Adversity and Prosperity

> I wish above all things that thou mayest prosper and be in
> health, even as thy soul prospereth.
>
> —3 JOHN 2

If Africa has been fertile soil for modern Protestantism, Asia has proved stonier ground. We have already seen the fruitless efforts of seventeenth-century missionaries in Sri Lanka and Taiwan. Their successors have not fared much better. Protestant churches in India, Japan, and elsewhere remain tiny in proportion to those countries' populations. In the next two chapters, we will turn to the two major exceptions to this rule.

The first Korean convert to Protestantism was baptized in 1879. A little over a century later, about ten million Koreans—20 percent or more of the population of South Korea—were Protestants. In the early twenty-first century, twenty thousand South Korean missionaries were working in more than 170 other countries around the world, making Korea second only to the United States as a Protestant missionary hub. Seoul is home to the largest church in the world, the Yoido Full Gospel Church, whose total congregation numbers more than 600,000, a feat that is managed by holding seven consecutive Sunday services in its main, 31,000-seat auditorium, which are also broadcast to worshippers in a dozen branch chapels across the country. Yet this is not a simple success story. Korean Protestantism has traveled a bumpy road, and its current prospects are uncertain.

Missionary Beginnings

Korea's turbulent recent history was preceded by long centuries of stasis. The pro-Chinese Chosŏn dynasty ruled the peninsula from 1392 to 1910 with a rigid Confucian orthodoxy. The Hermit Kingdom, as Western visitors called it, was even more firmly closed to outsiders than Japan. Even so, Catholicism was introduced in the seventeenth century and established a toehold. By 1800, there were perhaps ten thousand Korean Catholics, holding on despite considerable suspicion that they were foreign agents. Protestant missionaries were keen to follow. A German missionary tried and failed in 1832. In 1866, a Welsh missionary accompanied an American ship that tried to force its way upriver to Pyongyang, but he and the entire crew were killed. Yet no hermit could keep nineteenth-century imperialism at bay indefinitely. Korea was eventually compelled to open its borders, first to Japan in 1876 and then to the Western powers, chiefly the United States, in 1882.

By then, two Scots Protestant missionaries, John Ross and John McIntyre, had established themselves in the neighboring area of China, where the Korean population yielded a first handful of converts. Had they been working with Korea's educated classes, who used Chinese writing, Ross and McIntyre would no doubt have used existing Chinese Bibles, but as it was, they were compelled to produce a proper Korean translation. Luke's Gospel was printed in 1882 and a full New Testament in 1887. These were written not in Chinese pictographs but in Korea's *hangŭl* script. *Hangŭl*, once derisively called "women's writing," had no social status, but it is East Asia's only phonetic alphabet, and with it Korean became what one missionary called "the simplest language in the world" to learn.[1] More important, while *hangŭl* might have had plebeian associations, it was unmistakably Korean. This was cemented by the translators' choice of the Korean word *hananim* to translate "God"; the word was associated with indigenous traditions, not Confucian ideas. As Korea's centuries-old sense of identity was tottering, Protestant missionaries embraced a demotic, popular writing that would become central to the emerging Korean nationalism. In Korea today, *hangŭl* is a source of considerable national pride, and Protestantism credited with its revival.

Those earliest missionaries had modest hopes: to work quietly with marginalized and excluded groups, sending Bibles where they could not go themselves. Others were soon hatching more ambitious plans. In 1884, when missionaries were still banned from Korea, Horace Allen arrived as part of the American diplomatic legation. He was a medical doctor and hoped to begin missionary work under that cover. The gamble paid off. Allen's success in treating an injured court official later that year did more to smooth the way for missionary work in Korea than any other single event. Missionaries were permitted to establish a hospital in Seoul in April 1885, and by 1892 Seoul had four Protestant schools (two Presbyterian, two Methodist) and four hospitals (one Presbyterian and three Methodist). These institutions charged little or nothing and tried not to discriminate by gender or social status. The missionaries began to win a reputation.

They remained by law forbidden to proselytize, but they were playing a long game. Their first priority was to study Korea's language and customs and to win respect. The first few converts were unskilled laborers or outcasts such as butchers, especially in the country's rugged and politically marginalized northwest. In 1897, a missionary commented approvingly on "the independent, manly spirit of many of the mountain people. A man seems to be more of a man in the North than in the South."[2]

That hint of distaste for Korean culture was telling. These first missionaries—predominantly American Presbyterians and Methodists—were mostly conservative and evangelical, untroubled by modernist theology, making stern moral demands of their converts. Would-be Korean Protestants were expected not to smoke, drink, or gamble and to keep Sunday free from both worldly work and worldly pleasure. They were also expected to separate themselves sharply from certain key features of Korean society. The missionaries reviled Confucian ancestor veneration as abominable idolatry, saw the caste system as a gross offense to human dignity, and were particularly offended by the treatment of Korean women. Evangelical Protestants do not have a reputation for feminism nowadays, but defending human equality, including the rights of women, was a subject on which evangelical missionaries could be militant. "The sages of Korea," one (male) Methodist wrote in 1898, "taught the nation that woman is inferior to man. Christianity flatly contradicts this"—a claim that would have surprised most Christians in previous centuries.[3] Nor was this merely talk. Half of all the mission schools established before 1910 were girls' schools. The missionaries not only used "women's writing"; they taught women to use it and even required them to learn it as a condition for baptism. In 1912, one woman missionary saw this policy as crucial for spurring would-be converts to godliness, singling out for praise "one woman with actually only half an eye left, and yet she holds up her book against it and reads so well that she can teach a class."[4] Women evangelists would become Korean Protestantism's secret weapon.

Given this unapologetic assault on Korean values, it is no surprise that converts were slow in coming. By 1890, the Presbyterians claimed a hundred converts, and the Methodists only nine. The missionaries worried that even those few were mere "rice-Christians," attracted by charitable work or hopes for money. One exasperated missionary claimed that he could baptize three-quarters of the entire population if he offered them $5 apiece.[5] Following a scheme devised by one influential American missionary in Korea, John Nevius, many of them hoped to avoid this problem by outsourcing the real work of conversion to Koreans. The plan was to train up converts in leadership from the beginning. Bringing in a new convert was a condition for admission to full church membership. Once this method had bedded down, it had some striking effects. Koreans rapidly took over the leadership of their churches. Having the mission sustained by indigenous volunteers, not by rich foreigners, reduced the incentive for false conversions and— importantly—the cost of the whole enterprise. By distributing the Bible as widely as possible, emphasizing that believers should study it as the inerrant Word of God, and trusting them to do so with little or no guidance, the missionaries guaranteed that another perennial feature of Protestantism would take root in Korea: sectarianism and doctrinal innovations.

The Nevius method was a bold approach to a difficult problem but not a quick fix. It was not responsible for the sudden surge of growth from the 1890s onward. For it turned out that it was not only Americans who had a dim view of traditional Korean ways. So did influential Koreans.

Late Chosŏn Korea was a hothouse flower, a venerable state whose structures had become brittle as a leaf. China, Korea's traditional protector, was in a similarly parlous condition, and new imperial powers were on the march. Tsarist Russia was actively trying to expand in the Far East, and Japan pressed from the other direction. Meanwhile, the United States was building a Pacific empire, while only occasionally remembering its anticolonial ideals.

In 1894–95, a brief and decisive Sino-Japanese war left Korea within Japan's sphere of influence. Desperate for a counterweight, the Korean regime looked to America. The U.S. diplomatic resident in Seoul, John M. B. Sill, was an Episcopalian and amateur missionary, on whose watch the missionaries at court had become an important diplomatic back channel. One Presbyterian missionary was a confidante of Queen Min, whose political wiles far surpassed those of her amiable, pliable husband, King Kojong. So it was doubly shocking when shortly after the Japanese victory, the queen was brutally murdered in the royal palace on Japanese orders.

American missionaries were in the thick of the crisis that followed. The king had a pro-Japanese cabinet foisted on him; he was kept a virtual prisoner, and his son, the crown prince, was taken to Japan. Fearing that he would be poisoned, the king ate only eggs boiled in their shells or cans of condensed milk opened in his presence. He managed to smuggle pleas for help to American and Russian supporters. On the night of November 28–29, 1895, a daring rescue was planned. A group of American military advisers and three American missionaries assembled at the palace and waited in an antechamber, oiling their guns. The signal came at midnight: gunshots in the royal chamber. They ran through, only to find two cabinet ministers already there, moving the king to "safety." One of the missionaries, it turned out, had accidentally let slip what they were intending. When they arrived, however, the king physically clung to them, keeping them with him for the remainder of the night.[6] He knew that whatever the Japanese might do to him, they would not risk laying a finger on American citizens.

Unfortunately for the king, the United States had no intention of picking a quarrel with Japan either. The missionaries were allowed to walk away from the botched rescue, but Sill was severely reprimanded by his superiors in Washington. In the end, in February 1896, it was the

Russians who actually secured the king's freedom. By then, however, the incident had firmly established the American missionaries' reputation as true friends of Korea. In September 1896, while Kojong was still under Russian protection, American missionaries in Seoul organized a public birthday celebration for him, in the name of the "Christian citizens of Seoul." Nearly a thousand people attended. When the king was eventually restored to a measure of independence in 1897, he went out of his way to show favor to the missionaries, whether from genuine gratitude or in the hope that they might help him secure an American alliance.[7]

Presbyterian missionaries in Japan did manage to rescue the prince from his gilded captivity there, taking him to the United States to be educated, but they could not dictate American foreign policy. President Theodore Roosevelt, whose main concern was blocking Russian expansion, supported Japanese control over Korea. In 1905, after Japan won a stunning military victory against Russia, America and Japan concluded a secret agreement under which the Philippines became an American colony and Japanese control over Korea was assured. Koreans did not know about this betrayal, but they did know that America had failed them. Korea became a Japanese protectorate, and King Kojong a puppet. In 1907, Kojong was made to abdicate in favor of one of his other sons, who was an invalid. In 1910, Korea was finally annexed and placed under direct military rule. Newspapers were closed and public associations banned. Tens of thousands were detained without trial, and many of them tortured.

As this disaster unfolded, increasing numbers of Koreans put their hope in the Americans' religion. A new breed of Korean nationalist was struggling to modernize the country, which meant Christianizing it. A new national newspaper was established in 1896, published in English and in Korean *hangŭl,* edited by a Christian convert, and pointedly titled the *Independent.* Its agenda was not simply resistance against Japanese nationalism but moral and spiritual renewal. The most obvious source for this renewal was Christianity. Conversions now began in earnest. Presbyterian and Methodist membership rose from 109 in 1890 to 4,871 in 1900 and 17,624 in 1905: tiny numbers, but an impressive rate of growth. The mission finally had some wind in its sails.

Revival and Nationalism

Sudden growth made the missionaries uneasy. They wanted neither rice-Christians nor nationalists in Christian garb. Their converts were studious, but were they sincere? Bible classes are all very well, grumbled one American Methodist in 1906, but what the Korean church "needs just now more than anything else" was "a REVIVAL."[8]

There were already hints of it. In 1903, R. A. Hardie, a Canadian Methodist missionary at Wonsan, had been wrestling with discouragement over his apparently fruitless ministry. Hardie eventually had an experience of God's grace in which he was assured that he simply needed to place his trust wholly in Christ. When he told his congregation about this experience, he did so in the form of a confession, publicly lamenting his failings. Suddenly he found his people emulating him and pouring into Bible study and extended prayer meetings with a new intensity.[9]

Word of the Wonsan revival spread. After the Japanese protectorate was established in 1905, interest intensified. Conversions accelerated; between 1905 and 1907, the number of organized Korean Protestant congregations doubled to 642. In 1907, a ten-day-long conference was planned in Korea's second city, Pyongyang, in Korean Protestantism's northern heartland. Fifteen hundred men attended a meeting on January 6 (women's meetings were held separately). One astonished witness wrote,

> Man after man would rise, confess his sin, break down and weep, and then throw himself on the floor and beat the floor with his fists in a perfect agony of conviction. . . . They would break out into uncontrollable weeping and we would all weep together. We couldn't help it.

The following night, matters were the same, only more so:

> Every sin a human being can commit was publicly confessed that night. Pale and trembling with emotion, in agony of mind and body, guilty souls, standing in the white light of their judgment, saw themselves as God saw them. . . . The scorn of men,

the penalty of the law, even death itself seemed of small consequences if only God forgave.[10]

As the conference ended, the revival rippled out, sparking copycat
meetings across the country. Thirty thousand Koreans applied for baptism that year.

It was a turning point. The missionaries' suspicions were finally
allayed, as one admitted with unusual frankness:

> Until this year I was more or less bound by that contemptible
> notion that the East is East and West, West and that there can
> be no real affinity or common meeting ground between them.
> With others I had said the Korean would never have a religious
> experience such as the West has. These revivals have taught
> me . . . that . . . the Korean is at heart, and in all fundamental
> things, at one with his brother of the West.

To remove the spectacles of subtle but pervasive racism with which
Westerners of this generation viewed the world was remarkably difficult, but this man was so impressed by the piety he had seen that he
now thought "the East not only has many things, but profound things,
to teach the West, and until we learn these things we will not know the
full-orbed Gospel of Christ."[11]

The revivals accelerated the transfer of control from the missionaries to Korean leadership. The last non-Korean moderator of Korea's
Presbyterian church stepped down in 1919. As missionary influence was
sidelined, Korean Protestantism's distinctive features began to emerge.
One practice that dates back to 1907 remains common in Korean
churches: unison prayer, in which all those present pray aloud at the
same moment, each offering his or her own individual prayer. The
voices blend to form a kind of collective speaking in tongues, such that
secrets can be spoken aloud but remain unheard, and repentance is
both individual and profoundly corporate. Some of the new leaders
were also pioneering new Korean practices. The Presbyterian revivalist
preacher Kil Sŏnju's extreme Biblicism led him to memorize the entire
book of Revelation and recite it aloud more than ten thousand times.

The prominence of the book of Revelation reflects an aspect of

Korea's theological inheritance from America: premillennial dispensationalism. This is a variant on classic Protestant premillennialism, which expects that the world will be overwhelmed by the forces of Antichrist before, finally, when all seems lost, Christ will return in glory to establish his kingdom. The dispensationalist variant, a nineteenth-century innovation, comes with several additions. Among these is the belief that before the worst of the tribulation begins, an event called the Rapture will take place. Believers will be caught up bodily into heaven, sparing them the sufferings that the rest of the world will endure before the end.

Korean Protestants have embraced these doctrines more enthusiastically than their co-religionists anywhere else in the world. Premillennialism was a perfect fit to Korea's early twentieth-century predicament. Japan's grip seemed unbreakable. Protestants said there was no worldly hope of improvement, and they seemed to be right. Their proposed solution was deep, heartfelt repentance. They blamed the national crisis not on Japan but on the firm, loving discipline of God, and so ultimately on something Koreans could do something about: their own sins. Even if they could not save the whole nation by repentance, they could certainly save themselves from the coming wrath.

Initially, these revivals disavowed any political purpose. Premillennialists, who see the world as a ship holed below the waterline, typically waste little attention on the politics of the ship's deck-chair arrangements. Yet Protestantism's very success in channeling Korean nationalism meant that it could not avoid becoming an anti-Japanese force. The Japanese regime even helped this. Wary of antagonizing America, and convinced by assurances that Protestantism was apolitical, the Japanese exempted religious entities from a 1907 ban on all Korean associations or organizations. Koreans wanting to organize or resist now had only one place to turn.

Protestants' apolitical stance became harder to maintain. Perhaps, as one preacher argued in 1910, Japan was not a legitimate ruling power but actually Antichrist, and Christians should stand against it. "If you muster enough Christians in the country to demand your legitimate rights by proper means, no evildoers can silence you!"[12] Not that the means were always proper. When a plot to assassinate the pro-Japanese prime minister was uncovered in 1909, Christians formed a majority of those arrested. There might be no earthly hope of standing against Japanese power, but not all hope is earthly. The biblical story of David and Goliath was much expounded; the Japanese eventually banned it as subversive. Koreans prayed that God would use them, "a despised people, the weakest nation on the earth . . . to show forth Thy glory in Asia."[13]

That was still some way off. For all their growth, the churches remained small. An overoptimistic evangelistic campaign in 1909–10, the Million Souls for Christ movement, fell far short of its hyperbolic goal. By 1918, Protestants numbered no more than 300,000, about 2 percent of Korea's population. But this far underplays their influence. The Protestant churches' prominence and national scope made them unique in occupied Korea. In a world of colonial empires, Christianity was generally the religion of the conquerors. In Korea, alone in the world, it was the religion of resistance.

We can see what this meant in the memoirs of Kim San, who later became a Communist guerrilla. Kim remembered how during the 1910s he attended a Christian school and thought that "the Christian church was the best institution in Korea," but he was never a believer and dismissed prayer as futile. A Christian teacher tried hard to win him over, arguing that "Christianity provides the only unity in Korea today and that it has been a great educational force [and] a movement for human emancipation."[14] The young Kim, however, thought that turning the other cheek to Japanese oppression seemed impractical.

The crisis came for him, and for Korea, in 1919. World War I was over, and the victorious Allies (including Japan) were meeting in Paris to shape a new world. Koreans were stirred by the American president Woodrow Wilson's vision of national self-determination and an end to imperialism. Plans were quietly spread through the churches' national networks. On March 1, a declaration of independence was published, signed by thirty-three Korean leaders, sixteen of them Protestants, including Kil Sŏnju. It was accompanied by coordinated, scrupulously peaceful public demonstrations across the country. Apocalyptic preachers had been speaking for years of "the time" and "the day." Now it had come.

Kim San's teacher proudly read the secretly circulated declaration to his class that very day. He said,

They cannot refuse to listen to the voice of a whole nation. President Wilson is fighting at the Peace Conference for the principle of self-determination of nations and for the principle of democracy. . . . America will not permit Japan to enslave Korea.

Then, Kim remembered, he led the students into the street "with thousands of other students and townspeople and paraded through the city, singing and shouting slogans. I was so happy I thought my heart would burst. . . . I ran through the streets all day and joined every passing demonstration, shouting until my voice was too hoarse to be heard."[15] The crowds sang (translated) Western hymns: "Onward, Christian Soldiers," "Stand up, Stand up for Jesus." It was Korea's moment.

The Japanese were taken by surprise, and for the first day the demonstrators held the streets. Then the reprisals came. There were tens of thousands of arrests. Protestants were specifically targeted. Kil Sŏnju was held in solitary confinement for two years. The general secretary of the Seoul Young Men's Christian Association (YMCA) was arrested, because the YMCA had been instrumental in distributing the declaration. He was asked whether he knew who was the head of the independence movement. He said he did:

They pounced on him like tigers. Who? Tell us. . . . God, he replied. God is at the head, and 20 million Koreans are behind.[16]

Hundreds were shot, churches were seized, and religious gatherings were forbidden. Kim San saw soldiers publicly crucifying a Christian leader "so he can go to heaven." For Kim, the shock of these days was life-changing:

I learned the meaning of force and the futility of nonviolence. At first the Christian spirit of martyrdom seemed very heroic to me; then it appeared stupid. Several times I saw Japanese soldiers fire on groups of Christian women gathered in the street singing hymns and songs of national independence. . . . The women did not run but stood quietly and raised their eyes to the skies as they redoubled their prayers.[17]

Weeks later, the news arrived from Paris that Korea's pleas would be ignored. National self-determination applied only to the subjects of the defeated powers.

The heroic catastrophe of the March First Movement was a turning point for Korea, and also for Korean Protestantism. Until this point, nationalism and faith had marched in lockstep. One Christian activist wrote in 1919, "We accepted Christianity for we hoped independence lay in the church. It is only through Christ's intervention that an opportunity at hand is before us."[18] In other words, this man had real faith in the power of God in Christ, but that faith was directed toward a specific, worldly end. And now it appeared to have failed.

For some, like Kim San, nationalism now trumped faith. Communism replaced Christianity as the most promising route to liberation. The churches' membership dropped in 1919 for the first time, and while growth resumed thereafter, it was at a gentler pace than before. During the 1920s and 1930s, numbers never topped half a million. A new, subtler Japanese governor-general appointed after the shock of 1919 softened the occupation, lifting the blanket ban on newspapers and associations, which ended the churches' monopoly of public organization. Much of Korea's propertied class now fell reluctantly into line with their occupiers, many church leaders among them. Japan's investment in education also helped to make Korean Protestantism's staunch conservatism look antiscientific: a religion of the past, not of the future. In 1930, one missionary wondered glumly, "Is it possible that the great Church in Korea may go the way of other Churches which had their day and ceased to be?"[19]

It was not quite that bad. What the churches did achieve in this period was to flush out nationalism in Christian garb. Kim Insŏ, a Christian journalist who had been imprisoned after 1919, was blunt with those who thought Protestantism meant liberation and reform. "One who loves his nation more than Christ is not fit for Christ. . . . One who loves society more than Christ is unfit for Christ."[20] A truism, perhaps, but one that before 1919 might have been discreetly left unsaid. Christianity could no longer be treated as a means to a worldly end.

The churches of this era were accused of collaborating with Japan, but they were not so much apolitical as apocalyptic. They rejected worldly political activism but did not hesitate to denounce the Japanese regime. The Exodus story, in which God miraculously delivered his people from their slave masters, was much discussed. Kil Sŏnju renounced his former activism, instead urging Christians to repent, to "keep awake and ready, to stand fast in the faith, and to wait in hope and joy" for their deliverance.[21] In the meantime, their priority should be to save souls. The premillennialist theologian Park Yune-Sun compared the world to a sinking ship: "It is stupid to put new paint on it."[22] Better to get as many people as possible into the lifeboats.

Such churches would neither resist Japan nor bow to it. As the occupation darkened in the 1930s, conflicts became impossible to avoid. Certain Christian theological themes were increasingly intolerable to the Japanese. Talk of the kingdom of God sounded like treason, and the claim that all humans are sinners was a direct slander on the emperor himself. In 1932, a new governor-general began to require Koreans to participate in Japan's state-sponsored Shinto rites. The regime claimed that these rites were not religious but a matter of political obedience. To plenty of Christians, they looked less like obedience and more like idolatry.

In 1937, when Japan invaded China proper, the use of the Korean language—especially *hangŭl*—in schools and newspapers was banned. By then, Shinto rites were being enforced on Christian schools with rigor. The Methodists (and indeed the Catholics) reluctantly accepted this, but the Presbyterians decided to close their schools rather than conform. Japan now set out to break the Presbyterians' resistance. Their General Assembly in 1938 was flooded with armed police, who compelled the moderator to propose a motion approving Shinto rites. The delegates dared not protest, and the vote was passed. In 1939, the same assembly was forced to cede full control over the church to the Japanese state. Foreign missionaries were pressured to leave, and the few who remained were interned when Japan went to war with the Western powers in December 1941. Some two hundred churches of various denominations were simply closed.

Total church membership fell by nearly half from its 1937 peak to barely 200,000 in 1943. This is not an index of apostasy so much as a recognition that the churches had been taken captive by the Japanese state. They were now forbidden to refer to God's or Christ's kingship, and the apocalyptic biblical books of Daniel and Revelation were banned. In 1943, in a gesture to its Nazi allies, Japan banned the entire Old Testament. It also required Shinto shrines to be constructed within churches. In July 1945, the Presbyterians and Methodists were forced into a merger.

There was some open resistance. A pastor named Ju Ki-Cheul preached against Shinto rites in a set-piece sermon, titled "Dare to Die," at Pyongyang Seminary in 1935. He died in prison in 1944. In 1941, a group of Koreans in Manchuria prepared a covenant against idolatry whose signatories and sympathizers were pursued with some energy. Korean Protestantism has understandably treasured these heroes, but like their brethren in Germany, Korean Protestants were late in discerning the nature of the threat they faced and slow to stand against it. They emerged from the war years with martyrs to celebrate but also with compromises to explain away.

South Korea's Journey

Throughout the occupation, Korean Protestants had looked forward to providential deliverance, which would come as a gift from God rather than by their own hands, and so it proved. Korea did not liberate itself. Instead, following Japan's surrender, it was occupied by Allied forces: the Soviet Union north of the 38th parallel of latitude, the United States to the south. That division is still in place.

The crucial years 1945–53 determined modern Korea's political and religious contours. The two occupation regimes were hostile to each other and to any Koreans who tried to build institutions covering the whole country. In the South, the American military government, and then the new Republic of (South) Korea set up in 1948, worked to flush out enemy agents. Anti-Communist paramilitary squads, many of them northern refugees, killed tens of thousands. In the North, the chief lightning rods for the burgeoning conflict were Protestants. The northern regime was not necessarily and inevitably anti-Christian. Kim Il Sung, the guerrilla who emerged as the Communist leader in the North, had been raised Christian, had once taught in a Methodist Sunday school, and counted Protestant ministers among his close advisers. But principled Communist atheism was reinforced by the suspicion that Protestantism was irredeemably American and bourgeois. An attempt in 1945–46 to form a Christian-led anti-Communist political movement, the Korean Democratic Party, led the Soviet occupiers to require that all northern Christians join a new, official Christian League of Korea. The league, soon renamed the Christian Federation, seized all church property and reduced seminary enrollment by 80 percent. Soon any Christian practice outside the Christian Federation was illegal, and as of April 1948 the federation refused to admit new members. Christianity had been put in a ghetto, where it was expected to die quietly.

In 1950, North Korea launched a surprise attack and quickly took most of the peninsula. Seoul was occupied for three months. Christians were targeted; churches were destroyed and pastors (among many others) imprisoned. An American-led United Nations force eventually mounted a counterattack, recapturing Seoul and briefly threatening to destroy the northern regime altogether, before Chinese intervention turned the war into a very bloody three-year slog. The stalemate ended with an armistice in 1953. There has yet to be an actual peace. The border between the two Koreas was established where it still stands, the world's most heavily militarized frontier.

The new South Korea was an impoverished, devastated, militarized state yoked into an unequal alliance with a superpower. It hosted some five million northern refugees, plenty of Protestants among them. The total Protestant population was still a sliver of the whole, but it was nationally prominent as never before. Rhee Syngman, South Korea's first president and soon its first dictator, was a Methodist elder who had Christian prayers said at the opening of the new National Assembly. Christians were vastly overrepresented in his government. The distinction between "Christian" and "anti-Communist" was being blurred, both north and south of the border.

South Korea's Protestants, finding themselves under an openly friendly government for the first time, did what comes naturally to Protestants: they quarreled. The wounds of the Japanese occupation were still raw. After the Presbyterian seminary in Pyongyang closed to avoid conforming to Shinto rites, a more theologically liberal Presbyterian group had founded the Chosŏn Theological Seminary in Seoul in 1940. There had been whispers of liberalism in Korea before, introduced by ministers who had met it while training abroad, but it had always been firmly suppressed. In 1934, a Presbyterian minister who dared question whether Moses wrote the book of Genesis was formally condemned by the General Assembly. The new seminary's modest openness to modernism was tame by Western standards, but plenty of Presbyterians were dismayed to have it as their only training institution, not least because its compromises were a poor contrast to the heroism of the Pyongyang seminarians. In 1947, a group of fifty-one students at Chosŏn formally protested: "We deplore modern theological thought and higher criticism. We refuse to have anything to do with liberal theology and rational theology." The petition led to the dismissal of the seminary's most controversial liberal teacher, Kim Chaejun. In 1953, he left the Presbyterian church altogether to form a new denomination, the Christ Presbyterian Assembly, or *kijang* church. Its founding principles were "freedom of faith and conscience" and an opposition to a "slavish" literalism that it called "Pharisaism."[23] The *kijang* church, unlike most other Korean denominations, engaged enthusiastically with the World Council of Churches. It looked as if Korean Protestantism might be ready to join the modern world.

During the 1970s, a new theological movement led by the *kijang* church sparked excitement in liberal theological circles around the world. *Minjung* theology was an Asian, Protestant counterpart to the Marxist-influenced liberation theology emerging among Catholics in Latin America. *Minjung* is a term for oppressed people, of any kind and class: those at the bottom of the social heap. *Minjung* theologians set out to build "a church for and of the *minjung*" and thereby to remake Korean society. As the so-called Korean Christian Declaration of 1973 put it, their intention was to "follow the footsteps of our Lord, living among our oppressed and poor people, standing against political oppression, and participating in the transformation of history, for this is the only way to the Messianic Kingdom."[24]

Those were not cheap sentiments. Rhee Syngman's authoritarian regime had been toppled by a student-led revolution in 1960. The brief prospect of a functioning democracy was ended by a military coup in 1961. Park Chung-hee, the coup leader, made himself president in 1963. After he came uncomfortably close to losing the 1971 presidential election, he openly seized dictatorial powers and freely used arbitrary arrest, imprisonment without trial, and torture to suppress opposition of any kind. Park himself was assassinated amid political protests in 1979, but military rule persisted. Despite considerable pressure both inside and outside South Korea, genuinely free elections were not held until 1987, and a civilian president not elected until 1992.

Given Korean Protestants' history of opposing Japanese rule, we might imagine that they would have led opposition to the dictatorship too. This was precisely the role the *kijang* church and the *minjung* theologians took on, especially in the 1970s. The 1973 declaration, issued on Easter Sunday, insisted that "the resurrection of Jesus Christ is the resurrection of democracy." On March 1, 1976—consciously echoing the famous date in 1919—twenty dissidents, most of them Christians, signed a Declaration for the Restoration of Democracy. All of those involved in these events suffered lengthy prison terms, and their courage won admirers across the world.[25]

Except, that is, in South Korea. Having begun as a small splinter group, the *kijang* church grew at a sickly rate compared with its denominational rivals. Between 1974 and 1979, when Protestant numerical expansion was at its fastest and radical Protestant political resistance at its plainest, the membership of the main Presbyterian denominations grew by 70 percent or more, while the *kijang* church's membership rose by a mere 11 percent. For all their courage, the *minjung* theologians did not attract much interest from the *minjung* themselves. And while democratic Korea may now remember their cause kindly, there has still been no flocking of converts to their banner.

In retrospect, *minjung* theology looks both nationalist and patriarchal. The first stirrings of *kijang* political activism, in the 1960s, were not to promote democracy but to oppose the restoration of diplomatic relations with Japan and to campaign against "the influence of foreign powers." *Minjung*-centered rewritings of history have the same chauvinist flavor. Contemporary Korean liberal theologians now argue that *minjung* theology took too much from traditional Confucian values and was an essentially political religion, led by male elites concerned with public affairs. Whether this is fair to the brave campaigners of the 1970s is almost beside the point. In the story of postwar Korean Protestantism, the *kijang* church and *minjung* theology are, for all their prominence, a sideshow.

For most South Korean Protestants living under the shadow of partition, there was for decades one simple political priority: anti-Communism. With the luxury of hindsight, and the knowledge that Korea's armed peace has endured for six decades, this can seem paranoid. Those living in Seoul in the 1960s and 1970s, thirty miles from the frontier, can be forgiven for thinking differently. *Minjung* theology was tainted with Marxist associations. Korea's largest Presbyterian denomination, the *hapdong* church, refused even to join the World Council of Churches, on the grounds that churches from Communist countries were represented there. Those churches were widely suspected of being puppets of their countries' regimes, and the *hapdong* had no wish to lend them legitimacy.

Park Chung-hee's regime certainly did its best to co-opt the Protestant churches. Members of his government, and on one occasion Park himself, attended prayer breakfasts hosted by sympathetic pastors. A new umbrella body for Korean Protestants, the Korean Christian Association for Anti-Communism, was openly friendly to the regime. Alongside the crackdowns on Christian opposition in 1973–74, the regime funded a series of mass rallies by friendly Protestant denominations, who were happy to play their part.

Most Korean Protestants did not actively support the dictatorships. Their stance was classically apolitical. In practice, that was tantamount to supporting the status quo, but there is reason to believe they did not like what was happening. According to a revealing 1982 survey of Korean Protestants, only 6 percent believed that churches should "actively and collectively" oppose corruption or human rights violations. The number who recommended simply ignoring these problems, however, was equally tiny. Instead, 32 percent believed that the churches should respond "through criticism and evangelism"—trying to convert the whole of society, to infuse the values of the Gospel at every level—while 43 percent recommended responding chiefly with prayer. That position appears weak only if you assume that prayer is not an effective means of intervening in worldly affairs.[26]

In the same survey, 89 percent of Protestants said they expected Christ's second coming "very soon." Because their premillennial theology told them to expect the world to grow ever worse, it was futile to try to save it. When the *kijang* church's Kim Chaejun claimed that a church should be "an organization of strength, awakening each citizen

to a sense of sovereignty and letting him speak," the Protestant majority countered that this might be admirable but it did not sound much
like a church.[27] Most Korean Protestants believed that politics was not
their business. They were on earth to save souls, which they were now
doing at an astonishing rate. The proportion of Protestants in the South
Korean population rose from 2.5 percent in 1960 (some 600,000 people),
to 10 percent in 1970, 19 percent in 1980, and as high as 27 percent in
1990—nearly twelve million believers. Almost all of the growth was in
rigorously conservative evangelical churches.

One vital context for this blistering growth is economic. It was the
minjung theologians' misfortune to be preaching justice for the poor at
a moment when the condition of the poor was changing faster than ever
before in human history. In 1960, the two Koreas were as poor as each
other and as much of contemporary Africa. Park Chung-hee's regime set
out on a deliberate dash for industrialization, involving massive, rapid
urbanization and enormous physical rebuilding. Between 1962 and 1989,
South Korea's economy grew from $2.7 billion to $230 billion, an average
of 8 percent per year across nearly three decades. At that time, only the
three other Asian "tigers," Taiwan, Singapore, and Hong Kong, had ever
managed sustained economic growth like this, and South Korea was the
largest of them. Within a generation, it went from subsistence poverty
to become one of the world's richest countries.

These two periods of breakneck growth, in Protestantism and in
economic output, virtually coincided. It is hard not to conclude that
they were connected in some way. To see how, we need to leave national statistics behind and visit South Korea's most famous church.

Full Gospels

In 1907, the year of the Pyongyang revival, the newly founded Holiness
Church (a Methodist offshoot) coined the word *sunbogeum* to describe
itself. *Sunbogeum* can be translated as "Full Gospel" or "Pure Gospel,"
implicitly dismissing other gospels as impure or incomplete. It was a
sign that this church was aligning itself with the global Pentecostalist
movement we will meet in the final chapter. The "Full" Gospel meant
that, as well as preaching personal redemption and the promise of
Christ's imminent return, the Holiness Church offered miraculous

healing. Healing became a steady undercurrent of Korean Protestantism, resurfacing regularly during the 1920s and 1930s. When the Pentecostal denomination the Assemblies of God founded its first church and
seminary in Korea in 1953, it readily adopted the *sunbogeum* label. The
Full Gospel churches have not, however, emphasized classic Pentecostal spiritual gifts such as speaking in tongues. Their focus has been on
healing, and beyond.

In 1958, two graduates of that Full Gospel Seminary founded a tent
church in Seoul. Choe Ja-Sil was raised Christian, and her faith had
been conventional until a series of personal and financial disasters over-
took her in 1953. In 1956, she attempted to starve herself to death but
instead experienced a new conversion and entered the seminary. There
she met a twenty-year-old man named Cho Yonggi, half her age, who
had been raised Buddhist but had converted following a miraculous
delivery from tuberculosis in 1954. The healing was never complete,
however, and he remained sickly. Choe, a former nurse, first met him
as a patient. They became a remarkable team, a partnership sealed
when Cho married Choe's daughter in 1965.

What set their church apart was their commitment to the power of
prayer. Choe developed a practice of "triple prayer," combining prayer
in tongues, prayer while fasting, and nightlong prayer vigils, which in
her experience produced miracles. She trained the church's members
in the same method. Her leadership in this is no accident. Korea's Presbyterian and Methodist establishments no longer permitted women the
prominence they had held in the first generation, but women healers
and evangelists were still as important as ever on Korean Protestantism's wilder fringes, as they were elsewhere in the broad world of Pentecostalism. To this day, more than 80 percent of the Full Gospel
Church's cell-group leaders are women, and women outnumber men
among its formal ministers—even as the church restricts public preaching and pastoring to men.

Cho, Choe's younger disciple, had a different practice: "specific
prayer." Rather than generalized pleas for renewal, Cho believed that
God wished him to pray for very specific outcomes. Early in his ministry (so the story goes), he prayed for a bicycle, and a desk and chair for
his office. God told him to be more precise. So he prayed for "a desk out
of Philippine mahogany, a chair with a steel frame and little wheels on

the bottom, and a bicycle made in the USA." The following day, he preached that by God's blessing he had actually received those things— which, as of that moment, he had not. His congregation, knowing he was as near destitute as they were, were incredulous. By the time he was challenged to produce the objects, donors had provided them.[28]

It did not stop with bicycles. Cho regularly spent whole nights, ten hours or more, in prayer. "I poured all my strength and cried out to God. . . . I became hoarse and could not even speak after prayer"—so much so that passengers at the bus station near the tent church com- plained about the noise.[29] He was praying for healing, because he in- sisted that Christians who neither teach nor experience physical healing have defective faith. Choe insisted that at their church "cancer, arthri- tis, tuberculosis, neuralgia, heart trouble, gallstones, asthma, epilepsy, and diabetes are healed by God's miraculous power."[30] But Cho also prayed for worldly wealth for himself and his community. Citing the obscure New Testament verse that is this chapter's epigraph, Cho ar- gued that God does not want his people to be poor. Christians should not be materialistic or covetous, but they should prosper and have enough money to give to others. Christians should pray for this pros- perity, and according to Cho's principle of specific prayer they should expect to receive it.

This "prosperity gospel" has been widely condemned. It is certainly different from Martin Luther's insistence that Christians follow Christ in suffering or from the conventional Christian view that to be poor is to be blessed. "Putting your faith to work for a successful life," as one of Cho's bestselling books urged, is a reversal of priorities that looks less like Protestantism than a gimcrack self-improvement scheme. There have been accusations of heresy and of financial scandal, and in 2014 Cho was found guilty of tax evasion and given a suspended prison sen- tence. For all these criticisms, the "prosperity gospel" still has a power- ful logic behind it. For centuries, Christians have taken Christ's offhand comment—"ye have the poor with you always"—as self-evident truth. Never before the modern period had any human society discovered an economic model that could lift entire societies out of poverty, and never had any done so as fast as South Korea. The Full Gospel Church was founded among destitute people who did not know that they stood on the cusp of one of the most extraordinary economic booms in human history. Even secular economists used the word "miracle." Cho's people could hardly be blamed for agreeing. These uprooted city workers prayed for prosperity, and it rained down on them. How could they not thank God?

Thanking God for prosperity, importantly, also meant sharing it. For example, as early as 1961, the church began a ministry to the deaf, and by 1964 it had ten separate congregations for the deaf comprising some five hundred individuals, under the care of seventeen dedicated ministers. There were naturally reports of deaf believers being healed, but those whose deafness was lifelong also found a community offering more support and welcome than any church before it. Having no interest in political activism does not make a church uncaring.[31]

As well as offering "specific prayer" for healing and prosperity, Cho asked God for church growth. The tent church opened in 1958, had 600 members by 1961 and 3,000 by 1964. The leap came in 1972, when Cho set about constructing a vast new church building on the island of Yeouido in central Seoul, opposite the National Assembly building. The story goes that this move was made well before there was any realistic prospect of paying for it. The money arrived at the very last moment, just in time to save the church from collapsing into bankruptcy and disgrace. Once the new building was opened, God told Cho to pray for 1,000 new church members per month. In 1978, the number rose to 3,000. And they came; the congregation topped 100,000 by 1979, 200,000 by 1981, and 500,000 by 1985. It was the first modern megachurch. Like the nation, the crowds were no longer destitute. The prosperity Cho had promised had arrived.

Minjung theology's failure and the Full Gospel Church's success are mirror images. The *minjung* theologians, establishment churchmen from comfortable backgrounds, attracted worldwide attention with their bold attempt to give the poor dignity and freedom. The Full Gospel Church, formed amid the very poor with women prominent in its ranks, had an even bolder agenda: that the poor need not be poor at all. It offered, and delivered, a liberation from bondage that combined the spiritual and the practical. It is no surprise that one enterprise turned into an elitist backwater and the other produced the largest church in human history.

The Full Gospel Church was a brash upstart whose emphasis on healing and prosperity alarmed more conventional Protestants, but it never strayed too far from orthodoxy. Other groups have ventured much further, using the Bibles that the missionaries circulated so widely as springboards to fresh revelations of their own. During and since the Japanese occupation, a tangle of quasi-Protestant sectarian groups has sprung up, each led by its own prophets. Among many others was Hwang Gukju, who in the 1920s claimed that Jesus' head had literally been grafted onto his own neck and who gathered a few dozen followers, many of them, detractors claimed, young and female. At least, unlike the Victory Altar movement of the 1990s, he was not accused of murdering them. A more endearing alternative was the Inside Belly Church, whose founder, Heo Ho-Bin, interpreted her own drawn-out phantom pregnancy in the late 1930s as a sign of Christ's return. She warned that the poverty of Christ's first coming must not be repeated. So, charmingly, her group set itself to making beautiful clothes for the soon-to-return Christ to wear. Unhappily, the church was based in northern Korea. After the Communist takeover, its members were rounded up, Heo was shot, and the now-enormous stockpile of clothes was burned. Another northern Protestant, Moon Sun-Myung, managed to escape south during the Korean War and then received the progressive revelations that led him to found the Unification Church, the only Korean sect to achieve international reach. Moon claimed, rather obliquely, to be the Messiah sent to complete the work that Jesus' premature death had left unfinished. Universal peace would be brought about through pure marriages, through which believers could escape the curse of original sin and give birth to a new, pure generation of humanity.

Korea's Protestant establishment reviles these sects, but they are part of its extended family. They draw on its distinct spirituality: healing, mountain retreats, unison prayer, heroic Bible memorization, nightlong prayer meetings. There is also a shared apocalypticism, indeed a sense of Korea itself as an apocalyptic nation, claiming a late but crucial place in the world's salvation history. To outsiders, it may seem a little self-centered for this small, embattled peninsula to claim such a role, but ancient Israel, too, was oppressed and insignificant. God chooses the weak to confound the powerful.

Northern Fears and Hopes

In modern Korea, of course, a certain measure of apocalypticism is entirely rational. South Korea has built its prosperity while confronting the world's last Stalinist dictatorship, now nuclear armed. Northern Korea was once Protestantism's heartland. What, if anything, remains of that tradition is a mystery.

The North Korean regime and its detractors tell almost completely contradictory stories about Protestantism. We do not need to entertain the official position, that citizens of the People's Democratic Republic of Korea enjoy freedom of religion. The restrictions of 1945–50 gave way to fierce persecution of Protestants, especially those with any American connections, during the Korean War. Kim Il Sung claimed that American wartime atrocities had permanently alienated the population from Christianity, and therefore that those who persisted in their faith must of necessity be counterrevolutionaries. In the regime's telling, though, this hard line was quickly softened. Christians who were plainly Communist and anti-American were welcome. A few pro-Communist Christian ministers did remain visible; one was vice president from 1972 to 1982. The official Christian Federation opened a seminary in 1972 and published an approved hymnbook in 1983. There were, however, no actual churches. The Christian Federation blamed this on war damage from the 1950s. North Korean Protestants would, it insisted, be free to open churches but preferred to meet in private homes. It claimed that there were ten thousand believers meeting in house churches in the mid-1980s. Foreign visitors who were taken to such meetings found congregations eager to affirm the federation's views. In 1988, to much fanfare, two churches (Protestant and Catholic) were built in Pyongyang, and a second Protestant church was added in 1992. After a slow start, they established decent congregations. North Korean observers began to attend the World Council of Churches. In 1992 and 1994, no less a visitor than Billy Graham was invited to Pyongyang, where he preached at the Protestant church and met Kim Il Sung at his private residence. The official Protestant body, now titled the Chosŏn Christian Alliance, has been an important conduit for the distribution of humanitarian aid to the North since the devastating famines of the early 1990s.[32]

The majority of South Korean Protestants believe this is all a sham: the new churches purely for show, the official bodies arms of the state whose purpose is to attract foreign aid. During the 1980s, the southern churches lined up along a predictable political spectrum. The smaller, more liberal churches were willing to work through the North's official channels, while more conservative bodies refused to give comfort to the enemy. However, since the North's humanitarian need became acute in the 1990s, most of the southern churches have swallowed their principles and worked with the northern church bodies. At the same time, they formed the North Korean Church Reconstruction Committee, whose purpose is to prepare to rebuild northern Christianity from the ground up when the northern regime collapses. In the meantime, it works with the growing number of refugees seeping out of the North.

The refugees have given new glimpses of life within the northern state. Skepticism about their claims is in order. These people are by definition alienated. Their claims are usually unverifiable and have sometimes been discredited. Even so, a broadly consistent picture emerges. Only rarely do refugees describe any direct encounter with Protestantism or indeed any other religious group in North Korea, although they have usually been exposed to a good deal of anti-Christian propaganda. The closest most had ever come to religious practice in the North was reverence for the Kim family, the intensity of which surpasses any mere personality cult. The official churches—the public buildings in Pyongyang and the supposed house churches—are routinely dismissed by refugees as fakes, their pews filled by party agents and their families. Some reports from visitors to the Pyongyang churches, which describe congregations unable to sing hymns, locate Bible verses, or recite the Lord's Prayer, seem to support this. It would seem that if any real Protestant life exists in the North, it does so on a very small scale and in great secrecy. A handful of refugees describe tiny groups meeting to pray, usually members of the same family. Where we have evidence of larger groups, it is because they were detected. In one refugee's words, "There is a chance that two people pair up and hold their hands together to pray. However, a gathering of three or more is dangerous."[33]

"Dangerous" is a euphemism. The North Korean regime's treatment of offenders of all kinds is unparalleled. Arrest and imprisonment is typically arbitrary and based on suspicion or association rather than on any notion of defined offenses. Possession of a Bible can have an entire extended family "sent to the mountains," that is, the prison camps. It is normal for three generations of a family to be imprisoned together. Sentences are equally arbitrary, although some camps are by design institutions whose inmates are worked to death rather than released. It is said that such camps are almost free from rats; if any appear, the inmates will eat them. Religious offenders mingle with anyone else who has triggered the regime's unsleeping suspicion. Several defectors who had formerly worked in the security services have testified that the regime is intensely interested in Protestantism, which is seen as a front for American and South Korean subversion. "In a way," one defector claimed, "all threats are related to religion." Suspected Protestants can often expect execution, not so much for belief in God as "for not following the One and Only Guidance System." To the northern regime, Protestantism is a faith with political consequences.[34]

Former security officials consistently allege that the regime actively attempts to infiltrate Christian groups, going so far as to set up wholly false "clandestine" churches to flush out Protestant sympathizers. Naturally, this sows distrust among believers and keeps larger groups from forming. One witness described a remarkable visit to a high-ranking official's house, at which the two of them and a third official "worshipped together . . . with the curtains drawn." They read the Bible aloud and prayed for Kim Jong Il, North Korea's leader. The newcomer asked how they reconciled their faith with their official position:

> They said that it was a heartbreaking job to catch Christians while they, too, were Christians, but they had to stay in their positions because their situation could turn even worse if an evil-minded person was in that position to ferret out believers. So they keep their positions and sometimes advise people to run away.[35]

Hardly heroic, but it is all too easy to cry "coward" from a position of safety. At any rate, this tale of compromised loyalties and measured courage seems to me to ring true.

Refugees have been a particular focus of the regime's anxiety. Since the 1994–95 famine, there has been a significant movement of North Korean refugees into China. Some have managed to escape to the wider world, helped by South Korean missionaries or by criminal gangs, groups that can sometimes overlap alarmingly. Many others have been forcibly returned to North Korea by China. Such people are treated with intense suspicion by the North Korean security services. Testimony from returnees who have subsequently escaped again is unanimous on one key point: all returnees are asked if they had any contact with Christians. The consequences of a yes, or of being caught carrying contraband such as a Bible, are not absolutely clear, but most witnesses believe that such people are either "sent to the mountains" or simply killed. One refugee who was forcibly repatriated in 1999 described how two brave or naive women among their group confessed that they had converted to Christianity while in China. They were immediately taken away, and the rest of the group were told they had been shot. One escaped security official confirmed that such people "are as good as dead."[36]

All of these claims are unverifiable, but we do know that large numbers of northern refugees have converted to Protestantism during or since their escape. For South Korean missionaries in China engaged in people-smuggling, Christian preaching is part of the package, and sometimes this involves a degree of coercion. There have been scandals over missionaries' withholding food from refugees who refuse religious instruction. Those who eventually reach South Korea find that churches provide what little social support there is, for refugees often assimilate poorly into southern society, whose rules and mores they struggle to understand. And it is understandable that the trauma of escape might trigger a spiritual crisis.

Most South Korean Protestants hope that one day Christian North Korea will rise from the old regime's ashes. It may not happen. Protestantism remains potent in the North's imagination, but its practice has been driven into dark corners. Those refugees who convert rarely do so quickly or without complications. But then, South Korea's own Christian future is also now in doubt.

Since 1990, when South Korea's economic expansion slowed to a more sedate, rich-world pace, Protestantism's expansion has ground to a halt. From the mid-1990s, the number of Protestants has declined slightly, while Catholicism has rapidly expanded (from a much lower base). The Yoido Full Gospel Church remains the world's largest, claiming more than 800,000 members, but the congregation, once young and hungry, has arrived at the middle-aged prosperity that the church promised and is no longer growing. As numerical growth has stalled, the churches' focus on it has only sharpened. The huge number of missionaries sent abroad by Korean churches is a source of considerable pride, even though many of these people are the surplus graduates of Korea's oversupply of unaccredited seminaries. The abduction of twenty-three Korean missionaries and students in Afghanistan in 2007, two of whom were murdered, shocked the country's missionary agencies into greater professionalism. Even so, the tendency to measure success in numbers is pervasive. An opinion poll in 1997 found that 71 percent of South Koreans believed that the Protestant churches were more interested in expansion than in the truth. Only 32 percent said this of Catholics.[37]

That judgment is symptomatic of a deeper problem: a widespread stereotype of Protestantism as intolerant, authoritarian, and narrow-minded. Occasional iconoclastic attacks on Buddhist temples and icons have not helped to dispel this. To be Protestant was once a political asset: President Kim Young Sam (1993–98), a Presbyterian elder, was elected on the back of Protestant support. But President Lee Myung-bak (2008–13), who declared that he saw Seoul as a Christian city, was damaged by accusations of sidelining non-Protestants. His successor, Park Geun-hye, did her best to make a political virtue of having no religious affiliation.

Some of these problems are ephemeral. Once the huge twentieth-century influx of converts has been digested, Korea's Protestant churches may emerge less inclined to triumphalist head counting. Deeper problems will persist, however. The authoritarian structures of many Protestant churches, focused on charismatic ministers, are unappealing to a good many Koreans and periodically produce financial or sexual scandals. Some North Korean refugees have rejected Christianity on the grounds that this structure seems unpleasantly familiar.

More fundamentally still, Korean Protestantism's staunch and remarkably uniform theological conservatism faces the same crisis of modernity that confronts Protestants across the contemporary world. Most Korean Protestants simply reject Darwinism or biblical criticism.

In what is now a highly educated society, this is becoming an obstacle to conversion. Yet any softening of this line risks muddying the clarity of the Full Gospel and weakening its countercultural magnetism.

So the switchback ride of Protestantism in its first Asian stronghold is not over. Its future both north and south is very uncertain. The odds may be that Korean Protestantism's heroic days are past. But Korean Protestants have spent more than a century beating the odds. There is no reason to think they will stop now.

CHAPTER 15

Chinese Protestantism's
Long March

Be ye not unequally yoked together with unbelievers: for
what fellowship hath righteousness with unrighteousness?

—2 CORINTHIANS 6:14

There are two stories of Protestantism in China. One is a story of
missionaries and their churches: a story of great efforts and uncertain rewards and of promising beginnings cut short. Behind this is another, more distinctively Chinese story, much of which is now hidden
or lost, with a more surprising ending: at present, Protestantism is winning more converts in the People's Republic of China than anywhere
else on Earth.

The Chinese and Roman empires were formed in the same era, but
unlike Rome, China has endured. One reason for that is a remarkable
ethnic and cultural unity, within which the preservation of the state is
valued very highly. By the same token, China has historically been a
society in which religion knows its place: in the spirit mediums and
household gods of the peasantry, in Islam's safe ethnic subgroups, or in
the more pervasive traditions of Buddhism and Daoism, which have
generally worked with the statist traditions of Confucianism.

Christianity established a toehold in China late in the first millennium but was suppressed by the tenth century. Roman Catholic missionaries in the sixteenth century began again from scratch and
managed, painstakingly, to persuade the Chinese establishment that
their religion was sufficiently intellectually respectable and politically
obedient to be permitted. It was a virtuoso balancing act and never altogether stable. The brilliant missionary Matteo Ricci published a

Chinese summary of Christian doctrine that devoted only one short paragraph to Jesus and did not mention his death at all—much less the fact that he was executed by an imperial official worried about sedition. When the pope tried to impose uniformity on his small Chinese flock in 1724, the emperor responded with the outrage due to any meddling foreigner. The missionaries were expelled, and Catholicism was labeled an "evil cult" and driven underground.

The Qing dynasty, who were Manchurian in origin, were themselves seen as foreigners. In turn, their instinct was to shut out the world. The eighteenth- and nineteenth-century world, however, would not be shut out. The brash, scrappy maritime empires pouring out of Europe were felling ancient kingdoms around the globe. They never actually conquered China. The sclerotic Qing state could not beat off its European predators, but it remained an elephant harried by dogs, too strong even in its senescence to be defeated outright. At worst it would be tamed for a while, and that turned out to be quite bad enough. The Western powers pried open China's slammed door, imposing a trading relationship on their own terms. When Protestants first met it, China was a hobbled giant.

Dreams and Visions

China's pioneering Protestant missionary was Robert Morrison, who came from the northern English town of Morpeth, a few miles from my own home. In 1807, he reached Canton, the one Chinese port where foreign visitors were permitted. There he secretly studied the language, which was forbidden for foreigners. He and a colleague produced the first English-Chinese dictionary and the first portions of the Bible in Chinese.

Missionaries would not have to be so tentative for long. The turning point was the Opium War of 1839–42, when Britain humiliatingly forced China to open key ports to trade. Foreigners were now permitted not only to settle but to build churches in Shanghai and four other coastal cities (Canton, Ningbo, Fuchow, and Amoy). China was compelled to lift its ban both on Catholicism—*tianzhujiao,* "the religion of the Lord of heaven"—and on Protestantism, which went by the distinct name of *jidujiao,* "the religion of Jesus." There remains no common

Chinese equivalent to the generic term "Christianity." Protestantism and Catholicism are generally classed as separate religions.

The gates were now open. The buccaneering freelance missionary Karl Gützlaff hatched a bold scheme to flood China with newly printed Bibles and tracts. His Chinese Union was founded with twenty converts in 1844. By 1848, it boasted a thousand, including a hundred traveling preachers and book distributors. Gützlaff himself looked after fundraising and publicity. His tour of Europe in 1849–50 made the China mission front-page news, securing donations from no less a sponsor than the king of Prussia. While he was away, jealous missionary rivals uncovered a rather different story. Some of Gützlaff's preachers never left Hong Kong. Others sold their Bibles as scrap paper or, in one case, sold them to a book dealer who then sold them back to the Chinese Union. Gützlaff vigorously denied that he was either naive or duplicitous, but he died soon after the scandal broke, and with him died a certain rash optimism. Missionaries would long suspect that Chinese converts were neither sincere nor reliable.[1]

Yet some converts were very real. Liang Fa, a carver of printing woodblocks who worked for Robert Morrison, converted in 1815 and was baptized the following year. He was ordained in 1823, China's first ordained Protestant, and spent the rest of his life in energetic ministry, writing and printing Christian tracts, undeterred by periodic arrests and beatings. His pamphlet *Good Words to Admonish the Age,* published in 1832, was typical: a miscellaneous collection of biblical extracts mixed with Liang's own comments. Like Matteo Ricci, Liang said little about Jesus and less about the Holy Spirit, emphasizing instead a stern morality and God's absolute sovereignty. Fatefully, his missionary colleagues approved the text for publication.

Liang planned simply to distribute as many copies of his pamphlet as he could, targeting the crowds of educated young men who gathered for the ferociously competitive examinations used to select Confucian bureaucrats. It was a rather forlorn hope, but with Christianity still banned, there were few alternatives. Surely, one missionary argued romantically, all these thousands of faithfully printed and distributed pamphlets, cast like bread on the waters, were not forgotten by God? "May we not rather indulge the hope, that at this very time these tracts are . . .

carrying the true light from heaven into some heart that was lost in the darkness of paganism?"² In 1835, after yet another arrest, Liang moved to Malaya with his family, and the work was surreptitiously taken up by an American missionary, Edwin Stevens. When Stevens died of a fever in 1837, the quixotic tract distribution came to an end. Neither Liang nor Stevens could possibly have known what they had started.

One of the examination candidates who took a tract from Stevens in 1836 was a young man named Hong Huoxiu. He later claimed he only glanced at it. What we know is that he kept it, that he failed the examination, and that in his despair he fell into a dangerous illness during which he had an extraordinary vision. All accounts of his vision date from at least ten years after the fact, years during which he had been meditating intensively on the vision, so it presumably grew in the telling. According to those accounts, Hong was lifted into a heavenly realm. He was led before a throne on which sat an old man, the creator of the world, black-robed like a sage but with a golden beard like a foreigner. This old father lamented how humanity had abandoned itself to demon worship, and he commanded Hong to destroy demons and return the world to righteousness. For this purpose, he gave Hong a new name, Hong Xiuquan. Hong was also introduced to a mysterious middle-aged man who was described as his own elder brother.

On waking from his trance, Hong changed his name as he had been instructed, but he made no other attempt to enact his vision for another seven years. In 1843, he failed the civil-service examinations for the fourth time. Only then, while he was raging against the system in general and the tyranny of the foreign Qing dynasty in particular, did he rediscover the half-forgotten pamphlet he had been given years before. The vision and the pamphlet came together in Hong's mind as a dazzling, single truth whose two halves corroborated each other. The old father was God, or, as Liang's tract called him, *Shangdi,* the "Lord on High." The middle-aged man was evidently Jesus. And although Liang's pamphlet did once describe Jesus as *Shangdi*'s only son, plainly he had another: Hong himself, now aged thirty, as Jesus had been when he, too, was called from provincial obscurity to greatness. Hong's mission was to subdue an obstinate world to the stern morality and radical human equality that his Father required, summed up in the Ten Commandments. Liang's pamphlet told how, once before, *Shangdi* had sent a flood—in Chinese, a *hong*—to destroy the wicked and wipe the world clean.

Hong baptized himself, along with a cousin. They then had swords made for themselves, inscribed "for exterminating demons." To begin with, the battle was a spiritual one. Hong renounced his father, because he now had a new one. He destroyed shrines and household gods in his own home and, in 1844, destroyed the ancient Confucius tablet in the school where he worked, an act of desecration that had him and his few followers driven out of the region. They removed to the neighboring province of Guangxi, where Hong's preaching slowly built up a following. They called themselves the God-Worshipping Society.

In 1847, Hong visited Canton and met an American Baptist missionary named Issachar Roberts. The missionary and the visionary liked each other. Roberts believed Hong had received the Holy Spirit, and Hong was eager to learn the ways of other God-Worshippers. But neither man persuaded the other to conform to his own Gospel. Hong took away a good deal of Protestant literature, including (for the first time) a complete Bible, hymnbooks, and a Chinese copy of *Pilgrim's Progress*. But he would not question his own unique status.

By 1850, when Gützlaff's Chinese Union was implausibly claiming a thousand converts, Hong's God-Worshipping Society was some twenty thousand strong. Hong was a powerful preacher, and his vision made a compelling story. The God-Worshippers' attacks on the sacred objects that they called idols horrified many but convinced some of the power of their God. Their campaign became steadily less spiritual. While imperial officials dismissed them as harmless fanatics, Hong and his allies concluded that the chief demons were none other than the Qing emperors. The very word "emperor," *huangdi,* was a blasphemous usurpation of *Shangdi*'s unique status. The God-Worshippers began to offer a heady moral and political vision: a China of equality, prosperity, and righteousness, freed from the corrupt tyranny of the foreign Qing and restored to its rightful place in the world.

On January 1, 1851, the God-Worshippers' cadres, seeking to force their stern ethic onto reluctant villages, ran into a government force sent to subdue this nuisance and slaughtered them. Ten days later, on Hong's thirty-eighth birthday, he was crowned Heavenly King (pointedly avoiding the blasphemous term "emperor") and proclaimed a *Taiping Tienkuo,* or "Heavenly Kingdom of Eternal Peace."

"Peace" was a misnomer. The Taiping Rebellion of 1851–64 is estimated to have left about twenty million dead, making it one of the bloodiest wars in all human history. It subjected a swath of China's heartland first to messianic and apocalyptic rule and then to genocidal reprisals. The Taiping seized the city of Yongan in 1851 and in 1853 took the great prize, Nanjing, the ancient capital, which Hong declared to be the "heavenly capital" and which remained his base until the end. That was the moment of the rebellion's greatest geographic extent, and Hong's decision to consolidate in Nanjing, rather than to press on to Beijing, the "Demon's Den," may have cost him the war. Building the heavenly kingdom was itself a bloody business. Qing officials, Buddhist and Daoist priests, and other "demons" were slaughtered, along with the entire populations of strongholds that refused to submit. The Taiping drew heavily on the biblical book of Joshua, a reliable proof text for religious slaughter. A witness who asked a group of Taiping soldiers in 1861 why they were so ready to kill was told that it was God's will and, furthermore, that they as God's soldiers could distinguish the righteous from the wicked:

> Sometimes they felt an inner urge to kill a person, and sometimes it was just the opposite. Sometimes they were just about to kill a person but their sword would not hit, while another time the sword would, as if against their will, fall upon someone to his certain death.[3]

The soldiers themselves were subject to draconian discipline, such as beheading for making a noise during Sabbath worship. Likewise, disputes among the Taiping leaders were not resolved amicably. An 1856 palace coup by Hong against the most dangerous of his rivals ended with some twenty thousand of his opponents butchered.

Meanwhile, the Qing regime had other crises to handle. Renewed wars with Britain and France in 1856–60 ended with an Anglo-French force occupying Beijing and another round of iniquitous treaties giving foreigners freedom to trade and to preach. It was humiliating but also a turning point. The regime was now free to concentrate on the

Taiping menace, and the Western powers, keen to defend the new status quo, provided some critical military assistance. By 1864, Nanjing was besieged. Hong told the faithful to eat weeds, which he called manna, rather than give in. The city fell only after his death, which might have been suicide or murder. The regime decided to wipe out all remnants of the threat, destroying as much documentary and material evidence of the Taiping kingdom as it could and slaughtering whole populations suspected of ideological contamination.

Is this a part of Chinese Protestantism's history? Taiping religion was an extremely idiosyncratic sect whose distinctive features and breathtaking violence have no real Protestant parallels. Its modern equivalent is not any Chinese church but the Cultural Revolution of 1966–76. Yet it did contain plenty of disconnected Protestant fragments. The Taiping professed to respect the Bible and printed an amended version of it, although Hong insisted that only his own revelation was truly definitive. They welcomed a few Protestant missionaries, who generally arrived full of optimism about the Taiping, only to be appalled by what they found. The Taiping took the Ten Commandments immensely seriously, beheading soldiers who failed to memorize them. They assiduously smashed idols. They practiced baptism, used a version of the Lord's Prayer, and strictly kept the Sabbath. They sang Christian hymns to Western tunes. Hong even had an organ installed in his palace in Nanjing. Their most widely reported hymn included the refrain:

> Praise Shangdi, the Heavenly Holy Father, Praise Jesus, the Holy Lord of the world's salvation, praise the Holy Divine Wind, the Holy Spirit, praise three persons forming one united true God.[4]

The Taiping were not Protestant, but they were a sign of things to come. While the missionaries were breaking stony ground in the treaty ports, the Taiping Rebellion shows that when Protestant religious practices and preoccupations were mixed with authentically Chinese themes, they could find fertile soil.

Even so, the Taiping kingdom is usually seen as having no direct influence on later Chinese Protestantism, not least because most Taiping believers were simply exterminated. On this view, the rebellion's main legacy was political. It enfeebled the Qing regime, whose victory was won by provincial armies who kept their newfound independence. And it drummed an old lesson with fresh force into China's collective memory: religion, especially Christianity, can be mortally dangerous.

Yet the possibility of a hidden religious legacy will not go away. The Taiping heartland in the Yangzi River basin maps closely, although not perfectly, onto the areas of Protestant strength in China today. We know enough about the Taiping administration to be sure its surviving subjects would have some vivid memories. In the cities, the Taiping army led compulsory Sabbath worship in "Heavenly Father halls," modeled on Protestant practices like those Hong had seen in Canton in 1847. The people faced forward, knelt for prayers, listened to sermons, and sang hymns. Some meetings were lively, and there are even reports of speaking in tongues. These rites were more intermittent in rural areas, where the army's ministry was more like itinerant preaching, often on the theme of humanity's duty to a creator God—before requisitioning supplies and conscripts. The Taiping's rigid egalitarianism was also imposed in God's name. An 1853 decree laid out a vision of radical redistribution: "Land shall be farmed by all; rice, eaten by all; clothes, worn by all; money, spent by all. There shall be no inequality, and no person shall be without food or fuel."[5] This was never implemented, but the Taiping did, unprecedentedly, tax the rich as well as the poor and ban kowtowing as an offense to human dignity. They even preached the spiritual equality of the sexes, very much as Protestant missionaries did, and banned foot binding and bride-prices. All this was done in a spirit of apocalyptic moralism. Women's feet were forcibly unbound, which could be agonizing. For a time, absolute segregation between men and women was imposed; even spouses were kept apart. Hong made an exception for himself and his closest associates. By the time he entered Nanjing, he had eighty-eight wives.

Taiping religion reached deep into the household. The kingdom was supposedly divided into "congregations" of twenty-five households, each overseen by a sergeant charged with rationing, taxation, and religious compliance. A Qing spy reported that these men would "check up on city residents to make sure that they were reciting scriptures and chanting hymns. Their compliance was noted on household registers." Each household was given a copy of the Ten Commandments. The prayers said at meals were, the missionaries reported, based on the Lord's Prayer, although for most Christians that prayer does not include an exhortation to "kill the demons!"[6]

Some of the Taiping later converted to orthodox Protestantism, including one of Hong's cousins. The Hakka, Hong's ethnic group, have ever since remained an unusually Christianized group and retained a pride in the Taiping as a patriotic movement.[7] Many other Chinese republicans and revolutionaries also idolized the Taiping. It seems likely that if the Taiping had been a little more pragmatic, and a little less murderously apocalyptic, they could have won their war and set China on a modernizing road akin to nineteenth-century Japan's, radically changing the course of world history. It did not happen, but we can imagine that their brand of totalitarian equality primed China not only for Protestantism but also for Communism.

Protestants and Imperialists

With the Taiping defeated and the Qing regime humbled, China finally lay open to Protestant missionaries. In 1860, there were only about a hundred in China; by 1905, there were some 3,500, with a substantial infrastructure of schools and hospitals. Most of this activity was centered on the coastal cities, but there were serious attempts to reach China's vast interior, led by the China Inland Mission, a nondenominational enterprise founded in 1865 that aimed simply to preach rather than to build communities or to provide social services. By 1900, over a fifth of all Protestant missionaries were under its auspices, and it had reached into every province in China. All this effort had by then yielded about 100,000 converts, enough to keep missionaries busy, but still a negligible proportion of a vast country. It was also somewhat smaller than the Catholic community, which had a longer tradition in China to build on and which had revived vigorously with legalization and the arrival of missionaries. But the Catholics had had even less success than the Protestants in breaking out from outcast and socially marginal groups.

Both Christian groups' growth was hampered by the missionaries themselves. They could build churches and minister to communities, but they generally lacked either the language or the cultural credibility

actually to win converts. That tended to be the work of Chinese evangelists, who could travel freely, use ties of kinship, and discuss their
faith in teahouses or private conversations, rather than in the formal,
alienating setting of public preaching. Above all, the female evangelists
known as Bible women became Protestantism's spearhead. These were
typically poor widows, often scarcely educated, sometimes blind, as
likely to memorize sections of the Bible as actually to read it. Initially,
they were thought of as companions and translators for women missionaries, but it soon became plain that they could work at least as well
unsupervised. Some were converted through personal relationships
with missionaries; some by the promise of a heavenly recompense for
their earthly sufferings; some by the appeal of a God who might protect
them where their own traditions had failed. Like the Taiping, their
repertoire included theatrical demonstrations of the powerlessness of
traditional gods. One Bible woman in Shandong punched holes in the
image of a dragon god, proving to the alarmed villagers that her God
could protect her. Like the Taiping, Protestants emphasized women's
spiritual equality and made a particular point of criticizing foot binding. Many Bible women unbound their own feet, a declaration of spiritual independence as powerful as it was painful. By 1900, there were
forty training schools for Bible women across the country.[8]

None of this made Christians popular. Instead, they became China's
most visible symbol of foreign oppression. Even the Bible women depended on legal privileges that the Western powers had secured at gunpoint. Christians, according to rumor, practiced sodomy, infanticide,
and cannibalism, and used the eyeballs of murdered Chinese to make
silver by some secret alchemy—hence their insatiable zeal for converts.
Missionaries and converts frequently had to call on officials or foreign consuls to protect them or to exempt them from local taxes that
they claimed supported "idolatrous" rituals and practices. This ensured
that they were further resented as freeloaders who threatened the social order.

Occasional local outbreaks of violence became almost routine. After another predatory European power, Germany, seized the Shandong
peninsula in 1897, a movement of so-called Boxers sprang up, for whom
the meditative practices associated with traditional Chinese martial
arts became a symbol of patriotic defiance. In 1898, a palace coup in

Beijing installed a sharply antiforeigner regime. This febrile context, combined with two years of drought and famine for which Christians were all too easily scapegoated, produced a sudden explosion of violence in 1900. The Boxer Rebellion targeted foreigners in general and Christians in particular. Some thirty thousand believers, mostly Catholics, were killed, including two hundred missionaries.

There was no real doubt that the European powers would suppress the rising, and indeed, after a joint Western force occupied Beijing, there were massive reprisals. But with the Qing regime plainly unraveling, there was no return to the status quo. Ever since the disastrous war with Japan in 1894–95, some bold spirits in Beijing had been arguing that China must modernize, Westernize, and, perhaps, Christianize. Many Westernizing reformers had been educated at mission schools, and some of them were actually Christian believers—such as Sun Yat-sen, revolutionary, admirer of the Taiping, and future president of China. The restored Qing government embarked on some reforms but could not keep pace with what its educated subjects were now demanding. In 1912, a revolution turned China not into a heavenly kingdom but into a republic.

The new state adopted a Western-style constitution and promised full freedom of religion. In 1913, the new president, Yuan Shikai, publicly asked the country's Protestants to pray for him. But the excited mirage of a Protestant China quickly faded. As in Korea, Chinese nationalists who had looked admiringly to the United States and its religion felt bitterly betrayed when America sided with Japan in 1919 and were drawn instead to Russia and to Communism. The Chinese Communist Party, founded in 1921, saw Christianity as a tool of imperialism. The Anti-Christian Movement launched the following year denounced Christianity as obscurantist, antiscientific, and oppressive. Mission schools were nationalized in 1924–25. On May 30, 1925, police under British command opened fire on peaceful demonstrators in Shanghai and killed ten of them. The wave of anti-imperialist protest that followed was focused on churches.

Protestants still hoped to Christianize Chinese nationalism. Some looked to Feng Yuxiang, the "Christian General," who had been converted at an evangelistic rally in 1913 and who, from 1919 onward, invited revivalist preachers to work with his troops. In 1923, he was made commander in chief of the army and laid plans for a network of

Christian army chaplains. Again there was a moment of missionary excitement. Then, after the shootings in Shanghai, he joined in the antiforeigner sentiment. He was dismissed in 1926, and his interlude of highly public piety started to look as if it had only been a passing ploy.[9]

Another mirage appeared in 1927, when the Nationalist government staged an internal anti-Communist coup. The new regime's leader, Chiang Kai-shek, now married into a leading Shanghai Christian family. Three years later, he was himself baptized. He spoke of working with the churches to fight poverty. Again, however, the Nationalists were exploiting rather than supporting the Protestant cause. Chiang's campaign for moral renewal was a queasy mixture of Confucianism and puritanism with fascist overtones. Those Protestants who played along found themselves implicated in his increasingly authoritarian regime with very little to show for it.

The missionaries were, at least, now finally beginning to understand how badly Christianity was tainted by imperialism. Who wanted the Christians' heaven, some Chinese asked, if that meant "associating with foreigners for all eternity"?[10] Missionaries began to talk of the "three-self" ideal: that churches should be self-governing, self-propagating, and self-supporting. The slogan remains in use today.

Two routes beckoned. Establishment missionaries favored slow indigenization, led by Chinese Christians raised in mission schools. In 1910, one such pastor, Cheng Jingyi, gave an electrifying speech at the World Missionary Conference in Edinburgh, denouncing the sectarian divisions the missionaries had brought to China and calling for "a united Christian Church without any denominational distinctions." That call led directly to the formation of a merged interdenominational body, the Church of Christ in China (CCC), formally launched in 1927, which included about a third of all Chinese Protestants. Yet no matter how much the CCC trumpeted the three-self principle, it still looked like missionary Protestantism in Chinese clothes, and still leaned on foreign funds and personnel. Many of its leaders were trained in liberal American seminaries, and some of its elements—notably the YMCA/YWCA, one of the first missionary outfits to attain majority-Chinese leadership—were strongly associated with the left-leaning Social Gospel. Plenty of Chinese Protestants saw this as selling their Gospel birthright for a dangerous mess of secular ideologies.

For those who felt this way, there was another route to three-self Protestantism: new, independent Chinese churches, which sprang up in Shanghai, Beijing, and elsewhere from 1900 on, led by disenchanted mission-school graduates, self-taught evangelists, and Pentecostal missionaries. The 1930s revivalist John Sung, for example, delivered long, exuberant sermons, sometimes with a coffin onstage, sometimes breaking into extemporized song. He would also bring the sick to the stage for anointing, a sharp smack on the forehead, and a brisk declaration that they were now healed. The establishment called him a madman, but he got results.

Full-scale denominations soon emerged. The True Jesus Church, whose self-baptized prophet Wei Enbo wielded "the sword of the Holy Spirit to kill the demons," was faintly reminiscent of Taiping religion, but these demons were strictly spiritual, and Wei claimed to be the second Paul, rather than Jesus' brother. He died after only three years of ministry, ensuring that the sect that developed after his death was messianic rather than apocalyptic. By the mid-1930s, it was the second-largest Protestant church in China.

Two smaller groups are worth noticing. The Jesus Family was a utopian community that held all property in common, raised children collectively, and practiced strict gender segregation. Their authoritarian leader, Jing Dianying, claimed that his dogs could smell the difference between a true believer and a hypocrite. In the chronic insecurity of the 1920s and 1930s, the Family proved able not only to care for themselves but to minister to the wounded and displaced from all sides. A larger and subtler movement was the Little Flock, or Local Assemblies, whose founder, Ni Tuosheng (Watchman Nee), was China's first truly substantial Protestant theologian. He was a radical egalitarian, opposed to paid ministry and denominational structures. He flirted with Pentecostalism but taught something much closer to Martin Luther's theology of suffering, insisting that by embracing self-abnegation, believers would be filled with the "sweet savor of Christ."[11] The movement's moral authority, austere simplicity, and ability to find solace in rigor suited the needs of a war-torn age. By the end of the 1940s, it numbered some seventy thousand.

The independent churches were theologically conservative, avowedly apolitical, usually millenarian, and invariably focused on individual salvation rather than on the Social Gospel: not positions that the Protestant establishment believed were the future. Yet by the 1940s, they accounted for about a quarter of all Chinese Protestants and were growing fast. Some adopted the slogan "Back to Jerusalem," a dream that Christianity might spread westward from China along the old Silk Road to reconquer its ancient Middle Eastern heartland, incidentally putting China at the heart of Christianity's history. It was one sign of a Christianity keen to shake off the foreign taint and replace it with a message of stern morality and divine power. Soon that power would be needed.

In 1937, Japan invaded China, the real beginning of World War II. Initially, Japan treated churches with caution, even trying to claim that Christianity was an ally against Communism. But the Japanese liked neither the churches' studious neutrality nor their missionary leaders. As in Korea, missionaries were put under pressure and then, when the Western powers entered the Asian theater of war in 1941, interned. In 1942, the Japanese forcibly merged the surviving churches into the so-called China Christian Union. Most Protestants either submitted or fled to the Nationalist- or Communist-controlled regions. Their churches, still dangerously dependent on Western support, tottered. After Japan's surrender in 1945, the Church of Christ in China was reestablished, missionaries surged back, and a modest wave of Protestant revival followed in the liberated eastern cities. But the restored Nationalist regime was soon fighting for its life against a Communist insurgency. Urban Protestants had no great love for the Nationalists, but they mostly regarded the Communists with simple terror. As it became clearer how the struggle would end, some became openly apocalyptic. Watchman Nee called for all members of his Little Flock movement to sell their possessions in anticipation of the end. In the spring of 1949, when the Communists were poised to cross the Yangzi River and enter Shanghai, another Little Flock leader prayed that God would drown them all in the river as he had drowned Pharaoh in the Red Sea. Instead, the red sea overwhelmed the Nationalists, and China suddenly found itself in a new world.

Death and Resurrection in the People's Republic

By 1949, China's Communist Party had moved on from its early anti-Christian stance. During the war with Japan, it had adopted a "united front" policy, which meant working alongside other "patriotic" forces. Communists had cooperated with missionaries and had recognized that they shared some principles with communitarian groups like the Jesus Family. For their part, many Protestants were now willing to give the Communists the benefit of the doubt. Patriotic hearts could take comfort in the fact that an inept and grossly corrupt regime had been replaced by a strong, genuinely independent central government. The Qing, the Taiping, the Boxers, the Republicans, and the Nationalists had been unable to deliver that for a century and a half. It was a situation Chinese Protestants had never known before.

Plenty of Protestants, especially those inclined to the Social Gospel, genuinely hoped that the Communists might confront the sins of corruption, imperialism, and poverty. As the young Anglican bishop K. H. Ting (Ding Guangxun) put it, at such a moment it was better to "err on the side of naivety rather than cynicism." To be sure, the Communists were committed to strict atheism, but as the new premier, Zhou Enlai, explained, that need not mean open conflict:

> We think your beliefs untrue and false, therefore if we are right, the people will reject them, and your church will decay. If you are right, then the people will believe you, but as we are sure that you are wrong, we are prepared for that risk.[12]

The Protestant establishment accepted the challenge. The Communist-friendly YMCA leader Wu Yaozong drew up a short document known as the Christian Manifesto in consultation with Zhou. This denounced the entire missionary enterprise as an imperialist plot but implied that a Protestantism purged of foreign influences could expect a secure place in the new China. It was a test of loyalty, and most Protestants accepted it, even if we doubt the official claim that it eventually amassed 400,000 signatures.

This dream of Christian-Communist harmony was probably always unattainable, but it was definitively broken by the Korean War. From October 1950 onward, Chinese and American forces were in open battle, and China's anti-imperialist rhetoric took on a sharper edge. China's remaining missionaries were expelled as agents of what Mao Zedong called "spiritual aggression." Churches were then forced to publicly denounce imperialist "running dogs" in their ranks. Denunciation meetings consisted of public attacks on certain scapegoated individuals mixed, in a weird echo of Protestant revivalism, with melodramatic public repentance. It was theater, of course, yet some of the penitence was genuine. In the patriotic fervor of the war, with a new social and political order being formed, the world no longer looked as it once had.

With both foreign missionaries and foreign funds gone, Protestants made a virtue of necessity and appealed to the long-touted three-self principle. In 1951, a new body was formed under Wu Yaozong's leadership called, awkwardly, the China Christian Resist-America Help-Korea Three-Self Reform Movement. In 1954, this became the more manageable Three-Self Patriotic Movement (TSPM), which to this day is the centerpiece of Chinese government policy toward Protestantism. It quickly became clear that only churches that joined the TSPM would be allowed to survive.

The TSPM's defenders, then and now, claimed it was the best means of defending Protestants' freedoms while ensuring that they served the patriotic interest. Wu worked to keep the movement open to theologically conservative and apolitical Protestants, with some apparent success. Watchman Nee, pointing out that his Little Flock was an exemplar of the three-self principle, preached a Christian duty to obey duly established political authority, as Luther had done four centuries earlier. He also passed up a chance to go into exile, a decision that would cost him dearly.

This wishful thinking mistook the Communist Party's united front policy for a genuine partnership. It was in fact long-standing Communist Party policy to place party members secretly within "united front" organizations, and churches were no exception. A recently discovered internal party document from 1950 orders party members (atheists by definition) to take up church posts under cover and work toward leadership.[13] How much this really happened is uncertain, but in 1966 a former YMCA minister and general secretary of the TSPM was revealed as just such a double agent. It seems unlikely that he was the only one. China's churches were not facing a state that could be trusted.

All religious groups faced ratcheting pressures. The Protestant churches, cut off from foreign funds, were now of necessity self-supporting, but they would not be permitted to be self-governing, and, as for self-propagation, the state actively restricted proselytization. The

Jesus Family was suppressed in 1952 and its leaders imprisoned. Watchman Nee was arrested that year on charges of corruption; he died in a labor camp in 1972. The Little Flock movement itself was banned in 1956. Wang Mingdao, a formidable Beijing preacher who had become famous for defying the Japanese, now refused to join the TSPM, which he called a "party of unbelievers." He was arrested in 1954, was forced into a confession that he quickly repudiated, and was then imprisoned until 1979. By then, he was almost eighty and nearly blind, but his stubbornness was undimmed; he refused to accept release without an apology. In the end, he was tricked into leaving prison by an exasperated government with no wish to refight the battles of a bygone age.

The TSPM's leaders still had hopes. During the Hundred Flowers movement of 1957, when the regime briefly encouraged public criticism, some religious-affairs officials suggested legalizing prayer in public places, allowing churches to hold Sunday schools, and permitting the baptism of people under eighteen (all of which are still illegal in China). The "Anti-Rightist" backlash that followed made a mockery of such hopes. The Communist state now set out to suffocate organized religion. In 1958, during the catastrophic Great Leap Forward that caused one of the worst famines in recorded history, several regions were declared officially atheist, in which no religious activity was permitted. In the rest of the country, Protestants were forced into a single united structure, jettisoning "imperialist" denominational categories, a process that radically reduced the number of churches. Shanghai had more than two hundred churches in 1949, twenty-three by the end of 1958, and eleven by 1965. Only four of Beijing's sixty-five prerevolutionary churches survived. Wu himself, head of the party's officially approved Protestant organization, was banned from traveling to Beijing in 1960, having not yet sufficiently "exposed his thinking."[14]

Nor were these few churches crowded. In Shanghai, Sunday attendance fell by more than half from 1959 to 1965. In 1963, not a single baptism took place in the city, and only four in 1964–65. The numbers of clergy were capped and "redundant" ministers placed in laboring jobs. Church buildings were used for compulsory political meetings, frequently on Sundays. Workers found it difficult to secure time off work to attend worship, and services became anodyne and studiously inoffensive. Known Christians risked arrest or having their careers blocked. Many were compelled to attend political study sessions, where they learned about how science had disproved religion and were forced to denounce fellow believers as "Rightists."

It turned out that this was a prelude. In 1966, Mao Zedong mobilized a new quasi-volunteer youth movement of "Red Guards" to implement a "Cultural Revolution." The targets were the "four olds": old customs, old cultures, old habits, and old ideas, all of which would now be forcibly stamped out. The result was a ten-year spasm of physical destruction and violence comparable to the Taiping Rebellion. The death toll was more modest—perhaps not even a million—but the Cultural Revolution's impact was pervasive, on religious life as on everything else.

In August 1966, all churches and temples across China were closed. Red Guards stormed the TSPM's headquarters. A poster reading WE ARE ATHEISTS; WE BELIEVE ONLY IN MAO ZEDONG was slapped onto the YMCA building in Beijing. Churches were looted, pastors beaten, and educated people of all kinds sent into internal exile or forced into manual labor jobs. One Shanghai pastor was imprisoned for two years, was severely whipped, had his house ransacked repeatedly, and was forced to wear a tunic bearing the words "Down with God." A woman from his congregation who had posted copies of the TSPM's official newsletter to a former missionary in America was beaten and kept under house arrest for four years.

Christianity was hardly the Cultural Revolution's main target. Even in the religious realm, Buddhism and Islam had much deeper roots in Chinese society and were therefore more serious potential rivals to Maoism. Christianity was an enfeebled imperialist legacy, already shrinking fast. Scattered and silenced, the last Protestant generation could be expected to die soon enough. Their faith might well die sooner. Under a relentless barrage of propaganda that made Maoist atheism seem the only honest, scientific, and patriotic stance, some embattled Protestants repented and admitted that their imperialist superstition could have no place in China's future. The end seemed inevitable.

Yet the Cultural Revolution now seems to have been the making of Chinese Protestantism. Daniel Bays, one of the foremost historians of Chinese Christianity, believes that the number of Protestants in China increased five- or sixfold during this period.[15] When the churches were reopened from 1979 onward, they swiftly filled with patient old believers and earnest new converts. The hidden story now becomes the main narrative.

When the Little Flock was suppressed in the 1950s, informal communities of believers persisted in the absence of the denominational bureaucracy. As one Shanghai leader put it, "We simply say that we are Christians in Shanghai. That was the original way we spoke of ourselves in the 1920s and 1930s." As members of the mainstream churches were squeezed out, they likewise began to meet privately in their homes. To begin with, these house churches were on the margins, but between 1966 and 1979, when all public worship in Communist China was illegal, they had the stage to themselves. Reconstructing their story is difficult, beneath anecdotes, legends, and a pervasive habit of secrecy. In 1974, K. H. Ting told an American academic who was permitted to visit him that Chinese Christians now met privately in homes simply to avoid the stigma of imperialist associations, which may say more about his own high-stakes political balancing act than about the real state of contemporary Protestantism. He claimed that there were twenty-five such groups in Nanjing.

It may be that in the old Taiping capital the Taiping practice of household worship came naturally. By contrast, oral history work in Shanghai has so far uncovered no evidence at all of underground Protestant groups meeting during the Cultural Revolution. Shanghai Protestants who are willing to discuss the period testify that they would simply "pray very quietly" or "keep my faith alive in my heart." At most, two or three members of a single family might meet in near silence to pray or to recite memorized portions of their now-illegal Bibles. One Nanjing community salvaged a Communion table from a ransacked church and collected savings for the day when a new church could be built. That took both faith and courage, but it also suggests urban Protestants could do no more than hunker down and wait for the world to change.[16]

Their rural brethren needed less patience. The scattering of urban believers to internal exile across China seeded Protestantism in previously untouched regions. Rural Protestants also built on older foundations, with communities of the True Jesus Church and Jesus Family reemerging. A formidable network of underground congregations emerged in the early 1970s in Henan province, an old stronghold of the China Inland Mission and the Little Flock. In the 1980s, Protestant growth in the province sparked official alarm about "Christianity fever."

The main architect of Protestantism's new success, ironically, was the Communist Party. The purges and denunciations of the 1950s had achieved their aim: they broke the association between Christianity and foreign imperialism. The TSPM argues, somewhat self-servingly, that this is the primary reason for Protestantism's modern success. Kicking away the churches' missionary crutches was not kindly meant, but they discovered that they could still stand. Protestantism still remains associated with America and the West, but no longer damagingly so. Its status is like that of so-called Chinese food in the modern West: it feels exotic but is in practice wholly assimilated. In 1996, one rural Protestant even told a researcher she was surprised to learn there were any Protestants outside China.[17] By forcing the Protestant churches to stop being imperialist running dogs, the party inadvertently did them a great favor.

The Cultural Revolution itself directly benefited the Protestant cause, in three ways. First, the movement's brutality was counterproductive. As Maoism slowly lost credibility, Protestantism was, for the first time in its Chinese history, unambiguously the religion of the oppressed rather than of imperialists or collaborators. Second, the sheer chaos of the Cultural Revolution created new freedoms in practice even as they were being denied in theory. The Red Guards' onslaught was terrifying but hardly systematic. Any movement that targets the educated is unlikely to have an efficient bureaucracy. By 1968, different Red Guard factions were close to civil war. Local officials had, in practice, a great deal of discretion and could sometimes be persuaded to turn a blind eye to religious gatherings—whether for reasons of bribery, kinship, conscience, or simply a wish to avoid attracting central government attention. In rural areas especially, while the stakes remained dangerously high for Protestants, the odds of being left alone were also surprisingly good.

Third, in one critical sense, the Red Guards were on Protestantism's side. The "four olds"—customs, cultures, habits, and ideas—were as much an obstacle to Protestantism as to Communism. The Red

Guards, like the Taiping before them, uprooted religious practices and patterns of all kinds. The resulting scorched earth was a unique opportunity for invasive species, especially those whose seeds had already been widely distributed. The proliferation of capitalism in post-Maoist China may owe a good deal to the brutal ground clearing of 1966–76. Protestantism was also well placed to colonize the bare soil. As one Chinese academic disapprovingly put it, the Cultural Revolution "caused a vacuum to form in the minds of many people, giving an opportunity for religion, which takes advantage of this weak point."[18]

So some shards of evidence suggest. In Fuzhou, an area that had been occupied by the Taiping and then targeted by Anglican missionaries, Christianity had apparently been wholly suppressed by 1966. In the early 1970s, however, a woman who swiftly became known as "the madwoman" began telling her neighbors, "You should believe in Jesus and get rid of superstitious things, and thus the Lord will protect you and give you peace." She sang hymns and taught them to anyone who would learn. Years later, one of her converts recalled how the madwoman visited her house and denounced the "stove" gods, the household deities that, unlike the more public gods of traditional Chinese religion, had not been systematically destroyed by the Cultural Revolution. Traditional pieties involved sacrificing small amounts of money to the stove gods each month. The madwoman's host, resenting the expense, threw away the stove gods and professed a belief in Jesus. The madwoman came to her house to teach her songs. The little group of converts did not do anything so rash as meet for worship, but they sometimes visited an elderly Christian who told them Bible stories from memory. Perhaps twice a year, traveling Christians came through the village, telling stories of healings, prophecies, and exorcisms. One convert recalled how she was given miraculous foreknowledge of which fishing boats would gather a good catch, a practical demonstration of God's power that helped to convert her fisherman husband.[19]

Glimpses like this are all we have, but they are suggestive enough. As this story demonstrates, Protestantism's resurgence was led from the villages and was overwhelmingly female. Plenty of other testimony confirms that miracles were critical in attracting converts and convincing skeptics—much more so than nebulous concepts such as eternal salvation, which is not a significant theme in Chinese traditional religion. Traditional bulwarks against Protestantism such as communal and ancestral loyalty had been badly damaged by the Cultural Revolution. Only the stove gods, the lowliest members of the celestial bureaucracy, had escaped, a vulnerable cultural fragment whose expense could easily seem pointless. By contrast, Protestantism had a unique advantage: its weightlessness. Unlike all of its religious rivals, including Catholicism, Protestantism had no ritual or material requirements, cost no money, needed no professionals, and left no evidence. It did not even need Bibles (which was fortunate, because there were none), so long as people could remember the stories or their shortwave radios could pick up transmissions from Hong Kong, Taiwan, and the Philippines. It needed prayers, and songs, and the name Jesus. One traveling exorcist and storyteller of the time, interviewed thirty years later, sounded almost wistful for those heroic days. The miracles that had once flowed so plentifully, she observed, had become far fewer, but that was only to be expected:

> Now we don't need those works anymore, for now we have the Bible, the hymnbook, and pastors who preach. At that time, we didn't have any of these. The only thing was that God spoke to you directly.[20]

We should not romanticize this era. Some Protestant survivors of the Cultural Revolution will admit that it fostered renewed faith, but it was a decade of destruction and pervasive fear, and the experience has marked Chinese Protestantism. A hymn written in 1973 gives a flavor of this:

> The harder the circumstances, the brighter my soul.
> I beg the Lord for the strength to survive a while longer
> The one who comes will redress injustice for the innocent. . . .
> Fellow Christians are separated by thousands of miles and
>   mountain ranges
> Separated in body, but we meet in spirit
> When the last trumpet is sounded, in an instant

> Saints from all times and all places will meet together and
>   never part.

Other verses from the same era affirm a fierce faith in God's goodness amid suffering. "There is sweetness in the bitter, kindness in the severe." Finding renewed strength in persecution, and stubbornly insisting that redemption is drawing ever nearer, are themes as old as Christianity itself. They would serve Chinese Protestantism well.[21]

Believing in Modern China

The Cultural Revolution as such finally ended in 1976, with Mao Zedong's death and the arrest of the "Gang of Four" who had sought to define Maoism. The truly decisive shift followed Deng Xiaoping's accession to the supreme leadership in December 1978. In April 1979, a church was reopened in Ningbo, where underground Protestant congregations had been prominent. A few other Protestant churches elsewhere followed from September onward. Catholic churches followed later, and Daoist temples later still. By the middle of 1980, there were thirty-five Protestant churches across China. Two years later, there were five hundred, and by 1987 nearly three thousand, more than a third of which were newly built. The TSPM, too, was revived, now paired with a new organization, the China Christian Council, which was supposed to be focused more on spiritual matters. Both entities were led by the same man, the wily old campaigner K. H. Ting, until his death in 2012. They continue to function as a single body.

The reversal was part of Deng's general policy of withdrawing from detailed regulation of individuals' lives while retaining overall control. The regime had abandoned the hasty utopianism of the Cultural Revolution, but not Marxism-Leninism. Therefore, it preferred to keep religion where it could see it. Because it continued to believe that history's inexorable forces doomed religion to extinction, it could afford to be patient. In the meantime, in traditional Chinese fashion, it saw religion as dangerous only if it posed a political threat of some kind. In 1991, a senior Communist official vented his exasperation with the various excuses journalists, intellectuals, or religious believers offered for

disobeying the state: the public interest, freedom of thought, conscience. "From our point of view these excuses are all irrelevant. We
treat these people as an administrative problem." Those who obey are
left alone. Those who do not are not.[22]

In 1982, the Communist Party issued a directive, the so-called Document 19, which forms the basis of religious policy down to the present. The
document permits five recognized religions—Buddhism, Daoism, Islam,
Catholicism, and Protestantism—on the grounds that they will eventually
and inevitably wither away. However, it permits only "normal" religious
activity, a usefully opaque category that allows for supposedly subversive
religious movements to be suppressed relentlessly. In the case of Protestantism, "normal" means the revived TSPM, but Document 19 does consider the phenomenon of "Protestants gathering in homes for worship
services." With masterful ambiguity, it declares that "in principle this
should not be allowed, yet this prohibition should not be too rigidly enforced." The TSPM ought to persuade such house churches "to make more
appropriate arrangements."[23]

The Protestantism that has grown up under these rules is often
described as falling into two mutually suspicious halves. There is a
TSPM church operating within tight legal constraints, seen by its enemies as compromised or indeed as an utter sham. And there are "underground" or "house" churches, seen by their advocates as defiant
heroes of conscience and by their detractors as subversive groups peddling fundamentalism and serving as conduits for hostile foreign influences. When we step away from the partisan name-calling, it seems
plain that the two sides' stories are deeply entwined.

TSPM churches face real restrictions. Because Document 19 bans
proselytization outside approved religious premises, the only places in
China where it is possible to buy Bibles or other Christian literature
legally are TSPM churches. Churches are barred from youth work of
any kind, although breaches of this rule have become more common
since the turn of the millennium. The ban on baptizing those under
eighteen is more strictly enforced. Local officials also impose formal or
informal quotas on the number of baptisms. The numbers of official
churches remain strictly controlled and are grossly inadequate to
hugely increased numbers of believers. Shanghai still has fewer official
Protestant churches than it did in 1949, and they suffer from severe

overcrowding. The numbers of seminaries and ministers are also tightly capped. The state's Religious Affairs Bureau vets all ordinations. There is not much evidence to support the fear that the ministers are political stooges, and openly political sermons are rare, but TSPM ministers scrupulously avoid any hint of controversy. They also have to attend frequent, lengthy meetings for political study, and some TSPM churches feel the need to offer such meetings for their congregations periodically—not that they are well attended.

Western Protestants, who now regard separation between church and state as normal, find all this dismaying, but few of their sixteenth- and seventeenth-century forebears would have understood the fuss. The TSPM's relationship to the Communist state is very much that of classic Lutheran churches to their princes, albeit in this case the state itself makes no claim to be Christian. Because almost all Chinese Protestants accept the Communist state as legitimate, the TSPM's claim to be "patriotic" has genuine appeal. The TSPM is undoubtedly politically compromised, but compromises cut both ways. Within its unified structure, the TSPM has increasingly found space for different Protestant traditions—allowing Seventh-day Adventists to worship on Saturdays and giving houseroom to once-banned groups such as the Little Flock. A Little Flock elder even became the TSPM's national chair in 2002. Most remarkably, in a country where Bibles were once illegal, the TSPM's Amity Foundation has, since 1985, printed and distributed some fifty million Bibles, making the Bible (after the works of Mao) the second-most-published book in China. They can only be bought legally on TSPM premises, but the long-standing assumption by foreign Protestants that China suffers a Bible famine is badly out of date.

Above all, TSPM churches are living Protestant communities. When Moore Memorial Church in Shanghai reopened in September 1979, the building had been a school for thirteen years. The nave was dominated by a huge portrait of Mao, discreetly covered with a cloth for the first service. A crowd had been gathering outside, singing hymns, since before dawn. During the service, people swayed and wept. Twelve hundred came the first week, sixteen hundred the next week, and twenty-two hundred the week after.[24] The persistent overcrowding in TSPM churches ever since tells its own story. And while the TSPM itself is under tight political control, the day-to-day life of its churches is not overtly politicized. Researchers who visited one church in the late 1980s noticed that it dutifully subscribed to the TSPM's official magazine but it moldered unread. Copies were wedged under a pulpit to stop it from wobbling on an uneven floor.[25]

For all the nationalistic "three-self" language, TSPM churches remain strikingly Western Protestant in character. Even newly built churches imitate Western architectural norms. Many TSPM churches remain dominated by Western hymnody. "If you don't let them sing foreign hymns, they will feel that they are not really singing hymns at all," one frustrated Chinese hymn writer commented, comparing himself to Luther persuading reluctant Germans to sing German hymns.[26] Worship is usually structured much like a Methodist, Baptist, or Presbyterian service from missionary times, although typically without any symbolic exchange of greetings. The TSPM is somewhat more liberal in theology than most house churches and, in its self-image at least, better educated.

The TSPM is also, of course, vividly aware of the non-TSPM churches. It no longer makes sense to call these "house" churches, because many of them now own church buildings and meet in the open. Nor are many of them "underground" or even, strictly speaking, illegal. "Unregistered" is closer to the mark. Whatever we call it, all observers agree that the unregistered sector is significantly larger than the TSPM. The two are rivals, but sometimes also allies. Some TSPM ministers are hostile to their unregistered brethren, but others have worked to protect them from local officialdom. The TSPM's own strongest argument for greater freedoms is that it needs to remain competitive. Without the unregistered churches, its prospects would undoubtedly be bleaker.

The reverse is also true. Some unregistered churches are essentially overflow communities from the TSPM. Others try to maintain cordial relations with the local TSPM churches and take little trouble to hide themselves. In Wenzhou, which in 1958 was made China's first fully atheistic city but is now known as China's Jerusalem, unregistered churches progressed from the 1990s habit of placing paper crosses on the doors of private houses to, twenty years later, building substantial churches topped defiantly by highly visible crosses.

These bold enterprises always remain vulnerable. Wenzhou has seen a crackdown and a spate of demolitions since 2014. Most unregistered churches take pains to remain discreet. Amid enormous local variation and constantly changing political weather, unregistered churches are often able to operate as long as they avoid attracting attention. Some are open secrets, others genuinely concealed. Groups rotate between several prearranged meeting places, buy single-use mobile phones to contact each other, take care to stagger arrival and departure times, or install soundproofing, hiding places, and secret exits in their houses. Keeping noise to a minimum is a particular priority.

Unregistered churches that break these unwritten rules can face persecution ranging from harassment, arrests, and beatings to significant prison sentences or, occasionally, execution. Public proselytizing and distributing Bibles or other Christian literature outside TSPM churches are harshly repressed. So, too, are foreign contacts or any hint of political dissidence. Unregistered churches commonly vet new would-be converts, hoping to exclude undercover police but also political dissidents who might bring trouble down on the entire group.

This is more than just prudence. Most unregistered churches argue, like sixteenth-century Anabaptists, that Christians should avoid politics as a matter of conscience. They sharply criticize the TSPM for its politicization, sometimes in terms that feel less like apolitical withdrawal and more like a challenge to the Communist state. This is what one unregistered church leader had to say about the TSPM in the early 1980s:

> I do not question their faith, but it's . . . one thing to pray and preach. And quite another thing to pray and preach under the so-called tolerance of an atheistic power. To participate in that is to participate in a clown show. There is no option but to separate ourselves for holiness. . . . I am not a political man. I support the People's Government as everybody does. But as a Christian, I can have no consort with atheistic communism.[27]

The unregistered churches remember that the Communist Party has turned on believers before, and they know that its continued commitment to atheism is more than lip service. If religion is an opium habit of which the people refuse to break themselves, eventually the state may decide to do it for them.

These were the forces that determined Protestants' part in the greatest political crisis of post-Mao China, the pro-democracy protests that ended in the Tiananmen Square massacre of June 4, 1989. The TSPM was caught up in the liberalizing mood. Its head, K. H. Ting, cautiously supported the demonstrators. He admitted that the TSPM had in the past "done some things which Christians find despicable" and predicted that it would soon be abolished, leaving Protestants free to operate without official registration. Then came the crackdown. Ting's response was, under the circumstances, both honorable and courageous. While he affirmed his support for the regime, he remained surprisingly outspoken on issues of religious freedom and of corruption. Others in the TSPM responded differently. One of Ting's main rivals, Shen Yifan, lambasted unregistered churches as foreign-inspired counterrevolutionaries who "steal money, rape women, destroy life and health, spread rumors and destroy social order." When a young man walked into a TSPM church in Shanghai soon after June 4 and asked the pastor to pray for the students killed in Beijing, the pastor refused, on the grounds that the students were not Christians. He then asked the young man for a list of names of pro-democracy Christians. The visitor left and did not return.[28]

The irony is that the pastor was mostly right. Most Protestants stayed out of the pro-democracy movement, true to their apolitical principles. The Protestant seminary in Beijing was one of the very few educational institutions in the city unrepresented in Tiananmen Square. Protestantism's opportunity was not the protests but the disillusionment that followed. With political hopes crushed, withdrawal into another sphere became more appealing. Many TSPM churches experienced a surge in baptisms between 1990 and 1993. Some claimed to have "lost" their baptismal records during this period, fearful of the trouble that rapid growth might attract. The unregistered sector presumably fared at least as well.

The regime is inclined to worry about "evil sects" in the unregistered churches. Official accounts of groups reminiscent of the Taiping—theocratic, polygamous, and murderous—have been used to justify arrests and executions. These allegations are mostly unfounded. The "Shouters," a quasi-Pentecostal group that the regime sees as the prototypical sect, are accepted by many other Protestants as reasonably orthodox. Most unregistered churches teach a more or less recogniz-able conservative or Pentecostal Protestantism in which healings, exor-cisms, and prophecies remain commonplace. Miracle stories flourish in an environment of censorship that prevents any open claims for, or open scrutiny of, signs and wonders.

That Spirit-led dimension colors these churches' relationship with the Bible. Members of one rural unregistered church of the 1990s, the "Apostolic Church," reportedly knew their Bibles well but insisted that only the Holy Spirit allowed them to interpret the Bible truly:

> Very often, they study the Bible, and wait for the Holy Spirit to reveal to them the hidden spiritual meaning of the Scripture. Once they receive such revelation, they would look for other verses with similar themes and associate these verses to un-cover further hidden spiritual lessons.[29]

In this church, the Bible was used inspirationally rather than polemically, with the open-ended potential of the process controlled by a "discerning group" of church leaders who kept interpretation within acceptable bounds. Chinese Protestants routinely affirm the inerrant authority of the Bible, and indeed of the 1919 Chinese translation, the Union Version. Yet they often interpret their Bibles allegorically or spiritually, rather than embracing scholarly fundamentalism of the American or Korean variety. Because the Bible is there to guide believers, obscure passages must neces-sarily be allegorical—so, for example, the book of Leviticus's rules exclud-ing the deformed or disabled from the Jewish priesthood may be interpreted as describing how certain moral defects can hamper Chris-tians' prayers.[30] The TSPM's educated theologians may mock this as sim-plistic, but it is a supple religion that has met believers' practical and spiritual needs and has formed the seedbed for Protestantism's growth far beyond its rural base.

China's Protestant Future

It is impossible to say how many Chinese Protestants there are today. Somewhere between fifty and a hundred million—the larger figure seems unlikely, but the trends of the past few decades suggest it will be passed before too long. There are at least fifty thousand registered TSPM churches and preaching places. In 2014, the TSPM claimed that there were at least twenty-three million Protestants in China, up from three million in 1982 and ten million in 1995. These numbers only include adult members of TSPM churches, and in any case are widely assumed to be serious underestimates. Local officials' strong incentive is to downplay religious activities in their areas, and the Communist Party is said to have a long-standing policy of keeping China's total number of reported religious believers below a hundred million. The TSPM statistics, such as they are, show that Protestants are not spread evenly across the country but concentrated in the provinces south and east of Shanghai, roughly the territory once held by the Taiping. About 70 percent of them are women. Whether these patterns have any bearing on the unregistered churches is unclear, although it is universally acknowledged that they outnumber the TSPM by a factor of two, three, or possibly even four to one.[31]

The numbers game is in any case a distraction. China now has a great many Protestants, but they certainly remain fewer than 10 percent of its enormous population. Even if an accurate count were possible, it is unclear quite who should belong. One unregistered church leader, asked to estimate the numbers in his congregation, replied that they were like the stars in the sky—in the sense that "when the weather is good, you can see more; when it is a cloudy . . . day, they all disappear."[32] Rather than trying to divide China's population sharply into Protestants and non-Protestants, we should ask, why has this phenomenal growth happened, and where is it likely to be going next?

The Protestant revival in the 1960s and 1970s was based on its offer of miracles, but in post-Mao China this was only ever going to be a niche market. Protestantism's more fundamental miracle is the moral transformation it has offered. Chinese Protestants have managed to attract a reputation for outstanding moral rectitude. A non-Christian Chinese sociologist studying rural Protestant growth in 1987 remarked on converts' moral transformation, from healing ancient quarrels, through abandoning alcohol and tobacco, to returning money to shopkeepers who had given them too much change. "People from all walks of life, including numerous cadres (despite the fact that they are nonbelievers), all speak well of these people."[33] Christians in many ages have aspired to this reputation. Few have succeeded. Why they have done so in China is hard to say. But as well as the power of the message itself, and its fruitful interweaving with both Confucian and Communist moral principles, it is clear that harsh persecution in the 1960s and 1970s, and intermittent pressure ever since, have managed to keep Chinese Protestantism honest.

One sign of this is a firm ethic of nonresistance—a prudent way of dealing with an overbearing state, but one that also carries real moral authority. Unregistered churches have a reputation for punctilious co-operation with the police, an approach that can make them seem soft targets for official extortion but can also win them sympathizers or even converts. That 1987 study quoted a Chinese hymn called "Keep One's Way":

> When struck, I do not strike back.
> When abused, I do not retort
> nor do I get upset and sulk.
> I smile when rebuked.

This authentically Christian ethic echoes traditional Confucian teaching on forgiveness. It is also a very practical response to Protestants' situation.[34]

This moral appeal was important as Protestantism spread from country to city in the years after 1990. A religion previously centered on poor, elderly women began to win younger, better-educated converts of both sexes. There has been a good deal of excitement about what K. H. Ting called "cultural Christians," a term applied to Chinese scholars interested in Christianity but not formally attached to a church. Whether such people can meaningfully be called Christians is not clear. Some are trying to construct secular ethics drawing on Christianity or are interested in Christianity simply as students of Western culture. Some are believers who find it prudent to mask their convictions with scholarship or who find the churches' Christianity crass. If they are significant, it is not because they are themselves converts but because they have helped to make Protestantism intellectually respectable.[35]

The actual urban converts, by contrast, tend to be from the younger generations who have come of age in the new China. Some speak of being drawn initially by curiosity or by the Western church music to which Chinese churches remain so loyal. One Shanghai convert recalled thinking, "It really struck me that people were there voluntarily, not like a big political meeting that you have to go to and listen to boring speeches. There must be something to this."[36] The most recurrent theme of these narratives, however, is of young, dislocated city dwellers scrabbling for security in a fast-changing world. Protestantism gives these converts community, the hope of divine assistance, and inner peace. Crucially, it gives meaning to their own life stories. If it has all happened under God's providence, they can not only make sense of the chaos of their lives up to that point but see that story as useful both to themselves and to others.[37] We have often observed Protestantism's extraordinary ability to adapt. In contemporary China, it is showing its parallel ability to integrate all the disparate elements of converts' experience into a single narrative.

Protestant enthusiasts are once again talking of a Christian China, but this seems no more likely now than it has ever been. Protestantism's growth depends on a very particular mix of toleration and persecution. Most Protestants have quite a lot of freedom most of the time, but they face significant restrictions, occasional bouts of much sharper repression, and no long-term security. The result is enough freedom to allow Protestantism to grow but enough persecution to keep it lean. The TSPM and unregistered churches between them provide spaces for being either loyally semidetached or apolitically withdrawn from an overbearing state. Either way, the symbolic exclusion of believers from the Communist Party gives them the invaluable status of outsiders. A century ago, the Qing and Republican regimes were defending churches against popular demands to demolish them. Now the Communist regime is demolishing unregistered churches built by local people. Protestantism no longer suffers from being associated with foreign imperialism but still benefits from the exotic air that hangs around it— its link to modernity, freedom, and America. It has enough of a track record to have acquired moral authority, but not yet enough to have acquired a reputation for corruption. It also has the momentum, novelty, and excitement that cluster around a growing movement.

Some of this may continue. It is hard to see how the Communist regime could shift dramatically toward either tolerance or repression.

But Chinese Protestantism cannot remain in its current sweet spot forever. Perhaps, as in Korea, when the era of breakneck economic growth is over, Protestantism's growth will also fizzle. One thing is already changing. Post-Mao Chinese Protestantism, for all its growth, remained remarkably invisible. Before 1949, a far smaller Protestant population had a much higher profile. Until recently, religious communities were entirely excluded from the public square, and even TSPM churches were discreet or entirely unseen. Yet growing numbers and confidence have made the invisibility trick harder and less urgent. Since 2000, the old dream of "Back to Jerusalem" has resurfaced, and unregistered churches have begun trying to carry the Gospel into China's western provinces. The change became unmistakable after an earthquake struck Sichuan province on May 12, 2008, killing more than eighty thousand people. In the chaotic aftermath, many of the first responders came from churches and made no secret of the fact. Since then, Chinese Protestants have become increasingly prominent in human rights campaigning. Rumor has it that a third or more of China's embattled human rights lawyers are now Protestants.

This new prominence might have helped precipitate a renewed clampdown that began in 2013 and is still continuing at the time of writing, part of President Xi Jinping's broader assault on independent civil society. In 2014, an official national-security think tank warned that "the infiltration of overseas religions has already extended its tentacles to reach all domains of Chinese society." A leaked 2014 policy paper from the government of Zhejiang province, where the crackdown is at its sharpest, expressed alarm that "religious development has been too fast . . . there are too many religious sites and 'overheated' religious activities."[38] The campaign has focused on publicly visible Christian symbols. Hundreds of crosses atop churches have been removed across Zhejiang province and elsewhere. Some entire churches, both TSPM and unregistered, have been demolished. Christianity has also been targeted in universities, with even secularized celebrations of Christmas banned and students threatened with expulsion for holding private prayer meetings.

The campaign has, in turn, been met with unprecedented resistance. It has also pushed the registered and unregistered sectors closer together. TSPM churches have been the primary targets of cross demolitions and appear now to have presumed too much from their quasi-official status. Some TSPM officials have dared to speak out against the campaign and have lost their positions as a result. Some unregistered church leaders have been openly defiant. In mid-2015, a thirty-strong group called Lawyers for the Protection of the Cross announced itself in Beijing. Some crosses have been rebuilt after demolition. In at least one case, when an unregistered church building was sealed, the congregation met for worship outside it and its leader spoke of suing the government. In August 2015, Wang Yi, a prominent pastor who identifies himself with the Calvinist tradition, even published a set of "ninety-five theses" for the unregistered sector, citing the example of "Martin Luther, a servant of God." These theses not only reject any political interference in Christian life, but urge Christians facing "illegal infringements from the government . . . to use any and all legal means to express their protest . . . and exercise proper self-defense." Luther would not necessarily have approved.[39]

How or indeed whether this particular campaign will end, we do not yet know. Regardless, there is as yet little sign of "overheated" Protestant growth cooling down. China is becoming a country with a substantial, energetic, and growing Protestant minority. How that minority, and the country at large, deal with that unprecedented situation—that is perhaps *the* question for global Protestantism in the twenty-first century.

CHAPTER 16

Pentecostalism: An Old Flame

Quench not the Spirit.

—I THESSALONIANS 5:19

The early twentieth century was an extraordinary moment in world history, and Protestants knew it. According to one traditional view, the world had been created around 4000 B.C. and was expected to last about six thousand years, so this new century might well be the world's last. As it dawned, almost the entire planet had been conquered or subdued by Europeans or their descendants. Europeans and North Americans believed not only that they could shape the entire world's fate but that it was their responsibility to do so. Two very different Protestant movements set out to fulfill that responsibility.

The first brought the most passionate, courageous, and intellectually engaged leaders of a swath of Protestant churches together to an unprecedented World Missionary Conference in Edinburgh in 1910, under the slogan "The evangelization of the world in this generation." The conference's focus was on healing denominational rifts, and from it flowed a series of agreements and even mergers between churches, culminating in the creation in 1948 of the World Council of Churches. A century on, however, this ecumenical project has run its course. Interdenominational relationships are much improved, but the World Council of Churches is no nearer to full Christian reunion than the United Nations is to establishing world peace.

The other early twentieth-century initiative bubbled up across the wilder fringes of Protestant revivalism. Its own mythology traces its founding to Los Angeles in 1906, but in fact it came from multiple sources on at least five continents. It was a very traditional Protestant revivalist movement, fired by a new conviction that the Gospel had to be taken to the entire world and that God was empowering his people to do it. Protestant establishments were slow to take this new movement seriously, and the Edinburgh conference's organizers paid it no attention at all. Yet nearly a tenth of all humanity and more than a quarter of all Christians now belong to this Pentecostal movement, broadly defined. It is the most dramatic religious success story of modern times.

A Tangle of Origins

Pentecostalism teaches Christians to seek a further step beyond conversion, known as baptism by the Holy Spirit. This Spirit-baptism is manifested through various "gifts" of the Holy Spirit, in particular through the experience that Pentecostals call speaking in tongues. The Pentecostal movement that crystallized in Los Angeles in 1906 and surged out across the world thereafter generally took speaking in tongues to be an essential marker of Spirit-baptism. Since the 1960s, however, it has been clear that this narrow definition of Pentecostalism is inadequate. The "charismatic" movement which began in that decade saw similar spiritual experiences taking root within the older Protestant denominations, and indeed in the Catholic Church. Then, from the 1980s, "third wave" Pentecostal/charismatic churches mushroomed in Africa, Latin America, and elsewhere, mostly independent of any denominational ties. These later movements now have far more adherents than do the classical Pentecostal denominations such as the Assemblies of God or the Apostolic Faith Mission. Some of them have adopted classic Pentecostal doctrines of Spirit-baptism and the centrality of speaking in tongues, but many more have not. What unites them is not a doctrine so much as an experience: the thrilling, rapturous, transformative inner encounter with the Holy Spirit which these churches help believers to achieve.

The problem with tracing Pentecostalism's origins is that ecstatic inner encounters with the Holy Spirit are nothing new for Christians. The New Testament seems to regard such experiences, including speaking in tongues, as normal. Overwhelming spiritual experiences of various kinds have been described through the centuries by Christians of every sort. Churches have usually tried to manage or restrain these experiences, but Protestantism has regularly broken through such restraints in its quest for a direct, unmediated encounter with God.

Although there is scant evidence of Protestants' actually speaking in tongues before the twentieth century, there is no shortage of other ecstatic manifestations. Plenty of Protestants have implicitly or explicitly claimed direct prophetic inspiration. Sixteenth- and seventeenth-century Protestants routinely wept profusely or groaned loudly during prayer, phenomena that they treasured as signs of the Holy Spirit working within them. The radical Presbyterians of early seventeenth-century Scotland and Ulster told tales of healings, resurrections, strange lights, and preachers inspired to deliver sermons of which they later had no memory. We are told that congregations continued in prayer without food or sleep for days at a stretch, or fell into "high breathing and panting, as those do who have run too long."[1] During the age of Britain's civil wars, radical groups trembled, roared, or foamed at the mouth. Quakers quaked. Shakers shook. The French Prophets, the Moravians, and other eighteenth-century revivalists experienced trances, fainting, visions, miracles, and ecstasies. In the United States, these experiences moved in from the margins. At the great Cane Ridge revival in Kentucky in 1801, people were seen "with a piercing scream, [to] fall like a log on the floor, earth, or mud, and appear as dead." The revival's leader described manifestations that would fit directly into a modern Pentecostal meeting:

> The laughing exercise . . . [A] loud, hearty laughter, but . . . the subject appeared rapturously solemn, and his laughter excited solemnity in saints and sinners. . . . [T]he singing exercise . . . The subject in a very happy state of mind would sing most melodiously, not from the mouth or nose, but entirely in the breast, the sounds issuing from thence. Such music silenced every thing, and attracted the attention of all. It was most heavenly.[2]

In 1821, Charles Finney, who would go on to be the century's greatest revivalist preacher, experienced something "like a wave of electricity, going through and through me. Indeed it seemed to come in waves and waves of liquid love. . . . I literally bellowed out the unutterable gushings of my heart." He called this "a mighty baptism of the Holy Spirit." Most revivalist preachers were concerned to tamp this sort of thing down. Billy Sunday was an electrifying preacher, but one shout of "Amen!" or "Hallelujah!" in one of his meetings would get you a warning, and two would have you thrown out.[3]

The first Protestant group who unabashedly embraced these phenomena came out of American Methodism. John Wesley had, controversially, taught that some Christians might by God's grace attain moral perfection. Theologically, this was awkward, but it made sense of what some believers had experienced. By the late nineteenth century, "holiness" movements pursuing this spiritual gift were teaching ever more austere moral codes—rejecting not merely alcohol and tobacco but sugar and that diabolical monument to male vanity, the necktie. They began to split from their denominations' lax, tie-wearing establishments and go their own way. In 1885, a Holiness Assembly in Chicago declared that holiness was a "second definite stage in Christian experience," bestowed "by the baptism with the Holy Spirit."[4] At "holiness" meetings in the 1890s, believers were "slain in the Spirit"; that is, they fell in an insensate trance, a practice and phrase that have passed into Pentecostal usage. Others laughed for an hour at a time, shouted, wept, or saw visions.

Pursuing this holiness through Spirit-baptism gave fresh purpose to earnest and enthusiastic Protestants who were not content simply to live their whole lives as an epilogue to their conversions. All it did, however, was to push the problem back. What were believers to do once that second definite stage had been attained, other than subsist in holy bliss? Some began to suspect that beyond the "second blessing" lay a third, a "baptism of fire." One holiness preacher developed no fewer than six stages, including a baptism of dynamite.[5]

The alternative to this infinite regression was developed by a group of English evangelicals who in 1875 began an annual conference in the Lake District town of Keswick. They shared the holiness believers' interest in dramatic spiritual experiences but rejected Wesley's perfectionism. Instead, their framework was apocalyptic. They recalled the original Pentecost, when, after the risen Christ ascended to heaven, the Holy Spirit was given to the first apostles and filled them with power. As the world's end drew near, they believed, there would be a new

Pentecost, in which God would empower his church's ministry once again. Citing an opaque Old Testament verse, they looked for a "latter rain" of the Holy Spirit to fall after a centuries-long drought.[6] Where the holiness movement thought of this Spirit-baptism as making believers perfect, the Keswickers expected it to make them powerful. It would equip them to fan out across the godless world that European empires had providentially conquered and bring it to the true faith before the end.

It was a potent idea. The Spirit would empower every believer, regardless of nationality, age, sex, or education. Preaching this message sparked revivals in Australia in 1901, in Estonia in 1902, in Sweden in 1905. A spin-off of the Keswick convention was set up in the Welsh border town of Llandrindod Wells in 1903, and in 1904–5 revival fever swept Wales, under the leadership of a young miner and trainee minister named Evan Roberts. Eighty-seven thousand people were said to have been converted. There were prophecies. Believers prayed and sang in Welsh and English simultaneously, in a holy Babel. Roberts declared that the "latter rain" had come. News of the Welsh revival was devoured all over the world. Readers from the United States to Korea prayed for the same Spirit to fall on them.

There was one problem with the thesis that this was a new Pentecost. In his popular 1895 manifesto for the Keswick movement, *The Baptism with the Holy Spirit,* Reuben A. Torrey pointed out the awkward fact that biblical accounts of baptism with the Holy Spirit invariably also mention speaking in tongues. Yet, despite all the other manifestations of the Spirit in the churches around him, he admitted, "I saw no one so speaking." Did this mean that the Spirit was not truly at work? Torrey was sanguine. Speaking in tongues was prominent in the early church, but that was no reason to believe it was essential. The Spirit's empowerment need not produce any outward manifestation at all. But the problem was not so easily dismissed.[7]

The New Testament passages describing "speaking in tongues" appear to describe two distinct phenomena. One is a straightforward miracle. On the Jewish feast of Pentecost, when the Holy Spirit filled the first apostles, a crowd present who were drawn from every nation under heaven each heard the message spoken in his or her own language. The curse of the Tower of Babel was reversed.[8] The second phenomenon, which St. Paul discussed at some length, is of believers speaking in an "unknown tongue," a divinely inspired utterance that neither the speaker nor any of those hearing understands, unless someone should be given the separate spiritual gift of interpreting it. He appears to imply that these believers speak the language of angels.[9]

This second variety fits tolerably well with a phenomenon, shared by Pentecostal Christians and several non-Christian peoples, which anthropologists call glossolalia: ecstatic and apparently involuntary utterances that sound like, but are not, a human language. This appears to be a naturally occurring phenomenon, which of course does not preclude the possibility that God uses it. While Torrey had not come across it, the phenomenon had occasionally surfaced in Protestantism's earlier history. A few of the French Prophets had claimed the miraculous ability to speak Latin, Greek, or Hebrew, but more had spoken in languages which no one could identify. Over a century later, in 1830, a dangerously ill Scottish girl named Mary Campbell suddenly sat up in bed, spoke "melodiously in an unknown tongue," and prophesied for a quarter of an hour. Others in nearby communities followed, in a contagion that eventually led a daring London Presbyterian minister named Edward Irving to permit speaking in tongues in his church and to the formation of the so-called Catholic Apostolic Church, the first charismatic Protestant denomination. Irving, incidentally, was an enthusiast for the French Prophets.[10]

There was also some tongue-speaking among the holiness movements of the 1890s. A hundred and thirty people were reported to have spoken in tongues at one North Carolina camp meeting in 1896. At a meeting in St. Louis, Missouri, in 1904, one man was said to have been inspired to speak in three different languages, and another "laughed in a manner resembling the laughter of several other nations."[11] It is not clear whether there was speaking in tongues during the Welsh revival—to most English listeners, Welsh might as well have been the language of angels—but some Welsh delegates at the 1905 Keswick convention began speaking in tongues, to the alarm of their colleagues.

The Welsh revival also helped to trigger tongue-speaking farther afield. In late 1904, one veteran evangelist in the American Midwest discovered that the mere act of reading about the Welsh revival was enough to set him speaking in tongues. A Los Angeles minister who visited Wales in 1905 found that his Baptist colleagues rejected the spiritual gifts he had brought back with him. He formed a splinter congregation, which a local newspaper reported was speaking "unintelligible jargon."[12]

Maybe the most remarkable reader of Welsh tales was Pandita Sarasvati Ramabai, a campaigner for nationalism and women's rights in her native India. She converted to Christianity as a young widow in the early 1880s but in about 1894 had what she called a "new experience of God's power . . . the personal presence of the Holy Spirit in me." She already ran a women's refuge but now refounded it as an explicitly evangelical project.[13] When she heard of the events in Wales, she sent her American sidekick Minnie Abrams and her own daughter to see for themselves. The two women returned in January 1905 aglow with excitement. On their advice, Ramabai set up daily early-morning meetings to pray for "the true conversion of all the Indian Christians including ourselves." After six months, the fire caught. The revival that swept through her refuge lasted for a year and a half, marked by ecstatic prayer meetings, miraculous healings, more than a thousand baptisms, and about seven hundred young women going out as missionary preachers. During late 1905, some of them also began speaking in tongues. It is not clear whether Ramabai herself spoke, but she was characteristically robust in denying that it was merely a matter of "hysterical women." "I wish," she wrote, "that all of us could get this wonderful and divine hysteria." She believed that speaking in tongues had renewed the women's moral character and empowered them to preach and pray.[14]

The emerging pattern, then, was that linked revivals were bubbling up across the world, that some of them included speaking in tongues, and that the phenomenon was not seen as having any particular importance. There was at first no reason to think that Charles Parham's case was any different. Parham was a Kansas evangelist who in the late 1890s experienced Spirit-baptism "like a stroke of lightning . . . thrilling every fiber of my being; making me know by experimental knowledge what Peter knew of old, that He was the Christ." In 1899, he became convinced that God would restore what he called the gift of "missionary tongues," the miraculous ability to preach in foreign languages. The following year, he heard tongue-speaking for the first time and opened a Bible school in Topeka, Kansas, attracting a small group of holiness types searching for something more. He primed his students to expect the gift of tongues. In December, one of them, a barely educated twenty-nine-year-old consumptive named Agnes Ozman, let slip a few words that she could not understand, but this was premature. Parham had a timetable in mind. On January 1, 1901, the first day of history's final century, the little community spent the day in prayer. Now, when Parham laid hands on Ozman's head in prayer, a fluent stream of syllables poured out of her. For the next three days, she spoke only in what she believed was Chinese. Parham and the rest of the community received the gift two days later. As he described it, "There came a slight twist in my throat, a glory fell over me and I began to worship God in the Swedish tongue."[15]

It was not the epoch-making event Parham imagined. Topeka was an unlikely new Jerusalem, and the Bible school soon broke up. Nor was Parham satisfied with his students' tongue-speaking. He wanted verified abilities to speak actual foreign languages, not ecstatic gibberish. He was also increasingly caught up in another fashionable idea: Anglo-Israelitism, a form of racist mysticism founded on the belief that the Anglo-Saxons were descended from the lost tribes of Israel and were therefore God's chosen people.

It is ironic, then, that when Parham's message finally bore spectacular fruit, it did so through two African American preachers. First was Lucy Farrow, the leader of a holiness congregation in Houston, Texas, who in 1905 was employed by the Parham family as a cook and nanny. Convinced by his preaching, she sought, and received, the gift of tongues. She then persuaded a young holiness preacher named William Joseph Seymour to attend another of Parham's pop-up Bible schools, although he was compelled to sit in the corridor and listen through an open door rather than join the other, white students in the classroom. Seymour became convinced of the importance of tongue-speaking but did not, yet, receive the gift himself. Instead, he was invited by a small holiness church in Los Angeles to come and serve as its pastor. In March 1906, he went, against Parham's advice, and it was a fiasco. He immediately told his new congregation that they must seek the gift of tongues as the only certain sign of Spirit-baptism, and they promptly threw him out. He was left destitute, meeting in private houses with a handful of those whom he had persuaded. They were a tiny group, poor, black, mostly women—considered the very dregs of humanity.

They met; they prayed. One of them, Edward Lee, had a vision in which the apostles "lifted their hands to heaven and they began to shake under the power of God and began to speak in other tongues." Yet none of them actually received the gift. So they embarked on a desperate project: they would fast for ten days, hoping to wrestle the gift of tongues from the Spirit by brute force. What rescued the situation was Lucy Farrow's arrival in Los Angeles, on the second day of the fast. The following evening, April 9, she met Lee. He was in bad shape, having done a full day's manual labor despite spending three days without food. He begged Farrow to lay hands on him to pray for the gift. She was initially reluctant, having just met him, but his demeanor eventually persuaded her that he was in earnest, and she did as he asked. Finally, "the power fell."[16]

As often happened, once tongues were first heard, they spread swiftly. Seymour's own longed-for Spirit-baptism finally followed three days later. The little community began to grow, and they moved into a fire-damaged, half-derelict Methodist church at 312 Azusa Street. "Azusa Street" became a name to conjure with. The revival gathered pace that summer, with daily congregations topping five hundred, and remained in full force for three years, attracting worldwide attention. Experiential, ecstatically Spirit-led Christianity did not begin at Azusa Street, but Pentecostalism as a denominational identity, and the use of the word "Pentecostal" in the modern sense, did. All of the classical Pentecostal denominations can trace their roots there. Fires had been lit all over the world, but this was the one caught by the wind.

The Pentecostal Experience

Two linked questions hang over this peculiar story. Why, given that ecstatic phenomena and Spirit-baptism had been current among revivalists for decades, did this one outbreak in Los Angeles explode across the world, where the others had burned themselves out? And why did the experience of bursting into unintelligible sounds suddenly become so important?

Azusa Street took off because it was the right place and the right time. Ecstatic outbreaks had been springing up across the world. If this one had fizzled, another would have come along. It is no great surprise it happened in Los Angeles, the Western world's outermost edge, the United States' fastest-growing city, a seething mixture of peoples unburdened by old ecclesiastical establishments. The city was already awash with revivalists, and the mood was made all the more febrile when, on April 18, 1906, the very morning that the *Los Angeles Times* ran its first report on the WEIRD BABEL OF TONGUES at Azusa Street, a massive earthquake flattened the city of San Francisco and shook Los Angeles itself. God was apparently trying to tell California something. One holiness preacher, who would soon himself become a Pentecostal, rushed out a tract simply titled *The Earthquake!!!* It ran through 125,000 copies within a month.

Seymour and Farrow added their own particular ingredients to this cocktail. Azusa Street was multiracial but black-led, an extremely unusual pattern in the United States. This gave it a cosmopolitan ethos, and it might have eased the path to ecstatic phenomena. Parham certainly thought so. When he finally visited Azusa Street in October 1906, he was horrified. It made him, he said, "sick at my stomach . . . to see white people imitating unintelligent, crude negroism of the Southland, and laying it on the Holy Ghost."[17] Others who do not share his racism have wondered whether deep traditions of African religious practice, preserved through generations of slavery, were surfacing in this revival. That notion seems implausible, but it is certainly true that ecstatic religion was more typical of contemporary black churches than white ones. In that sense at least, this community was a unique crossing point. Azusa Street took great pride in being inclusive of all peoples and all languages.

The meetings themselves took place every day, from around ten in the morning until late into the night, and entirely ignored conventional church rules. The outside of the building was marked only by the roughly painted words APOSTOLIC FAITH GOSPEL MISSION. Inside, people sat on planks balanced on empty kegs or brought their own chairs. The bare earth floor was strewn with straw. A makeshift pulpit of packing crates was jammed in under the low ceiling. The room swarmed with flies. In one corner stood a discreet offering box, because Seymour refused to pressure his people by passing a collection plate. The offerings that clustered around the box were wordless testimonies to trans-formed lives: abandoned tobacco pipes, bottles of liquor, and crutches.[18] The meetings themselves fit their surroundings. For many months, there were no musical instruments to accompany the singing. There was not much formal preaching, only occasional short exhortations from Seymour. Most of the meetings consisted of believers' taking turns to testify about the Spirit's work in their lives, glorifying God, and encouraging one another, keeping the meetings at a rolling boil. Ecstatic outbreaks were almost continuous. Someone would be speak-ing, one witness remembered, and

> suddenly the Spirit would fall upon the congregation. God himself would give the altar call. Men would fall all over the house like the slain of battle. . . . The scene often resembled a forest of fallen trees.[19]

Sometimes an outsider wandered in, a gawker come to see the "holy rollers." Seymour would welcome the newcomer, call for everyone present to pray, and before too long the visitor too "went down under the power."[20]

Some visitors remained immune. One Los Angeles pastor called Azusa Street "a disgusting amalgamation of African voudou supersti-tion and Caucasian insanity." A reporter described seeing a middle-aged woman, "the typical old-maid school teacher," standing up in front of the meeting and, without preliminaries, saying, "Ippy, Ippy, ippisit, ip-pley, catty catis, clak, claky." They thought she was speaking in tongues, the reporter added, but "it sounded more like an old speckled hen had laid an egg in the corner of the barn and wanted everyone to know it." Some at Azusa Street took to writing in tongues, and the *Los Angeles Daily Times* printed a sample of the resulting unintelligible script, which it called "chicken tracks on paper."[21] If the secular press saw this as sim-ply lunatic fun, however, the holiness journals took it more seriously. The curious, the hostile, and the hungry all began to make their way to Azusa Street, many to be reconfirmed in their hostility, some to be struck down and won over.

Not that Seymour's congregation waited for visitors to come to them. The longed-for "latter rain" was falling, and a new Pentecost had come. As the fast-growing community acquired an ethic of making self-sacrificial offerings, they chose not to prettify their building but to pour all their resources into spreading the word. In September 1906, the community produced the first issue of a newspaper audaciously titled *The Apostolic Faith*. Five thousand copies were printed, mostly for free circulation to anyone who might be interested. "The real revival," that first issue declared, "has only started, as God has been working with His children mostly, getting them through to Pentecost, and laying the foundation for a mighty wave of salvation among the unconverted." The second issue doubled its print run to ten thousand. Circulation peaked at eighty thousand in 1908 and declined thereafter only because imitators were springing up around the world. As daughter churches took root, they too refused to sink funds into fixed assets. Typically, they rented anonymous accommodations, often preferring meeting spaces above ground level, for the Spirit had fallen on the first disciples in an upper room. They plowed all they had into camps, Bible schools, and above all newspapers, sometimes bankrupting themselves with massive free distributions.[22] The movement proliferated and, by the 1920s, had splintered into a series of makeshift denominations. As early as 1909, many of the Azusa Street congregation had scattered. Seymour himself fell out acrimoniously with much of the community in 1911–12 and was frozen out of a movement that was becoming increasingly white led. He died in obscurity in 1922.

At the center of all this publicity was the phenomenon of speaking in tongues. The simplest and least interesting reason for this was that, as Parham had argued, a new Pentecost had to be marked by the same spiritual gifts as the first one. The problem with this explanation is that, despite the gift of tongues, Azusa Street did not fit the biblical model terribly well. The Pentecost story describes tongues being used to preach the Gospel. Azusa Street's pattern, however, was to use tongues in worship meetings even though no one present understood them, a phenomenon that St. Paul explicitly discouraged.[23]

A second reason for focusing on tongues was more practical and urgent. If taking the Gospel to the whole world was conceivable now as it had never been before, that task was still pretty daunting. The entire Keswick movement was based on the conviction that God would empower his people to tackle such an impossible task. Of all the practical obstacles would-be missionaries faced, the single most formidable was language. How could a mighty wave of salvation sweep the world if missionaries had to spend years learning every single language first? The problem, Bible believers knew, dated back to the Tower of Babel, when God had cursed humanity with mutually incomprehensible languages. So perhaps he might now lift the curse? Speaking in tongues was more than a sign of the Holy Spirit's presence. It was the single most practical and urgent gift God could give to his church.

This was Parham's innovation. Most others who heard tongue-speech thought it was meaningless, but Parham, and after him the Azusa Street community, believed that these incomprehensible sounds were real human languages that no one present happened to understand. The first issue of *The Apostolic Faith* claimed that at Azusa Street

> The Lord has given languages to the unlearned: Greek, Latin, Hebrew, French, German, Italian, Chinese, Japanese, Zulu and languages of Africa, Hindu and Bengali and dialects of India, Chippewa and other languages of the Indians, Esquimaux, the deaf mute language, and, in fact the Holy Ghost speaks all the languages of the world through His children.[24]

To speak in tongues was to be commissioned by God to preach the Gospel to some particular nation. It was simply a matter of discovering what language you had been given. This was not easy. An inner conviction, a confident assertion from someone who had once heard a language spoken, a few syllables that sounded like particular words—this was often the best that could be done. Ecstatic gestures might look like inspired sign language, even if, as in one early case, that convert signed "with such rapidity that the eye could not trace or record the different signs given."[25] On the back of such slender evidence, untrained missionaries equipped only with burning faith and the miracle of tongues headed to the Middle East, China, India, Africa, and elsewhere. Lucy Farrow herself set off for Liberia. "God," the first edition of *The Apostolic Faith* declared, "is solving the missionary problem, sending out new-tongued missionaries on the apostolic faith line, without purse or scrip."[26]

It ought to have been a disaster. Aside from the lack of funds and structures, which left a great many would-be missionaries destitute and contributed to an alarmingly high death rate, the gift of tongues turned out not to be what those first believers imagined. A few cases of supposedly miraculous speech are recorded. At Mukti, in India, one Marathi girl who we are assured had no previous knowledge of English suddenly prayed in English, "idiomatically, distinctly and fluently." Sophia Hansen, a Pentecostal missionary in China, claimed that six months after her arrival in the country she was suddenly and miraculously given the Chinese language, albeit only for the purpose of preaching the Gospel. Multiple witnesses confirmed her story.[27] Whatever we make of such tales, they were exceptional. Most Pentecostal missionaries traveled the world, only to discover, devastatingly, that the people to whom they preached understood them no better than they understood themselves.

The truly remarkable thing is how little this disappointment daunted the movement's spirit. Some missionaries continued searching for the elusive tribe who might understand them, but most concluded that in fact they were not going to be understood. One missionary who took himself to India discovered on his arrival that, as he put it, his languages had changed. But he reflected,

> Whether or not I was speaking an Indian language in Los Angeles does not shake my faith or even cause me anxiety. I know that God was talking through me, and what it was He knew all about it, and that was quite enough for me. . . . I supposed He would let us talk to the natives of India in their own tongue, but He did not, and as far as I can see, will not . . . but will employ the gifts—such as wonderful signs of healing and other powers, that the heathen can see for themselves.

When he returned to the United States, he taught other would-be Pentecostal missionaries that there was no shortcut to language learning. By 1917, the newly formed Missionary Council of the Assemblies of God was requiring two years' preliminary language study from its recruits. Some Pentecostal students were still convinced that the Holy Spirit helped them in the ordinary grind of language learning. And the Spirit sometimes provided inspired understanding. One Pentecostal missionary in South Africa preached in English to Xhosa audiences, before his words were "interpreted" by a Xhosa preacher who himself spoke no English.[28]

Most of the converts whom these early Pentecostal missionaries actually made were other Protestant missionaries. Missionary networks linked to the holiness movement, like the China Inland Mission or the Christian and Missionary Alliance, were readily available entry points for Pentecostals. By converting missionaries who had already done the tedious linguistic groundwork, Pentecostals found that they could jump the language barrier after all. In 1906, an Azusa Street missionary heading to Jerusalem to test her gift of Arabic met and converted the British pastor of a Methodist church in Norway. He took Spirit-baptism back with him and made Oslo into ground zero for European Pentecostalism; Norwegian missionaries fanned out across four continents. In South Africa, where holiness-style revivalism was already well established, Pentecostals were pushing at an open door. John G. Lake—a convert of Parham's rather than of Azusa Street's—was first on the scene in 1908 and caused a stir by publicly embracing and kissing a black minister named Elias Letwaba. Letwaba would spend the next fifty years building up South African Pentecostalism.

Another story was unfolding closer to home. California had been Mexican territory until 1848, within living memory, and there were Hispanic converts at Azusa Street well placed to take the message south. A Pentecostal mission was established in Guatemala by 1911. One Mexican convert took the Gospel back to her home at Chihuahua, splitting the town's small Protestant community. Italian American Pentecostal missionaries went to the Italian immigrant communities in Argentina and Brazil from 1909 onward. São Paulo's Italian community was a million strong, and the church founded among them, the Congregation of Christ, is now one of Brazil's largest. The Swedish American Pentecostals who in 1910 were led by the Spirit to Belém, in the northern Brazilian state of Pará, had stonier ground to plow, but there was a small Swedish mission church there, where they met with a handful of enthusiasts to pray for revival. By the time they were thrown out, they had picked up enough Portuguese to manage, and Belém became a mission center for the country. The most dramatic success in Latin America, however, was sparked not by Azusa Street but by Pandita Sarasvati Ramabai's revival in India. When Willis and May Louise

Hoover, American Methodist missionaries in Chile, read about the Indian revival in 1909, they prayed to emulate it. The alarmed Methodist hierarchy condemned the ensuing ecstatic revival, and the Hoovers left to form the Methodist Pentecostal Church. Within five years, their church had twelve hundred members in twelve cities. Chile's main Pentecostal churches today are its descendants.

One reason for the Chilean movement's success was that—unlike the churches that trace their descent from Azusa Street—it never taught a strict doctrine of "initial evidence." That doctrine, which Parham had formulated, held that speaking in tongues was not merely a gift of the Spirit but an infallible sign of Spirit-baptism. That is, anyone who has never spoken in tongues has not received the baptism of the Holy Spirit. Even if redeemed and destined for salvation, such a person is something of a second-class Christian. Non-Pentecostals have always loathed this doctrine, not least because nobody likes being a spiritual also-ran. It has also been controversial within Pentecostalism. Seymour himself eventually rejected it, one of the reasons why he became alienated from the emerging Pentecostal establishment. Modern Pentecostalism has also left it behind in many parts of the world. Speaking in tongues has faded in southern African Pentecostalism and has never been a feature of the Pentecostal-style churches of Korea. Those examples suggest that tongue-speaking is not in fact necessary for Pentecostalism to succeed as a missionary movement. So, if speaking in tongues was neither a missionary nor a theological necessity, why did early Pentecostals make it so central to their life? The answer lies not in the theory of tongue-speaking but in the experience.

The act of uttering a stream of incomprehensible syllables might be of limited theological significance, but the experience is profound, both for speakers and for hearers. For hearers, it is a sharp challenge. The initial-evidence doctrine is implicit in the act itself. If you have never spoken in tongues yourself (and I should add that I have not), hearing someone else do so sets that person apart. It sounds like evidence of an entirely new spiritual experience, a conversation from which you are excluded. You may feel alienated and decide that this eruption of incomprehensibility is evidence of mental imbalance or of malign spiritual forces. Alternatively, you may long to share the experience. A middle position, treating tongues with indifference, is hard to maintain when actually facing the phenomenon.

Those who longed for it often had a long wait, and for some it never came.[29] A few received it in isolation. It was and remains much more common, however, to "catch" tongues from another speaker. There were certainly cases of deliberate, conscious attempts by believers to churn out the best attempt at gibberish they could manage. This could be deliberate fakery, but it was sometimes also recommended as a route to the real thing. If you can trundle along the runway fast enough, the Spirit may put enough of a breath under your wings to lift you into the air.

When liftoff came, it was and is, all witnesses agree, an astonishing, transformative experience. The speech itself was a mere side effect. "My tongue," Agnes Ozman said, "began to get thick and . . . my mouth was filled with a rush of words." An early Azusa Street convert named Burke recalled that "something began to get hold of my jaw bones and tongue." For both of them, the point was not the sounds they made but that "a great joy came into my soul," "a music band of a thousand instruments was set up within me." Both used the image of floodwaters. "I just let the praise come as it would in the new language given, with floodgates of glory wide open," said Ozman. The Spirit, Burke said, "came like the outpouring of water on the crown of my head and it went through my entire body to the very tips of my toes and fingers and my heart seemed to expand ten times larger."[30] Others used the biblical image of fire burning within them, or added a modern twist by talking of electricity. The South African missionary John G. Lake received "shocks of power" that "increased in rapidity and voltage." One North Carolina Pentecostal received "such a shock from heaven's battery that he could not stop talking in an unknown tongue all the way home." An Azusa Street convert who felt the Spirit's power shoot through him like "electric needles" wrote that the experience left him as "sweet and clean" as if he had been through a washing machine.[31]

Tongue-speaking matters not for itself but for the inner experience that accompanies it: an immediate, ecstatic, and settled sense of God's presence and power. We have seen throughout this book that Protestantism is about the sometimes reckless pursuit of an unmediated love affair with God. In that sense, Pentecostalism is profoundly and authentically Protestant. The Pentecostal missionaries who took their tongues across the world did so not chiefly because they believed that they would be understood but because they *felt* empowered. It was a feeling that brimmed over from them in words they could not understand.

Protestants have often been uneasy about wordless, contemplative prayer or set, liturgical prayer, seeing this kind of spirituality as elitist, idolatrous, or hypocritical. Nineteenth-century Anglophone Protestantism in particular was a religion of the plain unvarnished English Word. Bursting into "words" that were not words was perhaps the only way such Protestants could explore this spiritual territory. A clear sign of this was how readily tongue speech slipped into music, a practice with no explicit biblical backing. On April 9, 1906, the very night the Azusa Street revival began, one of the first tongue-speakers sang in her new language to an improvised tune. "Singing in the Spirit," "singing in tongues," "the heavenly choir," and "the heavenly chorus" were everyday matters at Azusa Street. Some listeners found the tuneful harmony of unrehearsed, independently inspired song to be the single most persuasive proof that the whole revival was the work of the Holy Spirit. Describing this singing, the revival's most important chronicler emphasized that

> No one had preached it. The Lord had sovereignly bestowed it. . . . The effect was wonderful on the people. It brought a heavenly atmosphere as though the angels themselves were present and joining with us. . . . It seemed to still criticism and opposition, and it was hard even for wicked men to gainsay or ridicule.[32]

This was not about preaching to the nations but about joining in a rapturous experience of God's presence.

What carried Pentecostalism around the world was a transporting experience that could manifest itself in any number of ways: speaking, singing, writing, gesturing, trembling, dancing, laughing, or falling insensate. Whether described as flood, fire, electricity, or dynamite, it was experienced as a taste of heaven, and it could radically change lives. Pentecostalism's achievement is to have harnessed the power of that inner experience to surge across the planet. Half a billion converts suggest it is a hard offer to beat.

Becoming a Global Faith

The early Pentecostals attracted plenty of opponents. Their wild abandon symbolized disorder, immorality, and madness, and their "demonic imitation of the apostolic gift of tongues" looked to many like the devil's work.[33] It did not help that women were so prominent in the leadership, nor that so many early Pentecostals were rootless people with no education or social standing. There were scandals; this was and remains a movement in which ambitious preachers can rise quickly by raw talent and without oversight, with predictable results. Worst of all, for those early American critics, Pentecostals were multiracial. Without exception, the Pentecostals were thrown out of the established churches. The Fundamentalists, in the depths of their own disarray in the late 1920s, still anathematized "tongues-talkers and faith healers."[34] Meeting places and homes were pelted with stones and glass, or even burned. In the Appalachians, some preachers were tarred and feathered.

Slowly, unwillingly, they formed themselves into denominations, splitting along both doctrinal and racial lines in the process. Their emerging structures helped to stamp out some scandals but also clamped down on the movement's exuberant creativity. By midcentury, the Pentecostal denominations seemed to have settled down into a niche. Their insistence on the central importance of tongues was a wall separating them from the remainder of the Christian world. It had given them their identity and allowed them to endure, but it meant they had very little to offer outsiders.

Then, in the 1950s, as America's mainstream Protestant churches were searching so earnestly for "authenticity," Pentecostal-type manifestations began to bubble to the surface again. Individual cases had been quietly popping up for some time before one caught public attention. Once again, it happened in Los Angeles. In July 1959, Dennis Bennett, Episcopalian rector in the suburb of Van Nuys, was leading prayers when "my tongue tripped, just as it might when you are trying to recite a tongue twister, and I began to speak in a new language!"[35] The revival that followed split the church. A generation earlier, Bennett and his converts would have been thrown out and would have either joined a Pentecostal church or set up their own. Now, however, he was merely moved to an Episcopalian mission in inner-city Seattle, where he continued preaching the power of spiritual gifts. As the movement spread within the Episcopal Church, bishops were reported to be "keenly interested." Soon this "charismatic renewal" received the same wary, measured acceptance in Methodist and Presbyterian churches.

Ironically, the now-established Pentecostal churches were less sanguine, reluctant to admit that the Spirit would work through the dead "Churchianity" of the mainline denominations. The leading Assemblies of God minister David du Plessis was expelled from his church for supporting the ecumenical charismatic renewal, although he was eventually reinstated. In 1964, du Plessis even attended the Roman Catholic Church's Second Vatican Council as an ecumenical observer, which most of his former colleagues would have seen as a capitulation to Antichrist. His instincts were not wrong. In 1965, the council ended the use of Latin in the liturgy for most Catholics, so worship suddenly no longer involved uttering syllables that most believers did not understand. Less than two years later, a student prayer weekend at a Catholic university in the United States took an unexpected turn. "Some praised God in new languages," one witness recalled; "others quietly wept for joy." The movement spread to other Catholic universities and then into some parishes. Once again, there was circumspect support from the hierarchy and even, in 1975, very cautious and limited encouragement from Pope Paul VI.[36]

In this way, Pentecostal and charismatic Christianity has become a part of the mainstream in Europe and North America. It has also, so far, remained a relatively minor player. Elsewhere, the story has been sharply different. We have already seen the growth of renewalist churches, some of them deeply indebted to Pentecostalism, in modern China and Korea. In Africa, the "charismatic renewal" arrived in the 1960s, just as the European colonial empires were disappearing. Many of the newly independent countries nationalized schooling, and because schools had been the backbone of the Christian denominations' presence in much of Africa, their networks were badly weakened. Into the gap moved cross-denominational Christian education organizations such as Scripture Union, ready conduits for charismatic renewal. Before long, these Western-led forms of Pentecostalism were overtaken by a throng of competing homegrown churches. In 2010, it was estimated that there were more than 177 million Pentecostals in Africa, spread between independent churches, classic Pentecostal denominations, and "charismatic" movements in the old denominations. The 2010 study estimated that 47 percent of South Africans, 48 percent of Zimbabweans, and 36 percent of Ghanaians were Pentecostals. In Nigeria, the proportion was slightly lower, at 30 percent, but that still comes to more than forty-eight million people.[37]

Africa's total is pipped by Latin America's estimated 181 million. Many of those are "charismatic" Catholics, but the dramatic story of Latin American religion in the past half century is the growth of Pentecostal-led Protestantism. Much of the world still thinks of Latin America as Catholic. In the early twentieth century, the region's Protestant population was indeed tiny and mostly non-Hispanic. By 1935, there was a modest Protestant presence of around two and a half million. Thirty years later, this had swollen to fifteen million, of whom around two-thirds were Pentecostals, and a surge was beginning. By 1985, there were around forty million Protestants, three-quarters of them Pentecostals. Polling in 2014 indicated that an astonishing 19 percent of Latin America's people are now Protestants, a proportion that rises to 26 percent in Brazil and over 40 percent in some Central American countries. Over half of those Protestants, 10 percent of the region's entire population, were converts from Catholicism. Of those converts, 81 percent cited the desire for a personal relationship with God as a decisive factor in their conversion.[38] This wave of Latin American converts is one of the most dramatic religious shifts in modern history.

Certain social patterns recur throughout Pentecostalism's global expansion. Converts tend to be young, and they tend to cluster; Pentecostalism is nothing if not communal. Small communities sometimes struggle for years to put down roots and only begin rapid expansion once they have an established presence. Converts are also disproportionately likely to have moved from the region of their birth, often to burgeoning megacities. These factors go some way to explaining why

Pentecostalism has thrived during half a century of dislocating economic and social change across much of the planet but struggled amid the more muted social shifts of modern Europe and North America. Pentecostalism has become the religion of the uprooted: an instant community blithely indifferent to ethnicity whose thousands of varieties include something for everyone.

Pentecostalism also offers very practical benefits: power to defeat demons and heal the sick. Many modern Christians have downplayed or allegorized the Bible's talk of demons and condemned the spirit beliefs common to many cultures as superstition. But Pentecostals expect to wrestle with demons in prayer and have happily absorbed spirit beliefs of all kinds. Large majorities of Pentecostals in Latin America and Africa testify to having witnessed exorcisms and healings; one study of South Africa's Zion Christian Church found that every single believer questioned claimed to have witnessed miraculous healings. One of the sparks for Pentecostal growth in 1980s Nicaragua was a much-repeated account of a Sandinista soldier's being raised from the dead. In the 1970s, Chile saw a bizarre spate of dental miracles, in which sufferers from toothache prayed and received fillings. One missionary explained that the fillings "just seem to grow there overnight or over a period of time. . . . This is generally the first thing to be shown to foreign visitors, a parade of young people pass by with open mouths." What was actually going on here is less important than the mood it exemplifies. The longing for divine healing may seem simple enough—toothache makes for heartfelt prayer—but healing is not merely a medical transaction. It is a spiritual event whose inner blessing can be life-changing even if the bodily effects turn out to be disappointing or illusory. Bodily need can be a route to the transformative inner encounter with the Holy Spirit that has been at Pentecostalism's heart from the beginning.[39]

There is a historic irony here. Early Protestants disdained Catholicism for its miracle-mongering, took delight in debunking miracle claims, and argued that the age of miracles had passed with the first apostles. That claim—that God once performed miracles but has now stopped—was always odd and seems chiefly to have been polemical opportunism, a way to discredit one of Catholicism's most potentially attractive features. It also came at a cost. Protestants found it hard to defend biblical miracles from the pervasive skepticism they had deliberately nurtured. One possible result, the Enlightenment's drift to unbelief, we have already seen. The alternative, which Pentecostalism has taken, is to free miracles from their biblical confinement and once again expect them here and now. So while sixteenth-century European Protestants converted Catholics by denying miracles, twentieth-century Latin American Protestants have converted Catholics by offering miracles with more verve than a bureaucratic church with a global reputation to protect can possibly match.

The Politics of Pentecostalism

Pentecostals' unabashed supernaturalism can seem crass to outsiders, but there is another, more serious criticism. Pentecostals, especially but not only in Latin America, are widely accused of supporting right-wing, imperialist, neocolonialist, or authoritarian political movements. The truth is more interesting than that.

From their beginnings, Pentecostals (unlike Fundamentalists) made a virtue of being apolitical. As one historian puts it,

> One can read through the Pentecostal journals that appeared between the early 1930s and the late 1940s . . . and get no sense that any events took place in the world other than the wonder-working, soul-saving miracles of the Holy Ghost.[40]

Some early American Pentecostals refused to vote at all. Others reluctantly took part when there was a particularly important issue at stake, such as Prohibition. As one early leader bluntly put it, most simply believed that "politics is rotten."[41] Its corruption and compromises offered nothing of value or interest to God's people. This is not the principled separatism of Anabaptists or Jehovah's Witnesses, for whom refusing to touch this world's anti-Christian regimes is a matter of conscience. Instead, it is a grimly realistic variant of Luther's doctrine of the two kingdoms. The kingdom of this world is legitimate, but in a sinful world it has little to offer Christians. It simply does not matter very much.

In Latin America, this principle was reinforced by self-interest. The region's defining twentieth-century ideological struggle was between Marxism and right-wing parties that claimed the mantle of Catholicism. The small Protestant minority made a virtue of being above the fray. Across the continent, Pentecostals were advised by their pastors to limit their political participation to voting and to limit their participation in trade unions to membership. A survey taken during Chile's most politically febrile period, the presidency of the socialist Salvador Allende, found that 60 percent of Pentecostals believed that "political participation did not really lead anywhere," and that Pentecostals were less likely than the general population to read newspapers and more likely to disdain regional or national politics as a trade in lies, controversy, and hatred.[42]

In 1973, Chile's Marxist experiment was abruptly ended by a coup. Augusto Pinochet swiftly became one of South America's nastiest dictators. In 1974, a joint declaration by thirty-two Chilean Pentecostal and evangelical denominations stated that his coup was "God's answer to the prayers of all the believers who recognized that Marxism was the expression of satanic power." Pinochet repaid the compliment, becoming an active patron of the Pentecostal Methodist Church. He used its huge Jotabeche Church in Santiago as the site of his annual national thanksgiving service and even asked its pastor to serve as a minister in his government.[43] All this in an era when many Latin American Catholics were embracing a Marxist-inflected liberation theology and opposing authoritarian regimes throughout the region, often at fearsome personal risk.

Hence the accusation that Pentecostals' political neutrality is a sham—the same accusation leveled at dictators' Protestant friends in South Africa and Korea. Refusal to participate while working meekly with whoever happens to be in power is not "neutral." It systematically favors oppressive and authoritarian regimes. The presumption that politics is corrupt is itself inherently right-wing, because many left-wing policies depend on active government intervention. In 2014, nearly twice as many Latin American Catholics as Protestants thought it was important to lobby for government activity to support the poor, and significantly more Catholics than Protestants (50 percent as against 37 percent) emphasized the importance of charitable support for the poor. By contrast, 47 percent of Protestants but only 24 percent of Catholics argued that the best way to help the poor was to bring them to Christ.[44]

In 1986, the Brazilian Anglican Robinson Cavalcanti, a future bishop, said that "the irrelevance of Protestantism [is] so great that, if the Rapture occurred today, Brazilian society would take a week to notice that the believers were no longer there."[45] It was meant as a bitter criticism, and that itself is revealing. Since the eighteenth century, European and European-derived societies have done something unusual in human history: they have paid sustained attention to politics. Mass movements of all kinds have proposed political solutions to human problems, solutions that have turned out to vary from the effective to the catastrophic. It is that context which makes Pentecostals' lack of interest in pursuing such solutions look irresponsible. This is their most profoundly countercultural stance: they simply do not particularly value social relevance. When they engage politically—and they do, increasingly so—it is on other grounds.

The alignment between Pentecostals and right-wing, anti-Marxist movements is real, but there is more to it than meets the eye. As the rhetoric of the declaration for Pinochet in 1974 suggests, many Pentecostals have a deep-seated suspicion of Marxism, one that is strongly reciprocated. In other words, while they will not be lured into politics by utopian hopes, they certainly can be mobilized to oppose specific evils, a category in which they would put Marxism's totalizing claims. Being grateful that God had used Pinochet to defeat a satanic threat did not necessarily mean approving of the man himself, and indeed the pastor whom Pinochet invited into his government refused the offer. Nor is Marxism the only perceived threat. Nigerian Pentecostals have been drawn into politics by fear of Islamization. Under the Nigerian dictators Ibrahim Babangida (1985–93) and Sani Abacha (1993–98), who were both Muslims, several Nigerian states adopted sharia law, and there were rumors that the government was facilitating attacks on Christians. The confident assertion by a senior Muslim cleric in 1989 that Muslims would never permit Nigeria to have a non-Muslim ruler provoked the Christian Association of Nigeria to call for "properly born-again Christians, filled with the Holy Spirit," to stand for election.[46] You do not need to agree with Pentecostals' anti-Marxist or anti-Islamic views to see the point. In both cases, Pentecostals entered the political arena not because they were advancing a right-wing agenda as such but because they were facing ideologies that they feared (rightly or wrongly) posed an existential threat.

By contrast, in the 1980s, Nicaragua, one of Latin America's most Protestant countries, was governed by the soft-Marxist Sandinistas, who were facing an insurgency from the U.S.-backed contra rebels. Most Pentecostal leaders loudly condemned the contras, proclaimed their apolitical stance, and avowed loyalty to the regime. Their chief concern was neither revolution nor counterrevolution but being able to preach and enact their Gospel untroubled by the kingdom of this world. The Sandinistas, as one scholar puts it, "found it hard to understand why, at a time when the poor needed to defend their gains against the United States and counter-revolution, so many were spending their nights clapping and singing to no apparent purpose."[47] But they were willing to permit it.

Religious liberty of this kind has been Pentecostals' key, nonnegotiable political demand from the beginning. It is limited and self-centered. They do not pay much attention to wider society's welfare so long as their community has its safe space. In that sense, it is easy for most oppressive regimes to buy Pentecostal loyalty. But in a one-party state, such as modern China, demanding a safe and genuinely independent religious space is highly subversive. In this regard, modern Pentecostals have faithfully followed the trail blazed by the Nazi-era Confessing Church. They have not openly opposed repressive regimes but have pretty stoutly attempted to defend their own domain. As with the Confessing Church, this stance is not heroic, but it has integrity and even a degree of honor.

Pentecostals, then, are loyal to repressive regimes, but only insofar as those regimes are willing to leave them alone. But they do also have a genuine affinity with center-right socioeconomic policies. Because they teach that the Holy Spirit empowers believers, they naturally emphasize individual or communal self-help rather than secular government initiatives. The stereotypical Pentecostal conversion produces moral transformation: new believers stop drinking and gambling, focus on providing for their families, and internalize an ethic of purposeful labor. The practical benefits that arise from these changes are taken to be blessings. A 2014 study in Brazil suggested that Protestant conversion is indeed associated with increased income, especially for less educated or nonwhite Brazilians. This may reflect Protestant churches' role as economic self-help networks as much as any ethical transformation. Although a higher proportion of Latin American Catholics approve in the abstract of charitable work to fight poverty, a much higher proportion of Protestants actually engages in charitable work of some sort themselves.[48] It makes theological sense. A community empowered by the Holy Spirit ought to be able to solve its own problems more effectively than godless and corrupt outsiders. As one Nigerian Pentecostal pastor put it in 2010,

> People make government too powerful in our country. They do not realize that the most powerful form of government is self-government. When God gives you a revelation of who you are, that is where change begins.[49]

This focus on private initiative and individual moral renewal may be compatible with authoritarian as well as with democratic center-right politics, but that does not make it illegitimate.

Yet some modern social problems cannot be solved by private initiative. Since the 1990s, Pentecostals worldwide have gradually been coming to terms with this and engaging more openly in politics, in their own distinctive way. They begin from the conviction that the Holy Spirit has called and empowered them, and therefore that the single most direct and practical way to effect political change is prayer. They know from their own lives that they can overcome demonic forces by God's power, and are ready to see corruption or other nebulous evils as literal demons that need to be confronted and cast out in the same way. In 1990, a Nigerian Pentecostal pastor published *A Call to Prayer for Nigeria,* summoning his readers to join him in

> the battle of translating the victory of Jesus over the Devil into the everyday, natural realities of our personal lives and also of our political, religious, economic and social systems. . . . Prayer—militant, strategic and aggressive prayer—must be our weapon of warfare at this time.

Since then, national bodies like Prayer for the Nation, Intercessors for Nigeria, and Nigeria Prays have emerged. According to Intercessors for Nigeria's founder, "When you pray prophetically, you are in the place of governmental authority. . . . It can change laws. It can cancel what politicians have said." Nigeria Prays even claims that prayer has averted civil war.[50]

Political prayer is more than a plea for God to intervene. It is itself a political act. Like a street demonstration, it asserts a community's concerns and deepens the participants' own commitment. In the early years of the twenty-first century, Pentecostal prayer camps—hybrids between demonstrations and revivalist meetings—became a regular feature of Ghanaian politics. In 2009, the newly elected president, John Mills, himself a Pentecostal, said, "I wish Ghana were a prayer camp," with the whole nation joined in one spiritual purpose. Not everyone agreed, but before long the opposition party was organizing prayer camps of its own.[51]

Once people are praying, they usually also start to act. Pentecostals' classic critique of politics is that it is a rotten business. In many countries, this is not a theological claim but a statement of the blindingly obvious. Pentecostals' political ambition, then, is to pull their countries neither to the left nor to the right but toward heaven. As in the personal, so in the political: what is needed is moral renewal and the Spirit's power. This means electing politicians who are personally morally irreproachable, and ideally ones who are Pentecostal. As one 1990s Nigerian Pentecostal pastor argued, "Politics . . . is not dirty; it is the players that are dirty. If you have good people in politics, it will change the nation."[52] In much of Africa, political candidates now commonly make a virtue of their Pentecostal piety. The deeper point, however, is not to put people in office but to sacralize a nation's political culture. In 1991, the Pentecostal Frederick Chiluba was elected president of Zambia. He promptly and controversially declared that Zambia was a "Christian nation," an assertion that was incorporated into the 1996 Zambian constitution. For Chiluba, it was both a reflection of his personal commitment and a means of ensuring God's blessing for his country. It also helped him to embrace, on Zambia's behalf, the purgative moral rigor of a neoliberal structural-adjustment program.

This ambition for national moral renewal strikes a chord in many modern democracies, where it is easy to change politicians but much harder to change the political culture. Yet the problems are obvious. Hypocrisy is easily mistaken for piety; piety is a poor substitute for competence; and power corrupts. Pentecostal politicians have not in fact been noticeably more honest than their rivals. Chiluba tried to cling to office beyond his mandated term. In Côte d'Ivoire, President Laurent Gbagbo, who explicitly linked his political movement to Pentecostalism, lost an election to a Muslim opponent in 2010. He rejected the result and fought a brief, nasty civil war that ended with his ejection and indictment by the International Criminal Court. Pentecostal churches elsewhere have been drawn uncomfortably close to ruling parties. Shortly before Nigeria's 2011 election, President Goodluck Jonathan was invited to a million-strong rally of the Redeemed Christian Church of God, addressed the audience, and knelt for a blessing from the pastor, a photo opportunity that made its way onto most national front pages.[53] As Pentecostals have always said, politics is a mucky business, and it is hard to play the game without getting dirty. But if Pentecostalism becomes a factional identity, it risks losing much of its power.

Pentecostalism's unique selling point is that it values the personal and the private over the political and the public. The comparison with its historic rival, Marxism, is instructive. Marxism calls the poor to struggle for a future revolution that is defined by public events. It has tended to spread in the workplace and other public spheres, and to be led by men. It dismisses religion as the opium of the people, a "false consciousness" capable of luring working people away from their own true interests. On this view, Pentecostalism is the crack cocaine of the people, a fiendishly strong drug that herds the poor into conformity with the right-wing forces that exploit them. By contrast, Pentecostalism offers neither a chance to sacrifice yourself for a future revolution nor the proverbial pie in the sky when you die, but baptism by the Holy Spirit today. It spreads in the private sphere, through households and families, and very often through women's agency. It offers solutions to the actual troubles that dominate most human lives: health, the security of families, drug or alcohol dependence, money worries. In practice, it does not solve all of these problems all of the time, but it comes close enough that for millions of people it looks more credible than any secular utopia. For underpinning all of these other blessings, and giving them their value, it offers a love affair with God, consummated in ecstatic worship. It promises not to revolutionize the world in the future but to change your life here and now.

The Protestant Future

Protestantism has had an eventful first five centuries and is not yet settling down into a dignified middle age. If anything, it is embarking on a footloose adolescence. This makes it a good moment to tackle the traditional adolescent problem: identity. What, actually, is Protestantism?

It is not a doctrine or a theology. Defining it that way is usually an attempt to exclude people, by arguing, for example, that anti-Trinitarians, Quakers, liberals, or Pentecostals have crossed some red line that has been drawn for the purpose. Nor is it a purely genealogical category, of people who share a common descent from Martin Luther's act of defiance but are now split into such a wild variety of branches that their only connection is historical. Some movements that are clearly descended from Protestantism have equally clearly become something different. Mormons, for example, have overlaid so much that is fundamentally new onto their Protestant heritage that they cannot meaningfully be called Protestant. Or, to take a darker case, there was not much Protestantism left in the Nazi-era "German Christians." Protestantism helped to seed all these movements, as it helped to seed a great deal that we now think of as purely secular: rationalism, capitalism, Communism, democracy, political liberalism, feminism, pluralism. Even some forms of atheism have Protestant fingerprints all over them. But if we stretch the word to encompass everything that bears its influence, Protestantism will embrace almost the entire world.

My argument throughout this book has been that Protestants are best treated as a family: a sprawling, diverse, and extremely quarrelsome family, to be sure, but one that is tied together by more than accidents of birth. As in many families, similar traits keep recurring from generation to generation. These characteristics are hard to pin down, but you know them when you see them. Protestants are divided from one another by their beliefs but tied together by a deeper unity of mood and emotion. Their tradition began in Martin Luther's ravishing love affair with the God he met in the Bible. It was a love for which he was willing to sweep aside any tradition or power structure that stood in his way. Since his day, Protestants have pursued that love in radically different ways: individually or through institutions, intellectually or emotionally, tolerantly or violently, calmly or restlessly, apocalyptically or idealistically, working within older traditions or radically rejecting them. Often that old flame has been reduced to a simmer or doused altogether, sometimes it has blazed beyond any control, but it is the same fire. To understand Protestantism's enormous impact on our world, we need to understand the restless burning it has kindled and rekindled in generations of believers.

Old Quarrels and New

So where is this fire going next? Predicting the future is a fools' game that everyone plays. Of course we will not get it right, but the themes and patterns we have seen play out over five centuries suggest some parameters. None of these guesses will be entirely correct, and some will be wildly wrong. But what follows is a description, not of what I want to happen, but of what I think will happen whether I like it or not.

Protestantism's formal and informal divisions are not about to heal. Protestants will not run out of things to argue about, and while some arguments will simmer down, others will flare up. Formal denominational structures will continue to weaken. There will be more independent, self-governing congregations, and where denominations hold together, they will do so by becoming loose confederations. The reality of a democratic age is that churches are answerable to the footloose believers who fund them. Those that try to deny this fact are swimming against the tide.

Proliferating divisions will continue to distress many Protestants but will not damage their prospects. From the nineteenth-century United States to modern Africa, Protestantism has thrived most when it is most divided, with sects and preachers vying for converts. Stagnation or decline is much more likely when a single church dominates, as in much of Protestant Europe, or where several churches are brought together into formal or informal alliances in which they avoid competing with one another, as in America's "mainline" or the Church of Christ in China before 1949.

Division can become dangerous if rivalry turns into violent hostility, but in this next period of Protestant history, there will not be much effort to impose orthodoxies by force. Dominant denominations or movements will not be able to call on the power of the state to support them against their rivals, and few will want to try. Historically, many Protestants have wanted to make their own views normative for entire societies, whether by imposing civil penalties for blasphemy or bans on alcohol. Protestant political activism will certainly continue, but not in this form. Few Protestants will have the stomach for forcing their own moral disciplines onto entire societies, often preferring to use those disciplines to differentiate themselves. Where they do campaign for coercive legislation, they will do so on secular grounds. This withdrawal from coercion will only make intra-Protestant arguments more intractable.

The main driver of continued division will be Protestantism's knack for adaptation. Protestantism will continue to fit itself promiscuously to cultures and subcultures across the globe. Nobody will like all of the results, many of which will simply entrench divisions that are already wearyingly familiar. But Protestantism's arguments never stay in the same spot for long.

In the late twentieth and early twenty-first centuries, a knot of issues around gender and sexual ethics has been bitterly divisive. In many countries, social norms on these issues have changed with astonishing speed, and Protestants have had to scramble to keep up. This has been all the harder because the changes have not been spread evenly across the world. The resulting, highly charged debates have created the impression that contemporary Protestantism is irrevocably divided between repressive, patriarchal dinosaurs and wild, freewheeling libertines. In fact, the gaps between the various sides are less significant than the speed with which the whole debate's center of gravity has shifted.

Since the eighteenth century, most Protestant churches, especially the most energetic among them, have been predominantly female.

Women in congregations have sometimes outnumbered men by three to two or more. Until the past half century, women were generally excluded from leadership roles, but that pattern has now largely collapsed. It is true that many churches continue, formally and informally, to restrict the central role in leading public worship to men. Given Protestants' mulish stubbornness when challenged, those restrictions will not change fast and may for a time become points of defiant countercultural pride. Even so, Protestantism's institutional patriarchy is being hollowed out. At every other level of Protestant churches, the numbers and energy of the female majority will make itself felt. Female leadership in everything apart from formal public worship has been the norm for Pentecostalism from the beginning and will increasingly become the norm for Protestantism as a whole. Some Protestants, men and women, will continue to worry that their religion is being feminized. This is a legitimate concern for a religion that aspires to convert men as well as women, but there is no reason to suspect that being female dominated will harm Protestantism. It may, indeed, be an excellent adaptation to a changing world.

On sexual ethics, the gaps are also less dramatic than they appear, because Protestants find it hard to defy social consensus. Protestant preachers who, for example, join the Roman Catholic Church in opposing artificial contraception are inciting their congregations to ignore them or to defect to more realistic rivals. An impassioned moral and theological argument was once made against contraception, but the cause is lost in most of the world. Most Protestants have given up fighting it.

A similar transition is well under way on the one sexual issue that we might imagine would be nonnegotiable for Christians. The New Testament does not record Jesus having much to say about sexual ethics, but he adamantly opposed divorce, and especially remarriage after divorce. Protestants have questioned that standard from the beginning, often allowing for divorce in cases of domestic violence or even simple adultery. In many contemporary societies, even this watered-down version of the traditional standard has become almost impossible to apply. Most modern Protestants find themselves holding a middle position: disapproving of or lamenting divorce in the abstract while acknowledging it as a social fact and accepting the reality of remarriage. Sometimes this is done joyfully, sometimes grudgingly, but rarely with demands that couples separate or that children be treated as illegitimate. For good or ill, much of the world now lives in an age of serial monogamy. Protestantism has had to get used to the fact.

Having swallowed that camel, it will not strain at a few further gnats, although it may take a little time to digest them. One longstanding issue that has not gone away is polygamy. Christians have since ancient times insisted on exclusive monogamy as the only legitimate form of marriage and have developed theological and ethical arguments for this, but the biblical basis for it is pretty shaky. A couple of New Testament verses require Christian ministers to be monogamous, and the rest of the New Testament seems to assume that monogamy is normal, but the Old Testament is full of divinely approved polygamists. As we have seen, the question has periodically resurfaced through Protestantism's history, even if we discount the example of Mormonism. Luther burned his fingers on the issue. John Milton wrote a treatise defending polygamy but thought better of publishing it. Various radical and utopian groups have practiced it. The main reason it has been rare among Protestants is simply that it has been rare in most of their host societies. In parts of Africa and Asia, however, polygamy is a well-established social reality, and the rise of Protestantism in these regions has made the question unavoidable.

It was a missionaries' dilemma for decades. In 1888, the Anglican Communion's international assembly, the Lambeth Conference, hewed as best it could to a traditionalist line: polygamists cannot be baptized unless they renounce all but one of their wives. This amounted to a demand that women be cast off and their children disowned, although it was accepted that wives might be baptized while remaining in their plural marriages. The predictable result was that polygamous converts withdrew to form churches of their own, such as the United Methodist Church in Nigeria. Twentieth-century Anglicans struggled to reconcile their monogamous principles with the social realities missionaries were confronting. The official line progressively softened. The 1988 Lambeth Conference finally accepted that polygamists may be baptized but forbade them to contract further plural marriages after baptism.[1] Even this line will prove hard to defend. Protestant converts who do not wish to abandon polygamous social norms will find churches to endorse this, just as converts in societies where divorce and remarriage are common expect churches to work with that reality. South Africa's Nazaretha Church admits polygamists to high office and has publicly defended President Jacob Zuma's polygamy.[2] Some churches will resist this pressure. Some will succumb reluctantly to it. Others will proudly embrace it. Converts will choose what suits them best.

At present, the single most explosive divide is over homosexuality. The speed of change in the Western democracies has been astonishing. Many countries have moved from criminalization to full legal equality within half a century, with a parallel shift in cultural norms from loathing to an almost banal acceptance. Churches have struggled to find their voice. The majority have tried to maintain their traditional condemnations, some enthusiastically, some simply wishing that these distasteful people would go away. A minority have embraced gay rights and developed theologies to fit. Most Protestants in societies that accept gay rights will eventually—over a generation or two—find ways of coming to terms with that reality, whether cheerfully or grudgingly. Some will continue to hold out, making a virtue of being countercultural, bolstered by links with societies around the world where gay rights have as yet gained little ground. But the reality is that both sides of this argument are driven by society, not theology. As long as some societies accept gay rights while others find them anathema, Protestants will be divided, in roughly the same proportions and for roughly the same reasons.

Are Protestants, then, doomed simply to tag along behind social shifts, finding justifications for them after the fact? Very often, yes. We have seen plenty of occasions when Protestants have embraced the beliefs their host societies needed, from the God-given status of slavery in the American South to the divine summons to battle on all sides of World War I. But Protestantism is more than a vessel waiting to be filled. There are some social norms it revolts at. In contemporary disputes over sexual ethics, the issue of abortion stands out. Abortion is now socially normalized in much of the world, but few even of the most liberal or pro-feminist Protestants have been able to bring themselves to accept the practice. If they support legal abortion, it tends to be on the grounds of minimizing harm. The breadth of the antiabortion consensus is particularly striking because it has such weak biblical foundations. It is a moral intuition, not a textual deduction. It seems unlikely either that that intuition will falter or that the broader move toward legal abortion around the world will slow.

This issue is a reminder that Protestants can discover and pursue ethical principles apart from the rest of society. Sometimes they do so believing that they have history on their side, but the self-conscious Protestant attempt to get prophetically out in front of history has a mixed track record. Slave-trade abolitionism, or the antiapartheid cause, have been vindicated by time. Alcohol prohibition, or the attempt to create "religionless Christianity," not so much. Protestants will keep on trying to embrace the future. Some will make promises of a "second Reformation," a phrase that has surfaced repeatedly through Protestant history and, like most sequels, is a reliable marker of a lack of any real ideas.

Protestants' thoughts about the future, however, will mainly be apocalyptic in mood. One might imagine that predictions of Christ's imminent return would, by now, be salted with a recognition that it might not happen just yet—indeed, that Christianity's history may still only be getting started. But Protestants have a poor track record of thinking that way, and this is not about to change. Our individual intuition that we each stand at the crux of world history is too strong, and is only reinforced by the Protestant doctrine that we all stand directly before God. The secular world's all-too-plausible apocalyptic anxieties, from climate change and nuclear weapons to the impact of artificial intelligence, will continue to lend credence to this pattern of Protestant thought. It will lead some Protestants to withdraw in despair from society, others to engage urgently with it, and a few to try to precisely predict or, worse, to precipitate the coming end.

That is a perennial theme, but what new causes will animate and divide the next generation of Protestants? My guess is that some Protestants will rediscover the spiritual importance of food. Protestantism is unusual among world religions in making no dietary prescriptions of any kind, although many churches still frown on alcohol and the Seventh-day Adventists go further. There are almost too many reasons for more Protestants to be drawn to dietary self-regulation. Fasting and self-denial have ample biblical justification, are perennial spiritual disciplines, and are also potent marks of identity. In consumer societies, they have a countercultural cachet, and where Protestants are competing with other religious groups, they are ways to assert recognizable piety. Because Protestants do not like managing their piety with calendars, self-denial is less likely to mean cycles of temporary fasts than indefinite regimes of self-discipline: in particular, full or partial vegetarianism, a practice whose modern history is entwined with Protestantism's.[3] This may be justified on health grounds, as a way of honoring the bodies God gave us. It may be justified with reference to the Old Testament's dietary laws, for which some Protestants have always hankered. It may be justified on the grounds of the environmental damage or the use of scarce food resources that are associated with animal husbandry. It may be justified on animal-centered grounds, whether the specific cruelties of industrialized farming or the wider intuition that killing and consuming fellow creatures is wrong. It will also be opposed, both on classic grounds of Christian freedom and also, of course, because many people like eating meat.

Beneath these disputes and many others will be the Bible. Throughout this book, we have seen that Protestants use the Bible both devotionally and polemically, as lovers and as fighters. Twentieth-century disputes between conservative and modernist theologies rarely recognized this basic fact. Those two parties disagreed bitterly about how and indeed whether to use the Bible polemically, but in practice their use of it devotionally and as a source of inspiration was shared ground. This dispute will not be resolved in the twenty-first century, but it will move on. Twentieth-century textual conservatism, like seventeenth-century Protestant Orthodoxy, was a defensive stance, and a successful one, as the collapse of various liberal and radical Protestantisms during the same period shows. But it also involved formidable problems, especially where a no-surrender textual absolutism trapped Protestants in scientific or historical claims that look very implausible or in ethical stances that are painfully countercultural. In the coming decades, that hard defensive line will soften.

The fundamental reason for this is the rise of Pentecostalism, now global Protestantism's main engine. Pentecostals will continue joyfully to affirm the Bible as a touchstone of faith. However, their openness to the Holy Spirit's continued promptings gives them a means of sidestepping textual stumbling blocks while still affirming faith in the Word. Their tradition makes it easier to read the Bible as a love letter and less necessary to read it as a treatise. The great Pentecostal ecumenist David du Plessis was as loyal to the Bible as anyone could wish, but in a 1986 memoir he reflected that "as Jesus predicted, I can write a Book of the Acts of the Holy Spirit in my lifetime that would eclipse the Acts of the Apostles."[4] The Bible is the Word of God, but not the last word.

For one example of what is possible, consider the Friday Masowe Church in contemporary Zimbabwe, whose members proudly describe themselves as "the Christians who don't read the Bible." As one of their preachers explained in 1999,

> Here we don't talk of Bibles. What is the Bible to me? Having it is just trouble. Look, why would you read it? It gets old. Look again. After keeping it for some time it falls apart, the pages come out. . . . We don't talk Bible-talk here. We have a true Bible here.

He indicated his heart. In fact, it is clear that the Masowe church's leaders do know their Bibles, and even learned their disdain for the Bible from the Bible. They believe that "the Bible is the Word of God, but it is not always relevant to the needs of Africans today." So they look to the Holy Spirit for direct guidance.[5] It is an extreme example, but once you have accepted the possibility that the Holy Spirit can act and speak here and now, this is where it can lead.

The ever more exuberant variety of Protestantism will itself weaken textual fundamentalism. It is not simply that a cacophony of different interpretations undermines any simple notion of being a "Bible believer." The Bible itself is becoming increasingly varied. Most Protestant cultures formed around a single biblical translation. These texts—the Luther Bible in German, the King James Bible in English, the Union Version in Chinese—came to be venerated or even, like some ancient translations, treated as inspired texts in their own right. This made shared Protestant vernacular cultures in those languages possible and gave believers the immediate contact with the Word that they craved. But it had its drawbacks.

One, ironically, is the sheer quality of those iconic Bibles. The King

James Bible is a literary masterpiece, and I have used it for the epigraphs throughout this book. But it renders the Bible's exuberant mixture of literary styles and voices into the same somberly magnificent register, making it easier to mistake "the Bible" for a single voice. It also masks a feature of the Bible that was immediately apparent to its ancient readers. The Greek of the New Testament is not somberly magnificent but blunt, simple marketplace language. Many ancient readers found the claim that this was God's Word shocking or laughable. Christians typically replied that it was indeed shocking, as shocking as God choosing to become a human baby. That salutary shock is something that few Protestants have ever been able to feel. The explosion of new biblical translations, permanently breaking the monopolies of those old, iconic versions, has helped to break down Protestantism's unified cultures, for good or ill. It makes it harder for Protestants to know, collectively, what "the Bible says." It may also make it easier for them to hear, individually, what the Bible is saying.

Protestants in the World

Protestant growth in China and sub-Saharan Africa will continue for the time being, although the blistering pace will ease. This will not produce a new rash of "Protestant countries," like Germany or Britain of old. In some countries, as seems to be the case in South Korea, Protestants will strike a ceiling beyond which it is hard to expand further. More complete dominance is possible in Africa, where there may be more self-proclaimed "Christian countries" like Zambia. But there as elsewhere, the speed of Protestantism's spread raises the possibility that it may ebb as quickly as it has flowed. It has become a preachers' truism in Africa that African Christianity is a mile wide and an inch deep. It is not at all clear that African Christians deserve such disparaging comments, but certainly the Christian identities of first- and second-generation converts are not yet settled and stable. Settled stability may not be something our age has to offer.

Pentecostalism's growth in Latin America is also set to continue, a success with wider significance. This is the first instance in modern times of Protestants' converting Catholic populations wholesale, or indeed of any of the world's major religions winning large numbers of converts from another. Where might Pentecostalism go next? The country to watch is India. Despite enormous missionary effort over several centuries, India's Christian population remains in the region of 2–3 percent. But if India achieves the sustained economic growth and urbanization to which it aspires, the resulting social dislocation could create the kinds of conditions in which Pentecostalism has thrived elsewhere in the world. It is possible that over the coming decades Pentecostalism may make significant inroads, especially if borne by Latin American or East Asian missionaries. And while Hindu identity is a formidable obstacle, alienation from Hindu nationalism may provide an opening.

South Asia is also a likely site of conflict with one of Protestantism's two great global competitors: Islam. The two great global religious movements of the past half century, Pentecostalism and jihadist Islam, are strange twins. Where Pentecostalism has spread almost unnoticed, jihadist Islam has made itself spectacularly visible. How these two movements' very different trajectories will intersect is one of the key questions of the twenty-first century. I hesitate to make any predictions at all, because the answer will depend less on developments within Protestantism than on how the bitter, switchback conflicts within the Islamic world play out. Some factions will triumph, some will be suppressed, some will discredit themselves, but although the rest of the world has a considerable stake in these struggles, it will not have very much influence on them.

Protestantism's competition with Islam will be focused on frontier zones, above all the southern Sahara and central Africa. This is likely to be a bruising and defensive battle, a struggle involving a good deal of actual violence, and also a race for the moral high ground. Here, if anywhere, Protestants will feel the need to hold to textual precision and to austerely traditionalist views of gender and sexual ethics. This struggle will not see many conversions in either direction. Its outcome—which may well be a grim stalemate—will be determined by violence, as Muslim and Christian rivals try to drive each other out of particular territories, and by demographics, as it becomes clear which group is outbreeding the other. It is not a cheerful prospect.

Protestantism will also confront Islam in Europe, but here the decisive factor is the presence of its other great global competitor. Not

Catholicism, whose ancient rivalry with Protestantism has become friendlier and less existentially threatening, but secularism. Secularism has made decisive inroads in Europe in the past half century and is also a formidable force in North America. In the wake of World War II, Europe's and America's white Christians were forced to accept a new and essentially secular set of ethical norms. Their old cultural hegemony has gone and they have not yet found a way to assert a role for themselves in this new world. They tend to feel that they represent the past rather than the future, whether they express that feeling through abashed nostalgia or conservative defiance.

What has complicated this long-running drama in Europe is jihadist Islam. Jihadist rhetoric labels the Western democracies as "Christian" or indeed as "Crusaders," and some right-wing elements in both Europe and America have embraced this notion of a clash of cultures between Christian and Muslim. For others, especially in Europe, the sensible desire to avoid any notion of a war against Islam has meant confronting jihadism through a wider skepticism about religion of any kind in public life. Whether Europe's historic religions can find a way out of this cross fire remains to be seen.

If European Protestantism has a future, it will likely be newly built, rather than a revival of historical denominational establishments. There are two reasons to suspect this may happen. One is immigration; Europe's combination of wealth, proximity to poor and conflict-prone regions, and sharp demographic downturn mean that, one way or another, its flow of immigrants is unlikely to slow markedly. As well as Middle Eastern Muslims, a great many of these immigrants will be African Christians.

European and American politics may contribute, too. The Western democracies have been undergoing a slow crisis of legitimacy, in which growing numbers of voters have become disenchanted with their political systems and with the centrist technocracies they tend to produce. This often manifests itself as anger with "politicians" as a class, and as a conclusion that politics is inherently corrupt. It can either bolster unconventional politicians who promise to change the entire political culture, or foster disgusted withdrawal from political life. These alarming conditions are similar to those in which Pentecostalism has thrived elsewhere in the world. A new political hegemony for Protestantism in the Western democracies is plainly unattainable, but Protestantism's long-standing claim that politics is of strictly limited importance is well suited to our times. Communities that disdain the corruption of public life, and offer spiritual rather than political power, may find that their message resonates. It is even possible that a new Pentecostal politics may emerge, aspiring less to a particular policy agenda than to changing the political culture with a new moralism, although promises like that are easier to make than to keep. It is not at all clear that a development like this would be good for the Western democracies, nor even that it would bolster Protestantism. It does, however, seem likely that the Western democracies' moribund and transactional political culture will find a new moral compass at some point. There are many worse options available.

As Protestants continue to play their parts in these and other dramas over the decades ahead, it will be important to remember what Protestantism is. It is an identity, indeed a whole family of squabbling identities, that people define themselves by, hold to, fight for, and sometimes abandon. It is also a family of cultures and practices, which set the patterns of individuals' and communities' lives. It is also a set of institutions with a persistent presence across a wide range of human societies and a set of doctrines and ideas. But before it is any of these things, it is that old love affair: a direct encounter with God's power, whether as a lived experience, a memory, or a hope. That is not what it is for every Protestant, of course, but without that underpinning, the identities, cultures, institutions, and doctrines would all collapse. That heartbeat, however muffled, is beneath it all. It is through that promise to change lives that Protestantism has changed the world.

Acknowledgments

This book has been knocking around my head for more than twenty years. I would trace its first beginnings back to 1994, when, as a new postgraduate studying the Reformation, I was also avidly following the story of South Africa's democratic transition. It struck me then that the Dutch Reformed Church's part in South Africa's struggles was absolutely of a piece with the Reformation conflicts we were discussing in classes every week. Perhaps Protestantism was the common thread. I've been tugging at that thread ever since, and the results—so far—are in your hands.

I was told that this would be an impossible book to write. Embracing that fact and doing it anyway is one of the things that has made the process so enjoyable. The other is the enormous help and encouragement I have received on the way. Most of this book was written while I was serving as head of the Department of Theology and Religion at Durham University, and if I had had less excellent colleagues, writing it really would have been impossible. The department also provided me with postgraduate research assistants who helped to map out unknown terrain for me—JiSeong Kwon, Hyuksang Kwon, and, my single most important collaborator on this project, Susan Royal. Friends and colleagues around the world have read drafts and given gently unsparing criticism: Benjamin Baker, Tony Claydon, Scott Dixon, Bob Fu, David Gehring, Jeremy Gregory, Mathew Guest, Ann Hughes, Hugh McLeod, Jenny Moberly, Mike Snape, David Trim, and Ryu Dae Young. I also have to thank audiences who have helped me knock some of these ideas into shape, chiefly at the Royal Historical Society, at Washington Adventist University, and especially at Gresham College. Among the others who have helped me along the way I need to thank Sarah Apetrei, Sheila Burdett, John Coffey, and Hans Hillerbrand. Mary Jane Haemig introduced me to New Sweden; Yuri Nishikawa taught me about the Taiping Rebellion, when I should have been teaching her. During the final six months, Jane Heath was an invaluable source of both encouragement and sharp insight. The book would never have happened at all without Felicity Bryan's support and advocacy, and would not have taken the shape it has without Joy de Menil's editorial eye. The entire editorial family at the *Journal of Ecclesiastical History* has humored me through my many enthusiasms as I wrote: I've come to depend on James Carleton Paget's support. Without Diarmaid MacCulloch's, the whole thing would have been unthinkable anyway.

Throughout the interminable genesis of my "Big Book of Protestants," Victoria, Ben, and Adam have had unstinting and sometimes excessive faith in me. But my deepest debt, and the book's dedication, is to my father. One of the last real conversations he and I had, before Parkinson's disease closed its vise on him, was about my plan for this book. His sense of excitement has buoyed me through the process. I hope he would have enjoyed it.

Glossary

Abolitionist. One who believes that slavery, or at least the slave trade, ought to be abolished, either gradually or immediately: see chapter 8.

Adventist. One in the *Millerite* or post-Millerite tradition who expects the imminent return of Christ, but without naming a specific date. In modern usage generally refers to *Seventh-day Adventists:* see chapter 9.

Anabaptist. Literally "rebaptizer." A hostile term for sixteenth-century and later radicals who practiced adult rather than infant baptism and generally withdrew from wider society: see chapters 1 and 4.

Anglican. An adherent of the liturgical Christianity typified by the Church of England, especially after 1660, which sometimes aspires to be a middle way between Catholicism and Protestantism: see chapters 2, 5, 10, 12.

Apocalyptic. Expecting the imminent end of the world, a belief that sometimes involves taking action to help the process along.

Arminian. A *Calvinist* dissident who rejects predestination. The movement is Dutch in origin but was later very influential in England and the United States: see especially chapters 3, 5, 7.

Baptist. Follower of a tradition originating in seventeenth-century England but now present worldwide, typically combining a broadly *Calvinist* or *Arminian* theology with a rejection of infant baptism. Distinct from *Anabaptists* in origins and beliefs: see chapter 5.

Calvinist. The dominant variety of *Reformed Protestant,* often strongly associated with the doctrine of predestination: see chapter 3.

Congregationalist. A Protestant, usually in the *Reformed* tradition, whose individual congregation elects its own minister and manages its own affairs without oversight. Traditionally strong in the northeastern United States.

Deist. One who believes in a distant or impersonal creator God who makes no day-to-day interventions in the universe, and who is typically skeptical toward the Bible: see chapter 7.

Dispensationalist. Follower of a *premillennial* doctrine formed in the United States in the nineteenth century that sees the world's history as falling into distinct stages, with believers taken directly to heaven (the Rapture) before the world endures a final period of tribulation.

Ecumenist. One who pursues reconciliation, perhaps including formal re-union, between different Christian denominations, especially in the twentieth century.

Erastian. One who believes that Protestant churches ought to be subject to the authority of the state: see chapter 2.

Evangelical. Protestants who stress biblical authority and the need for individual conversion, especially from the eighteenth century onward: see chapter 7.

Fifth Monarchist. A seventeenth-century English *apocalyptic* movement that aimed to establish a perfect kingdom of the saints: see chapter 5.

Fundamentalist. Properly, a member of an *evangelical* movement emerging in the United States in the early twentieth century, opposed to *modernism* and claiming *inerrant* verbal inspiration of the entire Bible. Also used more generally for inerrantists: see chapter 12.

German Christians. Protestants who allied with Nazism and attempted to produce a "de-Judaized" Christianity: see chapter 11.

Gnesio-Lutheran. A late sixteenth-century *Lutheran* who insisted on a strict adherence to Luther's teaching, in opposition to *Philippists:* see chapter 3.

Inerrantist. One who believes that the Bible is entirely and literally free from error of any kind, in opposition to *modernists:* see chapter 12.

Liberal. In Protestant theology, a broad term for believers from the late eighteenth century on who are willing to adapt or reinterpret doctrine and who often have an optimistic view of humanity: see chapter 10.

Lutheran. The tradition, looking directly to Martin Luther, that became established in state churches in Germany and Scandinavia: see chapters 1, 3, 7.

Methodist. A type of *evangelical* Protestant, initially a subgroup of *Anglicans* in the eighteenth century, later in independent churches. Mostly *Arminian* in theology: see chapter 7.

Millerite. Follower of a movement in the northeastern United States that predicted Christ's return for the year 1844: see chapter 9.

Modernist. A Protestant who accepts and incorporates scientific worldviews, the results of biblical scholarship, and other modern critiques of traditional Christian beliefs. Opposed to *inerrantists:* see chapters 10, 12.

Moravian. Member of a small but influential eighteenth-century *revivalist* movement, extremely active in missionary work: see chapter 7.

Mormon. A member of a Protestant-influenced religion founded in the nineteenth-century United States, claiming its own priesthood, prophets, and extensive authoritative revelations: see chapter 9.

Neo-orthodox. A descriptor for anti*liberal* twentieth-century Protestantism, insisting on the absolute need for Christ's redemption but without rejecting *modernist* views wholesale: see chapters 11, 12.

Orthodox. A generic term for correct belief, often applied specifically to the defensive, scholarly Protestant establishments of the seventeenth and eighteenth centuries: see chapter 7.

Pentecostal. A Christian who teaches the ecstatic presence of the Holy Spirit in believers *or,* more precisely, a member of a denomination of this kind founded in the early twentieth century, most of which particularly emphasize speaking in tongues: see chapter 16.

Philippist. A late sixteenth-century Lutheran who followed Philip Melanchthon's teaching and was accused of leaning toward *Calvinism.* Opposed to *Gnesio-Lutheranism:* see chapter 3.

Pietist. Member of a movement originating in seventeenth-century *Lutheranism* that stressed inner union with Christ and spiritual renewal, both by individual believers and by mutually encouraging groups of laypeople: see chapter 7.

Premillennialist. An *apocalyptic* Protestant who believes that the world will degenerate into sin and tyranny before Christ's imminent return, making efforts at social or political reform futile: see chapter 14.

Presbyterian. A *Calvinist* who takes the view that churches ought to govern themselves through a hierarchy of councils while remaining independent of state control: see chapters 3, 5.

Progressive. In the United States, a Protestant *liberal* who emphasized the *Social Gospel* and the perfectibility of human society: see chapter 10.

Puritan. Follower of a *Calvinist* movement originating in England that emphasized the pursuit of both outward holiness and inner piety: see chapters 5, 7.

Quaker. Member of a radically antihierarchical movement originating in seventeenth-century England that stressed direct spiritual experience of the "inner light" over the Bible or traditional theology: see chapter 5.

Reformed Protestant. Early Protestants distinct from Lutheranism, who emerged in Switzerland and southern Germany. Sometimes known misleadingly as *Calvinist:* see chapter 3.

Revivalist. An *evangelical* who seeks an emotionally charged conversion experience, often through camp meetings or other mass gatherings: see especially chapters 7, 9, 16.

Seventh-day Adventist. Member of an *Adventist* church teaching renewed holiness during this final phase of the world's history, distinguished by observation of Saturday as the Sabbath: see chapter 9.

Social Gospel. The *liberal* belief that Christians should concern themselves more with combating social or economic evils than with preaching a "spiritual" gospel of redemption from sin. Often a term of abuse: see chapters 10, 12, 15.

Socinian. A *Reformed Protestant* who denies the doctrine of the Trinity and does not believe Christ is divine: see chapter 3.

Spiritualist. A term *either* for radicals in early Protestantism and *Anabaptism* who emphasized the direct inspiration of the Holy Spirit, *or* for adherents of the non-Christian practice of attempting to speak with spirits of the dead, widespread in the nineteenth and twentieth centuries: see chapters 1, 10.

Unitarian. A Protestant who denies the Trinity and the divinity of Christ; part of a movement that was an early stronghold of *liberalism:* see chapter 10.

Notes

Introduction

1. E. Gordon Rupp and Philip S. Watson, eds., *Luther and Erasmus: Free Will and Salvation; Erasmus: De Libero Arbitrio; Luther: De Servo Arbitrio* (London: SCM Press, 1969), 37.
2. John Knox, *On Rebellion*, ed. Roger Mason (Cambridge, U.K.: Cambridge University Press, 1994), 119.
3. Max Weber, *The Protestant Ethic and the Spirit of Capitalism*, trans. Talcott Parsons (London: Routledge, 1992).
4. Ibid., 70.
5. William Chillingworth, *The Religion of Protestants: A Safe Way to Salvation* (Oxford: Leonard Lichfield, 1638), 375.
6. John Calvin, *Institutes of the Christian Religion*, ed. John T. McNeill, trans. Ford Lewis Battles (Philadelphia: Westminster Press, 1960), 78–81 (my emphasis).
7. Martin Luther, *Three Treatises* (Philadelphia: Fortress Press, 1970), 274; Sears McGee, ed., *The Miscellaneous Works of John Bunyan, vol. 3, Christian Behavior; The Holy City; The Resurrection of the Dead* (Oxford: Clarendon Press, 1987), 72.
8. Brian A. Gerrish, "The Word of God and the Words of Scripture: Luther and Calvin on Biblical Authority," in *The Old Protestantism and the New: Essays on the Reformation Heritage* (Chicago: University of Chicago Press, 1982), 55.

Chapter 1: Luther and the Fanatics

1. Desiderius Erasmus, *Christian Humanism and the Reformation: Selected Writings*, ed. John C. Olin (New York: Harper & Row, 1965), 97–108.
2. This is spelled out most clearly in Luther's 1520 tract "The Freedom of a Christian," in *Three Treatises*, 261–316.
3. Alister E. McGrath, *Luther's Theology of the Cross: Martin Luther's Theological Breakthrough*, 2nd ed. (Chichester, U.K.: Wiley-Blackwell, 2011), 222.
4. Mark U. Edwards Jr., *Printing, Propaganda, and Martin Luther* (Berkeley: University of California Press, 1994), 17, 21, 22, 26–27.
5. Scott H. Hendrix, *Martin Luther: Visionary Reformer* (New Haven, Conn.: Yale University Press, 2015), 101; Edwards, *Printing, Propaganda, and Martin Luther*, 1, 30.
6. Peter Marshall, *1517: Martin Luther, the 95 Theses, and the Invention of the Reformation* (Oxford: Oxford University Press, 2017).
7. Every Luther biography narrates these events; in my view, the best recent study is Hendrix, *Martin Luther*, 55–85.
8. Martin Luther, *Luther's Works*, vol. 32, *Career of the Reformer II*, ed. George W. Forell (Philadelphia: Fortress Press, 1958), 106.
9. Martin Luther, *Luther's Works*, vol. 48, *Letters I*, ed. Gottfried G. Krodel (Philadelphia: Fortress Press, 1963), 200.
10. Luther, *Career of the Reformer II*, 108.
11. Martin Luther, *Luther's Works*, vol. 43, *Devotional Writings II*, ed. Gustav K. Wiencke (Philadelphia: Fortress Press, 1968), 65; Luther, *Letters I*, 307.

12. Luther, *Career of the Reformer II*, 113.

13. In, for example, Alister E. McGrath, *Christianity's Dangerous Idea* (London: SPCK, 2007); Brad S. Gregory, *The Unintended Reformation: How a Religious Revolution Secularized Society* (Cambridge, Mass.: Harvard University Press, 2012).

14. Reinhold Seeberg, *Textbook of the History of Doctrines*, trans. Charles E. Hay, 2 vols. (Grand Rapids, Mich.: Baker Book House, 1958–61), 2:300–301; Martin Luther, *Luther's Works*, vol. 54, *Table Talk*, ed. and trans. Theodore G. Tappert (Philadelphia: Fortress Press, 1967), 79–80, 373, 452.

15. Martin Luther, *Luther's Works*, vol. 35, *Word and Sacrament I*, ed. E. Theodore Bachmann (Philadelphia: Fortress Press, 1960), 361–62, 397; Luther, *Table Talk*, 424; Martin Luther, *Luther's Works*, vol. 34, *Career of the Reformer IV*, ed. Lewis W. Spitz (Philadelphia: Muhlenberg Press, 1960), 317.

16. Martin Luther, *Luther's Works*, vol. 14, *Selected Psalms III*, eds. Jaroslav Pelikan and Daniel E. Poellot (St. Louis: Concordia, 1958), 36.

17. Gerrish, "The Word of God and the Words of Scripture," 55.

18. An argument made powerfully in Scott H. Hendrix, *Tradition and Authority in the Reformation* (Aldershot, U.K.: Variorum Collected Studies, 1996), 2:147.

19. Luther, *Letters I*, 307.

20. Ibid., 225.

21. Martin Luther, *Luther's Works*, vol. 45, *The Christian in Society II*, ed. Walther I. Brandt (Philadelphia: Fortress Press, 1959), 70–71; Martin Luther, *Luther's Works*, vol. 51, *Sermons I*, ed. John W. Doberstein (Philadelphia: Fortress Press, 1959), 77.

22. Luther, *Table Talk*, 50.

23. Mark U. Edwards Jr., *Luther and the False Brethren* (Stanford, Calif.: Stanford University Press, 1975), 7–17.

24. Martin Luther, *Luther's Works*, vol. 46, *The Christian in Society III*, ed. Robert C. Schultz (Philadelphia: Fortress Press, 1967), 51.

25. Rupp and Watson, *Luther and Erasmus*.

26. Walter Klaassen, Frank Friesen, and Werner O. Packull, eds., *Sources of South German/Austrian Anabaptism* (Kitchener, Ont.: Pandora Press, 2001), 19, 44.

Chapter 2: Protectors and Tyrants

1. Luther, *Three Treatises*, 13–14.

2. Eric Lund, ed., *Documents from the History of Lutheranism, 1517–1750* (Minneapolis: Fortress Press, 2002), 56.

3. Ibid., 58.

4. Alec Ryrie, *The Age of Reformation: The Tudor and Stewart Realms, 1485–1603* (Harlow, U.K.: Pearson, 2009), 110–29.

5. Luther, *Table Talk*, 384; Ryrie, *Age of Reformation*, 145n8.

6. Luther, *Christian in Society II*, 66.

7. David C. Steinmetz, *Luther in Context* (Bloomington: Indiana University Press, 1986), 124; Thomas A. Brady, "Luther and the State: The Reformer's Teaching in Its Social Setting," in *Luther and the Modern State in Germany*, ed. James D. Tracy (Kirkville, Mo.: Sixteenth Century Journal Publishers, 1986), 40.

8. Luther, *Christian in Society II*, 89, 109, 111–14.

9. Timothy George, *Theology of the Reformers* (Nashville: Broadman Press, 1988), 110.

10. C. Scott Dixon, "The Princely Reformation in Germany," in *The Reformation World*, ed. Andrew Pettegree (New York: Routledge, 2000), 151–53.

11. Lund, *Documents from the History of Lutheranism*, 71; Luther, *Table Talk*, 382.

12. Hughes Oliphant Old, *The Shaping of the Reformed Baptismal Rite in the Sixteenth Century* (Grand Rapids, Mich.: Eerdmans, 1992), 56; Susan Royal, "John Foxe's 'Acts and Monuments' and the Lollard Legacy in the Long English Reformation" (PhD diss., Durham University, 2014).

13. James M. Stayer, *Anabaptists and the Sword* (Lawrence, Kans.: Coronado Press, 1976), 141.

14. Matthew 18:15–17.

15. Philip Benedict, *Christ's Churches Purely Reformed: A Social History of Calvinism* (New Haven, Conn.: Yale University Press, 2002), 460–89.

16. William G. Naphy, *Calvin and the Consolidation of the Genevan Reformation* (Manchester, U.K.: Manchester University Press, 1994).

17. Knox, *On Rebellion*, 119.

18. Robert Pitcairn, ed., *The Autobiography and Diary of Mr. James Melvill* (Edinburgh: Wodrow Society, 1842), 370.

19. Cynthia Grant Shoenberger, "The Development of the Lutheran Theory of Resistance, 1523–1530," *Sixteenth Century Journal* 8 (1977): 68–70.

20. Ibid., 61–76; Quentin Skinner, *The Foundations of Modern Political Thought*, vol. 2, *The Age of Reformation* (Cambridge, U.K.: Cambridge University Press, 1978).

21. J. Craigie, ed., *The Basilikon Doron of King James VI* (Edinburgh: Scottish Text Society, 1944), 1:75.

22. Lund, *Documents from the History of Lutheranism*, 57.

Chapter 3: The Failure of Calvinism

1. Thomas Brady, *Turning Swiss: Cities and Empire, 1450–1550* (Cambridge, U.K.: Cambridge University Press, 1985).

2. Bruce Gordon, *The Swiss Reformation* (Manchester, U.K.: Manchester University Press, 2002), 40–42, 46–51.

3. Matthew 26:26–28.

4. Lee Palmer Wandel, *The Eucharist in the Reformation: Incarnation and Liturgy* (Cambridge, U.K.: Cambridge University Press, 2006), 94–207.

5. Amy Nelson Burnett, "Basel and the Wittenberg Concord," *Archiv für Reformationsgeschichte* 96 (2005): 33–56.

6. Bruce Gordon, *Calvin* (New Haven, Conn.: Yale University Press, 2009), vii.

7. Timothy George, "John Calvin and the Agreement of Zurich (1549)," in *John Calvin and the Church: A Prism of Reform* (Louisville, Ky.: Westminster John Knox Press, 1990), 42–58.

8. Thomas J. Davis, *The Clearest Promises of God: The Development of Calvin's Eucharistic Teaching* (New York: AMS Press, 1995), 41–48.

9. Bruce Gordon, "Wary Allies: Melanchthon and the Swiss Reformers," in *Melanchthon in Europe: His Work and Influence Beyond Wittenberg*, ed. Karin Maag (Grand Rapids, Mich.: Baker Books, 1999), 45–67.

10. Timothy Wengert, "'We Will Feast Together in Heaven Forever': The Epistolary Friendship of John Calvin and Philip Melanchthon," in Maag, *Melanchthon in Europe*, 19–44.

11. George, "John Calvin and the Agreement of Zurich (1549)," 55.

12. Robert Kolb, *Luther's Heirs Define His Legacy: Studies on Lutheran Confessionalisation* (Aldershot, U.K.: Variorum, 1996), 1:1–14.

13. Ibid., 1:8–9.

14. Robert Kolb, "Luther, Augsburg, and the Concept of Authority in the Late Reformation: Ursinus vs. the Lutherans," in *Controversy and Conciliation: The Reformation and the Palatinate, 1559–1583*, ed. Derk Visser (Allison Park, Pa.: Pickwick, 1986), 36.

15. Robert Kolb, "Altering the Agenda, Shifting the Strategy: The Grundfest of 1571 as Philippist Program for Lutheran Concord," *Sixteenth Century Journal* 30, no. 3 (1999): 705–26.

16. Wiktor Weintraub, "Tolerance and Intolerance in Old Poland," *Canadian Slavonic Papers* 13 (1971): 21–44.

17. Paul Douglas Lockhart, *Frederick II and the Protestant Cause* (Leiden: Brill, 2004), 158–73.

18. Elsie Anne McKee, "A Lay Voice in Sixteenth-Century 'Ecumenics': Katharina Schütz Zell in Dialogue with Johannes Brenz, Conrad Pellican, and Caspar Schwenckfeld," in *Adaptions of Calvinism in Reformation Europe*, ed. Mack P. Holt (Aldershot, U.K.: Ashgate, 2007), 81–110.

19. Jerome Friedman, *Michael Servetus: A Case Study in Total Heresy* (Geneva: Librairie Droz, 1978); Gordon, *Calvin*, 217–32.

20. Alec Ryrie, "The Afterlife of Lutheran England," in *Sister Reformations: The Reformation in Germany and England,* ed. Dorothea Wendebourg (Tübingen: Mohr Siebeck, 2011), 213–34.

21. Diarmaid MacCulloch, *Thomas Cranmer: A Life* (New Haven, Conn.: Yale University Press, 1996), 501–3, 518–20.

22. Graeme Murdock, *Beyond Calvin: The Intellectual, Political, and Cultural World of Europe's Reformed Churches* (Basingstoke, U.K.: Palgrave, 2004), 16.

23. W. B. Patterson, *James VI and I and the Reunion of Christendom* (Cambridge, U.K.: Cambridge University Press, 1997), 165–80.

24. J. Minton Batten, *John Dury: Advocate of Christian Reunion* (Chicago: University of Chicago Press, 1944), 29–30.

25. Thomas S. Freeman, "Dissenters from a Dissenting Church: The Challenge of the Freewillers, 1550–1558," in *The Beginnings of English Protestantism,* eds. Peter Marshall and Alec Ryrie (Cambridge, U.K.: Cambridge University Press, 2002), 151–52.

26. Nicholas Tyacke, *Anti-Calvinists: The Rise of English Arminianism, c. 1590–1640* (Oxford: Clarendon Press, 1987), 87, 103.

27. Batten, *John Dury*, 38.

28. Diarmaid MacCulloch, "Calvin: Fifth Latin Doctor of the Church?," in *Calvin and His Influence, 1509–2009,* eds. Irena Backus and Philip Benedict (Oxford: Oxford University Press, 2011), 33–45.

Chapter 4: Heretics, Martyrs, and Witches

1. William Monter, "Heresy Executions in Reformation Europe, 1520–65," in *Tolerance and Intolerance in the European Reformation,* eds. Ole Peter Grell and Bob Scribner (Cambridge, U.K.: Cambridge University Press, 1996), 48–64.

2. Richard Rex, "The English Campaign Against Luther in the 1520s," *Transactions of the Royal Historical Society,* 5th ser., 39 (1989): 85–106.

3. Craig D'Alton, "The Suppression of Lutheran Heretics in England, 1526–29," *Journal of Ecclesiastical History* 54 (2003): 228–53.

4. Greg Walker, "Saint or Schemer? The 1527 Heresy Trial of Thomas Bilney," *Journal of Ecclesiastical History* 40 (1989): 223.

5. David Bagchi, "Luther and the Problem of Martyrology," in *Martyrs and Martyrologies,* ed. Diana Wood, Studies in Church History, vol. 30 (Oxford: Blackwell, 1993), 209–20.

6. Elizabeth Evenden and Thomas S. Freeman, *Religion and the Book in Early Modern England* (Cambridge, U.K.: Cambridge University Press, 2011).

7. Patrick Collinson, "John Foxe and National Consciousness," in *John Foxe and His World,* eds. Christopher Highley and John King (Aldershot, U.K.: Ashgate, 2002), 10–34.

8. R. Po-chia Hsia, *The World of Catholic Renewal, 1540–1770* (1998; Cambridge, U.K.: Cambridge University Press, 2005).

9. Mark Greengrass, *The French Reformation* (Oxford: Blackwell, 1987), 43.

10. Natalie Zemon Davis, "The Rites of Violence," *Past and Present* 59 (1973): 51–91.

11. Barbara Diefendorf, *Beneath the Cross: Catholics and Huguenots in Sixteenth-Century Paris* (New York: Oxford University Press, 1991); Philip Benedict, "The St. Bartholomew's Massacres in the Provinces," *Historical Journal* 21 (1978): 201–25.

12. Philip Benedict, *Rouen During the Wars of Religion* (Cambridge, U.K.: Cambridge University Press, 1981), 125–134; Andrew Pettegree, *The Invention of News: How the World Came to Know about Itself* (New Haven, Conn.: Yale University Press, 2014), 146.

13. Peter Marshall, "Papist as Heretic: The Burning of John Forest, 1538," *Historical Journal* 41 (1998): 351–74.

14. Leo Damrosch, "Nayler, James (1618–1660)," *Oxford Dictionary of National Biography* (Oxford: Oxford University Press, 2004), accessed March 11, 2016, www.oxforddnb.com/view/article/19814.

15. Martin Luther, *Luther's Works,* vol. 40, *Church and Ministry II,* ed. Conrad Bergendoff (Philadelphia: Fortress Press, 1958), 57, 230.

16. Alan Levine, ed., *Early Modern Skepticism and the Origins of Toleration* (Lanham, Md.: Lexington Books, 1999), 7–9; John Dunn, "The Claim to Freedom of Conscience: Freedom of Speech, Freedom of Thought, Freedom of Worship?," in *From Persecution to Toleration: The Glorious Revolution and Religion in England,* eds. Ole Peter Grell, Jonathan I. Israel, and Nicholas Tyacke (Oxford: Clarendon Press, 1991), 171–93.

17. Peter van Rooden, "Jews and Religious Toleration in the Dutch Republic," in *Calvinism and Religious Toleration in the Dutch Golden Age,* eds. R. Po-chia Hsia and Henk van Nierop (Cambridge, U.K.: Cambridge University Press, 2002), 132–47; Nigel Smith, ed., *The Poems of Andrew Marvell* (Harlow, U.K.: Pearson, 2007), 253.

18. Judith Pollmann, "The Bond of Christian Piety: The Individual Practice of Tolerance and Intolerance in the Dutch Republic," in Hsia and Nierop, *Calvinism and Religious Toleration in the Dutch Golden Age,* 56.

19. Gary K. Waite, *Eradicating the Devil's Minions: Anabaptists and Witches in Reformation Europe, 1525–1600* (Toronto: University of Toronto Press, 2007), 132–36.

20. Christopher Marsh, *The Family of Love in English Society, 1550–1630* (Cambridge, U.K.: Cambridge University Press, 1994).

21. Samme Zijlstra, "Anabaptism and Tolerance: Possibilities and Limitations," in Hsia and Nierop, *Calvinism and Religious Toleration in the Dutch Golden Age,* 112–31.

22. Waite, *Eradicating the Devil's Minions,* esp. 17, 69, 77.

23. Ibid., 134–36, 154; Luc Racaut, *Hatred in Print: Catholic Propaganda and Protestant Identity During the French Wars of Religion* (Aldershot, U.K.: Ashgate, 2002), 62.

24. Waite, *Eradicating the Devil's Minions,* 3, 140, 145–46.

25. David Wootton, "Reginald Scot / Abraham Fleming / The Family of Love," in *The Languages of Witchcraft,* ed. Stuart Clark (Basingstoke, U.K.: Macmillan, 2000), 119–138.

Chapter 5: The British Maelstrom

1. Keith Lindley, ed., *The English Civil War and Revolution: A Sourcebook* (London: Routledge, 2013), 48, 50.

2. Thomas N. Corns, *Uncloistered Virtue: English Political Literature, 1640–1660* (Oxford: Clarendon Press, 1992), 18.

3. Ann Hughes, *Seventeenth-Century England: A Changing Culture* (London: Ward Lock, 1980), 1:76.

4. Henry Burton, *The Protestation Protested* (1641), sig. A3r.

5. Robert von Friedeburg, "The Continental Counter-Reformation and the Plausibility of Popish Plots, 1638–42," in *England's Wars of Religion, Revisited,* eds. Charles W. A. Prior and Glenn Burgess (Farnham, U.K.: Ashgate, 2011), 58.

6. David Booy, ed., *The Notebooks of Nehemiah Wallington, 1618–1654: A Selection* (Aldershot, U.K.: Ashgate, 2007), 226.

7. Burton, *Protestation Protested,* sigs. C3v–4r.

8. John Milton, *The Prose Works* (London: Westley and Davis, 1835), 104, 117.

9. Hughes, *Seventeenth-Century England,* 1:134.

10. J. P. Kenyon, ed., *The Stuart Constitution* (Cambridge, U.K.: Cambridge University Press, 1986), 276.

11. Andrew Sharp, ed., *The English Levellers* (Cambridge, U.K.: Cambridge University Press, 1998), 93; Jason Peacey, "Radicalism Relocated: Royalist Politics and Pamphleteering of the Late 1640s," in *Varieties of Seventeenth- and Early Eighteenth-Century English Radicalism in Context,* eds. Ariel Hessayon and David Finnegan (Farnham, U.K.: Ashgate, 2011), 61.

12. Hughes, *Seventeenth-Century England,* 1:172–73; John Saltmarsh, *Sparkles of Glory; or, Some Beams of the Morning-Star* (London: Giles Calvert, 1647), sig. A5r–v.

13. Margaret A. Judson, *From Tradition to Political Reality: A Study of the Ideas Set Forth in Support of the Commonwealth Government in England, 1649–1653* (Springfield, Ohio: Conference on British Studies, 1980), 5.

14. Jane Baston, "History, Prophecy, and Interpretation: Mary Cary and Fifth Monarchism," *Prose Studies* 21, no. 3 (1998): 3.

15. B. S. Capp, *The Fifth Monarchy Men: A Study in Seventeenth-Century English Millenarianism* (London: Faber & Faber, 1972), 151–52.

16. Andrew Bradstock and Christopher Rowland, eds., *Radical Christian Writings: A Reader* (Oxford: Blackwell, 2002), 123–25, 132.

17. Nigel Smith, ed., *A Collection of Ranter Writings from the 17th Century* (London: Junction Books, 1983), 86–87, 89, 105–7.

18. Ibid., 181.

19. John Holland, *The Smoke of the Bottomlesse Pit* (London: for John Wright, 1651), sigs. A2v, A4r; Smith, *Collection of Ranter Writings from the 17th Century*, 185.

20. David Booy, ed., *Autobiographical Writings by Early Quaker Women* (Aldershot, U.K.: Ashgate, 2004), 81–91.

21. Holland, *Smoke of the Bottomlesse Pit*, sig. A3v; A. L. Morton, *The World of the Ranters: Religious Radicalism in the English Revolution* (London: Lawrence & Wishart, 1970), 82.

22. Morton, *World of the Ranters*, 91; Booy, *Autobiographical Writings by Early Quaker Women*, 116.

23. Kenneth L. Carroll, "Early Quakers and 'Going Naked as a Sign,'" *Quaker History* 67, no. 2 (1978): 69–87.

24. Mary Howgill, *A Remarkable Letter of Mary Howgill to Oliver Cromwel, Called Protector* (London, 1657), sig. A2r.

25. Sylvia Brown, "The Radical Travels of Mary Fisher: Walking and Writing in the Universal Light," in *Women, Gender, and Radical Religion in Early Modern Europe* (Leiden: Brill, 2007), 38–64.

26. Robert South, *Interest Deposed, and Truth Restored* (Oxford: A.L. for Tho. Robinson, 1660), sig. D2r.

27. Kenneth Fincham and Stephen Taylor, "Vital Statistics: Episcopal Ordination and Ordinands in England, 1646–60," *English Historical Review* 126, no. 519 (2011): 319–44.

28. Judith Maltby, "'Extravagances and Impertinencies': Set Forms, Conceived and Extempore Prayer in Revolutionary England," in *Worship and the Parish Church in Early Modern Britain*, eds. Natalie Mears and Alec Ryrie (Farnham, U.K.: Ashgate, 2013), 221–43.

Chapter 6: From the Waters of Babylon to a City on a Hill

1. Rudolph P. Almasy, "Tyndale Menedemus," in *Word, Church, and State: Tyndale Quincentenary Essays*, eds. John T. Day, Eric Lund, and Anne M. O'Donnell (Washington, D.C.: Catholic University of America Press, 1998), 134–39.

2. Hannibal Hamlin, *Psalm Culture and Early Modern English Literature* (Cambridge, U.K.: Cambridge University Press, 2004), 219.

3. Matthew 10:23.

4. Andrew Pettegree, *Foreign Protestant Communities in Sixteenth-Century London* (Oxford: Oxford University Press, 1986), 234, 239–40.

5. M. F. Backhouse, "Guerilla War and Banditry in the Sixteenth Century: The Wood Beggars in the Westkwartier of Flanders (1567–1568)," *Archiv für Reformationsgeschichte* 74 (1983): 232–51.

6. Geert H. Janssen, "Exiles and the Politics of Reintegration in the Dutch Revolt," *History* 94, no. 313 (2009): 36–52.

7. Richard L. Greaves, "Macalpine, John (d. 1557)," *Oxford Dictionary of National Biography* (Oxford: Oxford University Press, 2004), accessed March 11, 2016, www.oxforddnb.com/view/article/17329.

8. Hans R. Guggisberg, *Basel in the Sixteenth Century* (St. Louis: Center for Reformation Research, 1982), 49–52.

9. Mark Taplin, *The Italian Reformers and the Zurich Church, c. 1540–1620* (Aldershot, U.K.: Ashgate, 2003), 81–108.

10. Lorna Jane Abray, *The People's Reformation: Magistrates, Clergy, and Commons in Strasbourg, 1500–1598* (Oxford: Basil Blackwell, 1985), 93–100, 132–37.

11. Leland Harder, ed., *The Sources of Swiss Anabaptism: The Grebel Letters and Related Documents*, Classics of the Radical Reformation, vol. 4 (Scottdale, Pa.: Herald Press, 1985), 451.

12. Silvia Shannon, "Villegagnon, Polyphemus, and Cain of America: Religion and Polemics in the French New World," in *Changing Identities in Early Modern France*, ed. Michael Wolfe (Durham, N.C.: Duke University Press, 1996), 325–44.

13. Benjamin Franklin French, ed., *Historical Collections of Louisiana and Florida: Including Translations of Original Manuscripts Relating to Their Discovery and Settlement* (New York: J. Sabin and Sons, 1869), 165–362, esp. 237.

14. William Symonds, *Virginia: A Sermon Preached at White-Chappel* (London: I. Windet for Eleazar Edgar and William Welby, 1609), 6; *New Englands First Fruits* (London: Henry Overton, 1643), sig. B6r.

15. Keith L. Sprunger, *Dutch Puritanism: A History of the English and Scottish Churches of the Netherlands in the Sixteenth and Seventeenth Centuries* (Leiden: Brill, 1982), 3, 91, 134, 139.

16. Susan Hardman Moore, *Pilgrims: New World Settlers and the Call of Home* (New Haven, Conn.: Yale University Press, 2007), 33–34.

17. Samuel Danforth, *A Brief Recognition of New Englands Errand into the Wilderness* (Cambridge, Mass.: S.G. and M.J., 1671), 10; Avihu Zakai, *Exile and Kingdom: History and Apocalypse in the Puritan Migration to America* (Cambridge, U.K.: Cambridge University Press, 1992), 144; Revelation 12:6.

18. Hardman Moore, *Pilgrims*, 31; Matthew 5:14.

19. Hardman Moore, *Pilgrims*.

20. *Winthrop Papers*, vol. 2, *1623–30* (Boston: Massachusetts Historical Society, 1931), 117; Trygve Skarsten, "Johan Campanius, Pastor in New Sweden," *Lutheran Quarterly* 2, no. 1 (1988): 54.

21. *New Englands First Fruits*, sig. A2r.

22. William Crashaw, *A Sermon Preached in London Before the Right Honorable the Lord Lawarre* (London: for William Welby, 1610), sig. D4r; *Winthrop Papers*, vol. 2, *1623–30*, 145; Alexander Young, *Chronicles of the First Planters of the Colony of Massachusetts Bay, from 1623 to 1636* (Boston: Little and Brown, 1846), 142.

23. *A Collection of Voyages and Travels*, 4 vols. (London: for Awnsham and John Churchill, 1704), 3:799, 803–4, 810–11, 901; C. R. Boxer, *The Dutch Seaborne Empire, 1600–1800* (London: Hutchinson, 1965), 140–41.

24. William Campbell, ed., *An Account of Missionary Success in the Island of Formosa* (London: Trübner, 1889), esp. 170; Chiu Hsin-hui, *The Colonial "Civilizing Process" in Dutch Formosa, 1624–1662* (Leiden: E. J. Brill, 2008).

25. Skarsten, "Johan Campanius, Pastor in New Sweden," 47–87; Thomas Campanius Holm, trans., and Peter S. Du Ponceau, ed., *Description of the Province of New Sweden* (Philadelphia: McCarthy & Davis, 1834), 140–41.

26. Francis Jennings, *The Invasion of America* (New York: W. W. Norton, 1976), 230–31; J. William T. Youngs Jr., "The Indian Saints of Early New England," *Early American Literature* 16, no. 3 (1981–82): 244–45.

27. Richard W. Cogley, *John Eliot's Mission to the Indians Before King Philip's War* (Cambridge, Mass.: Harvard University Press, 1999).

28. Ibid., 5, 45–51.

29. *The Day-Breaking, if Not the Sun-Rising of the Gospell with the Indians in New-England* (London: Richard Cotes for Fulk Clifton, 1647), 15.

30. Matthew 28:19; James A. Scherer, *Gospel, Church, and Kingdom: Comparative Studies in World Mission Theology* (Minneapolis: Augsburg, 1987), 67–69.

31. Cogley, *John Eliot's Mission to the Indians Before King Philip's War*, 9–21.

32. Thomas Thorowgood, *Ievves in America* (London: William Hunt for Thomas Slater, 1650), 54–55; Cogley, *John Eliot's Mission to the Indians Before King Philip's War*, 83–90;

Isak Collijn, "The Swedish-Indian Catechism: Some Notes," *Lutheran Quarterly* 2, no. 1 (1988): 92.

33. Lund, *Documents from the History of Lutheranism*, 170.

34. *Collection of Voyages and Travels*, 3:802; *Winthrop Papers*, vol. 2, *1623–30*, 114; *New Englands First Fruits*, sig. B2r–v.

35. *Collection of Voyages and Travels*, 3:800; Charles L. Cohen, "Conversion among Puritans and Amerindians: A Theological and Cultural Perspective," in *Puritanism: Transatlantic Perspectives*, ed. Francis Bremer (Boston: Massachusetts Historical Society, 1993), 244–45; *The Day-Breaking, if Not the Sun-Rising of the Gospell with the Indians in New-England*, 15.

36. Scherer, *Gospel, Church, and Kingdom*, 69.

37. Cogley, *John Eliot's Mission to the Indians Before King Philip's War*, 178–80, 208–22; Jennings, *Invasion of America*, 233.

Chapter 7: Enthusiasm and Its Enemies

1. W. R. Ward, *The Protestant Evangelical Awakening* (Cambridge, U.K.: Cambridge University Press, 1992), 99.

2. D. G. Hart, *Calvinism: A History* (New Haven, Conn.: Yale University Press, 2013), 141–43.

3. Jack B. Rogers and Donald K. McKim, *The Authority and Interpretation of the Bible: An Historical Approach* (San Francisco: Harper & Row, 1979), 172–84.

4. Philip Jacob Spener, *Pia Desideria*, trans. and ed. Theodore G. Tappert (Philadelphia: Fortress Press, 1964), 36, 49, 52, 56–57, 98–100.

5. Ian Green, *Print and Protestantism in Early Modern England* (Oxford: Oxford University Press, 2000), 348–50; Ward, *Protestant Evangelical Awakening*, 10–13.

6. Spener, *Pia Desideria*, 89–92.

7. Edmund Calamy, *A Caveat against New Prophets* (London, 1708), 37.

8. *Praise out of the Mouth of Babes* (London: J. Downing, 1708), 7–8, 14.

9. Ward, *Protestant Evangelical Awakening*, 127.

10. Ibid., 136–37.

11. Jon Sensbach, "'Don't Teach My Negroes to Be Pietists': Pietism and the Roots of the Black Protestant Church," in *Pietism in Germany and North America, 1680–1820*, eds. Jonathan Strom, Hartmut Lehmann, and James Van Horn Melton (Farnham, U.K.: Ashgate, 2009), 189.

12. Jon Sensbach, *Rebecca's Revival: Creating Black Christianity in the Atlantic World* (Cambridge, Mass.: Harvard University Press, 2005), esp. 46, 77–79, 99, 105–6, 151.

13. Ibid., 158–233.

14. *An Extract of the Rev. Mr. John Wesley's Journal* (Bristol: Felix Farley, 1743), 30.

15. Colin Podmore, *The Moravian Church in England, 1728–1760* (Oxford: Clarendon Press, 1998), 59–60.

16. William Adams, *The Necessity of the Pouring out of the Spirit from on High upon a Sinning Apostatizing People* (Boston: John Fester for William Avery, 1679), sig. A2r, p. 13; Thomas S. Kidd, *The Great Awakening: The Roots of Evangelical Christianity in Colonial America* (New Haven, Conn.: Yale University Press, 2007), 2.

17. Leigh Eric Schmidt, *Holy Fairs: Scottish Communions and American Revivals in the Early Modern Period* (Grand Rapids, Mich.: Eerdmans, 2001).

18. Jonathan Edwards, *A Faithful Narrative of the Surprizing Work of God in the Conversion of Many Hundred Souls in Northampton* (London: John Oswald, 1737), 11, 26–27, 87–89, 109–15, 122.

19. David Harlan, *The Clergy and the Great Awakening in New England* (Ann Arbor, Mich.: UMI Research Press, 1980), 50–51.

20. Kidd, *Great Awakening*, 48–49.

21. David Hempton, *Methodism: Empire of the Spirit* (New Haven, Conn.: Yale University Press, 2005), 78.

22. Marilyn J. Westerkamp, "Taming the Spirit: Female Leadership Roles in the American Awakenings, 1730–1830," in *The Rise of the Laity in Evangelical Protestantism*, ed. Deryck W. Lovegrove (London: Routledge, 2002), 102; John A. Hargreaves, "Fletcher, Mary (1739–1815)," *Oxford Dictionary of National Biography* (Oxford: Oxford University Press, 2004), accessed March 27, 2014, www.oxforddnb.com/view/article/40209.

23. Catherine A. Brekus, *Strangers and Pilgrims: Female Preaching in America, 1740–1845* (Chapel Hill: University of North Carolina Press, 1998), 59–63.

24. Ibid., 23–26.

25. Keith Edward Beebe, ed., *The McCulloch Examinations of the Cambuslang Revival (1742): A Critical Edition: Conversion Narratives from the Scottish Awakening*, 2 vols. (Woodbridge, U.K.: Scottish History Society, 2013), 1:65.

26. A slogan attributed to the fourth-century theologian St. Ambrose; first coined in those terms in English by the Puritan Robert Bolton, in his *Some Generall Directions for a Comfortable Walking with God* (London, 1626), 245; and endlessly repeated thereafter.

27. Beebe, *McCulloch Examinations of the Cambuslang Revival*, 1:107, 113, 175, 217, 2:44, 122.

28. Kidd, *Great Awakening*, 153–54.

29. Harlan, *Clergy and the Great Awakening in New England*, 57.

30. Hans Otte, "The Pietist Laity in Germany, 1675–1750: Knowledge, Gender, Leadership," in Lovegrove, *Rise of the Laity in Evangelical Protestantism*, 49.

31. Jonathan Edwards, *The Distinguishing Marks of a Work of the Spirit of God* (Boston: S. Kneeland, 1741), 18.

32. Hymn 14, accessed March 14, 2016, www.anngriffiths.cardiff.ac.uk/hymns .html#xiv.

Chapter 8: Slaves to Christ

1. Victor Enthoven, "Early Dutch Expansion in the Atlantic Region, 1585–1621," in *Riches from Atlantic Commerce: Dutch Transatlantic Trade and Shipping, 1585–1817*, eds. Johannes Postma and Victor Enthoven (Leiden: Brill, 2003), 40n73.

2. Michael Craton, *Testing the Chains: Resistance to Slavery in the British West Indies* (Ithaca, N.Y.: Cornell University Press, 2009), 273.

3. J. Albert Harrill, *The Manumission of Slaves in Early Christianity* (Tübingen: Mohr Siebeck, 1995), 21.

4. Seymour Drescher, *Abolition: A History of Slavery and Antislavery* (Cambridge, U.K.: Cambridge University Press, 2009), 69–70.

5. Robin Blackburn, *The Making of New World Slavery: From the Baroque to the Modern, 1492–1800* (London: Verso, 2010), 75.

6. Karen O. Kupperman, *Providence Island, 1630–41: The Other Puritan Colony* (Cambridge, U.K.: Cambridge University Press, 1993), 157–72; Drescher, *Abolition*, 74.

7. Samuel Sewall, *The Selling of Joseph: A Memorial* (Boston: Bartholomew Green and John Allen, 1700), 1; Mary Turner, *Slaves and Missionaries: The Disintegration of Jamaican Slave Society, 1787–1834* (Urbana: University of Illinois Press, 1982), 9.

8. J. R. Oldfield, "Lay, Benjamin (1681–1759)," *Oxford Dictionary of National Biography* (Oxford: Oxford University Press, 2004), accessed March 17, 2016, www.oxforddnb .com/view/article/16216.

9. Jacobus Elisa Johannes Capitein, *The Agony of Asar: A Thesis on Slavery by the Former Slave Jacobus Elisa Johannes Capitein, 1717–1747*, ed. and trans. Grant Parker (Princeton, N.J.: Markus Wiener, 2001), 49.

10. Ibid., 93, 112–13.

11. James Walvin, *Black Ivory: Slavery in the British Empire* (Oxford: Blackwell, 2001), 165; Travis Glasson, *Mastering Christianity: Missionary Anglicanism and Slavery in the Atlantic World* (Oxford: Oxford University Press, 2012), 100–104.

12. Morgan Godwyn, *The Negro's & Indians Advocate, Suing for Their Admission into the Church* (London: J.D., 1680), 108.

13. Thomas Ingersoll, "'Releese Us out of This Cruell Bondegg': An Appeal from Virginia in 1723," *William and Mary Quarterly,* 3rd ser., 51, no. 4 (1994): 782.

14. Sensbach, *Rebecca's Revival,* 83, 149, 155–56.

15. Ibid., 141–42.

16. Godwyn, *Negro's & Indians Advocate,* 128.

17. Edwin B. Bronner, "An Early Antislavery Statement: 1676," *Quaker History* 62, no. 1 (1973): 50.

18. Kidd, *Great Awakening,* 216.

19. Godwyn, *Negro's & Indians Advocate,* 38.

20. Sensbach, *Rebecca's Revival,* 144; Walvin, *Black Ivory,* 160.

21. Kidd, *Great Awakening,* 222.

22. Molly Oshatz, *Slavery and Sin: The Fight against Slavery and the Rise of Liberal Protestantism* (Oxford: Oxford University Press, 2012), 19.

23. Leland J. Bellot, "Evangelicals and the Defense of Slavery in Britain's Old Colonial Empire," *Journal of Southern History* 37 (1971): 28.

24. Glasson, *Mastering Christianity,* 69.

25. Kenneth Morgan, *Slavery and the British Empire: From America to Africa* (Oxford: Oxford University Press, 2007), 174.

26. Glasson, *Mastering Christianity,* 186–87.

27. Frederick Douglass, *Narrative of the Life of Frederick Douglass, an American Slave, Written by Himself* (New York: Anchor Books, 1973), 77–78, 81.

28. John Coffey, "'Tremble, Britannia!': Fear, Providence, and the Abolition of the Slave Trade, 1758–1807," *English Historical Review* 127, no. 527 (2012): 844–81.

29. Richard Huzzey, "The Moral Geography of British Anti-slavery Responsibilities," *Transactions of the Royal Historical Society,* 6th ser., 22 (2012): 116; Coffey, "'Tremble, Britannia!,'" 862–65.

30. Holger Lutz Kern, "Strategies of Legal Change: Great Britain, International Law, and the Abolition of the Transatlantic Slave Trade," *Journal of the History of International Law* 6, no. 2 (2004): 233–58.

31. Craton, *Testing the Chains,* 273–90.

32. Ibid., 321.

33. Douglass, *Narrative of the Life of Frederick Douglass,* x–xi.

34. John R. McKivigan, *The War against Proslavery Religion: Abolitionism and the Northern Churches, 1830–1865* (Ithaca, N.Y.: Cornell University Press, 1984), 65–69.

35. Oshatz, *Slavery and Sin,* 46.

36. Douglas Ambrose, "Religion and Slavery," in *The Oxford Handbook of Slavery in the Americas,* eds. Robert L. Paquette and Mark M. Smith (Oxford: Oxford University Press, 2010), 393.

37. *Memoir of Old Elizabeth, a Colored Woman* (Philadelphia: Collins, 1863), in *Six Women's Slave Narratives,* ed. William L. Andrews (New York: Oxford University Press, 1988), 16.

38. Oshatz, *Slavery and Sin,* 13, 40, 45, 80.

39. Aileen S. Kraditor, *Means and Ends in American Abolitionism: Garrison and His Critics on Strategy and Tactics, 1834–1850* (New York: Pantheon Books, 1969), 93; John Ernest, "Crisis and Faith in Douglass's Work," in *The Cambridge Companion to Frederick Douglass,* ed. Maurice S. Lee (Cambridge, U.K.: Cambridge University Press, 2009), 61.

40. William L. Andrews, ed., *Sisters of the Spirit: Three Black Women's Autobiographies of the Nineteenth Century* (Bloomington: Indiana University Press, 1986), 98.

41. José Carlos Barbosa, *Slavery and Protestant Missions in Imperial Brazil,* trans. Fraser G. MacHaffie and Richard K. Danford (Lanham, Md.: University Press of America, 2008), 92, 97.

Chapter 9: Protestantism's Wild West

1. Winthrop S. Hudson, "A Time of Religious Ferment," in *The Rise of Adventism: Religion and Society in Mid-Nineteenth-Century America,* ed. Edwin S. Gaustad (New York: Harper & Row, 1974), 2–3.

2. Nathan O. Hatch, *The Democratization of American Christianity* (New Haven, Conn.: Yale University Press, 1989), 4.

3. Sydney E. Ahlstrom, *A Religious History of the American People* (New Haven, Conn.: Yale University Press, 1972), 433.

4. Hatch, *Democratization of American Christianity*, 69–70, 74.

5. Wayne R. Judd, "William Miller: Disappointed Prophet," in *The Disappointed: Millerism and Millenarianism in the Nineteenth Century*, eds. Ronald L. Numbers and Jonathan M. Butler (Knoxville: University of Tennessee Press, 1993), 18–19.

6. Matthew 24:36; Ecclesiastes 1:9.

7. David T. Arthur, "Joshua V. Himes and the Cause of Adventism," in Numbers and Butler, *Disappointed*, 39; Brekus, *Strangers and Pilgrims*, 320–23.

8. Arthur, "Joshua V. Himes," 50.

9. Numbers and Butler, *Disappointed*, 214–15, 226.

10. Jonathan M. Butler, "The Making of a New Order: Millerism and the Origins of Seventh-Day Adventism," in Numbers and Butler, *Disappointed*, 196; Arthur, "Joshua V. Himes and the Cause of Adventism," 51–53.

11. Numbers and Butler, *Disappointed*, 211, 215.

12. Ibid., 221.

13. Everett N. Dick, "The Millerite Movement, 1830–1845," in *Adventism in America*, ed. Gary Land (Berrien Springs, Mich.: Andrews University Press, 1998), 25.

14. Hudson, "Time of Religious Ferment," 11–12; Robert V. Hine, "Communitarianism," in Gaustad, *Rise of Adventism*, 74–75.

15. Lawrence Foster, *Religion and Sexuality: The Shakers, the Mormons, and the Oneida Community* (Urbana: University of Illinois Press, 1984), 66–68.

16. Numbers and Butler, *Disappointed*, 182, 224.

17. Laurence Foster, "Had Prophecy Failed? Contrasting Perspectives of the Millerites and Shakers," in Numbers and Butler, *Disappointed*, 183.

18. Numbers and Butler, *Disappointed*, 215–16.

19. Ronald L. Numbers, *Prophetess of Health: A Study of Ellen G. White*, 3rd ed. (Grand Rapids, Mich.: Eerdmans, 2008), 56.

20. John B. Blake, "Health Reform," in Gaustad, *Rise of Adventism*, 42–43.

21. Numbers, *Prophetess of Health*, 230–36.

22. Ibid., 132, 208.

23. Ibid., 159.

24. Robert Crompton, *Counting the Days to Armageddon: The Jehovah's Witnesses and the Second Presence of Christ* (Cambridge, U.K.: James Clarke, 1996), 37–41; cf. Revelation 7:4.

25. Crompton, *Counting the Days to Armageddon*, 66, 131.

26. *Jehovah's Witnesses in the Divine Purpose* (Brooklyn: Watchtower Bible and Tract Society, 1959), 17.

27. Crompton, *Counting the Days to Armageddon*, 135, 139–40.

28. M. James Penton, *Apocalypse Delayed: The Story of Jehovah's Witnesses* (Toronto: Toronto University Press, 1997), 145.

29. Moroni 10:4, Alma 32:33 (Book of Mormon); Leonard J. Arrington and Davies Bitton, *The Mormon Experience: A History of the Latter-Day Saints* (London: Allen & Unwin, 1979), 23.

30. Terryl L. Givens, *People of Paradox: A History of Mormon Culture* (Oxford: Oxford University Press, 2007), 17–18, 31. Brigham Young University in Salt Lake City is ranked 66th out of 280 national universities in the United States at the time of writing: http://colleges.usnews.rankingsandreviews.com/best-colleges/best-colleges/rankings/national-universities, accessed Aug. 31, 2016.

31. R. Laurence Moore, *Religious Outsiders and the Making of Americans* (Oxford: Oxford University Press, 1986), 34.

32. Eugene E. Campbell. *Establishing Zion: The Mormon Church in the American West, 1847–1869* (Salt Lake City: Signature Books, 1988), 224–25.

33. Arrington and Bitton, *Mormon Experience*, 195–204.

Chapter 10: The Ordeals of Liberalism

1. Friedrich Schleiermacher, *On Religion: Speeches to Its Cultured Despisers,* ed. Richard Crouter (Cambridge, U.K.: Cambridge University Press, 1996), 3, 11–12.

2. Anthony John Harding, ed., *Coleridge's Responses: Selected Writings of Literary Criticism, the Bible, and Nature,* vol. 2, *Coleridge on the Bible* (London: Continuum, 2007), 4–5.

3. Richard M. Gamble, *The War for Righteousness: Progressive Christianity, the Great War, and the Rise of the Messianic Nation* (Wilmington, Del.: ISI Books, 2003), 43–44.

4. Harding, *Coleridge on the Bible,* 177.

5. Gary Dorrien, *The Making of American Liberal Theology: Imagining Progressive Religion, 1805–1900* (Louisville, Ky.: Westminster John Knox Press, 2001), 9.

6. Eda Sagarra, *A Social History of Germany, 1648–1914* (New York: Holmes & Meier, 1977), 205–6.

7. Schleiermacher, *On Religion,* 13–15, 27, 49–50.

8. Ibid., xiii, 22, 25, 28, 30, 33, 44, 49–50, 78–81.

9. Dorrien, *Making of American Liberal Theology,* 48–49, 99.

10. Sagarra, *Social History of Germany,* 213–14; Dorrien, *Making of American Liberal Theology,* 102–4.

11. John Rogerson, "History and the Bible," in *The Cambridge History of Christianity,* vol. 8, *World Christianities, c. 1815–c. 1914,* eds. Sheridan Gilley and Brian Stanley (Cambridge, U.K.: Cambridge University Press, 2006), 181–96; Owen Chadwick, *The Secularization of the European Mind in the Nineteenth Century* (Cambridge, U.K.: Cambridge University Press, 1975), 179.

12. Harding, *Coleridge on the Bible,* 108, 175; Dorrien, *Making of American Liberal Theology,* 28.

13. Schleiermacher, *On Religion,* 50; Dorrien, *Making of American Liberal Theology,* 276.

14. Timothy Larsen, "Bishop Colenso and His Critics: The Strange Emergence of Biblical Criticism in Victorian Britain," in *The Eye of the Storm: Bishop John William Colenso and the Crisis of Biblical Inspiration,* ed. Jonathan A. Draper (London: T&T Clark, 2003), 49.

15. Gerald Parsons, "Biblical Criticism in Victorian Britain: From Controversy to Acceptance?," in *Religion in Victorian Britain,* vol. 2, *Controversies* (Manchester: Manchester University Press, 1988), 245–55.

16. J. M. I. Klaver, *Geology and Religious Sentiment: The Effect of Geological Discoveries on English Society and Literature between 1829 and 1859* (Leiden: Brill, 1997), 6, 20, 31, 43.

17. Ibid., 11–12, 25.

18. Ibid., xi, 179–81.

19. Ibid., 182, 186; Schleiermacher, *On Religion,* 13.

20. Chadwick, *Secularization of the European Mind in the Nineteenth Century,* 166.

21. James R. Moore, *The Post-Darwinian Controversies* (Cambridge, U.K.: Cambridge University Press, 1979); G. Blair Nelson, "'Men Before Adam!': American Debates over the Unity and Antiquity of Humanity," in *When Science and Christianity Meet,* eds. David C. Lindberg and Ronald L. Numbers (Chicago: University of Chicago Press, 2003), 161–81.

22. Moore, *Post-Darwinian Controversies,* 263.

23. Dorrien, *Making of American Liberal Theology,* 320.

24. Ibid., 317.

25. Moore, *Post-Darwinian Controversies,* 223–24.

26. Nicholas Hope, *German and Scandinavian Protestantism, 1700–1918* (Oxford: Clarendon Press, 1995), 590.

27. A. J. Hoover, *God, Germany, and Britain in the Great War: A Study in Clerical Nationalism* (New York: Praeger, 1989), 4, 12.

28. Ibid., 14.

29. Ibid., 14, 98.

30. Ibid., 3.

31. Ibid., 9.

32. Ibid., 24–25.

33. Gamble, *War for Righteousness,* 30, 38, 53.
34. Ibid., 143.
35. Ibid., 159.
36. Ibid., 146, 162–63.
37. Ibid., 153.
38. Jeffrey P. Moran, *The Scopes Trial: A Brief History with Documents* (Boston: Bedford/St. Martin's, 2002), 16; George M. Marsden, *Fundamentalism and American Culture,* 2nd ed. (Oxford: Oxford University Press, 2006), 142.

Chapter 11: Two Kingdoms in the Third Reich

1. *Hitler's Table Talk, 1941–1944,* trans. Norman Cameron and R. H. Stevens (London: Weidenfeld and Nicolson, 1953), 59, 61, 343, 625; Peter Matheson, ed., *The Third Reich and the Christian Churches* (Edinburgh: T. & T. Clark, 1981), 1.
2. Robert P. Ericksen, "Assessing the Heritage: German Protestant Theologians, Nazis, and the 'Jewish Question,'" in *Betrayal: German Churches and the Holocaust,* eds. Robert P. Ericksen and Susannah Heschel (Minneapolis: Fortress Press, 1999), 25.
3. Susannah Heschel, *The Aryan Jesus: Christian Theologians and the Bible in Nazi Germany* (Princeton, N.J.: Princeton University Press, 2008), 2.
4. Friedrich Weber and Charlotte Methuen, "The Architecture of Faith under National Socialism: Lutheran Church Building(s) in Braunschweig, 1933–45," *Journal of Ecclesiastical History* 66, no. 2 (2015): 343.
5. Hermann Beck, "Anti-Semitic Violence 'from Below': Attacks and Protestant Church Responses in Germany in 1933," *Politics, Religion, and Ideology* 14, no. 3 (2013): 410; Matheson, *Third Reich,* 12–15.
6. Matheson, *Third Reich,* 15; Karl Barth, *The German Church Conflict,* ed. T. H. L. Parker, trans P. T. A. Parker (London: Lutterworth Press, 1965), 75.
7. Dietrich Bonhoeffer, *Letters and Papers from Prison,* ed. Eberhard Bethge (London: Collins, 1959), 135–37.
8. Barth, *German Church Conflict,* 72.
9. Ericksen, "Assessing the Heritage," 23–25.
10. Samuel Koehne, "Nazi Germany as a Christian State: The 'Protestant Experience' of 1933 in Württemberg," *Central European History* 46 (2013): 112.
11. Victoria Barnett, *For the Soul of the People: Protestant Protest Against Hitler* (Oxford: Oxford University Press, 1992), 84.
12. Matheson, *Third Reich,* 96.
13. Ibid., 28.
14. Ibid., 6; Doris L. Bergen, *Twisted Cross: The German Christian Movement in the Third Reich* (Chapel Hill: University of North Carolina Press, 1996), 68.
15. Bergen, *Twisted Cross,* 24, 26.
16. Matheson, *Third Reich,* 39.
17. Ibid., 75.
18. *Hitler's Table Talk,* 6, 59, 625.
19. Bergen, *Twisted Cross,* 24, 26.
20. Ibid., 47.
21. Heschel, *Aryan Jesus,* 150.
22. Matheson, *Third Reich,* 29.
23. Bergen, *Twisted Cross,* 113–17.
24. Matheson, *Third Reich,* 50.
25. Theodore N. Thomas, *Women against Hitler: Christian Resistance in the Third Reich* (Westport, Conn.: Praeger, 1995), 39–40.
26. Matheson, *Third Reich,* 50.
27. Barth, *German Church Conflict,* 75.
28. Matheson, *Third Reich,* 76.
29. John Bowden, *Karl Barth* (London: SCM Press, 1971), 74.

30. Christine Elizabeth King, *The Nazi State and the New Religions* (New York: Edwin Mellen Press, 1982), 154, 160.

31. Matheson, *Third Reich*, 62.

32. Kenneth C. Barnes, "Dietrich Bonhoeffer and Hitler's Persecution of the Jews," in Ericksen and Heschel, *Betrayal*, 123; Barnett, *For the Soul of the People*, 144–46.

33. Gilbert Woodrow Scharffs, "History of the Church of Jesus Christ of Latter-Day Saints in Germany Between 1840 and 1968" (PhD diss., Brigham Young University, 1969), 125–28.

34. Matheson, *Third Reich*, 97–98.

35. Ibid., 99.

36. Ibid., 94.

37. *Hitler's Table Talk*, 555.

Chapter 12: Religious Left and Religious Right

1. Marsden, *Fundamentalism and American Culture*, 152, 158–59.

2. Kelly J. Baker, *Gospel According to the Klan: The KKK's Appeal to Protestant America, 1915–1930* (Lawrence: University Press of Kansas, 2012), 39, 43.

3. Ibid., 61–62.

4. Marsden, *Fundamentalism and American Culture*, 221.

5. Ibid., 169.

6. Moran, *Scopes Trial*, 49.

7. Mark Edwards, "Can Christianity Save Civilization? Liberal Protestant Antisecularism in Interwar America," *Journal of Religious History* 39, no. 1 (2015): 61–63.

8. Michael Snape, *God and Uncle Sam: Religion and America's Armed Forces in World War II* (Woodbridge, U.K.: Boydell Press, 2015), 579.

9. Hugh McLeod, *The Religious Crisis of the 1960s* (Oxford: Oxford University Press, 2007), 34–36.

10. Joel A. Carpenter, *Revive Us Again: The Reawakening of American Fundamentalism* (Oxford: Oxford University Press, 1997), 24.

11. Ibid., 225.

12. Mark Silk, *Spiritual Politics: Religion and America Since World War II* (New York: Simon & Schuster, 1988), 101.

13. Ibid., 105.

14. Stewart J. Brown, "W. T. Stead and the Civic Church, 1886–1895: The Vision Behind 'If Christ Came to Chicago!,'" *Journal of Ecclesiastical History* 66, no. 2 (2015): esp. 324, 331, 336.

15. Bonhoeffer, *Letters and Papers from Prison*, 91.

16. Ibid., 93, 95, 125.

17. Doug Rossinow, *The Politics of Authenticity: Liberalism, Christianity, and the New Left in America* (New York: Columbia University Press, 1998), 55, 60, 70–71.

18. Bergen, *Twisted Cross*, 87.

19. His movement between those two worlds remains the most plausible explanation for the fact that his PhD thesis and other academic writings included elements of plagiarism, apparently due to slipshod academic and note-taking practice rather than deliberate dishonesty.

20. James Melvin Washington, ed., *A Testament of Hope: The Essential Writings and Speeches of Martin Luther King Jr.* (New York: HarperCollins, 1986), 38.

21. Stewart Burns, ed., *Daybreak of Freedom: The Montgomery Bus Boycott* (Chapel Hill: University of North Carolina Press, 1997), 17, 134–35.

22. Ibid., 22, 164, 169, 172; Washington, *Testament of Hope*, 38.

23. Burns, *Daybreak of Freedom*, 24, 154, 168.

24. Ibid., 17.

25. Silk, *Spiritual Politics*, 114.

26. David L. Chappell, *A Stone of Hope: Prophetic Religion and the Death of Jim Crow* (Chapel Hill: University of North Carolina Press, 2004), 94.

27. Ibid., 5–6, 97, 108–10, 141–43; Washington, *Testament of Hope*, 299.

28. Washington, *Testament of Hope*, 300.

29. Sam Brewitt-Taylor, "From Religion to Revolution: Theologies of Secularization in the British Student Christian Movement, 1963–1973," *Journal of Ecclesiastical History* 66, no. 4 (2015): 793–94, 798–800.

30. Ibid., 800, 803–4, 806.

31. Ibid., 803.

32. Risto Lehtonen, *Story of a Storm: The Ecumenical Student Movement in the Turmoil of Revolution* (Grand Rapids, Mich.: Eerdmans, 1998), 307, 310, 314.

33. Jill K. Gill, *Embattled Ecumenism: The National Council of Churches, the Vietnam War, and the Trials of the Protestant Left* (DeKalb: Northern Illinois University Press, 2011), 359–60.

34. Hugh McLeod, *The Religious Crisis of the 1960s* (Oxford: Oxford University Press, 2007), 90.

35. John A. T. Robinson, *Christian Freedom in a Permissive Society* (London: SCM Press, 1970), 227–28, 239.

36. Silk, *Spiritual Politics*, 137–41.

37. Gayraud S. Wilmore, *Black Religion and Black Radicalism: An Interpretation of the Religious History of Afro-American People* (Maryknoll, N.Y.: Orbis Books, 1983), 212–13.

38. Jason S. Lantzer, *Mainline Christianity: The Past and Future of America's Majority Faith* (New York: New York University Press, 2012), 54.

39. Donald Heinz, "The Christian World Liberation Front," in *The New Religious Consciousness*, eds. Charles Y. Glock and Robert N. Bellah (Berkeley: University of California Press, 1976), 147.

40. William M. Newman and William V. D'Antoni, "'For Christ's Sake': A Study of Key '73 in New England," *Review of Religious Research* 19, no. 2 (1978): 139–40.

41. Brian Stanley, *The Global Diffusion of Evangelicalism: The Age of Billy Graham and John Stott* (Nottingham: Inter-Varsity Press, 2013), 156, 164.

42. David R. Swartz, *Moral Minority: The Evangelical Left in an Age of Conservatism* (Philadelphia: University of Pennsylvania Press, 2012), 218.

43. "This Tea Party Lawmaker Said Obama Shouldn't Quote the Bible Because Republicans Own It," *Yahoo News*, Jan. 14, 2016, accessed Feb. 9, 2016, http://news.yahoo.com/tea-party-lawmaker-said-obama-134939060.html.

44. Swartz, *Moral Minority*, 227.

45. Ibid., 239.

46. Maxine Phillips, "Moral Minority: The New Protestant Left," *Dissent* 62, no. 1 (2015): 106.

47. Buzz Aldrin, "Guideposts Classics: Buzz Aldrin on Communion in Space," *Guideposts*, accessed March 21, 2016, www.guideposts.org/faith/stories-of-faith/guideposts-classics-buzz-aldrin-on-communion-in-space?nopaging=1; Elizabeth Diaz, "The Secret Communion on the Moon: The 44-Year Anniversary," *Time*, July 20, 2013, accessed Mar. 21, 2016, http://swampland.time.com/2013/07/20/the-secret-communion-on-the-moon-the-44-year-anniversary/.

Chapter 13: Redeeming South Africa

1. Jonathan Neil Gerstner, *The Thousand Generation Covenant: Dutch Reformed Covenant Theology and Group Identity in Colonial South Africa, 1652–1814* (Leiden: Brill, 1991), 246; Richard Elphick, *Kraal and Castle: Khoikhoi and the Founding of White South Africa* (New Haven, Conn.: Yale University Press, 1977), 206.

2. Elphick, *Kraal and Castle*, 107–9.

3. Ibid., 203.

4. Gerstner, *Thousand Generation Covenant*, 248.

5. Bengt Sundkler and Christopher Steed, *A History of the Church in Africa* (Cambridge, U.K.: Cambridge University Press, 2000), 344, 430, 433.

6. John W. de Gruchy, *The Church Struggle in South Africa*, 2nd ed. (Grand Rapids, Mich.: Eerdmans, 1986), 19.

7. Donald Harman Akenson, *God's Peoples: Covenant and Land in South Africa, Israel, and Ulster* (Ithaca, N.Y.: Cornell University Press, 1992), 74.

8. Richard Elphick, *The Equality of Believers: Protestant Missionaries and the Racial Politics of South Africa* (Charlottesville: University of Virginia Press, 2012), 46, 319.

9. De Gruchy, *Church Struggle in South Africa*, 8.

10. Akenson, *God's Peoples*, 88.

11. De Gruchy, *Church Struggle in South Africa*, 31.

12. Sundkler and Steed, *History of the Church in Africa*, 818.

13. C. C. Saunders, "Tile and the Thembu Church: Politics and Independency on the Cape Eastern Frontier in the Late Nineteenth Century," *Journal of African History* 11 (1970), 553–70.

14. Sundkler and Steed, *History of the Church in Africa*, 424.

15. T. Dunbar Moodie, *The Rise of Afrikanerdom: Power, Apartheid, and the Afrikaner Civil Religion* (Berkeley: University of California Press, 1975), 190, 209, 215, 223.

16. Ibid., 218–21.

17. Elphick, *Equality of Believers*, 51.

18. Ibid., 229.

19. Ibid., 228–29, 232.

20. P. Eric Louw, *The Rise, Fall, and Legacy of Apartheid* (Westport, Conn.: Praeger, 2004), 35.

21. Elphick, *Equality of Believers*, 235–36.

22. Ibid., 236.

23. De Gruchy, *Church Struggle in South Africa*, 172.

24. Elphick, *Equality of Believers*, 300.

25. Christoph Marx, "From Trusteeship to Self-Determination: L. J. du Plessis' Thinking on Apartheid and His Conflict with H. F. Verwoerd," *Historia* 55, no. 2 (2010): 63.

26. De Gruchy, *Church Struggle in South Africa*, 56, 60.

27. Elphick, *Equality of Believers*, 308.

28. Piet Meiring, "Remembering Cottesloe: Delegates to the Cottesloe Consultation Tell Their Stories," in *Reformed Churches in South Africa and the Struggle for Justice: Remembering 1960–1990*, eds. Mary-Anne Plaatjies-Van Huffel and Robert Vosloo (Stellenbosch: Sun Press, 2013), 43; Hans S. A. Engdahl, *Theology in Conflict: Readings in Afrikaner Theology* (Frankfurt: Peter Lang, 2006), 39.

29. De Gruchy, *Church Struggle in South Africa*, 94.

30. Ibid., 118.

31. Hermann Giliomee, *The Afrikaners: Biography of a People* (London: Hurst, 2011), 629.

32. Akenson, *God's Peoples*, 297–99.

33. Ibid.; Giliomee, *Afrikaners*, 619, 625.

34. Conor Cruise O'Brien, "South Africa: An Ominous Lull," *New York Review of Books*, Sept. 27, 1979, 28.

35. J. J. F. Durand, "Bible and Race: The Problem of Hermeneutics," *Journal of Theology for Southern Africa* 24 (1978): 7.

36. Brian Johanson, "Race, Mission, and Ecumenism: Reflections on the Landman Report," *Journal of Theology for Southern Africa* 10 (1975): 52–53, 56.

37. Durand, "Bible and Race," 8.

38. Johan van der Merwe, "The Dutch Reformed Church from *Ras, Volk en Nasie* to *Kerk en Samelewing*," in Plaatjies-Van Huffel and Vosloo, *Reformed Churches in South Africa and the Struggle for Justice*, 58.

39. "Confession of Belhar," Reformed Church in America, accessed Mar. 22, 2016, www .rca.org/resources/confession-belhar?pid=304.

40. Van der Merwe, "Dutch Reformed Church from *Ras, Volk en Nasie* to *Kerk en Samelewing*," 59.

41. Ibid., 62.

42. Sundkler and Steed, *History of the Church in Africa*, 991.

43. Gustav Gous, "From the Church Struggle to a Struggling Church: A Tale of Three Conferences: Cottesloe, Rustenburg, and Cape Town," *Missionalia* 21, no. 2 (Nov. 1993): 260.

44. Frits Gaum, "From *Church and Society* (1986) to Rus nburg (1990): Developments within the Dutch Reformed Church," in Plaatjies-Van Huffel and Vosloo, *Reformed Churches in South Africa and the Struggle for Justice,* 69.

45. David Chidester, "Stories, Fragments, and Monuments," in *Facing the Truth: South African Faith Communities and the Truth & Reconciliation Commission,* ed. James Cochrane, John de Gruchy, and Stephen Martin (Cape Town: David Philip, 1999), 134.

46. Joel Cabrita, *Text and Authority in the South African Nazaretha Church* (Cambridge, U.K.: Cambridge University Press, 2014), 323; Robin M. Petersen, "The AICs and the TRC: Resistance Redefined," in Cochrane, de Gruchy, and Martin, *Facing the Truth,* 117.

47. Allan Anderson, *Bazalwane: African Pentecostals in South Africa* (Pretoria: University of South Africa, 1992), 38, 47.

48. Petersen, "The AICs and the TRC," 115, 118, 121.

49. Anderson, *Bazalwane,* 19.

Chapter 14: Korea in Adversity and Prosperity

1. George D. Chryssides, *The Advent of Sun Myung Moon: The Origin, Beliefs, and Practices of the Unification Church* (New York: St. Martin's Press, 1991), 71.

2. Chung-Shin Park, *Protestantism and Politics in Korea* (Seattle: University of Washington Press, 2003), 27.

3. Ibid., 56.

4. Timothy S. Lee, *Born Again: Evangelicalism in Korea* (Honolulu: University of Hawai'i Press, 2010), 137.

5. Dae Young Ryu, "The Origin and Characteristics of Evangelical Protestantism in Korea at the Turn of the Twentieth Century," *Church History* 77, no. 2 (2008): 388.

6. Dae Young Ryu, "Religion Meets Politics: The Korean Royal Family and American Protestant Missionaries in Late Joseon Korea," *Journal of Church and State* 55, no. 1 (2013): 121–22.

7. Ibid., 123.

8. Ryu, "Origin and Characteristics of Evangelical Protestantism in Korea at the Turn of the Twentieth Century," 393.

9. Young-Hoon Lee, "Korean Pentecost: The Great Revival of 1907," *Asian Journal of Pentecostal Studies* 4, no. 1 (2001): 73–75.

10. Ibid., 77.

11. Eunsik Cho, "The Great Revival of 1907 in Korea: Its Cause and Effect," in *Missiology* 26, no. 3 (1998): 296.

12. Park, *Protestantism and Politics,* 32.

13. Chang Han Kim, "Toward an Understanding of Korean Protestantism: The Formation of Christian-Oriented Sects, Cults, and Anti-cult Movements in Contemporary Korea" (PhD diss., University of Calgary, 2007), 138.

14. Nym Wales and Kim San, *Song of Ariran: A Korean Communist in the Chinese Revolution* (San Francisco: Ramparts Press, 1941), 74, 83.

15. Ibid., 75–78.

16. Ung Kyu Pak, *Millennialism in the Korean Protestant Church* (New York: Peter Lang, 2005), 128.

17. Wales and Kim, *Song of Ariran,* 78.

18. Park, *Protestantism and Politics,* 133.

19. Kim, "Toward an Understanding," 143.

20. Park, *Protestantism and Politics,* 147.

21. Ibid., 61.

22. Pak, *Millennialism in the Korean Protestant Church,* 238.

23. Park, *Protestantism and Politics,* 70, 82–83.

24. Choo Chai-Yong, "A Brief Sketch of a Korean Christian History from the Minjung Perspective," in *Minjung Theology: People as the Subjects of History* (London: Zed Press, 1981), 79.

25. David Kwang-Sun Suh, "Korean Theological Development in the 1970s," in *Minjung Theology*, 41.

26. Lee, *Born Again*, 119–20.

27. Park, *Protestantism and Politics*, 84.

28. Ig-Jin Kim, *History and Theology of Korean Pentecostalism:* Sunbogeum *(Pure Gospel) Pentecostalism* (Zoetermeer, Netherlands: Uitgeverij Boekencentrum, 2003), 127.

29. Ibid., 130.

30. Kim, "Toward an Understanding," 199.

31. Kim, *History and Theology of Korean Pentecostalism*, 138, 154.

32. For a more positive view of Christianity in the North, see Dae Young Ryu, "Religion, Politics, and Church Construction in North Korea," *Theology Today* 63 (2007): 493–99.

33. *A Prison Without Bars: Refugee and Defector Testimonies of Severe Violations of Freedom of Religion or Belief in North Korea* (United States Commission on International Religious Freedom, 2008), 23.

34. Ibid., 23, 34.

35. Ibid., 23.

36. Ibid., 38; David Hawk, *The Hidden Gulag: The Lives and Voices of "Those Who Are Sent to the Mountains": Exploring North Korea's Vast System of Lawless Imprisonment* (Washington, D.C.: Committee for Human Rights in North Korea, 2012), 137.

37. Lee, *Born Again*, 147.

Chapter 15: Chinese Protestantism's Long March

1. Jessie G. Lutz and R. Ray Lutz, "Karl Gützlaff's Approach to Indigenization: The Chinese Union," in *Christianity in China from the Eighteenth Century to the Present*, ed. Daniel H. Bays (Stanford, Calif.: Stanford University Press, 1996), 269–91.

2. Jonathan Spence, *God's Chinese Son: The Taiping Heavenly Kingdom of Hong Xiuquan* (London: Flamingo, 1997), 18.

3. Rudolf G. Wagner, *Reenacting the Heavenly Vision: The Role of Religion in the Taiping Rebellion* (Berkeley, Calif.: Institute of East Asian Studies, 1982), 91.

4. Thomas H. Reilly, *The Taiping Heavenly Kingdom: Rebellion and the Blasphemy of Empire* (Seattle: University of Washington Press, 2004), 127.

5. J. C. Cheng, ed., *Chinese Sources for the Taiping Rebellion, 1850–1864* (Hong Kong: Hong Kong University Press, 1963), 40.

6. Reilly, *Taiping Heavenly Kingdom*, 119; P. Richard Bohr, "Taiping Religion and Its Legacy," in *Handbook of Christianity in China*, vol. 2, *1800 to the Present*, ed. R. G. Tiedemann (Leiden: Brill, 2010), 383.

7. Nicole Constable, "Christianity and Hakka Identity," in Bays, *Christianity in China from the Eighteenth Century to the Present*, 163.

8. Jessie G. Lutz, ed., *Pioneer Chinese Christian Women: Gender, Christianity, and Social Mobility* (Bethlehem, Pa.: Lehigh University Press, 2010), esp. 251–52.

9. Lian Xi, *Redeemed by Fire: The Rise of Popular Christianity in Modern China* (New Haven, Conn.: Yale University Press, 2010), 91–94.

10. Ibid., 7.

11. Kim-Kwong Chan and Alan Hunter, eds., *Prayers and Thoughts of Chinese Christians* (London: Mowbray, 1991), 90.

12. Ryan J. Dunch, "Autonomous Churches and the Question of Religious Freedom," in Tiedemann, *1800 to the Present*, 886–87.

13. Fuk-Tsang Ying, "The CPC's Policy on Protestant Christianity, 1949–1957: An Overview and Assessment," *Journal of Contemporary China* 23, no. 89 (2014): 889–90 and n25.

14. John Craig William Keating, *A Protestant Church in Communist China: Moore Memorial Church Shanghai, 1949–89* (Bethlehem, Pa.: Lehigh University Press, 2012), 130.

15. Daniel H. Bays, *A New History of Christianity in China* (Chichester, U.K.: Wiley-Blackwell, 2012), 186.

16. Philip L. Wickeri, *Seeking the Common Ground: Protestant Christianity, the Three-Self Movement, and China's United Front* (Maryknoll, N.Y.: Orbis Books, 1988), 164, 186; Keating, *Protestant Church in Communist China*, 150–51, 154–55.

17. Ryan Dunch, "Protestant Christianity in China Today: Fragile, Fragmented, Flourishing," in *China and Christianity: Burdened Past, Hopeful Future*, eds. Stephen Uhalley Jr. and Xiaoxin Wu (Armonk, N.Y.: M. E. Sharpe, 2001), 207.

18. Donald E. MacInnis, *Religion in China Today: Policy and Practice* (Maryknoll, N.Y.: Orbis Books, 1989), 329.

19. Chen-Yang Kao, "The Cultural Revolution and the Emergence of Pentecostal-Style Protestantism in China," *Journal of Contemporary Religion* 24, no. 2 (2009): esp. 176–77.

20. Ibid., 178.

21. Chan and Hunter, *Prayers and Thoughts of Chinese Christians*, 20, 28.

22. Daniel H. Bays, "Chinese Protestant Christianity Today," in *Religion in China Today*, ed. Daniel L. Overmyer (Cambridge, U.K.: Cambridge University Press, 2003), 186.

23. Alan Hunter and Kim-Kwong Chan, *Protestantism in Contemporary China* (Cambridge, U.K.: Cambridge University Press, 1993), 88.

24. Keating, *Protestant Church in Communist China*, 172–73.

25. Hunter and Chan, *Protestantism in Contemporary China*, 184.

26. Keating, *Protestant Church in Communist China*, 210.

27. Chan and Hunter, *Prayers and Thoughts of Chinese Christians*, 99.

28. Hunter and Chan, *Protestantism in Contemporary China*, 94, 98; Keating, *Protestant Church in Communist China*, 185.

29. Zhong Min and Chan Kim-Kwong, "The 'Apostolic Church': A Case Study of a House Church in Rural China," in *Christianity in China: Foundations for Dialogue*, eds. Beatrice Leung and John Young (Hong Kong: University of Hong Kong, 1993), 254–55.

30. Ji Tai, "Hermeneutics in the Chinese Church," *Chinese Theological Review* 12 (1998): 145–46; cf. Leviticus 21:16–23.

31. Fenggang Yang, *Religion in China: Survival and Revival Under Communist Rule* (Oxford: Oxford University Press, 2012), 92–96; "Nation Plans Establishment of Christian Theology," *China Daily*, Aug. 7, 2014, accessed Sept. 12, 2016, www.chinadaily.com.cn/cndy/2014-08/07/content_18262770.htm.

32. Zhong and Chan, "'Apostolic Church,'" 252.

33. MacInnis, *Religion in China Today*, 328.

34. Ibid., 327.

35. Zhuo Xinping, "Discussion on 'Cultural Christians' in China," in Uhalley and Wu, *China and Christianity*, 283–300.

36. Keating, *Protestant Church in Communist China*, 181.

37. Fenggang Yang, "Lost in the Market, Saved at McDonald's: Conversion to Christianity in Urban China," *Journal for the Scientific Study of Religion* 44 (2005): 435.

38. Verna Yu, "Wenzhou's Removal of Crosses and Actions Elsewhere May Signal Wider Crackdown," *South China Morning Post*, Sept. 7, 2014, accessed Jan. 29, 2016, www.scmp.com/news/china/article/1586751/wenzhous-removal-crosses-and-actions-elsewhere-may-signal-wider-crackdown?page=all.

39. China Partnership, "95 Theses: The Reaffirmation of Our Stance on the House Church," Aug. 30, 2015, accessed Oct. 13, 2016, www.chinapartnership.org/blog/2015/08/95-theses-the-reaffirmation-of-our-stance-on-the-house-church?rq=95%20theses.

Chapter 16: Pentecostalism: An Old Flame

1. W. K. Tweedie, ed., *Select Biographies Edited for the Wodrow Society, Chiefly from the Manuscripts in the Library of the Faculty of Advocates*, vol. 1 (Edinburgh: Wodrow Society, 1845), e.g. 146.

2. Ahlstrom, *Religious History of the American People*, 434–35.

3. Allan Anderson, *Spreading Fires: The Missionary Nature of Early Pentecostalism* (London: SCM Press, 2007), 23; Robert Mapes Anderson, *Vision of the Disinherited: The Making of American Pentecostalism* (Oxford: Oxford University Press, 1979), 38.
4. Anderson, *Vision of the Disinherited,* 39.
5. Ibid., 35.
6. Joel 2:23; cf. Acts 2:1–21; James 5:7.
7. Anderson, *Vision of the Disinherited,* 42.
8. Acts 2:1–21: cf. Genesis 11:1–9.
9. 1 Corinthians 13–14.
10. Lionel Laborie, *Enlightening Enthusiasm: Prophecy and Religious Experience in Early Eighteenth-Century England* (Manchester, U.K.: Manchester University Press, 2015), 98–99; Larry Christenson, "Pentecostalism's Forgotten Forerunner," in *Aspects of Pentecostal-Charismatic Origins,* ed. Vinson Synan (Plainfield, N.J.: Logos International, 1975), 26. The title "Catholic" is a reminder that Protestants contest the Roman Catholic Church's right to be seen as the true "catholic," that is, universal, Christian church.
11. Anderson, *Vision of the Disinherited,* 35.
12. Anderson, *Spreading Fires,* 48.
13. Ibid., 79.
14. Ibid., 85.
15. Anderson, *Vision of the Disinherited,* 47, 54.
16. Cecil M. Robeck Jr., *The Azusa Street Mission and Revival: The Birth of the Global Pentecostal Movement* (Nashville: Thomas Nelson, 2006), 66–67.
17. Anderson, *Spreading Fires,* 59.
18. Robeck, *Azusa Street Mission and Revival,* 73; Anderson, *Vision of the Disinherited,* 66.
19. Anderson, *Vision of the Disinherited,* 69.
20. Christenson, "Pentecostalism's Forgotten Forerunner," 29.
21. Robeck, *Azusa Street Mission and Revival,* 9, 113, 157.
22. Anderson, *Spreading Fires,* 49; Anderson, *Vision of the Disinherited,* 74–75.
23. 1 Corinthians 14:6–19.
24. Anderson, *Spreading Fires,* 53, 58.
25. Grant Wacker, *Heaven Below: Early Pentecostals and American Culture* (Cambridge, Mass.: Harvard University Press, 2001), 39.
26. Anderson, *Spreading Fires,* 58.
27. Ibid., 63, 80.
28. Ibid., 62–63.
29. Wacker, *Heaven Below,* 38.
30. Robeck, *Azusa Street Mission and Revival,* 183–84; Anderson, *Vision of the Disinherited,* 53–54; Wacker, *Heaven Below,* 36.
31. Daniel Woods, "The Royal Telephone: Early Pentecostalism in the South and the Enthusiastic Practice of Prayer," in *Religion in the American South: Protestants and Others in History and Culture,* eds. Beth Barton Schweiger and Donald G. Mathews (Chapel Hill: University of North Carolina Press, 2004), 136; Wacker, *Heaven Below,* 36–39.
32. Robeck, *Azusa Street Mission and Revival,* 149–53.
33. Horace S. Ward, "The Anti-Pentecostal Argument," in Synan, *Aspects of Pentecostal-Charismatic Origins,* 104.
34. William W. Menzies, "The Non-Wesleyan Origins of the Pentecostal Movement," in Synan, *Aspects of Pentecostal-Charismatic Origins,* 85.
35. Joshua R. Ziefle, *David du Plessis and the Assemblies of God: The Struggle for the Soul of a Movement* (Leiden: Brill, 2013), 111.
36. Ibid., 121.
37. Todd M. Johnson, "Counting Pentecostals Worldwide," *Pneuma* 36 (2014): 281–83.
38. David Martin, *Tongues of Fire: The Explosion of Protestantism in Latin America* (Oxford: Blackwell, 1990), 50–51; Pew Research Center, "Religion in Latin America," Nov. 13,

2014, accessed April 24, 2016, www.pewforum.org/2014/11/13/religion-in
-latin-america.

39. Pew Research Center, "Religion in Latin America"; Anderson, *Bazalwane,* 100; David
    Stoll, *Is Latin America Turning Protestant? The Politics of Evangelical Growth* (Berkeley:
    University of California Press, 1990), 100, 112.

40. Moore, *Religious Outsiders and the Making of Americans,* 142.

41. Anderson, *Vision of the Disinherited,* 208.

42. Martin, *Tongues of Fire,* 238–40.

43. Stoll, *Is Latin America Turning Protestant?,* 112, 316.

44. Pew Research Center, "Religion in Latin America."

45. Stoll, *Is Latin America Turning Protestant?,* 315.

46. Richard Burgess, "Pentecostalism and Democracy in Nigeria: Electoral Politics, Pro-
    phetic Practices, and Cultural Reformation," *Nova Religio* 18, no. 3 (2015): 43.

47. Stoll, *Is Latin America Turning Protestant?,* 100.

48. Joseph E. Potter, Ernesto F. L. Amaral, and Robert D. Woodberry, "The Growth of
    Protestantism in Brazil and Its Impact on Male Earnings, 1970–2000," *Social Forces* 93,
    no. 1 (2014): 125–53; Pew Research Center, "Religion in Latin America."

49. Burgess, "Pentecostalism and Democracy in Nigeria," 55.

50. Ruth Marshall, *Political Spiritualities: The Pentecostal Revolution in Nigeria* (Chicago:
    University of Chicago Press, 2009), 1; Burgess, "Pentecostalism and Democracy in
    Nigeria," 46.

51. Andreas Heuser, "Encoding Caesar's Realm—Variants of Spiritual Warfare Politics in
    Africa," in *Pentecostalism in Africa: Presence and Impact of Pneumatic Christianity in Post-
    colonial Societies,* ed. Martin Lindhardt (Leiden: Brill, 2015), 279–81.

52. Burgess, "Pentecostalism and Democracy in Nigeria," 48.

53. Ibid., 39.

Epilogue: The Protestant Future

1. Timothy Willem Jones, "The Missionaries' Position: Polygamy and Divorce in the
   Anglican Communion, 1888–1988," *Journal of Religious History* 35, no. 3 (2011): 393–408.

2. Cabrita, *Text and Authority in the South African Nazaretha Church,* 121, 342.

3. I. Miller, "Evangelicalism and the Early Vegetarian Movement in Britain c. 1847–
   1860," *Journal of Religious History* 35 (2011): 199–210; Samantha Calvert, "A Taste of
   Eden: Modern Christianity and Vegetarianism," *Journal of Ecclesiastical History* 58
   (2007): 461–81. Full disclosure: in 2012, I became pescatarian myself for some of the
   reasons discussed here.

4. Ziefle, *David du Plessis and the Assemblies of God,* 105.

5. Matthew Engelke, *A Problem of Presence: Beyond Scripture in an African Church* (Berkeley:
   University of California Press, 2007), 2–3, 6–7.

Index